# The
# Cambridge History *of*
# American Literature

*EDITED BY*

WILLIAM PETERFIELD TRENT

JOHN ERSKINE

STUART P. SHERMAN

CARL VAN DOREN

*IN THREE VOLUMES*

3 Vein one

New York : The Macmillan Company
Cambridge, England : at the University Press
1956

# The
# Cambridge History of
# American Literature

* *

EDITED BY

WILLIAM PETERFIELD TRENT

JOHN ERSKINE

STUART P. SHERMAN

CARL VAN DOREN

IN THREE VOLUMES

* *

*New York: The Macmillan Company*
*Cambridge, England: at the University Press*
1956

# THE CAMBRIDGE HISTORY

## OF

# AMERICAN LITERATURE

## Volume I

Colonial and Revolutionary Literature

Early National Literature: Part I

# The Cambridge History

of

# American Literature

Edited by

William Peterfield Trent

John Erskine

Stuart P. Sherman

Carl Van Doren

In Three Volumes

Colonial and Revolutionary Literature
Early National Literature: Part I

New York: The Macmillan Company
Cambridge, England: at the University Press

PRINTED IN THE UNITED STATES OF AMERICA

# PREFACE

IT was a hard saying of a Spanish aphorist of the seventeenth century that "to equal a predecessor one must have twice his worth." We should deprecate the application of that standard to *The Cambridge History of American Literature*, yet we are not without hope that the work, of which we here present the first volume, will be found to mark some progress in the right direction. We would call attention to the following as perhaps its chief distinctive features: (1) It is on a larger scale than any of its predecessors which have carried the story from colonial times to the present generation; (2) It is the first history of American literature composed with the collaboration of a numerous body of scholars from every section of the United States and from Canada; (3) It will provide for the first time an extensive bibliography for all periods and subjects treated; (4) It will be a survey of the life of the American people as expressed in their writings rather than a history of *belles-lettres* alone. The significance of these features may be emphasized by some reference to the characteristic merits and defects of previous works in this field, to which we are under obligations too extensive for detailed mention.

The earliest and the latest historians of a literature have great advantages: the earliest, that he has no predecessors; the latest, that he has many. It is a pleasure to remember Samuel L. Knapp, who in the preface to his *Lectures on American Literature*, published in 1829, easily justified the publication of that interesting and patriotic overture: "We have very good histories—narrative, political, military, and constitutional; but I know none, as yet, that can be called literary—meaning by the term, a history of our literature, and of our literary men." "You are aware," he continues, "that it has been said by foreigners, and often repeated, that there was no such thing as American literature; that it would be vain for anyone to seek for proofs of taste, mind, or information, worth possessing, in our early records; and some of our citizens, who have never examined these matters, have rested so quietly after these declarations, or so fondly denied them, that the bold asserters of these libels have gained confidence in tauntingly repeating them. The great epoch in our history—the revolution of 1775—seemed sufficient, alone, to many of the present generation, to give us, as a people, all the celebrity and rank, among the nations of the earth, we ought to aspire to, without taking the trouble to go back to the previous ages of heroick virtue and gigantick labours. Many of the present generation are willing to think that our ancestors were a pious and persevering race of men, who really did possess some strength of character, but, without further reflection, they are ready to allow that a few pages are 'ample room and verge enough' to trace their character and their history together: I have ventured to think differently";—and the editors of the present work are at this point in accord with Knapp.

Knapp, however, illustrates a temptation which has beset investigators of American literature from his day to ours, namely, the temptation to relinquish the unremunerative project of adequate scholarly publication and to compensate oneself by producing a text-book adapted to the means and the minds of school-boys. "My plan," he says, in a passage which throws an illuminating beam down the whole pathway of American literary scholarship—"My plan when I commenced my researches was an extensive one, and I gathered copious materials to carry it into effect. For several years past I have had access to libraries rich in American literature; but when I sat down to work up the mass I had collected, the thought suggested itself to my mind, that no adequate compensation could ever be reasonably expected for my pains. . . . Still I could not be persuaded to relinquish altogether my design, and I therefore set about abridging my outlines, dispensing with many of my remarks, and giving up many elaborate finishings I had promised myself to make in the course of my work. And another thought struck me most forcibly, that a heavy publication would not be readily within the reach of all classes of youth in our country, but that a single volume of common size, in a cheap edition, might find its way into some of our schools, and be of service in giving our children a wish to pursue the subject of our literary history as they advanced in years and knowledge." The philosophic observer may here remark that our historian, like his innumerable successors, follows the way of all flesh in that when he has abandoned his ideal immediately there bolts into his mind an excellent reason for abandoning it.

A second temptation of the American historian, which appeared long before Knapp and persisted long after him, is to magnify the achievements of one's own parish at the expense of the rest of the country. In Governor Bradford's *History of Plymouth Plantation* there is hardly a trace of inflation; throughout that grave and noble narrative the Governor cleaves to his purpose to write "in a plain style, with singular regard unto the simple truth in all things." But in Cotton Mather one finds already a local pride that looks disdainfully upon the neighbour colonies and deigns only to compare the New England worthies with the prophets and apostles of Palestine. In the more temperate passages of the *Magnalia Christi Americana* he cultivates the just self-esteem of his section with considerations like these: "I will make no odious comparisons between Harvard College and other universities for the proportion of worthy men therein educated; but New England, compared with other parts of America, may certainly boast of having brought forth very many eminent men, in proportion more than any of them; and of Harvard College (herein truly a Sion College) it may be said, *this and that man were bred there;* of whom not the least was Mr. Thomas Shepard." The local pride, more or less justifiable, which renders tumid the periods of this energetic old Puritan, was a useful passion at a time when literature was obliged to develop independently in widely separated colonies. It is a useful passion still in a country of a hundred million inhabitants separated by such spatial and spiritual intervals as lie between Boston, New York, Richmond, Chicago, New Orleans, and San Francisco. It has stimulated the production of our innumerable "local-colorists" in poetry and prose fiction. It underlies many entertaining books and articles on the New England School, the Knickerbocker School, the Southern School, the Hoosier School, and the rest; but it is not conducive to the production of a quite unbiassed history of American literature.

Many of our historians who escaped from the colonial or provincial illusion succumbed, especially in the period before the Civil War, to the temptation of national pride. There was much provocation and incitement both at home and abroad. Transatlantic critics enquired tauntingly, "Who reads an American book?" and challenged the American authors to show reasons why sentence of death should not be pronounced against them. It no longer sufficed to say with the colonial divines of New England: We have created in the wilderness of the western world a commonwealth for Christ, a spiritual New Jerusalem. It no longer served to declare with the Revolutionary Fathers: We have established the political Promised Land, and have set up the lamp of Liberty for a beacon light to all nations. What was demanded early in the nineteenth century of the adolescent nation was an indigenous independent national literature. The wrong answer to this demand was given by the enthusiastic patriots who, after the Revolution, advocated the abrogation of English in "these States" and the invention and adoption of a new language; or compiled, to silence their skeptical English cousins, pretentious anthologies of all our village elegists; or offered Dwight's *Conquest of Canaan* as an equivalent to Milton's *Paradise Lost*, Barlow's *Columbiad* as an imposing national epic, Lathrop's poem on the sachem of the Narragansett Indians, *The Speech of Caunonicus*, as heralding the dawn of a genuinely native school of poetry. Our pioneer historian Knapp discreetly hesitates to say "whether she of 'the banks of the Connecticut' [Mrs. Sigourney], whose strains of poetic thought are as pure and lovely as the adjacent wave touched by the sanctity of a Sabbath's morn, be equal to her tuneful sisters, Hemans and Landon, on the other side of the water." But Knapp, who is a forward-looking man, anticipates the spirit of most of our *ante-bellum* critics and historians by doing what in him lies to give to his fellow countrymen a profound bias in favor of the autochthonous. "What are the Tibers and Scamanders," he cries, "measured by the Missouri and the Amazon? Or what the loveliness of Illysus or Avon by the Connecticut or the Potomack?—Whenever a nation wills it, prodigies are born. Admiration and patronage create myriads who struggle for the mastery, and for the olympick crown. Encourage the game and the victors will come." In some measure, no doubt, *Rip Van Winkle*, the Indian romances of Cooper, the philosophy of Emerson and Thoreau, the novels of Hawthorne, Longfellow's *Evangeline, Miles Standish*, and *Hiawatha* were responses to this encouragement of the game— to the nation's willing an expression of its new American consciousness.

Against the full rigour of the demand for an independent national literature there was, by the middle of the last century, a wholesome reaction represented in Rufus Wilmot Griswold's introduction to his *Prose Writers of America* (1847). Since this old demand is still reasserted from year to year, it may not be amiss to reprint here Griswold's admirable reply to it. "Some critics in England," he says, "expect us who write the same language, profess the same religion, and have in our intellectual firmament the same Bacon, Sidney, and Locke, the same Spenser, Shakespeare, and Milton, to differ more from themselves than they differ from the Greeks and Romans, or from any of the moderns. This would be harmless, but that many persons in this country, whose thinking is done abroad, are constantly echoing it, and wasting their little productive energy in efforts to comply with the demand. But there never was and never can be an exclusively national literature. All nations are indebted to each other and to preceding ages for the means of advancement; and our own, which from our various origin may be said to be at the confluence of the rivers of time which have swept through every country, can with less justice than any other be looked to for mere novelties in art and fancy. The question between us and other nations is not who shall most completely discard the Past, but who shall make best use of it. It cannot be studied too deeply, for unless men know what has been accomplished, they will exhaust themselves in unfolding enigmas that have been solved, or in pursuing *ignes fatui* that have already disappointed a thousand expectations." With more intelligent conceptions than many of his predecessors possessed of what constitutes a national literature, Griswold was still a proud nationalist. His valuable collections of American prose and poetry are mainly illustrative of writers who flourished in the first half of the nineteenth century. Of the work of that period he forms in general estimates tempered by his confidence that something better is yet to come.

In 1855 something better came in the shape of the two large volumes of the *Cyclopædia of American Literature* by Evert A. and George L. Duyckinck, a work of extensive research, designed, in the words of the authors, "to bring together as far as possible in one book convenient for perusal and reference, memorials and records of the writers of the country and their works, from the earliest period to the present day." Here for the first time were presented, in something like adequate measure and proportion, materials for the study of our literature in what the compliers recognized as three great periods: "the Colonial Era," "the Revolutionary Period," and "the Present Century." Disclaiming any severe critical pretentions, they exhibited the breadth of their historical interests in the declaration that "it is important to know what books have been produced, and by whom; whatever the books may have been or whoever the men." A similar breadth of historical interest animated Moses Coit Tyler in the production of his notable and still unsurpassed history of American literature from 1607 to 1783. Free from the embarrassment of the early historians who had advanced to their task with a somewhat inflamed consciousness that they were defending the Stars and Stripes, Tyler had still a clear sense that he was engaged upon a great and rewarding enterprise. In his opening sentence he strikes the note which every historian of a national literature should have in his ear: "There is but one thing more interesting than the intellectual history of a man, and that is the intellectual history of a nation." If Tyler had been able to carry his narrative down to the present day in the spirit and manner of the portion of his work which he brought to completion, the need for our present undertaking would have been less obvious.

Unhappily the next noteworthy historian, Charles F. Richardson, whose *American Literature 1607–1885* was published in 1886–8, is rather a protest against the work of Tyler than a supplement to it. His leading purpose is not historical enquiry and elucidation but æsthetic judgment. "We have had enough description," he declares; "we want analysis." He opens his account with a definition of literature well framed to exclude from his consideration most of the important writing in America before the nineteenth century: "Literature is the written record of valuable thought, having other than merely practical purpose." Under this definition he is justified in asserting that "if a certain space be devoted to the colonial literature of America, then, on the same perspective ten times as much is needed to bring the record down to our day. . . . I believe that the time has come for the student to consider American literature as calmly as he would consider the literature of another country." Under this calm consideration the seventeenth and eighteenth centuries dwindle into a sombre little vestibule before the wide edifice which contains the writers who flourished through the middle years of the nineteenth century—Hawthorne is the latest novelist who receives extended notice. Richardson was not immune from the influence of the Zeitgeist of the eighties. What he does is, in short, to create the idea of what we may call the American Victorian Age, before and after which there is little that merits the attention of the dispassionate critic.

Professor Barrett Wendell in his interesting *Literary History of America*, published in 1900, presents with even sharper emphasis than Professor Richardson his similar conception of a closed "classical" period existing through the middle years of the last century. As we view the Americans from the beginning of their history, "we can instantly perceive," he declares, "that only the last, the Americans of the nineteenth century, have produced literature of any importance. The novelists and the historians, the essayists and the poets, whose names come to mind when American literature is mentioned, have all flourished since 1800." This is the somewhat restricted point of view established in the Introduction. In the composition of the history, the survey of the field, one suspects, was still further restricted by the descent upon Professor Wendell of the spirit of Cotton Mather; for the total effect of the narrative is an impression that the literary history of America is essentially a history of the birth, the renaissance, and the decline of New England.

The *Cambridge History* marks a partial reversion to the

position of the earlier historians who looked into the past
with interest and into the present and future not without hope.
Following in general the plan of *The Cambridge History of
English Literature* and of our encyclopædic Duyckinck, we
have made it our primary purpose to represent as adequately
as space allowed all the periods of our national past, and to
restore the memory of writers who are neglected because they
are forgotten and because they are no longer sympathetically
understood. To write the intellectual history of America
from the modern æsthetic standpoint is to miss precisely what
makes it significant among modern literatures, namely, that
for two centuries the main energy of Americans went into
exploration, settlement, labour for subsistence, religion, and
statecraft. For nearly two hundred years a people with the
same traditions and with the same intellectual capacities as
their contemporaries across the sea found themselves obliged
to dispense for the most part with art for art. But the long
inhibition and belated expansion of their purely æsthetic
impulses, unfavourable as it was to the development of poetry
and fiction, was no serious handicap to the production of a
prose competently recording their practical activities and expressing their moral, religious, and political ideas. Acquaintance with the written record of these two centuries should
enlarge the spirit of American literary criticism and render it
more energetic and masculine. To a taste and judgment
unperverted by the current finical and transitory definitions
of literature, there is something absurd in a critical sifting
process which preserves a Restoration comedy and rejects
Bradford's *History of Plymouth;* which prizes a didactic poem
in the heroic couplets and despises the work of Jonathan Edwards; which relishes the letters of some third rate English
poet, but finds no gusto in the correspondence of Benjamin
Franklin; which sends a student to the novels of William
Godwin, but never thinks of directing him to *The Federalist.*
When our American criticism treats its facile novelists and
poetasters as they deserve, and heartily recognizes and values
the works in which the maturest and wisest Americans have
expressed themselves, its references to the period prior to
1800 will be less apologetic.

For the nineteenth century, too, without neglecting the

writers of imaginative literature who have been most emphasized by our literary historians, we have attempted to do a new service by giving a place in our record to departments of literature, such as travels, oratory, memoirs, which have lain somewhat out of the main tradition of literary history but which may be, as they are in the United States, highly significant of the national temper. In this task we have been much aided by the increasing number of monographs produced within the past quarter of a century upon aspects of American literary history. Such collections as *A Library of American Literature*, edited by Edmund Clarence Stedman and Ellen M. Hutchinson in 1889–90, and the *Library of Southern Literature* (1908–13), compiled by various Southern men of letters, have been indispensable.

In the actual preparation of the work we have been indebted for many details to the unsparing assistance of Mrs Carl Van Doren, who has also compiled the index.

1 June, 1917.

W. P. T.
J. E.
S. P. S.
C. V. D.

The bibliography mentioned in the above preface is not included in this edition.

# CONTENTS

## BOOK I

## COLONIAL AND REVOLUTIONARY LITERATURE

## CHAPTER I

### TRAVELLERS AND EXPLORERS, 1583–1763

By GEORGE PARKER WINSHIP, A.M., Librarian of the Harry Elkins Widener Collection, Harvard University.

PAGE

## CHAPTER II

### THE HISTORIANS, 1607–1783

By JOHN SPENCER BASSETT, Ph.D., Professor of American History in Smith College.

## CHAPTER III

### THE PURITAN DIVINES, 1620–1720

By VERNON LOUIS PARRINGTON, A.M., Professor of English in the University of Washington.

# Contents

# CHAPTER VIII

## AMERICAN POLITICAL WRITING, 1760–1789

By WILLIAM MACDONALD, Ph.D., Professor of History in Brown University.

PAGE

# CHAPTER IX

## THE BEGINNINGS OF VERSE, 1610–1808

By SAMUEL MARION TUCKER, Ph.D., Professor of English in the Brooklyn Polytechnic Institute.

# BOOK II

# EARLY NATIONAL LITERATURE

# CHAPTER I

## TRAVELLERS AND OBSERVERS, 1763–1846

By LANE COOPER, Ph.D., Professor of English in Cornell University.

# CHAPTER II

## THE EARLY DRAMA, 1756–1860

By ARTHUR HOBSON QUINN, Ph.D., Dean of the College, University of Pennsylvania.

# Contents

## CHAPTER III

### EARLY ESSAYISTS

By GEORGE FRISBIE WHICHER, Ph.D., Associate Professor of English in Amherst College.

## CHAPTER IV

### IRVING

By MAJOR GEORGE HAVEN PUTNAM, Litt.D.

## CHAPTER V

### BRYANT AND THE MINOR POETS

By WILLIAM ELLERY LEONARD, Ph.D., Assistant Professor of English in the University of Wisconsin.

#### I. BRYANT

#### II. MINOR POETS

## CHAPTER VI

### FICTION I: BROWN, COOPER

By CARL VAN DOREN, Ph.D., Head Master of The Brearley School, Associate in English in Columbia University.

# Contents

## CHAPTER VII

### FICTION II: CONTEMPORARIES OF COOPER

### By CARL VAN DOREN

## CHAPTER VIII
### TRANSCENDENTALISM

### By HAROLD CLARKE GODDARD, Ph.D., Professor of English in Swarthmore College.

## CHAPTER IX
### EMERSON

### By PAUL ELMER MORE

# Book I

## CHAPTER I

## Travellers and Explorers, 1583-1763

THE English folk who became Americans during the early years of the seventeenth century kept the language of the relatives and friends whom they left, and with it their share in the literary heritage of the race. They owed much to the influences surrounding them in their new homes, but such skill in writing as they possessed came with them from the other side of the Atlantic. The names of an earlier group of adventurers are associated with the New World because they made a voyage along its coastline or resided for a little while at some seaside settlement. Sir Humphrey Gilbert on his homeward voyage from the New-found-land in 1583, sitting abaft with a book in his hand, while the *Golden Hind* was tossed by "terrible seas breaking short and high pyramidwise," is the finest type of the seamen who made the English occupation of America possible. The narrative of Gilbert's fatal voyage, written by Edward Haie, found a place in the ample store-house of adventurous records which makes all who love good reading and virile English the debtors of Richard Hakluyt.

It is an accident of geography which gives American readers a valid claim upon Humphrey Gilbert and his precursors and successors who told their straightforward tales for Hakluyt or for the booksellers who issued the scores of thin pamphlets in which Londoners first read about the trans-Atlantic voyage. These were in their day only a few among the many pamphlets which entertained the frequenters of St. Paul's churchyard with experienres in odd corners of the Mediterranean or of the Indian Ocean, or along the Arctic route to Central Asia.   They all shared in developing the British Empire and English literature.   Martin Frobisher and North-West-Foxe beyond the polar circle, Thomas Hariot inside the Carolina sandspits, and Sir Richard Hawl·ins in the Gulf of Mexico are by this chance of geography given a place at the beginning of the annals of American literature, instead of sharing the scant notice allotted to their equally deserving contemporaries whom fate led elsewhere.   The same fate sent Francis Drake to sojourn for a time on the California coast, and it likewise set in motion the economic and political forces which two centuries later transferred this region into the keeping of the English race, thereby adding the great circumnavigator to the American roll.   Later came one whom Americans have adopted as a folk hero, Captain John Smith.[1]   He risked his life with equal abandon in Flanders and Turkey and Poto-watomy's land, but Virginia claims him as her own.   He may have been, as it was once the fashion to proclaim, an inordinate liar, but whatever the historians say, the certain fact is that what he wrote was read in his own day and has ever since been read by thousands who have identified him with the first English colony.

"And this is as much as my memory can call to mind worthie of note; which I have purposely collected, to satisfie my friends of the true worth and qualitie of Virginia."   So John Smith wrote at the end of his "Description" of that colony published in 1612.

Yet some bad natures will not sticke to slander the Countrey, that will slovenly spit at all things, especially in company where they can find none to contradict them.   Who though they were scarse ever 10 miles from *James* Town, or at the most but at the falles; yet holding it a great disgrace that amongst so much action, their actions were nothing, exclaime of all things, though they never adventured to knowe any thing; nor ever did any thing but devoure the fruits of other mens labours.   Being for most part of such tender educations and small experience in martiall accidents, because they found not English cities, nor such faire houses, nor at their

[1] See also Book I, Chap. II.

owne wishes any of their accustomed dainties, with feather beds
and downe pillowes, Tavernes and alehouses in every breathing
place, neither such plenty of gold and silver and dissolute liberty
as they expected, [they] had little or no care of any thing, but to
pamper their bellies, to fly away with our Pinnaces, or procure their
means to returne for England. For the Country was to them a
miserie, a ruine, a death, a hell, and their reports here, and their
owne actions there according.

Straightforwardness of narrative was characteristic of the
period. This quality, and the absence of literary consciousness,
distinguish the accounts written by these English seafarers
from the productions of the rival French and Spanish voyagers.
Each adapted his style to the public which he sought to influence. They were all alike trying to start or to accelerate the
stream which was to transform the Western hemisphere into
a part of the European world. Consequently the English
tracts rarely possess qualities which separate them from the
rest of the mass of seventeenth-century travel-books. Another
result is that nearly all of them are more easily read, three
centuries later, than the Continental output of the same
period.

The corner of the New-found-land which retained this
distinctive name exerted an especial attraction in the earlier
days upon the adventurers who felt a longing to express themselves in literary form. Humphrey Gilbert was accompanied
thither by the learned Stephen Parmenius of Buda, whose
Latin verses "Ad Thamesin" are preserved on Hakluyt's pages.
One of the first Englishmen to establish an American residence
was William Vaughn, a Welshman and the composer of an
amazing volume called *The Golden Fleece . . . Transported
from Cambrioll Colchos, out of the Southermost Part of the Iland
commonly called the Newfoundland, By Orpheus Junior*, to
London, where it was printed in 1626. This work has long
been the butt of despairing historians, who have sought for the
Ariadnean thread which should guide them through its 350
pages of puerile fancies, discursive theology, significant episodes,
and rhymed prose. For the reader who skips casually from
paragraph to paragraph, the volume yields an entertaining
notion of what was talked about in the fishing shacks on the

northern coast, and of how the leader of one band of adventurers amused himself. It contains a parody of the Litany which is said to have been sung by four of the "Fraternitie attired in long white Robes," and may have been part of an embryo pageant wherewith the days were whiled away.

Vaughn had a "deare Friende and Fellow-Planter, Master Robert Hayman, who with Pen and Person" prepared "more roome for Christians in the Newfound-World," and who published in 1628 a volume of *Quodlibets, lately come over from New Britaniola, All of them Composed and done at Harbor-Grace in Britaniola, anciently called Newfound-Land*. The verses which fill its pages passed current with the similar output of his age. A number, and by no means the least rhythmical, were inspired by his associates on the western shores of the Atlantic. One of these is addressed "To the right Honourable, Sir George Calvert, Knight, Baron of Baltamore, and Lord of Avalon in Britaniola, who came over to see his Land there, 1627"; it compares Baltimore to the Queen of Sheba.

The repayment of the drafts made upon the literature of the motherland was not long delayed. It is more than probable that Shakespeare found in the reports of some New World voyagers one of his most momentous inspirations. Hugh Peters and the younger Harry Vane were only two of the temporary Americans who returned to take a lively part in the pamphleteering conflicts of the Protectorate. Roger Williams divided his controversial activities equally between the old and New England, and his *Key into the Languages of America* was cast into shape while he was on his way from one to the other.

Robert Sedgwick, one of the worthiest of those New Englanders who were recalled to serve the mother country, obtained a place for himself in literary annals by the reports which he addressed to Cromwell from the West Indies, where he was in charge of an expedition against the Spaniards. Carlyle, wearied of "the deadly inextricable jungle of tropical confusions" through which he struggled in "the Stygian quagmires of Thurloe's Collection of the State Papers from 1638 to 1661," found Sedgwick's letters "of all others the best worth reading on this subject." Sedgwick was a prospering settler at Charlestown in Massachusetts, speculating in land

and customs duties, an organizer of the Ancient and Honourable Artillery Company, when his worldly career was diverted
by a chance meeting with Cromwell. The Lord Protector
recognized a man after his own model, and sent him in quick
succession against the Dutch on the Hudson River, the French
at Acadia, and the Spanish of the Island Colonies. In one of his
reports from his last expedition to Jamaica he begs the Protector
to pardon his

prolix and rude expressions. I am apt sometimes to think I shall
write no more. I am sometimes sick, and think I may fall among
the rest of my countrymen; and durst do no other than plainly
to let your highness know our state and condition.

Plainly and simply, and most convincingly, he set forth the
deplorable situation of Jamaica and of the English soldiers
who were dying there.

On the North American mainland, settlement followed
exploration and colonization. For half a century there was
little record of travelling beyond the limits of the outlying
pasture lands and adjoining home sites. Occasionally some-
one bolder than his neighbours pushed a canoe up-stream to
the head of navigation, or wandered into the valleys beyond
the surrounding ridges, but very rarely were observations or
physical experiences committed to paper. The impulse to
print the reports of travellers did not come until there was
land to be sold. The seventeenth-century promoters of
speculation carried on the practice of distributing tracts
telling about the property they wished others to buy. The
little pamphlets issued by the Virginia Company, by the
Massachusetts Agents, by William Penn in German, Dutch, and
French as well as in English, by the Scots Proprietors of the
Jerseys, and by the Lords of Carolina, are today worth more
money than many of the acres that they describe. Most of
these early tracts were written by men who had travelled
through the regions of which they wrote. Rarely is there
any substantial reason for doubting the honesty of what was
reported as the result of actual observation. "What I write,
is what I have proved," remarks one of the frankest of these
promoters of a New World settlement in which he hoped to
make his fortune, Edward Bland, Merchant. On 27 August,

1650, Bland set forth from the head of "Appamattuck River"
in Virginia in search of the Falls of Blandina. His journey
took him across broad stretches of "very rich Champian Land,"
"a pleasant Country, of temperate Ayre, and fertile Soyle."
The beauty of the country, the heaps of bones which led the
native guides to relate tales of valorous deeds, and the preservation of the party through "information our Guide told us he
had from a woman that was his Sweet-heart," offered opportunities that a later-day reader wishes might have been improved
with some of the appreciation of literary possibilities which a
Frenchman could hardly have neglected. Bland's narrative
goes steadily forward toward the goal and home again, without
digression for any merely entertaining purpose from each day's
march and the nightly watch against surprise.

The natives supplied the picturesque element for most of
the writing of colonial times. To them also were due a number
of involuntary journeyings, the accounts of which make an
important part of American literature. There is nothing in
English, or in any other language, that surpasses these narratives of Indian captivities in vividness or in the bare statement
of physical suffering and of mental torment. They held the
attention of readers who knew the writers, and the stream of
successive reprintings is still going on, to supply an unabated
demand.

The first and the best known of these narratives is that
of Mrs. Mary Rowlandson.[1] She was the wife of the minister
at Lancaster, Massachusetts, where the natives seized her when
they burned the town during King Philip's War. The record
of her subsequent "Removes" has seldom been equalled as a
direct appeal for human sympathy. The hours following her
capture may well have been

the dolefullest night that ever my eyes saw. Oh the roaring, and
singing, and dancing, and yelling of those black creatures in the
night, which made the place a lively resemblance of hell . . .
There remained nothing to me but one poor wounded Babe, and it
seemed at present worse than death, that it was in such a pitiful
condition, bespeaking Compassion, and I had no refreshing for it,
nor suitable things to revive it.

[1] 2d ed. 1682. The date of the first edition is unknown.

Mrs. Rowlandson's narrative is matched by that of John Gyles of Pemaquid (1736), who collected from his minutes

these private Memoirs, at the earnest Request of my Second Consort; that we might have a Memento ever ready at Hand to excite, in our selves Gratitude & Thankfulness to GOD; and in our Offspring a due Sense of their Dependance on the SOVEREIGN of the Universe.

Gyles was captured in 1689, and spent the ensuing nine years with the Indians along the Penobscot River and with the French in Canada. The natives soon tired of the too easy amusement of seeing him suffer, and as he managed to avoid death by drowning and frost-bite, he gradually made a place for himself by the humblest usefulness.

The natives of the woods of Maine and those of the everglades of Florida were equally skilful in devising methods of terrifying strangers who were thrown by chance or indiscretion amongst them. The account of *God's Protecting Providence In the Remarkable Deliverance of Robert Barrow, Faithfully Related by Jonathan Dickenson* (1699), is in many respects the best of all the captivity tracts. Driven ashore by a storm on the Gulf coast of Florida, late in September, 1696, the survivors, among them Dickenson's wife with their baby at her breast, six weeks later reached St. Augustine. For most of this interval, the wanderers were in hourly expectation of death. As is frequently the case, the record of these experiences is so undemonstrative that it is unconvincing, until the whole story is reread from the beginning. It was only after the more desperate dangers were over, and the prospect began to favour their escape, that Dickenson's narrative became pathetic. When the Spanish outposts were reported to be only two marches away, the fugitives

had a great Loss; having a Quart of Berries whole, and as much pounded to mix with Water, to feed our Child with; the Fire being disturbed, the Cloth which we had our Food in was burn'd.

This was a loss which might easily have proved, to persons emaciated and weakened by suffering, the fatal last straw; but in spite of a driving storm and freezing weather, all but two of the party managed to drag their blood-caked bodies through the sand to the Spanish garrison. At St. Augustine the Commandant and the other residents divided their scanty supplies with the fugitives, and nursed them until they were fit to be sent on their way to the Carolinas. The aged Quaker, Robert Barrow, survived all these experiences just long enough to greet the Friends who were awaiting him at Philadelphia. There he died three days later, on 4 April, 1697,

having passed through great Exercises, in much Patience; and in all the times of our greatest Troubles, was ready to Counsel us to Patience, and to wait what the Lord our God would bring to pass: And he would often express, That it was his Belief, that our Lives should be spared, and not be lost in that Wilderness, and amongst those People, who would have made a Prey of us.

The same fundamental religious impulse which sustained Robert Barrow on the storm-swept Florida beaches had settled the New England Puritan colonies. This same overwhelming impulse drove into these colonies, half a century after their permanent establishment, a succession of groups of wanderers whose peregrinations left a broad and often blood-stained trail the length of the continent and seaward to the islands. The men and women who made up these groups, called in derision Quakers, wrote as freely as they discoursed, and the spirit that animated them brooked no interference with either speech or progress. The names of several, Mary Dyer, Marmaduke Stevenson, and George Fox, whom Roger Williams "digg'd out of his Burrowes," to wit Edward Burroughs, are better known, but none of them wrote more forcefully than Alice Curwen. In the year 1660, "hearing of the great Tribulation that the Servants of the Lord did suffer in *Boston*, of cruel Whippings, of Bonds and Imprisonments, yea, to the laying down of their natural Lives," Mistress Curwen felt the call to go and profess in that bloody town. "Having this Testimony sealed in my Heart," she writes, "I laboured with my Husband day and night to know his Mind, but he did not yet see it to be required of him," he having but just returned from the Lancashire gaol in which he had been confined for refusing to pay the tythe. The call reached him in season to enable him to embark on the vessel on which his wife had taken passage for America. Journeying to Boston, they missed imprisonment through a legal technicality, and went on their way to the eastward. They were more fortunate on their return, for the constables drove them "all along the Street, until they came to the Prison, whereinto they thrust us; but the Lord was with us, and our Service there was great; for many people, both rich and poor, came to look upon us."

Another traveller who did his best to scour the colonists of heretical opinions, his own opinions being as pronounced when he was directed by the Quaker spirit as when he followed the Anglican order, was George Keith. He knew the controversially-minded Americans better than anyone else at the end of the seventeenth century. The descriptions of his opponents which are scattered through his hundred-odd publications are an invaluable elucidation of the state oⱼ mind which fructified in the revivals of forty years later, when George Whitefield and Jonathan Edwards came to make plain the way to salvation. Whitefield[1] kept a diary during his constant journeyings between England and America and through the mainland colonies. These personal records were published at the close of each important stage of his wanderings, and the seven pamphlets in which they appeared were reprinted in numerous editions. They contributed largely to the success of the great revivalist's ministry. Upon the reader of two hundred years later they still leave the impression of a dominating spirit, and of a sweet nature unconscious of its power. Worn out by wordy wrestlings with a recalcitrant sinner, Whitefield would cheerfully get out of a sick bed to preach to the Free Masons, "with whom I afterwards dined, and was used with the utmost civility."

An elemental fondness for rhyme and rhythm was responsible for the preservation of a few records of travellings not in themselves as remarkable as the effusions for which they gave the occasion. Two of these were *A Monumental Memorial* of *A Late Voyage from Boston in New-England To London, Anno 1683. In a Poem. By Richard Steere*, and a broadside, *A Journal of the Taking of Cape-Breton, Put into Metre By L. G., One of the Soldiers of the Expedition*, in 1745.

The eighteenth century brought economic independence

[1] See also Book I, Chap. v.

and settled social conditions to the older English colonies. With these went the leisure and comfort which prepare a community for the conscious enjoyment of literature. These changing circumstances are reflected in the keen observations and amusing descriptions preserved by one of the sprightliest of New England matrons, Madame Sarah Knight. During the winter of 1704–5, Mrs. Knight was obliged to go to New York to attend to some business affairs. The trip from Boston followed the shore line, and was accomplished as expeditiously as her energetic nature, bored by the humdrum happenings along the way, could hurry it along, but five months elapsed before she regained her own fireside and warming pan. From the first stopping place, where she found the other guests "tyed by the Lipps to a pewter engine," and the next day's guide, whose "shade on his Hors resembled a Globe on a Gate post," there was scarcely a stage of her journey which did not provide its subject for entertaining comment.

An equal appreciation of the fact that mileage and food are not the only things worth recording by those who go abroad gives permanent value to the diaries kept by the second William Byrd of Westover in 1732 and 1733, when he followed the course of Edward Bland in searching for the likeliest Virginian land-holdings. Byrd was a model for all who journey in company, for he "broke not the Laws of Travelling by uttering the least Complaint" at inopportune torrents or "an impertinent Tooth . . . that I cou'd not grind a Biscuit but with much deliberation and presence of mind." He "contriv'd to get rid of this troublesome Companion by cutting a Caper," with a stout cord connecting the tooth and the snag of a log. "This new way of Tooth-drawing, being so silently and deliberately perform'd, both surprized and delighted all that were present, who cou'd not guess what I was going about."

Byrd has been made known for his "happy proficiency in polite and varied learning." He was not peculiar, however, among the gentlemen of his generation for a style which shows an acquaintance with what is recognized as literature. Most of the people who possessed inherited wealth and established position were able to spell correctly, and they obeyed the laws of English grammar. Many of Byrd's contemporaries in the New World could not do either of these things, and it has come to be the fashion among their descendants to excuse those eminently respectable and often brave and prosperous men and women, because of a belief that their short-comings were in accord with the practice, or lack thereof, of their own day. Byrd's writings, and even more clearly those of the Maryland physician Alexander Hamilton, furnish the best of evidence that illiteracy was ignorance due to a lack of education as truly in 1700 as it is two centuries later.

Dr. Hamilton, who is not known to have been related to the more eminent publicist of the same name, in 1744 followed his own advice and sought to rid himself of a persistent indisposition by a change of climate and companions. Except for this health-seeking incentive, his journey from Annapolis to Portsmouth in New Hampshire was a pleasure trip, probably the earliest recorded in America.

Reading was easily the first of Dr. Hamilton's pleasures. On his journey he picked up from the Philadelphia book stalls the latest English novels, and in New York he bought a new edition of a classical favourite. When his own supply of reading matter gave out, he rummaged through the inn or explored his host's book shelves. The tavern keeper at Kingston in Rhode Island convinced him that it was unlawful, and therefore inexpedient, to travel on the Sabbath, and so he loitered about all day, "having nothing to do and no books to read, except it was a curious History of the Nine Worthies (which we found in Case's library) a book worthy of that worthy author Mr. Burton, the diligent compiler and historian of Grub Street." The scenery, luckily, furnished a partial compensation for the dearth of literary pastime, for he noted as he approached this hostelry that it brought to his mind "some romantic descriptions of rural scenes in Spenser's *Faerie Queene.*"

The day following his arrival at Boston being Sunday, he attended meeting, where he heard "solid sense, strong connected reasoning and good language." For the rest of this day's entry in his journal he records "staid at home this night, reading a little of Homer's First Iliad." As he does not say, we can only guess whether he took his Homer in the original or through a translation. With Latin we know that he was on intimate terms, even without the evidence of his Scottish medical degree. While at Newport he writes:

I stayed at home most of the forenoon and read Murcius [Meursius], which I had of Dr. Moffatt, a most luscious piece, from whom all our modern salacious poets have borrowed their thoughts. I did not read this book upon account of its lickerish contents, but only because I knew it to be a piece of excellent good Latin, and I wanted to inform myself of the proper idiom of ye language upon that subject.

On his return to New York he notes that a day

passed away, as many of our days do, unremarked and trifling. I did little more than breakfast, dine and sup. I read some of Homer's twelfth Iliad, and went to the coffee-house in the afternoon.

Back in Philadelphia, he found the September air

very sharp and cold for the season, and a fire was very grateful. I did little but stay at home all day, and employed my time in reading of Homer's Iliad.

His next forenoon was

spent in reading of Shakespear's *Timon of Athens, or Manhater*, a play which tho' not written according to Aristotle's rules, yet abounds with inimitable beauties, peculiar to this excellent author.

With such saddle-bag friends to accompany him, Dr. Hamilton was well prepared to pass judgment upon the casual acquaintances who crossed his path. When he first looked about him in Philadelphia, he

observed several comical, grotesque Phizzes in the inn where I put up, which would have afforded variety of hints for a painter of Hogarth's turn. They talked there upon all subjects,—politicks, religion, and trade,—some tolerably well, but most of them ignorantly.

The next morning the Doctor kept his room, reading Montaigne's *Essays*, "a strange medley of subjects, and particularly entertaining." On Sunday he was asked out to dinner, but found "our table chat was so trivial and trifling that I mention it not. After dinner I read the second volume of *The Adventures of Joseph Andrews*, and thought my time well spent."

Dr. Hamilton, one of the most entertaining of American travellers, appears to advantage even beside the urbanity of Byrd and the sprightliness of Mrs. Knight. Bent upon no special errand, he observed freely, and all the more so, one suspects, because of his detachment. Such a quality was not so easy during the next generation, when the wars between the French and English in America, the beginnings of colonial, and then national, pride, the growth of natural science, and the coming of the romantic spirit of solitude and love of nature furnished new motives. Then travelling became a fad, a profession, a duty, and led to the production of an extensive literature which may more properly be discussed with the work of men who were no longer colonials but citizens of the new republic.

# CHAPTER II

# The Historians, 1607–1783

"IN these five moneths of my continuance here," wrote John Pory, of Virginia, in 1619, "there have come at one time or another eleven sails of ships into this river; but fraighted more with ignorance, than with any other marchansize." The writer was a Cambridge graduate, a man of good standing in England, and had crossed the Atlantic to find that Virginia was not the Virginia of his dreams. Ten years earlier all the incoming ships brought well-born adventurers to Jamestown; now they held only those who intended to produce tobacco. Henceforth the future of the colony was with those who could clear the forests, establish plantations, and withstand the agues of the mosquito-infested lowlands. The leaves of fate for Virginia were not to be thumbed in a book. They stood broad and strong over the rich bottom-lands, where the summer sun seemed to the onlooker to deck their oily surfaces with a coat of silver. In the days of the gentlemen adventurers nine men wrote about the history of the colony; in the days of the tobacco growers a century could not show as many.

The earliest Virginians were full of enthusiasm and wished to tell the coming generations how the colony of Virginia was founded. Their enterprise was popular in England, and he who wrote about it was sure of readers. The men who planted tobacco were prosaic. They were poor men become rich, or well-born men become materialistic, and it was only after many years that any of the forms of culture appeared among them. One of these forms was literature, but it was ever a plant of spindling growth.

The first historian in Virginia, the first in the British colonies, was Captain John Smith. He was twenty-seven years old and a soldier of fortune when he landed at Jamestown in 1607. He was a member of the council, and the council was lawmaker, executive, and judge under the authority of the Company which sent the colony out. According to the enthusiasts who preached colonization three tasks awaited the men of Jamestown: to discover mines as the Spaniards had discovered them in Mexico, to convert the Indians to Christianity, and to plant another England in the New World. The third only was accomplished, and it was accomplished chiefly through the efforts and good sense of Smith.

Of the one hundred and five colonists thirty-five were gentleman adventurers, leaders of the enterprise but useless in the forest. They waited in idleness while labourers built houses and constructed a fort. Then illness came, agues and fluxes, and it seemed that Jamestown would share the fate of Roanoke Island. Smith saved it by turning trader. Going to the Indians with trinkets he secured enough corn to last through the critical years of 1607 to 1609. Some of the high-born adventurers approved of Smith's leadership, but others found him intolerable. He was the son of a Lincolnshire copyholder; and how should he give orders to his betters? Moreover, he was boastful. From mere boyhood he had been seeking his fortune with sword in hand, in France, Italy, and southeastern Europe. He told many stories of what he had done, romantically coloured and tending to proclaim his glory. Posterity does not accept them as true, and we may not be surprised if his companions in the colony found them unbelievable. Thus he had his enemies as well as his friends. In the shifting of parties his own friends became triumphant and Smith was recognized as president for more than a year.

Late in 1609 he returned to England. He had lost the confidence of the Company, and nothing he could do sufficed to regain it. In 1614 he induced some London merchants to send him to the northern coasts with a fishing expedition. While the sailors sought the cod at Monhegan, he sailed along the coast, making an excellent map, and giving names to bays headlands, and rivers. At his request the Prince of Wales gave the name New England to this region, and to New England Smith transferred his affections, seeking support for a colony he wished to plant there. A large expedition was promised, and he received the title "Admirall of New England"; but nothing came of his hopes save the title, which he invariably attached to his name thereafter.

It was evidently by accident that Smith became a historian. In the spring of 1608 Wingfield, one of his opponents at Jamestown, a cousin by marriage to the Earl of Southampton, departed for England, his mind full of his wrongs. Two months later another ship departed, carrying a long letter from Smith to his friends filled with a hopeful account of the colony. This letter was handed about among the members of the Company and late in the year came into the hands of one who had it published with the title, *A True Relation of Such Occurrences and Accidents of Noate as Hath Hapned in Virginia since the First Planting of that Collony*. A preface explained: "Somewhat more was by him written, which being as I thought (fit to be private) I would not adventure to make it publicke." The *True Relation* is the first printed American book, and of all Smith's writings it is the one which posterity most esteems. It is not boastful, or controversial, although it is very personal. The style is direct, vivid, and generally simple. It was well received, and seems to have awakened literary ambitions in its author.

Smith's second effort was made in 1612, when he published *A Map of Virginia. With a Description of the Countrey*. It contained a good map of the shores of the Chesapeake Bay, and an account of the natural history of Virginia, together with supplementary chapters on events in the colony from June, 1608, to the end of 1609. These accounts were written by some of his friends and are in his praise. Smith calls them "examinations" and had them taken down while their authors were in London. They were evidently prepared to revive his waning fortunes. In 1616, after his return from New England, he published *A Description of New England*, and in 1620 *New Englands Trials*, a tract on the fisheries. The *Trials* was brought down to date in 1622, and an account of the colony at Plymouth was included in it.

Smith was now a confirmed hack writer. Possibly he had Purchas and Hakluyt in mind when in 1624 he gave to the world a book containing all that he knew about Virginia. It was a narrative drawn from several sources. First, he used his own works, and when they were exhausted he reproduced, or culled from, any relation he had at hand. The whole bore the title *The Generall Historie of Virginia, New-England, and the Summer Isles*. Relatively an unimportant part of it is written by Smith, but he does not pretend to have written the parts he did not write. Three other books completed his literary career. One was called *An Accidence or the Path-way to Experience*, a tract which appeared in 1626 and was reissued several times, not always with the same title. It contained a description of the most observable features of a ship of war, and was designed for young seamen. In 1630 was published *The True Travels, Adventures, and Observations of Captaine Iohn Smith;* and in 1631 came another tract, *Advertisements for the Unexperienced Planters of New-England*. In the year it was published, 21 June, he died in London and was buried in St. Saviour's Church.

Two serious charges of falsification have been brought against Smith, one in connection with the Pocahontas incident, and the other in reference to his *True Travels*. Late in 1607 he made a trading expedition among the Indians and was captured and carried before Powhatan. In the *True Relation* he says he was well treated by the great chief and sent back to Jamestown with all kindness. In the *Generall Historie*, he says that he was about to be slain by the order of Powhatan, when Pocahontas, the chieftain's daughter, threw her arms over his prostrate body and begged for his life so effectively that he was set free. The case is unpleasant for Smith. Not only is the matter omitted from his early works, but it is not mentioned by any other writer of the comparatively large group of contemporary historians of Virginia. Even Hamor, who has much to say about Pocahontas, says nothing about a rescue of Captain Smith. It is conceivable that Smith may have omitted the story from the *True Relation*, lest it should produce a bad effect in England, but he could hardly have kept it from the other settlers at Jamestown, and if the story was once current there, where Pocahontas was well known, it must have been repeated by one of the other writers. By every canon of good criticism we must reject the story. Smith has also been accused of inventing most of the incidents which reflect his glory in the *True Travels*. The charge rests on an alleged misuse of geographical names and on the alleged impossible form of a grant of a coat of arms which Smith said was given him by Sigismund of Transylvania and which was accepted as genuine at the Heralds' College in London. The criticism[1] is very sweeping. If it is well taken our historian degenerated in the latter part of his career to a literary mountebank, but the matter may still await a more judicious investigation than it has yet received.

Turning from Virginia[2] we shall not find any considerable early historian in another colony outside of New England. So far as the region south of the Hudson is concerned idealism in regard to planting colonies exhausted itself with the splendid dreams of Raleigh, Hakluyt, and Edward Sandys. Lord Baltimore and Penn, it is true, attempted to revive it in Maryland and Pennsylvania, but their colonists did not respond to their efforts. These colonies were settled by as practical a class of farmers and traders as those who brought the river bottoms of Virginia under the sway of King Tobacco. Throughout this region literature had to wait on material prosperity before it could find a home.

The New Englanders, however, were idealists from the beginning. This, of course, means that their ministers and leading men were idealists. The majority of the inhabitants were as matter of fact as the majority in any other colony. But the ruling class were committed to the defence of an idealistic theory, and they naturally wished its history preserved. Out of this impulse came several historical works which we could ill afford to lose. All things considered, the Puritans made better historians than the Virginians. It is true their writings abound in superstition, but the superstitions were honestly set down as they were honestly held by the people of the age.

---

[1] Its most notable champion is Mr. Lewis L. Kropf, who asserts that when he communicated a copy of Smith's patent to the Hungarian Heraldic Society it was received with an outburst of laughter. Mr. Kropf pronounces Smith "an impudent forger." See Kropf, Lewis L., *Captain John Smith of Virginia, Notes and Queries*, London, 1890, Seventh Series, vol. ix; also *American Historical Review*, vol. iii, p. 737. A series of letters by the Rev. Edward D. Neill and William Wirt Henry, beginning in the Richmond *Dispatch*, 12 July, 1877, and continuing through several weeks, threshed out this controversy without settling anything.

[2] For the works of the early minor Virginia historians see the Bibliography.

They are, therefore, a necessary part of the history of the times. Moreover, the Puritans, ministers and godly laymen alike, wrote a solid and connected kind of history, and they wrote enough of it to furnish a good picture of the times.

Two minor authors introduce the early group of New England historians. The real name of the first is not known, but his book is called, from its publisher, "Mourt's" *Relation*, a description of affairs at Plymouth from its settlement until the date of publication, 1622. The other book, which appeared in 1624 with the title *Good News from New England*, was by Edward Winslow, one of the leading colonists. They are both short accounts of the daily doings of the men who planted the first permanent New England colony; and they are comparable in style and scope to Smith's *True Relation*, and to any of the other early narrations of Virginia or Maryland. They were written to inform friends in England of the progress of the Pilgrim settlements.

After "Mourt" and Winslow we come to two historians whose excellence entitles them to first rank among the earliest writers of their kind. They wrote quite as much as Captain John Smith, and their writings are more to be esteemed. No one has cast doubts on the accuracy of William Bradford, of Plymouth, or of John Winthrop, of Massachusetts Bay. While not historical compositions as such, their books are, in vivid and sustained human interest, as well as in the power of depicting the conditions of the first settlements, a most adequate and successful kind of history. Each is a journal written by a man who stood at the head of affairs, whose life was so important in his day that we have in it a reflection of the progress of the important things of the colony in which he lived.

William Bradford was one of the *Mayflower* passengers whose sober judgment and integrity had won for him the confidence of the Pilgrims ere they sailed for America. In 1621 he was chosen governor, and he held the office by annual re-election until his death in 1657, except for five years when, as Winthrop said, "by importunity he gat off." He believed it his duty to write about what he had seen and known of the trial and success of the men who, under divine guidance, had made Plymouth a fact. He began to write about 1630 and proceeded at so leisurely a gait that in 1646 he had only reached the year 1621. Four years later his account had come to the year 1646, but here his efforts ceased. His work is known as *The History of Plymouth Plantation*.

Neither Bradford nor his immediate successors made an effort to publish the history. They seem to have considered it a document to be kept for the use of future historians. It was, in fact, freely used for this purpose by his nephew, Nathaniel Morton, in a book called *New England's Memorial*, published in 1669. It remained in the hands of the family of the author for a hundred years and finally came into the possession of the Rev. Thomas Prince, who used it in writing his *Chronological History*, published in 1736. Hutchinson also used it in preparing his *History*. When Prince died he left the manuscript, with many other valuable writings, in the tower of the Old South Church, in Boston. During the Revolution the British troops used this church for a riding school, and Prince's carefully collected library was dispersed. The British gone, such books as could be found were gathered together, but no trace of Bradford's manuscript was discovered. It was long believed to be lost, but it found its way to London, where it came at last to the library of the Bishop of London, and for many years lay unnoticed at Fulham Palace. In 1844 Wilberforce published a book on the Protestant Church in America, in which he referred to the manuscript. Four years later appeared Anderson's *History of the Colonial Church*, an English work, and in it also was a reference to the manuscript. Seven years later two gentlemen of Boston came across the reference in Anderson's book. An investigation was made, and the identity of the Fulham manuscript with Bradford's was completely established. The Bishop of London held that only an act of Parliament could restore it to the place whence it had been taken. He made, however, no objection to a request that the Massachusetts Historical Society be allowed to publish the manuscript, and in 1856 that society gave the world the first complete publication of Bradford's book. It was enriched with annotations by the learned Charles Deane. In 1867 another request was made that the bishop should surrender the manuscript, but the reply was the same as in the first instance. In 1896 the then Bishop of London relented, and Bradford's manuscript was given up without an act of Parliament. It was received in Boston with high honour and much joy on the part of learned men and was placed in the State Library, a chief ornament of the archives of the Commonwealth of Massachusetts. In 1912 it was published in a final and authoritative form by the Massachusetts Historical Society.

*The History of Plymouth Plantation* is a Puritan book in the best sense. Its author was a man of intelligence, whose moderate educational opportunities had been supplemented by earnest and industrious private studies. He knew the Latin, Greek, and Dutch languages, and in his old age taught himself Hebrew so that he might read the oracles of God in the form in which they originally appeared. His *History* is loosely annalistic, but a direct and simple style gives charm, as a sincere faith in Puritanism gives purity, to the entire book. He who would understand the spirit of old Plymouth would do well to read Bradford through.

What Bradford's *History* is to Plymouth, John Winthrop's journal is to the Massachusetts Bay Colony. The author, more than any other man, was the founder of the colony. He was an earnest Puritan, a supporter of the ideas of Hampden and Pym, and by natural ability he was a leader of men. He left Cambridge before graduation, married at seventeen, became a justice of the peace at eighteen, and was soon a man of note in his shire, Suffolk, where he was lord of the manor of Groton. In 1630 he gave up all this, as well as a lucrative position as attorney in the Court of Wards, and threw in his lot with the men who were to settle Massachusetts. He was the colony's first governor, and through annual re-elections served it for twelve years, finally dying in office in 1649. Rev. John Cotton described him as

a governour . . . who has been to us as a brother, not usurping authority over the church; often speaking his advice, and often contradicted, even by young men, and some of low degree; yet not replying, but offering satisfaction also when any supposed offences have arisen; a governour who has been to us as a mother, parent-like distributing his goods to bretheren and neighbours at his first coming; and gently bearing our infirmities without taking notice of them.

The life of John Winthrop was worthy of this tribute in all respects.

Introspection was a Puritan trait, and the first governor at Boston had his share. Early in life he kept a little diary which he called *Experiencia*, a record of very deep spirituality. His letters show that he thought God directed his love and marriage. It was in the spring of 1630 that he embarked for Massachusetts, and while aboard ship, "riding at the Cowes, near the Isle of Wight," on Easter Monday, he began a journal which he kept faithfully until a few months before his death. It is filled with colony affairs, but its title, *A History of New England*, is misleading. It says little about any other colony than that over which the writer ruled, and the form is not that of history proper. Yet it is a valuable record of the life of the time, and presents good expositions of most of the problems of the early colony. While it is not written in so interesting a style as Bradford's book, it is in a fair diary manner, rarely becoming tedious to a reader who has the taste for the fine points of a contemporary document. It is Puritan in a liberal sense. Some New England writers can never forget their peculiar type of religion; but Winthrop discusses business matters like a man of business and public affairs like a man accustomed to weigh the fortunes of state in an even scale.

Like the early Virginia historians, Bradford and Winthrop were English-bred. Their culture was English and it was superior to that which the succeeding generation, born in America, could be expected to have. Two historians, however, Captain Edward Johnson and Nathaniel Morton, stand between them and the historians who are of purely American birth and training. Both were born in England, but they arrived in Massachusetts at such an early age that they were colony-trained to all intents and purposes.

Johnson was a man of strong natural traits, self-made, and representing the middle class in colonial society. He was a ship-wright by trade, and showed ability in leadership. He was the chief founder of the town of Woburn and its representative in the General Court. He gave loyal allegiance to the ministers, and was dazzled by their piety and learning. Puritanism offered him complete satisfaction, and he willingly accepted its dogmas. "You are not set up for tolerating times!" he exclaimed in the face of certain signs that the hold of the system was weakening. To preserve the influence of the early doctrines he wrote *Wonder-Working Providences of Zion's Saviour in New England*, published in 1654. We read it to-day to learn to what degrees of credulity the early New Englanders went in their acceptance of the power of the supernatural over human affairs. To the author and his contemporaries the book was plain history, a record of the actualities of life. The chief merit of the *Providences* for those who rightly value a human document is that it is a picture of early Puritan life as seen by an average man. Winthrop and Bradford lived at the centre of things. The problems of governors and assemblies concerned them. Johnson was interested in the planting of churches, the life of the towns, and the affairs of ordinary people, and it has been well said that while he "shows little precision in anything but his creed; yet his book is one of the most curious that an inquirer into the manners and institutions of our fathers can peruse."[1]

Nathaniel Morton was a trusted nephew of Governor Bradford and became secretary of the Plymouth colony. Possessed of fair ability, he was long a man of note and a preserver of Plymouth tradition. In 1669 he published, as we have seen, *New England's Memorial*, a history of the colony. For the early years he drew directly on his uncle's book, transcribing large portions of it. Until the discovery of the Fulham manuscript, Morton's book was the best source for Bradford's text. The part which was concerned with the years following Bradford was written by Morton himself, and is meagre and disappointing, but Johnson and he were long the standard historians for the average New Englander. They may be considered the last of the early group, and in their manner and purposes they looked forward to the second group, men who were either born in America or who arrived after the American ideals were well enough formed to master the newcomers.

The second group, then, was American in a sense unknown to the first group. Its subjects were events rooted in American life, and save as American government and conditions were

[1] Winthrop, *History of New England*, ed. Savage, vol. I, p. 100 n.

dependent on relations with the mother country, this phase of history had no relation to England. It opened, naturally, with treatments of the most striking incidents of the day, Indian wars and internal disorders. Here were struggles calling for the best efforts of the settlers, struggles in which horrors and signal victories had followed one another in dramatic swiftness. Historians arose to write about them with marked ability; and their books were read far and wide. Then a generation followed during which the colonies grew in wealth and refinement. A leisure class was developed, the struggles of the assemblies against the king's prerogative gradually caused the formation of colony parties with colony ideals and aspirations, and in due time men appeared who undertook to tell the stories of colony development. These men belong to the later colonial period. In reflection and the power of dealing with materials, they are superior to the mere depicters of episodes. If their works are less readable, it must be remembered that their tasks are more difficult. It is easier to describe the Deerfield raid and the fate of the captured inhabitants than to trace the development of a political unit.

New England did not have the only Indian wars in America, but she alone had worthy historians of them. The struggles of 1622 and 1642 in Virginia, the Tuscarora War in North Carolina, and the Yemassee War in South Carolina, to say nothing of the wars of the Iroquois in New York, were as worthy of historical description as the struggle known as King Philip's War in New England, but they found no pen to describe them for the contemporary public. Bacon's rebellion in Virginia was well narrated for posterity, but the narratives long remained in manuscript; and the important struggles between South Carolina and Georgia on the one side and Spanish Florida on the other have not to this day been made the subjects of adequate treatment in a readable form.

In New England, on the other hand, historical effort for popular information was fairly abundant. Seven men appeared to describe the horrors of savage warfare, filling their pages with thrilling stories which the public read with eagerness. The first was Captain John Mason, whose *History of the Pequot War*, based upon his own experience, was published in 1677. It is written in cold-blooded indifference to the feelings of compassion, and we shiver today at the vengeance of the whites; but it raised no qualms in the men of the seventeenth century, who were brought up on sterner ideas. In the same year was published the Rev. William Hubbard's *Narrative of the Troubles with the Indians of New England*. Like the author's *History of New England*, it abounds in errors, but it was widely read. It appeared as Philip's War was drawing to a close, at a time when the people were especially excited against the savages. It had a worthy companion in Benjamin Church's *Entertaining Passages Relating to Philip's War*, published in 1716, a powerful book by one who took a leading part in the struggle he describes. Another work that was widely read was Samuel Penhallow's *Wars of New England with the Eastern Indians*, 1726. The author was chief justice of New Hampshire.

With 1690, when the French and Indian wars began, a new kind of warfare fell on the colonies. Bands of Indians, sometimes accompanied by Frenchmen, came out of Canada, destroyed isolated settlements, and escaped to the north with large trains of captives. The victims suffered much from the strenuous marches of their captors, and from actual cruelty. Most of them were redeemed after years of exile, and they returned with thrilling stories in their mouths. Here was a new field for the historian, and it was well worked.[1]

A distinct place must be reserved for Daniel Gookin, a Virginia Puritan who moved to Massachusetts to escape the persecutions of Governor Berkeley. He was made superintendent of Indians in his new home and showed a humane and intelligent interest in the natives that entitles him to rank with John Eliot. The retaliation of the whites in Philip's War grieved him sorely, but the tide of wrath was so strong that his protests only made him unpopular. He wrote two books on the Indians, *Historical Collections of the Indians in New England*, written in 1674 (published 1792), and *The Doings and Sufferings of the Christian Indians*, completed in 1677 (published 1836). Gookin also wrote a *History of New England* which remained in manuscript and was unhappily destroyed without having been published. The author was a man of great breadth of mind and not deeply touched by the

[1] See also Book I, Chap. I.

narrow ecclesiasticism of the day. He was also in a position to know about the public events of his time. His history of New England, had it been published, must have given us an important view of the subject.

Another historian of the Indians was Dr. Cadwallader Colden, a man of learning and high position in Philadelphia and New York. He settled in New York in 1710, where he enjoyed the confidence of the authorities and was promoted to important offices. He had a deep interest in the superior organization of the Iroquois and wrote about them in his *History of the Five Indian Nations* (1727–47). Through great industry he collected a large amount of valuable information about these Indians, and the book is still a mine of facts, although the research of later times has rendered many of its statements unsatisfactory. In this connection mention should be made of John Lawson's *History of North Carolina*, published first as *New Voyage to Carolina* in 1709. It was written by a man of excellent sense who had opportunity to know the Indians and natural resources of North Carolina, but it contains little about civil affairs. Lawson was English born and bred, and lived only a few years after his arrival, but he had a right to the name "American," since he gave his life to the service of the colony. He was murdered by the Indians in 1711.

It seems certain that most of the books on the Indians were written in answer to a popular demand. The same could not be said of the political histories, which began to appear in the first half of the eighteenth century. The impulse behind such works is perhaps best stated in the words of Stith, of Virginia, who said that he began to write his history as "a noble and elegant entertainment for my vacant hours, which it is not in my power to employ more to my own satisfaction, or the use and benefit of my country." Few of the historians of this class had a large number of readers. Two wrote about Virginia, Robert Beverley and the Rev. William Stith. The former was a wealthy planter who saw while in London a poor account of the colony by the British historian and pamphleteer, John Oldmixon, and undertook to write a better. His book, *A History of Virginia* (1705), was hastily prepared without any study of documents or other respectable sources. Its chief value lies in the shrewd and just observations the author made on Virginia life and history out of his own knowledge. Stith was connected with prominent persons in the colony and had been president of William and Mary College. His *History of the First Discovery and Settlement of Virginia* was published in 1747. The volume brought the story of the colony down to the fall of the London Company, 1624. It was accurate and based on the records of the Company, and is one the most modern of our colonial histories in its method. But Stith had no sense of proportion. His book was so full of details that his subscribers found it unreadable and failed to continue their support. No second part was published.

For the middle colonies we have two histories still remembered by posterity, a *History of New York* (1757), by William Smith and a *History of New Jersey* (1765) by Samuel Smith. The author of the former was a high official in New York and had much ability. He was a tory, and the unpopularity he acquired on that account was shared by his book. Unable to read Dutch, he had an inadequate idea of the early history of the colony; but for the English period the book has maintained an honourable position to this day. It is well written and, making due allowances, it is equal to the standard of historical literature in England before Hume. Samuel Smith was an industrious and conscientious Quaker, and his history was written from the point of view of the middle class of society. It is still regarded as reliable but the style is heavy.

In New England during this period political history did not engage the attention of historians as much as Indian history. Besides Gookin, whose unpublished history has been mentioned, three men deserve notice. One was the already noticed Rev. William Hubbard, whose *General History of New England* did not find a publisher until 1815. The earlier part is taken with the slightest amount of change from Morton's *Memorial* and Winthrop's journal. After these two sources are exhausted the book becomes meagre and inaccurate.

A much better writer was the Rev. Thomas Prince, of Boston, whom we have encountered in connection with Bradford's manuscript. The preservation of documents and rare pamphlets was to him a labour of love, and by industry he collected a large library of valuable materials. Many of the books are now preserved in the Boston Public Library. Prince's devotion to history is recognized in the name of the Prince Society, of Boston, one of the most honoured of American historical organizations. The result of his efforts at writing history was a *Chronological History of New England, in the Form of Annals*, the first volume of which appeared in 1736. It began with the creation of man on the sixth day and proceeded rapidly to the landing of the Pilgrims at Plymouth. Then it moved with great detail through the events of the succeeding decade, until a hint from the publisher that the book was becoming too large brought it to an end with 7 September, 1630. The poor sale of the volume discouraged the author, who did not resume his work until 1755. He then began a continuation in serial parts at sixpence each; but the sale was so small that he gave up the project after three numbers had been issued.

Prince's work is a delight to the genealogist and the antiquarian, for precision marks every step he took.

"I cite my vouchers to every passage," he said, "and I have done my utmost, first to find out the truth, and then to relate it in the clearest order. I have laboured after accuracy; and yet I dare not say that I am without mistake; nor do I desire the reader to conceal any he may possibly find."

No modern scientific historian could speak better. If Prince lacked literary ability, the want was made up in his strict sense of accuracy; and we should remember that it is rare that the world has a man who is endowed with both characteristics.

Both Hubbard and Prince were ministers and wrote with a full sense of the importance of the churches in the New England life. Their outlook was biased, although not intentionally so. From them we turn at the very close of the colonial period to a New England historian as free from this influence as Colden or William Smith. Thomas Hutchinson was descended from Mrs. Anne Hutchinson, who was exiled from Massachusetts in 1638 because she defied the Puritan hierarchy, and he was quite free from religious narrowness. Born in 1711, he graduated from Harvard in 1727 and began a prosperous career as a merchant. He won the confidence of the Boston people, who sent him to the assembly, where he distinguished himself by opposing the issue of paper money. He was for a long time the most popular man in the colony, and he was promoted from one high office to another, becoming lieutenant-governor in 1758, chief justice in 1760, acting governor in 1769, and governor in 1771.

Hutchinson loved Massachusetts, but he was intellectually a conservative, and he did not accept the theory on which the colonists rested their resistance to the king and Parliament. He wished to preserve the Empire undivided, and hoped that some plan might be found by which America might have home rule without renouncing the name British. He was opposed in principle to the Stamp Act, but disapproved of the violence with which it was received. A Boston mob, angered by false reports against him, wrecked his house, destroyed his furniture, and scattered his books and papers through the streets. The assembly paid him for the property loss, but he never recovered the good will of Boston. He tried to reconcile king and colony, but neither was in a mood to be reconciled. Early in 1774 he went to England, giving place to General Gage. He was well received, and the king allowed him a handsome pension, while Oxford conferred upon him the degree of *Doctor Civilis Juris*. But as the months passed and the war became inevitable, Hutchinson's pleas for peace made him unpopular. King, ministers, and society generally were for punishing the disobedient colonies. The protests of the exiled governor became weaker and weaker, and he finally retired from public notice. With his family he led an unhappy existence in London until his death in 1780.

In the eighteenth century history was an honored branch of literature. Hume, who published his great history between 1754 and 1761, was made independent by the sales, while Robertson, who was just coming into his fame, found himself both flattered and wealthy. History had not yet fallen into the hands of those who were to reduce it to a dull statement of facts which nobody reads except those who wish to incorporate them in other statements of fact. Nor had the world yet been submerged by the modern deluge of imaginative literature. It was in 1764, while Hume and Robertson were at the height of their freshly won fame, that Hutchinson published the first volume of his *History of the Colony of Massachusetts Bay*. The second was in preparation when the Stamp Act mob destroyed

the house of the author.  Among the debris recovered from
the streets was the soiled manuscript of this volume.  It was
completed and published in 1767.  The third volume was
not written until the governor had taken up his residence in
London, and it was not published until 1828.  Hutchinson's
*History* is not faultless.  He was bitterly denounced by Otis
and Samuel Adams, and he did not show an ability to appreciate them.  He left untouched some important phases of
Massachusetts history, and was indifferent to social and industrial changes.  In spite of these faults, for which excuses can
be made, he was the best American historian of his time.  He
treated narrative history in a philosophical manner and wrote
simple and natural sentences whose charm endures to this
day.  After he left our shore many a year passed before we
had a historian who could equal him in the power to understand
and narrate the story of American political life.

## CHAPTER III

# The Puritan Divines, 1620–1720

NEW ENGLAND Puritanism—like the greater movement of which it was so characteristic an offshoot—is one of the fascinating puzzles in the history of the English people. It phrased its aspirations in so strange a dialect, and interpreted its programme in such esoteric terms, that it appears almost like an alien episode in the records of a practical race. No other phase of Anglo-Saxon civilization seems so singularly remote from every-day reality, so little leavened by natural human impulses and promptings. Certain generations of Englishmen, seemingly for no sufficient reason, yielded their intellects to a rigid system of dogmatic theology, and surrendered their freedom to the letter of the Hebrew Scriptures; and in endeavouring to conform their institutions as well as their daily actions to self-imposed authorities, they produced a social order that fills with amazement other generations of Englishmen who have broken with that order. Strange, perverted, scarce intelligible beings those old Puritans seem to us—mere crabbed theologians disputing endlessly over Calvinistic dogma, or chilling the marrow of honest men and women with their tales of hell-fire. And we should be inclined to dismiss them as curious eccentricities were it not for the amazing fact that those old preachers were not mere accidents or by-products, but the very heart and passion of the times. If they were listened to gladly, it was because they uttered what many were thinking; if they were followed through tribulation and sacrifice by multitudes, it was because the way which they pointed out seemed to the best intelligence of their hearers the divinely approved path, which, if faithfully followed, must lead society out of the present welter of sin and misery and misrule into a nobler state. For the moment religion and statecraft were merged in the thought of Englishmen; and it was because the Puritan ministers were statesmen as well as theologians—the political quite as much as the religious leaders—that the difficult task of social guidance rested for those generations with the divines. How they conducted themselves in that serious business, what account they rendered of their stewardship, becomes therefore a question which the historian may not neglect.

It was to set up a Kingdom of God on earth that the Puritan leaders came to America; and the phrase should enlighten us concerning their deeper purpose. But no sooner was their work well under way than the conception of a kingdom of God tended to merge in the newer conception of a commonwealth of Christ, and this in turn found itself confronted by the still newer conception of a commonwealth of free citizens; and it is the painful wrestling with these changing ideals, with all that was implied in each to the several classes and institutions of society, that gives historical significance to the crabbed writings of the New England divines. As political thinkers they inherited a wealth of political speculation, accumulated during more than a hundred years of extraordinary intellectual activity; and if we would understand the matter as well as the manner of their disputations, we must put ourselves to the trouble of translating the obsolete phraseology into modern equivalents, and conceive of Puritanism as the expression of current English radicalism. It was the English beginning of the great modern social readjustment which goes under the name of the democratic revolution; and its total history, covering a long period of a hundred and forty years, constitutes a noble chapter in the struggle for human freedom. If the evolution of modern society falls into two broad phases, the disintegration of the old caste society into free citizens, and the regrouping of the free citizens into a new social democracy, the significance of Puritanism becomes clear—it was a disruptive force that served to destroy the cohesion of the ancient caste solidarity resolving society into its individual members. It was the rebellion of the many against the overlordship of the few; a rebellion that proposed to coerce the freedom of men by the law of God alone; a challenge of existing institutions and regnant philosophies, which if successful could not fail to bring about profound social changes.

Necessarily, therefore, the Puritan reformation was allied with political reformation, and the period of ecclesiastical reorganization was equally a period of political reorganization. Modern political parties were thrown up out of the ferment of religious dispute, and the inevitable cleavages of Puritan thought were determined broadly by the cleavages of political thought. The three parties in the ecclesiastical field, Anglican, Presbyterian, and Independent, reflected the current political ideals of tory, whig, and democrat. The first was monarchical in principle, the ecclesiastical expression of tory absolutism. It gathered to its support the hereditary masters of society, who held that there should be one authoritative church, to which every subject of the crown must belong, to the support of which all must contribute, and in the governance of which only the appointed hierarchy should share. The second party was aristocratic in principle, the expression of the rising ideal of whiggery, or government by property through the instrumentality of landed gentlemen. Country squires and prosperous London citizens desired a church system which they could control, and this system they discovered in Presbyterianism, newly brought over from Geneva, which gave the control of the parish to the eldership, composed of responsible gentlemen who should serve as trustees for the good of the whole. The third party was more or less consciously democratic in principle, the expression of the newly awakened aspirations of the social underling. The poor man wanted to be ruled neither by bishops nor by gentlemen, but preferred to club with the like-minded of his own class, and set up an independent church along democratic lines. That was the true Christian church, he believed, which withdrew from all communion with sinners and established a "Congregation of the Saints"; and so he called himself a Separatist. But whatever name he might call himself by, he was at bottom a democrat who demanded the right of self-government in the church, and who, when times were ripe, would assuredly assert the greater right of self-government in the state.

Broadly speaking, the Anglicans kept the situation pretty

2

well in hand up to the accession of Charles I. During the long disputes between Charles and the Parliament, the rising party of Presbyterians was organizing its forces to break the rule of the bishops, and the early years of Parliamentary sovereignty marked the culmination of the middle period, dominated by the Presbyterian ideal. But no sooner was the ruthless hand of tory absolutism struck down than the long gathering forces of social discontent came to a head and broke with the moderate party of Presbyterian reformers; whereupon there followed the real Puritan revolution which had been preparing since the days of Wyclif. The Separatists seized control of Parliament and set about the work of erecting a government that should be a commonwealth of free citizens; the voice of the democratic underling, for the first time in English history, was listened to in the national councils, and the army of the democrat stood ready to enforce his demands with the sword. But unfortunately the strong wine went to the head; unbalanced schismatics endeavoured to set up impossible Utopias; zeal outran wisdom; and the Puritan movement broke at last into a thousand sects and went to pieces. But not before its real work was done; not before the political principles, which hitherto had been obscurely entangled in theological disputation, were set free and held up to the view of Englishmen; not before the new democratic philosophy had clarified its fundamental principle, namely, that the individual both as Christian and citizen derives from nature certain inalienable rights which every church and every government is bound to respect.

It was during the decade of the thirties, at the moment when Presbyterianism was in the ascendancy, that the Puritan migration to New England took place; and the leaders of that notable movement were effectively Presbyterian in sympathies and policies. Possessed of ample means and of good social position, they were liberals rather than radicals, and they shared the common Presbyterian hope of capturing the ecclesiastical establishment as a whole instead of separating from it. But they had been preceded to America by the Plymouth congregation, a body of low-born Separatists, who had set up a church upon frankly democratic principles. In an unfortunate moment for Presbyterianism, the pioneer church at Salem came under the influence of the Plymouth example, and the following year, when the main body of Puritans came over with Winthrop, they fell in with the Salem example and set up the new churches on the Congregational principle, as seeming to provide the most suitable form for the development of a theocracy. The inconsistency of an arrangement by which an aristocratic leadership accepted a democratic church organization was obscured for the moment by the unanimity of ministers and congregation; but it was clearly perceived by the Presbyterians of the old country, and it was to prove the source of much contention in later years.

Out of this fundamental inconsistency sprang a large part of the literature with which we are concerned in the present chapter. The ministers, as the spokesmen of New England, soon found themselves embroiled in controversy. During the first ten years or more the controversy lay between New England and old England Puritans, and the burden upon the former was to prove to the satisfaction of English Presbyterianism that the "Congregational way" was not democratic Separatism, with its low stigma of Brownism, but aristocratic Presbyterianism. During the later years, when Presbyterianism had been definitely overthrown in England, the controversy lay between the theocratic hierarchy—which after the year 1637 was the dominant power—and the dissenting democracy; the former seeking to Presbyterianize the church away from its primitive Congregationalism, the latter seeking to maintain the purity of the Plymouth ideal. In dealing with the several ministers, therefore, we shall divide them into the emigrant generation and the native generations, and set the aristocratic Presbyterians over against the democratic Congregationalists, endeavouring to understand the chief points at issue between them.

The most authoritative representative of the ideals of the middle period of Puritanism—its aristocratic conservatism in the guise of theocratic polities—was the celebrated John Cotton, first Teacher to the church at Boston. Of good family and sound university training, he was both a notable theologian and a courteous gentleman. "Twelve hours in a day he commonly studied, and would call that a scholar's day," his grandson reported of him; and his learned eloquence was universally admired by a generation devoted to solid argumentative discourse. When he ascended the pulpit on Sundays and lecture days, he carried thither not only the wisdom of his beloved master Calvin but the whole Puritan theology to buttress his theses. Good men were drawn to him irresistibly by his sweetness of temper, and evil men were overawed by his venerable aspect. For all his severe learning he was a lovable man, with white hair framing a face that must have been nobly chiselled, gentle-voiced, courteous, tactful, by nature "a tolerant man," than whom none "did more placidly bear a dissentient," or more gladly discover a friend in an antagonist. If his tactful bending before opposition, or his fondness for intellectual subtleties, drew from his grandson the appellation "a most excellent casuist," we must not therefore conclude that he served the cause of truth less devotedly than the cause of party.

For in his mildly persistent way John Cotton was a revolutionist. A noble ideal haunted his thought, as Utopian as any in the long roll of Utopian dreams—the ideal of a Christian theocracy which should supersede the unchristian government which Englishmen had lived under hitherto. A devout scripturist, he accepted the Hebrew Bible as the final word of God, not to be played fast and loose with but to be received as a rule of universal application, perfect to the last word and least injunction. The sufficiency of the Scriptures to social needs was an axiom in his philosophy; "the more any law smells of man the more unprofitable," he asserted in his proposed draft of laws; and at another time he exclaimed, "*Scripturae plenitudinem adoro.*" He chose exile and the leaving of his beautiful English church rather than yield to what he regarded as the unscriptural practices of Laud, and now that he was come to a new land where a fresh beginning was to be made, was it not his Christian duty to "endeavour after a *theocracy*, as near as might be, to that which was the glory of Israel, the 'peculiar people'"? The old common law must be superseded by the Mosaic dispensation, the priest must be set above the magistrate, the citizen of the commonwealth must become the subject of Jehovah, the sovereignty of the state must yield to the sovereignty of God.

It was a frankly aristocratic world in which John Cotton was bred, and if he disliked the plebeian ways of the Plymouth democracy equally with the Brownist tendencies of Plymouth Congregationalism, it was because they smacked too much of popular sovereignty to please him. And when he found himself confronted by signs of democratic unrest in Boston his course of action seemed to him clear. The desire for liberty he regarded as the sinful prompting of the natural man, a godless denial of the righteous authority of the divinely appointed rulers. If democracy were indeed a Christian form of government, was it not strange that divine wisdom should have overlooked so significant a fact? In all the history of the chosen people nowhere did God designate the democratic as the perfect type, but the theocratic; was He now to be set right by sinful men who courted popularity by stirring the dirt in the bottom of depraved hearts? To a scripturist the logic of his argument was convincing:

It is better that the commonwealth be fashioned to the setting forth of God's house, which is his church: than to accomodate the church frame to the civill state. Democracy, I do not conceyve that ever God did ordeyne as a fit government eyther for church or commonwealth. If the people be governors, who shall be governed? As for monarchy, and aristocracy, they are both of them clearly approoved, and directed in scripture, yet so as referreth the soveraigntie to himselfe, and setteth up Theocracy in both, as the best forme of government in the commonwealth, as well as in the church.[1]

Holding to such views, the duty devolving upon him was plain—to check in every way the drift towards a more democratic organization, and to prove to old-world critics that the evil reports of the growing Brownism in New England, which were spreading among the English Presbyterians, were without foundation. The first he sought to accomplish by the strengthening of the theocratic principle in practice, busying himself in a thousand practical ways to induce the people to accept the patriarchal rulership of the ministers and elders, in accordance with the "law of Moses, his Judicials"; the second he sought to accomplish by proving, under sound scriptural authority, the orthodoxy of the New England way. His chief effort in this latter field was his celebrated work, *The Way of the Con-*

[1] Letter to Lord Say and Sele, Hutchinson, *Hist. of Mass. Bay Colony*, vol. I. p. 497.

*gregational Churches Cleared;* a treatise crammed, in the opinion of an admirer, with "most practical Soul-searching, Soul-saving, and Soul-solacing Divinitie," "not Magisterially laid down, but friendly debated by Scripture, and argumentatively disputed out to the utmost inch of ground." The partisan purpose of the book was to prove that Congregationalism, as practised in New England, was nearer akin to aristocratic Presbyterianism than to democratic Brownism; and of this purpose he speaks frankly:

Neither is it the Scope of my whole Book, to give the people a share in the Government of the Church. . . . Nay further, there be that blame the Book for the other Extreme, That it placeth the Government of the Church not at all in the hands of the People, but of the Presbyterie.[1]

Out of this same theocratic root sprang the well-known dispute with Roger Williams concerning toleration. Not freedom to follow the ways of sin, but freedom to follow the law of God—this was Cotton's restriction upon the "natural liberties" of the subject of Jehovah. There must be freedom of conscience if it be under no error, but not otherwise; for if freedom be permitted to all sinful errors, how shall the will of God prevail on earth? In this matter of toleration of conscience, it is clear enough today that the eyes of the great theocrat, "so *piercing* and *heavenly* (in other and precious Truths of God)"—as Roger Williams acknowledged—were for the moment sadly "over-clouded and bloud-shotten." But for this the age rather than the man was to blame. It was no fault of John Cotton's that he was the product of a generation still resting under the shadow of absolutism, unable to comprehend the more democratic philosophy of the generation of Roger Williams. He reasoned according to his light; and if he was convinced that the light which shone to him was a divine torch, he proved himself thereby a sound Puritan if not a good Christian.

The native sweetness and humanity of Cotton's character, despite his rigid theocratic principles, comes out pleasantly when the great preacher is set over against the caustic lawyer‐

[1] Part II, p. 15.

minister and wit, Nathaniel Ward of Ipswich, author of the strange little book, *The Simple Cobbler of Aggawam*, and chief compiler of the celebrated *Body of Liberties*. Born nearly two-score years before Roger Williams, he was well advanced in his sixties when he set foot in the new world, and upwards of seventy when he wrote the *Simple Cobbler*. More completely than any of his emigrant brethren he belonged to the late Renaissance world, which lingered on into the reigns of James and Charles, zealously cultivating its quaint garden of letters, coddling its odd phrases, and caring more for clever conceits than for solid thought. Faithful disciple of Calvin though he was, there was in him a rich sap of mind, which, fermented by long observation and much travel, made him the raciest of wits, and doubtless the most delightful of companions over a respectable Puritan bottle. "I have only Two Comforts to Live upon," Increase Mather reported him as saying; "The one is in the Perfections of Christ; The other is in The Imperfections of all Christians."

It is the caustic criticism of female fashions, and the sharp attack upon all tolerationists who would "hang God's Bible at the Devil's girdle," that have caught the attention of later readers of the *Simple Cobbler;* but it was as a "subtile statesman" that Ward impressed himself upon his own generation, and it is certainly the political philosophy which gives significance to his brilliant essay. Trained in the law before he forsook it for the ministry, he had thought seriously upon political questions, and his conclusions hit to a nicety the principles which the moderate Presbyterians in Parliament were developing to offset the Stuart encroachments. The insufficiency of the old checks and balances to withstand the stress of partisanship was daily becoming more evident as the struggle went forward. There must be an overhauling of the fundamental law; the neutral zones must be charted and the several rights and privileges exactly delimited. What was needed was a written constitution. Hitherto God "hath taken order, that ill Prerogatives, gotten by the Sword, should in time be fetcht home by the Dagger, if nothing else will doe it: Yet I trust there is both day and means to intervent this bargaine." To preserve a just balance between rival interests, and to bring all parties to a realization of their responsibility to God, were

the difficult problems with which Ward's crotchety lucubrations mainly concern themselves.

Authority must have power to make and keep people honest;
People, honesty to obey Authority; both, a joynt-Councell to keep
both safe.   Moral Lawes, Royall Prerogatives, Popular Liberties,
are not of Mans making or giving, but Gods: Man is but to measure
them out by Gods Rule: which if mans wisdome cannot reach,
Mans experience must mend:   And these Essentials, must not be
Ephorized or Tribuned by one or a few Mens discretion, but lineally
sanctioned by Supreame Councels.   In *pro-re-nascent* occurrences,
which cannot be foreseen; Diets, Parliaments, Senates, or account-
able Commissions, must have power to consult and execute against
intersilient dangers and flagitious crimes prohibited by the light of
Nature:   Yet it were good if States would let People know so
much beforehand, by some safe woven *manifesto*, that grosse Delin-
quents may tell no tales of Anchors and Buoyes, nor palliate their
presumptions with pretense of ignorance.   I know no difference
in these Essentials, between Monarchies, Aristocracies, or Demo-
cracies. . . .

He is a good King that undoes not his Subjects by any one of
his unlimited Prerogatives: and they are a good People, that undoe
not their Prince, by any one of their unbounded Liberties, be they
the very least.   I am sure either may, and I am sure neither would
be trusted, how good soever.   Stories tell us in effect, though not
in termes, that over-risen Kings, have been the next evills to the
world, unto fallen Angels; and that over-franchised people, are
devills with smooth snaffles in their mouthes . . . I have a long
while thought it very possible, in a time of Peace . . . for disert
Statesmen, to cut an exquisite thred between Kings Prerogatives,
and Subjects Liberties of all sorts, so as *Caesar* might have his due
and People their share, without such sharpe disputes.   Good
Casuists would case it, and case it, part it, and part it; now it, and
then it, punctually.

Nathaniel Ward was no democrat and therefore no Con-
gregationalist.   "For Church work, I am neither Presbyterian,
nor plebsbyterian, but an Interpendent," he said of himself.
But his Interpendency was only an individualistic twist of
Presbyterianism.   For the new radicals who were rising out
of the turmoil of revolution, he had only contempt; and for their
new-fangled notion of toleration, and talk of popular liberties,

he felt the righteous indignation of the conservative who
desires no altering of the fundamental arrangements of society.
Only the Word of God could justify change; and so when he
was commissioned to write a body of liberties for the new commonwealth, he presented as harsh and rigid a code as the sternest theocrat could have wished, a strange compound of the
brutalities of the old common law and the severities of the
Mosaic rule.   He was too old a man to fit into the new ways—
a fact which he recognized by returning to England to die,
leaving behind him as a warning to Congregationalism the
pithy quatrain:

> The upper world shall Rule,
>   While Stars will run their race:
> The nether world obey,
>   While People keep their place.

The more one reads in the literature of early New England
the more one feels oneself in the company of men who were
led by visions, and fed upon Utopian dreams.   It was a day
and a world of idealists, and of this number was John Eliot,
saintly apostle to the Indians, who, in the midst of his missionary
dreams and the arduous labours of supplying the bread of
life to his native converts, found time to fashion his brick for
the erection of that temple which the Puritans of the Protectorate were dreaming of.   The idols had been broken under the
hammer of Cromwell; the malevolent powers that so long had
held sway at last were brought low; it remained now only for
the people of God to enter into a solemn covenant to establish
a commonwealth after the true divine model.   That no mistake
should be made in so important a matter, John Eliot sent out
of the American wilderness the plan of a Christian Utopia,
sanctioned by Mosaic example and buttressed at every point
by chapter and verse, which he urged upon the people of
England as a suitable guide to their feet.

Naked theocracy is nowhere more uncompromisingly
delineated than in the pages of *The Christian Commonwealth*.
At the base of Eliot's political thinking were the two germinal
conceptions which animated his theocratic brethren generally:
the conception that Christ is King of Kings, before whom all
earthly authority must bow, and the conception that the

Scriptures alone contain the law of God. "There is undoubtedly a forme of civil Government instituted by God
himself in the holy Scriptures. . . . We should derogate from
the sufficiency and perfection of the Scriptures, if we should
deny it." From these main premises he deduced a system that
is altogether remarkable for its thorough-going simplicity.
Since the law has been declared once for all, perfect and complete, there is no need for a legislative branch of government;
and since Christ is the sole overlord and king, there is no need
for an earthly head of the state; it remains only to provide a
competent magisterial system to hear causes and adjudicate
differences. Society is concerned wholly with duties and not
at all with rights; government therefore begins and ends with
the magistrate. In order to secure an adequate magis-
tracy, Eliot proposed to divide society into groups of tens, fifties,
hundreds, and thousands, each of which should choose its rulers,
who in turn should choose their representatives in the higher
councils; and so there was evolved an ascending series of
magistrates until the supreme council of the nation was reached,
the decisions of which should be final.

The duties of all the Rulers of the civil part of the Kingdom of
Christ, are as followeth . . . to govern the people in the orderly and
seasonable practice of all the Commanders of God, in actions liable
to Political observations, whether of piety and love to God, or of
justice, and love to man with peace.

Far removed as *The Christian Commonwealth* was from the
saner thought of the Army democrats, it is the logical culmination of all theocratic dreams. The ideal of social unity, of
relentless conformity, according to which the rebel is a social
outlaw to be silenced at any cost, dominates this Christian
Utopia as mercilessly as it dominated the policy of Laud.
In setting up King Jesus for King Charles, there was to be no
easing of the yoke upon the rebellious spirit; and in binding
society upon the letter of the Scripture there was to be no room
for the democratic aspirations of the leveller. Curious as this
little work is—testifying rather to the sincerity of Eliot's
Hebraism than to his political intelligence or to his knowledge
of men—it is characteristic of the man who consecrated his

life to the dream of an Indian mission. How little disturbed he was by the perversities and limitations of facts, is revealed anew in the polity which he laid down for his Indian converts:

And this VOW I did solemnly make unto the Lord concerning them; that they being a people without any forme of Government, and now to chuse; I would endeavour with all my might, to bring them to embrace such Government, both civil and Ecclesiastical, as the Lord hath commanded in the holy Scriptures; and to deduce all their Lawes from the holy Scriptures, that so they may be the Lord's people, ruled by him alone in all things.

Which vow, considering the state of the Indian tribes to whom it was to apply, may serve to throw light upon the causes of the scant success of the Saints in dealing with the Indians.

Despite the logic of the theocrats, unanimity of opinion among the Saints was sadly lacking; and the peace of the new Canaan was troubled and the patience of the leaders sorely tried by pious malcontents, who were not content that God should rule through John Cotton, but themselves desired to be the Lord's vicegerents. The democrats were constantly prodding the ruling coterie of gentlemen; and the democratic conception of a commonwealth of free citizens intruded more and more upon the earlier conception of a kingdom of God. Capable leaders of the new radicalism were not lacking; and if we would comprehend the dissension and heart-burnings of those early times, we must set the figures of Roger Williams and Thomas Hooker over against John Cotton and the theocrats.

Roger Williams, advocate of toleration, was the most tempestuous soul thrown upon the American shores by the revolution then griping England, the embodiment and spokesman of the new radical hopes. He was an arch-rebel in a rebellious generation, the intellectual barometer of a world of stormy speculation and great endeavour. A generation younger than the Boston leaders, he came to maturity at the beginning of the wave of radicalism that was to sweep England into civil war. Older ties of class and custom he put aside easily, to make room for the new theories then agitating young Englishmen; and these new theories he advocated with an importunity disconcerting to practical men more given to weighing times and occasions. The kernel of his radicalism was the ideal of a democratic church in a democratic society. The more closely we scrutinize the thought of the great Separatist, the more clearly we perceive that the master principle of his career was Christian—the desire to embody in his life the social as well as the spiritual teachings of Christ. He put aside tradition and went back to the foundation and original of the gospel, discovering anew the profoundly revolutionary conceptions that underlie the philosophy of Jesus. He learned to conceive of men literally as the children of God and brothers in Christ, and out of this primary conception he developed his democratic philosophy. It was to set up no Hebraic absolutism that he came to America; it was to establish a free commonwealth of Christ in which the lowest and meanest of God's children should share equally with the greatest. But before there could be a free commonwealth there must be free churches; the hand of neither bishop nor presbytery must lie upon the conscience of the individual Christian; and so Roger Williams threw himself into the work of spreading the propaganda of Separatism. Not only did he protest in New England against the tyranny of the magistrates, but he flung at the heads of all enemies of freedom the notable book on toleration in which he struck at the root of the matter by arguing that "conscience be permitted (though erroneous) to be free."

In an earlier age he would have become a disciple of St. Francis; but in the days when the religious movement was passing over into a political movement, when it was being talked openly that both in church and state "the Originall of all free Power and Government" lies in the people, he threw in his lot with the levellers to further the democratic movement. As early as 1644 he had formulated his main principles:

From this *Grant* I infer . . . that the *Soveraigne, originall,* and *foundation* of *civill power* lies in the *people* . . . And if so, that a People may erect and establish what *forme* of *Government* seemes to them most meete for their *civill condition:* It is evident that such *Governments* as are by them erected and established, have no more *power,* nor for no longer time, then the *civill power* or people consenting and agreeing shall betrust them with. This is cleere not only in *Reason,* but in the experience of all *commonweales,* where the people are not deprived of their *naturall freedome* by the power of *Tyrants.*[1]

Clearly the radical times, his own experience, and his discussions with Sir Harry Vane had carried Roger Williams far into the field of political speculation, and confirmed his prepossessions of broader political rights for the common people from whom he had sprung. In all his later thinking there stood sharply before his mind the figure of the individual citizen, endowed with certain inalienable rights, a free member of a free commonwealth; and it was this profoundly modern conception which he transported to the wilderness of Rhode Island, providing there a fit sanctuary for the ark of the democratic covenant which was soon to be roughly handled by the tory reaction of Restoration England.

A courageous and unselfish thinker was this old-time Separatist and democrat. The friendliest of souls, time has brought him the friends which his restless intellect drove from him in his own day. However hopelessly we may lose ourselves in the tangle of his writings, confused by the luxuriance of his Hebraic tropes, we can plainly discern the man, the most charitable, the most open-minded, the most modern, amongst the notable company of Puritan emigrants—the sincerest Christian among many who sincerely desired to be Christians. His own words most adequately characterize him: "*Liberavi animam meam:* I have not hid within my *breast*, my *souls* belief." Naturally such a man could not get on with the Presbyterian leaders of Boston Bay; the social philosophies which divided them were fundamentally hostile; and the fate which Roger Williams suffered was prophetic of the lot that awaited later zealots in the democratic cause—to be outcast and excommunicate from respectable society.

A man of far different mettle was old Thomas Hooker of Hartford. The sternest autocrat of them all, a leader worthy to measure swords with the redoubtable Hugh Peters himself, a man of "mighty vigour and fervour of spirit" who, to further "his Master's work, would put a king in his pocket," he would seem to be the very stuff out of which to fashion a dictator

---

[1] *Narr. Club Pub.*, III., 249.

for the snug Presbyterian Utopia. Nevertheless there was some hidden bias in the old Puritan's nature that warped him away from Presbyterianism, and made him the advocate of a democratic Congregationalism. The great schism which rent the early theocracy, carrying off three congregations into the Connecticut wilderness, was an early witness to the antagonisms which lurked in the ambitions of diverse-minded enthusiasts. The seceders had other notions of church organization, it appears, than those held by the dominant group; but they were moderates, who believed that everything should be done decently and in order, and instead of setting up a clamour and bringing confusion upon God's work, they withdrew quietly under the leadership of Thomas Hooker and set up their new church at Hartford.

Concerning the "grave and juditious Hooker" surprisingly little is known, notwithstanding the work that he did and the influence that he wielded during a masterful life. He was a man evidently regardless of fame, who took small pains to publish his virtues to the ears of posterity; nevertheless it is clear that he was a better democrat than the Boston leaders— the father of New England Congregationalism as it later came to be when the Presbyterian tendency was finally checked. For his pronounced democratic sympathies some ground may be discovered in his humble origin. He was sprung of a plain yeoman family, got his education by the aid of scholarships, married a "waiting-woman" to the wife of his patron, and lived plainly, untroubled by social ambitions. He was a self-made man who had risen by virtue of strength of character and disdained to be a climber. He was evidently one of the greatest preachers of his time in either England, and he had early been marked by Laud's spies as one of "the people's creatures" "who blew the bellows of their sedition." He drew young men to him—among others John Eliot; and even though he should be silenced, his influence would remain "His genius will still haunte all the pulpits in ye country, where any of his scholars may be admitted to preach," one of the sycophants reported of him. Such a man must be reckoned with; and when in New England he found the ways too autocratic to suit him, he threw himself into the work of quickening the democratic unrest. "After Mr. Hooker's coming over," said Hubbard, "it was observed that many of the freemen grew to be very jealous of their liberties."

He was more concerned with experimental religion than with theology, more the pastor than the teacher. Nevertheless, when the Massachusetts leaders were troubled by attacks of old-world Presbyterians directed against "the New-England way," they drafted Hooker to write a defence. This was the origin of his *Survey of the Summe of Church Discipline*, a knotty book vigorous in thought and phrase, the most important contribution of New England Congregationalism to the great disputes of the time. The old champion went straight to the heart of the matter, seizing upon the political principles involved:

> But whether all Ecclesiasticall power be . . . rightly taken in to the Presbytery alone: Or that the people of the Particular Churches should come in for a share . . . This is left as the subject of the inquiry of this age, and that which occasions great thought of heart of all hands: Great thoughts of hearts in the Presbytery, as being very loth to part with that so chief priviledge, and of which they have taken possession so many years. Great thoughts of heart amongst the churches, how they may clear their right, and claim it in such pious sobriety and moderation, as becomes the Saints: being unwilling to loose their cause and comfort, meerly upon a nihil dicit: or forever to be deprived of so precious a legacy, as they conceive this is, though it hath been withheld from them, by the tyranny of the Pope, and prescription of times. Nor can they conceive it lesse, then a heedlesse betraying of their speciall liberties . . . by a carelesse silence, when the course of providence, as the juncture of things now present themselves, allows them a writt Ad melius inquirendum. . . . These are the times when people shall be fitted for such priviledges, fit I say to obtain them, and fit to use them. . . . And whereas it hath been charged upon the people, that through their ignorance and unskilfulnesse, they are not able to wield such priviledges, and therefore not fit to share in any such power, The Lord hath promised: To take away the vail from all faces in the mountain, the weak shall be as David, and David as an Angel of God.[1]

If the Presbyterianizing party found the path they were treading thorny and rough, it was due in no small part to

[1] Introd.

Thomas Hooker, who liberally bestrewed their path with impedi-
ments. Hebraist and theocrat though he professed to be, his
Hebraic theocracy was grounded upon the people, and pointed
straight towards the sovereignty of the individual congregation.
"The Lord hath promised to take away the vail from all faces
in the mountain"—and if the veil be removed and the people
see, shall not the people judge concerning their own causes?
In this faith Thomas Hooker lived and laboured, thereby
proving his right to be numbered among the stewards of our
American democracy.

The fibre of the emigrant leaders had been toughened by
conflict with old-world conservatism and turned radical by the
long struggle with an arrogant toryism. By a natural selective
process the stoutest-hearted had been driven overseas, and the
well-known words of William Stoughton, "God sifted a whole
Nation that he might send choice grain over into this wilder-
nes,"[1] were the poetic expression of a bitter reality. But
seated snugly in the new world, in control of church and state,
the emigrant radicalism found its ardour cooling. The Synod
of 1637 set a ban upon Antinomianism and other heretical
innovations, and thereafter Massachusetts settled down to a
rigid orthodoxy. The fathers had planted, was it not enough
for the sons to water and tend the vine, and enjoy the fruit
thereof? And so the spirit of conservatism took possession of
the native generation, the measure of excellence being accounted
the fidelity with which the husbandmen revered the work of the
emigrant pioneers. Translated into modern terms, it means
that the native ministers, having inherited a system of which
they were the beneficiaries, discovered little inclination to
question the title deeds to their inheritance, but were mainly
bent on keeping them safe. To preserve what had been gained,
and as far as possible to extend the Presbyterian principle,
became their settled policy; and so in all the life of New England—in the world of Samuel Sewall, as well as in that of
Cotton Mather—a harsh and illiberal dogmatism succeeded
to the earlier enthusiasm.

The indisputable leader of the second generation was

[1] From a sermon entitled, *New-Englands true interests; not to lie: Or, a Treatise declaring . . . the terms on which we stand, and the tenure by which we hold
our . . . precious and pleasant things.* Cambridge, 1670.

Increase Mather, son of Richard Mather, and father of Cotton, the most vigorous and capable member of a remarkable family. After graduating at Harvard, he entered Trinity College, Dublin, where he proceeded Master of Arts. He spent some years in England, preaching there to the edification of many, until the restoration of Charles sent him back to America to become the guiding spirit of the New England hierarchy. He was by nature a politician and statesman rather than a minister, the stuff of which frocked chancellors were made; and he needed only a pliant master to have become another Wolsey or Richelieu. He liked to match his wit in diplomacy with statesmen, and he served his native land faithfully and well in the matter of wheedling Dutch William into granting a new charter to Massachusetts. A natural autocrat, he was dictatorial and domineering, bearing himself arrogantly towards all underlings, unyielding in opposition to whoever crossed his will. And in consequence he gathered about his head such fierce antagonism that in the end he failed of his ambitions, and shorn of power he sat down in old age to eat the bread of bitterness.

Skill in organization was the secret of his strength. In no sense a creative thinker, wholly lacking in intellectual curiosity and therefore not given to speculation, he built up a compact hierarchical machine, and then suffered the mortification of seeing it broken to pieces by forces that lay beyond his control. If the theocratic ideal of ecclesiastical control of secular affairs were to maintain itself against the growing opposition, the ministers must fortify their position by a closer organization. They must speak as a unit in determining church policies; above all they must guard against the wolves in sheep's clothing who were slipping into the pulpits to destroy the flocks. To effect such ends Synods were necessary, and Increase Mather was an ardent advocate of Synodical organization. He prompted the calling of the "Reforming Synod" of 1679–80, served as Moderator, dominated the debates, and drafted the report; and the purpose which underlay such work was the substitution of a Presbyterian hierarchy for the older Congregationalism. The church must dominate the state; the organized ministers must dominate the church; and Increase Mather trusted that he could dominate the ministers—such in brief was the dream of this masterful leader of the second generation.

The source of his power lay in the pulpit, and for sixty-four years the Old North Church was the citadel of Mather orthodoxy. His labours were enormous. Sixteen hours a day he commonly studied. Among many powerful preachers he was reckoned "the complete preacher," and he thundered above his congregation with an authority that must have been appalling. His personal influence carried far, and doubtless there were many good men in Boston who believed—as Roger Williams said of John Cotton—that "God would not suffer" Increase Mather "to err." Those whom his voice could not reach his pen must convince, and the busy minister set a pace in the making and publishing of books which only his busier son could equal. He understood thoroughly the power of the press, and he watched over it with an eagle eye; no unauthorized or godless work must issue thence for the pollution of the people; and to insure that only fit matter should be published he was at enormous pains to supply enough manuscript himself to keep the printers busy. The press was a powerful aid to the pulpit in shaping public opinion, and Increase Mather was too shrewd a leader not to understand how necessary it was to hold it in strict control. He was a calculating dictator, and he ruled the press with the same iron hand with which he ruled the pulpit. He was no advocate of freedom, for he was no friend of democracy.

Of the odium which an obstinate defence of a passing order gathered about the name of Mather, the larger share fell to the lot of Cotton Mather, whose passionately distorted career remains so incomprehensible to us. One may well hesitate to describe Cotton Mather; the man is unconceivable to one who has not read his diary. Unlike Increase, he was provincial to the core. Born and bred in Boston, his longest trips into the outer world carried him only a few miles from the Old North Meeting-house, where for years he served as co-labourer with his father. Self-centred and self-righteous, the victim of strange asceticisms and morbid spiritual debauches, every circumstance of his life ripened and expanded the colossal egotism of his nature. His vanity was daily fattened by the adulation of silly women and the praise of foolish men, until the insularity of his thought and judgment grew into a disease. His mind was clogged with the strangest miscellany of truth and fiction; he laboured to acquire the possessions of a scholar, but he listened to old wives' tales with an amazing credulity. In all his mental processes the solidest fact fell into grotesque perspective, and confused itself with the most fantastic abortions. And yet he was prompted by a love of scientific investigation, and in the matter of inoculation for smallpox showed himself both courageous and intelligent.

Living under the shadow of his father, he was little more than a reduced copy of the Mather ambitions, inheriting a ready-made theology, a passion for the ideals of the emigrant generation, an infallible belief in the finality of the Mather conclusions. The masterfulness of old Increase degenerated in the son into an intolerable meddlesomeness; and in the years of reaction against ecclesiastical domination the position of Cotton Mather was difficult. He was exposed to attack from two sides; the tories with whom he would gladly have affiliated, and the democrats whom he held in contempt, both rejected the archaic theocracy. As his meddlesomeness increased, the attacks of his enemies multiplied, wounding his self-esteem bitterly—"having perhaps the Insults of contemptible People, the Assaults of those insignificant *Lice*, more than any man in *New-England*," as his son testifies. "These troublesome but diminutive Creatures he scorn'd to concern himself with; only to *pity* them and *pray* for them." He would die willingly, he believed, to save his erring people from their sins, but he obstinately refused to be dictated to by them.

Of the content of his innumerable writings the accompanying Bibliography will give sufficient indication. A man of incredible industry, unrestrained by any critical sense, and infatuated with printer's ink, he flung together a jumble of old saws and modern instances and called the result a book. Of the 470 odd titles, the *Magnalia* alone possesses some vitality still, the repository of much material concerning early days in Massachusetts that we should not willingly lose. "In his *Style*, indeed," according to a contemporary critic, "he was something singular, and not so agreeable to the Gust of the Age. But like his *manner of speaking*, it was very *emphatical*."

The emphasis, it must be confessed, is now gone from his pages, and the singularity remains, a singularity little agreeable to the gust of today.

The party of conservatism numbered among its adherents every prominent minister of the greater churches. The organization propaganda of the Mathers spread widely, and in 1705 a group of men put forth a series of "Proposals" looking to a closer union of the churches, and greater control of the separate congregations by the ministerial association.[1] Seven years later John Wise, pastor of the second church of Ipswich, published his *Churches Quarrel Espoused*, and in 1717, his *Vindication of the New England Churches*. The two works were a democratic counterblast to the Presbyterian propaganda, and stirred the thought of the churches so effectively as to nullify the Proposals, and put an end to all such agitation in Massachusetts.

Posterity has been too negligent of John Wise hitherto. Although possessed of the keenest mind and most trenchant pen of his generation of Americans, he was untainted by any itch of publicity, and so failed to challenge the attention of later times. Nevertheless, what we know of him is to his credit. An independent man, powerful of body, vigorous of intellect, tenacious of opinion, outspoken and fearless in debate, he seems to have understood the plain people whom he served, and he sympathized heartily with the democratic ideals then taking shape in the New England village. Some explanation of his democratic sympathies may be discovered in his antecedents. His father was a self-made man who had come over to Roxbury as an indented servant—most menial of stations in that old Carolinian world. There he doubtless taught his son independence and democratic self-respect, which stood John Wise in good stead when he later came to speak for the people against the arbitrary tax of Andros, the encroachments of the Mathers, or the schemes of the hard-money men.

When, in response to the challenge of the Presbyterians, he turned to examine critically the work of the fathers, he found in it quite another meaning than Cotton Mather found.

[1] For an account of the movement, see Walker's *History of the Congregational Churches in the United States*, pp. 201–213.

It was as a radical that he went back to the past, seeking to recover the original Congregational principle, which, since the conservative triumph in the Synod of 1637, had been greatly obscured. The theme of his two books is the same, a defence of the "venerable New-English constitution"; but the significance of them in the history of democratic America lies in the fact that he followed "an unbeaten path," justifying the principles of Congregationalism by analogy from civil polity. Seemingly alone amongst the New England clergy of his day he had grounded himself in political theory; and the doctrine upon which he erected his argument was the new conception of "natural rights," derived from a study of Puffendorf's *De Jure Naturae et Gentium,* published in 1672. This was the first effective reply in America to the old theocratic sneer that if the democratic form of government were indeed divinely sanctioned, was it not strange that God had overlooked it in providing a system for his chosen people? But Wise had broken with the literal Hebraism of earlier times, and was willing to make use of a pagan philosophy, based upon an appeal to history, a method which baffled the followers of the old school. They found difficulty in replying to such argument:

That a democracy in church or state, is a very honourable and regular government according to the dictates of right reason, And, therefore . . . That these churches of New England, in their ancient constitution of church order, it being a democracy, are manifestly justified and defended by the law and light of nature.

With the advance of the democratic movement of modern times, the life and work of John Wise take on new interest. After a spirited contest lasting for three-quarters of a century, theocratic Puritanism merged in ecclesiastical democracy. For two generations it had remained doubtful which way the church would incline. Dominated by gentlemen, it was warped toward Presbyterianism; but interpreted by commoners, it leaned towards Congregationalism. The son of a plebeian, Wise came naturally into sympathy with the spirit of radical Separatism, bred of the democratic aspirations of the old Jacobean underlings; and this radical Separatism he found justified by the new philosophy, as well as by the facts of the

New England village world. The struggle for ecclesiastical democracy was a forerunner of the struggle for political democracy, which was to be the business of the next century; and in justifying his ecclesiasticism by political principles, John Wise was an early witness to the new order of thought.

Judged by the severest standards, the Puritan ministers were a notable group of men; the English race has never bred their superiors in self-discipline and exalted ideals, and rarely their equals in consecration to duty. Their interests might be narrow and their sympathies harsh and illiberal; nevertheless men who studied ten to sixteen hours a day were neither boors nor intellectual weaklings. A petty nature would not have uttered the lament of Increase Mather:

not many years ago, I *lost* (and that's an afflictive *loss* indeed!) several moneths from study by sickness. Let every God-fearing reader joyn with me in prayer, that I may be enabled to redeem the time, and (in all wayes wherein I am capable), to serve my generation.[1]

From the long hours of reading they acquired a huge mass of learning; out of the many books they read they made still other books of like nature and purpose. The way of printer's ink was the path of celebrity and authority, and the minister who had not a goodly number of volumes to his credit was an unprofitable servant, lacking ambition to glorify his Lord. Though they denied themselves in other things, they did not stint their library. In 1686 John Dunton numbered eight book-shops in the village of Boston; and in 1702 Cotton Mather described his study, "the hangings whereof, are Boxes with between two and three thousand Books in them."

According to present taste it was an uninviting library; works of pure literature were as lacking as books of history and political philosophy and science. Nevertheless, though their reading was narrow, the ministers in many respects were in advance of their times. For all his grotesque lack of scientific method, Cotton Mather was more nearly a scientist than any other man of his day in Boston,—a weakness which laid him open to criticism. Under date of 23 December, 1714, Sewall noted in his diary:

[1] Preface to *Remarkable Providences*.

> Dr. C. Mather preaches excellently from Ps. 37. Trust in the Lord, etc., only spake of the Sun being in the centre of our system. I think it inconvenient to assert such problems.

His membership in the Royal Society, to which he forwarded his *Curiosa Americana*, encouraged him to keep abreast of current scientific thought; and it was from this source that he got the idea of inoculation for smallpox, which he urged upon the people of Boston so insistently that a war of pamphlets broke out. When we remember that during ninety years only two books on medicine were published in New England—one a popular pharmacopeia and the other a hand-book on smallpox prevention—it is suggestive that within a few months sixteen papers on inoculation came from the press. In this case the minister was in advance of the physicians.

If the influence of the ministers was commanding, it was due in part to their indisputable vigour, and in part, it must be acknowledged, to their control of the means of publicity. The complete domination of the press they regarded as their perquisite; and they swayed public opinion sometimes by means not wholly to their credit. Those who opposed their policies experienced difficulties in gaining a hearing. Thus Robert Calef, who attacked the Mathers because of the witchcraft business, found it desirable to send his manuscript to London for publication, and John Wise probably sent his manuscript of *The Churches Quarrel Espoused* to New York.[1] Complaints were heard that the press was closed. In the preface to *The Gospel Order Revived*, by T. Woodbridge and other malcontents, published in New York in 1700,

> The Reader is desired to take Notice that the Press in *Boston* is so much under the aw of the Reverend Author, whom we answer, and his Friends, that we could not obtain of the Printer there to print the following Sheets, which is the true Reason why we have sent the Copy so far for its Impression and where it was printed with some Difficulty.

When James Franklin spoke out roundly against the tyranny of the ministers, they induced the magistrates to teach him respect by throwing him into the common gaol. It was

[1] See Bibliography on this point.

a serious matter to offend the hierarchy, even in the days of its decline, and far more serious to attack. But the days of its domination were numbered, and after 1720 the secular authority of the Puritan divines swiftly decayed. The old dream of a Kingdom of God was giving way, under pressure of economic circumstance, to the new dream of a commonwealth of free citizens. The theological age was to be followed by a political age, and in this later world of thought the Puritan divines were unfitted to remain leaders of the people.

# CHAPTER IV

# Edwards

J ONATHAN EDWARDS was born at Windsor, Connecticut, in 1703. He belonged, unlike his great contemporary Franklin in this, to the "Brahmin families" of America, his father being a distinguished graduate of Harvard and a minister of high standing, his mother being the daughter of Solomon Stoddard, a revered pastor of Northampton, Massachusetts, and a religious author of repute. Jonathan, one of eleven children, showed extraordinary precocity. There is preserved a letter of his, written apparently in his twelfth year, in which he retorts upon certain materialistic opinions of his correspondent with an easiness of banter not common to a boy; and another document, from about the same period, an elaborate account of the habits of spiders, displays a keenness of observation and a vividness of style uncommon at any age.

He studied at Yale, receiving his bachelor's degree in 1720, before his seventeenth birthday. While at college he continued his interest in scientific observations, but his main concern was naturally with theology and moral philosophy. As a sophomore he read Locke *On the Human Understanding*, with the delight of a "greedy miser" in "some newly discovered treasure." Some time after reading Locke and before graduation he wrote down a series of reflections, preparatory to a great metaphysical treatise of his own, which can be compared only with the *Commonplace Book* kept by Berkeley a few years earlier for the same purpose. In the section of "Notes on the Mind" this entry is found: "Our perceptions or ideas, that we passively receive by our bodies, are communicated to us immediately by God." Now Berkeley's *Principles* and his *Hylas and Philonous* appeared in 1710 and 1713 respectively, and the question has been raised, and not answered, whether this Berkeleian sentiment was borrowed from one of these books or was original with Edwards. Possibly the youthful philosopher was following a line of thought suggested by the English disciples of Malebranche, possibly he reached his point of view directly from Locke; in any case his life-work was to carry on the Lockian philosophy from the point where the Berkeleian idealism left off.

After graduation Edwards remained for two years at Yale, preparing for the ministry. In 1722 he was called to a Presbyterian church in New York. Here he preached acceptably for eight months, returning then to his father's house, and later to New Haven, where he held the position of tutor in the college. In 1727 he went to Northampton as colleague, and became in due time successor, to his grandfather. Almost immediately after ordination he married Sarah Pierrepont, like himself of the Brahmin caste, whom he had known as a young girl, and whose beauty of body and soul he had described in a passage of ecstatic wonder.

"They say," he began, being himself then twenty and the object of his adoration thirteen, "there is a young lady in New Haven who is beloved of that great Being who made and rules the world, and that there are certain seasons in which this great Being, in some way or other invisible, comes to her and fills her mind with exceeding sweet delight."

The marriage, notwithstanding this romantic rapture, proved eminently wise.

Like a good many other men of his age Edwards lived his inner life, so to speak, on paper. There is therefore nothing peculiar or priggish in the fact that at the beginning of his religious career he should have written out a set of formal resolutions, which he vowed to read over, and did read over, at stated intervals in order to keep watch on his spiritual progress. A number of these resolutions have been printed, as has also a part of the diary kept at about the same time. Neither of these documents, the time of their writing considered, contains anything remarkable. But it is quite otherwise with the private reflections which he wrote out some twenty years later (about 1743) at Northampton, apparently on some occasion of reading over his youthful diary. In these we have an autobiographical fragment that, for intensity of absorption in the idea of God and for convincing power of utterance, can be likened to the *Confessions* of St. Augustine, while it unites to this religious fervour a romantic feeling for nature foreign to the Bishop of Hippo's mind and prophetic of a movement that was to sweep over the world many years after Edwards's death. A few extracts from this document (not so well known as it would have been if it had not been printed with the works of a thorny metaphysician) must be given for their biographical and literary interest:

From my childhood up, my mind had been full of objections against the doctrine of God's sovereignty, in choosing whom he would to eternal life, and rejecting whom he pleased; leaving them eternally to perish, and be everlastingly tormented in hell. It used to appear like a horrible doctrine to me. But I remember the time very well, when I seemed to be convinced, and fully satisfied, as to this sovereignty of God. . . . I have often, since that first conviction, had quite another kind of sense of God's sovereignty than I had then. I have often since had not only a conviction, but a delightful conviction. The doctrine has very often appeared exceeding pleasant, bright, and sweet. Absolute sovereignty is what I love to ascribe to God. But my first conviction was not so.

The first instance that I remember of that sort of inward, sweet delight in God and divine things that I have lived much in since, was on reading those words, *Now unto the King eternal, immortal, invisible, the only wise God, be honour and glory for ever and ever, Amen.* As I read the words, there came into my soul, and was as it were diffused through it, a sense of the glory of the Divine Being. . . .

Not long after I first began to experience these things, I gave an account to my father of some things that had passed in my mind. I was pretty much affected by the discourse we had together; and when the discourse was ended, I walked abroad alone, in a solitary place in my father's pasture, for contemplation. And as I was walking there, and looking up on the sky and clouds, there came into my mind so sweet a sense of the glorious *majesty* and *grace* of God, that I know not how to express. I seemed to see them both in a sweet conjunction; majesty and meekness joined together; it was a sweet and gentle, and holy majesty; and also a majestic meekness; an awful sweetness; a high, and great, and holy gentleness.

This is not the Edwards that is commonly known, and indeed he put little of this personal rapture of holiness into his published works, which were almost exclusively polemical in design. Only once, perhaps, did he adequately display this aspect of his thought to the public; and that was in the *Dissertation on the Nature of Virtue*, wherein, starting from the definition of virtue as "the beauty of the qualities and exercises of the heart," he proceeds to combine ethics and aesthetics in an argument as subtle in reasoning as it is, in places, victorious in expression. One cannot avoid the feeling, when his writings are surveyed as a whole, that in his service to a particular dogma of religion Edwards deliberately threw away the opportunity of making for himself, despite the laxness of his style, one of the very great names in literature.

It should seem also that he not only suppressed his personal ecstasy in his works for the press, but waived it largely in his more direct intercourse with men. He who himself, like an earlier and perhaps greater Emerson, was enjoying the sweetness of walking with God in the garden of earth, was much addicted to holding up before his people the "pleasant, bright, and sweet" doctrine of damnation. Nor can it be denied that he had startling ways of impressing this sweetness on others. It is a misfortune, but one for which he is himself responsible, that his memory in the popular mind today is almost exclusively associated with certain brimstone sermons and their terrific effect. Best known of these is the discourse on *Sinners in the Hands of an Angry God*, delivered at Enfield, Connecticut, in the year 1741. His text was taken from Deuteronomy: "Their foot shall slide in due time"; and from these words he proceeded to prove, and "improve," the truth that "there is nothing that keeps wicked men at any moment out of hell, but the mere pleasure of God." He is said to have had none of the common qualities of the orator. His regular manner of preaching, at least in his earlier years, was to hold his "manuscript volume in his left hand, the elbow resting on the cushion or the Bible, his right hand rarely raised but to turn the leaves,

and his person almost motionless"; but there needed no gesti-
culation and no modulation of voice to convey the force of his
terrible conviction, when, to an audience already disposed to
accept the dogma, he presented that dogma in a series of
pictures like the following:

> The God that holds you over the pit of hell, much as one holds a
> spider, or some loathesome insect, over the fire, abhors you, and is
> dreadfully provoked; his wrath towards you burns like fire; he looks
> upon you as worthy of nothing else, but to be cast into the fire;
> he is of purer eyes than to bear to have you in his sight.

The congregation of Enfield, we are told, was moved almost
to despair; "there was such a breathing of distress and weeping"
that the speaker was interrupted and had to plead for silence.
Sincerity of vision may amount to cruelty, and something is
due to the weakness of human nature.

The result was inevitable. The people of Northampton
listened to Edwards for a time; were rapt out of themselves;
suffered the relapse of natural indolence; grew resentful under
the efforts to keep them in a state of exaltation; and freed
themselves of the burden when it became intolerable. At
first all went well. Stoddard, in whose declining years the
discipline of the church had been somewhat relaxed, died in
1729, and the fervour of his successor soon began to tell on the
people. In 1733, as Edwards notes in his *Narrative of Surprising
Conversions*, there was a stirring in the conscience of the young,
who had hitherto been prone to the awful sin of "frolicking."
The next year the sudden conversion of a young woman,
"who had been one of the greatest company keepers in the
whole town," came upon the community "like a flash of
lightning"; the Great Awakening was started, which was to
run over New England like a burning fire, with consequences
not yet obliterated. The usual accompaniments of moral
exaltation and physical convulsions showed themselves.
Edwards relates with entire approbation the morbid conversion
of a child of four. The poor little thing was overheard by her
mother in her closet wrestling with God in prayer, from which
she came out crying aloud and "wreathing her body to and
fro like one in anguish of spirit." She was afraid she was
going to hell!

It was inevitable that such a wave of superheated emotion should subside in a short time. In fact the enthusiasm had scarcely reached its height when it began to show signs of perversion and decay. Immediately after the story of the young convert Edwards notes that "the Spirit of God was gradually withdrawing" and "Satan seemed to be let loose and raged in a dreadful manner." An epidemic of melancholy and suicidal mania swept over the community, and multitudes seemed to hear a voice saying to them: "Cut your own throat, now is a good opportunity." Strange delusions arose and spread, until common sense once more got the upper hand.

It was an old tale, told in New England with peculiar fury. The saddest thing in the whole affair is the part played by Edwards. Other leaders saw the danger from the first, or were soon awakened to it; but Edwards never, either at this time or later, wavered in his belief that the Awakening, though marred by the devil, was in itself the work of the Divine Spirit. His *Thoughts on the Revival of Religion* and his *Marks of a Work of the True Spirit* are both a thoroughgoing apology for the movement, as they are also an important document in his own psychology. The jangling and confusion he admits; he recognizes the elements of hysteria that were almost inextricably mixed up with the moral exaltation of conversion; but his defence is based frankly on the avowal that these things are the universal accompaniments of inspiration—they attended the founding of the church in the Apostolic age, they were to be expected at the instauration of religion. Often the reader of these treatises is struck by a curious, and by no means accidental, resemblance between the position of Edwards and the position of the apologists of the romantic movement in literature. There is the same directness of appeal to the emotions; the same laudation of sheer expansiveness, at the cost, if need be, of judgment or measure or any other restraint. Prudence and regularity may be desirable in the service of God, yet it is still true that "the cry of irregularity and imprudence" has been mainly in the mouths of those who are enemies to the main work of redemption. Perturbation, in truth, is not properly so called when it is the means of rousing the cold and indifferent from their lethargy; we are bound to suppose that not even the man "of the strongest reason and greatest learning" can remain master of himself if "strongly impressed with a sense of divine and eternal things." It comes in the end to this, that, notwithstanding his verbal reservations, Edwards had no critical canon to distinguish between the order and harmony governed by a power higher than either the imagination or the emotions, and the order and harmony that are merely stagnation.

One factor in his confidence was a belief that the discovery of America, coinciding as it did with the beginning of the Reformation, came by Providence for "the glorious renovation of the world"; nay more, that the humble town in which he was preaching might be the cradle of the new dispensation, from whence it should spread over the whole earth. His language may even seem to betray a touch of spiritual pride over the part he himself should be called upon to play as the instrument of Grace in this marvellous regeneration. That vice of the saints was indeed a subject much in his meditations, and one of the finest pieces of religious psychology in his works is the passage of the *Revival* in which he tracks it through the labyrinthine deceits of the human heart. It was a sin against which he had probably to keep particular ward in these years, but we should not say that he ever, in any proper sense of the word, lapsed from the virtue of Christian humility. If he seemed to set himself above other men as an exigent judge, this was rather due to a faulty sympathy, an inability to measure others except by the standard of his own great faculties. Thus, for all his emotionalism, he lived under the control of an iron will, and he could not comprehend how the over-stimulation of terror and joy in a weaker disposition would work moral havoc. Nor from his own constant height could he understand how brief and fitful any mood of exaltation must be among ordinary men in their ordinary condition. Hence he not only failed to see the gravity of the actual evils at the time of the Awakening, but failed also, with more grievous results for himself, to recognize the impossibility of flogging the dead emotion into new life.

The issue came on a point of church discipline. Edwards believed that religion was essentially a matter of the emotions or affections. A man might have perfect knowledge of divine things, as indeed the devil had, but unless the love of God was implanted in his heart by the free act of Grace he had no lot with the faithful. To develop this theme he wrote his great *Treatise Concerning Religious Affections*, a work which may without exaggeration be said to go as far as the human intellect can go in the perilous path of discriminating between the purely spiritual life and the life of worldly morality. Now even the simple statement of the difference between the condition of Grace and the condition of nature is hard for the natural man to follow; but when Edwards, with the acumen of a genius and the doggedness of a scholar, imposed his distinction on all the intricate feelings of life, the natural man was dazed; and when he attempted to make it the criterion of admission to the Lord's Table, the natural man who thought himself a Christian rebelled. Stoddard had held it right to admit to communion all those who desired honestly to unite themselves with the church. Edwards protested that only those who had undergone a radical conversion and knew the affections of supernatural love should enjoy this high privilege. His congregation sided with their old guide against him.

The quarrel was further embittered by another issue. It came to light that certain young folk of the church were reading profane books which led to lewd conversation. Edwards called for public discipline of the sinners; the congregation supported him until investigation showed that the evil was widespread and would bring discredit on most of the better families of the town, and then they blocked further proceedings. If tradition is correct in naming *Pamela* as one of the guilty books, we may admire the literary taste of youthful Northampton, yet think that their pastor was justified in condemning such reading as incendiary. However that may be, when, on 22 June, 1750, a public vote was taken whether Edwards should be dismissed from his pastorate, a large majority was counted against him. Northampton has the distinction of having rejected the greatest theologian and philosopher yet produced in this country. The behaviour of Edwards when the crisis actually came was simple, dignified, and even noble. His *Farewell Sermon*, with its dispassionate and submissive appeal from the tribunal of men to that final judgment which shall be given in knowledge and righteousness, cannot be read today without a deep stirring of the heart.

At the age of forty-six Edwards was thrust upon the world, discredited, in broken health, with a large family to support, but undaunted. Then befell a strange thing. This philosopher, whose thoughts and emotions ranged beyond the ken of most educated men, was sent to the frontier town of Stockbridge as a missionary to the Indians. There for six years he laboured faithfully and, at least in the practical management of affairs, successfully. It must have been one of the memorable sights of the world to see him returning on horseback from a solitary ride into the forest, while there fluttered about him, pinned to his coat, the strips of paper on which he had scribbled the results of his meditations. His days were little troubled, and not overburdened with work, peaceful it is thought; and now it was he wrote the treatise on the *Freedom of the Will* upon which his fame chiefly depends.

In 1757 his son-in-law, the Rev. Aaron Burr, died, and Edwards was chosen by the Trustees of the College of New Jersey to succeed him as president. Edwards hesitated, stating frankly to the Trustees his disabilities of health and learning, but he finally accepted the offer. He left his family to follow him later, and arrived in Princeton in January, 1758. Smallpox was in the town, and the new president was soon infected. His death took place on 22 March, in the fifty-fifth year of his age. His last recorded words were: "Trust in God and ye need not fear."

The child was indeed father of the man, and it was peculiarly fitting that he who from youth upward had been absorbed in the idea of God should have died with the sacred word on his lips. But what shall be said of the fearlessness—and there is no reason to question the perfect sincerity of his spiritual joy —in the breast of one who had made terror the chief instrument of appeal to men and had spent his life in fighting for a dogma which the genial author of *The One-Hoss Shay* thought no decent man could hold without going crazy? To understand that charge properly we must throw ourselves back into the age in which Edwards lived.

Now the Edwardian theology was a part of the great deistic debate which took its root in the everlasting question of the

origin of evil in the world.  It was a three-cornered contest.  The
Calvinists and the infidels both believed in a kind of determinism, but differed over the nature of the determining cause.   The
Calvinists found this cause in a personal Creator, omnipotent
and omniscient, to whom they did not scruple to carry up all
the evil as well as all the good of the universe—"c'est que
Dieu," as Calvin himself states categorically, "non seulement a
preveu la cheute du premier homme, et en icelle la ruine de toute
sa posterité, mais qu'il l'a ainsi voulu."   The deists, who at
this time formed the fighting line of the infidels, while verbally
acknowledging the existence of God and theorizing on the
nature of evil, virtually regarded the universe as a perfectly
working machine in which there was no room for a personal
governor or for real sin.   To the Arminians, including the
bulk of the orthodox churchmen, the alliance between Calvinism and deism seemed altogether to outweigh the differences.
As Daniel Whitby declares in the preface to his discourses
*On the Five Points of Calvinism* (1710; reprinted in America),
to hold God responsible for evil is to play directly into the
hands of the atheists.  And so the age-old dispute between
Augustinian and Pelagian, and between Calvinist and Arminian,
took on a new life from the deistic controversy, and there
sprang up a literature which undertook to preserve the idea of
an omnipotent personal Creator and at the same time to
save his face, if the expression may be tolerated, by attributing to men complete free will and accountability for their
actions.

    It was in answer to Whitby's book and one or two others
of the kind that Edwards composed his *Freedom of the Will*.
His argument has a psychological basis.   In the *Treatise
Concerning Religious Affections* he had divided the soul into
two faculties: one called the understanding, by which it dis-
cerns, views, and judges things; the other called the heart
or will, being nothing else but the inclination of the soul
towards or the disinclination from what is discerned and
judged by the understanding.   In the *Freedom of the Will*
he starts with Locke's statement that "the Will is perfectly
distinguished from Desire, which in the very same action may
have a quite contrary tendency from that which our Wills
set us upon."   This theory Edwards analyses and rejects, and

then proceeds to show that a man's desire and will are virtually the same faculty of the soul. It follows from this that the will at any moment is determined by the strongest motive acting upon the soul; we are free in so far as no obstacle is presented to our willing in accordance with our inclination, but our inclination is determined by what at any moment seems to us good. In his attack on the common arguments for the freedom of the will Edwards is magnificently victorious. If the psychology by which the Arminians sought to relieve God of the burden of evil in human life is pushed into a corner, it shows itself as nothing more than this: Man's will is a faculty absolutely indeterminate in itself and entirely independent of his inclinations. When, therefore, a man errs, it is because, the choice between evil with its attendant suffering and good with its attendant happiness being presented to him, the man, having full knowledge of the consequences and being impelled by no momentary preponderance of the one or the other from his innate disposition, deliberately and freely chooses what is evil and painful. Such an account of human action is monstrous, inconceivable; it offered an easy mark for so sharp a logician as Edwards.

But whence arise the conditions by which a man's inclination is swayed in one direction or the other? Edwards carries these unflinchingly up to the first cause,—that is, as a Christian, to God. Berkeley had made the world to consist of ideas evoked in the mind of man by the mind of God; Edwards accepts the logical conclusion, and holds God responsible for the inclination of the human will which depends on these ideas. Calvin did not hesitate to attribute, in the bluntest language, the source of evil to God's will, but at the same time he warned men against intruding with their finite reason into this "sanctuary of the divine wisdom." The mind of Edwards could not rest while any problem seemed to him unsolved. Confronted with the mystery of the divine permission of evil, he undertakes to solve it by applying his psychology of man to the nature of God. (He himself would put it the other way about: "Herein does very much consist that image of God wherein he made man.") The passage in which he develops this thesis, though generally overlooked by his critics, is of the first importance:

We must conceive of Him as influenced in the highest degree, by
that which, above all others, is properly a moral inducement, viz.,
the moral good which He sees in such and such things: and therefore
He is, in the most proper sense, a moral Agent, the source of all
moral ability and Agency, the fountain and rule of all virtue and
moral good; though by reason of his being supreme over all, it is
not possible He should be under the influence of law or command,
promises or threatenings, rewards or punishments, counsels or
warnings. The essential qualities of a moral Agent are in God,
in the greatest possible perfection; such as understanding, to perceive the difference between moral good and evil; a capacity of
discerning that moral worthiness and demerit, by which some
things are praiseworthy, others deserving of blame and punishment;
and also a capacity of choice, and choice guided by understanding,
and a power of acting according to his choice or pleasure, and
being capable of doing those things which are in the highest sense
praiseworthy.

In other words, the will of God is precisely like the will of
man; it is merely the inclination, or *moral inducement*, to act
as he is *influenced* by external power. The fatal mystery of
good and evil, the true cause, lies above and beyond him; he
is, like ourselves, a channel, not the source. The only difference is that God has complete knowledge of the possibilities of
being, and therefore is not moved by threats and blind commands but, immediately, by what Edwards elsewhere calls the
"moral necessity" of governing in accordance with the best of
the "different objects of choice that are proposed to the Divine
Understanding." By such a scheme God is really placed in
about such a position as in the Leibnitzian continuation of
Laurentius Valla's *Dialogue on Free Will and Providence*,
where he is naïvely portrayed as looking upon an infinite variety
of worlds piled up, like cannon balls, in pyramidal form before
him, and selecting for creation that one which combines the
greatest possible amount of good with the least possible admixture of evil.

From this pretty sport of the imagination Edwards would
no doubt have drawn back in contempt, and indeed in his
ordinary language God is merely the supreme Cause, without further speculation. One of the Leibnitzian inferences,
moreover, is utterly excluded from his philosophy. He was no

optimist, was in fact the last man to infer that, because this world is the best possible conceivable, evil is therefore a small and virtually negligible part of existence. On the contrary the whole animus of his teaching springs from a deep and immediate hatred of evil in itself and apart from any consideration of its cause.

"The thing," he says, "which makes sin hateful, is that by which it deserves punishment; which is but the expression of hatred. . . . Thus, for instance, ingratitude is hateful and worthy of dispraise, according to common sense; not because something as bad, or worse than ingratitude, was the cause that produced it; but because it is hateful in itself, by its own inherent deformity."

To the charge of the Arminians that the doctrine of pre-destination leaves no place for the punishment of sin, this is an adequate and practical reply. But the consequences of this principle of common sense are, in another way, peculiar and even disastrous to the Edwardian theology. If we are right, as we indubitably are right, in detesting evil in itself and where-ever seen, and if we hold with Edwards that the will of God, like the will of man, is merely the inclination towards the best object presented to its choice, and there is no power either in God or in man above the will, in what essential way, then, does the act of God in creating a world mixed with evil differ from the act of Judas in betraying God, and how are we relieved from hating God for the evil of his work with the same sort of hatred as that which we feel for Judas? Edwards had terrified the people of Enfield with a picture of God treading down sinners till their blood sprinkled his raiment, and exulting in his wrath. The retort is obvious, and unspeakable. Nor can he, or any other Predestinarian, escape the odium of such a retort by hiding behind the necessity of things which all men must, in one way or another, admit. There is a war between the nations, he will say, and suddenly a bomb, drop-ping upon a group of soldiers, themselves innocent of any crime, horribly rends and mangles them. Here is a hideous thing, and by no twisting of the reason can we avoid carrying the responsibility for this evil back to the first great cause of all. Shall we be held impious for saying metaphorically that the blood of these soldiers is sprinkled on the raiment of that

Cause?—Aye, but the difference to us morally if we leave that cause in its own vast obscurity, unapproached by our reason, untouched by our pride; or if we make it into an image of ourselves, composed only of understanding and inclination like our own, and subject to our reprobation as surely as to our love!

Edwards had riddled and forever destroyed the arguments for free will commonly employed by the Arminians; is there no alternative for the human reason save submission to his theological determinism or to fatalistic atheism?

One way of escape from that dilemma is obvious and well known. It is that which Dr. Johnson, with his superb faculty of common sense, seized upon when the Edwardian doctrine came up in conversation before him. "The only relief I had was to forget it," said Boswell, who had read the book; and Johnson closed the discussion with his epigram: "All theory is against the freedom of the will, all experience for it." That is sufficient, no doubt, for the conduct of life; yet there is perhaps another way of escape, which, if it does not entirely silence the metaphysical difficulties, at least gives them a new ethical turn. Twice in the course of his argument Edwards refers to an unnamed Arminian[1] who placed the liberty of the soul not in the will itself, but in some power of suspending volition until due time has elapsed for judging properly the various motives to action. His reply is that this suspension of activity, being itself an act of volition, merely throws back without annulling the difficulty; and as the argument came to him, this refutation is fairly complete. But a fuller consideration of the point at issue might possibly indicate a way out of the dilemma of free will and determinism into a morally satisfying form of dualism within the soul of man himself. At least it can be said that the looseness of the Arminian reasoning leaves an easier loophole of escape into a human philosophy than does the rigid logic of the Predestinarians.

Yet for all that, though we may follow Edwards's logical system to the breaking point, as we can follow every meta-

[1] Edwards, it should seem, had immediately in mind the *Essay on the Freedom of Will in God and the Creature* of Isaac Watts; but the notion had been discussed at length by Locke (*Essay* II, xxi), and at an earlier date had been touched on with great acumen by John Norris in his correspondence with Henry More.

physical system, and though we may feel that, in his revulsion from the optimism of the deists, he distorted the actual evil of existence into a nightmare of the imagination,—yet for all that, he remains one of the giants of the intellect and one of the enduring masters of religious emotion. He had not the legal and executive brain of Calvin, upon whose *Institutes* his scheme of theology is manifestly based, but in subtle resourcefulness of reasoning and still more in the scope of his spiritual psychology he stands above his predecessor. Few men have studied Edwards without recognizing the force and honesty of his genius.

## CHAPTER V

# Philosophers and Divines, 1720–1789

AN old-time classification of the human faculties will serve
to explain the development of American thought in the
eighteenth century, a development which led to the
overthrow of high Calvinism. As there were three divisions
of the human mind—intellect, sensibility, and will, so were there
three divisions among the enemies of orthodoxy. Those who
followed the intellect were the rationalists, or deists. Those
who followed sensibility were the "hot" men, or enthusiasts.
Those who followed the will were the ethical reformers, who
emphasized the conscious cultivation of morality rather than
a divinely wrought change in man's nature. This last group
constituted the Arminians, the first in order of time in leading
the assault upon embattled tradition. When Jonathan Edwards, in 1734, complained of the "great noise in this part of
the country about Arminianism," he showed his alertness to
the preliminary attack of the enemy. That attack was especially directed against the middle of the five points of Calvinism.
It was not so much against particular redemption, or the perseverance of the saints, as against irresistible grace that the
battle-cry was raised. The reason given was that such grace
was bound to destroy man's free agency and convert him into a
mere machine. This explains why Edwards threw up as a
counterscarp his massive work upon the freedom of the human
will wherein that freedom was virtually denied.

Meanwhile, the second group, the men of feeling, came into
action. Received as allies, they turned out to be anything but
a help to the cause. After the religious revival and the great
awakening of 1734, Edwards the logician became, in a measure,
Edwards the enthusiast. But calling in the aid of evangelists

like George Whitefield carried sensibility beyond the limits of sense. To argue against the Arminians that, because of irresistible grace, men lack all native moral power, was to make men altogether passive in conversion and to run the risk of being carried away in a flood of feeling. So while Edwards warmed up his system by his writings on the *Religious Affections*, Whitefield had to be cautioned by the Connecticut divine for his too great dependence upon impulse. Brought in as an ally, Whitefield thus became an unconscious underminer of high Calvinism. It was one thing to preach irresistible grace; it was another to lack the restraining grace of common sense.

It was this lack which brought in the third group, those who sought the test of intellect. Agreeing with the Arminians as to the importance of the will, and opposing the enthusiasts for their extravagance of feeling, they had behind them the whole weight of the age of reason. But here a paradox appears. While, in general, our eighteenth-century thought went through the three phases of the conventional classification of man's powers, the development of that thought was anything but conventional. Before the problems of the will and of the feelings could be determined by the orderly processes of reason, the controversy was complicated by the irruption of a foreign force. George Whitefield was the disturber of the peace, and through him the question of morals lapsed into a question of manners. It was not denied that the evangelist did some good. The fault lay in the way in which he did it. Against this inspired son of a tavern keeper the New England clergy united in using the adjective "low," and naturally, as leaders of provincial society, they damned anything that was low. This staid and proper body, priding themselves upon dignity in deportment and rationality in religion, were, moreover, outraged at the conduct of an itinerant preacher who held forth in fields and barns and preferred emotional tests to cool conviction. New England now saw revealed the old struggle between masses and classes, between town and gown. Against the enthusiasts and ranters the clergy and the college authorities were speedily arrayed. Whitefield decidedly made a tactical blunder when he brought railing accusations against divines like Charles Chauncy (1705–1787), pastor of the First Church in Boston, and Edward Wigglesworth (1693–1765), professor

of divinity in Harvard College.   On his first visit to the colonies,
Whitefield had made some unhappy remarks about the provincial universities as "abodes of darkness, a darkness which
could be felt," and about the collegians at Cambridge as
"close Pharisees, resting on head knowledge."   On his second
visit, he added insult to injury by saying that on account of
these "unguarded expressions" a few "mistaken, misinformed,
good old men were publishing half-penny testimonials against
the Lord's Anointed."

The reference here is, among others, to Wigglesworth.   The
latter, in his reply, does not deign to defend the college against
the charge of being a seminary of paganism, but proceeds to
attack its defamer: first, because of his manners, next, because
of his ways of making money, and lastly, because of the
evil fruits of enthusiasm.   He grants that an itinerant, who
frequently moves from place to place, may have a considerable
use in awakening his hearers from a dead and carnal frame.
But while such an exhorter may have a manner which is very
taking with the people, and a power to raise them to any
degree of warmth he pleases, yet in thrusting himself into
towns and parishes he destroys peace and order, extorts
money from the people, and arouses that pernicious thing—
enthusiasm.

This attack was to be expected.   The New England clergy, as
chosen members of a close corporation, abhorred the disturbers
of their professional etiquette and were alarmed at poachers
upon their clerical preserves.   It not only threatened their
social pedestals but it touched their pockets to have these
"new lights" taking the people from their work and business
and leading them to despise their own ministers.

This aspect of the Whitefield controversy shows that the
causes of the opposition were largely social and economic, the
same causes which worked—though in the other direction—in
the opposition to the establishment of English episcopacy in the
land.   When the New England fathers had both "pence and
power," as Tom Paine would say, it was natural that they
should not relish the loss of either, at the expense of high
churchmen or low itinerants.   But a cause deeper than the
economic lay in this outraging of the spirit of the times.   This
was the age of reason, and the leaders of church and college

prided themselves on being of a cool and logical temperament.
Hence Wigglesworth's most serious charge against Whitefield
is that of irrationality. Enthusiasm, he explains, is a charge of
a higher nature than perhaps people are generally aware of.
The nature of enthusiasm is to make a man imagine that
almost any thought which bears strongly upon his mind is
from the Spirit of God, when at the same time he has no
proof that it is. In short, to be of an enthusiastic turn is no
such innocent weakness as people imagine.

This was Wigglesworth's caveat to the public. Whitefield
might have made it out a mere halfpenny testimonial had it not
been succeeded by the formidable work of Charles Chauncy.
This was the volume entitled *Seasonable Thoughts on the State
of Religion in New England* (1743). That state, in the eyes of the
pastor of the First Church in Boston, was, in one word, bad.
The preaching of "disorderly walkers," especially their well-
advertised preaching in other men's parishes, it was argued,
would lead, should it become the general practice, to the entire
dissolution of our church state. But besides the evil effect upon
the body politic, there was that upon the human body. With
remarkable acumen, Chauncy points out the abnormalities in
the practices of revivalism. The new lights, he recounts, lay
very much stress on the "extraordinaries," such as agitations,
outcries, swoonings, as though they were some marks of a just
conviction of sin. This is their inference, but the real fact is
that the influence of awful words and fearful gestures is no
other than "a mechanical impression on animal nature."
And the same natural explanation holds for the joy of the new
lights. It may have its rise in the animal nature, for some have
made it evident, by their after lives, that their joy was only a
sudden flash, a spark of their own kindling. And when this
is expressed among some sorts of people by singing through
the streets and in ferryboats, from whatever cause it sprang it
is certainly one of the most incongruous ways of expressing
religious joy.

It must not be inferred from these strictures that Chauncy
was a sour Puritan, averse to people's happiness. The contrary was the truth. His objections lay in the superficial and
ephemeral character of the religious emotions among the new
lights. Their joy was evidently but the reaction of relief from

the fearsome tenets of their preachers.    The doctrines of total
depravity and eternal damnation struck terror into the heart
of the sinner.    Now it was by a sort of incantation, by a
promise of immediate assurance of salvation, that the itinerant removed this terror.    It was, then, in a skilful way that
Chauncy met such practices.    The places where the revivalists
had been at work were called the burnt-over districts.    To
prevent future conflagrations it was then necessary to start a
back-fire.    This Chauncy did by removing the unreasoning
terror of the old doctrines.    But it was necessary to do more.
In place of the old faith, which, though a painful thing to hold,
men were loath to abandon, there must be brought a new and
emollient doctrine.    New England's nervous diathesis called
for something to soothe the system.    This came to be found in
the exchange of pessimism for optimism; in the replacing of
a dread judge by a benevolent deity, belief in whom would give
a  steady  and  lasting  satisfaction.    By  1784  Chauncy, as
opposer of the new lights, had learned his lesson.    The heart
must be appealed to as well as the head.    So his argument is
built up from below, benevolence being first defined as "that
quality, in the human mind, without which we could not be
the objects of another's esteem."

With this hint taken from the learned English divine, Samuel
Clarke, his American disciple shows how the old doctrines will
dissolve of themselves.    Out of the five points of Calvinism
two were obviously inconsistent with benevolence.    One of
these was irresistible grace, as the correlate of irresistible power;
the other was eternal damnation, as the correlate of total
depravity.    One reason, therefore, why Chauncy attacked the
ranters was that they were reactionaries.    But the cruel old
penal view was bound to pass away of itself.    Men's minds
had entered the deistic drift.    The arguments of rationality
became the telling arguments.

"Some later writers"—and the remark is evidently directed
against Edwards—"might make the infinitely benevolent God,
the grand and only efficient, who has so connected a chain of
causes that His final result should be the everlasting damnation of
a great number of the creatures His hands had formed. . . .    But
such metaphysical reasoning does not stand the test of experience.
There is too much skill and contrivance displayed in the forma-

tion of this and other globes, too numerous the creatures formed with the capacities of enjoyment to lead to a jaundiced view of the Creator and His attributes. And so many creatures brought into existence according to a settled uniform course of nature, and with a variegated capacity for happiness, preclude the notion of an inscrutable or malevolent deity."[1]

This sort of argumentation reminds one of the discussion of Square and Thwackum on the eternal fitness of things. But with the exception of an occasional hack-writer like Thomas Paine, it was the method generally employed by scholars of the upper class. The method betrays a certain weakness in the middle of Chauncy's work, since it must have gone over the heads of men of the class reached by Whitefield, son of the innkeeper, or by Tennent, promoter of log-cabin learning.

Such an optimistic purview, embracing earth, sun, and moon, dry land and water, became stale, flat and unprofitable. The argument that things as they are, including disease and death, disclose no defect of benevolence in the deity, is not helped by the disclaimer that we "know not the intire plan of heaven and are able to see but a little way into the design of the Deity." This was naught but the old argument of a learned ignorance, much used by the upholders of the scheme of inscrutable decrees.

The strong part of Chauncy's work lies in his attack upon absolute causation. The net of necessity in which the framer of the Berkshire divinity was caught, was escaped by Chauncy through an appeal to common sense.

"The abettors of this scheme," argues the Bostonian, "must clearly and fully perceive its inconsistency with men being free agents, and that it totally destroys the idea of moral good and evil. . . . The argument may hold for beasts of the field, whose whole conduct is the effect of previous choice and pleasure; but for human beings the unbroken concatenation of causes would deprive them of free agency."

And so would it be with that other prop of Puritanism, the belief in divine intervention.

An infinitely benevolent being might interpose, as occasion required, to prevent the mischief that would otherwise take place,

[1] *Benevolence of the Deity*, pp. 32, 53, 55, 61.

but possibly the method of communicating good by general laws, uniformly adhered to, is, in the nature of things, a better adapted one to produce the greatest good, than the other method of inter- positions continually repeated.[1]

In a life that nearly spanned the eighteenth century, Chauncy affords an excellent example of the double reaction of the age of reason against the doctrines of irrationalism. His works had these two merits; they undermined the harsh doctrines of Calvinism which the new lights had utilized to strike terror into the hearts of the unthinking; and they afforded a substitute for sentimentalism, for, in place of violent joy, one could gain a placid contentment in the ways and works of Providence.

Another thinker of ability, but of a less noble and elevated style, was Chauncy's younger contemporary, Jonathan May- hew (1720–1766), a graduate of Harvard in 1744, and best known for his lively attacks upon the Tory doctrines of passive obedience and non-resistance. Mayhew gained a reputation for bringing a new style and manner into preaching. The son of a father who argued with ingenuity in behalf of human liberty, he was reputed to be a cheerful, liberal man, opposed to the gloomy doctrines of former times. Thus he early de- clared total depravity both dishonourable to the character of God and a libel on human nature. Mayhew's opposition to the five points of Calvinism was considered so imprudent that, at his ordination over the West Church, the Boston clergy declined the invitation to dine with the council, and one cautious cleric advised his barber not to go and hear such a heretic. Mayhew was really that, for he violently resisted the doctrine of irresistible grace, and entirely rejected the doctrine of the Trinity as taught by the Athanasian and Nicene creeds. In this he pointed the way to the coming Unitarianism, and that almost two generations before the Unitarian manifesto of 1819.

Although on the "new side," Mayhew was opposed to the "new lights." Long before the coming of Whitefield, he had been present at a religious revival in Maine, noticed its ex- travagance and fanaticism, and the people's violent gestures and shrieks. From this early experience, he came to value

[1] *Benevolence of the Deity*, pp. 132, 133.

"rational religion" the more highly. The phrase is significant. Upon the arrival of Whitefield in Boston in 1749, Mayhew claimed that the evangelist's hearers were chiefly "of the more illiterate sort," and that the discourse itself was "confused, conceited and enthusiastic."

The old term of reprobation reappears. So, like Chauncy himself, Mayhew offers the same antidote. In place of a God of wrath and terror, he would put the Scriptural God who is represented "under the characters of a father and a king, the wisest and best father, the wisest and best king." This sentiment eventuated in two Thanksgiving sermons *On the Nature, Extent and Perfection of the Divine Goodness.* In these the argument is ingenious. While Chauncy held that wisdom without goodness might be good, Mayhew held that goodness without wisdom might be bad. The political writer now appears in the doctrinal and shows that his God is no easy-going monarch whose goodness is to be considered mere good nature.

"As we recall certain well intentioned governors," he argues, "who, despite their paternal affection, have wrought prodigious mischief to the State, so we may in some measure conjecture, if we are not afraid even to think, what might be the consequence of boundless power, though accompanied with universal benevolence, but not adequate wisdom, extending itself at will thro-out the universe."[1]

But the argument must not lead to the Calvinistic *cul-de-sac*, whereby there is no other end for punishment, on the part of the king of heaven, save his own glory. As Mayhew in his *Discourse Concerning Unlimited Submission and Non-Resistance to the Higher Powers* (1750) had remonstrated against the orders from Whitehall, so here he remonstrates against the immutable decrees of the Westminster Confession. His reasoning leads to a literal *reductio ad absurdum*.

Tho' God is, in the highest sense, an absolute sovereign; yet in *that* ill-sense, he is not certainly an arbitrary Being. . . . For what glory could possibly redound to any being acting unreasonably, or contrary to the dictates of true goodness? It is peculiarly absurd to suppose that He, who accounts *goodness* his glory, should aim at advancing it by *such* a conduct.[2]

[1] *Divine Goodness*, p. 16.      [2] *Ibid.*, p. 26.

With the same caustic irony with which he had flavoured his celebrated *Reflections on the Resistance Made to King Charles I*, Mayhew seeks to prove that the king of heaven, though absolute, is not arbitrary.

"The Earthly Prince," he continues, "may take off the head of the traitor, robber, or murderer, not to gratify his own anger, but for the common good. Contrariwise, punitive justice may be a branch of goodness, but how far from goodness it would be to condemn the bulk of mankind to eternal misery."[1]

The amiable heretic of Massachusetts may here be contrasted with the rigid Calvinist of Connecticut. Edwards, in his dreadful Enfield sermon, implied that the majority of his hearers were in danger of hell fire. Mayhew calmly carried out that implication. He had taken as an appropriate text for his Thanksgiving sermon, "The Lord is good to all." But this, for the sake of the argument, he is willing to change to, "The Lord is good to three-fourths of His creatures, and His tender mercies are over three-fourths of all His works,"—and so on down to the smallest fraction of mankind.

Mayhew is a master of ironic attack. He discloses this in his political discourses, ranging from that against Non-Resistance to that against the Stamp Act. But when it comes to defending his views, he is weak. He declaims effectively against the terrible punishment to be meted out by the Calvinistic judge of all mankind, but, in upholding benevolence, he outdoes the most complacent deist of his day. The first of his Thanksgiving sermons contends that the nature of divine goodness admits of strict application *a priori*. The companion sermon attempts to make that goodness of universal extent, and goes to such extremes as praising December weather in the town of Boston. But though the arguments are forced, these provincial writings have a certain interest as being prototypes of those hollow documents, the Thanksgiving proclamations of governors and presidents.

Through the two Massachusetts divines, Chauncy and Mayhew, one may traverse, by parallel paths, the whole controversy between old and new lights, a controversy beginning with a narrow emotionalism and ending with a rationalistic trend

[1] *Divine Goodness*, p. 38.

towards universalism. A similar course of thought, but expressed with far higher literary skill, may be pursued in the writings of the Connecticut scholar Samuel Johnson (1696–1772), a graduate of Yale College in 1714, a disciple of George Berkeley when he came to Rhode Island in 1729 and, in 1754, the first head of King's College,[1] New York. Especially does Johnson's *Elementa Philosophica* strike a balance between extremes. Like the *Alciphron* of Berkeley, to whom the *Elements* was dedicated, Johnson's work was directed against both fatalists and enthusiasts. The author's situation was logically fortunate. He was familiar with both "predestination and fanatical principles" and avoided the excesses of each. Brought up in Yale College, under the rigid Rector Clap, he came to dislike the severities of Puritanism. Acquainted with the ways of "that strange fellow Whitefield," he was also opposed to the doctrines of grace, as preached in the revivals. Strict Calvinism, as he contended against Jonathan Dickinson, "reflects dishonour upon the best of Beings"; while this "odd and unaccountable enthusiasm," as he wrote to Berkeley, "rages like an epidemical frenzy" and, by dividing the dissenters, proves to them a source of weakness rather than of strength.

Johnson's position was that of a moderate man. Add to that his cheerful and benevolent temper, and he appears one of the most attractive of the colonial thinkers. His education in Connecticut, his trip to England, his friendship with Benjamin Franklin, were all part and parcel of his training in letters. Educated at New Haven at a time when the old lights framed the policy of the college, Johnson, as he says in his autobiography, "after many scruples and an intolerable uneasiness of mind" went over to "that excellent church, the Church of England." This change, which necessitated a public disavowal of his former faith, was due in large measure to browsing in forbidden fields. Before Johnson's graduation, some of the speculations and discoveries of Descartes, Boyle, Locke, and Newton had been heard in the Connecticut colony. But the young men were cautioned against these authors, as well as against a new philosophy which was attracting attention in England. The reason given was that the new thought would

---

[1] Now Columbia University.

corrupt the pure religion of the country and bring in another system of divinity.

It was characteristic of Johnson, brought up in the darkened chambers of Calvinism, to attempt to obtain a glimpse into the brighter world outside. He had partially done this in reading a rare copy of Lord Bacon's *Advancement of Learning*, with the consequence of finding himself "like one at once emerging out of the glimmer of twilight into the full sunshine of open day." For himself this result was reflected in a manuscript entitled *The Travails of the Intellect in the Microcosm and Macrocosm*. For the benefit of others who might be lost in the "palpable obscure" of scholasticism, Johnson next drafted *A General Idea of Philosophy*. In this, philosophy is artfully described as "The Study of Truth and Wisdom, *i. e.* of the Objects and Rules conducing to true Happiness." Such a definition was in marked contrast with the atmosphere of the college of Connecticut, where, as Johnson's earliest biographer put it, "the metaphysics taught was not fit for worms."

In 1731 Johnson had enlarged this "Cyclopaedia of Learning," into an *Introduction to the Study of Philosophy*. The purpose of this tract was to set before young gentlemen a general view of the whole system of learning in miniature, "as geography exhibits a general map of the whole terraqueous globe." The plan of the tract was likewise noteworthy. Instead of making man's chief end to glorify God, it made the happiness of mankind to be God's chief end. In the meantime, for the purpose of obtaining Episcopal ordination, Johnson had made a trip to England. There the young colonial had the distinction of meeting Alexander Pope at his villa, and the English Samuel Johnson. He also visited Oxford and Cambridge universities, from both of which he was later to be honoured with the doctorate of divinity. But, as he subsequently wrote to his son, who made a similar literary pilgrimage, he confessed that, though he liked "to look behind the gay curtain," he preferred "ease and independence in the tranquil vales of America." On his return home, Johnson found neither ease nor tranquillity. Coming back to the land of the blue laws, he felt obliged to preach and write against current Calvinism. Thus one parish sermon was directed against absolute predestination, "with its horror, despair, and gloomy apprehension," while one pamphlet contended that the "Doctrine of Divine Sovereignty as implying God's eternal, arbitrary and absolute determination . . . is contrary to the nature and attributes of God, because inconsistent with the very notion of His being a moral governor of the world."[1] Yet even in this discussion against the Presbyterian Jonathan Dickinson, Johnson exhibits a lightness of touch which relieves the subject of much of its soberness:

Suppose some unhappy wretch entirely in the power of some arbitrary sovereign prince. Suppose the sovereign had beforehand absolutely resolved he should be hanged, but for the fancy of the thing, or purely to please himself, and gratify a capricious humour of his, commands him to lift a weight of ten thousand pounds and heave it to the distance of a mile, and tells him if he will do this he will give him an estate of ten thousand a year, and if he will not do it he shall certainly be hanged. At the same time he promises and designs him no manner of help or means whereby he might be enabled to accomplish it. It is true he speaks very kindly to him, and gives him several great encouragements expressed just like promises. He tells him if he will be up and doing he will be with him, and that if he will try and strive and pray for help, his labour shall not be in vain. However, the truth of the matter at the bottom is that he never intends to help him, having beforehand absolutely resolved he shall be hanged, and without help he can no more stir the weight than create a world. Now I humbly conceive that this unhappy wretch is under a necessity of disobeying and being hanged.[2]

Johnson's skilfulness was shown better in his constructive than in his controversial writings. If he rendered Calvin absurd by his use of the satirical paraphrase, he rendered Berkeley plausible by the glamour of his style. He was first attracted to the Irish idealism because it supplied him with the strongest arguments against the doctrine of necessity. But when Berkeley himself came to America, the neophyte fell in love with the author and his system at the same time. It was then that Johnson, according to his best biographer, became a convert to the "new principle," which he regarded, when rightly understood, as the true philosophical support of faith. The

[1] *Letter from Aristocles*, 10 September, 1744.
[2] *Letter . . . in defence of Aristocles*, pp. 14–20.

denial of the absolute existence of matter, a whimsical paradox
to the superficial thinker, he found to mean nothing more than
a denial of an inconceivable substratum of sensible phenomena.
The affirmation of the merely relative existence of sensible
things was to him the affirmation of orderly combinations of
sensible phenomena, in which our corporeal pains and pleasures
were determined by divine ideas that are the archetypes of
physical existence.

The correspondence between Johnson and Berkeley was the
most notable in the history of early American thought.   It is
a great literary loss that not all of Berkeley's letters have been
recovered, for in them, as Johnson wrote, one can gather "that
Candour and Tenderness which are so conspicuous in both your
writings and conversation." From these *disjecta membra* of
Johnson, however, one can reconstruct the very form of that
idealism which rescues us from the absurdity of abstract ideas
and the gross notion of matter, takes away all subordinate natural causes, and accounts for all appearances by the immediate
will of the Supreme Spirit.    From Johnson's correspondence, then, one can gather Berkeley's own notions as to archetypes, ectypes, space, spirits and substance.   The fragments
throw a flood of light upon subjects of high interest to the metaphysician, but the effect upon the mind of the disciple was more
important, for through such veritable Berkeleian handbooks
as were Johnson's, the seeds of idealism attained a lodgment in
the American mind.   Fruition did not occur until the time of
Emerson, but for sheer literary skill in the presentment of a
system deemed impossible by most men of that day, Johnson's
*Elements* was remarkable.   The good bishop, to w om the
volume was dedicated, did not live to see it, but, as was remarked by Berkeley's son, this little book contained the wisdom
of the ages and showed the author to be very capable of spreading Berkeley's philosophy.

The spreading of that system, however, was checked by
untoward circumstances.   When a French critic observed that
Anglo-Americans of the late eighteenth century were unfit to
receive or to develop true idealism, he probably had in mind the
commercialism of the day and the threatening political state of
affairs between the colonies and the mother country.   Indeed,
in both places immaterialism found the times out of joint.

From Philadelphia, then the literary centre of the country, Franklin, the printer of the book, wrote that those parts of the *Elements of Philosophy* that savoured of what is called Berkeleianism are "not well understood here." And in London one can imagine the reception that would be given to a colonial production, from the anecdote recounted of the son of the American Samuel Johnson when he met the great lexicographer. The latter, after speaking harshly of the colonials, exclaimed, "The Americans! What do they know and what do they read?" "They read, Sir, the *Rambler*," was the quick reply.

Like son, like father. The elder Johnson was able to extricate himself from even such difficulties as those offered by the Berkeleian system. He also had the boldness to apply the principles of the new rationalism not only to all men, but to all ages of man. Intellectual light, he argues, is common to all intelligent beings, a Chinese or Japanese, a European or an American. It is also to be found in children. In contrast to such an opinion as that of Jonathan Edwards that infants were "like little vipers," Johnson asserted that we ought to think them of much more importance than we usually apprehend them to be. Considering their achievements in learning not only the mother tongue but the divine visual language, we should apply to them the good trite old saying, *Pueris maxima reverentia debetur*.

Considerations such as these were so contrary to the spirit of the times as to arouse opposition from both sides. To consider children worthy of reverence was opposed to the Puritan view of them as born in sin, and to consider that man as such is assisted by an inward intellectual light "perpetually beaming forth from the great fountain of all light" ran counter to the common sense of the day. Thus William Smith, provost of the College of Philadelphia, who held the place once offered by Franklin to Johnson, argues against these very issues as presented in the *Elements*. "Our author," he explains, "from a sincere zeal to vindicate the rights of the Deity, and a just abhorrence of the absurd system of the materialists, has gone farther towards the opposite extreme than will be justified by some philosophers."[1] The extreme here referred to was, of course, Berkeleianism, against which the Philadelphian argues

---

[1] Preface to the *Elements*.

in substance as follows: The Dean, while at Newport, might have been justified in putting into his *Minute Philosopher* rural descriptions exactly copied from those charming landscapes that presented themselves to his eye in the delightful island at the time he was writing,—that was all very well; but for the Dean's disciple to attempt to introduce into the schools and infant seminaries in America this unadulterated Irish idealism was another thing. Doctor Johnson, explains his critic, only pretends to teach logic and moral philosophy; his logic and his morality are very different from ours. There is no matter, by his scheme; no ground of moral obligation. Life is a dream. All is from the immediate impressions of the Deity. Metaphysical distinctions which no men, and surely no boys, can understand . . . will do much to prevent the fixing of virtue on her true bottom.[1]

Such was the ironical fate that befell Johnson. Though he had done good service against the enthusiasts, and had written the best ethical treatise of colonial times, he was nevertheless charged with being fantastical, and his work with undermining morality.

A similar fate befell the last of our colonial thinkers, John Woolman (1720–1772), the Quaker, a sort of provincial Piers Plowman, whose visions of reform were far ahead of his day. In his *Journal*, the humble tailor of New Jersey takes up, in order, the evils of war and of lotteries, of negro slavery and excessive labour, of the selling of rum to the Indians, of cruelty to animals. Moreover, like the visions of the Plowman, Woolman's work might be called a contribution to the history of English mysticism. Whittier described the *Journal* as "a classic of the inner life"; Channing, as "beyond comparison the sweetest and purest autobiography in the language"; while Charles Lamb urged his readers to get the writings of Woolman "by heart."

These writings are in marked contrast to the controversial spirit of their time. They avoid entangling alliances with either the old or new divinity, and have little to do with the endless quarrels between Calvinists and Arminians. In place of doctrine and formal creed come "silent frames" and

---

[1] Letter to the Rev. Richard Peters, July 18, 1754, from the original in the Pennsylvania Historical Society.

the exercises of the interior or hidden life. The contrast is like that portrayed by Woolman himself when he said that "while many parts of the world groaned under the heavy calamities of war, our habitation remains quiet, and our land fruitful."

In Woolman, then, we have the fruits of quietism as contrasted with the fruits of controversy. Duties rather than doctrine are emphasized, and all with that air of innocent simplicity held so desirable by the Society of Friends. Because of his candour and his fervour, Woolman might be called a socialist unconscious of his socialism, except for the fact that his efforts were exerted in a private capacity, and that he offended not even those with whom he laboured—soldiers, slave owners, dealers in goods which were to be looked upon as contraband to Christianity. He accomplished his results upon the Quaker principle of natural sensibility. In marked contrast to the Calvinist principle of the depravity of the human heart, he argues upon the possibilities of the human mind towards good: —"that as the mind was moved, by an inward principle, to love God as an invisible, incomprehensible being; by the same principle it was moved to love Him in all His manifestations in the visible world."[1]

Armed with this gentle logic, he began to set down, not his programme of reforms, but a recital of certain "heavenly openings" in respect to the care and providence of the Almighty over his creatures. The first of those creatures for whom Woolman was concerned was a slave. Here there arose a conflict between the logic of compassion and the logic of commerce, for when his employer obliged him to write a bill of sale for a poor negro woman, he was much afflicted in mind. As was his wont, Woolman now began to gather reasons for his feeling of uneasiness. That which was against conscience he now finds to be against logical conviction, especially when in a journey to the Southern provinces he meets with slave owners. To their arguments in favour of fetching negroes from Africa for slaves because of the wretchedness occasioned by their intestine wars, he replies that liberty is the natural right of all men equally. But this general principle—a commonplace of the age of reason—is not so effective as one more particular:

[1] *Journal*, p. 9.

There is great odds on what principle we act. If compassion on the Africans, in regard to their domestic trouble, were the real motives of our purchasing them, that spirit of tenderness being attended to, would incite us to use them kindly. But to say they live unhappy in Africa is far from being an argument in our favour; our real views in purchasing them are to advance ourselves, and, while our buying captives taken in war animates those parties to push on the war and increase desolation amongst them, we too are putting upon our shoulders a burthensome stone, a burden that will grow heavier and heavier till times change in a way disagreeable to us.[1]

Upon this argument, presented with a kindly shrewdness, many of Woolman's slave-owning hearers looked serious. It was a prophecy of the irrepressible conflict between slave-holders and free-holders, and that over a century before that conflict came. So the prospect of a road lying open to degeneracy in some parts of this newly settled land of America, now drove Woolman to publish, and at his own expense, *Some Considerations on the Keeping of Negroes Recommended to the Professors of Christianity of every Denomination* (1754-62). The author is troubled with a weight of distress because, instead of the spirit of meekness, gentleness, and heavenly wisdom, a spirit of fierceness and a love of dominion too generally prevails. Yet it is not criticism, but compassion, that furnishes Woolman with his strongest lever against that great building "raised by degrees, from small beginnings in error." In a series of indirect questions, the logician of the heart brings the matter home. Drawing upon contemporary accounts of the slave trade, he argues in this fashion:

Should we consider ourselves present as spectators, when cruel negroes privately catch innocent children, who are employed in the fields; hear their lamentable cries, under the most terrifying apprehensions; or should we look upon it as happening in our own families, having our children carried off by savages, we must needs own, that such proceedings are contrary to the nature of Christianity.[2]

In the light of such disclosures, Woolman might have attacked the accursed institution with directness and bitterness, but his method is ever indirect, ever imbued with a sweet reasonableness.

[1] *Journal*, p. 60.   [2] *Keeping of Negroes*, p. 317.

"The English government," he continues, "hath been commended by candid foreigners for the disuse of racks and tortures, so much practiced in some states; but this multiplying slaves now leads to it; for where people exact hard labour of others, without a suitable reward, and are resolved to continue in that way, severity to such who oppose them becomes the consequence. . . . These things are contrary to the true order of kind providence. Admit that the first negro man and his wife did as much business as their master and mistress, and that the children of the slaves have done some more than their young masters. . . . It follows, that in equity these negroes have a right to a part of this increase. . . . Again, if we seriously consider that liberty is the right of innocent men; that the Almighty God is a refuge for the oppressed; that in reality we are indebted to them . . . to retain them in perpetual servitude, without present cause for it, will produce effects, in the event, more grievous than setting them free would do."[1]

And so in a final passage breathing the very spirit of the Society of Friends, the Quaker liberator presents the fundamental objection to the keeping of the poor blacks in servitude:

There is a principle, which is pure, placed in the human mind, which in different places and ages hath had different names; it is, however, pure and proceeds from God.—It is deep, and inward, confined to no forms of religion, nor excluded from any, where the heart stands in perfect sincerity. In whomsoever this takes root, and grows, of what nation soever, they become brethren.[2]

[1] *Keeping of Negroes*, p. 298.          [2] *Ibid.*, p. 325.

## CHAPTER VI

# Franklin

IN a respectful and indeed laudatory notice of Franklin for *The Edinburgh Review* of July, 1806, Lord Jeffrey employed the case of the "uneducated tradesman of America" to support his contention that "regular education is unfavourable to vigour or originality of understanding." Franklin attained his eminence, so runs the argument, without academical instruction, with only casual reading, without the benefit of association with men of letters, and "in a society where there was no relish and no encouragement for literature." This statement of Franklin's educational opportunities is manifestly inadequate; but it so pleasantly flatters our long-standing pride in our self-made men that we are loath to challenge it. The hero presented to the schoolboy and preserved in popular tradition is still an "uneducated tradesman of America": a runaway Boston printer walking up Market Street in Philadelphia with his three puffy rolls; directing his fellow shopkeepers the way to wealth; sharply inquiring of extravagant neighbours whether they have not paid too much for their whistle; flying his kite in a thunderstorm; by a happy combination of curiosity and luck making important contributions to science; and, to add the last lustre to his name, by a happy combination of industry and frugality making his fortune. This picturesque and racy figure is obviously a product of provincial America, the first great Yankee with all the strong lineaments of the type: hardness, shrewdness, ingenuity, practical sense, frugality, industry, self-reliance. The conception of the man here suggested is perhaps sound enough so far as it goes, being derived mainly from facts supplied by Franklin himself in the one book through which he has secured an eternal life in literature. But the popular notion of his personality thus derived is incomplete, because the *Autobiography*, ending at the year 1757, contains no record of the thirty-three years which developed a competent provincial into an able, cultivated, and imposing man of the world.

The Franklin now discoverable in the ten volumes of his complete works is one of the most widely and thoroughly cultivated men of his age. He had not, to be sure, a university training, but he had what serves quite as well: sharp appetite and large capacity for learning, abundance of books, extensive travel, important participation in great events, and association through a long term of years with the most eminent men of three nations. In touch as printer and publisher with the classic and current literature produced at home and imported from abroad, he becomes in Philadelphia almost as good a "Queen Anne's man" as Swift or Defoe. His scientific investigations bring him into correspondence with fellow-workers in England, France, Germany, Italy, Holland, and Spain. Entering upon public life, he is forced into co-operation or conflict with the leading politicians, diplomats, and statesmen of Europe. In his native land he has known men like Cotton Mather, Whitefield, Benjamin Rush, Benjamin West, Ezra Stiles, Noah Webster, Jay, Adams, Jefferson, and Washington. In England, where his affections strike such deep root that he considers establishing there his permanent abode, he is in relationship, more or less intimate, with Mandeville, Paine, Priestley, Price, Adam Smith, Robertson, Hume, Joseph Banks, Bishop Watson, Bishop Shipley, Lord Kames, Lord Shelburne, Lord Howe, Burke, and Chatham. Among Frenchmen he numbers on his list of admiring friends Vergennes, Lafayette, Mirabeau, Turgot, Quesnay, La Rochefoucauld-Liancourt, Condorcet, Lavoisier, Buffon, D'Alembert, Robespierre, and Voltaire. It is absurd to speak of one who has been subjected to the moulding of such forces as a product of the provinces. All Europe has wrought upon and metamorphosed the Yankee printer. The man whom Voltaire kisses is a statesman, a philosopher, a friend of mankind, and a favourite son of the eighteenth century. With no softening of his patriotic fibre or loss of his Yankee tang, he has acquired all the common culture and most of the master characteristics of the Age of Enlightenment—up to the point where the French Revolution injected into it a drop of madness: its emancipation from authority, its regard for reason and nature, its social consciousness, its progressiveness, its tolerance, its cosmopolitanism, and its bland philanthropy. Now this man deserves his large place in our literary history not so much by virtue of his writings, which had little immediate influence upon *belles-lettres,* as by virtue of his acts and ideas, which helped liberate and liberalize America. To describe his most important work is to recite the story of his life.

In reviewing his own career Franklin does not dwell on the fact that he who was to stand before kings had emerged from a tallow chandler's shop. To his retrospective eye there was nothing miraculous nor inexplicable in his origin. On the contrary he saw and indicated very clearly the sources of his talents and the external impulses that gave them direction. Born in Boston on 6 January, 1706, he inherited from his long-lived parents, Josiah and Abiah Folger Franklin, a rugged physical and mental constitution which hardly faltered through the hard usage of eighty-four years. He recognized and profited by his father's skill in drawing and music, his "mechanical genius," his "understanding and solid judgment in prudential matters, both in private and publick affairs," his admirable custom of having at his table, "as often as he could, some sensible friend or neighbour to converse with," always taking care "to start some ingenious or useful topic for discourse, which might tend to improve the minds of his children." Benjamin's formal schooling was begun when he was eight years old and abandoned, together with the design of making him a clergyman, when he was ten. He significantly remarks, however, that he does not remember a time when he could not read; and the subsequent owner of one of the best private libraries in America was as a mere child an eager collector of books. For the two years following his removal from school he was employed in his father's business. When he expressed a firm disinclination to become a tallow chandler, his father attempted to discover his natural bent by taking him about to see various artisans at their work. Everything that Franklin touched taught him something; and everything that he learned, he used. Though his tour of the trades failed to win him to any mechanical occupation, it has ever since been a pleasure to me [he says] to see good workmen handle their tools; and it has been useful to me, having learnt so much by it as to be able to do little odd jobs myself in my house . . . and to construct little machines for my experiments, while the intention of making the experiment was fresh and warm in my mind.

Throughout his boyhood and youth he apparently devoured every book that he could lay hands upon. He went through his father's shelves of "polemic divinity"; read abundantly in Plutarch's *Lives;* acquired Bunyan's works "in separate little volumes," which he later sold to buy Burton's *Historical Collections;* received an impetus towards practical improvements from Defoe's *Essay upon Projects* and an impetus towards virtue from Mather's *Essays to do Good.* Before he left Boston he had his mind opened to free speculation and equipped for logical reasoning by Locke's *Essay Concerning Human Understanding,* the Port Royal *Art of Thinking,* Xenophon's *Memorabilia,* and the works of Shaftesbury and Collins.

Franklin found the right avenue for a person of his "bookish inclination" when his brother James, returning from England in 1717 with a press and letters, set up in Boston as a printer, and proceeded to the publication of *The Boston Gazette,* 1719, and *The New England Courant,* 1721. Benjamin, aged twelve, became his apprentice. It can hardly be too much emphasized that this was really an inspiring "job." It made him stand at a very early age full in the wind of local political and theological controversy. It forced him to use all his childish stock of learning and daily stimulated him to new acquisitions. It put him in touch with other persons, young and old, of bookish inclination. They lent him books which kindled his poetic fancy to the pitch of composing occasional ballads in the Grub Street style, which his brother printed, and had him hawk about town. His father discountenanced these effusions, declaring that "verse-makers were generally beggars"; but coming upon his son's private experiments in prose, he applied the right incentive by pointing out where the work "fell short in elegance of expression, in method, and in perspicuity." "About this time," says Franklin in a familiar paragraph, "I met with an odd volume of the *Spectator.*"

Anticipating Dr. Johnson's advice by half a century, he gave his days and nights to painstaking study and imitation of Addison till he had mastered that style—"familiar but not coarse, and elegant but not ostentatious"—which several generations of English essayists have sought to attain. All the world has heard how Franklin's career as a writer began with an anonymous contribution stealthily slipped under the door of his brother's printing-house at night, and in the morning approved for publication by his brother's circle of "writing friends." Professor Smyth[1] inclined to identify this contribution with the first of fourteen humorous papers with Latin mottoes signed "Silence Dogood," which appeared fortnightly in *The New England Courant* from March to October, 1722. In this year Benjamin was in charge of the *Courant* during his brother's imprisonment for printing matter offensive to the Assembly; and when, on repetition of the offence, the master was forbidden to publish his journal, it was continued in the name of the apprentice. In this situation James became jealous and overbearing, and Benjamin became insubordinate. When it grew evident that there was not room enough in Boston for them both, the younger brother left his indentures behind, and in 1723 made his memorable flight to Philadelphia.

Shortly after his arrival in the Quaker city, he found employment with the second printer in Philadelphia, Samuel Keimer, a curious person who kept the Mosaic law. In 1724, encouraged by the facile promises of Governor Keith, Franklin went to England in the expectation that letters of credit and recommendation from his patron would enable him to procure a printing outfit. Left in the lurch by the governor, he served for something over a year in two great London printing-houses, kept free-thinking and rather loose company, and, in refutation of Wollaston's *Religion of Nature*, upon which he happened to be engaged in the composing-room, published in 1725 his suppressed tract *On Liberty and Necessity*. Returning to Philadelphia in 1726, he re-entered the employ of Keimer; in

[1] *The Writings of Benjamin Franklin.* Collected and edited by Albert Henry Smyth. New York, 1907. Vol. II, p. 1. The Dogood Papers were claimed by Franklin in the first draft of his *Autobiography*, and they have been long accredited to him; but they were first included in his collected works by Professor Smyth.

1728 formed a brief partnership with Hugh Meredith; and in 1730 married and set up for himself. In 1728 he founded the famous Junto Club for reading, debating, and reforming the world—an institution which developed into a powerful organ of political influence. Shortage of money in the province prompted him to the composition of his *Modest Inquiry into the Nature and Necessity of Paper Currency* (1729), a service for which his friends in the Assembly rewarded him by employing him to print the money—"a very profitable job and a great help to me." Forestalled by Keimer in a project for launching a newspaper, Franklin contributed in 1728–9 to the rival journal, published by Bradford, a series of sprightly "Busy-Body" papers in the vein of the periodical essayists. Keimer was forced to sell out; and Franklin acquired from him the paper known from 2 October, 1729, as *The Pennsylvania Gazette.* To this he contributed, besides much miscellaneous matter, such pieces as the *Dialogue between Philocles and Horatio concerning Virtue and Pleasure*, the letters of "Anthony Afterwit" and "Alice Addertongue," *A Meditation on a Quart Mug*, and *A Witch Trial at Mount Holly.* In 1732 he began to issue the almanacs containing the wit and wisdom of "Poor Richard," a homely popular philosopher, who is only the incarnation of common sense, and who is consequently not, as has been carelessly assumed, to be identified with his creator.

By the time he was thirty Franklin gave promise of becoming, by a gradual expansion of his useful activities, the leading Pennsylvanian. In 1736 he was chosen clerk of the General Assembly, and in the following year was appointed postmaster of Philadelphia. He made both these offices useful to his printing business and to his newspaper. In compensation, he used his newspaper and his business influence to support his measures for municipal improvements, among the objects of which may be mentioned street-sweeping, paving, a regular police force, a fire company, a hospital, and a public library. As his business prospered, he expanded it by forming partnerships with his promising workmen and sending them with printing-presses into other colonies. In 1741 he experimented with a monthly publication, *The General Magazine and Historical Chronicle for all the British Colonies in America;* this monthly, notable as the second issued in America, expired with the sixth number. In 1742 he invented the stove of which he published a description in 1744 as *An Account of the New Invented Pennsylvanian Fire Places*. In 1743 he drew up proposals for an academy which eventually became the University of Pennsylvania, and in 1744 he founded the American Philosophical Society. In 1746 he witnessed Spence's electrical experiments in Boston, bought the apparatus, and repeated the experiments in Philadelphia, where interest in the new science was further stimulated that year by a present of a Leyden jar given to the Library Company by the English experimenter Peter Collinson. To this English friend Franklin made extended reports of his earlier electrical investigations in the form of letters which Collinson published in London in 1751 with the title *Experiments and Observations in Electricity, made at Philadelphia in America, by Mr. Benjamin Franklin.* In 1752 he showed the identity of lightning and electricity by his kite experiment, and invented the lightning rod. In 1748, being assured of a competency, he had turned over his business to his foreman David Hall, and purposed devoting the rest of his life to philosophical inquiries. But he had inextricably involved himself in the affairs of his community, which, as soon as it found him at leisure, "laid hold" of him, as he says, for its own purposes—"every part of the civil government, and almost at the same time, imposing some duty upon me." He was made a justice of the peace, member of the common council, and alderman, and was chosen burgess to represent the city of Philadelphia in the General Assembly. In 1753 he was appointed jointly with William Hunter to exercise the office of postmaster-general of America. In 1754 as a member of the Pennsylvania commission he laid before the colonial congress at Albany the "Plan of Union" adopted by the commissioners. In 1755 he displayed remarkable energy, ability, and public spirit in providing transportation for General Braddock's ill-fated expedition against the French; and in the following year he himself took command of a volunteer military organization for the protection of the north-west frontier. In 1757 he was sent to England to present the long-standing grievances of the Pennsylvania Assembly against the proprietors for obstructing legislation designed to throw upon them a fair share of the expense of government.

Though Franklin's political mission was not wholly successful, his residence in England from 1757 to 1762 was highly profitable to him. It developed his talent as a negotiator of public business with strangers; it enabled him to consider British colonial policies from English points of view; and it afforded him many opportunities for general self-improvement. After a fruitless effort to obtain satisfaction from the representatives of the Penn family, dismissing as impractical the hope of procuring for Pennsylvania a royal charter, he appealed to the Crown to exempt the Assembly from the influence of proprietary instructions and to make the proprietary estates bear a more equitable proportion of the taxes. To get the Assembly's case before the public, he collaborated with an unknown hand on *An Historical Review of the Constitution and Government of Pennsylvania*, published in 1759. The result was a compromise which in the circumstances he regarded as a victory. His interest in the wider questions of imperial policy he exhibited in 1760 by aspersing the advocates of a hasty and inconclusive peace with France in his stinging little skit, *Of the Meanes of disposing the Enemies to Peace*,[1] which he presented as an extract from the work of a Jesuit historian. In 1760, also, he was joint author with Richard Jackson of a notably influential argument for the retention of Canada, *The Interest of Great Britain Considered with Regard to Her Colonies;* to which was appended his *Observations Concerning the Increase of Mankind, Peopling of Countries*, etc. In the intervals of business, he sat for his portrait, attended the theatre, played upon the harmonica, experimented with electricity and heat, made a tour of the Low Countries, visited the principal cities of England and Scotland, received honorary degrees from the universities, and enjoyed the society of Collinson, Priestley, Price, Hume, Adam Smith, Robertson, and Kames. He returned to America in the latter part of 1762. In 1763 he made a 1600-mile tour of the northern provinces to inspect the postoffices. In the following year he was again in the thick of Pennsylvania politics, working with the party in the Assembly which sought to have the proprietary government of the province replaced by a royal charter. In support of this movement he published in 1764 his *Cool Thoughts*

[1] See *Writings*, ed. Smyth, Vol. IV, pp. 89–95.

*on the Present Situation of our Public Affairs* and his *Preface to the Speech of Joseph Galloway*, a brilliant and blasting indictment of the proprietors, Thomas and Richard Penn.

In the fall of 1764 Franklin was sent again to England by the Assembly to petition for a royal charter and to express the Assembly's views with regard to Grenville's Stamp Act, then impending. On 11 July, 1765, after the obnoxious measure had been passed by an overwhelming majority, Franklin wrote to Charles Thomson:

> Depend upon it, my good neighbour, I took every step in my power to prevent the passing of the Stamp Act. . . . But the Tide was too strong against us. The nation was provoked by American Claims of Independence, and all Parties joined in resolving by this act to settle the point. We might as well have hindered the sun's setting.

This letter and one or two others of about the same date express a patient submission to the inevitable. As soon, however, as Franklin was fully apprised of the fierce flame of opposition which the passage of the act had kindled in the colonies, he caught the spirit of his constituents and threw himself sternly into the struggle for its repeal. In 1766 he underwent his famous examination before the House of Commons on the attitude of the colonies towards the collection of the new taxes. The report of this examination, which was promptly published, is one of the most interesting and impressive pieces of dramatic dialogue produced in the eighteenth century. After the repeal, Franklin received recognition at home in the shape of new duties: in 1768 he was appointed agent for Georgia; in 1769, for New Jersey; in 1770, for Massachusetts. In the summer of 1766 he visited Germany; the following summer he visited Paris; and he was in France again for a month in 1769. His pen in these years was employed mainly in correspondence and in communications to the newspapers, in which he pointedly set forth the causes which threatened a permanent breach between the mother country and the colonies. In 1773 he published in *The Gentleman's Magazine* two little masterpieces of irony which Swift might have been pleased to sign: *An Edict by the King of Prussia* and *Rules by which a Great Empire may be Reduced to a Small*

*One.* In 1774, in consequence of his activity in exposing Governor Hutchinson's proposals for the military intimidation of Massachusetts, Franklin was subjected before the Privy Council to virulent and scurrilous abuse from Attorney-General Wedderburn. This onslaught it was, accentuated by his dismissal from the office of postmaster-general, which began to curdle in Franklin his sincere long-cherished hope of an ultimate reconciliation. It is a curiously ominous coincidence that in this year of his great humiliation he sent with a letter of recommendation to his son-in-law in Philadelphia one Thomas Paine, an obscure Englishman of whiggish temper, two years later to become the fieriest advocate of American independence. In disgrace with the Court, Franklin lingered in England to exhaust the last possibilities of amicable adjustment: petitioning the king, conferring with Burke and Chatham, and curiously arranging for secret negotiations with the go-betweens of the Ministry over the chessboard of Lord Howe's sister. He sailed from England in March, 1775, half-convinced that the Ministry were bent upon provoking an open rebellion. When he arrived in Philadelphia, he heard what had happened at Lexington and Concord. On 5 July, 1775, he wrote a letter to an English friend of thirty years' standing, William Strahan, then a member of Parliament; it was shortened like a Roman sword and sharpened to this point:

> You and I were long Friends:—You are now my Enemy,—and I am
>
>          Yours,
>
>             B. FRANKLIN.

As Franklin was sixty-nine years old in 1775, he might fairly have retreated to his library, and have left the burden of the future state to younger hands. He had hardly set foot on shore, however, before the Pennsylvania Assembly elected him delegate to the first Continental Congress, where his tried sagacity was enlisted in organizing the country's political, economic, and military resources for the great conflict. On 7 July, 1775, the old man wrote to Priestley:

> My time was never more fully employed. In the morning at six, I am at the Committee of Safety, appointed by the Assembly

to put the province in a state of defence; which committee holds till near nine, when I am at the Congress, and that sits till after four in the afternoon.

In the period slightly exceeding a year previous to his departure for France, he served on innumerable committees of the Congress, was made Postmaster-General of the colonies, presided over the Constitutional Convention of Pennsylvania, was sent on a mission to Canada, assisted in drafting the Declaration of Independence, and signed it.

In October, 1776, he sailed for France on a commission of the Congress to negotiate a treaty of alliance, which was concluded in February, 1778, after the surrender of Burgoyne had inspired confidence in the prospects of the American arms. In September, 1778, he was appointed plenipotentiary to the Court of France. Clothed with large powers, he transacted in the next few years an almost incredible amount of difficult business for his country. He obtained from the French government the repeated loans which made possible the carrying on of a long war; he made contracts for clothing and ammunition; he dissuaded or recommended to Congress foreign applicants for commissions in the colonial army; he arranged exchanges of prisoners-of-war; he equipped and to some extent directed the operations of privateers; he supplied information to many Europeans emigrating to America; he negotiated treaties of amity and commerce with Sweden and Prussia. With all this engrossing business on his hands, he found time to achieve an immense personal popularity. He was not merely respected as a masterly diplomat; he was lionized and idolized as the great natural philosopher, the august champion of liberty, and the friend of humanity. In the press of public affairs, never losing interest in scientific matters, he served on a royal French commission to investigate Mesmerism; sent to his foreign correspondents ingenious geological and meteorological conjectures; and transmitted to the Royal Society reports on French experiments in aeronautics. He entertained with a certain lavishness at his house in Passy; and he was a frequent diner-out, adored for his wit and good humour in the intimate coteries of Mme. Helvetius and Mme. Brillon. He set up for the amusement of himself and his friends a private press in Passy, on which he printed a number of *bagatelles* of an accomplished and charming levity: *The Ephemera* (1778), *The Morals of Chess* (1779), *The Whistle* (1779), *The Dialogue between Franklin and the Gout* (1780.) In 1784 he resumed work on his unfinished autobiography, and published *Advice to such as would remove to America* and *Remarks Concerning the Savages of North America.* In his residence in France he began seriously to feel the siege of gout, the stone, and old age. In 1781, in reply to repeated supplications for leave to go home and die, Congress had appointed him a member of the commission to negotiate a treaty of peace between England and the United States. This last great task was completed in 1785. In midsummer of that year he said a regretful farewell to his affectionate French friends, received the king's portrait set in four hundred diamonds, and in one of the royal litters was carried down to his point of embarkation at Havre de Grace.

Franklin arrived in Philadelphia in September, 1785, resolved to set his house in order. He was soon made aware that, like the hero in *The Conquest of Granada*, he had not "leisure yet to die." He was overwhelmed with congratulations; or, as he put it with characteristic modesty of phrase in a letter to his English friend Mrs. Hewson: "I had the happiness of finding my family well, and of being very kindly received by my Country folk." In the month after his arrival he was elected President of the State of Pennsylvania; and the honour was thrust upon him again in 1786 and in 1787. In a letter of 14 November, 1785, he says:

I had not firmness enough to resist the unanimous desire of my country folks; and I find myself harnessed again in their service for another year. They engrossed the prime of my life. They have eaten my flesh, and seem resolved now to pick my bones.

In 1787 he was chosen a delegate to the convention to frame the Constitution of the United States—an instrument which he deemed not perfect, yet as near perfection as the joint wisdom of any numerous body of men could bring it, handicapped by "their prejudices, their passions, their local interests, and their selfish views." In 1789, as President of the Abolition Society, Franklin signed a memorial against slavery which was laid before the House of Representatives; and on 23 March, 1790, less than a month before his death, he wrote for *The Federal Gazette* an ironical justification of the enslaving of Christians by African Mohammedans—quite in the vein of the celebrated *Edict of the King of Prussia.* As the shadows thickened about him, he settled his estate, paid his compliments to his friends, and departed, on the seventeenth day of April, 1790, in his eighty-fifth year.

In the matter of religion Franklin was distinctly a product of the eighteenth-century enlightenment. He took his direction in boyhood and early manhood from deistical writers like Pope, Collins, and Shaftesbury. At various periods of his life he drew up articles of belief, which generally included recognition of one God, the providential government of the world, the immortality of the soul, and divine justice. To profess faith in as much religion as this he found emotionally gratifying, socially expedient, and conformable to the common sense of mankind. He would have subscribed without hesitation to both the positive and negative dogmas of the *religion civile* formulated by Rousseau in the *Contrat Social.* In his later years he was in sympathetic relations with Paine, Price, and Priestley. He was, however, of a fortunately earlier generation than these English "heretics," and certain other circumstances enabled him to keep the temper of his heterodoxy sweet while theirs grew acidulous, and to walk serenely in ways which for them were embittered by the *odium theologicum.* His earlier advent upon the eighteenth-century scene made possible the unfolding and comfortable settlement of his religious ideas before deism had clearly allied itself with political radicalism and edged its sword for assault upon inspired Bible and established church as powers federate with political orthodoxy in upholding the ancient régime. Among the diverse denominational bodies in Pennsylvania his perfectly genuine tolerance and his unfailing tact helped him to maintain a friendly neutrality between parties which were far from friendly. Like Lord Chesterfield, he sincerely believed in the decency and propriety of going to church; and he went himself when he could endure the preachers. He advised his daughter to go constantly, "whoever preaches." He made pecuniary contributions to all the leading denominations in Philadelphia; respectfully acknowledged the good features of each; and undertook to unite in his own creed the common and, as he thought, the essential features of all. Man of the world as he was, he enjoyed the warm friendship of good Quakers, good Presbyterians, Whitefield, the Bishop of St. Asaph, and his French abbés. His abstention from theological controversy was doubtless due in part to a shrewd regard for his own interest and influence as a business man and a public servant; but it was due in perhaps equal measure to his profound indifference to metaphysical questions unrelated to practical conduct. "Emancipated" in childhood and unmolested in the independence of his mind, he reached maturity without that acrimony of free thought incident to those who attain independence late and have revenges to take. He was consistently opposed to the imposition of religious tests by constitutional authority. But in the Constitutional Convention of 1787 he offered a motion in favour of holding daily prayers before the deliberations of the assembly, for, as he declared, "the longer I live, the more convincing proofs I see of this Truth, *that* God *governs in the Affairs of Men.*" With his progress in eminence and years, he seems to have been somewhat strengthened in Cicero's conviction that so puissant a personality as his own could not utterly perish, and he derived a kind of classical satisfaction from the reflection that this feeling was in concurrence with the common opinions of mankind. A few weeks before his death he admitted, in a remarkable letter to Ezra Stiles, a doubt as to the divinity of Jesus; but he remarked with his characteristic tranquillity that he thought it "needless to busy myself with it now, when I expect soon an Opportunity of knowing the Truth with less Trouble." Not elate, like Emerson, yet quite unawed, this imitator of Jesus and Socrates walked in this world and prepared for his ease in Zion.

Franklin set himself in youth to the study of "moral perfection," and the work which only great public business prevented his leaving as his literary monument was to have been a treatise on the "art of virtue." His merits, however, in both the theory and practice of the moral life have been seriously called in question. It is alleged that his standards were low and that he did not live up to them. It must be conceded on the one hand that he had a natural son who became governor of New Jersey, and on the other hand that industry and frugality,

which most of us place among the minor, he placed among the
major virtues. When one has referred the *"errata"* of his
adolescence to animal spirits, "free thinking," and bad company; and when one has explained certain laxities of his
maturity by alluding to the indulgent temper of the French
society in which he then lived; one may as well candidly admit
that St. Francis made chastity a more conspicuous jewel in his
crown of virtues than did Dr. Franklin. And when one has
pointed out that the prudential philosophy of *Poor Richard's
Almanac* was rather a collection of popular wisdom than an
original contribution; and when one has called attention to the
special reasons for magnifying economic virtues in a community
of impecunious colonists and pioneers; one may as well frankly
acknowledge that there is nothing in the precepts of the great
printer to shake a man's egotism like the shattering paradoxes
of the Beatitudes nor like the *Christian Morals* of Sir Thomas
Browne to make his heart elate. Franklin had nothing of what
pietists call a "realizing sense" of sin or of the need for mystical
regeneration and justification—faculties so richly present in
his contemporary Jonathan Edwards. His cool calculating
reason, having surveyed the fiery battleground of the Puritan
conscience, reported that things are properly forbidden because
hurtful, not hurtful because forbidden. Guided by this
utilitarian principle, he simplified his religion and elaborated
his morality. His system included much more than maxims
of thrift and prudent self-regard, and to insinuate that he set
up wealth as the *summum bonum* is a sheer libel. He commended diligence in business as the means to a competency;
he commended a competency as a safeguard to virtue; and he
commended virtue as the prerequisite to happiness. The
temple that he reared to Moral Perfection was built of thirteen
stones: temperance, silence, order, resolution, frugality, industry, sincerity, justice, moderation, cleanliness, tranquillity,
chastity, and humility—the last added on the advice of a
Quaker. He wrought upon the structure with the method
of a monk and he recorded his progress with the regularity of a
bookkeeper. The presiding spirit in the edifice, which made it
something more than a private oratory, was a rational and
active benevolence towards his fellow-mortals in every quarter
of the earth. The wide-reaching friendliness in Franklin may

be distinguished in two ways from the roseate humanitarian
enthusiasm in the Savoyard Vicar. It was not begotten by a
theory of "natural goodness" nor fostered by millennial
expectations, but was born of sober experience with the utility
of good will in establishing satisfactory and fruitful relations
among men. It found expression not in rhetorical periods
but in numberless practical means and measures for ameliorating the human lot. By no mystical intuition but by the common light of reason the "prudential philosopher" discovered
and acted upon the truth that the greatest happiness that can
come to a man in this world is to devote the full strength
of body and mind to the service of his fellow-men. Judged
either by his principles or by his performance, Franklin's moral
breadth and moral elevation have been absurdly under-
estimated.

It is perhaps in the field of politics that Franklin exhibits
the most marked development of his power and his vision.
A realistic inductive thinker, well versed in the rudiments of his
subject long before the revolutionary theorists handled it,
he was not rendered by any preconception of abstract rights
indocile to the lessons of his immense political experience. He
formulated his conceptions in the thick of existing conditions,
and always with reference to what was expedient and possible
as well as to what was desirable. He served his apprenticeship
in the Philadelphia Junto Club, which at its inception was
little more than a village improvement society, but which threw
out branches till it became a power in the province, and a
considerable factor in the affairs of the colonies. In this
association he learned the importance of co-operation, mastered
the tactics of organization, practised the art of getting propaganda afoot, and discovered the great secret of converting
private desires into public demands. In proposing in 1754
his plan for a union of the colonies he was applying to larger
units the principle of co-operative action by which he had
built up what we might call to-day his "machine" in Pennsylvania. Writers like Milton and Algernon Sidney had re-
enforced his natural inclination towards liberal forms of government. But he had in too large measure the instincts and the
ideas of a leader, and he had too much experience with the
conflicting prejudices and the resultant compromises of popular

assemblies, to feel any profound reverence for the "collective wisdom" of the people. "If all officers appointed by governors were always men of merit," he wrote in his *Dialogue Concerning the Present State of Affairs in Pennsylvania*, "it would be wrong ever to hazard a popular election." That his belief in popular representation was due as much to his sense of its political expediency as to his sense of its political justice is suggested by a passage in his letter on the imposition of direct taxes addressed to Governor Shirley, 18 December, 1754: "In matters of general concern to the people, and especially where burthens are to be laid upon them, it is of use to consider, as well what they will be apt to think and say, as what they ought to think." His sojourn in England widened his horizons, but not beyond the bounds of his nationality. As agent, he felt himself essentially a colonial Englishman pleading for the extension of English laws to British subjects across the sea, and playing up to the Imperial policy of crushing out the colonizing and commercial rivalry of France. The ultimate failure of his mission of reconciliation effected no sudden transformation of his political ideas; it rather overwhelmed him with disgust at the folly, the obstinacy, and the corruption rampant among English politicians of the period. He returned to the arms of the people because he had been hurled from the arms of the king; and he embraced their new principles because he was sure that they could not be worse applied than his old ones. His respect for the popular will was inevitably heightened by his share in executing it in the thrilling days when he was helping his fellow-countrymen to declare their independence, and was earning the superb epigraph of Turgot: *Eripuit fulmen coelo, sceptrumque tyrannis.* His official residence in France completely dissolved his former antagonism to that country. In the early stages of the conflict his wrath was bitter enough towards England, but long before it was over he had taken the ground of radical pacificism, reiterating his conviction that "there is no good war and no bad peace." He who had financed the Revolution had seen too much non-productive expenditure of moral and physical capital to believe in the appeal to arms. If nations required enlargement of their territories, it was a mere matter of arithmetic, he contended, to show that the cheapest way was purchase. "Justice," he declared, "is as strictly due between neighbour Nations as between neighbour Citizens, . . . and a Nation that makes an unjust War, is only a *great Gang*." So far as he was able, he mitigated the afflictions of noncombatants. He proposed by international law to exempt from peril fishermen and farmers and the productive workers of the world. He ordered the privateersmen under his control to safeguard the lives and property of explorers and men of science belonging to the enemy country; and he advocated for the future the abolition of the custom of commissioning privateers. In the treaty which he negotiated with Prussia he actually obtained the incorporation of an article so restricting the "zone of war" as to make a war between Prussia and the United States under its terms virtually impossible. His diplomatic intercourse in Europe and his association with the Physiocrats had opened his eyes to the common interests of all pacific peoples and to the inestimable advantages of a general amity among the nations. His ultimate political ideal included nothing short of the welfare and the commercial federation of the world. To that extent he was a believer in "majority interests." It may be further said that his political development was marked by a growing mastery of the art of dealing with men and by a steady approximation of his political to his personal morality.

For the broad humanity of Franklin's political conceptions undoubtedly his interest in the extension of science was partly responsible. As a scientific investigator he had long been a citizen of the world; and for him not the least bitter consequence of the war was that it made a break in the intellectual brotherhood of man. If he had not been obliged to supply the army of Washington with guns and ammunition, he might have been engaged in the far more congenial task of supplying the British Academy with food for philosophical discussion. He could not but resent the brutal antagonisms which had rendered intellectual co-operation with his English friends impossible, and which had frustrated his cherished hope of devoting his ripest years to philosophical researches. A natural endowment he certainly possessed which would have qualified him in happier circumstances for even more distinguished service than he actually performed in extending the frontiers of knowledge. He had the powerfully developed curiosity of the explorer and the inventor, ever busily prying into the causes of things, ever speculating upon the consequences of novel combinations. His native inquisitiveness had been stimulated by a young civilization's manifold necessities, mothering manifold inventions, and had been supplemented by a certain moral and idealizing passion for improvement. The practical nature of many of his devices, his interest in agriculture and navigation, his preoccupation with stoves and chimneys, the image of him firing the gas of ditch water or pouring oil on troubled waves, and the celebrity of the kite incident, rather tend to fix an impression that he was but a tactful empiricist and a lucky dilettante of discovery. It is interesting in this connection to note that he confesses his lack of patience for verification. His prime scientific faculty, as he himself felt, was the imagination which bodies forth the shapes and relations of things unknown—which constructs the theory and the hypothesis. His mind was a teeming warren of hints and suggestions. He loved rather to start than to pursue the hare. Happily what he deemed his excessive penchant for forming hypotheses was safeguarded by his perfect readiness to hear all that could be urged against them. He wished not his view but truth to prevail—which explains the winsome cordiality of his demeanour towards other savants. His unflagging correspondence with investigators, his subscription to learned publications, his active membership in philosophical societies, and his enterprise in founding schools and academies all betoken his prescience of the wide domain which science had to conquer and of the necessity for co-operation in the task of subduing it. Franklin was so far a Baconian that he sought to avoid unfruitful speculation and to unite contemplation and action in a stricter embrace for the generation of knowledge useful to man. But in refutation of any charge that he was a narrow-minded utilitarian and lacked the liberal views and long faith of the modern scientific spirit may be adduced his stunning retort to a query as to the usefulness of the balloons then on trial in France: "What is the use of a new-born baby?"

Of Franklin's style the highest praise is to declare that it reveals the mental and moral qualities of the man himself. It is the flexible style of a writer who has learned the craft of expression by studying and imitating the virtues of many

masters: the playful charm of Addison, the trenchancy of
Swift, the concreteness of Defoe, the urbanity of Shaftesbury,
the homely directness of Bunyan's dialogue, the unadorned
vigour of Tillotson, and the epigrammatic force of Pope.  His
mature manner, however, is imitative of nothing but the
thoroughly disciplined movement of a versatile mind which
has never known a moment of languor or a moment of un-
controllable excitement.  Next to his omnipresent vitality,
his most notable characteristic is the clearness which results
from a complete preliminary vision of what is to be said, and
which in a young hand demands deliberate preconsideration.
To Franklin, the ordering of his matter must have become
eventually a light task as, with incessant passing to and fro
in his experience and with the daily habit of epistolary communication, he grew as familiar with his intellectual terrain as
an old field marshal with the map of Europe.  For the writing
of his later years is marked not merely by clearness and force
but also by the sovereign ease of a man who has long understood the interrelations of his ideas and has ceased to make
revolutionary discoveries in any portion of his own nature.  His
occasional wrath does not fluster him but rather intensifies
his lucidity, clarifies his logic, and brightens the ironical smile
which accompanies the thrust of his wit.  The "decent plainness and manly freedom" of his ordinary tone—notes which
he admired in the writings of his maternal grandfather Peter
Folger—rise in parts of his official correspondence to a severity
of decorum; for there is a trace of the senatorial in the man,
the dignity of antique Rome.  He is seldom too hurried, even
in a private letter, to gratify the ear by the turning and cadence
of sentence and phrase; and one feels that the harmony of his
periods is the right and predestined vesture of his essential
blandness and suavity of temper.  His stylistic drapery, however, is never so smoothed and adjusted as to obscure the
sinewy vigour of his thought.  His manner is steadily in
the service of his matter.  He is adequate, not copious; for
his moral "frugality and industry" prompt him to eschew
surplusage and to make his texture firm.  His regard for
purity of diction is classical; he avoids vulgarity; he despises
the jargon of scientific pedants; but like Montaigne he loves
frank and masculine speech, and he likes to enrich the language

of the well bred by discreet drafts upon the burry, homely, sententious, proverbial language of the people. Like Lord Bacon and like many other grave men among his fellow-countrymen, he found it difficult to avoid an opportunity for a jest even when the occasion was unpropitious; and he never sat below the Attic salt. When his fortune was made, he put by the pewter spoon and bowl of his apprenticeship; his biographers remind us that he kept a well stocked cellar at Passy and enjoyed the distinction of suffering from the gout. With affluence and years he acquired a "palate," and gave a little play to the long repressed tastes of an Epicurean whom early destiny had cast upon a rock-bound coast. The literary expression of his autumnal festivity is to be found in the *bagatelles*. *The Ephemera* proves that this great eighteenth-century rationalist had a fancy. It is no relative, indeed, of that romantic spirit which pipes to the whistling winds on the enchanted greens of Shakespeare. It is rather the classic Muse of eighteenth-century art which summons the rosy Loves and Desires to sport among the courtiers and philosophers and the wasp-waisted ladies in a *fête champêtre* or an *Embarkment for Cythera* of Watteau. The tallow chandler's son who enters on the cycle of his development by cultivating thrift with Defoe, continues it by cultivating tolerance and philanthropy with Voltaire, and completes it with Lord Chesterfield by cultivating "the graces."

# CHAPTER VII

# Colonial Newspapers and Magazines, 1704-1775

THE development of the colonial press coincides with a period often regarded as narrowly provincial in American literature. That spirit of adventure which enlivens the early historical narratives had settled into a thrifty concern with practical affairs, combined with an exaggerated interest in fine-spun doctrinal reasoning. The echoes of Spenser and other Elizabethans to be heard in some few Puritan elegies and in Anne Bradstreet's quaint imagery, had died away. Knowledge of Europe had become so casual that the colonial newspaper often found it necessary to describe Dresden or Berlin as "a fair, large, and strong city of Germany," and to insert other geographical notes of the simplest sort.

These limitations in the colonial point of view, however, had several striking effects on the early journalism between 1704 and 1750, or thereabouts. The reader who examines the small, ill-printed, half illegible news sheets is surprised to find them more varied in many ways, and more distinctly literary than modern journalism aims to be. The simple fact of the matter is that the dearth of news at length forced the editorial mind to become inventive and even, in some instances, creative. When we remember that European news failed entirely during the long winters; that intercolonial communication was irregular and unsystematic; that criticism of the government in political editorials meant an official inquiry followed by the forced discontinuance of the paper, if not by a trial for libel; that the public already had enough religious exhortation from the pulpit and from pamphlets on *The Fatal Consequences of Unscriptural Doctrine or Twenty Considerations against Sin,*—remembering these things it will not seem so extraordinary that the newspapers turned to the spectacle of the actual life about them, and, to convey it, sought their models in the world of letters so little known in the colonies.

It was James Franklin, Benjamin Franklin's older brother, who first made a news sheet something more than a garbled mass of stale items, "taken from the Gazetts and other Publick Prints of London" some six months late. Franklin, "encouraged by a number of respectable characters, who were desirous of having a paper of a different cast from those then published, . . . began the publication, at his own risk, of a third newspaper, entitled *The New England Courant.*"[1] These respectable characters were known as the Hell-Fire Club; they succeeded in publishing a paper "of a different cast," which, although it shocked New England orthodoxy pretty thoroughly, nevertheless proved vastly entertaining and established a kind of literary precedent.

For instead of filling the first page of the *Courant* with the tedious conventionalities of governors' addresses to provincial legislatures, James Franklin's club wrote essays and satirical letters after the manner of *The Spectator* just ten years after the first appearance of *The Spectator* in London. How novel the whole method would be to New England readers may be inferred from the fact that even the Harvard library had no copies of Addison or Steele at this period. Swift, Pope, Prior, and Dryden would also have been looked for in vain. Milton himself was little known in the stronghold of Puritanism. But the printing office of James Franklin had Shakespeare, Milton, Addison, Steele, Cowley, Butler's *Hudibras*, and *"The Tail of the Tub"*[2] on its shelves. All these were read and used in the editor's office, but *The Spectator* and its kind became the actual model for the new journalism.

As a result, the very look of an ordinary first page of the *Courant* is like that of a *Spectator* page. After the more formal introductory paper on some general topic, such as zeal or

---

[1] Isaiah Thomas, *History of Printing in America.* In *Transactions and Collections of the American Antiquarian Society*, vol. v, p. 110.

[2] The spelling of the *Courant.*

hypocrisy or honour or contentment, the facetious letters of imaginary correspondents commonly fill the remainder of the *Courant's* first page. Timothy Turnstone addresses flippant jibes to Justice Nicholas Clodpate in the first extant number of the *Courant*. Tom Pen-Shallow quickly follows, with his mischievous little postscript: "Pray inform me whether in your Province Criminals have the Privilege of a Jury." Tom Tram writes from the moon about a certain "villainous Postmaster" he has heard rumours of. (The *Courant* was always perilously close to legal difficulties and had, besides, a lasting feud with the town postmaster.) Ichabod Henroost complains of a gadding wife. Abigail Afterwit would like to know when the editor of the rival paper, the *Gazette*, "intends to have done printing the Carolina Addresses to their Governour, and give his Readers Something in the Room of them, that will be more entertaining." Homespun Jack deplores the fashions in general, and small waists in particular. Some of these papers represent native wit, with only a general approach to the model; others are little more than paraphrases of *The Spectator*. And sometimes a *Spectator* paper is inserted bodily, with no attempt at paraphrase whatever.

Benjamin Franklin, a mere boy at this time, contributed to the *Courant* the first fruits of his days and nights with Addison. The fourteen little essays from Silence Dogood to the editor are among the most readable and charming of Franklin's early imitations, clearly following *The Spectator*, yet at rather long range and with considerable adaptation to the New England environment. Silence rambles on amiably enough except for occasional slurs on the New England clergy, in regard to whom the *Courant* was always bitter, and often scurrilous. For the Hell-Fire Club never grasped the inner secret of Mr. Spectator, his urbane, imperturbable, impersonal kindliness of manner. Instead, they vented their hatred of dogmatism and intolerance in personalities so insolent as to become in themselves intolerant. Entertaining, however, the *Courant* is, from first to last, and full of a genuine humour and a shrewd satiric truth to life.

Offensive as the *Courant* certainly was to New England orthodoxy, its literary method was seized upon and used in the new paper established under the influence of the Boston clergymen Mather Byles and Thomas Prince. This was *The New*

*England Weekly Journal*, and Mather Byles, hailed at the time as "Harvard's honour and New England's hope," who "bids fair to rise, and sing, and rival Pope"[1] contributed largely to the verse and prose on the first page of the paper. A series of "Speculations" is announced, in exact and close imitation of *The Spectator;* even a fictitious author, Proteus Echo, appears as a new Spectator of men and manners, to banter a folly by representing it in a glass. He forms a club, and sketches the members for us in his second essay, which proceeds exactly as the second number of *The Spectator*.

These characters of Proteus Echo's "Society" show some good strokes. There is Mr. Timothy Blunt, an amusing New England version of Sir Roger de Coverley. He lives at some distance from the town of Boston, but rides in every week, often bringing his "Wallet ballanced with two Bottles of Milk, to defray his necessary Expenses. . . . His Periwigg has been out of the Curl ever since the Revolution and his Dagger and Doublet are supposed to be the rarest Pieces of Antiquity in the Country." If it had not been for an unlucky stroke to his "Intellectuals" in his infancy, "he would have stood the fairest of any of his Contemporarys to have found out the Philosopher's Stone." The "wonderful Mr. Honeysuckle, the Blossom of our Society, and the beautiful Ornament of Litterature," is nothing less than Will Honeycomb translated into a poet.

On the whole, however, such work is rare in the *Journal*. Strictly moral essays, of which even *The Spectator* has its full share, soon follow the more creative touches, and we find the ordinary eighteenth-century treatment of merit, covetousness, idleness, the vapours, and so on. Such essays came to be the accepted "filling" for the first page of many newspapers up to 1740 and sometimes after that date. Jeremy Gridley's *Rehearsal* (1743–6), for instance, has a series of speculations rather above the common order, yet requiring no especial notice for their originality or their importance except as a type.

Benjamin Franklin's later journalism amply fulfilled the promise contained in the Silence Dogood papers. When he finally established himself in Philadelphia, shortly before

[1] See Book I, Chap. IX.

1730, the town boasted two wretched little news sheets, Andrew Bradford's *American Mercury*, and Keimer's *Universal Instructor in all Arts and Sciences, and Pennsylvania Gazette*. This instruction in all arts and sciences consisted of weekly extracts from Chambers's *Universal Dictionary*, actually commencing with A, and going steadily on towards Z, followed by instalments of Defoe's *Religious Courtship*, called by the editor "a scarce and delightful piece of History." Franklin quickly did away with all this when he took over the *Instructor*, and made it *The Pennsylvania Gazette*. The *Gazette* soon became Franklin's characteristic organ, which he freely used for satire, for the play of his wit, even for sheer excess of mischief or of fun.

From the first he had a way of adapting his models to his own uses. The series of essays called *The Busy-Body*, which he wrote for Bradford's *American Mercury* in 1729, followed the general Addisonian form, modified already to suit homelier conditions. The thrifty Patience, in her busy little shop, complaining of the useless visitors who waste her valuable time, is related to the ladies who address Mr. Spectator. The Busy-Body himself is a true Censor Morum, as Isaac Bickerstaff had been in the *Tatler*. And a number of the fictitious characters, Ridentius, Eugenius, Cato, and Cretico, represent traditional eighteenth-century classicism. Even this Franklin could use for contemporary satire, since Cretico, the "sowre Philosopher," is evidently a portrait of Franklin's rival, Samuel Keimer.

As time went on, Franklin depended less on his literary conventions, and more on his own native humour. In this there is a new spirit,—not suggested to him by the fine breeding of Addison, or the bitter irony of Swift, or the stinging completeness of Pope. The brilliant little pieces Franklin wrote for his *Pennsylvania Gazette* have an imperishable place in American literature. It is none the less true that they belong to colonial journalism.

*The Pennsylvania Gazette*, like most other newspapers of the period, was often poorly printed. Franklin was busy with a hundred matters outside of his printing office, and never seriously attempted to raise the standards of his trade. Nor did he ever properly edit or collate the chance medley of stale items which passed for news in the *Gazette*. His influence on the practical side of journalism was very small. On the other hand, his advertisements of books show his very great interest in popularizing secular literature. Undoubtedly his paper contributed to the broader culture which distinguished Pennsylvania from her neighbours before the Revolution. Starting with the custom of importing a stray volume or two along with stationer's supplies, Franklin gradually developed a book shop in his printing office. There was nothing unusual in this fact, by itself. His rival, Andrew Bradford, and many other printers in the colonies had odd collections for sale. But while Bradford was advertising the *Catechistical Guide to Sinners*, or *The Plain Man's Path-way to Heaven*, along with an occasional *Spectator*, Franklin's importations, listed in the *Gazette* for sale, included works of Bacon, Dryden, Locke, Milton, Otway, Pope, Prior, Swift, Rowe, Defoe, Addison, Steele, Arbuthnot, Congreve, Rabelais, Seneca, Ovid, and various novels, all before 1740. The first catalogue of his Library Company shows substantially the same list, with the addition of Don Quixote, and the works of Shaftesbury, of Gay, of Spenser, and of Voltaire. These latter were probably for sale in the printing office as well.

Advertisements of merchandise in all the colonies throw a good deal of light on the customs of the time, and, incidentally, also on the popular taste in reading. We find that Peter Turner has "Superfine Scarlet Cloth, Hat Linings, *Tatlers*, *Spectators*, and Barclay's *Apology*"[1]; that Peter Harry imports "Head Flowers in Boxes, Laces and Edgings, Psalm-books, Play-books, the *Guardians* in 2 vol., Women's Short Cloaks, Men's Scarlet Great Coats"[2] and other apparel. The ship *Samuel*, from London, brings over "sundry goods, particularly a very choice collection of printed Books, Pictures, Maps and Pickles, to be Sold very reasonable by Robert Pringle."[3]

Franklin's influence in journalism was not confined to Pennsylvania. He often assisted young journeymen in the establishment of newspapers in distant towns. Thomas Whitemarsh, for instance, went to Charleston, South Carolina,

[1] See *The American Mercury*, No. 1010, 3 May, 1739.
[2] See *The South Carolina Gazette*, February, 1734.
[3] *Ibid.*, No. 511, 9 January, 1744.

in 1731, as Franklin's partner in a new enterprise, which soon included a new paper, *The South Carolina Gazette*. Naturally, Whitemarsh filled his front page with essays, sometimes reprinted from *The Spectator*, but often original, with a facetious quality suggesting Franklin. A few burlesques such as the papers of a certain Meddlers' Club are little better than nonsense, rarely enlivened by a flash of wit. Once we find an odd bit of local colour, when a member of this club criticizes the fair ones of Charleston for promenading too much along the bay. "I have heard," he says, "that in Great Britain the Ladies and Gentlemen choose the Parks and such like Places to walk and take the Air in, but I never heard of any Places making use of the Wharfs for such Purpose except this." Essays of one sort or another were always popular in *The South Carolina Gazette*. Here may be found interesting notices of the various performances (probably professional) of Otway's *Orphan*, Farquhar's *Recruiting Officer*, and other popular plays of the period which were given at the Charleston theatres for twenty or thirty years before the first wandering professional companies began to play in the Northern colonies. Here, too, we find in the issue of 8 February, 1735, what is probably the first recorded prologue composed in the colonies.

Early theatrical notices may also be followed in *The Virginia Gazette*, a paper of unusual excellence, edited by William Parks in Williamsburg, the old capital of Virginia. Here *The Busy-Body*, *The Recruiting Officer*, and *The Beaux-Stratagem* were all performed, often by amateurs, though professionals were known as early as 1716 in Williamsburg. Life in Williamsburg in 1736 had a more cosmopolitan quality than in other towns. A sprightly essay-serial called *The Monitor*, which fills the first page of *The Virginia Gazette* for twenty-two numbers, probably reflects not only the social life of the capital, but also the newer fashion in such periodical work. It is dramatic in method, with vividly realized characters who gossip and chat over games of piquet or at the theatre. *The Beaux-Stratagem*, which had been played in Williamsburg three weeks before, is mentioned as delightful enough to make one of the ladies commit the indiscretion of giggling. *The Monitor* represents a kind of light social satire unusual in the colonies.

Satire of a heavier sort when attempted by newspaper

writers was never long sustained above mere invective, though
it sometimes began with tolerable Hudibrastic or Popean
couplets. *The Dunciad* and *Hudibras* were well known and often
quoted in such bitter controversies as the famous Whitefield
warfare in Charleston between 1740 and 1745. *A Tale of a
Tub* and *Gulliver's Travels* also furnished admirable epithets for
one's foes. Occasionally some journalist tried to moderate the
heat of battle by recurring to the dignity of Addison. In
political controversy, especially if he happened to be a liberal,
he preferred *Cato's Letters*,[1] Locke, or Algernon Sidney, throughout the early period. Thus it was that the colonists from
Boston to Savannah were constantly imbibing advanced
British constitutional theories.

After 1750, general news became accessible, and the newspapers show more and more interest in public affairs. The
literary first page was no longer necessary, though occasionally
used to cover a dull period. A new type of vigorous polemic
gradually superseded the older essay. A few of the well-known
conventions were retained, however. We still find the fictitious
letter, with the fanciful signature, or a series of papers under a
common title, such as *The Virginia-Centinel*, or Livingston's
*Watch-Tower*. The former is a flaming appeal to arms, running
through *The Virginia Gazette* in 1756, and copied into Northern
papers to rouse patriotism against the French enemy. The
expression of the sentiment, even thus early, seems national.
This whole series, though somewhat florid in style, shows the
familiarity of the cultivated Southerner with his favourite
English poets,—Young, Pope, Shakespeare. Livingston's well-
known *Watch-Tower*,[2] a continuation of his pamphlet-magazine
*The Independent Reflector*, has already the keen edge of the
Revolutionary writings of fifteen and twenty years later. The
fifty-second number even has one of the popular phrases of the
Revolution: "Had I not sounded the Alarm, Bigotry would
e'er now have triumphed over the *natural Rights of British
Subjects.*"[3]

This expression "natural rights," occurring so early as 1755

---

[1] *Cato's Letters* or *The British Cato*, a series of political papers by Thomas Gordon
and John Trenchard, published in London from 1720 to 1723.
[2] Appearing in Gaine's *Mercury* in 1754–1755.
[3] The italics are not in the original.

in Livingston's paper, is probably accidental or vague, but the full political theory of Rousseau, with all its abstractions regarding mankind in general, was soon added to the definite and always cherished belief in the constitutional privileges of Englishmen. The ideas of the French philosophers were in the air, and there is plenty of evidence in the colonial newspapers for fifteen or twenty years before the Revolution that the French influence was increasing. Even during the French and Indian war, booksellers advertised French texts, grammars, and dictionaries in the papers, while courses in French were often announced. Before the close of the war, we find *The Boston Gazette* printing extracts from Montesquieu's *Spirit of Laws*, with an apology and the expressed hope that it may not be "political Heresey" to suppose that "a Frenchman may have juster Notions of Civil Liberty than some among ourselves." This was in the days when "Gallic perfidy" was the popular note.

After 1760 all the important works of Rousseau, Montesquieu, and the Encyclopedists as well as many other French books were advertised for sale in the colonial press. Such advertisements indicate the taste of the reading public more accurately than do catalogues of private libraries, which represent individual preferences. Voltaire had long been known in the colonies. Rousseau's *Social Contract* was advertised as a *Treatise on the Social Compact, or The Principles of Political Law*. He himself is referred to again and again as "the ingenious Rousseau," or "the celebrated Rousseau." And *Émile* and *La Nouvelle Héloïse* were evidently in demand. The famous *Letters of a Farmer in Pennsylvania* by John Dickinson belong to the colonial press in a very special way, since not only did they first appear in *The Pennsylvania Chronicle, The Pennsylvania Journal*, and *The Pennsylvania Gazette* almost simultaneously in the winter of 1767–1768, but they were reprinted in nearly every newspaper on the continent, from Nova Scotia to Georgia.[1] The *Letters* were soon known in France, where they were translated by Jacques Barbeu Dubourg, with a preface of glowing compliment.

Reports of French interest in America inclined the colonists still more to the French philosophy of government. As a

[1] See also Book I, Chap. VIII.

matter of fact, from the time of the Stamp Act, political essays
of every description filled the newspapers, and what one paper
published was soon reprinted in others. Thus the influence of
the press in this critical period can hardly be overrated. If
the "pumpkin Gentry" of New England (to use a tory phrase)
took offence at some encroachment, gentlemen planters of the
South were sure to read the whole case in a few weeks and, in
spite of their differing civilization, to sympathize with the
Northern firebrands. When Dr. Arthur Lee sent home to
*The Virginia Gazette* his *Monitor*, a series of essays describing
hostile conditions in London, and urging his countrymen to
non-importation, it was not by any means his countrymen of
Virginia alone who heard the call. The *Monitor* has something
of the distinguished style of the *Farmer*, and it is natural that
the two should have been published together in a Williamsburg edition. Revolutionary Virginia burgesses always toasted
the *Farmer's* and *Monitor's* letters together. But essays of an
entirely different type also appeared constantly. Republicans
and Loyalists fought violent battles under assumed classical
names. Constitutionalis, Massachusettensis, Senex, Novanglus, Pacificus, Caesariensis, Amicus Publico, Cunctator, Vir-
ginius, Mucius Scaevola, Cato, Scipio, Leonidas, Brutus, and
many more argued hotly and often powerfully the whole
question of allegiance, on abstract grounds.

Isaiah Thomas's *Massachusetts Spy* shows the course
of this long battle. Constantly on the verge of being suppressed, from its establishment in 1770 to the Revolution, it
carried radicalism to its logical conclusion. When the *Spy*
began to be reprinted in other papers, as "the most daring
production ever published in America," the country as a whole
was ready for Tom Paine's *Common Sense*.

In regard to other forms of periodical literature before the
Revolution, it is often difficult to draw precise distinctions.[1]
Newspapers are easily enough distinguished in general by the
attempt to give items of current news. Outside the regular
news sheets, there is a strange assortment of colonial productions usually classed as magazines, but in many cases hardly

[1] Mr. Albert Matthews notes this difficulty in his bibliography of New England
magazines. See his *Lists of New England Magazines*, in *Publications of the Colonial
Society of Massachusetts*, vol. XIII, pp. 69–74.

recognizable as such. For instance, William Livingston's *Independent Reflector, or Weekly Essays* and also Andrew Oliver's *Censor*, are nothing more than single essays published serially. The *Censor* was published in weekly reply to "Mucius Scaevola" and other writers of the *Spy*. The very meaning of the word "magazine" in the eighteenth century makes classification difficult. It was literally a "storehouse," being applied to literature as a "collection"; almost any assemblage of writings, especially if published serially, could be referred to as a "magazine." Even the regular London magazines of the period were made up largely of excerpts from weekly reviews and periodicals, along with a summary of the news of the month. A department called "Poetical Essays" was usually more original, but on the whole both *The Gentleman's Magazine* and *The London Magazine* could be described fairly enough as collections of material from various sources.

There were a few magazines of this standard English type in America before the Revolution. Franklin, as usual, led the way, though it happened that his rival Andrew Bradford actually published the first magazine in the colonies. Franklin's soon followed, and these two little periodicals brought out the same month in Philadelphia, 1741, clearly indicate the attempt to transplant the English type, with some adaptations, for colonial readers. Franklin's title, *The General Magazine and Historical Chronicle for all the British Plantations in America*, shows his intention of giving a review of colonial news rather than of British. He did, as a matter of fact, use *The Virginia Gazette* and other weeklies for articles and verse, but he also took European items whenever he could get them. Both magazines were evidently premature, however, for Bradford's existed only three months, and Franklin's only six.

The next attempt at this sort of periodical came from Boston two years later. Jeremy Gridley was the able editor of *The American Magazine and Historical Chronicle*. It is an excellent piece of work for that date, both in general arrangement and in details of printing. There is very little original material, however, since the editor not only imitated *The London Magazine* very closely in plan, but boldly copied most of the essays, articles, and verse from it or from *The Gentleman's Magazine*. An occasional translation from the classics by a Harvard student, a burlesque by "Jonathan Weatherwise" on the absurd weather signs of the country folk, or perhaps a timely article from a "neighbouring colony" does not suffice to impart a native flavour to the magazine as a whole. It is distinctly "imported." The attempt was nevertheless creditable, and certainly kept readers in touch with the best English reviews. The magazine continued for three years.

A dozen years later *The New England Magazine of Knowledge and Pleasure* announced its motto, "Alluring Profit with Delight we blend," but it confined itself to hackneyed essays on old models. In the same year, however, at Philadelphia, a magazine of decided originality and of genuine importance in colonial literature was coming out month by month with the first provost of the new college as its editor and guiding spirit. The Rev. William Smith, called to America from Aberdeen in 1752, brought a great love of letters to his new work and soon succeeded in imparting his own literary enthusiasms to a group of young students. It is largely due to his constant encouragement that a strain of lyric poetry at length sounded in clear, welcome notes, a strain all too short and slight, but of real beauty. These young poets belonged to the generation after that of Franklin's famous Junto, one of the college group being a son of Franklin's friend Thomas Godfrey, the mathematician. Thomas Godfrey, Jr., needed all the active help of the provost, since poetical gifts did not meet with favour in the Godfrey household. Francis Hopkinson, Joseph Shippen, and Nathaniel Evans were also introduced to the public by Smith.

The interesting thing about William Smith's own literary enthusiasms is his love of eighteenth-century romanticism. In a thoroughly romantic temper he made himself a retreat by the falls of the Schuylkill, which he describes under the guise of Theodore, the Hermit, in his *American Magazine*, noting "the singular gloom of its situation," hidden by "a romantic tuft of trees," and made more lonely by surrounding waters. He could soon announce in his magazine that he had almost too many poems to draw from. Practically all the verse in its thirteen numbers is original, although at times, especially in the long poems of James Sterling, the most conventional eighteenth-century manner is amusingly evident. The essays, with very few exceptions, were not only written in the colonies but were often well adapted to the problems of the day, the war on the border, the Indians, the public policies of the government. The pride in "this young country" is everywhere evident, combined with perfect loyalty to Great Britain. In this year 1758 the successor of *The American Magazine*, called *The New American Magazine*, continued the same general policy, without securing the same originality. William Smith had been called to England, and the new venture lacked his power. It had the honour of publishing Nathaniel Evans's fine *Ode on the late General Wolfe*, however, in probably its earliest and simplest form.

With the next magazines we are again on the eve of the revolution. "The town has met," and we read instructions, articles, orations, odes, and satires on the situation, sometimes reprinted from the newspapers, sometimes written for the magazine, but always inflammatory, since the two noteworthy periodicals of this period, *The Pennsylvania Magazine* and *The Royal American Magazine*, were edited respectively by the two firebrands, Thomas Paine and Isaiah Thomas. Paine's magazine did not lack pungent wit of one kind or another, although for the more strictly literary sections both he and Isaiah Thomas drew freely on conventional English sources which, in theory, they should have rejected. Thomas's *Royal American Magazine* is enlivened by the famous Paul Revere engravings and is otherwise interesting, particularly for its confident belief in the new country soon to be the United States.

# CHAPTER VIII

# American Political Writing, 1760–1789

A MERICAN history between 1760 and 1789—from the end, that is, so far as military operations were concerned, of the Seven Years' War to the inauguration of the new government under the Federal Constitution—falls naturally into three well-marked periods. The first, comprising the development of the constitutional struggle with Great Britain over taxation and imperial control, reaches its culmination in the armed collision between the British and the patriot forces at Lexington, 19 April, 1775. The second period covers the eight years of war, ending with the peace treaty of September, 1783; while the third embraces the so-called "critical period" of the Confederation, and the formation and adoption of the Constitution.

Such a time of storm and stress, of revolution and evolution, is pretty certain, especially in a new country, if it bring forth literature at all, to bring forth such as is predominantly political in content, style, and purpose. The Revolutionary leaders who have left a large and permanent impress upon American literature were concerned chiefly with such weighty matters as the nature of the British constitution, the formulation of colonial rights, and the elaboration of schemes of government and administration; and it was of these things that they chiefly wrote. It is a striking tribute to the classical education of the age, to the moulding power of closely-reasoned theological and legal treatises on which ministers and lawyers fed,[1] and to the subtle, pervasive influence of the English Bible, that the best political writing of the Revolutionary period attained a dignity and

[1] See Book I, Chap. VII, for evidence as to the knowledge of French radical books in the colonies after 1760

impressiveness of style, a noble power of rhetorical form, and a telling incisiveness of phrase which won the instant admiration of English critics, and which stamp the political literature of American national beginnings as superior to the similar literature of any other people anywhere.

Of the first notable contribution to the literary history of the Revolution we have, unfortunately, only a second-hand report. When, in 1761, following the death of George II and the accession of George III, the surveyor-general of customs at Boston applied to the Superior Court of Massachusetts for the reissuance of writs of assistance,[1] granting authority to search for and seize uncustomed goods, some merchants of Boston and others combined to oppose the application. James Otis the younger, for ten years past one of the leaders of the Massachusetts bar, and lately advocate-general, who, unable to support the application for the writs, had resigned his office, made the leading argument for the petitioners. In a great speech, the substance of which has survived only in notes taken at the time by John Adams,[2] then a young lawyer, and more fully written out many years later, Otis challenged the writs as "the worst instrument of arbitrary power, the most destructive of English liberty and the fundamental principles of law, that ever was found in an English law-book." At once general in its terms and perpetual in its operation, lacking the exact specification of place and circumstance which a search-warrant ought to contain, such a writ was on both accounts illegal. The freedom of one's house was violated by it; the only precedent for it belonged to the days of arbitrary power under Charles II. "No acts of Parliament can establish such a writ. . . . An act against the constitution is void."

Otis could impede, but he could not defeat, the application, and the writs were eventually issued. He had, however, raised the important question of the application of English law to the colonies, and the nature and extent of the "rights of Englishmen" which the colonial charters, in express terms, had guaranteed. Elected a member of the House of Representatives, he presently led an attack upon Governor Bernard for fitting

---

[1] A form of writ is given in W. MacDonald, *Select Charters*, 259–261. The best account of the subject is in Quincy, *Massachusetts Reports*, 395–540.

[2] *Works*, II, 124 note, 521–525; X, 246–249, 274–276.

out an armed vessel without the approval of the House; drafted a communication in which the governor was charged with "taking from the House their most darling privilege, the right of originating all taxes"; and late in 1762 published his first political pamphlet, *A Vindication of the Conduct of the House of Representatives of the Province of the Massachusetts-Bay*, in which, mixed with extreme praise of the King of Great Britain and denunciation of the King of France, and vague suggestions as to the nature of human rights, the privileges of the colonies under the British constitution were stoutly maintained. Neither historically nor legally was the argument beyond question, and the claim of right was a call to the future rather than an interpretation of the past. What was said, however, was said with vigour and incisiveness, and to Otis's provincial audience carried weight.

The treaty of Paris, ceding to Great Britain all the vast possessions of France on the mainland of North America, together with Florida and other Spanish territory east of the Mississippi, was concluded 10 February, 1763. On the 23d of that month, Charles Townshend became first lord of trade, with the oversight of colonial administration, in the short-lived ministry of Bute, and some far-reaching changes in the colonial system were presently announced. The salaries of governors and judges, hitherto paid by the colonial assemblies, were now to be paid by the crown, thus insuring, it was believed, a better enforcement of the trade laws and a proper revenue from customs; and a standing army of ten thousand men was to be maintained in America, in anticipation of an attempt by France to recover what it had lost, the expense of the troops to be met by parliamentary taxation of the colonies. Grenville, who became prime minister in June, supported the plan. In March, 1764, Grenville gave notice of his intention to impose stamp duties; laying the matter over for a year, however, in order that the colonies might be consulted. In April a Sugar Act imposed new colonial customs duties.

The prospect of direct taxation by Parliament aroused widespread apprehension in America, and called forth in July the ablest and best-known of Otis's pamphlets, *The Rights of the British Colonies Asserted and Proved*. With notable moderation and restraint, and in a tone pervadingly judicial rather than partisan, Otis argued the case for the colonies, appealing as before to the British constitution as he understood it, and to the logic of right, liberty, and justice. A colony being an integral part of the mother country, though territorially separated from it, its people are, "by the law of God and nature, by the common law, and by act of Parliament . . . entitled to all the natural, essential, inherent, and inseparable rights of our fellow-subjects in Great Britain." Among these rights was that of freedom from taxation save with their own consent, and of representation in the supreme or some subordinate legislature. Parliament admittedly possessed a general supervisory authority over the colonies, but if, under the guise of regulation, it were to infringe upon the right of taxation through duly elected representatives, it would be guilty of an arbitrary violation of the constitution. Forcible resistance, however, even to an unconstitutional act, was not to be thought of.

There would be an end of all government, if one or a number of subjects or subordinate provinces should take upon them so far to judge of the justice of an act of Parliament, as to refuse obedience to it. . . . Therefore let the Parliament lay what burdens they please on us, we must, it is our duty to submit and patiently bear them, till they will be pleased to relieve us.

Otis voiced effectively the first impulse of thoughtful, patriotic Americans as they contemplated the prospect of parliamentary taxation. The proposed act violated the constitution whose benefits the colonists claimed, but forcible resistance would be treason. The same line of argument, more systematically and cogently put, characterized Oxenbridge Thacher's *Sentiments of a British American* (1764). Thacher was a fellow townsman of Otis, and the two had been associated in the case of the writs of assistance. Like Otis, Thacher's legal argument closes with a strong profession of loyalty to the crown, and there is no good ground for thinking that in either case the profession was insincere. Argument and dissent were an Englishman's right, and the constitution had grown by protest against abuses.

An even more effective statement of the American case is found in *The Rights of Colonies Examined*, a pamphlet written by Stephen Hopkins, governor of Rhode Island, and pub-

lished at Providence in 1765. Admitting the right of Parliament to regulate the affairs of the whole empire, Hopkins not
only claims for the colonies "as much freedom as the mother
state from which they went out," but dwells forcibly upon the
dangerous tendency of the new policy, the widespread apprehension which it has already aroused, and the absence of any
clear necessity for raising an American revenue by parliamentary fiat.

What motive . . . can remain, to induce the parliament to abridge
the privileges, and lessen the rights of the most loyal and dutiful
subjects; subjects justly intituled to ample freedom, who have long
enjoyed, and not abused or forfeited their liberties, who have used
them to their own advantage, in dutiful subserviency to the orders
and interests of Great-Britain?

Such reasoning as that of Otis, Thacher, and Hopkins, however convincing to the popular mind, avoided, but did not settle,
the important and difficult constitutional question of the ultimate authority of Parliament over the colonies. On that
question the wisest were certain to differ, and a presentation
of the other side of the case was speedily forthcoming. In
February, 1765, there appeared at Newport *A Letter from a
Gentleman at Halifax, to his Friend in Rhode-Island*, published
anonymously, but written by Martin Howard, a Newport
lawyer of repute. In this temperate, logical, and readable
pamphlet, the "Gentleman at Halifax," replying to Hopkins's
"labored, ostentatious piece," puts his finger on the primary
defect in the whole colonial argument, namely, the claim "that
the colonies have rights independent of, and not controulable by
the authority of parliament." If they derived their political
rights from Parliament, were not those rights subject to interpretation or abridgement by Parliament? A lively controversy
ensued. Hopkins defended himself in a series of articles in the
Providence *Gazette*, while Otis, his zeal for debate knowing no
provincial bounds, printed *A Vindication of the British Colonies
against the Aspersions of the Halifax Gentleman*. Howard
retorted with *A Defence of the Letter from a Gentleman at Halifax,
to his Friend in Rhode-Island*, to which Otis responded with
*Brief Remarks on the Defence of the Halifax Libel on the British-
American-Colonies*. The tide of patriotism was rising, however,

and the populace presently took a hand. Before the summer was over Howard, after being hanged and burned in effigy at Newport, fled to England, and the "rights of the colonies" were both "asserted and proved."

No substitute for the stamp tax having been agreed upon by the colonial assemblies, the Stamp Act became a law (March, 1765). In the interval between the approval of the act and the date (1 November) at which it was to go into effect, disorderly bodies calling themselves "Sons of Liberty" organized a campaign of forcible resistance; with the result that, when the first of November arrived, stamps and stamped paper were not to be had. Meantime, the newspaper and pamphlet controversy continued. To a pamphlet written by Soame Jenyns, a member of Parliament, published in 1765, entitled *The Objections to the Taxation of Our American Colonies, by the Legislature of Great Britain, Briefly Considered*, Otis replied with *Considerations on Behalf of the Colonies, in a Letter to a Noble Lord*, the argument of which, save in its plea for leniency and consideration on the part of Great Britain in view of the extent and importance of the colonies, does not differ materially from that which the author had previously advanced. John Adams, "with the exception of Jefferson . . . the most readable of the statesmen of the Revolutionary period," now entered the lists with a series of four essays, published anonymously and without title in the Boston *Gazette* in August, 1765. Beginning with an examination of the "ecclesiatical and civil tyranny" which he found exemplified in the canon and feudal law, and of which the Stamp Act was held up as the consummate illustration, Adams traced the course of the historical struggle between corporate oppression and individual liberty and self-assertion. "Admitting we are children, have not children a right to complain when their parents are attempting to break their limbs, to administer poison, or to sell them to enemies for slaves?" Adams had read his history with a Puritan obsession, and neither his interpretation of facts nor his reasoning did him here much credit. The essays had influence, however. Reprinted in *The London Chronicle*, they were finally published in 1768, in revised form, under the misleading title of *A Dissertation on the Canon and the Feudal Law*.[1]

[1] *Works*, III, 445–464.

With the resolutions,[1] memorials, and petitions of the Stamp
Act Congress (October, 1765), we reach the first of the series of
great state papers which, while of supreme value for the proper
understanding of the constitutional position of the colonies, are
also, in some respects, the most characteristic literary product
of the Revolutionary period. Nowhere else in American
literature does the peculiar gift of formal expression and logical
exposition in politics show itself on so large a scale or in so great
a cause, and in no country in the world has such expression
moved so long and so consistently on a high plane, or voiced
itself with so much dignity, condensed forcefulness, or formal
beauty. For the most part the work of a few hands, and in
some cases of composite authorship, the state papers of the
American Revolution became, through their force of argument
and sweep of phrase, the accepted statements of political
faith, first for the patriot party, and then for the American
people.

Of the important papers agreed to by the Stamp Act Congress, two—a declaration of rights and grievances and a petition to the king—were mainly the work of John Dickinson of
Pennsylvania, whose notable career as a political writer, already
begun in the controversial atmosphere of his own colony, was
to earn for him the title of "the penman of the Revolution."
At the end of the year 1765 Dickinson also published at Philadelphia a pamphlet entitled *The Late Regulations respecting
the British Colonies on the Continent of America Considered,
in a Letter from a Gentleman in Philadelphia to his Friend in
London*,[2] which was reprinted in London and attracted favourable notice. A notable pamphlet, published anonymously,
by Daniel Dulany of Maryland, one of the ablest of colonial
lawyers, entitled *Considerations on the Propriety of Imposing
Taxes in the British Colonies, for the Purpose of Raising a
Revenue, by Act of Parliament*, in which the notion of the "vir-
tual representation" of the colonies in Parliament was conclusively denied, appeared while the Stamp Act Congress was in
session, and was also republished in London.

The repeal of the Stamp Act (March, 1766) caused a sudden
cessation of the agitation in America; and the ominous Declara-

---

[1] Text in W. MacDonald, *Select Charters*, 314, 315.

[2] *Writings*, ed. Ford, I, 211–245.

tory Act, asserting for the first time the right of Parliament "to bind the colonies and people of America, subjects of the crown of Great Britain, in all cases whatsoever," received little attention. In June, 1767, however, the New York assembly was suspended by act of Parliament for its refusal to comply with the requirements of an act for the quartering of troops; while the Townshend acts, which followed immediately, laid duties upon a number of colonial imports, established resident customs commissioners in America, legalized writs of assistance, and readjusted the tea duties in the interest of the hard-pressed East India Company. The colonies, in resisting the Stamp Act, had dwelt upon the unconstitutionality of internal taxation by a Parliament in which they were not represented. Townshend now sought to turn the tables by imposing the external taxes which he professed to think the colonies, by inference, had conceded the right of Parliament to impose.

The passage of the Townshend acts revived, though to a less wide extent, the controversy over colonial rights. Of the writings which attended this phase of the discussion, easily the most important is John Dickinson's *Letters from a Farmer in Pennsylvania to the Inhabitants of the British Colonies.*[1] First published in a Philadelphia newspaper in 1767–68,[2] and reproduced from thence in most of the newspapers then issued in the colonies, they were in 1768 collected in a pamphlet, of which some eight editions appeared in America, two in London, one in Dublin, and a French version in Amsterdam. Without the legal mastery of Thacher or Dulany, but, fortunately, also without the discursiveness and extravagance of Otis or the intellectual and religious bias of John Adams, Dickinson reviewed, earnestly and directly, the colonial case; warned the colonies of the grave danger of admitting any form of parliamentary taxation, external or internal; sustained the right of protest and petition, and urged economy, thrift, and the development of American industry. Forcible resistance, indeed, is with him not to be thought of, and the idea of independence is spurned; yet at the same time Dickinson insists

that we cannot be happy, without being free; that we cannot be free, without being secure in our property; that we cannot be secure

[1] *Writings*, ed. Ford, I, 307–406.    [2] See also Book I, Chap. VII.

in our property, if, without our consent, others may, as by right, take it away; that taxes imposed on us by parliament, do thus take it away.

On the whole, it is the form rather than the substance of the *Letters from a Farmer* that is most original.　Dickinson wrote as a cultivated, prosperous gentleman, addressing an audience of intelligent, but plain, people the soil of whose minds had been already somewhat prepared.　What Dickinson did, and did with effective skill, was to present in attractive literary form the best of what had already been said and thought on behalf of the colonial claims, and to adapt the argument to the new crisis presented by the Townshend programme.　Too patriotic to submit without a protest, and too thoughtful to rebel, he voiced more successfully, perhaps, than any other American publicist of his day, the sober second-thought of the great body of colonists who were ready to carry resistance to any point short of separation and war.

The Massachusetts Circular Letter[1] (11 February, 1768), prepared by Samuel Adams for a committee of the House of Representatives, and addressed to the speakers of other representative houses throughout the colonies, introduces to us the man who, more zealously and persistently than anyone else, devoted himself to achieving American independence.　Holding the humble office of tax-collector in Boston, Adams's devotion to public causes, joined to a rare talent for political organization, had already made him the master of the Boston town-meeting and the leading spirit in the provincial House of Representatives.　In the course of the bitter fight which he waged against Governor Bernard and Governor Hutchinson, and in furtherance of his relentless insistence upon the right of complete local self-government for the colonies, Adams drafted, in whole or in part, most of the resolutions and reports which made Massachusetts the leader in the constitutional struggle, and which also marked it for special punishment later at the hands of Parliament.

The Circular Letter, studiously dignified and respectful in tone, is the best summary statement of the colonial argument which had thus far been put forward.　Admitting the supreme

---

[1] Text in W. MacDonald, *Select Charters*, 331–334.

legislative authority of Parliament over the whole empire, it rests its case on the

essential, unalterable right, in nature, engrafted into the British constitution, as a fundamental law, and ever held sacred and irrevocable by the subjects within the realm, that what a man has honestly acquired is absolutely his own, which he may freely give, but cannot be taken from him without his consent.

So precious is the right of representation, and so great the "utter impracticability" of actually being represented in Parliament, that

this House think that a taxation of their constituents, even without their consent, grievous as it is, would be preferable to any representation that could be admitted for them there.

Devotion to naked principle could go no farther, nor indicate more clearly the desired goal of independence.

The Townshend Revenue Act remained in force until April, 1770. The act produced an inappreciable revenue, necessitated extraordinary expenditures for its enforcement, and had no other effect upon the situation in America than to reawaken and solidify the colonial opposition to parliamentary taxation, and stimulate interest in the development of colonial manufactures and in the concerted non-importation and non-consumption of British goods. One of the first steps of the North ministry was to repeal it (1770), except the tax of three pence a pound on tea, retained to assert the principle of the Declaratory Act of 1766. For the next two years and more the agitation was not actively kept up, and even such violent disorders as the Boston Massacre (March, 1770) and the burning of the revenue schooner *Gaspée* (1772) occasioned hardly more than local excitement. Colonial newspapers continued to print essays on American rights, and houses of assembly embodied their views in resolutions; but these occasional writings, while doubtless not without their influence upon public opinion, hardly constitute a political literature of importance.

To this early period of revolutionary agitation belong also the first two volumes of Thomas Hutchinson's *History of the Colony of Massachusetts Bay* (1764–67)[1] and the famous Hut-

[1] See also Book I. Chap. II.

chinson "Letters," which, although not made public until 1773,
date from 1768–69. Written by Hutchinson, previous to his
governorship, to a friend in England, the "Letters" discuss
events in Massachusetts from the point of view of a loyalist
official who, deeply attached to the colony, was also deeply concerned at the grave course which affairs were taking, and who
could honestly declare:

I wish the good of the colony when I wish to see some further
restraint of liberty rather than the connexion with the parent state
should be broken; for I am sure such a breach must prove the ruin
of the colony.

By means never divulged, Franklin, in 1773, got possession of
the letters and sent them to friends in Boston, where their
publication greatly intensified the hostility to Hutchinson and
precipitated his recall.

With the destruction of the tea at Boston (16 December,
1773), the controversy between the colonies and the mother
country entered upon the stage which was to lead to a declaration of independence and to war. In February, 1774, at a
hearing before the Privy Council on a petition from Massachusetts for Hutchinson's removal, Franklin was bitterly denounced for his connection with the Hutchinson letters, and
was presently removed from his office of deputy postmaster-
general for North America. In March, the port of Boston was
by statute closed to commerce, except in food, after 1 June,
until compensation should be made to the East India Company
for the loss of the tea. In May, the charter of Massachusetts
was so altered by act of Parliament as largely to deprive the
colony of self-government, while by another statute provision
was made for the trial in England, or in another colony, of
persons accused of murder or other capital offence because of
anything done by them in suppressing riots or enforcing the
revenue laws. In June, more stringent regulations were en-
acted for the quartering of troops. General Gage had already
arrived at Boston as military governor, and the coercion of the
colony began.

The first Continental Congress, which met at Philadelphia
5 September, adopted a set of "Declarations and Resolves,"[1]

[1] Text in W. MacDonald, *Select Charters*, 357–361.

similar in tone and general argument to those of the Stamp Act Congress, but containing a significant admission of the right of Parliament to regulate the external trade of the colonies, provided the aim were regulation and not taxation. A petition to the king and an address to the inhabitants of Canada, both drafted by Dickinson, were also adopted, together with a memorial to the inhabitants of British America, drawn by Richard Henry Lee of Virginia, and an eloquent address to the people of Great Britain, the work of John Jay of New York, later the first chief-justice of the United States Supreme Court. An agreement known as the "Association"[1] pledged the people of the colonies to commercial non-intercourse with Great Britain, and to the encouragement of industry, economy, and neighbourly kindness. Copies of these various state papers were separately printed and widely circulated.

The passage of the coercive acts, and the assembling of a Congress to consider plans of united resistance, stirred anew the fires of literary controversy. In May, 1774, the same month that saw the arrival of Gage and the British troops at Boston, Josiah Quincy published at that place his *Observations on the Act of Parliament, commonly called the Boston Port-Bill; with Thoughts on Civil Society and Standing Armies.* Quincy was a brilliant young lawyer, who, in company with John Adams, had chivalrously defended the British soldiers indicted for participation in the Boston Massacre, in 1770. A competent critic[2] has suggested that the larger part of the pamphlet, dealing with "civil society and standing armies," had been carefully prepared some time before, advantage being taken of the Port Act to publish the work with an expanded title. Quincy's pamphlet was shortly followed by James Wilson's *Considerations on the Nature and the Extent of the Legislative Authority of the British Parliament*, an ingenious rejection of such authority in favour of allegiance to the king alone. The writer, a young lawyer of Philadelphia, was later to contribute powerfully to the acceptance of the Federal Constitution by Pennsylvania.

Not all who entered the lists, however, agreed so unreservedly with the sentiments of Congress or of the patriot

[1] Text in W. MacDonald. *Select Charters*, 362–367.
[2] Tyler, *Literary History of the American Revolution*, I, 272 note.

leaders. A series of papers in *The Pennsylvania Packet*, reprinted in a pamphlet with the title *A Few Political Reflections Submitted to the Consideration of the British Colonies, by a Citizen of Philadelphia*, and attributed to Richard Wells, urged compensation for the tea and the abandonment of violent protest, at the same time arguing for united rejection of the claim to taxation on the ground that the colonies were too old and too strong to be kept in leading-strings. An anonymous *Letter from a Virginian*, addressed to the Congress at Philadelphia, went further and frankly questioned the constitutional soundness and political wisdom of the arguments put forth by the Congress.

No history of the American Revolution, or of the political literature to which it gave birth, would be complete without consideration of the loyalists. That independence was in fact the work of a minority, and that the methods by which the loyal majority was overawed and, in part, expelled were as highhanded and cruel as they were active and vigorous, must be freely conceded. Weighty as was the colonial argument, force and violence were freely employed to give effect to it. But the great loyalist party, numbering among its leaders many of the ablest, most devoted, and wealthiest men in colonial life, was not crushed without a struggle; and the arguments with which its adherents defended their cause and sought to defeat that of their opponents were not less ably put or trenchantly phrased than those of the patriots themselves.

Soon after the "Association" agreement of the Continental Congress was adopted (October, 1774), there was published in New York the first of four pamphlets by a "Westchester Farmer." The author was the Rev. Samuel Seabury, then and for some time rector of St. Peter's Church, Westchester, and later, by time's curious working, first bishop of the Protestant Episcopal Church in the United States. The four pamphlets, entitled respectively *Free Thoughts on the Proceedings of the Continental Congress*, *The Congress Canvassed*, *A View of the Controversy between Great-Britain and her Colonies*, and *An Alarm to the Legislature of the Province of New-York*, were a powerful attack upon the aims and policy of the Congress and the patriot leaders, and a plea for such adjustment as would assure to the colonies local self-government, on the one hand, with full recognition of parliamentary authority on the other. For writing the pamphlets Seabury was mobbed, imprisoned, and hounded until in 1776 he took refuge within the British lines.

It was in reply to the first of Seabury's pamphlets that Alexander Hamilton, then a college student of seventeen, made anonymously his first essay in authorship with *A Full Vindication of the Measures of the Congress, from the Calumnies of their Enemies* (1774) and *A Farmer Refuted* (1775). None of the pamphleteers of the Revolutionary period excels Hamilton in the logical acumen and expository power which he here displays, and none approached him in his clear discernment of the theatre and character of the war, if war must be. Yet even Hamilton, with all his precocious intellectual power, failed to point out beyond peradventure how union with the Empire under allegiance to the king comported with a denial of the legislative power of Parliament. The only outcome for the colonies was independence, and independence was the word which, as yet, most colonial leaders appeared anxious to avoid.

Before the attacks of the "Westchester Farmer" had ceased, Daniel Leonard, a Boston lawyer of social prominence, began the publication in a loyalist newspaper, over the pen-name of "Massachusettensis," of a series of seventeen letters, *To the Inhabitants of the Province of the Massachusetts-Bay* (1774–75). Seabury had emphasized the impracticability and political unwisdom of the recommendations of the Congress. Leonard assailed the unconstitutional arguments of the patriots, and the revolutionary character of their attacks upon parliamentary enactments and crown officers.

The task of combating the influence of "Massachusettensis" was undertaken by John Adams, who, early in 1775, published in the Boston *Gazette*, over the signature of "Novanglus," a series of letters traversing Leonard's argument. Twelve articles had appeared when the battle of Lexington (19 April, 1775) intervened. Adams did not lack legal knowledge or logical proficiency, but he was no match for Leonard in debate, nor could he keep to the point; and although the republication of the letters in London, and a reprint many years later in the United States, gave some vogue to the name "Novanglus," the essays won no permanent distinction either for themselves or for their author. It was as a hard-working member of the Continental Congress, and not as a writer or political philosopher, that Adams made his worthiest contribution to the American cause.

To a different class belong the numerous writings of Joseph Galloway, a delegate from Pennsylvania to the first Continental Congress. Already prominent in the politics of his colony, Galloway submitted to the Congress a *Plan of a Proposed Union between Great Britain and the Colonies.* Read in the light of the present day, the scheme seems like a suggestive anticipation of later British colonial policy; but the Congress, after debating it at length, and rejecting it by the narrow majority of a single vote, trampled it under foot, and ordered all reference to it expunged from the printed journal. Galloway later published the plan in *A Candid Examination of the Mutual Claims of Great Britain and the Colonies* (New York, 1775). In 1778, after two years spent with the British forces, Galloway went to England, where he was thought sufficiently important to be examined before the House of Commons, and where he continued to publish pamphlets on America until the end of the war.

Another New York loyalist, President Myles Cooper of King's College (now Columbia), gifted with wit and sarcasm above most of his fellows, entered the lists in 1774 with two anonymous pamphlets—*The American Querist: or, Some Questions Proposed relative to the Present Disputes between Great Britain and her American Colonies,* and *A Friendly Address to all Reasonable Americans.* In August, 1775, a mob stripped and mutilated him, but he contrived to escape to a British ship-of-war, and thence to England, where he obtained ecclesiastical preferment. Charles Lee, soon to be numbered among the renegades and traitors, but at the moment in the enjoyment of a repute as a military expert which he had done little to earn, replied to Cooper with some cleverness in *Strictures on a Pamphlet, entitled a 'Friendly Address to all Reasonable Americans'* (1775)—the only contribution of Lee's to the patriot cause for which he may be appreciatively remembered.

Although not published until 1797, by which time the author had been for more than twenty years resident in England, Jonathan Boucher's *A View of the Causes and Consequences of the American Revolution* may perhaps be included in our enumeration of loyalist writings. From 1762 to 1775 Boucher was rector of parishes in Maryland and Virginia, finding time, however, to take an active part in colonial politics. The volume referred to, dedicated to Washington and prefaced by an extended introduction, consists of thirteen sermons preached to his American congregations, and forms as a whole the best presentation of the loyalist cause as embraced and championed by an Anglican minister. For his boldness, however, his parishioners drove him into exile, in common with many another clergyman who held similar views.

Mention should also be made here of the poems of Philip Freneau and John Trumbull, although the fuller discussion of their literary significance belongs elsewhere in this work.[1] The first of Freneau's poems of the Revolution, *On the Conqueror of America Shut up in Boston* and *General Gage's Soliloquy*, were published in the summer of 1775, while the siege of Boston was in progress. Trumbull, whose muse had already responded to some of the earlier incidents of the war, published the first canto of *McFingal* in January, 1776. Grounded, as were the writings of both of these authors, in a clear, popular understanding of the points at issue, and foreshadowing, in Freneau's case, the ultimate attainment of independence, the satirical humour of the poems confirmed the faithful and strengthened the wavering quite as effectively as state papers or pamphlet treatises.

The great influence of Benjamin Franklin, covering the entire period of the revolutionary struggle, was exerted chiefly through the customary channels of diplomacy, and in a voluminous correspondence with friends and public men on both sides of the Atlantic; and his contemporary publications, comparatively few in number, carried weight because of their directness and sturdy common sense, and of the fame of their writer as a scientist or as the author of *Poor Richard's Almanac* or as the skilful champion of the colonial cause in England, rather than because of their literary merit or their substantive contribution to the American argument. The report of his *Examination*[2] before the House of Commons (1766), while the repeal of the Stamp Act was under discussion, showed a states-

---

[1] See Book I, Chap. IX.      [2] *Writings*, ed. Smyth, IV, 412–448.

manlike knowledge of American conditions, and dexterity and boldness in defending the patriot cause. In January, 1768, he contributed to *The London Chronicle* an article entitled *Causes of the American Discontents before 1768*, and later in the year he wrote a short preface for a London reprint of Dickinson's *Letters from a Farmer*.

For the next five years Franklin was occupied with his duties as colonial agent of Massachusetts, Georgia, and other colonies. His writings during that period consist almost wholly of letters, and of articles on electricity and economic subjects. Then, in September, 1773, he attacked the colonial policy of Hillsborough in *Rules by which a Great Empire may be reduced to a Small One*, following this, early in 1774, with an article *On the Rise and Progress of the Differences between Great Britain and Her American Colonies*. The publication of the Hutchinson letters, although it brought official censure and cost Franklin the loss of a remunerative office, did not materially affect his reputation or weaken his influence; but a *Tract relative to the Affair of Hutchinson's Letters*, written in 1774, was, possibly from prudential reasons, not published.[1]

That persistent opposition to Parliament, whether through elaborated constitutional arguments or by such practical devices as commercial non-intercourse, might in the end raise the issue of independence, had early been perceived; and the earnest protestations of loyalty to the crown which are found in the resolutions of the Stamp Act Congress or the declaration and resolves of the First Continental Congress, if read chiefly in the light of subsequent events, do not seem entirely unequivocal. Not until late in 1775, however, after armed collisions had occurred at Lexington, Concord, and Bunker Hill, after Gage had been hopelessly besieged at Boston, and after a second Continental Congress, assuming the general direction of affairs, had begun the organization of a revolutionary government, appointed Washington commander-in-chief, and taken the first steps toward obtaining foreign aid, did the demand for independence, or even the disposition seriously to consider it, become general.

Of the writings which contributed immediately to the final break, the foremost place must be given to Thomas Paine's

[1] For Franklin, see also Book I, Chap. VI.

*Common Sense* (1776). Paine, after an unimportant and not wholly respectable career in England, came to America in 1774, in his thirty-eighth year, armed with introductions from Franklin, and settled at Philadelphia. His pamphlet *Common Sense*, published in January, 1776, seized the psychological moment. Brushing aside all legal and historical argument as no longer to the point, and resorting to the wildest exaggeration and misrepresentation for the purpose of discrediting England and its people, Paine laid his finger on the heart of the situation. The colonies had gone too far to turn back. They were already alienated. The British connection was no longer valuable to them, and reconciliation would be an evil rather than a good. Common sense dictated that they should be free. Enthusiastic acclaim from leaders and public, and a sale of over 100,000 copies within three months, attested the success and power of Paine's first essay in political pamphleteering.

Sweeping as Paine's success was, the course of events had nevertheless prepared the way. In February, 1775, Lord North had startled the House of Commons by introducing and passing a conciliatory resolution; but the offer, unsatisfactory less because of its terms than because of want of confidence in the ministry and the king, had been effectually prejudiced by the passage, in March and April, of bills restraining the trade of the colonies to Great Britain and the British West Indies, and by further provisions for the prosecution of the war. It was on the first of the restraining bills, that relating to New England, that Burke made his great speech on conciliation. In June came the battle of Bunker Hill and the appointment of Washington as commander-in-chief. On 6 July Congress adopted a *Declaration of the Causes and Necessity of Taking Up Arms*,[1] the joint work of Dickinson and Jefferson, and one of the greatest of the state papers of the Revolution. Still protesting that "we have not raised armies with ambitious designs of separating from Great Britain, and establishing independent states," the declaration reviewed, vigorously but with dignity, the course of recent events, protested in the name of liberty against a policy that would enslave the colonies, and proclaimed solemnly the intention of fighting until freedom was assured.

[1] Text in W. MacDonald, *Select Charters*, 374–381.

In our own native land, in defence of the freedom that is our birthright, and which we ever enjoyed till the late violation of it—for the protection of our property, acquired solely by the honest industry of our fore-fathers and ourselves, against violence actually offered, we have taken up arms. We shall lay them down when hostilities shall cease on the part of the aggressors, and all danger of their being renewed shall be removed, and not before.

Two days later (8 July) a last petition to the king once more protested loyalty and devotion, and prayed the interposition of the crown to bring about reconciliation. At the end of the month, however, in an elaborate report drawn by Jefferson, Lord North's offer of conciliation was emphatically, almost contemptuously, rejected. In August a royal proclamation declared the colonies in rebellion. Franklin, meantime, had quietly slipped out of England and returned to America, where he was at once elected to Congress. He had withstood to the last the encroachments of parliamentary authority in England, and was now to witness the passing of royal authority in America. With the rejection of petitions on the one side and of compromise on the other, Paine could well urge that the time had come to act.

For the writing of the Declaration of Independence (4 July, 1776) Jefferson had had some preparation, in a way, through two publications already favourably known to members of the Congress. In 1774 he had published at Williamsburg *A Summary View of the Rights of British America, Set Forth in Some Resolutions Intended for the Instruction of the Present Delegates of the People of Virginia now in Convention*, in which, with somewhat flamboyant boldness of phrase, he had offered to the king "the advice of your great American council," and had appealed to him to open his breast "to liberal and expanded thought," that the name of George the Third might not be "a blot in the page of history." In June, 1775, he had framed an *Address of the House of Burgesses*, on the subject of Lord North's conciliatory resolution, which was adopted by the house and served as the model for the report on the same resolution which was approved by the Congress in July. He had also, as we have seen, collaborated with Dickinson in the preparation of the *Declaration of the Causes and Necessity of Taking Up Arms*.

The real preparation, however, lay, not in Jefferson's training or skill as a writer, nor in the possession by him of extraordinary insight or prophetic vision, but in the succession of events for the fifteen years past and in the innumerable pamphlets and essays which those had called out.   The conduct of the king, the ministry, and the Parliament, the history and necessities of the colonies, and the constitutional foundations of empire had all been repeatedly and ably examined by lawyers and publicists, and the findings set forth by accomplished writers, long before Jefferson was called upon to say the final word.   Of all the criticisms that have been passed upon the *Declaration of Independence*, the least to the point is that it is not original.   The material was at hand, the argument had been elaborated, the conclusions had been drawn.   For originality there was as little opportunity as there was need.   What was required now was a concise summing up of the whole matter, full enough to give a clear impression of completeness, vigorous and bold enough to serve as a national manifesto, and polished, dignified, and incisive enough to catch the ear, to linger in the memory, and to bear endless repetition.   That Jefferson met this need with consummate success, working into one brief statement doctrine, accusation, argument, and declaration of freedom, was a demonstration that the hour and the man had met.

The period of active hostilities (1775–1781), which had already begun when the Declaration of Independence was adopted, was not characterized by literary activity.   On the American side, at least, the case had been fully stated, and with the decision of the Congress to accept no terms of conciliation that did not recognize independence, there was no longer an English-speaking audience to which to appeal; while to France and Holland, whose aid was sought, the appeal was necessarily diplomatic rather than literary.   With the recourse to arms, pamphleteers and essayists entered the army, or busied themselves with public service in Congress, state, or local community.   Dickinson, who had drawn back when independence severed allegiance to the crown, nevertheless shouldered a musket.   The loyalists were overawed or driven out, and their writings belong thereafter to the countries of their exile.   Newspapers were few, paper was scarce, mails were infrequent and precarious, schools and colleges were interrupted or suspended altogether.

Of publication and writing of certain sorts, on the other hand, there was a considerable volume. The *Journal of the Continental Congress*, published from time to time, with the exception of such parts as were thought to require secrecy,[1] is an invaluable record of proceedings, although it contains no report of debates. Numerous reports, resolutions, and other state papers of importance were, however, printed separately in broadside or pamphlet form for the use of members of Congress or for wider distribution. The acts and resolutions of the state legislatures, so far as such bodies were able to meet, were also printed, together with occasional proclamations and other public documents.

The letters of American statesmen, particularly Washington, Franklin, John Adams, Samuel Adams, John Jay, and Patrick Henry, published long afterwards in collected editions, existed for the most part only in manuscript; but their quasi-public character, together with their circulation from hand to hand, often gave to them, to an extent much greater than would be the case today, though within limited circles, the essential character of publications. Larger audiences, but still local, were reached by sermons, many of which, especially those of the New England clergy, dealt much with the war and the political issues of the time. Comparatively few of these, however, were printed contemporaneously. Of great importance to an understanding of the revolutionary struggle are the journals and letter-books of soldiers and officers, both American and British, and the controversial narratives and defences of Burgoyne, Cornwallis, Clinton, and others regarding the conduct of military affairs; but few of these are predominantly political in character, almost none were printed in America at the time, and the publication of nearly all of those by American authors dates from years long subsequent to the war.

Of the war-time pamphlets, the most important are the series to which the author, Thomas Paine, gave the title of *The Crisis*. The first issue of the series had its origin in the gloom and despondency occasioned by Washington's famous

---

[1] The material in the *Secret Journals*, 4 vols., Boston, 1821, is included in the Ford and Hunt edition of the *Journals* (see Bibliography).

retreat across New Jersey, in the fall and early winter of 1776; a retreat which to many seemed to presage the speedy collapse of the American cause. On 18 December, Washington, irritated and alarmed at the rapid dwindling of his army under the operation of short-term enlistment, wrote to his brother:

Between you and me, I think our affairs are in a very bad situation; not so much from the apprehension of General Howe's army, as from the defection of New York, Jerseys, and Pennsylvania . . . In a word, my dear Sir, if every nerve is not strained to recruit the new army with all possible expedition, I think the game is pretty near up.

The next day there issued from the press the first number of *The Crisis*, with its ringing call:

These are the times that try men's souls. The summer soldier and the sunshine patriot will, in this crisis, shrink from the service of his country; but he that stands it now, deserves the love and thanks of man and woman. . . . Up and help us; lay your shoulders to the wheel; better have too much force than too little, when so great an object is at stake. . . . The heart that feels not now, is dead.

Sixteen of these stirring pamphlets, produced as the hopes and fears, the successes and failures of the war gave occasion, were issued down to the end of 1783, when the series ended.

With the surrender of Cornwallis (October, 1781), the active military and naval operations of the war practically ceased. Nearly two years were to elapse before the treaty of peace (September, 1783) formally recognized the independence of the United States; but independence had been achieved in fact, and the way was now open for the discussion of new political problems. A frame of government, the *Articles of Confederation*, had gone into effect in March, 1781; and when fighting ended, Congress and the country turned their attention to the pressing questions of finance, the development and administration of the West, the restoration of normal conditions in industry, commerce, and social life, and the perfection of the Federal union. It is not without significance that, among the statesmen whose defence of colonial rights had developed both the theory and the practice of revolution, there were many who were now to set the United States forward in the next stage of its career.

For the replacement of the Articles of Confederation by the "more perfect" union of the Federal Constitution, private correspondence, as in the case of the Revolution, did much to prepare the way. Jefferson and John Adams were absent from the country on diplomatic service, the former in France, the latter at the Court of St. James; and Franklin, prince of American diplomatists, was not, in the larger field of government, a constructive statesman. But Washington, Madison, Jay, Hamilton, Patrick Henry, and other leaders were busy with their pens, discussing with one another, particularly in the interval from 1785 to 1787, the defects of the Articles, the need of a firmer national organization, and the practical possibilities of united action. Prominent in this epistolary discussion were such questions as the protection and encouragement of American commerce, retaliation against England for its imperfect observance of the terms of peace, the adjustment of the opposing interests of large and small states, and the provision of an adequate revenue for the payment of the revolutionary debt and the maintenance of the Federal establishment.

In May, 1787, the Federal Convention met at Philadelphia. In anticipation of its deliberations, Madison set down his opinion as to the *Vices of the Political System of the United States*,[1] and prepared a summary view *Of Ancient and Modern Confederacies*.[2] The former noted most of the important points around which the debate later turned, but there is nothing in the Constitution to show that the latter had influence with the convention. The convention was preëminently a practical body. The sources of the Federal Constitution are in the government of England, the constitutions of the states, the Articles of Confederation, and the experience of the country and of Congress under the Articles. The *Journal* of the convention comprises only a bare record of proceedings, and does not report debates; the proceedings, moreover, were behind closed doors. For our knowledge of what was said, as distinguished from what was voted, we are dependent upon Madison's elaborate *Notes*, taken down at the time and corrected and

---

[1] *Writings*, ed. Hunt, II, 361–369.          [2] *Ibid.*, II, 369–390.

supplemented by the journal; some *Minutes* of Yates, a New York delegate; a *Report* by Luther Martin to the Maryland assembly[1]; and the letters, many of them still unpublished, of members of the convention. The elaborate publication of documents, debates, and reports which commonly attends a modern state constitutional convention was conspicuously lacking.

While the convention was in session, there was published at Boston, New York, and Philadelphia, in separate editions, the first volume of John Adams's *Defence of the Constitutions of Government of the United States of America.* This work, written and first published in London, was occasioned, the author states, by Turgot's sweeping attack upon the American theory of government, contained in a letter to Dr. Richard Price, in 1778, and published by Price in his *Observations on the Importance of the American Revolution, and the Means of Making it a Benefit to the World* (1785). Two additional volumes appeared in 1788.[2] The prominence of the author gave the work, especially the first volume, some vogue; but the disorderly arrangement, the verbose and careless style, the many glaring inaccuracies and inconsistencies due to hasty writing and negligent proofreading, a political philosophy nowhere profound, and the characteristic temper of the advocate rather than of the expositor, did Adams no credit; while his frank criticisms of some features of American government opened the way for attacks upon his sincerity and loyalty which followed him throughout his life. To this disfavour the "worship of the Constitution" as a perfect instrument, which began soon after the successful establishment of the government under it, undoubtedly contributed.

With the adjournment of the Convention in September, and the submission of the Constitution to ratifying conventions in the states, the public became for the first time acquainted with the pending scheme of government; and the great debate on ratification began. The newspapers teemed with political essays, and pamphlets multiplied. The Constitution lacked neither friends nor foes. On the side of the Constitution were

[1] The foregoing are included in Elliott's *Debates* and Farrand's *Records of the Federal Convention* (see Bibliography).

[2] *Works*, IV, V.

James Sullivan of Massachusetts, with his eleven letters of *Cassius*; Oliver Ellsworth of Connecticut, with thirteen letters of *A Landholder;* Roger Sherman of the same state, who contributed five letters of *A Countryman* and two of *A Citizen of New Haven*; and John Dickinson, in his *Letters of Fabius*. The opposing views of the Anti-federalists were vigorously set forth by *Agrippa*, whose eighteen letters are probably to be ascribed to James Winthrop of Massachusetts; by George Clinton of New York, who published seven letters under the name of *Cato*; by Robert Yates, in two letters of *Sydney*; and in seven letters by Luther Martin.[1]

The pamphlet literature was equally important. Noah Webster, best known to later generations as a lexicographer, came to the support of the new instrument in *An Examination into the Leading Principles of the Federal Constitution;* as did John Jay, in *An Address to the People of the State of New York;* Pelatiah Webster of Philadelphia, in *The Weakness of Brutus Exposed*, a reply to the first of a series of sixteen essays ascribed to Thomas Treadwell of New York; Tench Coxe, in *An Examination of the Constitution*, written over the pseudonym of "An American Citizen"; and David Ramsay, in *An Address to the Freemen of South Carolina*. The opposition was represented by Elbridge Gerry's *Observations on the New Constitution;* Melanchthon Smith's *Address to the People of the State of New York*, and preëminently by Richard Henry Lee, in his *Observations leading to a Fair Examination of the System of Government proposed by the late Convention*, and by George Mason of Virginia, in his *Objections to the proposed Federal Constitution*, to the latter of whom James Iredell of North Carolina made an elaborate rejoinder.[2]

Incomparably superior, whether in content, or in form, or in permanent influence, to all the other political writing of the period are the eighty-five essays known collectively as *The Federalist*. The essays, the joint work of Hamilton, Madison, and Jay, appeared in the New York *Independent Journal* during the seven months beginning October, 1787. They had been preceded, and to a considerable extent called out, by a series of attacks upon the new Constitution contributed by Governor

[1] All the foregoing are reprinted in P. L. Ford, *Essays on the Constitution*.
[2] The foregoing are collected in P. L. Ford, *Pamphlets on the Constitution*.

George Clinton and Robert Yates to the New York *Journal*, over the pen-names of "Cato" and "Brutus" respectively. The authorship of a few of the essays has been an interesting problem of historical criticism, but four were the work of Jay, fourteen were certainly written by Madison, three are probably to be ascribed to Madison, nine are probably Hamilton's, three are the work of Hamilton and Madison jointly, and the remaining fifty-one are the work of Hamilton.[1] The plan was Hamilton's, moreover, and his influence undoubtedly dominated all the numbers of the series, whoever the particular author.

The papers of *The Federalist* are in part an account of the merits and defects of confederacies, and a discussion of the difficulties and advantages of union, and in part an examination of the weaknesses of the Articles of Confederation and a defence of the provisions of the proposed Constitution. Their actual influence upon the ratification of the Constitution in New York, which was the chief reason for writing them, has probably been overrated, nor are they free from partisan bias and the kind of popular argument likely to be effective in political debate. As the earliest contemporary exposition, in extended form, of the Constitution, however, they occupy a unique position. Written in the heat of controversy, and before the great structure of American constitutional law had even been begun, they forecast with extraordinary acuteness some of the most fundamental principles of constitutional interpretation which the federal courts were later to adopt, as well as some of the grave political issues on which party lines were to form. Judicial reference and quotation have given to *The Federalist* a weight of authority second only to that of the Constitution itself, and upon the authorship of the larger part of its pages the reputation of Hamilton as a publicist mainly rests.

[1] This follows the classification in Ford's edition.

# CHAPTER IX

# The Beginnings of Verse, 1610–1808

THE two centuries that cover the beginnings of American poetry may be divided into three periods. The first period is that of the early colonial verse which begins in 1610 with the publication of Rich's ballad on the settlement of Jamestown and ends with the seventeenth century. With 1700 begins the second period, which is one of transition in purpose, subject, and style. The third period, which is marked by the beginnings of nationalism, opens with the passage of the Stamp Act in 1765 and closes with the publication of Bryant's *Embargo* in 1808.

Even in the light of the unliterary conditions that prevailed in the Southern and Middle colonies it is surprising to find how little verse was produced south of New England before the middle of the eighteenth century. The Southern colonists were not of a literary class, and probably would have written little or nothing under any conditions; in the Southern colonies and, to a less degree, in the Middle colonies, conditions were distinctly unfavourable to literature; and in Virginia, especially, there were no schools, no printing presses, no literary centres, and few people who cared to write books or, apparently, to read them. Yet, though the New England of the seventeenth century left us many thousands of lines of verse of various kinds, as against the less than one thousand lines left by all the colonies to the south of that region, it was Virginia that produced what is perhaps the one real American poem of the seventeenth century. This is the epitaph on the insurrectionary leader Nathaniel Bacon, written "by his Man." The "Man" clearly was no menial but a reader and a poet. His brief elegy of forty-four lines is worthy of Ben

Jonson himself, and is indeed written in that great elegist's dignified, direct, and manly style:

> In a word
> *Marss* and *Minerva*, both in him Concurd
> For arts, for arms, whose pen and sword alike
> As *Catos* did, may admireation strike
> In to his foes; while they confess with all
> It was their guilt stil'd him a Criminall.

Maryland has even less to show than Virginia. The rhyming tags of verse appended to the chapters of George Alsop's *Character of the Province of Maryland* (1666) cannot be taken seriously. The description of Maryland contained in the *Carmen Seculare* of a certain Mr. Lewis shows that Pope had not yet reached Baltimore in 1732, however at home he may have been in Boston and Philadelphia. Of the same type is a *True Relation of the Flourishing State of Pennsylvania* (1686), by John Holme, a resident of that colony. The *True Relation* is utilitarian in purpose and homely in style, but on the whole its five hundred lines in various metres, with their catalogues of native animals and plants in the manner of William Wood's verses in his *New England's Prospect*, are rather pleasing. New York produced practically no English verse until the Revolution; and the Carolinas and Georgia continued barren until near the close of the eighteenth century, when Charleston became something of a literary centre. But Pennsylvania came to be fairly prolific early in the transition period, and continued so for almost a century until New York and Boston, as literary centres, finally displaced Philadelphia.

The earliest New England verse was as utilitarian and matter-of-fact as any prose. Narratives of the voyages, annals of the colonies, descriptions of flora, fauna, and scenery, written in the main for readers in the mother country, were versified merely for the sake of the jingle. Altogether this descriptive and historical verse amounts to less than a thousand lines. *A Looking Glass for the Times* (1677), by Peter Folger of Nantucket, derives interest from the fact that it was written by the maternal grandfather of Benjamin Franklin. Its four hundred lines in ballad quatrains are very bad verse, however, and, though it has been termed "A manly plea for toleration in an age of intolerance," there is still question as to whether it was actually published in the author's lifetime and, consequently, whether Folger ran any risk. The most important piece of historical verse in this period was the work of the first native-born American poet, Benjamin Tompson (1644–1714), who, as his tombstone at Roxbury informs us, was a "learned schoolmaster and physician and the renowned poet of New England," and is "mortuus sed immortalis." His chief production, *New England's Crises*, is a formal attempt at an epic on King Philip's War. The prologue pictures early society in New England and recounts the decadence in manners and morals that has brought about the crisis,—the war as God's punishment. The six hundred and fifty lines of pentameter couplets are somewhat more polished than those of the poet's contemporaries, and might suggest the influence of Dryden if there were any external reason for supposing that the Restoration poets gained admission to early New England. Tompson's classical allusions, part of his epic attempt, are in amusing contrast to his rugged and homely diction, but his poem as a whole has at least the virtue of simplicity, and is interesting as the first of a long line of narratives in verse which recount the events of the wars fought on American soil.

*A Brief Account of the Agency of the Honorable John Winthrop* [in obtaining a charter for Connecticut], though not published until 1725, belongs in purpose and style to the seventeenth century. The author, Roger Wolcott, afterwards governor of Connecticut, was little more of a poet than Governor Bradford, but his literary pretensions ally him with Benjamin Tompson. His couplets are rugged and his diction prosaic, in the main, but the heroic style of the battle scenes and the lofty similes employed by the hero as he recounts to Charles II the settlement and the history of the Colony, show that Wolcott too was consciously attempting an epic. His poem is a link between the unliterary historical and descriptive verse of early New England and the more pretentious epics that appeared so abundantly during the latter half of the eighteenth century.

The most characteristic poetic products of early New England are the memorial poems. Subsequent generations have made merry over their matter and style, and indeed little can be said in their favour if they are to be taken as an index to the poetic taste of the time and not simply as conventional tributes to the dead.    If, however, the New England elegy is to be judged on its literary merits, we should remember that it was not an isolated type, unique in the poverty of its matter and style, but that it simply reflected its English origin and was closely related to its English counterparts.    Unlike the English, though, the writers of New England did not evolve a better style of their own, the elegies at the close of the century being, if anything, worse than those at the beginning.    Perhaps Quarles was chiefly responsible for their pentameter couplets, rough with run-on lines and imperfect rhymes.    Despite occasional variety of form in six-line stanza or quatrain, there is little variety of tone or style; and in all these thousands of lines scarcely a line of genuine poetry, or a single poem worth preservation in its entirety.

The succession of these elegies is surprisingly unbroken for at least forty years.    Both authors and subjects are in the main the divines who controlled the destinies of New England and who provided its literature.    When such an elegy as that on the Rev. Thomas Shepard by the Rev. Urian Oakes, president of Harvard, is discovered amid this dreary elegiac waste, its merits are sure to be exaggerated.    This poem in fifty six-line stanzas, though commonplace in thought and style, is not without pathos, and gives an impression of sincerity.    But the Rev. Urian Oakes himself was not so fortunate in his elegist, no less a person than the Rev. Cotton Mather, the most prolific elegist of his time.    His elegy on Oakes reaches a length of over four hundred lines.    To adorn his subject he "ransacks the ages, spoils the climes"; his pentameters and his quatrains are mere doggerel, his rhymes are atrocious, and his lines rife with conceits and puns and classical and biblical allusions.    John Cleveland at his best could do no worse.    The real feeling that probably inspired Mather's writing is obscured by the laboured insincerity of his style.    But the nadir is reached by the Rev. Nicholas Noyes (1647–1717), who in his elegies on the Rev. John Higginson and the Rev. Joseph Green shows promising possibilities of bathos, but who in his poem on the Rev. James Brayley's attack of the stone revels in such a plethora of conceits and puns as to put to the blush his most

gifted English contemporaries.   The one elegiac poem of early
New England that may be worth preserving is the *Funeral
Song* (1709), written by the Rev. Samuel Wigglesworth, son of
Michael, on the death of his friend Nathaniel Clarke.   Together
with its real feeling, it exhibits a certain felicity of diction
that bespeaks Elizabethan models; and such phrases as "where
increate eternity's concealed," "solemn music," and "warbling
divinest airs," seem to show that Milton had reached New
England.   As a genre the elegy died with the decline of the
clergy, and passed as a fashion passes with changed conditions.

The most interesting as well as the most pleasing figure in
early New England verse is that of Anne Bradstreet, who was
"fathered and husbanded" respectively by Thomas Dudley
and Simon Bradstreet, both in their time governors of Massachusetts.   Born in London in 1612, she emigrated in 1630 with
her husband and died in 1672.   Although the mother of eight
children, she found time to write over seven thousand lines of
verse in what must have been, to her, peculiarly uncongenial surroundings.   Her brother-in-law, the Rev. John Woodbridge,
when on a visit to London in 1650, published without her knowledge her poems under the title of *The Tenth Muse, Lately
Sprung Up in America*, and a second edition followed in Boston
in 1678.   That her poems were read and admired is attested
by such poetic tributes as that of Nathaniel Ward, who affirms
that she was "a right Du Bartas girle," and represents Apollo
as unable to decide whether Du Bartas or the New England
Muse was the more excellent poet.   But Anne Bradstreet was
not a poet; she was a winsome personality in an unlovely age.
That she should have written verse at all was phenomenal,
but that it should have been poor verse was inevitable.   Her
*Exact Epitome of the Four Monarchies*, in several thousand lines
of bad pentameter couplets, is simply a rhyming chronicle of the
medieval type, the matter of which was supplied by Raleigh's
*History of the World*.   Her *Four Elements, Constitutions, Ages
of Man, and Seasons of the Year*, almost equally worthless as
poetry, is an interesting adaptation of Sylvester's translation of
the *Divine Weeks*.   She repeatedly states her admiration for Du
Bartas and her indebtedness to him.   Thirteen lines in the
second day of the first week of his poem suggested her theme,
and this she expands in the form of a medieval *debat*; other

passages from Du Bartas she condenses, expands, or merely paraphrases. She gives only about 1800 lines to the entire exposition of her elements, humours, ages, and seasons; hence she uses but a small part of the encyclopædic material of the French poem. The feeble New England imitation cannot compare with the original. Du Bartas, though often flat and prosaic, is immense in his range, and is at times even a poet; Anne Bradstreet's range is narrow; her allusions are merely to the best known historical and mythological characters; her descriptions of natural phenomena, though she might be expected to find original inspiration in her New England environment, are vague and conventional. In occasional lines of Sylvester's translation occurs something of Elizabethan spaciousness; the only meritorious lines of Anne Bradstreet's poem occur in the *Spring;*

> The fearfull bird his little house now builds
> In trees and walls, in Cities and in fields.
> The outside strong, the inside warm and neat,
> A natural Artificer compleat.

The verse of all her longer poems is precisely that of Sylvester—a couplet, not quite loose, but less compact than the heroic couplet, with the characteristic Elizabethan freedom in rhyme and with the shifting caesura. It is not, however, in these long, dreary, and purely didactic poems that Anne Bradstreet shows her real capacity. When she walks in happier paths, with a song in her heart, remembering Spenser and Giles Fletcher, she shows that perhaps in more fortunate times she might have written poetry. Her *Contemplations* is a meditative and descriptive poem in thirty-three seven-line stanzas, in which occur passages at least pleasing in suggestion and rhythm, however reminiscent of greater times and talents:

> When I behold the heavens as in their prime,
> And then the earth (though old) stil clad in green,
> The stones and trees, insensible to time,
> Nor age nor wrinkle on their front are seen;
> If winter come, and greeness then do fade,
> A Spring returns, and they more youthfull made;
> But Man grows old, lies down, remains where once he's laid.

Her lines to her husband, though not great poetry, are perhaps the most sincere, and are certainly the most human and touching she ever wrote; and her poem on the rearing of her eight children, while infelicitous in its barnyard metaphor, presents a happy and lovable picture. So lovely and pathetic is the figure of the woman herself, and so remarkable are her achievements in the light of her environment, that one finds it ungracious to speak harshly of her verse.

It is rather remarkable that so little purely religious verse was produced in early New England. Quarles, himself a Puritan, was prolific in hymns, divine songs, and paraphrases from the Bible. New England boasted a distinct literary class, not unfamiliar with great religious poetry; but its one biblical paraphrase and its one effort at writing religious song was *The Bay Psalm Book*. To meet the need for divine songs to sing in the churches, Richard Mather, Thomas Welde, and John Eliot supervised the preparation of a new metrical version of the Psalms. *The Bay Psalm Book*, as it came to be called, was the first book published on American soil, and passed through twenty-seven editions between 1640 and 1752, when it was superseded by John Barnard's *New Version of the Psalms of David*. It surpasses even Sternhold and Hopkins in uncouthness, and as a monument of bad taste has furnished an easy target for the ridicule of subsequent and less devout generations. It is unfair, however, to take *The Bay Psalm Book* as an index to the poetic taste of its period, or its subsequent popularity as indicating anything more than its usefulness. It was a makeshift, and they knew it was a poor one; an edition "revised and refined" by John Dunster and Richard Lyon followed in 1647. If these were "refined," then, as Timothy Dwight remarks, "a modern reader would almost instinctively ask, ' What were they before?'"

We still possess in its original crudity the "epic of New England puritanism," *The Day of Doom; or, a Poetical Description of the Great and Last Judgment*. This was the masterpiece of the Rev. Michael Wigglesworth (1631–1705), who was born in England, but emigrated to America, and graduated from Harvard at the age of twenty. He was a physician as well as a theologian and a poet, amiable and humane in character, and greatly beloved. The most widely read and perhaps the most representative poet of early New England, he was also, with the exception of Anne Bradstreet, the most prolific. In both subject-matter and style he is only too representative of his times. His *Day of Doom*, first published in 1662, versifies the scriptural passages concerning the last judgment, and adds to these a statement of the Calvinistic dogmas of eternal punishment. Its two hundred eight-line stanzas tell a story which still entertains the reader, even if it has lost its power to terrify. Relatively, no poem was ever more popular; the first edition of eighteen hundred copies was sold within a year; within the century after, ten subsequent editions were published; and its final passing was coincident only with the passing of the theology that gave it birth and rendered it tolerable. The opening stanzas of the poem show some imagination and power of description; but these are borrowed plumes; all that is good in *The Day of Doom* comes from the Bible. Wigglesworth had no real poetry in him; at no period and under no conditions would he have been a poet. His *God's Controversy with New England*, inspired by the great drought of 1662, deserves no consideration as poetry; but the poem that followed in 1669 is of greater interest. This is *Meat out of the Eater; or, Meditations concerning the Necessity, End, and Usefulness of Affliction unto God's Children*, a theological treatise in rhyme, over two thousand lines in length, in various metres and divided into many different sections. The reflections, with their references to biblical prototypes, the quaint and often fantastic style, point to Quarles's *Emblems* as their inspiration. Though even less poetic than *The Day of Doom*, the poem contains the only two good lines that Wigglesworth ever wrote:

> War ends in peace, and morning light
> Mounts upon Midnight's wing.

In his *Vanity of Vanities*, which was appended to the third edition of *The Day of Doom* in 1673, certain rather polished heroic quatrains suggest Davenant or Dryden as possible models. But, as Wigglesworth's library contained not one volume of English poetry, the poet must have found his model outside of his library; it is beyond belief that either he or any other New England versifier of his period could have originated or even improved any form of verse.

The years between the close of the seventeenth century and the passage of the Stamp Act in 1765 form a transition period in the development of American verse. It is interesting to note that the passing of the old century coincided almost exactly with the passing of the old models. About 1700 new literary influences came from England; the old forms of verse were discarded for others more polished; Quarles and Sylvester gave way, first to Waller, then to Pope. But the change was not one of form alone. The decline of clerical influence, the increase of security and comfort in the conditions of life, the more frequent intercourse with England—all these and other changes were reflected also in the subject-matter, the purpose, and the spirit of the new verse.

New England poets before 1700 learned nothing from the English poets of the latter half of the seventeenth century; for New England seems to have placed all the literature of the Restoration period under a rigorous embargo. There is no sufficient evidence that Dryden was known in America before 1700, in spite of some fairly regular quatrains by Michael Wigglesworth and an occasional polished couplet by Cotton Mather and Benjamin Tompson. If they knew even Milton they perhaps saw in him only the champion of divorce and of other heresies. But there are other and obvious reasons for this ignorance or neglect of Dryden and Milton. Although John Cotton had some correspondence with Quarles, there was not much literary communication of any kind between the colonies and England before the eighteenth century. New England was complete in itself.

Dr. Benjamin Colman (1673-1747), upon his return from England in 1699, brought with him both Blackmore and Waller. This decisive event in the history of American verse marked the beginning of a new era, that of the heroic couplet. But though Colman praises Waller and Blackmore and recommends both to his daughter Jane Turell, he himself, when he wrote his *Elijah's Translation* (1707) on the death of the Rev. Samuel Willard, imitated Dryden in his heroic couplets and his method of applying a Bible story as in *Absalom and Achito-*

*phel.* Jane Turell (1708–1735), whose literary tastes were formed by her father, admired the "Matchless Orinda," Blackmore, and Waller; but she wrote the couplet of Pope. Another and even earlier evidence of the influence of Pope is a poem by Francis Knapp, who was born in England in 1672, and at an uncertain date emigrated to America and settled as a country gentleman near Boston. In 1715 he addressed a poetical epistle to Pope beginning

> Hail! sacred bard! a muse unknown before
> Salutes thee from the bleak Atlantic shore,

which was included among the prefatory poems in a subsequent edition of Windsor Forest (first published in 1713). Thus promptly Pope crossed the Atlantic to begin his undisputed reign of almost a century. Knapp's heroic poem *Gloria Brittannorum* (1723), an obvious imitation of Addison's *Campaign*, celebrates "The most illustrious persons in camp and cabinet since the glorious revolution to the recent time," and is perhaps the earliest example of the patriotic narrative poem that was to become so common in American after the Revolution.

But a far more distinguished exponent of the style of Pope was the Rev. Mather Byles. "To let you see a little of the reputation which you bear in these unknown climates—I transmit to you the enclosed poems," Byles wrote to Pope in 1727. It was perhaps these poems that Byles published in a volume in 1736, and which were published anonymously in the somewhat celebrated volume of 1744, *Poems by Several Hands*. Mather Byles is a more eminent figure in the annals of American poetry than is at all warranted by his poems, which are few and altogether imitative. His reputation is due in part to the general poverty of the transition period—the barest era in our verse—and in part to his fame as a preacher and a wit. He was born in 1707, was educated at Harvard, and served as pastor of the Hollis Street church in Boston through the greater part of his ministerial life. After the Declaration, he became a staunch and vehement Tory, lost his former popularity, and died embittered and broken in 1788. He corresponded with Lansdowne, Pope, and Watts, took himself seriously as a poet, at least in his younger days; and in his attention to contemporary English literature and his setting up of something approaching an æsthetic standard in verse, represents a definite change from the point of view of the generation before him. But the Puritan is still at work in him, however modern may be his style. His most ambitious poem, *The Conflagration*, a description of the physical phenomena of the last day, and a shorter poem, *The Comet*, are both in the spirit of Wigglesworth, for all their heroic couplets and artificial diction. His elegies are unadulterated Pope; and his hymns are in imitation of Watts.

One of the first volumes of miscellaneous verse published in America was the *Poems by Several Hands* (Boston, 1744). All the poems are anonymous; and aside from humorous ballads probably by Joseph Green, they merely echo Pope, with a plethora of "amorous swains" and "blushing charms." Some were certainly written by Byles, and others are tributes to his genius. Indeed, the purpose of the volume was to extol Byles as a poet worthy to be mentioned with Homer and with his only modern rival, Pope. Already America was looking for its Homer, a search that was to continue with increasing assiduity throughout the century—and Boston found him in Byles.

More original and interesting than the poems of Byles are the humorous verses of his friend Joseph Green (1706–1780), a Boston distiller possessed of literary tastes, who ranked with Byles as a wit and social favourite. After the outbreak of the Revolution he too became a Tory, and finally found refuge in London, where he died. Though his poems seem to have been written for his own amusement and that of his friends, they are important as the first attempt to lighten the heavy Puritanism of early New England with some leaven of humour and wit. *An Entertainment for a Winter's Evening* is perhaps the earliest piece of Hudibrastic verse written in America. We have travelled far from Puritan New England when a Bostonian can find amusement in the godless spectacle of a drunken parson and his tipsy companions, and can edify his fellow townsmen with a burlesque account of their nocturnal adventures.

Associated with Byles and Green in *Poems by Several Hands* was the Rev. John Adams, a young clergyman of Boston who died in 1740 at the age of thirty-five. Five years after his death his friends published his *Poems on Several Occasions;*

*Original and Translated*, which contains among other pieces paraphrases from the Bible, translations from Horace, and half a dozen elegies, including one on Cotton Mather and one on Jane Turell. All these are written in the heroic couplet but in a diction more natural than Pope's. That Adams knew Milton's poems is apparent in his *Address to the Supreme Being*. Indeed these poems, though pervaded by the Puritan spirit, yet reveal a more purely æsthetic purpose and a more careful style than can generally be found before the later years of the century.

The almanacs of Nathaniel Ames, father and son, of Dedham, Massachusetts, had their part in disseminating throughout New England a knowledge of the English poets and perhaps also in fostering a taste for humorous poetry. The brief passages from Dryden, Pope, and James Thomson (yes, and Blackmore!), prefixed to the astronomical data, and the unpretentious humorous verses scattered through the other matter, were far more widely read than the laboured and ambitious poems of the literary group in Boston. An *Essay upon the Microscope* is an elaborate poem, by the elder Ames, which, if not poetic, is interesting as perhaps our first ode in irregular verse.

Boston was not the only literary centre of this transition period. Franklin tells us in his *Autobiography* that when he first entered the printing office of Samuel Keimer in Philadelphia in 1723, he found the printer laboriously composing in type an elegy on Aquila Rose, a young poet who had just died in that city—perhaps the worst elegy ever written. The poet elegized died in 1723 at the age of twenty-eight. Within the few years preceding his death he wrote the slight occasional poems in heroic couplets that were in 1740 published in a volume by his son. Probably at no time would Aquila Rose have been a poet, but his verses were quite the best that Philadelphia had yet produced, and were to remain so until Thomas Godfrey surpassed them a generation later. Furthermore, they show that the new influences from England had reached Philadelphia as well as Boston. George Webb, a member of Franklin's "Junto," wrote *Batchelors' Hall* in defence of the life led by himself and other young bachelors at their club near the city. Unconventional as that life may have been, Webb's heroic couplets are as conventional as could be desired, and, together with the verses written by other members of his circle, they recall the dominant hand of Pope. Intrinsically unimportant as was all the verse written in Philadelphia in this early period, it must have done its work in creating a literary atmosphere and in establishing traditions; for this city remained throughout the entire century the centre both for the writing and the publishing of American poetry.

During the whole of the eighteenth century the long poem, didactic, descriptive, and philosophic, flourished in England, and during the latter half of the same century its imitative progeny flourished in America. There could be no justification for cataloguing these imitative efforts, since not one of them still lives in our literature, and very few of them show any distinctive American traits. In the main, their method, their ideas, their imagery are as English as those of their prototypes; their heroic couplet is that of Pope or Goldsmith; their blank verse is that of Thomson or Young.

The tide set in with imitations of Pomfret, whose *Choice* (1700) appeared in at least four editions in America between 1751 and 1792. In 1747 William Livingston, who was to become the famous governor of New Jersey, expressed his ideal of existence in a direct imitation of Pomfret which he called *Philosophic Solitude, or the Choice of a Rural Life*. Ten years later a second imitation of Pomfret followed in *The Choice* by Dr. Benjamin Church of Boston, who longs for a home in the country, the right kind of wife, congenial friends, and leisure to read his favourite poets—Milton, Dryden, Gay, "awful Pope, unequalled bard," and "nature-limning Thomson." Though dwelling in a small American town, he sighs for solitude as longingly as he might have done in the midst of a world capital. Livingston and Church are half a century late in their sporadic imitations; and for a while Americans were simply catching up with almost a hundred years of English didactic poetry; but after the tide once turned, about the middle of the century, imitation was much more prompt and general and, after the Revolution, immediate and universal.

Goldsmith reached Americans almost at once, and appeared in nine editions between 1768 and 1791. His numerous imitators are all alike in using his method, his style, and even his very subject-matter. Among imitations of *The Deserted Village* may be mentioned Thomas Coombe's *Peasant of Auburn* (1775), which contains lines fine enough to save it from oblivion. Imitations of Thomson's *Seasons* began to appear soon after the first American edition was published in 1777, increased in number with the five successive editions up to 1792, and continued through at least the first decade of the nineteenth century. To read one of these is to know all, with their very fair verse, and their conventional and generalized descriptions of scenery that might as well be English as American. It is interesting to note, however, that the native element in our descriptive verse grows more pronounced in the decade preceding the first work of Bryant. The form is still that of Thomson, but the poet has at last opened his eyes to the distinctive beauty of American nature. In his *Descriptive Poems* (1802) John D. McKinnon wrote of the Hudson and the Mohawk Rivers and our own October landscape, as well as of

> th' illimitable plain
> Depastured by erratic buffaloes;

and some "Untaught Bard," writing under the influence of both Thomson and Young, in his *Spring* clearly foretells the coming of *Thanatopsis*. John Hayes, professor at Dickinson College, in the 2500 lines of blank verse of his *Rural Poems* (1807) celebrates American birds and flowers in spite of his imitation of Milton and Thomson. Still more interesting in this respect is *The Foresters* (1804) of the ornithologist Alexander Wilson, a poem in 2200 lines of heroic couplets which tell the story of a journey through New York and Pennsylvania to Niagara Falls. Wilson is a scientist rather than a poet, but he sees nature sympathetically and gives what he sees in a simple and direct style. At last the poet writes with his eye on American nature and not on conventional descriptions by English poets.

The one poem that sums up all the direct imitations of Goldsmith, and Thomson, and of Denham, Milton, Pope, and Beattie as well, is *Greenfield Hill*. Timothy Dwight (1752–1817), a grandson of Jonathan Edwards, at the age of nineteen graduated from Yale, where he then became a tutor. In 1777–1778 he served as chaplain in the army, and varied his duties by writing patriotic songs for the soldiers. In 1783 he became pastor of the church at Greenfield, Connecticut, and in 1795 was made president of Yale. He was the first of our great college presidents, and as theologian, scholar, patriot, and writer was one of the eminent personalities of his time. As a poet he belongs to a group of writers who during the last two decades of the eighteenth century formed a literary centre at New Haven and Hartford. The chief "Hartford Wits" were Timothy Dwight, John Trumbull, Joel Barlow, David Humphreys, Richard Alsop, Lemuel Hopkins, and Theodore Dwight, a brother of Timothy, all either graduates of Yale or associated with that college. Their contemporary reputation was immense. Dwight, Barlow, and Humphreys, indeed, were practical men of affairs, and all were more or less versatile. But the reading public looked upon them as geniuses; and Freneau was the only poet aside from the Hartford group who was ever mentioned in connection with them. Yet even as they were issuing their declaration of literary independence, they were in every line betraying their dependence upon English poetic style, ideas, and imagery. Their more ambitious and laboured poems, including almost all those by Dwight, Barlow, and Humphreys, are to the modern reader the least successful. Their best work, which they themselves and the public took less seriously, is in the form of satire, and was mainly written, singly or in collaboration, by Trumbull, Theodore Dwight, Alsop, and Hopkins. Yet the work of the "Hartford Wits" in fostering poetry in a period of political and social struggle and change deserves grateful recognition from the student of American literature.

Timothy Dwight's *Greenfield Hill* is a medley of echoes. The poet stands upon a hill in his Connecticut parish, and, like his English predecessors, describes the view, paints the social conditions of the country, recounts its history, and prophesies its future. The 4300 lines of the poem are divided into seven parts, written variously in heroic couplet, Spenserian stanza, blank verse, and octosyllabics. The poet's desire "to contribute to the innocent amusement of his countrymen and to their improvement in manners and in economic, political, and moral sentiments" results in a history, guide-book, and treatise on manners, morals, and government, but not in a poem. To say that *Greenfield Hill* is made to order and is inspired by morality and patriotism, is to state the genesis of all the serious work of the Hartford group.

Outrageously long poems on æsthetic subjects were rife in America toward the close of the century. At a time when society and politics were in a state of upheaval, when neither the domestic nor the foreign policy of the country had been settled, and when consequently there was so much of native interest to write about, it is incongruous to find so many poems suggested by Akenside's *Pleasures of the Imagination* and Brooke's *Universal Beauty*. Richard Alsop's *Charms of Fancy* in all its 2300 lines of heroic couplets contains not a fresh image or an original idea; but *The Powers of Genius* by John Blair Linn is at least the work of a man of taste and scholarship and compares favourably with all but the very best of its British counterparts. The extreme of dulness and futility is reached in the many poems on philosophy and religion for which Pope and Young were largely responsible. Somewhat stronger and more interesting than most of these is Timothy Dwight's *Triumph of Infidelity*, which purports to be a satire, and which with irony and abuse rather than logic attempts to refute the arguments of the eighteenth century "infidels," Voltaire included. Biblical paraphrases, too, multiplied after the Revolution, and appeared in large numbers between 1780 and 1810. These are supplemented by epics on biblical themes, the most celebrated of which is again the work of the indefatigable Timothy Dwight, written by the time he was twenty-two, but published when he was thirty-three and should have known better. *The Conquest of Canaan* (1785), in ten thousand lines of heroic couplets, owes its style to Pope's Homer and much of its method and imagery to Virgil and Milton. The epic as a whole is what might be expected when the poet's purpose is "to represent such manners as are removed from the peculiarities of any age or country, and might belong to the amiable and virtuous of any period, elevated without design, refined without ceremony, elegant without fashion, and agreeable because they are ornamented with sincerity, dignity, and religion." Into the heroic biblical narrative are woven the loves of Irad and Selima and of Iram and Mira, who take their evening strolls through the lanes and meadows of Connecticut. Though intolerably verbose, the poem contains purple passages which lift it to the level of the average eighteenth-century epic and which perhaps led Cowper to review it favourably. With a noble disregard of congruity, *The Conquest of Canaan* is, withal, distinctly patriotic, with its union of "Canaan and Connecticut" and its allusions to contemporary persons and events.

The third period of early American verse, which begins with 1765 and ends with 1808, is characterized by two remarkably coincident phenomena, one political, the other æsthetic. One of these is the beginning of the nationalism that produced our early patriotic poems and satires, and is marked by the passage of the Stamp Act. The other, also beginning about 1765, is the wholesale importation and reprinting of English poetry which worked with the growth of native culture to produce a great quantity of verse all more or less imitative of English models and largely independent of political conditions. All the poems of this period, whether springing from political or from purely æsthetic influences, are most conveniently treated under their various genres without regard to individual writers, though one poet, Philip Freneau, demands separate consideration.

The first ballad springing from American soil recounts a battle fought in 1725 between whites and Indians near Lovewell's Pond in Maine. Composed at the time of the event, it was for generations preserved only by word of mouth, and was not published for almost a century. Though unliterary, it tells its story with vigour and directness, and is of additional interest in that Longfellow in 1820 chose the same fight as the subject of his first poem, *The Battle of Lovell's Pond*.

Many fugitive verses on the French and Indian War[1] were published anonymously in the newspapers, the best of which are perhaps *The Song of Braddock's Men*, and the lines on Wolfe—

Thy merits, Wolfe, transcend all human praise.

Anti-British ballads began to appear immediately upon the

[1] The French and Indian War gave birth to a curious volume of *Miscellaneous Poems on Divers Occasions, Chiefly to Animate and Rouse the Soldiers* (1756), by Stephen Tilden, which, in spite of its wretched verse, is of some interest as the first of its kind in America.

passage of the Stamp Act, to continue until the close of the Revolution. These spring from the heat of the conflict, and are as replete with patriotism as they are deficient in literary merit. Yet they admirably fulfilled their purpose of arousing public spirit, and many of them were known and sung everywhere. John Dickinson's *Patriot's Appeal*, which begins

> Then join hand in hand, brave Americans all,
> By uniting we stand, by dividing we fall,

gave rise to a parody which was in turn parodied in the famous *Massachusetts Liberty Song*. Almost equally popular were John Mason's *Liberty's Call*, Thomas Paine's *Liberty Tree*, and Timothy Dwight's *Columbia*, with its refrain

> Columbia, Columbia, to glory arise,
> The queen of the world and the child of the skies.

But the one ballad that shows a spark of poetry is *Nathan Hale*, which commemorates the capture and death of the young American spy. It opens with a promise that is scarcely sustained throughout the poem:

> The breezes went steadily thro the tall pines,
> A saying "Oh! hu-sh," a saying "Oh! hu-sh,"
> As stilly stole by a bold legion of horse,
> For Hale in the bush, for Hale in the bush.

Best known of the purely humorous ballads is Francis Hopkinson's *Battle of the Kegs* (1778), which tells of the alarm felt by the British over some kegs that the Americans had charged with powder and had set floating in the Delaware River.

The hundreds of patriotic ballads, songs, and odes that appeared after the Revolution, though more ambitious and "literary," seem less spontaneous and sincere than the earlier verse, which called a nation to arms; and for all their flaunting of the stars and stripes, they leave the reader cold. Scarcely a poet who wrote between 1780 and 1807 failed to compose at least one such poem; but, it is safe to say, the only patriotic ballads of permanent merit written between 1725 and 1807 are the sea poems of Freneau.

The longer American patriotic poems of the later eighteenth century may take the form of narratives of battle, of personal eulogies, or, perhaps most characteristically, of philosophic statements of what today is called "Americanism." They increase in number toward the close of the century, when the air was full of American principles and ideals, and finally, in spite of their imitative style, they become in spirit at least a distinctive product without exact parallel in England. The best of them express a national aspiration that can still appeal to the patriotic reader. There is little of all this, however, in the early outbursts evoked by the French and Indian War, when the poets were generally loyal to Great Britain. On the accession of George the Third in 1761 the faculty and graduates of Harvard published a curious volume of congratulatory poems entitled *Pietas et Gratulatio Collegii Cantabrigiensis Apud Nov-Anglos*. The volume of one hundred and six pages includes thirty-one poems, three of which are in Greek, sixteen in Latin, and twelve in English. The poems in English are in the form of irregular odes or heroic couplets stilted and commonplace in subject and style. The modern reader may find amusement in such loyal lines as

> Bourbons to humble, Brunswicks were ordained:
> Those mankind's rights destroyed, but these regained.

But the patriotic poem was soon to transfer its allegiance. A truly remarkable quantity of narrative verse tells the story of the Revolution and celebrates its civil and military leaders. Almost everyone who wrote verse in America after the Revolution produced an ode or an epic to vindicate his patriotism. Literature was now democratic; nothing was needed but inspiration, and the air was full of that. Far above the average is the rather fine *Eulogium on Major-General Joseph Warren*, written by "A Columbian"; but the vast majority of these historic and eulogistic narratives serve but to exemplify the heights of patriotism and the depths of bathos. The elaborate and laboured elegies on Washington are as numerous and as futile as might be expected. The finest eulogy on Washington was written prior to his death by Dr. Benjamin Young Prime in a pindaric ode of 1400 lines entitled *Columbia's Glory, or*

*British Pride Humbled*, which, in spite of its conventional form and style and lack of imagination, contains passages of admirable rhetoric.

Closely related to the narratives and eulogies are the many and lengthy poems belonging to the philosophic and didactic "glory of America" type, of which Freneau seems to have been the originator. The most prolific poet of this school was Colonel David Humphreys (1753–1818), who graduated from Yale in 1771, served as aide-de-camp to Washington, and became a frequent guest at Mount Vernon. He was associated with the Hartford Wits after 1786; served as minister to Portugal in 1791, and as minister to Spain from 1797 to 1802. A versatile man like others of the Hartford group, he was not only soldier, diplomat, and poet, but also an experimenter in sheep-raising and wool-manufacture. His six patriotic poems vary in length from four hundred to one thousand lines of heroic couplets. "Every poet who aspires to celebrity strives to approach the perfection of Pope and the sweetness of his versification," says Humphreys. All his patriotic poems are the work of an experienced versifier with full command of his subject and with little poetic inspiration. The *Poem on the Happiness of America* celebrates liberty and democracy, American scenery, resources, achievements, and prospects, with a boundless belief in the possibilities of America and her divine mission.

No other member of the Hartford group, indeed no other man of letters of his time, lived a life so active and varied as Joel Barlow (1754–1812). After his graduation from Yale, he served as chaplain in the army, and in 1781 married and settled in Hartford as lawyer and editor. His philosophic poem *The Vision of Columbus*, published in 1787, was read and admired in France and England. Barlow later went to France as agent of the notorious Scioto Land Company, apparently in ignorance of its fraudulent character. In Paris he became a strong partisan of democracy, and for several years divided his time between France and England, writing political pamphlets and books, and making a fortune through commerce and speculation. While resident in Savoy in 1792, he wrote what is certainly his most original and enduring poem and also one of the best pieces of humorous verse in our early literature.

*Hasty Pudding* is a mock-heroic of the conventional eighteenth-century type, in four hundred lines of heroic couplets. Its three cantos describe the making of the famous New England dish, the eating of it, and the traits that render it delectable and worthy of eulogy. The pastoral scenes are native, not imitated, the diction is simple and natural, and the humour, though rather thin, is sufficiently amusing. Barlow rendered valuable service to his native land in 1795, when he went to Algiers and secured the release of American prisoners; and again in 1798 when he helped to avert war between France and America. He returned home in 1805, and two years later published his *Columbiad*. He again served his country well in 1811, when he was sent by President Madison as an envoy to Europe; but in journeying to meet Napoleon he was caught in the retreat from Moscow, and died and was buried in Poland. Though democrats in America celebrated his memory, he perhaps has never had justice done him as a patriot and typical American.

When *The Vision of Columbus* was published in 1787 it suited the taste of the time, and its author was hailed as a genius, not only by his fellow Hartford Wits but also by the public at large. Its subject and style gave it a reputation that it could not have attained even a decade later. Barlow was misled by his temporary success into the fatal error of expanding the 4700 lines into the 8350 lines of *The Columbiad*. But when the latter appeared in 1807, it failed to please the very public that had welcomed its predecessor. Its failure was due less to the changes in the poem than to the development of public taste during the poet's absence in Europe. Pope's dominance had been successfully contested, and the long philosophic poem itself was in its decline. Barlow's failure was all the more striking on account of his very audacity. His *Vision of Columbus* was simply a philosophic poem; his *Columbiad* was avowedly an epic, meant to have a vaster theme, a more refined style, and a higher moral purpose than Homer's. *The Columbiad*, however, remains merely a "geographical, historical, political, and philosophical disquisition." To Columbus, as he lies sick and in prison, there appears Hesper, the genius of the western world, and, with the purpose of setting forth all that Columbus and America have contributed to the welfare of the world, reviews the state of Europe in the middle ages, the voyages of discovery, conquests, and colonisation, and the war of the Revolution, with references to contemporary persons and events. He concludes with a prophecy of the future glories of America. This literary drag-net has drawn into itself nothing delicate or tender and little that is truly human, for such qualities are not compatible with its forced sublimity and its declamatory and gaudy rhetoric. To the worst vices of the conventional poetic diction, Barlow in a painful effort to achieve the grandiose, has added vile phrases of his own peculiar coinage. And yet, hidden away among these thousands of lines of laboured rhetoric, are pas-sages really fine and free in both conception and execution. Atlas, genius of Africa, prophesies to Hesper the ruin that must follow American slavery. In the chaos

> His own bald eagle skims alone the sky,
> Darts from all points of heaven her searching eye,
> Kens thro the gloom her ancient rock of rest,
> And finds her cavern'd crag, her solitary nest.

The most vigorous poems produced in America between 1765 and 1807 were the numberless satires that marked every stage of the fight with England and of the internal strife be-tween Whigs and Tories and, later, between Republicans and Federalists. *Hudibras*, *The Dunciad*, *The Rolliad*, *The Anti-Jacobin*, and the satires of Churchill, of Gifford, and of "Peter Pindar" bred in America songs, mock-heroics, burlesques, and satires of direct attack, in lyric measures, heroic couplets, and octosyllabics.

American political satire began with the Stamp Act. *The Times* (1765) by the Rev. Benjamin Church of Boston, which vigorously defends the colonists, imitates Churchill, who for four years had been famous in England as the most relentless satirist of the day, and is doubly interesting in that its author later changed his attitude and was expelled from Boston as a traitor. The Boston Port Bill evoked from John Trumbull an *Elegy on the Times* (1775), which uses the elegiac quartrains of Gray for satiric invective; but far more important is the same author's *McFingal*, the most effective satire of its time. Trumbull was born in what is now Watertown, Connecticut, in 1750, and graduated from Yale in 1767 in the same class with Timothy Dwight.   In 1772 he published his *Progress of Dullness*, a satire in Hudibrastic verse on the current educational system and the ignorance of the clergy which is still interesting.   After studying law in the office of John Adams in Boston, he returned to New Haven to practise, and in 1776 published the first two cantos of *McFingal*.[1]   In 1781 he published the third and fourth cantos, and in the same year removed to Hartford, where he became associated with the Hartford Wits and joined in writing *The Anarchiad*.   After serving as State's attorney, he became a judge of the Superior Court of Connecticut, and finally judge of the Supreme Court of Errors, a position which he held until 1819.   For some years he was the treasurer of Yale, from which he received the degree of LL.D. in 1818.   He removed to Detroit in 1825, and died there in 1831.

*McFingal*, Trumbull's chief work, is a political satire in favour of the whigs.   As much the guide as the child of public sentiment, the piece had thirty editions.   It is a burlesque epic in 3800 lines of Hudibrastic verse in four cantos, which parodies epic speeches in council, heroic encounters, and prophecy.   At a town meeting held in a New England village to discuss the question of rebellion against the mother country, the whigs, led by the impassioned Honorius, and the tories, headed by Squire McFingal, an officeholder under the Crown, engage in furious argument.   The whigs are finally victorious in speech and also in the battle which terminates the discussion.   Under threats, McFingal's tory constable recants, but the obdurate Squire is tarred and feathered and glued to the liberty pole, where he is left to meditate his misdeeds.   Escaping in the night, he convenes a meeting of fellow tories in the cellar, and relates to them the vision which he has gained through his gift of second sight, and which prophesies final victory for the whigs.   The meeting breaks up at the approach of the whigs and McFingal deserts his followers and escapes to the British.   The verse runs swiftly, with considerable comic force, and contains epigrammatic couplets that might have come from *Hudibras*:

[1] Published as Canto I, but since divided into two cantos.

> No man e'er felt the halter draw,
> With good opinion of the law,

and

> But optics sharp it needs, I ween,
> To see what is not to be seen.

The burlesque contrasts, the absurd figures of speech, the far-fetched allusions, are learned from Butler; and the verse, with its frequent elisions, its feminine rhymes, and its homely diction, is more nearly that of *Hudibras* than of any other satire. Churchill is responsible for such serious passages in the speeches as

> For ages blest thus Britain rose
> The terror of encircling foes;
> Her heroes ruled the bloody plain;
> Her conq'ring standard aw'd the main,

as also for the use of personifications and of the terrible:

> Around all stained with rebel blood,
> Like Milton's lazar house it stood,
> Where grim Despair attended nurse,
> And Death was gov'rnor of the house.

For all its indebtednesses *McFingal* remains the most entertaining satire in our early literature, and the only surviving poem by any member of the Hartford group.

The two most vigorous and prolific tory satirists were Joseph Stansbury (1750–1809), a merchant of Philadelphia, and the Rev. Jonathan Odell (1737–1818), of New Jersey. Their satires and satirical songs, odes, and ballads are generally alike both in matter and style, but Stansbury is the better poet, and has to his credit several satirical lyrics, quite as good as any of their time on either side of the water. He turns off an ode to the king, a comic ballad recounting an American reverse, or a loyal song, all with equal facility and with little of the invective characteristic of Odell. His *Town Meeting*, a satirical ballad of over one hundred and fifty lines, is typical, but his lyric, *To Cordelia*, addressed to his wife from Nova Scotia at the close of the Revolution, shows that he could also write a true poem.   Odell, whose satires were not only in the main longer and less original, but also more virulent, was the Freneau of the tory side.   Though possessed of little humour and less wit, he is at least vigorous and incisive and can give Freneau as good as he sends:

> Back to his mountains Washington may trot.
> He take this city?   Yes—when ice is hot.

That Churchill was his model appears in his *Feu de Joie;* his *Word of Congress* (1779), four hundred lines of politico-personal invective against the Continental Congress; and in the still longer *American Times* (1780), which attacked the leaders of the American cause with extreme bitterness and scurrility.

After the Revolution and before the adoption of the Constitution, social and political unrest produced *The Anarchiad, a Poem on the Restoration of Chaos and Substantial Night* (1786–1787), in which four of the Hartford group, Joel Barlow, John Trumbull, David Humphreys, and Lemuel Hopkins cleverly adapted their English original *The Rolliad* to the conditions that gave rise to Shays's Rebellion, paper money, demagogy, and other evils of the time.   *The Anarchiad* is in 1200 lines of heroic couplets, and is divided into fourteen parts that purport to be extracts from an ancient epic, lately discovered, which foretell conditions in the decade following the Revolution. The verse is that of Pope and Goldsmith, from whom many passages are paraphrased; the style is a parody of Homer, Dante, Milton, and Pope; and the mock-heroic method is conventional; yet the satire through its wit and good sense deserved its immense popularity.   The speech of Hesper in favour of a firm union of the states is fine and eloquent; and the brilliant satirical picture of the Land of Annihilation, though obviously suggested by *The Dunciad*, is not unworthy of its original.

The entire story of the strife between federalist and republican, Hamiltonian and Jeffersonian, can be read in the verse satire of the time.   No American shows this bitter partisanship more than Thomas Green Fessenden (1771–1837).   His *Terrible Tractoration*, written in England about English conditions, is not political but is chiefly aimed at the critics of

Perkins's "metallic tractors," an invention of which Fessenden was the agent. Its 1800 lines of Hudibrastic verse, full of references to contemporary persons and scientific matters, form a fair example of a not very admirable type of satire. Fessenden again displays his mental alertness and his indebtedness to "Peter Pindar" in *Democracy Unveiled, or Tyranny Stripped of the Garb of Patriotism*. This surprising production, in which he reaches the nadir of indecent personalities, attacks Jacobinism, democracy, and Jefferson in particular, with a virulence that disregards both good sense and good taste.

The political mock-epic appears in the anonymous *Aristocracy* (1795), which ridicules the alleged aristocratic notions of the federalists. Also political in a sense is *The Group* (1795), by William Cliffton, a satire on the men who hid from danger during the Revolution but who now claim the reward of patriots. Though its series of portraits in the mock-heroic style of Pope is not without vigour, it is less original and amusing than Cliffton's *Rhapsody on the Times*, several hundred lines of octosyllabics in the style of Prior, which contains narrative and descriptive satire against unrestricted immigration.

Before the nineteenth century our social and literary satires are amusing only as futile attempts to make something out of nothing. The society and literary productions of Philadelphia are satirized in a series of poems beginning in 1762 and extending on into the next century; such as *The Manners of the Times* (1762) by "Philadelphiensis"; the anonymous *Philadelphiad;* and the more vigorous but still conventional *Times* (1788) by Peter Markoe. Other Philadelphia satires of this type might be named without raising the average of merit. Fortunately, New York and Boston seem to have been somewhat less analytic in their attitude; though both cities were guilty of such conventional social and literary satires as Winthrop Sargent's *Boston* (1803). The inflated journalistic style of the last decade of the century suggested the one really clever and original literary satire of its time in America. *The Echo* was begun in 1791, was published serially, and appeared complete as a volume of three hundred pages in 1807. Its authors, who seem to have been Richard Alsop and Timothy Dwight, select some particularly bombastic passage from a current newspaper and travesty its style in heroic couplets with a result that has not yet quite lost its flavour. The satire probably owed something to the parodies of *The Anti-Jacobin*, though in this case the matter and not the form is burlesqued.

At the close of the century the long satiric poem in Hudibrastic verse or heroic couplet was already passing away in England, though American versifiers continued to imitate the outworn models. In the light of *The Biglow Papers* all these early beginnings seem faint and pale; but they are still significant as indications of the growth of national consciousness. It should also be noted that in average merit our early verse satire is probably not inferior to its counterpart in England. There is little to be said for the genre on either side of the water.

Volumes of miscellaneous short poems began to appear in 1765, but, owing to the Revolution and its attendant changes, ceased almost entirely between 1770 and 1790, and revived only during the last decade of the century. Though intrinsically of little merit, they show in the main that Pope and the long poem were not absolutely dominant and that Americans were reading English lyrical poetry and were learning to write graceful verse which certain of the public were ready to read. This public was small enough, however, for most of the volumes were published by subscription; and a remarkable number were issued by pious friends as memorials to young poets, and hence show little except that friendship may make unreasonable demands.

The poems of Thomas Godfrey (1736–1763) of Philadelphia were published two years after his death by his friend and fellow poet Nathaniel Evans. His work is highly imitative; pastorals in heroic couplet, after Pope; an *Ode to Friendship* and a *Dithyrambic on Wine* in the manner of Dryden's occasional odes; a *Night Piece* in elegiac quatrains, which shows the influence of Gray and Young; songs in the manner of Shenstone and Prior; and here and there a touch of Collins. His best as well as his most ambitious poem is *The Court of Fancy*, an allegory in heroic couplets, suggested by Chaucer's *House of Fame*. Though conventional in style, it is not without originality, and as the first truly imaginative poem written in America is of more than passing interest. Godfrey's imitative habit could not quite cloak his spontaneity, and had he come only a generation later he might have contributed more permanently to our poetry.

The poems of his friend and editor the Rev. Nathaniel Evans (1742–1767), also of Philadelphia, were issued five years after his death in a volume entitled *Poems on Several Occasions* which contains a number of unimportant occasional poems, and others imitative of Milton, Cowley, Prior, Gray, and Collins. Evans's most ambitious effort is his *Ode on the Prospect of Peace;* but more interesting is his tribute to Benjamin Franklin in praise of physical science. On the whole his poems show less native ability than Godfrey's and are equally imitative; but the work of both is significant as the beginning of our more purely lyrical verse.

Had not the Revolution interfered,[1] the publication of volumes of miscellaneous poems would probably have continued unbroken. When about 1790 it began again, to continue indefinitely, the awakening of national consciousness had produced no change in the matter and style of the short poem; it was still an echo. And Philadephia was still the centre for writing and publication. But new influences—such as Mrs. Radcliffe, Ossian, and the contemporary romantic ballads—are often apparent in the last decade of the century. The sentimental, the mysterious, the horrible, environed with appropriate scenery, appear here and there in the work of such poets as William Moore Smith (1759–1821), of Philadelphia, who gives evidence of this imported "romanticism" in *The Wizard of the Rock*, a blend of Parnell, Percy, and Goldsmith; and *Maria's Grave*, which is placed amid the romantic scenery pictured by the poet's originals across the Atlantic. Most distinguished personally of the Philadelphia poets was Judge Francis Hopkinson (1737–1791),[2] signer of the Declaration of Independence, whose many occasional poems are merely as good as the average of their kind, but whose songs, some of which are suggestive of Gay and Prior, are distinctly musical and pleasing. The Rev. John Blair Linn (1777–1804), who, like Godfrey and Evans, died young and left his work unfinished, wrote odes to solitude

---

[1] Aside from patriotic songs and ballads, not much lyrical verse was published between 1770 and 1786, and that little appeared in newspapers and magazines.

[2] See also Book II., Chap. II.

12

and melancholy, pastorals and elegies, and other echoes of
Shenstone, Gray, and even Mason. It is noticeable that the
songs and light social lyrics of the close of the century come from
Philadelphia, the social capital. The gifted and original
William Cliffton (1772–1799) was both a satirist and a lyrist.
His half-dozen lyrics, quite the two best of which are *To Fancy*
and *To a Robin*,[1] are not without grace and delicacy, which
he owes largely to his models, Gay, Prior, and Collins. Like
Freneau and other poets of the time, Cliffton found his surroundings unsympathetic:

> In these cold shades, beneath these shifting skies,
> Where Fancy sickens, and where Genius dies;
> Where few and feeble are the Muse's strains,
> And no fine frenzy riots in the veins.

So he characterizes his environment in his epistle to William
Gifford, which was prefixed to the American edition of the
*Baviad* and *Maeviad* in 1799. Gifford's stinging satire on the
"Della Cruscan" school of poetry was welcomed in America
by Cliffton, whose verse was at least manly and sincere.

It is not certain that Joseph Brown Ladd (1764–1786) wrote
his *Poems of Arouet* under Della Cruscan influence, for they
were published in the year in which the school took its rise in
Florence; they are at least an anticipation of its more languishing side. But whether or not the Della Cruscan mania had
reached Charleston, where Ladd was killed in a duel, in 1786, it
was certainly widespread in Boston less than a decade later.
Mrs. Sarah Wentworth Morton (1759–1846),[2] termed by her
admirers "The American Sappho," praises Della Crusca in a
fervid address prefixed to her narrative poem *Ouabi, or the Virtues of Nature* (1790), and as "Philenia" exchanged poetical
tributes with her "Menander," no less a celebrity than Robert
Treat Paine, Jr. (1773–1811).

Boston's craving for a native poet, the bad taste of the time,
and the poet's own wayward life combined to give Paine a
reputation surpassing that of any of his contemporaries. At
Harvard he was known by his occasional poems, and his

---

[1] The latter is written in the eight-line anapestic stanza greatly favoured
by Shenstone and later used by Cowper in his *Alexander Selkirk*, which occurs
with notable frequency in the lyrics of this period.

[2] See also Book II, Chap. VI.

patriotic song *Adams and Liberty* made him a celebrity. Though he practised law, he gave most of his time to the theatre and to poetry. Soon his reputation was such that he could command five dollars a line for his verse, a price never before approached in America and perhaps never since equalled. His marriage with an actress estranged him from his family, and after this event his life was that of a wastrel. His services, however, were in request upon all public occasions, from the opening of theatres to meetings of the Phi Beta Kappa. For such occasions he wrote the didactic poems, prologues, and odes in conventional but vigorous heroic couplets that form the greater part of his work. *The Ruling Passion*, for Phi Beta Kappa, and *The Invention of Letters*, for a Harvard commencement, were hailed as the spontaneous and original outbursts of genius, though both are merely laboured and conventional didactic poems of a type that was even then in its decline. In these and a few other of Paine's poems one finds rhetorical passages of some merit amid a waste of bombast and affectation but looks in vain for any imagination or real feeling. The diction embodies all the vices against which the new poetry rebelled. Della Crusca plus Pope would have crushed a more genuine talent than Paine's. His reputation is a curious evidence of the pathetic craving for a national poet and of the determination to force the birth of a genius. His *Works in Prose and Verse*, an octavo volume of over five hundred pages, was published one year after his death, with all the reverence due to a classic.

"The American Sappho" was not the only woman singer of Boston. Mrs. Susanna Rowson,[1] besides her plays and novels, wrote poems which unite "sensibility" and didacticism. Her odes, hymns, elegies, nature lyrics, and songs show little observation of life or nature, and scarcely any distinctive American quality. Of all these, the patriotic lyric *America, Commerce, and Freedom*, which is commonplace but not without spirit, alone has survived. The *Poems, Dramatic and Miscellaneous*, of Mrs. Mercy Warren (1728-1814)[2] include ponderous and solemn epistles and elegies that are merely belated echoes of Pope. New York also had its woman poet in Mrs. Ann Eliza Bleecker (1752–1783), whose melancholy

[1] See also Book II, Chaps. II and VI.     [2] See also Book II, Chap. II.

life is reflected in the tone of her sentimental elegies, epistles, descriptive poems, and religious lyrics, in the style of the English poets of the first half of the century. Her daughter, Mrs. Margaretta Faugeres, who published her own poems with those of her mother in 1793, shows in her poem on the Hudson the growing attention to native scenery. The inquiring reader may find all the imitative qualities of our early lyric poets if he will consult the very inclusive *Original Poems, Serious and Entertaining*, of Paul Allen (1775-1826), whose facile and graceful verse is indicative of English influences all the way from Prior to Cowper.

Aside from the lyrics of Freneau, the two original strains in our early lighter verse are the humorous poems of Thomas Green Fessenden and of Royall Tyler,[1] and the nature lyrics of Alexander Wilson. Fessenden contributed humorous poems of New England country life to Dennie's *Farmer's Weekly Museum*, and these were afterwards published in his *Original Poems*. To this same magazine and also to Dennie's *Port Folio*, Royall Tyler contributed pictures and studies in verse of American environment and character which are worth all the pretentious imitations of his contemporaries, The lyrics scattered throughout the pages of Alexander Wilson's *Ornithology* and afterwards printed in his collected poems merit more attention than they have heretofore received. Wilson was scientist and poet enough to celebrate the osprey, the Baltimore bird, the hummingbird, and the bluebird in true nature lyrics which, together with those of Freneau, are not unworthy forerunners of Bryant's.

Philip Freneau was born in New York of Huguenot ancestry in 1752, and died near Freehold, New Jersey, in 1832. His long and eventful life was spent in a variety of pursuits. After he graduated from Princeton in 1771, he was author, editor, government official, trader, and farmer. As regards the genesis of his poems, two facts in his life are especially important. His newspaper work encouraged a fatal production of the satirical and humorous verse that gave him reputation; and his trading voyages inspired poems descriptive of the scenery of the southern islands, and made possible what is perhaps his most original and distinctive work, his naval ballads.

[1] See also Book II, Chaps. II, III, and VI.

From the volumes of the most recent edition of Freneau's poems, aggregating 1200 pages, the reader gains the impression that had this poet written half as much he might have written twice as well. That he was something of the artist is shown by the care with which he revised his poems for five successive editions; but his revisions are sometimes actually for the worse. Yet Freneau surpassed all his contemporaries not only in quality but also in sheer quantity and in variety of subject and form. Furthermore, his work presents an almost unique combination of satiric power, romantic imagination, and feeling for nature. At one extreme is the bitter invective of his satires; at the other, the delicate fancy of his best lyrics. His early poems show the influence of Milton, as in *The Power of Fancy;* of Gray, as in *The Monument of Phaon* and *The Deserted Farm House;* and of Goldsmith, as in *The American Village*—all of which contain lines of original power and beauty; but in his *Pictures of Columbus*, he reaches complete originality. When the poet has Columbus exclaim in the face of death,

> The winds blow high; one other world remains;
> Once more without a guide I find the way,

he shows that at last the new world has produced a poet.

In his voyages Freneau found the tropical scenery of his descriptive poems. *The Beauties of Santa Cruz*, though unequal and crude, has a definiteness of imagery and a simplicity of diction that set it apart from the conventional school of Thomson. *The House of Night*, which combines description and narrative, is the most remarkable poem written in America up to its time. In the use of "romantic" scenery and of death as a theme, Freneau was not a pioneer; but in his supernaturalism and in the strange and haunting music of his lines, he stood alone, and, as has often been remarked, anticipated Coleridge and Poe. Although Freneau was known in England, it may be doubted whether he influenced the English romantic poets. More probably, both he and they were influenced by the same general tendencies; for the romantic movement was already well under way when he wrote the *The House of Night*. The poem is overlong, lacks unity of tone and matter, and altogether is disappointingly crude; but it contains such lines as

> so loud and sad it play'd
> As though all music were to breathe its last,
>
> I saw the infernal windows flaming red,

and

> Trim the dull tapers, for I see no dawn,

which are a source of astonishment to one who has followed the course of American poetry up to this point.   But unfortunately the romantic strain which promised so richly was soon lost.

Freneau's poems of the "glory of America" type, such as his *Rising Glory of America*, written in collaboration with H. H. Brackenridge[1] when the two were seniors at Princeton, were inspired by a great vision and still retain a certain eloquence. His burlesques of American scenes and characters, such as *Slender's Journey*, are less successful; but his satires in both quantity and variety surpassed all but *McFingal* in their day. "Poet of the American Revolution" is no misnomer, if the term is to include political events up to 1815.   Freneau's masters in satire are Dryden, Churchill, and "Peter Pindar"; and his tone ranges from burlesque to invective.   *The Political Balance* and *The British Prison Ship* are the most powerful and original satires of their time.   The royalist printers Rivington and Gaine were his chief targets during the last years of the Revolution. In his personal satires he uses the anapest, which he was the first to popularize in America.   His later satires, usually in lyrical stanzas, were suggested by "Peter Pindar"; the phrase "Peter Pindar of America" gives the key to his contemporary reputation.   That his finer work received no praise was to Freneau a source of discouragement and even of bitterness. His aspiration was lyrical; but he had fallen on evil days:

> On these bleak climes by fortune thrown,
> Where rigid reason reigns alone,
> Where lovely fancy has no sway,
> Nor magic forms about us play—
> Nor nature takes her summer hue,
> Tell me, what has the muse to do?[2]

Freneau's newspaper work, his political affiliations, and his business ventures operated unfavourably upon his lyrical poetry.

---

[1] For whom see also Book II, Chap. VI.          [2] *To an Author.*

Although his fervour was reawakened by the French Revolution and again by the War of 1812, almost all his best lyrics were written between 1775 and 1790. In the main these concern the American Indian, the smaller objects of nature, and the sea, and in subject at least are altogether original. *The Indian Burying Ground* is well known; *The Indian Student*, which curiously anticipates some phases of Wordsworth's *Ruth*, and *The Dying Indian*, are scarcely less fine. His nature lyrics, such as *The Wild Honeysuckle*, *The Caty-Did*, and *On the Sleep of Plants*, are the first to give lyrical expression to American nature. Their simplicity and restraint suggest Collins and Gray, but they are not imitative, and it is probable that Freneau is more original in even the style of his lyrics than has generally been acknowledged. *To a Man of Ninety* would at once be lighted upon as an imitation of Wordsworth had it not actually anticipated the *Lyrical Ballads*. The elegiac lyric *Eutaw Springs*, which Scott pronounced the best thing of its kind in the language, may have been suggested by Collins, but is still strongly original. However this may be, Freneau seems to merit all that his latest editor claims for him as a pioneer in the lyric of the sea. *On the Death of Captain Nicholas Biddle* (1779) has much of Campbell's spirit and power; *The Paul Jones* and *Captain Barney's Victory over the General Monk* deserve more than the mere credit given to the pioneer, for they are intrinsically fine.

There remains, then, out of Freneau's voluminous product, a small body of work of permanent interest. *The House of Night* deserves remembrance, not only for its pioneer romanticism but also for passages of intrinsic beauty and power; and a score of his lyrics, while far from perfect, are fine enough to deserve a permanent place in our anthologies. What his slender but genuine talent might have produced under more favourable conditions, even a generation later, can only be surmised, but even as it is we have in Freneau the only American poet before Bryant who possessed both imaginative insight and felicity of style.

A few general conclusions concerning early American poetry may be stated briefly. First, the sheer quantity of it is surprisingly large in proportion to the population. Again, it is not the product of a new civilization, but as a whole is the extremely sophisticated result of English literary traditions. In style at least it is highly imitative of English models, and in many instances it shows an immediate transmission of literary influences. Finally, in the average merit of its style, it is, at least in the eighteenth century, quite equal to all but the very best of its time in the mother country. Altogether, the first two centuries of American poetry prepared the soil for the truly native growth that was to come after 1812—a growth that was no sudden phenomenon but simply the inevitable result of the cumulative forces of two hundred years.

# Book II

## CHAPTER I

# Travellers and Observers, 1763–1846

THE literature of travel, fresh, varied, and cosmopolitan, doubtless owes its principal charm to its effect upon the sense of wonder, and hence in the last analysis is to be understood in its bearing upon imagination and poetic art; but its relation to history and geography is not superficial. Accordingly, we may first recall such dates and events as will suggest in outline the expanding region in which the second great division of American travellers range. With the close of the French and Indian War begins the supremacy of the English-speaking race in North America. Before twenty years had passed, the Colonies, no longer a mere fringe of population along the Atlantic, have achieved their independence, and possess a territory reaching inland to the Mississippi. Twenty years later, in 1803, comes the Louisiana Purchase, when the wily Napoleon, for a consideration, and to thwart his colonizing foe across the Channel, endowed the Americans with a tract of land extending from that great river north-west to the Rocky Mountains, the importance of which even Jefferson, with his westward-looking eyes, was unable to grasp in full. Another eight years, and there is a temporary check in the Astoria Settlement, later recorded by Irving. Then comes the War of 1812–14, and after it a rapid inrush of immigration. Of the native citizens, two generations have been born since the War of Independence; Revolutionary heroes are passing; and the new leaders are alien to England. The nation has become distinct. In 1819 Spain relaxes her feeble hold upon Florida.

In 1823, twenty years after the Louisiana Purchase, the utterance of the Monroe Doctrine announces to the world the position of the United States in the Occident. Meantime internal waterways and highroads have been developed; and subsequently, during the presidency of Jackson, the steam locomotive is introduced. The year 1845 marks the annexation of Texas; and with the cession of New Mexico and California in 1848, the country virtually assumes its present proportions. Almost a century has passed since the nondescript Captain Carver, immediately after the French and Indian War, conceived the idea of opening up the vast north-western tract to the enterprise of Great Britain. The interest of travellers has shifted from the character and habits of the roving Indian to the domestic manners of East and West, North and South; and science has moved from a less impersonal, yet fairly exact, observation of plants and animals, or of subterranean rivers in a terrestrial paradise, to the precise geology of a Featherstonhaugh or a Lyell.

This period of travel saw the rise of modern geography as an exact science, and the development of the ancillary sciences, geology, botany, zoology, and anthropology. If the great epoch of modern geographical discovery began with 1768 and the voyages of the Englishman Captain Cook, the scientific elaboration of results by Continental investigators also mainly occupied the second half of the eighteenth century. Linnæus was still alive, and had followers collecting specimens in America. Zimmermann, who translated the *Travels* of William Bartram into German, likewise ushered in the study of the geographical distribution of plants and animals as well as of mankind; while Blumenbach the anthropologist was making his famous collection of human skulls at Göttingen. The first work on physical geography ever published, that of the Swede Bergman, appeared in 1766, shortly before the time when books of American travel began to grow numerous. The influence of Continental science upon American observers is often obvious, as in the case of Linnæus, to which Zimmermann refers in his translation of Bartram. Indeed, a pupil of Linnæus, Pehr Kalm, who has been included among the botanists of Philadelphia, is remembered for his description of Niagara Falls. But the influence was pervasive and general, so that geography proper soon became domesticated in this country. The *Geography Made Easy* of Jedidiah Morse, first published at New Haven in 1784, quickly went through a number of editions and transformations. About 1796 President Dwight of Yale, in his *Travels*, records that a work of Morse is studied by both freshmen and sophomores, probably referring to a revision of the more extensive *American Geography* of 1789. Dwight himself made judicious use of it. The indefatigable Morse, though not a Humboldt, a Ritter, or a Leopold von Buch, was a lowly precursor of the European scientists who furnished the next generation with ideals in geography and travel.

If territorial expansion and the development of geographical science are to be noted in studying the literature of travel, the general background of eighteenth-century thought must not be forgotten. The so-called rationalism of the French, with its tendency to destroy traditional distinctions, to suppress imagination, and yet to end in a kind of deism, is too large a subject for more than passing notice. On the other hand, we may dwell for a moment upon the sentimental treatment of external nature in Rousseau, and upon his conception, in part derived from early American travellers, of the "natural" man in a terrestrial paradise. Such a being could, in fact, exist only in a tropical or sub-tropical environment such as the favoured regions in which the first American explorers and missionaries encountered the natives. Yet the transference of the idea to the Indians of North America was easy in an age when popular geography was vague; and the faith of the Jesuits in the potential goodness of the savage doubtless helped to propagate a general belief that the aborigines were noble. The idea, which seems rather to have come from the travellers than from Rousseau, but possibly is dormant in almost every educated mind, is well established in American literature from William Bartram to Fenimore Cooper. The related notion of social equality in a state of nature has a more solid basis. As in Crèvecœur's *American Farmer*, it grows out of the facts of life in a new agricultural settlement.

An opposite conception was also prevalent. Side by side with the ideal of an eloquent stoic, artless, magnanimous by nature, we find—often in the same book of travels—the cruel savage as he is, vengeful and impure. Montaigne, indeed, a predecessor of Rousseau in admiring the unlettered aborigines, had held that the European surpassed the savage in barbarity; yet when he turns from the ideal to the actual, there is but a step between Montaigne and Hobbes, who declares the life of nature to be "nasty, solitary, brutish, and short." And Hobbes merely anticipates Voltaire and Pauw, whose unedifying pictures of American natives were put together from the accounts of travellers. We have, then, in the literature of Europe the same opposition between observed fact and preconceived notion that we meet in Bartram or Carver. On the one hand, we have *La Jeune Indienne* of Chamfort, presented at the Théâtre Français in 1764, or Rousseau's *Chanson des Sauvages* and *Danse Canadienne*; on the other, a debate among the learned on the question whether the villainy of the Indians was original, or had been acquired through contact with civilization. In *De l'Amérique et des Américains*, published at Berlin in 1771, the anonymous author attacks the theories of Pauw, and vigorously contends that the savages were evil enough to begin with.

Man in a state of nature suggests solitude; and solitude, with its charms for the eighteenth-century poet, suggests the so-called "feeling for nature" that of late has been much discussed by literary students in dealing with that period. Though the point is not always made clear, the actual topic under discussion is the Neoplatonic doctrine of divine immanence. To a man who believes in this, the world, with its plants and animals, is no longer a work of art, shaped by the fingers of a Master-Artist; it is filled with a subtle spirit which is interfused in all material and living things, "rolls" through them, and is their principle of movement and pulsation. In one form or another, this notion of immanence, familiar in the earlier poems of Wordsworth, characterizes the reaction against the age of reason, and may be found in many observers of nature in America. Its origin is obscure; nor can one readily see why Neoplatonic ideas should cast a spell over minds so diverse as those of Rousseau, Goethe, Wordsworth, and the Quaker Bartram. The suggestion has been made that the writings of the mystic Boehme had an influence upon the Society of Friends. But the sources of the "feeling for nature" are likely to have been as various as the evidences of it in American travellers.

Against the background thus rapidly sketched we are to project a hundred years of travel and observation. The wealth and variety of material are very great. For the period in question, one bibliographer has recorded 413 titles of works bearing upon the single state of Illinois; for the same region between 1818 and 1865, he notes 69 British travellers, 53 American, and 31 German. For the country as a whole, a second writer has listed forty-five books of the sort by foreigners between 1789 and 1820. Whether of American or foreign origin, such books were not restricted to one volume; gradually there came to be two or three, and sometimes four. And commonly the route described was one of these: from New York to Albany, and thence across to Niagara Falls; from an eastern port south to Savannah by boat, then overland to Mobile and New Orleans, and up the Mississippi; from Philadelphia to Pittsburgh, down the Ohio to the Mississippi, and from the Mississippi up the Missouri to the North-west. Canadian travellers followed the St. Lawrence.

As the lists would indicate, the literature is cosmopolitan—an inference that is confirmed in other ways. Not only were the works of foreigners turned into English, but British and American observers were translated on the Continent: Bartram into French, German, and Dutch; Crèvecœur into French (by himself) and German; Weld into Italian, Dutch, and German; and so on. Again, the same work, as, for example, Bartram's, might be published in the same year at Philadelphia and at London or Dublin, or first in this country, and then abroad, or *vice versa*. And finally, the borrowings from earlier by later travellers, irrespective of tongues, are endless.

Confining ourselves as far as possible to British and American travellers, we may say that their motives were as various as their callings and station, and ran from the lust of a Daniel Boone for new solitudes, through the desire to promote the fur trade or immigration, and through semi-scientific or scientific curiosity, to the impulses of the literary artist or to the religious aims of the missionary. George Rogers Clark, Logan, and Boone were pioneers. Fearon, Darby, and Faux came to study conditions for emigrants. Bernard, Tyrone Power, and Fanny Kemble were actors. Wilson, Nuttall, and Audubon were professed ornithologists; the Bartrams and Michaux, botanists.

Schoolcraft was an ethnologist, Chevalier a student of political economy, Fanny Wright a social reformer. Grund, Combe the phrenologist, and Miss Martineau had a special interest in humanitarian projects. Richard Weston was a bookseller, John M. Peck a Baptist missionary, DeWitt Clinton, who explored the route of the future Erie Canal, a statesman. Many others had eyes trained in surveying. Boone was a surveyor, like Washington himself—and Washington may be classed with the observers and diarists. Buckingham, a traveller by vocation, had journeyed about the world for thirty years before visiting America; nor did he feel his obligation ended when he had published the customary three stout volumes. Crèvecœur actually was a farmer, though he was more, and Richard Parkinson, very definitely, a student of agriculture. The abusive Ashe came to examine the "western" rivers, and to observe the products and actual state of the adjacent country. Among transients from the Continent were Chastellux, the friend of Washington, Chateaubriand, with his youthful plan of helping Washington to discover the Northwest Passage, the Duc de la Rochefoucauld, a fair observer, and De Tocqueville, who wrote his classic treatise on America after a brief visit for the purpose of studying prisons. "Charles Sealsfield" (Karl Postl), whose several periods of residence were longer, who wrote in English, yet more in German, and whose tombstone in Switzerland calls him "*ein Buerger von Nordamerika*," is hard to classify.

The commonest type among these works seems to be the journal, which is the form used by William Bartram; but the epistolary type, represented by Crèvecœur, by Dwight, and by Wirt in his *Letters of the British Spy*, is very common. The general range of substance is displayed by circumstantial titles in the Bibliography. Among objects of interest to many were, in the early years of the Republic, the persons of Washington and Jefferson, and, in his time, the picturesque figure of Jackson; and among natural wonders, Niagara Falls, the "Rock Bridge" of Virginia, and the Mammoth Cave. This, after its discovery by Hutchins in 1809, took its place in the attractions of Kentucky with the furry cap of Boone. The Indians, of course, supplied an unfailing interest. Their habits, as in Bartram, speculation concerning their origin, as in Timothy

Dwight, and remarks upon their language, as in Carver, are stock material; so, too, such lists as Carver's of plants and animals. Another topic is seen in Gilbert Imlay's anticipations of states to be formed from the land to the north and west of the Ohio. Or an occasional enthusiast, possibly remembering Berkeley's project for educating the natives, will found an imaginary school of letters in a suitable landscape. Thus Stansbury in central New York, almost fifty years before the opening of Cornell University, deems the site of Ithaca most fitting for a college: "Inexhaustible stores for the study of natural history will always be at hand, and for all other sciences the scholar will be secluded in a romantic retirement which will give additional zest to his researches." The attention of others, as Fanny Kemble and Harriet Martineau, is drawn to the negro and his master in the South, more than ever, perhaps, after the anti-slavery agitation in England.

But the interest in slavery, in frontier life, and indeed in all the main topics of the later travellers, is not peculiar to them, partly because essentials are necessarily repeated, partly because subsequent observers have read, and often consciously imitate, their predecessors. Crèvecœur's ghastly picture of the slave in chains would impress any sensitive reader. But no where could imitation be clearer than in respect to impossible marvels, which even the steadiest early observers like Bartram are impelled to relate. We read in his description of an enraged alligator: "The waters like a cataract descend from his opening jaws; clouds of smoke issue from his dilated nostrils"; and, aware that this guileless traveller was merely yielding to custom, we are not led to undervalue his notes on sub-tropical fauna. Nor are we forced to discredit an entire later work, wherein adventures, like some of those in Ashe, may be altogether imaginary. Further, when unconscious imitation passes into extensive borrowing, as in Carver, we must recall the tolerance which the eighteenth century showed to this sort of indebtedness, and not condemn the debtor out of hand. So late as the year 1836, Irving could employ good sources in his own way, with a general acknowledgment of the fact in his Introduction.

For various reasons the earlier travels are more interesting; and it may be said that the best of them appeared, or were written, between 1775 and 1800. We may select as typical the

*Travels* of Carver (1778), the *Travels* of William Bartram (1791), and the *Letters from an American Farmer* of Crèvecœur (1782).

The dubious personal history of Carver, and questions as to the authenticity of his book, will excuse the introduction of certain details in his biography. Jonathan Carver, the ostensible author of *Travels through the Interior Parts of North America in the Years 1766, 1767, and 1768*, was not the great-grandson of the first colonial Governor of Connecticut, but was probably born in humble circumstances at Canterbury in that state. In 1746 he married Abigail Robbins, by whom he had seven children; he later contracted a bigamous marriage in England. The extent of his education has been disputed; but he seems to have had some knowledge of surveying and map-making, with perhaps a smattering of medicine. His title-page calls him "J. Carver, Esq., Captain of a Company of Provincial Troops during the Late War with France"; and he probably was captured with Burk's company of rangers in 1757, when he was "wounded in his Leg at the bloody Massacree of the unhappy Garrison of Fort William Henry at Lake George." The war over, he says he began to think of exploring the most unknown parts of England's new territory. In the opinion of a severe critic, Professor Edward G. Bourne, Carver's actual journey was limited to this: he went from Boston to Michilimackinac, thence by way of the Fox River and the Wisconsin to the Mississippi, and thence up the Minnesota; returning, he explored northern Wisconsin and the northern shore of Lake Superior. Failing in Boston to publish an account of his discoveries, in 1769 he went to England with a project for further exploration in the North-west. The pecuniary aid accorded him as a needy person by the Government would argue some recognition of his services. He evidently enlisted the sympathy of Dr. Lettsom and others who took an interest in his schemes, and, like many another, no doubt received help with the manuscript before his *Travels* were published in 1778. But he failed in his main endeavour, and is said to have "died in misery, in 1780, at the age of 48."

His book instantly became popular, and it so remained, as twenty-three editions and translations bear witness. The author or compiler, whoever he was, understood the public, was a man of some imagination, and knew how to combine

Carver's own material with observations from previous writers; nor does he fail to mention, in the casual way of the time, authorities like Charlevoix and Adair, from whom, as we now look at things, we must say he unblushingly filches. Here is one of the examples pointed out by Professor Bourne. Charlevoix had said of the Indians in the English translation:

> On the smoothest grass, or the hardest earth, even on the very stones, they will discover the traces of an enemy, and by their shape and figure of the footsteps, and the distance between their prints, they will, it is said, distinguish not only different nations, but also tell whether they were men or women who have gone that way.

And in Carver we read:

> On the smoothest grass, on the hardest earth, and even on the very stones, will they discover the traces of an enemy, and by the shape of the footsteps, and the distance between the prints, distinguish not only whether it is a man or woman who has passed that way, but even the nation to which they belong.

In spite of his borrowings, and in spite of incredible and monstrous stories, even worse than the sordid actualities of savage life, Carver maintains that he is strictly veracious:

> I shall in no instance exceed the bounds of truth, or have recourse to those useless and extravagant exaggerations too often made use of by travellers, to excite the curiosity of the public, or to increase their own importance. Nor shall I insert any observations but such as I have made myself, or, from the credibility of those by whom they were related, am enabled to vouch for their authenticity.

These false pretensions easily lead one to underestimate the element of truth in the narrative, and Carver's share in its production. Carver was not too uneducated to make notes and gather materials for a book. He could write a long coherent letter to his first wife, and specimens of his writing are not in the hand of an ignorant man. He, not less than his assistant or assistants in publication, could have met with the works of Charlevoix, Adair, and Lahontan in London book-stalls. But it was hardly his pen that made reference to Plato and Grotius.

The volume is dedicated "To Joseph Banks, President of the Royal Society." Then follows, in the second edition, a magniloquent Address to the Public. The journal proper occupies but a third of the volume. Next come seventeen chapters on the origin, physique, and dress of the Indians, their manners and customs, their government, their food, dances, methods of warfare and games, and their language. The eighteenth deals with animals, birds—as, for example, "the Whipperwill, or, as it is termed by the Indians, the Muckawiss" —fishes, reptiles, and insects; the nineteenth, with the vegetable kingdom. There is an Appendix on the future of discovery, settlement, and commerce. In his Introduction Carver says:

What I chiefly had in view, after gaining a knowledge of the Manners, Customs, Languages, Soil, and natural Productions of the different nations that inhabit the back of the Mississippi, was to ascertain the Breadth of that vast continent which extends from the Atlantic to the Pacific Ocean, in its broadest part between 43 and 46 Degrees Northern Latitude. Had I been able to accomplish this, I intended to have proposed to Government to establish a Post in some of those parts about the Straits of Annian, which, having been first discovered by Sir Francis Drake, of course belong to the English. This I am convinced would greatly facilitate the discovery of a North-West Passage, or a communication between Hudson's Bay and the Pacific Ocean. . . . A settlement on that extremity of America . . . would open a passage for conveying intelligence to China and the English settlements in the East Indies, with greater expedition than a tedious voyage by the Cape of Good Hope or the Straits of Magellan will allow of.

This was the dream that foreshadowed the present development of the entire North-west. It worked in the mind of Jefferson, took shape in the Lewis and Clark expedition and in the enterprise of John Jacob Astor, and reappeared in Irving's *Astoria*. Carver's volume still fastens upon the imagination, as it did in the time of Schiller, Wordsworth, and Chateaubriand.

Coleridge, who found pleasure in Carver's descriptions, doubtless set a higher value upon Bartram; he says in *Table Talk*: "The latest book of travels I know, written in the spirit of the old travellers, is Bartram's account of his tour in the Floridas. It is a work of high merit every way." The poet almost certainly refers, not to *A Journal Kept by John Bartram of Philadelphia, Botanist to His Majesty for the Floridas;* but to the volume of *Travels* by his son, William Bartram. Yet it is difficult to mention the son without reference to the father, whom Linnæus called the greatest self-taught botanist in the world. John Bartram, born in 1699, when almost seventy years old explored the St. John's River in Florida, accompanied by William, who in turn made a second journey to the region in 1773, "at the request of Dr. Fothergill, of London," the English naturalist being zealous "for the discovery of rare and useful productions . . . chiefly in the vegetable kingdom." Both father and son corresponded with European scientists, including Gronov and Dillen, but more particularly with Peter Collinson, through whom the elder Bartram came into relations with virtually all the distinguished naturalists of his time. The botanic garden for which the father began to collect in 1730, and which is now within the limits of Philadelphia, was justly famous. Here, it is said, Washington and Franklin were wont to sit and talk just prior to the Revolution; and Bartram's Garden is still an object of interest as the first establishment of its kind on this continent. From a local guide is extracted this description of its founder:

He was one of an early incorporated company to bank the Schuylkill and the Delaware, by which means he rescued, out of extensive swamps, arable land, and pasture for many cattle and horses; his crops of wheat challenge the farmer of to-day; he fertilized his orchard in an ingenious way that was a "miracle in husbandry." Besides, he was stone-mason; his interesting old house he built with his own hands, quarrying the stone on his estate in a remarkable manner; see, also, in the Garden the watering-trough and the cider-press, cut out of solid rock. And his record is fuller yet; he had to study Latin for his botany; he was enough acquainted with medicine and surgery to be of great help to his poorer neighbors; he delineated a plan for deep-sea soundings more than a hundred years before the *Challenger* expedition. His thirst for knowledge was insatiable. His joy in the revelations of nature was unbounded. What wonder that he was astonished when people complained that they were tired of time!

His son William, called by the Seminoles "Puc-Puggy" (Flower-Hunter), was born at Kingsessing, Pennsylvania, 1739, he and his twin-sister taking fifth place in the succession of children.  He grew up with the Garden, accompanied his father on collecting tours, travelled himself, and published his *Travels through North and South Carolina, Georgia, East and West Florida, the Cherokee Country, the Extensive Territories of the Muscogulges, or Creek Confederacy, and the Country of the Chactaws*, as well as "the most complete and correct list of American birds prior to the work of Alexander Wilson"; he lived in Philadelphia, unmarried, a student of science, caring for the Garden until his death in 1823.  A professorship was offered him in 1782 by the University of Pennsylvania, but failing health led him to decline it.   His manuscript work on the Indians was published by the American Ethnological Society in 1853.

The *Travels* reveal the enthusiasm of a man still young, with an eye that nothing escapes, not without poetical imagination or philosophical vision, and with a deep reverence for the Creative Spirit which he feels in all about him.  The volume is divided into four Parts.  In the first, the Introduction, he recounts the voyage by packet from Philadelphia to Savannah, whence he proceeds to the "Alatamaha" River.  The second describes East Florida, and the ascent of St. John's River in a small canoe.  On reaching Lake George, "which is a dilatation of the River St. Juan," his vessel "at once diminished to a nutshell on the swelling seas."  The Indian whom he engaged to assist him on the upper river becoming weary, Bartram continues on alone, to encamp at an orange grove, to battle with alligators, and to observe "a large sulphureous fountain."   Descending again, he is robbed by a wolf, and so, after sundry adventures, arrives at the lower trading-house.  He then "proceeds on a journey to Cuscowilla," where he meets with a friendly reception from the "Siminoles," and from there goes to view the "great bason" or sink, whose subterranean waters swarm with fish.  In Part III, having returned to Charleston, he sets out for the Cherokee territories and the "Chactaw" country, going as far as Mobile, from which, turning back, he accompanies a band of traders to visit the Creeks.  Again in the company of traders, he sets off for Georgia; from Augusta he revisits Savannah, whence he makes a "short excursion in the South of Georgia," adding to his collection, and gathering seeds of "two new and very curious shrubs."  At Charleston he began the overland journey northward through Virginia; he crossed the River Susquehanna on the ice, "next morning sat forward again towards Philadelphia," and in two days more arrived at his father's house on the banks of the River Schuylkill, having been absent nearly five years.

Though collecting as a botanist and observing as an ornithologist, Bartram thus far has mainly been occupied with the Indians. In Part IV he discusses their persons, character, and qualifications, noting that they have the "most perfect human figure," their government and civil society, their dress and amusements, property and occupations, marriage and funeral rites, and their language and monuments. The ready pencil of the naturalist provided the engraver with drawings of botanical and zoological subjects throughout the volume. The frontispiece represents "Mico Chlucco the Long Warrior, or King of the Siminoles," whose dancing crest of splendid feathers flashes again in Wordsworth's *Ruth*.

A bare survey does scant justice to the richness of form and colour in Bartram's pages. At one time he is struck with "the tall aspiring Gordonia lasianthus." "Its thick foliage, of a dark green colour, is flowered over with large milk-white fragrant blossoms, on long slender elastic peduncles, at the extremities of its numerous branches, from the bosom of the leaves, and renewed every morning"—the "budding, fading, faded flowers" of *Ruth*. Or again we see the solitary dejected "wood-pelican," alone on the topmost limb of a dead cypress; "it looks extremely grave, sorrowful, and melancholy, as if in the deepest thought"—an image used by Wordsworth in Book Third of *The Prelude*. Of the "Alatamaha" Bartram says: "I ascended this beautiful river, on whose fruitful banks the generous and true sons of liberty securely dwell, fifty miles above the white settlements." Allured by the "sublime enchanting scenes of primitive nature," and by "visions of terrestrial happiness," he wandered away to a grove at the edge of a luxuriant savannah:

How happily situated is this retired spot of earth! What an elysium it is! where the wandering Siminole, the naked red warrior, roams at large, and after the vigorous chase retires from the scorching heat of the meridian sun. Here he reclines and reposes under the odoriferous shades of Zanthoxylon, his verdant couch guarded by the Deity; Liberty, and the Muses, inspiring him with wisdom and valour, whilst the balmy zephyrs fan him to sleep.

The apostrophes and redundant descriptions, which the rigorous German translator pruned away, did not prevent Zimmermann from calling Bartram's volume one of the most instructive works of the time. The faults of an unpractised writer are relieved by a constant cheerfulness, candour, and animation; "cheerful," "cheering," and "social" are favourite epithets. The words "animate," "animating," "vibration," and the like, give a clue to his Neoplatonic and Hartleian philosophy, which subtly recommended him to contemporary European poets:

If, then, the visible, the mechanical part of the animal creation, the mere material part, is so admirably beautiful, harmonious, and incomprehensible, what must be the intellectual system? that inexpressibly more essential principle, which secretly operates within? that which animates the inimitable machines, which gives them motion, impowers them to act, speak, and perform, this must be divine and immortal?

There is a motion and a spirit in the environment itself: "At the reanimating appearance of the rising sun, nature again revives"; "the atmosphere was now animated with the efficient principle of vegetative life"; "the balmy winds breathed the animating odours of the groves around me." "At the return of the morning, by the powerful influence of light, the pulse of nature becomes more active, and the universal vibration of life insensibly and irresistibly moves the wondrous machine. How cheerful and gay all nature appears." In Bartram the "feeling for nature" is quite as distinct as the idea of the "natural" man. The social philosophy of the time is more apparent in Crèvecœur.

In a letter to Richard Henderson on the subject of immigrants, Washington writes (19 June, 1788):

The author of the queries may then be referred to the *Information for those who would wish to remove to America*, and [sic] published in Europe in the year 1784, by the great philosopher Dr. Franklin. Short as it is, it contains almost everything that needs to be known on the subject of migrating to this country. . . .

Of books at present existing, Mr. Jefferson's *Notes on Virginia* will give the best idea of this part of the continent to a foreigner; and the *American Farmer's Letters*, written by Mr. Crèvecœur (commonly called Mr. St. John), the French consul in New York, who actually resided twenty years as a farmer in that State, will afford a great deal of profitable and amusive information, respecting the private life of the Americans, as well as the progress of agriculture, manufactures, and arts in their country. Perhaps the picture he gives, though founded on fact, is in some instances embellished with rather too flattering circumstances.

"The name of our Family is St. Jean, in English St. John, a name as Antient as the Conquest of England by William the Bastard." So writes St. Jean de Crèvecœur, but he puts "J. Hector St. John" on the title-page of his imaginary *Letters from an American Farmer*. Born at Caen, 31 January, 1735, at the age of sixteen he went to England. A seven years' education there may explain the superiority of his English style over his French. Emigrating to Canada, he subsequently was resident in Pennsylvania, and in 1764 became a citizen of New York. After five years he settled as a farmer in Ulster County; at a mature age for the colonies he married Mehetable Tippet of Yonkers. He made journeys in New York and Pennsylvania, and to the west, to the south as far as Charleston—possibly to Jamaica, and into New England. In 1779, on attempting to return to France, he was imprisoned in New York City as a spy. When released, he went to England, sold his *Letters* for thirty guineas, and crossed to Normandy; we find him writing from Caen in 1781. Through the Countess de Houdetot of Rousseau's *Confessions* he was enabled to send a copy of his book to Franklin, then (1782) on a mission abroad. Instrumental in helping Americans in England to return to this country, when Crèvecœur himself came back, in 1783, it was to find his wife just dead, and his children in the care of strangers. Meanwhile he had been appointed French consul in New York. His travels with Franklin gave rise to a three-volume work, not so interesting as the *Letters*, entitled *Voyage dans la Haute Pennsylvanie*. From 1790 until his death at Sarcelles, 12 November, 1813, he lived in France.

The *Letters* of this "farmer of feelings" to a doubtless hypothetical "W. S. Ecuyer" are dedicated "to the Abbé Raynal, F.R.S.":

Behold, Sir, an humble American Planter, a simple cultivator of the earth, addressing you from the farther side of the Atlantic. . . . As an eloquent and powerful advocate, you have pleaded the cause of humanity in espousing that of the poor Africans; you viewed these provinces of North America in their true light, as the asylum of freedom, as the cradle of future nations, and the refuge of distressed Europeans.

Of the twelve, the Introductory Letter is intentionally rambling. A former European guest having asked for a detailed account of colonial life, "neighbour James" seeks counsel of the minister, who tells him: "He that shall write a letter every day of the week will on Saturday perceive the sixth flowing from his pen much more readily than the first." But the Farmer's wife dissuades him, unless the plan be followed secretly, so as not to arouse gossip. A chance allusion to the speeches of "friend Edmund," that is, of Burke, accords with the attention to style in the letters that follow. "If they be not elegant," says the minister, "they will smell of the woods, and be a little wild"; but he also assures the Farmer: "Nature hath given you a tolerable share of good sense . . . some perspicuity," and "a warmth of imagination which enables you to think with quickness." The second letter takes up the situation, feelings, and pleasures of an American farmer, and the third, on "What is an American?" relates the diverting experiences of Andrew the Hebridean, in his first meeting with Indians. In the fourth we pass to the Island of Nantucket, while the fifth describes the education and employment of the islanders. In the sixth, after an account of Martha's Vineyard and the whale fishery, the author returns to a discussion of manners and customs, this topic continuing in the seventh and eighth. The ninth transfers us to Charleston and the South, where slavery brings the author to "an examination of what is called civilized society." "Would you prefer the state of men in the woods to that of men in a more improved situation? Evil preponderates in both. . . . For my part, I think the vices and miseries to be found in the latter exceed those of the former." In the tenth, a special inquiry of the correspondent abroad is met with a dissertation on snakes and on the humming-bird. The eleventh is a letter "From Mr. Iw–n Al–z, a Russian Gentleman, describing the Visit he paid at my request to Mr. John Bertram, the celebrated Pennsylvania Botanist." The twelfth and last pictures the distress of a "frontier man"—menaced by the savages, and unsettled by the revolt of the colonies,—who "would chearfully go even to the Mississippi, to find that repose to which we have been so long strangers"; with his appeal to the Father of Nature, to the Supreme Being whose creative power inhabits "the immense variety of planets," the volume closes.

Crèvecœur's pretext of an inquiring foreigner mirrored the curiosity of Europe respecting the colonies, and the way in which that curiosity was satisfied, not merely through the multiplying books of travel, but also through the exchange and publication of formal letters. Such was the origin of Jefferson's *Notes on the State of Virginia; Written in the Year 1781, Somewhat Corrected and Enlarged in the Winter of 1782, for the Use of a Foreigner of Distinction, in Answer to certain Queries Proposed by Him.* This serious piece of scientific writing, perhaps the most frequently printed treatise that has emanated from the South, was compiled by Jefferson while he was Governor of Virginia, and sent to M. Barbé de Marbois, Secretary of the French Legation. It was first issued at Paris (1784–85). The arid statistics, the details of agriculture, and the generally dry geography, important in their time, now mean less to the reader than do Jefferson's occasional flights in a loftier style, represented in the following:

The Natural Bridge, the most sublime of nature's works, though not comprehended under the present head [Cascades and Caverns], must not be pretermitted. . . . Though the sides of this bridge are provided in some parts with a parapet of fixed rocks, yet few men have resolution to walk to them and look over into the abyss. You involuntarily fall on your hands and feet, creep to the parapet, and peep over it. Looking down from this height about a minute gave me a violent headache. If the view from the top be painful and intolerable, that from below is delightful in an equal extreme. It is impossible for the emotions arising from the sublime to be felt beyond what they are here; so beautiful an arch, so elevated, so light, and springing as it were up to heaven!

The influence of the *Notes*, of their author, and of Jeffersonian ideals, is constantly met in other works of description. The
allusions to Washington himself are scarcely more frequent.
In 1794 Henry Wansey, an English manufacturer, breakfasted
with Washington, and "was struck with awe and admiration";
but about the same time, Thomas Cooper, who, in a flying
visit, found "land cheap and labour dear," remarks that "the
government is the government *of* the people and *for* the people."
And when John Davis, the pedestrian, had from 1798 to 1802
"entered, with equal interest, the mud-hut of the negro and the
log-house of the planter," he dedicated his book to Jefferson.
Isaac Weld the Irishman, author of a widely read book on the
United States and Canada, wrote one of his thirty-eight letters
from Jefferson's then unfinished establishment at Monticello.
He made mediocre pencil sketches of Niagara Falls, and the
"Rock Bridge" of Virginia, but secured a picture of Mount
Vernon from a friend. He visited the Dismal Swamp, saw
Washington in a cheerful mood at a reception in Philadelphia,
and culled observations on the Indians, helping himself at need
from Carver and Jefferson. In Weld's account, the backsliding
of the educated savage Joseph Brant became heroic.

With Weld, the strictures of the British travellers upon
American life become sharp. A mild rejoinder to foreign de-
preciation soon appeared in the fictitious *Letters of the British
Spy* by the American jurist William Wirt, which purported
to derive from the abandoned manuscript of "a meek and
harmless" young Englishman of rank who was travelling in-
cognito. Composed in a formal Addisonian manner, this
defence of American statesmen and American eloquence is
overcharged with allusions to Cicero and Demosthenes. Nevertheless, some of the descriptions cling to the mind.[1] It is easy
to perceive why the booklet went through so many editions,
when one finds in it the leading men of the nation in 1803 under
a thin disguise. Here, for example, is President Jefferson:

The . . . of the United States is in his person tall, meagre,
emaciated; his muscles relaxed, and his joints so loosely connected
as not only to disqualify him, apparently, for any vigorous exertion

[1] See also Book II, Chap. III.

of body, but to destroy everything like elegance and harmony in his air and movement.

Wirt's young nobleman denies to the President the gift of poetical fancy; yet Jefferson allowed such imaginative faculty as he possessed to dally with the theme of western exploration. As early as 1784 he was devising names for ten suggested states to the northwest—"Sylvania," "Michigania," "Metropolitamia," etc.,—after the pseudo-classical taste of the day. He was therefore ready to promote discovery in the far North-west when the moment for action arrived. Indeed, before the Lewis and Clark enterprise, he had twice made plans for the same general undertaking. More particularly, while he was Vice-President of the American Philosophical Society, in 1793, he had arranged with the French botanist Michaux, then in this country, for an expedition which was to follow the Missouri and some tributary thereof to a point where these waters might communicate with the Columbia River, opening a way to the Pacific. The scheme fell through when Michaux became involved in a French marauding project against the Spanish, and lingered among the recruits in Kentucky. It seems that Meriwether Lewis, a young neighbour of Jefferson, had desired the position of leader in the great exploration.

Lewis, who in 1801 became private secretary to Jefferson, was born in 1774 of a prominent stock in Virginia. After five years at a Latin school, he studied botany on his mother's farm, then entered the army raised to quell the Whiskey Rebellion, and, serving as an officer under Wayne, rose to be a captain. In the eyes of Jefferson, Lewis was "brave, prudent, habituated to the woods, and familiar with Indian manners and character," besides possessing "a great mass of accurate observation on all the subjects of nature." When chosen to pilot the now famous expedition which bears his name, he further prepared himself by studying with competent scientists at Philadelphia; and feeling the need of a companion for the tour, he chose a friend of his boyhood, his elder by four years, Captain William Clark, also a soldier under Wayne, experienced in Indian warfare, and practised in the construction of forts. An unpolished, but staunch and friendly man, heartily returning the warm affection of Lewis, Clark accepted the opportunity

with spirit, and made ready to join him in seeking the information which Jefferson desired "for the benefit of our own country
and of the world." For a time it was Jefferson's pretence that
the undertaking was "a literary enterprise." But when the
sale of Louisiana was ratified, there was no further need of
concealing the interest of the Federal Government in the
project.

Lewis left Pittsburgh on 31 August, 1803, to meet Clark in
Kentucky. They wintered in Illinois, as Clark writes,

at the enterance of a Small river opposit the Mouth of Missouri
Called Wood River, where they formed their party, Composed of
robust helthy hardy young men.

In the spring the detachment of twenty-nine regular members
and sixteen supernumeraries began the slow progress up the
Missouri. They spent the next winter in a stockade in North
Dakota, proceeding in the spring of 1805 to the source of the
Jefferson Fork of the Missouri, and under many hardships
crossing over the barrier mountains toward the end of summer.
Going down the Columbia River, they reached the Pacific
at the close of the autumn, to pass the winter in their Fort
Clatsop—log huts enclosed by a palisade. Here they had
leisure to study the natives and to compile records. In March,
1806, they began the return journey. After surmounting the
difficult snow-clad barrier in June, the party divided, Lewis
making his way to the Falls of the Missouri, and exploring
Maria's River, Clark returning to the head of Jefferson Fork,
proceeding thence to the Yellowstone River, and following this
down to the Missouri. Coming together again in August, they
went to St. Louis in September, having consumed about two
and one-third years in the wilds.

The subsequent duties of Lewis as Governor of Louisiana
Territory, and of Clark as Superintendent of Indian Affairs,
delayed the preparation of the records, although Jefferson was
ardent for their publication. In 1809, Lewis, while on his way
to Washington and Philadelphia to take charge of the editing,
met his death, probably by violence, in Tennessee; whereupon
the unlettered Clark, at the urgent desire of Jefferson, undertook the task with the help of Nicholas Biddle of Philadelphia.

Biddle performed the major part of the editing, and then Paul Allen, a journalist, supervised the printing. After many vicissitudes, the work was published in February, 1814. Much of the scientific material, however, was not included; nor was a strictly accurate account of the expedition and its results ever given to the world until the recent edition (1904–1905) of the *Original Journals* by Dr. Thwaites. Of the first edition, about 1400 copies were circulated, from the sale of which Clark apparently received nothing. Though the authentic work became popular in America and Europe, being reprinted and translated, the initial delay in publication, and the presence of other diarists in the party, made room for more than one earlier account of the expedition—for example, the *Journal* of Patrick Gass, of which there were five editions before 1814, as well as a French and a German translation in that year. However made known, the achievement of Lewis and Clark has won greater fame than any other geographical exploration ever undertaken within the United States proper. The Government expedition from Pittsburgh to the Rocky Mountains in 1819, under the command of Major Long, was more fruitful in technical results; and with the vast, though unmethodical, accumulations of Schoolcraft the data on Indians in the records edited by Biddle are not to be compared in value. But the authorized account of Jefferson's great enterprise, published in the concluding year of the final war with England, marked the fulfilment of Carver's vision, and betokened the approaching establishment of the United States as the ruling power in the Western Hemisphere.

When the strife of arms was settled by the Treaty of Ghent in 1814, a literary war between Great Britain and America burst into flame. It had long been smouldering. In the *Travels* of the Rev. Andrew Burnaby, of the Church of England, there was little to offend the jealous or sensitive American. This genial clergyman went through the "Middle Settlements," beginning with Virginia, in 1759 and 1760. His slender volume, published in 1775, had reached a third edition by 1798, being revised and enlarged, and was still valued in 1812 when Pinkerton chose it for his collection of travels in all parts of the world. Burnaby's affection for the colonies is only second to his love of England. He balances the advantages and disadvantages of North and

South, and of Philadelphia, New York, and Boston. At "Prince-town" he finds "a handsome school and college for the education of dissenters, erected upon the plan of those in Scotland," with "about twenty boys in the grammar-school, and sixty in the college." There are "only two professors, besides the provost." He sees beautiful homes along the Raritan River, and handsome ladies at "Brunswick"; but the people of Rhode Island "are cunning, deceitful, and selfish"— though he adds: "After having said so much to the disadvantage of this colony, I should be guilty of injustice and ingratitude, were I not to declare that there are many worthy gentlemen in it, who see the misfortunes of their country, and lament them." The lower classes at Boston are insufferably inquisitive; yet "Arts and Sciences seem to have made a greater progress here than in any other part of America." By 1798 Burnaby might well have revised his prediction that "America is formed for happiness, but not for empire." Before this there had been critics more hostile, like J. F. D. Smyth; but in British travellers who really belong to the period about 1800, there is a new and characteristic note of displeasure. Weld remarks that the Pennsylvania farmers "live in a penurious style"; they are "greatly inferior to the English." The roads are "execrable," and the Americans in general are prying. In Ashe, who had expected too much, the reaction against both people and customs is violent; he grieves because at Carlisle, Pennsylvania, he "did not meet with a man of decent literature"; and this is the mildest of his abuse. Weld, Parkinson, Ashe, and Bradbury, in a line, raise and re-echo the note of censure. Before Bradbury's work was published, there was a dismal chorus from the great British periodicals. As early as 1814 *The Quarterly Review* was chiming in, to be duly followed by the *Edinburgh* and the *British*, and by *Blackwood's Magazine*. Both Gifford and Sydney Smith lent their voices, and Southey was supposed by the Americans to have produced one of the bitterest attacks upon them. Various causes exasperated the discussion—discontented emigrants, discontent in England at the emigration, vainglory in America, especially over the outcome of the second war, the sensitiveness of Americans to the charge of inquisitiveness and lack of reserve, and, by no means least, the pirating of English books by American publishers.

The strife was at its height from 1814 to 1825. "In the four quarters of the globe, who reads an American book? or goes to an American play? or looks at an American picture or statue?" Such were the cordial questions put by Sydney Smith in *The Edinburgh Review* for January, 1820. The sourness of the reviewers, great and small, reacted upon new books of travel, and prospective observers when they crossed the ocean came with the prepossession that democratic institutions in America had corrupted good manners. There was a recrudescence of the old theory, once formulated by Pauw, that everything deteriorated when transplanted from Europe. Fearon (1818) — "no lover of America," said Sydney Smith,—Harris (1821), Welby (1821), and Faux (1823) gave the English public the reading it enjoyed, and the publishers welcomed fresh manuscript. "Have a passage ready taken for 'Merriker," whispers Mr. Pickwick's friend Weller to Sam. "Let the gov'ner stop there till Mrs. Bardell's dead . . . and then let him come back and write a book about the 'Merrikins as 'll pay all his expenses, and more, if he blows 'em up enough." Evidently the painful animadversions had not ceased in 1837; they were perhaps generally mitigated after 1825. Captain Basil Hall in 1829, Fidler in 1833, Thomas Hamilton in 1833, Captain Marryat in 1839, and Thomas Brothers in 1840, keep up the unlucky strain, sometimes with more, and sometimes with less good humour. Brothers is of opinion that "there is in the United States more taxation, poverty, and general oppression than ever known in any other country." And in January, 1844, *The Foreign Quarterly* asserts that "As yet the American is horn-handed and pig-headed, hard, persevering, unscrupulous, carnivorous, . . . with an incredible genius for lying." Ere this, however, better sense was prevailing. Basil Hall, though preferring the manners of aristocratic England, was not unkindly, nor was Mrs. Trollope (1832) unsympathetic. Dickens himself, having followed the Ohio and the Mississippi to St. Louis, and having visited Looking-Glass Prairie, in 1842 published his *American Notes*, in which he "blows 'em up" with moderation. The courteous Sir Charles Lyell (1845) was unfortunately justified in a dislike of American boasting.

Meanwhile the Americans, sensitive as well as vainglorious,

or patriotic, on their part had not been idle, whether in the magazines or in books. *Niles' Weekly Register*, and *The North American Review*, with Edward Everett as editor, hurried to the defence, and Timothy Dwight, Irving, Fenimore Cooper, and Paulding were among those who, with or without finesse, parried the foreign thrusts.   Robert Walsh wrote *An Appeal from the Judgments of Great Britain respecting the United States* (1819), while John Neal of Portland carried the fight into the enemy's camp by contributing to *Blackwood's Magazine* from 1823 until 1826.  After Dwight's death his *Travels* in New England and New York were published, four substantial volumes, representing vacation journeys which he had taken for reasons of health from 1796 on.  They are full of exact information on every conceivable subject—on the prevailing winds, on the "excellencies of the colonists of New England," "their enterprise and industry, their love of science and learning, their love of liberty, their morality, their piety," on the superiority of soil and climate, etc.  But the serious vein was not the only one for such a contest, as Paulding was aware when he wrote the anonymous *John Bull in America, or the New Munchausen* (1825), which for its time was effective as an allegorical satire upon English opinion in relation to travellers.  It is now less amusing than the strictures that called it forth.  But there is something trivial about the whole episode.

The best kind of reply to the taunt of Sydney Smith was the literary work of Fenimore Cooper and Washington Irving, who are more fully treated elsewhere in this history.[1]  Of Cooper's novels, three more important ones had been produced before he was entangled in the controversies that occupied much of his life.  *The Pioneers* reflected his early experiences on the frontier; while *The Last of the Mohicans* deserves notice because it contains, in distinct types, both the idealized and the unidealized Indian that we have seen in the travellers.  Chingachgook is a true descendant of Montaigne's high-minded savage, and belongs to the family of Rousseau's "natural" man; whereas the base "Mingoes" are more like real aborigines. *The Prairie*, with its large element of description, was followed during the author's residence abroad by *Notions of the Americans Picked up by a Travelling Bachelor* (1828), a series of letters by

[1] See also Book II, Chaps. IV and VI.

an imaginary Englishman, in which there is an attempt to rectify prevailing European and British misconceptions of America, and to show the Americans how to be more refined, and how to suppress their self-satisfaction. A middle course pleased neither English nor Americans; nor did the criticism in *Homeward Bound* and *Home as Found* tend to pacify Cooper's fellow-countrymen. The turmoil of his later years did not prevent him from writing two of his most popular novels, *The Pathfinder* and *The Deerslayer*, which again disclose his conception of the forest and frontier.

Few have depicted that life with more truth and spirit than Irving. From the noisy disputes between John Bull and Jonathan we come back to him as to a contemplative traveller of some previous generation; and in truth he carries on the tradition of Carver, and of Lewis and Clark. Returning in 1832, after an absence in Europe of seventeen years, Irving found his countrymen expecting him to vindicate his patriotism, and American letters, by some work on a native theme. Instead of directly yielding to the call, he made "a wide and varied tour," joining a Government expedition to the Arkansas River, exploring the hunting-grounds of the stealthy Pawnees, witnessing the pursuit of the buffalo, and sharing the spoils of bee-hunters. The result was *A Tour on the Prairies* (1835), which represents but a part of the journey. "It is," he says, "a simple narrative of every-day occurrences"; but it describes the motley life of the border with fidelity—Osage Indians, "stern and simple in garb and aspect," with "fine Roman countenances, and broad deep chests"; gaily dressed Creeks, "quite Oriental" in appearance; and "a sprinkling of trappers, hunters, half-breeds, creoles, negroes of every hue, and all that other rabble rout of nondescript beings that keep about the frontiers, between civilized and savage life, as those equivocal birds, the bats, hover about the confines of light and darkness." Irving's next task was to write the history of John Jacob Astor's development and consolidation of the fur-trade in the North-west (after the Lewis and Clark expedition), in *Astoria, or Anecdotes of an Enterprise beyond the Rocky Mountains*, which appeared in 1836. The literary method here employed is characteristic of so many books of travel, beginning with Carver's, that Irving may be allowed to explain it in his own words:

a paradise nor yet a den of thieves but a good nurse for the farmer, did much in the third decade of the last century to stimulate emigration of a better sort from the mother country to the land of free endeavour. Possession of the soil, and the opportunity to gain more and more of it—as depicted by Crèvecœur—must always act as a stimulus to the human mind. Once reaching these shores, a mobile population would be allured to the West through the virile descriptions of the Mississippi Valley by a Timothy Flint, or through the animated sketches of life and manners by a James Hall. To the literature of travel may also be ascribed much of the attraction exerted by this country upon distinguished foreigners in seasons of stress or misfortune. Napoleon himself once spoke of America as a possible retreat. If Crèvecœur's portrait of the free and social colonist was "embellished with rather too flattering circumstances," it was not the less true in presenting an ideal that the Americans have striven to realize; it was real in the sense that it governed their better thoughts and actions. By disengaging and projecting the ideal form of American life, such works interpreted the new republic for England and the Continent. More than this, they interpreted one part of the new nation to another. No other class of books can have done so much to consolidate the people; their effect upon character and imagination can hardly be overestimated.

They gave wings to the imagination; and here they are especially significant for the history of literature. As the discovery of America was accompanied by an outburst of poetry in the Renaissance, other causes, naturally, contributing thereto—as the mind of a Shakespeare was caught by a chance description of the "still-vexed Bermoothes"; so the great advances in geographical discovery and natural science after the middle of the eighteenth century made themselves felt in another generation of poets, and American travels found a quick response in works of literary art. The place of the travellers in the movement known as "the return to nature" would require for adequate treatment nothing short of a dissertation; nor could one always discriminate between the literary preconceptions which the observers brought with them and the ultimate facts about man and his environment which they transmitted to the poets. Yet we recognize in the reports of American travel something ultimate, as did the poets and philosophers.

Scattered instances suffice for illustration. In the speech *On Conciliation with America*, Burke, who himself had a share in an *Account of the European Settlements* (1757), betrays an acquaintance with more recent works of a similar kind. To one of Carver's borrowed passages on Indian funeral customs Schiller owes the substance of the *Nadowessiers Todtenlied*, a poem greatly admired by Goethe. Still better known is the employment of what is striking and exotic in Carver and Bartram by Chateaubriand in the composite landscape of *René* and *Atala*, and his mingling of conventional with imaginary incidents in the *Voyage en Amérique*.

In American and English poets, also, one may see the connection between higher forms of literature and books of travel. Freneau translates the *Travels* of the Abbé Robin (Philadelphia, 1783), and writes *Stanzas on the Emigration to America and Peopling the Western Country* (*Poems*, 1786). Timothy Dwight's "Most fruitful thy soil, most inviting thy clime," in *Columbia*, echoes the sentiment of his *Travels*. Longfellow derives the myth of Hiawatha from Schoolcraft, and is said to have used Sealsfield's *Life in the New World*, and Frémont's *Expedition to the Rocky Mountains*, in *Evangeline*. In Bryant, the allusion to

> the continuous woods
> Where rolls the Oregon

has been traced to Carver. *Thanatopsis*, the lines *To a Waterfowl*, and *The Prairies* alike reveal the spirit of inland discovery.

The relation of English poets to American observers is most significant of all. Coleridge praises Cartwright, Hearne, and Bartram; "the impression which Bartram had left on his mind," says his grandson, "was deep and lasting." Lamb is enamoured of pious John Woolman, and eventually favours Crèvecœur, yielding to Hazlitt's recommendation. Southey commends Dwight, and employs Bartram in *Madoc*. In *Mazeppa*, Byron, an inveterate reader of travels, takes the notion of an audible aurora borealis from Hearne. But the most striking instance is Wordsworth. Commonly supposed to have refrained from describing what he had not seen with the

bodily eye, and to have read little save his own poetry, he was
in fact a systematic student in the field of travel and observation, for the ends of poetical composition.   Accordingly, he
writes to Archdeacon Wrangham, perhaps in 1811:   "You
inquire about old books; you might almost as well have asked
for my teeth as for any of mine.   The only modern books that I
read are those of travels, or such as relate to matters of fact—
and the only modern books that I care for."   What they meant
to him may be seen in *Ruth*, which is full of images from Bartram—the magnolia, the cypress, green savannas, and scarlet
flowers that set the hills on fire; in *The Complaint of a Forsaken
Indian Woman*, based on Hearne; in the address to Hartley
Coleridge, reminiscent of Carver; in Book Third of *The Prelude*, where the ideal environment for a university and its
students is clearly that of Bartram's "Alatamaha" River,
"where the generous and true sons of liberty securely dwell";
and in Book Third of *The Excursion*.   Here the Solitary, a returned American traveller, first relates his dissatisfaction with
the "unknit Republic," echoing Ashe, and English opinion in
the year 1814, and then tells of his vain search for the natural
man of Rousseau.   He found little more to please him than
"the Muckawiss," of Carver:

> So, westward, tow'rd the unviolated woods
> I bent my way; and, roaming far and wide,
> Failed not to greet the merry Mocking-bird;
> And, while the melancholy Muccawiss
> (The sportive bird's companion in the grove)
> Repeated o'er and o'er his plaintive cry,
> I sympathised at leisure with the sound;
> But that pure archetype of human greatness,
> I found him not.   There, in his stead, appeared
> A creature, squalid, vengeful, and impure;
> Remorseless, and submissive to no law
> But superstitious fear, and abject sloth.

The Solitary is not Wordsworth, but a dramatically conceived
malcontent.   The animating note that is characteristic of
American travel at its best was sounded, not by English poets
in the time of George the Third, but forty years before the

close of the French and Indian War in Berkeley's anticipatory
lines *On the Prospect of Planting Arts and Learning in America:*

> There shall be sung another golden age,
> The rise of empire and of arts . . .
> Westward the course of empire takes its way.

# CHAPTER II

# The Early Drama, 1756–1860

OUR native drama, even though it antedated the novel and the short story, has practically no history until the latter half of the eighteenth century. The first drama written in this country which is now in existence, the satirical farce, *Androborus*, was printed, it is true, in 1714. It was by Governor Richard Hunter[1] of New York, but as he was an Englishman, the interest in his work is limited to its representation of local conditions. *Androborus* was not acted, and had no influence in the development of an acting drama. The two forces which seem to have led to the production of a native play upon the stage were the indirect influence of the early performances of masques and of dramatic odes and dialogues at the colleges, and more directly, the acting of the first regular company of professional players.

The earliest college exercise, including original composition, that has survived, is Francis Hopkinson's revision of *The Masque of Alfred*, originally written by Thomson and revised by Mallet in 1751, which deals with the invasion of England by the Danes. It was performed, according to Hopkinson's statement,[2] several times during the Christmas holidays of 1756–7 in the College of Philadelphia.[3] Hopkinson's original lines number more than two hundred, besides a new prologue and epilogue, and new scenes are introduced so that the masque may be considered as in large measure original. What makes

---

[1] For a description of *Androborus*, see Ford, P. L., *The Beginnings of American Dramatic Literature* in *The New England Magazine*, Feb., 1894, New Series, vol. IX., No. 6, p. 674.

[2] See *The Pennsylvania Gazette*, 20 and 27 Jan.; 3 and 10 Feb., 1757, for a detailed account of the Masque, giving Hopkinson's lines.

[3] Now the University of Pennsylvania.

it of special interest is the fact that Thomas Godfrey, our first dramatist, who grew up under the tutelage of William Smith, Provost of the College, and who was a close friend of Hopkinson, was in all probability prompted to write by witnessing this and similar early attempts at dramatic composition.[1]

Among these college exercises others that have survived are *An Exercise Containing a Dialogue and Ode Sacred to the Memory of his late Gracious Majesty, George II*, performed at the public commencement in the College of Philadelphia, 23 May, 1761, the dialogue being by the Rev. Dr. William Smith, the first Provost, and the ode by Francis Hopkinson. A similar exercise on the accession of George III was performed at the public commencement on 18 May, 1762. The epilogue on this occasion was by the Rev. Jacob Duché, Hopkinson's classmate and afterwards chaplain of Congress. A similar entertainment, *The Military Glory of Great Britain*, was performed at the commencement in the College of New Jersey,[2] 29 September, 1762, while there is evidence of dramatic interest at Harvard College if not dramatic authorship as early as 1758.[3]

Of more direct influence, however, on early dramatic writing, were the performances of plays by the company under David Douglass. There seem to have been theatrical performances in this country since 1703,[4] but the permanent establishment of professional acting dates from the arrival of Lewis Hallam and his company from England in 1752. This company acted in Philadelphia in 1754, where Godfrey doubtless saw them, and it was to this company after its reorganization under Douglass in 1758 that he offered his play, *The Prince of Parthia*, which he had finished before the end of 1759. It was not performed at this time, but was acted on 24 April, 1767, at the Southwark Theatre, in Philadelphia, according to an advertisement in

[1] For Hopkinson, see also Book I, Chap. IX.

[2] Now Princeton University.

[3] Matthews, Albert, *Early Plays at Harvard, Nation*, vol. XCVIII, no. 2542, p. 295, 19 March, 1914.

[4] Sonneck, O. G., *Early Opera in America*, 1915, p. 7. See also, for the beginning of theatrical companies, Daly, Charles P., *When Was the Drama Introduced in America?* 1864, reprinted in *Dunlap Soc. Pub.*, Ser. 2, vol. I, 1896; Ford, P. L., *Washington and the Theatre, Dunlap Society Pub.*, Ser. 2, vol. VIII, 1899. For earlier performances by amateurs, see Bruce, P. A., *An Early Virginia Play, Nation*, vol. LXXXVIII, no. 2276, p. 136, 11 Feb., 1909, and Neidig, W. J., *The First Play in America, Nation*, vol. LXXXVIII, no. 2274, p. 86, 28 Jan., 1909.

*The Pennsylvania Journal and Weekly Advertiser* of 23 April, which contains a list of the players who were to take part. Godfrey did not live to see his play, but died in 1763, two years before it was published. This play, the first written by an American to be produced by a professional company, is a romantic tragedy, laid in Parthia about 200 B.C., and is written in blank verse of a flexible and dignified character. It is no unworthy beginning for American dramatic poetry, but it led at the time to no school of writing. It is interesting, however, to note that at a later period the most significant literary drama in this country was produced in the field of tragedy to which *The Prince of Parthia* belongs.

The Pre-Revolutionary period was purely a tentative one. The work of Charlotte Lenox, who was born here but whose plays were written and played in England, hardly concerns us, while such plays as *Ponteach*, by Major Robert Rogers (1766), or *The Disappointment* of Col. Thomas Forrest (1767), since they were not acted, fail to be significant, however tragic the recital of Indian wrongs in the former or however comic the hoax described in the latter may be. The *Conquest of Canada*, performed at the Southwark Theatre in Philadelphia, 17 February, 1773, has been sometimes referred to as "the second American play," but its author, George Cockings, was an Englishman, who wrote the play while in Boston, and it is in any case of little value either in matter or form.

On 20 October, 1774, the Continental Congress convened and passed a recommendation in its Articles of Association— that the colonists "discountenance and discourage all horse racing and all kinds of gaming, cock fighting, exhibitions of shows, plays and other expensive diversions and entertainments." Douglass and his "American Company," which had occupied the theatres in the colonies for almost a quarter century, left for the West Indies and the first period in the history of the American drama was closed.

During the Revolution a number of political satires were written, none of them, however, in strict dramatic form. The most important are *The Adulateur* (1773) and *The Group* (1775), by Mrs. Mercy Warren, of Boston, *The Fall of British Tyranny* (1776), by John Leacock, and the anonymous farce *The Blockheads* (1776), which has been attributed to Mrs.

Warren, but which internal evidence indicates is not by her. They paint the Tory officeholders and the British soldiers in very unflattering colours, but in no worse hues than the satirists on the loyalist side portray their enemies in such products as *The Americans Roused in a Cure for the Spleen* (1775?) or *The Battle of Brooklyn* (1776). There is no conclusive evidence that any of these were acted, though on the title page of *The Group* it is represented "as lately Acted, and to be Reacted, to the Wonder of all Superior Intelligences Nigh Head Quarters at Amboyne." The literary quality is not remarkable in any event, although Mrs. Warren at times writes a blank verse of considerable distinction, but their chief interest lies in their close relation to the great conflict they represent.[1]

The authority of Congress, except when ratified by action of the several states, did not extend beyond a recommendation to discontinue plays, but with the exception of a brief season in 1778 at the Southwark Theatre in Philadelphia, the activities of the Baltimore Company which began in 1781, and the later ventures of Ryan's Company in New York, the wishes of Congress were generally respected. With the coming of peace, the feeling against plays began to lessen. Lewis Hallam, the younger, returned to Philadelphia in 1784, and when he was coldly received there took to New York the reorganized American Company that was to be so closely associated with the history of the drama in that city. From the point of view of the production of dramatic writing, however, nothing is worthy of record until 1787.

In that year, dramatic performances were given by the American Company in New York, Philadelphia, Baltimore, and Annapolis. There was a more decided interest in things theatrical, but most important was the production in New York on 16 April, 1787, of *The Contrast* by Royall Tyler, the first American comedy to be produced by a professional company. As had been the case with Godfrey, the local company served as the inspiration for Tyler. The theme of the play is the contrast between simple native dignity as typified in Colonel Manly and imported foppery and follies represented by Dimple, Charlotte, and Letitia. The most important character, however, is that of Jonathan, the servant of Manly, who is the prototype of a

---

[1] For Mrs. Warren see also Book I, Chap. IX.

long succession of stage Yankees. Tyler also wrote a comic opera in two acts, *May Day in Town or New York in an Uproar*, performed 18 May, 1787, in New York, and after his return to Boston produced a dramatic satire entitled *A Georgia Spec. or Land in the Moon*, aimed at the rage for speculating in the Georgia lands of the Yazoo Purchase. It was played in Boston and New York in 1797.[1]

Important historically as Tyler was, this period is dominated by the personality of William Dunlap, whose first acted play, *The Father*, performed in New York on 7 September, 1789, was a comedy of manners inspired by the success of *The Contrast*. The success of this play and that of his drama *Leicester*, the second American tragedy, played first under the title of *The Fatal Deception*, on 24 April, 1794, inspired him to go on. According to his own statement he wrote fifty plays[2] "and other pieces unpublished," most of which were acted successfully. These include tragedy, comedy, melodrama, farce, opera, and interlude. He is especially significant as an adaptor of German and French plays, and it was through him that Kotzebue was introduced to the American stage. His first adaptation from Kotzebue, *The Stranger*, played on 10 December, 1798, was from an English version, but the success of this led him to study German, and he adapted and produced at least thirteen plays of Kotzebue, the most significant being *False Shame*, played in 1799, and *The Virgin of the Sun* and *Fraternal Discord*, both acted in 1800. He also adapted Zschokke's *Abaellino* in 1801 with great success, while his earlier adaptation of Schiller's *Don Carlos* in 1799 had been a failure. He did not neglect American themes, however, and one of his most popular plays, *André* (1798), afterwards rewritten as *The Glory of Columbia* (1803), represents the Revolutionary period. His career as manager of the American Company from 1796 to 1805 and the influence he had upon the development of the stage at that time make it fitting to close this period with the date at which financial difficulty forced him to shut his doors. He became connected with the theatre again from 1806 to 1811 and wrote even after that, but his later contribution was comparatively

---

[1] For Tyler, see also Book I, Chap. IX, and Book II, Chaps. III and VI.

[2] A complete bibliography of Dunlap records sixty-five plays. See Bibliography.

unimportant. This period is noteworthy also for the beginning of organized dramatic criticism in New York in the work of a group headed by Peter Irving and Charles Adams, who met after the play, wrote critiques in common, and secured their publication.

The next period begins naturally with the work of James N. Barker of Philadelphia and John Howard Payne of New York. Barker's first play, *Tears and Smiles*, was produced in 1807. This comedy continued the representation of contemporary manners started in *The Contrast* and reflected also the reproduction of recent events in the reference to the Tripoli pirates. In his dramatization of historical American life in *The Indian Princess* (1808), probably the first dramatic version of the Pocahontas story, and *Superstition* (1824), whose motif was the witchcraft delusion in New England, Barker represents the American playwright working with native material. Even in *Marmion* (1812) he put in King James's mouth a ringing speech which, while seeming to apply to Scottish conditions, actually reflected the feeling of America toward England in 1812. *Marmion* was played as late as 1848. Payne, unlike Barker, represents foreign influence. From 1806 when his *Julia, or The Wanderer*, was acted in New York, his dramatic work consisted largely of adaptation from English, French, and German sources. His complete bibliography[1] records sixty-four plays, of which nineteen were published. His most significant work was done in the field of tragedy, such as his *Brutus*, first played in London in 1818, or in comedy like *Charles II*, first performed in London in 1824, while the bulk of his work is composed of melodrama or farce. It was in his opera of *Clari* (1823) that the song *Home Sweet Home* was first sung. Payne's achievement can hardly be properly rated until it is ascertained how much of his work is original, and so far as his treatment of native material goes, he is not so significant as lesser dramatists such as M. M. Noah, who made a brave attempt to dramatize American history in *She Would Be a Soldier* (1819) and *Marion* (1821). *She Would Be a Soldier* was based on the battle of Chippewa in 1812. It proved popular; Forrest acted the Indian Chief in 1826, and it was repeated as late as 1848.

[1] See Bibliography.

There are several reasons why the year 1825 forms a convenient point of departure in the development of the drama. Up to about 1822, largely through the excellence of the company at the Chestnut Street Theatre where Jefferson, Warren, and Wood formed a triumvirate in comedy, Philadelphia had been the theatrical metropolis.[1] Then the growing importance of the port of New York brought an increasing number of foreign actors to that city and made it important for an actor to begin his career there. The year 1825–6, according to Ireland,[2] was remarkable in the history of the New York stage, since it witnessed the first attempt to establish Italian opera with a fully organized company, the beginning of Hackett's career as a comedian, and the combination of Placide, Hilson, Barnes, and Miss Kelly in comedy at the Park Theatre. Most important, this year marked the real beginning of Edwin Forrest's career, both in Philadelphia and in New York.

The very prominence of New York and its proximity to Europe, however much they added to its theatrical prestige, hindered the development of the drama. The succession of English actors who were brought over as "stars" resulted in little encouragement to native writers, while in Philadelphia, under the encouragement of Edwin Forrest and others, a group of dramatists arose whose work became widely known both at home and abroad. For the year 1829–30 Durang lists nine plays by American writers, among them *Pocahontas* by George Washington Custis and John Kerr's first draft of *Rip Van Winkle*.

In 1829 Forrest produced the Indian play of *Metamora* by John Augustus Stone, an actor who lived during his creative period in Philadelphia. The play was a bit bombastic and the speeches of Metamora show a curious mixture of Indian and Ossian, but they are at times very effective and some of the phrases of this play became bywords in the mouths of the people.

Forrest also inspired Robert Montgomery Bird of Philadelphia to write *The Gladiator* in 1831. It was played by Forrest in all parts of the Union and at Drury Lane in 1836. In this play Dr. Bird combined the principal sources of dramatic interest—self-preservation, love of wife, child, and brother, desire

---

[1] See Durang, C., *History of the Philadelphia Stage*, Second Series, Chap. III, and Wemyss, F. C., *Twenty-Six Years of the Life of an Actor-Manager*, vol. I, p. 74.

[2] Ireland, *Records of the New York Stage*, vol. I, p. 483.

for freedom, and personal loyalty—in one central character, expressed this combination of qualities and sentiments in
a vigorous personality, especially suited for Forrest, and
clothed the sentiments expressed in a dignified and flexible
blank verse, varied at times by prose. Bird's tragedy of Peru,
*Oralloossa* (1832), but more especially his *Broker of Bogota*
(1834), both produced by Forrest, are among the most significant
of American dramas. The character of Febro in *The Broker of
Bogota*, energetic, with a middle-class mind but courageous
and with a passion for his children, is admirably conceived.
Bird was also known as a novelist, and one of his romances,
*Nick of the Woods*, dramatized by Louisa Medina in 1838,
proved to be one of the most successful melodramas of the time.
His *Infidel* was dramatized by Benjamin H. Brewster and
played in Philadelphia in 1835, and *The Hawks of Hawk
Hollow* was put on the stage in 1841.[1]

Bird's fellow-citizen, Richard Penn Smith, while not so
great a dramatist, is significant on account of his laudable
attempts to treat native material. At least fifteen of his plays
were performed, eleven of which have been preserved in print
or in manuscript. Of his tragedy *Caius Marius*, in which
Forrest starred, we have only tradition and one scene. His
national plays, *The Eighth of January*, celebrating Jackson's
victory at New Orleans, *William Penn*, his drama of colonial
and Indian life, both played in 1829, and *The Triumph at
Plattsburg* (1830), concerned with McDonough's victory on
Lake Champlain, are vigorous plays and were well received.

Although Robert T. Conrad's historical play of *Jack Cade*,
first acted in Philadelphia in 1835, was not written originally
for Forrest, it was through his acting that it received its best
interpretation. This play was a worthy rival of Bird's dramas
for favour here and abroad. It has a deeper significance than
appears at first glance, for it was made a vehicle for the expression of democratic ideals, and this strengthened its hold on the
American people.

The most significant of this group of Philadelphia dramatists was George Henry Boker. His first play, *Calaynos*, is a
tragedy based on the hatred of the Spaniards for the Moors.
Previous to its performance in Philadelphia in 1851, it had a

[1] See also Book II, Chap. VII.

long run at the Sadlers Wells Theatre in London in 1849, where
Samuel Phelps played Calaynos and G. K. Dickenson, Oliver.[1]
His second tragedy, *Leonor de Guzman*, produced in 1853, was
also laid in Spain and is concerned with the revenge of the
injured Queen, Maria of Portugal. His comedy *The Betrothal*,[2]
produced successfully in Philadelphia and New York in 1850,
and played in England in 1853, is laid in Italy. With the exception of *Under a Mask*, a prose comedy, performed in Philadelphia in 1851, all of Boker's acted plays are of a distinguished
quality. His masterpiece, however, was his tragedy *Francesca
da Rimini*, first acted by E. L. Davenport in 1855 in New
York and Philadelphia, and revived by Lawrence Barrett in
1882 and by Mr. Otis Skinner in 1901. The art with which
the medieval Italian life is depicted, the music of the verse
and the noble conception of Lanciotto, the wronged husband
and brother, lift this tragedy to its deserved place in the first
rank of verse dramas written in the English language during
the nineteenth century.

It is not to be supposed that dramatic talent was limited to
Philadelphia. Epes Sargent and Julia Ward Howe in Boston,
Nathaniel Parker Willis of Boston and New York, Charlotte
Barnes Conner and Anna Ogden Mowatt of New York, and
George H. Miles of Baltimore, to mention only a few, wrote
plays that were definite contributions to literature as well as
practically adapted for the stage. From this point it becomes
necessary, however, owing to the wealth of material and the
imposed limits of the chapter, to treat the plays from the point
of view of types of the drama, rather than as the work of individuals, and this is also most productive of results. Examination of printed plays before 1860, combined with search through
the histories of the stage, discloses about seven hundred plays
by American writers actually placed upon the boards. These
figures are obviously incomplete,[3] but they show at least the

---

[1] *Calaynos*, Lond. ed., n.d., p. 8.

[2] The facts given here and in the Bibliography are based upon the manuscripts
of Boker, in the possession of his family.

[3] The histories of Dunlap, Durang, Wood, Ireland, Brown, Seilhammer, Clapp,
Wemyss, and the MSS. diary of Wood have been carefully examined in preparation
of these figures, but inaccuracies, confusions of titles of acted and printed plays,
difficulty of deciding in all cases as to the nationality of the playwright, etc., make
the statements only relatively exact.

wide activity of our early playwrights notwithstanding the difficulties under which they laboured, and to which one of them so vigorously refers.[1]

Of greatest distinction as literature are the tragedies. About eighty of these were performed, forty of which are extant, and they belong usually to the type known as romantic tragedy. In many cases there is an additional historical interest. Among those dealing with ancient history the most significant are Payne's *Brutus* (1818), Bird's *Gladiator* (1831), David Paul Brown's *Sertorius, the Roman Patriot*, acted by the elder Booth in 1830, and *Waldimar* by John J. Bailey, produced by Charles Kean in 1831 and based on the massacre at Thessalonica in the fourth century A.D. Dunlap's *Leicester* (1794), Barker's *Marmion* (1812), and Conrad's *Jack Cade* (1835) are the best of the dozen dealing with English history, while the historical interest is also definite in such tragedies as John Burk's *Female Patriotism or The Death of Joan D'Arc* (1798), Dunlap's *Virgin of the Sun* (1800), Mrs. Ellet's *Teresa Contarini* (1835), a Venetian tragedy, Epes Sargent's *Velasco*, laid in Burgos in 1046, and acted by E. L. Davenport in 1837, and *Bianca Visconti*, by Nathaniel Parker Willis, based on the career of Francesco Sforza. This play won the prize competition offered by Josephine Clifton, who produced it in 1837 in the principal cities of this country. It held the stage as late as 1852. George H. Miles's prize play of *Mohammed*, performed in 1851, and *Leonor de Guzman* and *Francesca da Rimini* of Boker belong also to this group. Even in the historical tragedies, however, it is the unhappy lot of the main character and the interest of the unfamiliar that hold the attention rather than the background, and there is no clear line to be drawn between those which are historical and those which are not. To the latter class belong Bird's *Broker of Bogota*, and a tragedy of peculiar interest, *Octavia Brigaldi*, by Mrs. Conner, in which she acted in the title rôle in 1837. The play was repeated often in this country and was successfully produced in London. It was based on the killing, in 1828, by Colonel Beauchamp of Kentucky, of Colonel Sharpe, who had seduced Beauchamp's wife before their marriage.[2] Mrs. Conner transferred the scene to Milan

---

[1] See "Letter from the Author" in *Moll Pitcher*, by Joseph S. Jones (1855).
[2] Trent, W. P., *William Gilmore Simms*, 1892, p. 117. W. G. Simms wrote

at the close of the fifteenth century. This preference for foreign scenes, especially in Spain or Italy, remains one of the significant features of this type of play. There has been a tendency to criticize these playwrights for failing to confine themselves to national themes, which in view of the existence of *Hamlet*, *Julius Caesar*, and *Othello* seems beside the point. But there is nothing so satisfactory in a review of our early drama as the steady progress in romantic tragedy from *The Prince of Parthia* in 1767 to *Francesca da Rimini* in 1855.

Little criticism, indeed, may be levelled at the quantity of the plays based upon native themes, historical or contemporary. Disregarding mere pantomime, theatrical history down to 1860 records performances of nearly two hundred plays with a national background, of which some forty are available for examination. First in point of time come the Indian dramas, of which the most important are Stone's *Metamora*, Bird's *Oralloossa*, and the series of plays dealing with the Pocahontas theme. The best of these are *The Indian Princess* by Barker (1808), *Pocahontas or The Settlers of Virginia* by George Washington Custis, first played in Philadelphia, 16 January, 1830, *Pocahontas*, by Robert Dale Owen, acted first 8 February, 1838, in New York, with Charlotte Cushman as Rolfe, and *The Forest Princess*, by Charlotte Barnes Conner, acted in Philadelphia, 16 February, 1848. They all emphasize the love story of Rolfe and Pocahontas and make John Smith a central character. Mrs. Conner alone takes Pocahontas to England, where she dies. Of the colonial dramas, Barker's *Superstition* (1824) and R. P. Smith's *William Penn* (1829) seem the most significant.

As was natural, the Revolution was the most appealing theme. Practically every great event from the Boston Tea Party to the Battle of Yorktown was dramatized. The treason of Arnold and André's capture was a favourite theme and it is to our credit that André usually is a heroic figure.[1] Marion and Franklin were also favourites, but everyone else runs a bad second to Washington so far as the stage is concerned. One of

---

two novels, *Beauchampe* (1842) and *Charlemont* (1856), upon this event, and C. F. Hoffman his *Greyslaer* (1840). *Beauchampe* was dramatized in 1856 by John Savage under the title of *Sybil*, which was frequently played.

[1] See Matthews, Brander, Int. to his reprint of *André* in *Dunlap Soc. Pub.,* Ser. 1, No. 4, 1887.

the most interesting scenes occurs in *Blanche of Brandywine* (1858) by J. G. Burnett, in which Howe deliberately puts himself in Washington's power in order, apparently, to offer him a dukedom. After refusing in terms which are refreshingly human, considering the usual vocabulary allotted to the Father of his Country in literature, Washington calmly lets his antagonist depart in peace. Patriotism must have covered a multitude of sins in this class of drama, for it otherwise is difficult to explain the success of John Burk's *Bunker Hill* (1797), hard to recognize as the work of the author of *Joan D'Arc*. Dunlap's *Glory of Columbia* is not bad, and such a play as *Love in '76* (1857) by Oliver Bunce must have given a good opportunity for a clever actress.

Leaving the Revolution, we find the troubles with the Barbary States celebrated in eight plays, beginning with Mrs. Rowson's *Slaves in Algiers* (1794), which is made a vehicle to express abolition sentiments in general. The War of 1812 was reflected in such popular plays as *She Would Be a Soldier* of Noah (1819), and R. P. Smith's *The Eighth of January* (1829), and *The Triumph at Plattsburg* (1830). As an illustration of the quick reflection of events upon the stage we find a statement in Durang[1] that on 8 December, 1812, there came news of the capture of the *Macedonian* by the *United States* and that on 11 December a patriotic sketch entitled *The Return from a Cruise* was performed at the Chestnut Street Theatre, in Philadelphia, including a part for Captain Decatur. Almost as prompt had been the dramatization of the victory of the *Constitution* over the *Guerrière*. The fight occurred on 31 August, 1812. On 9 September, William Dunlap's *Yankee Chronology* was played in New York, while on 28 September, the opening night, a play was on the stage in both Boston and Philadelphia. Clapp tells us[2] that "in the early days of the theatre, every public event of sufficient importance was immediately dramatized, and during the progress of the war, the spirit was kept up by the frequent production of pieces in honour of our naval victories."

The Mexican War furnished its quota of plays, none, however, of special significance. Nor was the ready appeal to the

---

[1] Durang, First Series, Chap. XLIX.
[2] Clapp, W. W., Jr., *Records of the Boston Stage*, 1853, p. 134.

stage limited to martial themes.   We find the Anti-Masonic
agitation represented in such a play as *Captain Morgan or The
Conspiracy Unveiled* (1827), while toward the close of our period
the adventures of Walker in Nicaragua, the Mormon emigration, and the California gold fever find dramatic expression.
Most important, of course, was the great question of abolition,
reflected in the run of G. L. Aiken's version of *Uncle Tom's
Cabin*, which was first acted at the Museum in Troy, New York,
in September, 1852, and after long runs there and elsewhere was
performed almost nightly in New York City from 18 July, 1853,
to 19 April, 1854.   Though it was not the first[1] stage version it
distanced all others as to popularity.   It follows the book quite
closely in its language but is melodramatic in the extreme and is
really a succession of scenes rather than a play.   The same
criticism may be applied to Mrs. Savage's *Osawattomie Brown*,
which placed on the stage of the Bowery Theatre on 16 December, 1859, a dramatic account of the raid of 1 November.

The line is not easy to draw between these patriotic spectacles, dealing with events that have now become historic, and
the comedies which reflected contemporary manners and
customs.   Both tend to become melodrama, and it would be
fruitless to classify rigidly the large number of melodramatic
comedies that are recorded as having had their day on the stage.
Among plays of which record of performance has been kept,
about four hundred in number, the largest group would be that
of comedy, and it was from this group that the most significant
plays from the point of view of stage development evolved.

In our first comedy, *The Contrast*, Tyler developed the
stage Yankee in Jonathan, and though J. Robinson's *Yorker's
Stratagem* (1792) and Barker's *Tears and Smiles* (1807) contain
Yankee characters, it was not till *The Forest Rose*, by Samuel
Woodworth, was placed on the stage in 1825 that a Yankee
character was developed which permanently held the boards.
The part of Jonathan Plowboy was played afterward by
Henry Placide, G. H. Hill, Joshua Silsbee, and others.   In the
preface[2] to the play it is stated that Silsbee played Jonathan for

[1] See Brown, T. A., *History of the New York Stage*, 1903, vol. 1, pp. 312–319,
for an interesting account of the different dramatizations of *Uncle Tom's Cabin*.
[2] Woodworth, S., *The Forest Rose*, Boston, 1854.   For Woodworth, see also
Book II, Chaps. v and vi.

over one hundred consecutive nights in London.　The comedy, which was accompanied by songs, is an interesting one, the action is quick and the conversation clever.　In 1829 J. H. Hackett transformed the character of Solomon Gundy in Colman's *Who Wants a Guinea?* into Solomon Swop and, re-christening the play *Jonathan in England*, made a great success in it.　Other well-known Yankee parts were Lot Sap Sago in *Yankee Land* (1834) and Deuteronomy Dutiful in *The Vermont Wool Dealer* (1839), both written by C. A. Logan, Jedediah Homebred in *The Green Mountain Boy* (1833) and Solon Shingle in *The People's Lawyer* (1839), both by Joseph S. Jones, and Sy Saco in John A. Stone's prize play of *The Knight of the Golden Fleece* (1834).　These plays are usually of the same type, a comedy or melodrama into which a Yankee comic character has been inserted.　He bears little relation to the play, but it is this very detachment that makes him important, for he is the one spot of reality among a number of stage conventions, and it is no doubt this flavour of earth that secured the warm reception which these plays received.　Read now, they seem hardly to justify it, but they point forward at least to a time when in the hands of an artist like James A. Herne this same material received a more significant treatment.

Another interesting development is represented in the local drama representing actual conditions, frequently of lower life, in the larger cities.　The date of the first production of such a play would be hard to determine.　Dunlap[1] speaks of a *Life in New York, or The Fireman on Duty*, before 1832.　As early as 1829 Hackett appeared in a play called *The Times or Life in New York*, in which he acted a Yankee character.　From the cast, however, as given in Ireland[2] it seems hardly likely that there was much realism in this play, however interesting it is as a point of connection with the species just described.　More promising is the description of *The New York Merchant and His Clerks*, performed in 1843, with scenery "representing the Battery, Wall St., Chatham Square and the Lunatic Asylum."　These plays, however, have not survived, but there can be little doubt that when F. J. Chanfrau made his great success in *A Glance at New York* in 1848, the public had been prepared to

---

[1] Dunlap, *History of the American Theatre*, London, 1833, vol. II, p. 381.

[2] Ireland, vol. I, p. 624.

enjoy the type of play he furnished. The story of the building of this play is an interesting one. It was written by Benjamin A. Baker, the prompter at the Olympic Theatre, who when Mitchell, the manager, had refused to produce it, insisted on its production at his own benefit and had the satisfaction of witnessing the tumultuous reception that Chanfrau received in the part of Mose, the New York fireman. Chanfrau had made a number of imitations of firemen before on the stage, and the play was, therefore, a growth. It is melodramatic, but there is a reality about the scenes in the dives and streets that points forward rather than backward. Baker continued in *New York as It Is* (1848) to exploit Mose, and the interest in that form of play was capitalized immediately by other writers and actors. *Philadelphia as It Is* appeared in 1849, and in Boston George Campbell produced in 1848 a local drama in which a scene in a police court was introduced.[1]

The vogue of these plays continued to the end of our period and beyond, and there is little distinction, so far as type is concerned, to be made between them and such a later play as Augustin Daly's *Under the Gaslight*. Such titles as *The Dry Goods Clerk of New York* (1851), *The Seamstress of New York* (1851), *New York by Gaslight* (1856), *The Poor of New York* (1857), *Life in Brooklyn, its Lights and Shades, its Virtues and Vices* (1858) illustrate the nature of the species perhaps sufficiently, while *Mose in California* (1849) and *Mose in China* (1850) show how cosmopolitan that gentleman became.

Much more important from the artistic standpoint were the comedies proceeding by means of social satire. Here, too, we turn back to our first comedy, *The Contrast*, for the beginning of the type, but while we note in 1841 the production of a "cutting satire upon fashionable life"[2] in the comedy of *Saratoga Springs*, which was very successful, it was not until the production of *Fashion* by Anna Ogden Mowatt on 24 March, 1845, at the Park Theatre in New York that we can chronicle a social satire of any distinction. *Fashion* is a good-humoured satire upon the artificial qualities of society in New York, and introduces the snob who is taken in by a French barber, the merchant ruined by his wife's extravagance, the confidential clerk who blackmails his employer, and as contrasts to these,

---

[1] Clapp, p. 457.      [2] Ireland, vol. II, p. 378.

the true-hearted farmer and his granddaughter who, by her efforts to save the daughter of the self-seeking social striver, almost loses her own lover. These are all types, to be sure, but they are made alive and the dialogue is clever. The play had a great success here and abroad,[1] and may be said to have founded a school of playwriting which lasts to this day. Its immediate successors, however, hardly came up to the standard set by *Fashion*. One of the best of them, *Nature's Nobleman*, produced in New York in 1851, was written by Henry O. Pardey, an English actor, who laid his scenes in Saratoga, Cape May, and a farm in New York State, and established quite well a contrast between American and English types. Mrs. Bateman's *Self*, E. G. Wilkins's *Young New York*, Cornelius Mathews's *False Pretences; or, Both Sides of Good Society*, all played in 1856, become caricature of a descending quality. Perhaps the most clever of the later comedies of social life is *Americans in Paris* by W. H. Hurlbert, performed in 1858.

In romantic comedy, there was very little that could compare with the achievement in romantic tragedy. *The Deformed*, played in 1830, by Richard Penn Smith, has some real merit, though it owes much to Dekker. *Tortesa, the Usurer*, by N. P. Willis, was played by J. W. Wallack in 1839 in New York and later in England, where Lester Wallack played Angelo to his father's Tortesa. It is an excellent play, and the last act, in which the usurer rises to the dignity of self-sacrifice, is especially appealing. Another play in which the two Wallacks were associated, *The Veteran* (1859), written by Lester Wallack, is an entertaining comedy laid in France and Algeria. Boker's *Betrothal* has already been mentioned. Mrs. Mowatt's *Armand, or The Child of the People*, produced in 1847 in New York and in 1849 in London, is a blank verse comedy of some merit. But here again the line between comedy and melodrama is hard to draw. Especially is this true in the plays dealing with Irish life, of which there are a number. One of the most interesting records in this connection is that describing the production, in 1842, after the playwright's death, of the adaptation of the novel of *The Collegians* by Louisa Medina. This play has not survived, but the

---

[1] For an interesting contemporary critique of *Fashion*, see Poe's *Works*, Virginia Edition, vol. XII, pp. 112–121 and 124–129.

As the journals, on which I chiefly depended, had been kept by men of business, intent upon the main object of the enterprise, and but little versed in science, or curious about matters not immediately bearing upon their interests, and as they were written often in moments of fatigue or hurry, amid the inconveniences of wild encampments, they were often meagre in their details, furnishing hints to provoke rather than narratives to satisfy inquiry. I have, therefore, availed myself occasionally of collateral lights supplied by the published journals of other travellers who have visited the scenes described, such as Messrs. Lewis and Clark, Bradbury, Brackenridge, Long, Franchère, and Ross Cox, and make a general acknowledgment of aid received from these quarters.

The work I here present to the public, is necessarily of a rambling and somewhat disjointed nature, comprising various expeditions by land and sea. The facts, however, will prove to be linked and banded together by one grand scheme, devised and conducted by a master spirit; one set of characters, also, continues throughout, appearing occasionally, though sometimes at long intervals, and the whole enterprise winds up by a regular catastrophe; so that the work, without any laboured attempt at artificial construction, actually possesses much of that unity so much sought after in works of fiction, and considered so important to the interest of every history.

While engaged upon *Astoria*, Irving had met at the house of Colonel Astor the picturesque Captain Bonneville, and learning that the Captain possessed a manuscript record of his experiences among the Rocky Mountain hunters, he secured it for a goodly sum, thereupon proceeding to rewrite and amplify it in the customary fashion. From the popular *Adventures of Captain Bonneville* (1837), one gains an indescribable sense of the buoyancy of spirit in the open prairies, and of high tension in the life of the mountaineers, sanguine and alert in the midst of dangers known or surmised.

The general influence of these travellers and observers upon commerce and immigration is rather the affair of the historian and economist. Unquestionably the effect of innumerable guides for emigrants, and statistical works on agriculture, was augmented by books of travel which in substance were not always distinct from these humbler compilations. The trenchant if malevolent Cobbett, glorying in a life of cheerful industry close to the soil, and representing America as neither cast[1] of characters is significant in view of the later dramatization of the same material in Dion Boucicault's *Colleen Bawn*.

The Gothic melodrama, illustrated by Dunlap's *Fontainville Abbey*, played in 1795, or his *Abaellino*, performed in 1801, was popular and in it he had a number of followers, some of whom, like S. B. Judah, in his *Rose of Aragon*, played in 1822, preserved the original meaning of the word Gothic. More interesting, if not more artistic, was the melodrama that dealt with contemporary events, such as Woodworth's *Lafayette or The Castle of Olmutz*, played in 1824, the year of Lafayette's visit to this country. Dunlap's importation of the domestic drama of Kotzebue had also its effect. Some of the dramas of this class, notably Noah's *Wandering Boys*, played first in Charleston in 1812 under the title of *Paul and Alexis*, were vastly popular. Most important in this class was the genesis of *Rip Van Winkle*. As early as 26 May, 1828, Thomas Flynn seems to have played a version of *Rip Van Winkle* in Albany. It was written by an native of Albany.[2] In October, 1829, there was produced in Philadelphia[3] a version written in whole or part by John Kerr, in which W. Chapman and later J. H. Hackett played Rip Van Winkle and "J. Jefferson" played Knickerbocker. This version was very popular and was afterward played in New York. A later play by Charles Burke is an adaptation of this one, with certain changes, notably the preservation of Dame Van Winkle, and the final version of Boucicault and Joseph Jefferson the younger is a development in its turn from Burke's play.

The farce as a species of comedy in the broader sense has already been spoken of in connection with the treatment of certain comic themes. Payne developed a form of farce largely from foreign sources, and W. E. Burton, by the development of farcical characters like the Toodles out of material whose history goes back to sentimental domestic drama, scored one of his greatest popular successes.

The dramatization of American novels calls for a word of comment here. The work of Cooper, W. G. Simms, J. P. Kennedy, C. F. Hoffman, R. M. Bird, T. S. Fay, Mrs. Stowe,

[1] Ireland, vol. II, p. 393.
[2] Phelps, H. S., *Players of a Century*, Albany, 1880.
[3] Durang, Second Series, Chap. L.

and others, was quickly placed on the stage.  It will be noticed that it was chiefly in the sphere of the romance that this was the case, Cooper being the prime favourite.  Though this work was rarely done by a dramatist of distinction, it was often popular.

What impresses one most in a survey of these types of drama is the evidence of organic growth.  It is possible to trace in the development of the drama in this country before the Civil War certain fairly distinct periods.  The first ends with the closing of the theatres in 1774 and has as its principal event the production of *The Prince of Parthia* in 1767.  The second, from 1774 to 1787, includes the Revolutionary satirists and is a transition period.  The third begins with the production of *The Contrast* in 1787 and closes with the termination of Dunlap's first period of managership in 1805.  It was a period of tentative effort, partly under the influence of German and French models.  The fourth period from 1805 to 1825 is one of development, with considerable native effort, but still largely under foreign influence, both English and Continental.  The fifth was a significant and creative period, from 1825 to the Civil War, with its climax in *Francesca da Rimini* in 1855.

This development was interrupted naturally by the Civil War.  What would have been its course had the war not occurred it is perhaps fruitless to speculate.  There were signs of a quickening of dramatic interest in the late fifties under the encouragement of such managers as Lester Wallack and Laura Keene, but the domination of the stage by Dion Boucicault and John Brougham, while it resulted in some significant plays, especially in a later period, was not an unmixed blessing from the point of view of the production of American drama.  The dramatization of English and French novels with resultant long runs, indeed the very success of Boucicault's original dramas, made for conditions in which the work of new playwrights became less in demand.  The old days in which a manager was willing to put on a play for a few nights were going fast, and with them went our early drama.  That its significance in the history of our literature has never been appreciated is due largely perhaps to the fact that some of its most important monuments are still unprinted.  But of its significance both in itself and for the later drama there is no shadow of doubt.

# CHAPTER III

# Early Essayists

I N anticipating Dr. Johnson's advice to fashion his prose style on the model of Addison, Franklin anticipated also the practice of American essay-writers for more than a generation. Like Franklin's *Dogood Papers*, the first essays printed in colonial newspapers were written with a conscious moral purpose. With some spice of wit Timothy Dwight and John Trumbull collaborated in an imitation of *The Spectator* in 1769–70, and between 1785 and 1800 nearly a hundred series of light periodical essays were contributed to various New England journals.[1] Those of the better sort like the "Neighbour" of *The Massachusetts Spy* or the "Metabasist" in *The Farmer's Journal* of Danbury, Connecticut, when not discussing politics, filled their columns with grave moralizing or racy satire on manners. They were widely copied and recopied by other papers, and a few such as Noah Webster's *Prompter* and Mrs. Judith Murray's *Gleaner* attained the distinction of separate publication by reason either of their plain common sense or their studied correctness. In general, the imitation of English models resulted in feeble literary replicas, or in strange patchworks of Yankee homespun with Addisonian finery.

During the first decade of the nineteenth century nearly every literary device and favourite character in the long line of British essayists was reproduced in this country. Isaac Bickerstaff owned an American cousin in Launcelot Langstaff of *Salmagundi*, memories of *l'Espion turc* were evoked by Wirt's *Letters of a British Spy*, and Goldsmith's Lien Chi Altangi dropped a small corner of his mantle on Irving's Mustapha Rub-a-Dub Kheli Khan and S. L. Knapp's Shahcoolen. The shade of Johnson dictated the titles of *The Traveller, The Rural*

[1] Ellis, H. M., *Joseph Dennie and his Circle*, p. 51.

*Wanderer*, *The Saunterer*, and *The Loiterer*, and such editorial pseudonyms as Jonathan Oldstyle, Oliver Oldschool, and John Oldbug were significant of the attempt to catch the literary tone of the previous age. But the essay of manners, a product of leisurely urban life, was not easily adapted to the environment of a sparsely settled, bustling young republic. "Perhaps, indeed," wrote the Rev. David Graham of Pittsburg, "it is impossible to give interest and standing popularity, to a periodical essay paper, constructed upon the model of the British Essayist, in an infant country."[1] Even in the populous cities "where the inhabitants amount to several thousand" there was little interest in the art of living. Reprehensible luxury and eccentric characters were hard to discover. But by dint of persistent attempts the essay of manners was made to grow in the new soil.

Perhaps the most successful "American Addison" was Joseph Dennie (1768–1812), who was "reasonably tinged with literature" while resisting a Harvard education, and after a short trial of the law, devoted his desultory talents to periodical writing until his death. He kindled the first sparks of a reputation by the *Farrago* essays, contributed to various country newspapers, but his *Tablet*, a hopeful weekly paper devoted to *belles lettres*, failed to set Boston ablaze. Yankee readers objected to his exercises in the manner of Goldsmith and Addison as "sprightly rather than moral." While a law-student, Dennie had supplemented his income by reading sermons in unsupplied churches, and now to gain a hearing he fitted each of his lucubrations with a text and tempered his sentiments ostensibly for the pulpit. *The Lay Preacher*, commenced in 1795, won immediate applause. Seven years later John Davis, the traveller, declared it the most widely read work in America, and its popularity contributed largely to the author's success as editor, first of *The Farmer's Weekly Museum* at Walpole, New Hampshire, and finally of that notable literary gazette, the Philadelphia *Port Folio*.

Though Dennie collaborated with his friend Royall Tyler in a mélange of light prose and verse "From the Shop of Messrs. Colon & Spondee," which later developed into a series

[1] *The Pioneer, consisting of Essays, Literary, Moral and Theological*, Pittsburg, 1812. P. 31.

of "Author's Evenings" reminiscent of men and books, his scattered writings were never collected or even completely identified, and his reputation must rest almost entirely upon *The Lay Preacher*. In these papers he sometimes dallied with a trifling subject, or to the indignation of severe critics applied a sacred text to the discussion of Mrs. Radcliffe's romances, or gave free rein to his eccentric humour in denouncing French innovations. But in the main he preserved a solemn front, dimming his wit with sobriety, as in the following extract from "Watchman, what of the night?"

Duty, as well as inclination, urges the Lay Preacher to sermonize, while others slumber. To read numerous volumes in the morning, and to observe various characters at noon, will leave but little time, except the night, to digest the one or speculate upon the other. The night, therefore, is often dedicated to composition, and while the light of the paly planets discovers at his desk the Preacher, more wan than they, he may be heard repeating emphatically with Dr. Young,

"Darkness has much Divinity for me."

He is then alone, he is then at peace. No companions near, but the silent volumes on his shelf, no noise abroad, but the click of the village clock, or the bark of the village dog. The Deacon has then smoked his sixth, and *last* pipe, and asks not a question more, concerning Josephus, or the Church. Stillness aids study, and the sermon proceeds.[1]

In reality, however, Dennie was as fond of conviviality as Steele, and as elegant in dress as Goldsmith. His literary pose had little in common with his actual habits of composition, as described by a former printer's devil of *The Farmer's Museum:*

One of the best of his Lay Sermons was written at the village tavern, directly opposite to the office, in a chamber where he and his friends were amusing themselves with cards. It was delivered to me by piece-meal, at four or five different times. If he happened to be engaged in a game, when I applied for copy, he would ask some one to play his hand for him, while he could "give the devil his due." When I called for the closing paragraph of the sermon, he said, "Call again in five minutes." "No," said Tyler, "I'll write

[1] *The Lay Preacher* (1796), p. 103.

the improvement for you." He accordingly wrote the concluding paragraph, and Dennie never saw it till it was in print.[1]

No trace of the "nights of mirth and mind" that he shared with "Anacreon" Moore, none of the ready puns that Irving learned to dread, can be found in the pious columns of *The Lay Preacher*. The wonder is, not that Dennie should be forgotten, but that, writing so evidently against the grain, he should have achieved his extraordinary vogue.

Among many young lawyers who found time to use their pens while waiting for briefs, Dennie is historically important as one of the first to adopt literature as a profession. Others who continued to write as an avocation were easily allured into religious or political controversy, for the renown of the *Federalist* papers was yet new. So Royall Tyler, author of several plays[2] and a series of periodical observations entitled *Trash*, besides a waggish account of Dennie's first appearance at the bar, became more a chief justice and less a man of letters after the publication of his novel, *The Algerine Captive*, in 1797.[3] David Everett, now barely remembered as the author of

> You'd scarce expect one of my age
> To speak in public on the stage,

wrote essays called *Common Sense in Dishabille* for *The Farmer's Museum*, but his inclination for *belles lettres* soon yielded to a maturer passion for writing political leaders and commentaries on the Apocalypse. Only the hardiest political writings could survive the frost of piety in New England.

Literary essays in the South were almost neglected in the general enthusiasm for forensic and pulpit oratory, or when written, reflected the formal style of public speeches. The most persistent essayist was William Wirt (1772–1834), who commenced lawyer with "a copy of Blackstone, two volumes of Don Quixote, and a volume of Tristram Shandy," gave sufficient attention to the first item of his library to become Attorney-General of the United States, and left as his chief literary monument a biography of Patrick Henry. *The Letters of a British Spy*, first printed in the Richmond *Argus* for 1803,

---

[1] J. T. Buckingham, *Specimens of Newspaper Literature* (1852), vol. II, p. 197.
[2] See also Book II, Chap. II.           [3] See also Book II, Chap. VI.

justly gained him a reputation as a critic and master of eloquence.[1] A temperateness, discernment, and sincerity unusual in the journalism of the day marked his observations on Virginia society and his strictures on the style of public men, and his descriptive powers, best illustrated in the striking picture of the Blind Preacher, elevated the *Spy* at once into the class of "elegant native classical literature." Later in conjunction with friends Wirt wrote ten essays, collected as *The Rainbow*, dealing with sundry political and social questions. These, like *The Old Bachelor*, in which he set himself to follow more closely the admired model of Addison, were too thickly studded with florid passages, oratorical climaxes, and didactic fulminations. Wirt's natural charm of manner survived only in his playful private letters.[2] Nothing of permanent mark came from the facile pen of William Crafts, editor of the Charleston *Courier*, and the ornate prose of Hugh Swinton Legaré is that of the scholar rather than of the familiar essayist.

New York and Philadelphia were comparatively free from the blight of theology and the bane of eloquence, though the latter city seems to have suffered from a constitutional profundity which even Dennie could not entirely overcome. It gave to the world nothing better than the *Didactics* of Robert Walsh. The commercial interests of Manhattan could claim little attention from young men of wit and spirit, but leisure and a society both cosmopolitan and congenial afforded them ample opportunity and provocation for literary *jeux d'esprit*. When the busy savant, Samuel Latham Mitchill, presided at the Sour Krout crowned with cabbage leaves or burlesqued his own erudition in jovial speeches at the Turtle Club, what wonder if Irving and the "lads of Kilkenny" found time to "riot at Dyde's on imperial champagne" or to sally out to Kemble's mansion on the Passaic—the original of Cockloft Hall—for a night of high fun and jollification. Dr. Mitchill's *Picture of New York*, with a wealth of geological and antiquarian lore travestied in the first part of the "Knickerbocker" *History*, records the numerous landmarks and traditions of

---

[1] An imitation called "The British Spy in Boston" appeared in *The Port Folio* for 3–24, Nov., and 22 Dec., 1804. An amusing parody of these followed on 26 Jan., 1805.

[2] See also Book II, Chaps. I and **XVII**.

the city. Corlaer's Hook was then something more than a memory, Hell Gate was still a menace to navigation, the Collect was not all filled up, and the tolls levied at Kissing Bridge formed a standing jest. In such an environment the tradition of Steele and Goldsmith culminated not unworthily with *Salmagundi*, a buoyant series of papers ridiculing the follies of 1807. Thereafter imitation of Addison could no further go. Moreover, in announcing with mock gravity their intention "simply to instruct the young, reform the old, correct the town, and castigate the age" the authors of *Salmagundi* exposed the prevailing overearnestness of the grim guardians of public virtue and taught their readers to expect entertainment as well as instruction from writers of the essay.

James Kirke Paulding (1779–1860), Washington Irving's chief assistant in this youthful venture, shared with his collaborator a love of English letters, a vivid recollection of the New York of their boyhood, and a keen eye for odd whimwhams and curiosities of character. So closely akin were they in spirit that to identify completely the contributions of either writer would be a hopeless task, but the papers known to have been written wholly or in large measure by Paulding indicate that his part in the undertaking was not inferior to Irving's. Nor was Paulding less a master of a graceful and vivacious style, formed by his boyish reading of *The Citizen of the World*. It was he who first sketched the characters of the Cockloft family, and in the case of "Mine Uncle John" he took the likeness of a real uncle as deftly as Irving portrayed the lively Mrs. Cooper in Sophie Sparkle or the fastidious Joseph Dennie in Launcelot Langstaff. Aunt Charity, who "died of a Frenchman," was apparently a joint production. The two writers might have acquired from Steele and his successors the art of drawing crotchety characters, if not the fondness for detecting them, but the inevitable urban setting of the British essays afforded few models for such studies of nature as the "Autumnal Reflections" of the seventeenth *Salmagundi* paper. There Paulding—who undoubtedly had a hand in it—discovered a happy talent for combining gentle melancholy with landscape description which remained one of the most attractive elements in his varied writings. Almost the only quotable passages in his pretentious poem, *The Back-*

*woodsman,*[1] have to do with wild and romantic scenery, and when in 1819 he revived the name, though not the sparkle of *Salmagundi*, the serious admonitory air of his continuation was sometimes freshened by vignettes of the Hudson valley or the frontier. After the second series of "Old Sal," Paulding wrote few essays except the unremarkable *Odds and Ends* contributed in his old age to *The Literary World*, but in his *Letters from the South*, in his tales and novels,[2] and even in his prose satires he found opportunities to manifest his delight in American scenes. Unlike Irving, he never travelled, and the beauties of his native land remained in his eyes unrivalled.

While the author of *Bracebridge Hall* and the *Alhambra* was cultivating his cosmopolitan fancy in many lands, Paulding grew more and more intensely local. In accepting the cares of a family and of official position—he was eventually Secretary of the Navy under Van Buren—he lessened his opportunities to develop his literary talent, and at the same time increased his desire to exalt the glory of American letters. Unusually sensitive to the faults of his fellow-countrymen, he too often went out of his way to rail at primogeniture, lotteries, French fashions, paper money, and the charities of "those venerable married ladies, and thrice venerable spinsters, who go about our cities like roaring lions, doing good." When in such works as in *Merry Tales of the Three Wise Men of Gotham* (1826), and the *New Mirror for Travellers* (1828), he undertook to quiz political or fashionable failings, his irony was not infrequently more severe than just. The same objection may be applied with double force to the acrimonious squibs which he hurled at British critics who dared sneer at American innovations.[3] Like many of his contemporaries Paulding could not refrain from using his stylus as a dagger whenever patriotically aroused, and he lost no opportunity to flaunt the merits of republican institutions before the "crowned heads" of Europe. He may best be remembered as an author whose faults and virtues combined to make him exclusively and eminently national.

*Salmagundi* was but one of a number of hopeful productions issued by two or three young men in combination or even by literary clubs after the traditional fashion of periodical essays.

---

[1] See also Book II, Chap. v.      [2] See also Book II, Chap. vii.
[3] See also Book II, Chap. i.

In 1818–19 a Baltimore society, which claimed Wirt as a member, printed a fortnightly leaflet called *The Red Book*, containing, besides verse, occasional papers by the future novelist, John Pendleton Kennedy.[1]   William Tudor, one of the Monthly Anthology Club of Boston, and first editor of *The North American Review*, collected his *Miscellanies* in 1821, and in that and the following year a more original member of the same coterie, the elder Richard Henry Dana,[2] edited and mainly wrote the six numbers of *The Idle Man*, perhaps the most notable competitor of Irving's *Sketch Book*.   Much of Dana's work may be paralleled elsewhere; the half-Shandean meditation on a suitable title for his periodical, the sketches of Ned Fillagree and Bob Brazen and of the whimsical old gentleman and his club, the eulogy of Kean's acting, and the plea for a more confident and independent criticism of American books—though this last does not lack vehemence—are not essentially different from such stuff as essays were usually composed of.   But the papers on " Domestic Life " and the "Musings" on the power of the imagination redeem their triteness of subject by a noble sincerity and depth of poetic insight not unworthy of a prose Wordsworth.   Three numbers of *The Idle Man* are taken up by tales of gloomy intensity which fall within the compass of this chapter only as they illustrate the ease with which the periodical essay might merge with the then unrecognized short story. Not a few contributions in the *Miscellanies* of Verplanck, Bryant, and Sands (originally published as *The Talisman* for 1828, 1829, 1830) were made of a descriptive or didactic essay prefixed to a simple tale, and the gleanings from numerous annuals included by the publisher, S. G. Goodrich, in *Sketches from a Student's Window* (1841), can hardly be classed except as an indistinguishable compound of essays and stories. In none of these cases are the narratives apologues or character sketches of the sort traditionally associated with the periodical essay.

Dana, though he continued to live in Cambridge, was intimately connected with Bryant and his set.   *The Idle Man* was printed in New York, and it was there, naturally enough, that the vein opened by Irving and Paulding in *Salmagundi* was most consistently followed by writers of the Knickerbocker group, many of them contributors at one time or another to

---

[1] See also Book II, Chap. VII.          [2] See also Book II, Chap. V.

Colonel Morris's *New York Mirror*. From that paper Theodore Sedgwick Fay, better known as the author of successful but mediocre novels, clipped enough of his occasional writings to fill two volumes entitled *Dreams and Reveries of a Quiet Man* (1832). Save for the lively satire of the *Little Genius* essays and a delicious travesty of Mrs. Trollope, there is little of other than historical interest in Fay's pictures of New York life. Distinctly in better form are the *Crayon Sketches* by William Cox, an English printer once in the employ of *The Mirror*. In his fondness for the theatre, his devotion to Scott, and his love of old English scenes and customs, Cox had much in common with Irving. Here too should be mentioned the editors, Park Benjamin of *The American Monthly Magazine* and *Brother Jonathan*, poet and miscellaneous writer; Lewis Gaylord Clark of *The Knickerbocker Magazine;* and his twin brother, Willis Gaylord Clark, a Philadelphia journalist whose "Ollapodiana" papers inherited something of Lamb and anticipated something of Holmes.[1]

Flashes of cleverness, geniality, and quiet humour, however, could not conceal the lack of originality and barrenness of invention that were becoming more and more apparent among the remoter satellites of Geoffrey Crayon. The stream of discursive literature was indeed running dry when Nathaniel Parker Willis (1806–61) burst into prominence like a spring freshet, frothy, shallow, temporary, but sweeping all before it. This prince of magazinists, precociously celebrated as a poet even before his graduation from Yale in 1823, and petted by society in this country and abroad, has suffered the fate of other ten days' wonders. Though the evanescent sparkle and glancing brilliance of his *A l'Abri*, less extravagantly known by its later title of *Letters from under a Bridge*, fully deserved Lowell's praise, though it is possible to understand the popularity of his vivid, vivacious glimpses of European society in *Pencillings by the Way* and the vogue of his clever "Slingsby" stories in *Inklings of Adventure*, yet it cannot be denied that Willis too often merited the charges of affectation and mawkishness which we still instinctively associate with the elaborately gilded backs of his many volumes. Unluckily he wrote himself out just at the time when his necessities compelled him to have

[1] See also Book II, Chap. xx.

continuous recourse to his pen for a livelihood. His later books sound like a parody of his true manner. It is unnecessary, therefore, to dwell upon the reasons for the decline of his immense reputation; they are obvious.

Nor is it needful to distinguish the paste from the genuine in the composition of the man himself; to defend him from the charge of puppyism by insisting upon his kindliness to younger authors. All that concerns us here is to indicate in what ways Willis inaugurated a temporary but essential phase in the development of the essay and indeed of American letters. The time had come to break with the smooth, dry, elegant style. Willis's romantic and sentimental ardour influenced more than his choice of subject; it dictated his whole manner. He was the most formless of writers. His eclectic, tentative genius readily expressed itself, and often with great charm, in amorphous informal blends of essay, letter, and story. Fleeting impressions, "dashes at life," ephemera, "hurry-graphs" were his forte. In an established form like the novel he was never successful. Striving to be original at all costs, he first embellished, then later mutilated the English language, sticking it full of foreign phrases, coined words, and oddities of diction culled from all times and localities. If these things seem intolerable when compared to the sure classic perfection of Irving's style, we must remember that fluidity is essential to the innovator. Willis followed no tradition, good or bad. That with no guide but his own not infallible taste he should have reached at his best an easy, supple grace of manner, never for a moment tedious, is an evidence of uncommon powers, and even his weaknesses, his not infrequent soft spots, show that at least he was independent of the methods of eighteenth-century prose.

In this respect Willis has been compared to Leigh Hunt, whom in several ways he certainly resembled, but he was not, like Hunt, an omnivorous reader. The social sense was stronger in him than literary instinct; the merits of his best work are the merits of lively chat. During his European wanderings he learned more from men than from books, and from women most of all. His Diotima was Lady Blessington, whose literary dinners and *soirées* were duly, in *The New York Mirror*, dashed at by his free pencil. At Gore House he heard gossip of Byron, saw D'Israeli in action, and met Rogers, Procter, Moore, and Bulwer, men of letters and men of the world. After such models Willis shaped his own career. He luxuriated in drawing-rooms and shone at dinners,

> The topmost bright bubble on the wave of The Town.

With his rapid glances into the kaleidoscope of society he combined—for his readers—views of famous places, anecdotes of travel, reflections by the way, descriptions of scenery, and observations on customs and characters, in all a delightfully varied mixture and exactly suited to his tastes and abilities. In America he wrote with the same minuteness and freshness of his rural life and rural neighbours at Glenmary and Idlewild, painted vivid word-pictures of such beauty spots as Nahant or Trenton Falls, or sketched fashionable life at Ballston and Saratoga in the days when those watering places were in their first glory. There where woods and streams were enlivened by flowered waistcoats, pink champagne, and the tinkle of serenades, Willis found a setting for some of his most characteristic writing. Jaunty and impermanent as the society it portrayed, his pages yet contain the most valuable deposit left by what Professor Beers has happily called the "Albuminous Age" of American literature.[1]

A more reserved, though hardly less voluminous writer than Willis, was the critic, biographer, and essayist, Henry Theodore Tuckerman, born in Boston in 1813 and from 1845 until his death in 1871 a resident of New York. As a young man he twice spent a year or two abroad, of which the fruits were an *Italian Sketch Book* in 1835 and several other volumes of travel. Meanwhile he had been reading widely, studying art, and meeting authors and painters. These things combined with a native fineness of temperament to preserve him from falling into the verbal excesses of Willis. Whatever else Tuckerman lacked, he was not wanting in good taste.

As a critic Tuckerman earned the praise of Irving for his "liberal, generous, catholic spirit." The solid merits of his *Thoughts on the Poets* were admired in Germany, where the

---

[1] Professor H. A. Beers has in every respect said the last word on Willis in his *Life* (*American Men of Letters*) and Introduction to *Selected Prose* (1885).

work was translated. But more popular in this country were *Characteristics of Literature* and *Essays, Biographical and Critical*, which illustrate various types of genius by little biographies of representative men. Addison, for instance, appeared—with no reference to Dennie—as the Lay Preacher. Many introductions, magazine articles on literature, and two books on American artists gave evidence of Tuckerman's critical versatility.

His cosmopolitan training is equally apparent in his familiar essays. *The Optimist* (1850) was nearly akin to the miscellaneous reflections sometimes imbedded in his early books of travel. It was followed by *The Criterion*, more appropriately known in England as *The Collector*, in 1866. Antiquarian in spirit, fond of mingling bits of book-lore with personal reminiscence, Tuckerman picks his meditative and discriminating way along the byways of literature and life. Authors, Pictures, Inns, Sepulchres, Holidays, Bridges, equally provoke his ready flow of illustrative anecdote and well-chosen quotation. With Longfellow and others, he did much to familiarize the American public with a wide range of literature. His cosmopolitanism, however, though of considerable service to his contemporaries, prevented him from interpreting the America that he knew to other countries or to after times. His pleasantly pedantic essays are no longer either novel or informing. Lowell and Whipple have left him scarcely a corner of his chosen field.

# CHAPTER IV

# Irving

WASHINGTON IRVING was born in William Street, New York City, 3 April, 1783. As this was the year in which the colonies finally achieved the independence for which they had been fighting for seven years, Irving may be regarded as the first author produced in the new republic.

The writer recalls that he visited Sunnyside with his father a year or two before the death of Irving and heard him narrate, doubtless not for the first time, how, when he was a youngster a year old, his nurse had held him up in her arms while Washington was passing by on horseback, in order that the General might place his hand on the head of the child who bore his name. "My nurse told me afterwards," said Irving, "that the General lifted me in his arms up to the pommel of his saddle and bestowed upon me a formal blessing." The listening boy looked, with reverential awe, at the head that had been touched by the first president, but when later he told his father about Irving's words, the father said: "You did not see the spot that Washington touched." "And why not?" was the natural question. "You goose," came the retort, "do you not know that Mr. Irving wears a wig?"

Washington Irving was prevented by poor health from following his two elder brothers to Columbia College. His formal training was limited to a course of a few years in the public schools of the day. He had always, however, encouraged in himself a taste for reading and an interest in human affairs so that his education went on steadily from year to year. His father, a Scotchman by birth, had built up an importing business and ranked well among the leading merchants of the city. The family comprised in all five sons and two daughters. The relations to each other of these brothers and sisters were always closely sympathetic, and throughout the record of Irving's career the reader is impressed with the loyal service rendered, first, by the elder brothers to the younger, and later, when the family property had disappeared and the earnings of the youngster had become the mainstay of the family, by Washington himself to his seniors, and to his nieces.

In 1804, Irving, who had just attained his majority, made his first journey to Europe. His father had died some years earlier, and the direction of the family affairs was in the hands of the eldest brother William. The trip seems to have re-established Washington's health, which had been a cause of anxiety to his brothers. After a voyage of forty-two days he landed in Bordeaux, whence he journeyed to Paris. He then travelled by way of Marseilles to Genoa, from which point he went by stage-coach through some of the picturesque regions in Italy. It was on these trips that he secured his first impressions of the Italian hill country and of the life of the country folk, impressions that were utilized later in the *Tales of a Traveller*. From Naples, crossing to Palermo, he went by stage to Messina, and he was there in 1805 when the vessels of Nelson passed through the straits in their search for the combined French and Spanish fleet under Villeneuve, a search which culminated in the great victory at Trafalgar.

Journeying in Europe during those years of war and of national upheaval was a dangerous matter. Irving was stopped more than once, and on one occasion was arrested at some place in France on the charge of being an English spy. He seems to have borne the troublesome interruptions with a full measure of equanimity, and he used each delay to good purpose as an opportunity for a more leisurely study of the environment and of the persons with whom he came into touch. He returned to New York early in 1806, shortly after Europe had been shaken by the battle of Austerlitz.[1]

Irving was admitted to the bar in November, 1806, having previously served as attorney's clerk, first with Brockholst Livingston and later with Josiah Ogden Hoffman. The law

---

[1] During these journeys he took notes, wrote them out in a full journal, portions of which are shortly to be published, and utilized his material in elaborate letters to his relations.

failed, however, to exercise for him any fascination, and his practice did not become important. He had the opportunity of being associated as a junior with the counsel who had charge of the defence of Aaron Burr in the famous trial held in Richmond in June, 1807. The writer remembers the twinkle in the old gentleman's eye when he said in reply to some question about his legal experiences, "I was one of the counsel for Burr, and Burr was acquitted." In letters written from Richmond at the time, he was frank enough, however, to admit that he had not been called upon for any important service. During Irving's brief professional association with Hoffman, he was accepted as an intimate in the Hoffman family circle, and it was Hoffman's daughter Matilda who was the heroine in the only romance of the author's life. He became engaged to Matilda when he was barely of age, but the betrothal lasted only a few months, as she died suddenly at the age of seventeen. At the time of Irving's death it was found that he was still wearing on his breast a locket containing her miniature and a lock of hair that had been given to him half a century before.

The first literary undertaking to which Irving's pen was devoted, apart from a few ephemeral sketches for one of the daily papers, was a serial publication issued at irregular intervals during 1807–08, under the title of *Salmagundi*. In this work, Irving had the collaboration of his brother William and his friend James K. Paulding.[1] The *Salmagundi* papers, reissued later in book form, possess, in addition to their interest as humorous literature, historical value as pictures of social life in New York during the first decade of the nineteenth century.

The famous *History of New-York* was published in 1809. The mystery surrounding the disappearance of old Diedrich Knickerbocker, to whom was assigned the authorship, was preserved for a number of months. The first announcement of the book stated that the manuscript had been found by the landlord of the Columbian Hotel in New York among the effects of a departed lodger, and had been sold to the printer in order to offset the lodger's indebtedness. Before the manuscript was disposed of, Seth Handaside, the landlord, inserted in New York and Philadelphia papers an advertisement describing

[1] See also Book II, Chaps. I, III, V, VII.

Mr. Knickerbocker and asking for information about him. When acknowledgment of the authorship of the book was finally made by Irving, it was difficult for his fellow New Yorkers to believe that this unsuccessful young lawyer and attractive "man about town" could have produced a work giving evidence of such maturity and literary power. He had secured an excellent position in New York society, a society which in the earlier years of the century was still largely made up of the old Dutch families. In the "veracious chronicle" of Mr. Knickerbocker free use was made of the names of these historic families, and it is related that not a few of the young author's Dutch friends found it difficult to accord forgiveness for the liberty that had been taken with their honourable ancestors in making them the heroes of such rollicking episodes.

After a brief editorial experience in charge of a Philadelphia magazine called the *Analectic*, to which he contributed some essays later included in *The Sketch Book*, Irving enjoyed for a few months the excitement of military service. He was appointed a colonel on the staff of Governor Tompkins, and during the campaign of 1814 was charged with responsibilities in connection with the defence of the northern line of New York.

In 1810, Irving had been taken into partnership with his two brothers, Peter and Ebenezer, who were carrying on business as general merchants and importers; and on the declaration of peace in 1814 he was sent by his firm to serve as its representative in Liverpool. If the business plans of that year had proved successful, it is possible that Irving might for the rest of his life have remained absorbed in commercial undertakings, but in 1818 the firm was overtaken by disaster and the young lawyer-merchant (never much of a lawyer and by no means important as a merchant) found himself adrift in England with small funds and with no assured occupation or prospects. He had already come into friendly relations with a number of the leading authors of the day, a group which included Scott, Moore, Southey, and Jeffrey. Scott had in fact sought him out very promptly, having years earlier been fascinated by the originality and the humour shown in *The History of New-York*.

After a couple of years of desultory travelling and writing, Irving completed a series of papers which were published in

New York in 1819–20 and in London in 1820, under the title of *The Sketch Book*. It is by this volume that he is today best known among readers on both sides of the Atlantic. The book has been translated into almost every European tongue, and for many years it served, and still serves, in France, in Germany, and in Italy as a model of English style and as a text-book from which students are taught their English. In this latter rôle, it took, to a considerable extent, the place of *The Spectator*.

The publication by Murray of *The Sketch Book*, and two years later of *Bracebridge Hall*, brought Irving at once into repute in literary circles not only in Great Britain, but on the Continent. In 1826, after a year or two chiefly spent in travelling in France, Germany, and Italy, he was appointed by Alexander Everett, at that time Minister to Spain, attaché to the Legation at Madrid, and this first sojourn in Spain had an important influence in shaping the direction of Irving's future literary work. In July, 1827, he brought to completion his biography of Columbus, later followed by the account of the *Companions of Columbus* (1831). The *Columbus* was published in London and in Philadelphia in 1828 and secured at once cordial and general appreciation. Southey wrote from London: "This work places Irving in the front rank of modern biographers"; and Edward Everett said that "through the Columbus, Irving is securing the position of founder of the American school of polite learning." Irving continued absorbed and fascinated with the examination of the Spanish chronicles. He made long sojourns in Granada, living for a great part of the time within the precincts of the Alhambra, and later he spent a year or more in Seville. He occupied himself collecting material for the completion of *The Conquest of Granada*, published in 1829, and for the *Legends of the Alhambra*, published in 1832.

In 1828, Irving declined an offer of one hundred guineas to write an article for *The Quarterly Review*, of which his friend Murray was the publisher, on the ground, as he wrote, "that the Review [then under the editorship of Gifford] has been so persistently hostile to our country that I cannot draw a pen in its service." This episode may count as a fair rejoinder to certain of the home critics who were then accusing Irving (as half a century later Lowell was, in like manner, accused) of having become so much absorbed in his English sympathies as to have lost his patriotism.

In 1829, Irving was made a member of the Royal Academy of History in Madrid, and having in the same year been appointed Secretary of Legation by Louis McLane, he again took up his residence in London. Here, in 1830, the Royal Society of Literature voted to him as a recognition of his "service to history and to literature" one of its gold medals. The other medal of that year was given to Hallam for his *History of the Middle Ages*. A little later Oxford honoured Irving with the degree of Doctor of Laws. The ceremony of the installation was a serious experience for a man of his shy and retiring habits. As he sat in the Senate Hall, the students saluted him with cries of "Here comes old Knickerbocker," "How about Ichabod Crane?" "Has Rip Van Winkle waked up yet?" and "Who discovered Columbus?"

In 1832, Irving returned to New York, having been absent from his country for seventeen years. His fellow citizens welcomed him, not a little to his own discomfiture, with a banquet given in the City Hall, where the orator of the evening addressed him as the "Dutch Herodotus." Later in the year, he made a journey through the territory of the Southwest, an account of which he published under the title of *A Tour on the Prairies* (1835). His description of St. Louis as a frontier post and of the great wilderness extending to the west of the Mississippi still makes interesting reading. Returning from his journey by way of New Orleans, he visited Columbia, South Carolina, where he was the guest of Governor Hamilton. The Governor, who had just transmitted to the legislature the edict of nullification, insisted that the author must repeat his visit to the state. "Certainly," responded the guest, "I will come with the first troops."

In 1834, Irving declined a Democratic nomination for Congress, and in 1838 he put to one side the Tammany nomination for mayor of New York and also an offer from President Van Buren to make him Secretary of the Navy. In 1842, he accepted from President Tyler the appointment of Minister to Spain. The suggestion had come to the President from Daniel Webster, at that time Secretary of State. The succeeding five years were in large part devoted to the collection of material relating to the history and the legends of Spain during the Moorish occupation.

On his return to New York in 1846, he met with a serious disappointment. His books were out of print, at least in the United States, and his Philadelphia publishers assured him that, as there was no longer any public demand for his writings, it would be an unprofitable venture to put new editions upon the market. They explained that the public taste had changed, and that a new style of authorship was now in vogue. The books had in fact been out of print since 1845, but at that time Irving, still absent in Spain, had concluded that the plan for revised editions might await his return. To be told now by publishers of experience that *The Sketch Book*, *Knickerbocker*, *Columbus*, and the other books, notwithstanding their original prestige, had had their day and were not wanted by the new generation, was a serious shock to Irving not only on the ground of the blow to his confidence in himself as an author, but because his savings were inconsiderable, and he needed the continued income that he had hoped to secure from his pen.

His personal wants were few, but he had always used his resources generously among his large circle of relatives, and having neither wife nor child he had made a home at Sunnyside for an aged brother Ebenezer, and at one time for no less than five nieces. Some western land investments, which in later years became profitable, were at this time liabilities instead of resources, and his immediate financial prospects were discouraging. He had taken a desk in the office of his brother John Treat Irving, and to John he now spoke, possibly half jestingly, of the necessity of resuming the practice of the law. He was at this time sixty-five years of age, and as it was forty years since he had touched a law book, it is hardly likely that he could have made himself of much value as a counsellor.

One morning early in 1848, he came into the office in a joyful frame of mind. He tossed a letter over to his brother saying: "John, here is a fool of a publisher willing to give me $2000 a year to go on scribbling." The "fool of a publisher" was the late George P. Putnam, who had recently returned from London where he had for eight years been engaged in the attempt to induce the English public to buy American books. Mr. Putnam now proposed to issue a uniform revised

edition of all of Irving's writings, with which should be associated the books that he might later bring to completion, and
to pay to the author a royalty on each copy sold, guaranteeing
against such royalty for a term of three years a sum increasing
with each year. It may be mentioned as evidence of the accuracy of the publisher's judgment that the payments during the
years in which this guaranty continued were always substantially in excess of the amounts contracted for.

In 1849, the London publisher Bohn began to print unauthorized editions of the various books of Irving. A series of
litigations ensued, as a result of which the authorized publishers,
Murray and Bentley, discouraged with a long fight and with
the great expense incurred in securing protection under the
existing copyright regulations, accepted the offer of the pirate
for the use, at a purely nominal price, of their publishing rights,
and Irving's works came thus to be included in Bohn's Library
Series. Copyright in Great Britain, as in the United States,
was in 1850 in a very unsatisfactory condition, and it was not
easy to ascertain from the provisions of the British statute just
what rights could be maintained by alien authors. So far as
American authors were concerned, this uncertainty continued
until, through the enactment of the statute of 1891, an international copyright relation was secured.

As one result of the transfer to Bohn of the control of the
English editions of Irving's earlier volumes, the author found
that he could not depend upon any material English receipts
for his later works. For the right to publish the English edition
of the *Life of Washington* (a work comprised in five volumes)
Bentley paid the sum of £50, which was a sad reduction from
the £3000 that Murray had given him for the *Columbus*.

In December, 1852, Irving wrote to his American publisher
a letter of thanks, which is notable as an expression both of the
sense of fairness and of the modest nature of the man. That
this expression of friendship was not a mere empty courtesy,
he had opportunity of making clear a few years later. In 1857,
partly because of the mismanagement of his financial partner
and partly because of the general financial disasters of the
year, Mr. Putnam was compelled to make an assignment
of his business. Irving received propositions from a number of
other publishers for the transfer of his books, the commercial

value of which was now fully appreciated. From some of these propositions he could have secured more satisfactory returns than were coming to him under the existing arrangement. He declined them all, however, writing to his publisher to the effect that as long as a Putnam remained in the publishing business, he proposed to retain for his books the Putnam imprint. He purchased from the assignee the plates and the publishing agreements; he held these plates for a year or more until Mr. Putnam was in a position to resume the control of the publication, and he then restored them to his publisher. He waived the larger proceeds to which, as the owner of the plates, he would have been entitled, and insisted that the old publishing arrangement should be resumed. Such an episode is interesting in the long and somewhat troubled history of the relations of authors with publishers, and it may be considered equally creditable to both parties.

The final, and in some respects the greatest of Irving's productions, the *Life of Washington*, was completed on his seventy-sixth birthday, 1859, and a month or two later he had the pleasure of holding in his hands the printed volume. His death came on 29 November, of the same year, and he was laid to rest in the beautiful little graveyard of the Sleepy Hollow Church. The writer has in his memory a picture of the great weather-beaten walls of the quaint little church with the background of forest trees and the surroundings of the moss-covered graves. Beyond on the roadside could be seen the grey walls of the mill, in front of which Ichabod Crane had clattered past, pursued by the headless horseman. The roadside and the neighbouring fields were crowded with vehicles, large and small, which had gathered from all parts of the countryside. It was evident from the words and from the faces of those that had come together that the man whose life was closed had not only made for himself a place in the literature of the world, but had been accepted as a personal friend by the neighbours of his home.

Washington Irving occupied an exceptional position among the literary workers of his country. It was his good fortune to begin his writing at a time when the patriotic sentiment of the nation was taking shape, and when the citizens were giving their thoughts to the constructive work that was being done by their selected leaders in framing the foundations of the new state. It was given to Irving to make clear to his countrymen that Americans were competent not merely to organize a state, but to produce literature. He was himself a clear-headed and devoted patriot, but he was able to free himself from the local feeling of antagonism toward the ancient enemy Great Britain, and from the prejudice against other nations, always based upon ignorance, that is so often confused with patriotism. Irving's early memories and his early reading had to do with the events and with the productions of colonial days. Addison and Goldsmith are the two English writers with whose works his productions, or at least those relating to English subjects, have been most frequently compared. His biography of Goldsmith shows the keenest personal sympathy with the sweetness of nature and the literary ideals of his subject. Irving's works came, therefore, to be a connecting link between the literature of England (or the English-inspired literature of the colonies) and the literary creations that were entitled to the name American, and they expressed the character, the method of thought, the ideals, and the aspiration of English folk on this side of the Atlantic.

The greatest intellectual accomplishment to be credited to New York during the first years of the republic was the production of *The Federalist*. It is fair to claim, however, that with Irving and with those writers immediately associated with his work during the first quarter of the nineteenth century, began the real literature of the country. Partly by temperament and by character, and partly, of course, as a result of the opportunities that came to him after a close personal knowledge of England, with a large understanding of things Continental, Irving, while in his convictions a sturdy American, became in his sympathies a cosmopolitan. His first noteworthy production, *The History of New-York*, is so distinctive in its imagination and humour that it is difficult to class. It is purely local in the sense that the characters and the allusions all have to do with the Dutch occupation of Manhattan Island and the Hudson River region, but, as was evidenced by the cordial appreciation given to the book on the other side of the Atlantic, the humour of Mr. Knickerbocker was accepted as a contribution to the literature of the world.

In the production of *The Sketch Book*, Irving was able not only to enhance his fame by a charming contribution to literature, but to render a special service to two countries, England and America. The book came into print at a time when the bitterness of the war which closed in 1814 was still fresh in the minds of both contestants. It was a time when it was the fashion in America to use Great Britain as a bugaboo, as a synonym for all that was to be abominated in political theories and in political action. The word "British" was associated in the minds of most Americans with an attempt at domination, while in England, on the other hand, references to the little Yankee nation were no more friendly, and things American were persistently decried and sneered at.[1]

It was of enormous value that at such a period, first in the list of patriotic Americans who through sympathetic knowledge of England have come to serve as connecting links between the two countries, Irving should have been a resident in England and should have absorbed so thoroughly the spirit of the best that there was in English life. It was in part because men honoured in Great Britain, writers like Scott, Southey, Rogers, Roscoe, Moore, men of affairs like Richard Bentley, John Murray, and many others, came not only to respect, but to have affectionate regard for, the American author, and it was in part because the books written by this man showed such sympathetic appreciation of things and of men English, that England was brought to a better understanding of the possibilities of America. If there could come from the States a man recognized as one of nature's gentlemen, and to be accepted as a companion of the best in the land, a man whose writings on things English won the highest approval of the most authoritative critics, it was evident that there were possibilities in this new English-speaking state. If one American could secure friendships in Great Britain, if one American could make a noteworthy contribution to the literature of the English tongue, the way was thrown open to other Americans to strengthen and widen the ties and the relations between the two countries. An American critic who might have been tempted to criticize some of the papers in *The Sketch Book* as unduly English in their sympathies and as indicating a surrender by the author of his American

[1] See also Book II, Chap. I.

principles, was estopped from any such folly by the fact that the same volume contained those immortal legends of the Hudson, *Rip Van Winkle* and *The Legend of Sleepy Hollow*. In these stories, poems in prose, the author utilized, as the pathway and inspiration for his imagination, the great river of which he was so fond. If Irving's descriptions of rural England were to give fresh interest to American readers in the old home of their forefathers, the skill with which he had utilized the traditional legends of the Catskill Mountains and had woven fanciful stories along the roadway of Sleepy Hollow made clear to readers on the other side of the Atlantic that imagination and literary style were not restricted to Europe.

The work begun in *The Sketch Book* was continued in *Bracebridge Hall*. Here also we have that combination (possibly paralleled in no other work of literature) of things English and things American. Squire Bracebridge is, of course, a lineal descendant of Sir Roger de Coverley. It is not necessary, however, because Irving was keenly sympathetic with Addison's mode of thought, to speak of Irving's hero as an imitation. England has produced more than one squire, and Bracebridge and the family of the Hall were the creations of the American observer. The English home of the early nineteenth century is presented in a picture that is none the less artistic because it can be accepted as trustworthy and exact. In this volume we have also a characteristic American study, *Dolph Heyliger*, a fresh romance of Irving's beloved Hudson River.

The *Tales of a Traveller*, the scenes of which were laid partly in Italy, show the versatility of the author in bringing his imagination into harmony with varied surroundings. Whether the subject be in England, in France, or in Italy, whether he is writing of the Alhambra or of the Hudson, Irving always succeeds in coming into the closest sympathy with his environment. He has the artist's touch in the ability to reproduce the atmosphere in which the scenes of his stories are placed.

The *Life of Columbus* may be considered as presenting Irving's first attempt at history, but it was an attempt that secured for him at once a place in the first rank among historians. In this biography, Irving gave ample evidence of his power of reconstituting the figures of the past. He impresses upon the reader the personality of the great discoverer, the idealist, the man who was so absorbed in his own belief that he was able to impress this upon the skeptics about him. We have before us a vivid picture of the Spanish Court from which, after patient effort, Columbus secured the grudging support for his expedition, and we come to know each member of the little crew through whose service the great task was brought to accomplishment. Irving makes clear that the opposition of the clerics and the apathy of King Ferdinand were at last overcome only through the sympathetic support given to the project by Queen Isabella.

In the *Conquest of Granada*, the narrative is given in a humorous form, but it represents the result of very thorough historic research. By the device of presenting the record through the personality of the mythical priestly chronicler, Fray Agapida, blindly devoted to the cause of the Church, Irving is able to emphasize less invidiously than if the statements were made direct, the bitterness, the barbarism, and the prejudices of the so-called Christianity of the Spaniards. Through the utterances of Agapida, we come to realize the narrowness of Ferdinand and the priestly arrogance of Ferdinand's advisers. The admiration of the reader goes out to the fierce patriotism of the great Moorish leader, El Zagal, and his sympathies are enlisted for the pathetic career of Boabdil, the last monarch of Granada. *Granada* was Irving's favourite production, and he found himself frankly disappointed that (possibly on the ground of the humorous form given to the narrative) the book failed to secure full acceptance as history and was not considered by the author's admirers to take rank with his more popular work.

The *Alhambra*, which has been called the "Spanish Sketch Book," is a beautiful expression of the thoughts and dreams of the author as he muses amid the ruins of the Palace of the Moors. The reader feels that in recording the great struggle which terminated in 1492 with the triumph of Spain, Irving's sympathies are not with the conquering Christians but with the defeated Moslems.

The *Life of Mahomet* and the supplementary volume on the successors of Mahomet followed in 1849–50. The biographies constitute good narrative and give further examples of the author's exceptional power of characterization. If they fail to reach the high standard of the *Columbus*, it is doubtless because Irving possessed no such close familiarity with the environment of his subjects. In Spain he had made long sojourns and had become imbued with the atmosphere of the Spanish legends and ideals. He knew his Italy, in like manner, from personal observation and from sympathetic relations with the peasants no less than the scholars, but Arabia was to him a distant land.

The writing of *Columbus* prepared the way for Irving's chief historical achievement. The *Life of Washington* is not only a biography presenting with wonderful precision and completeness the nature and career of a great American, but a study, and the first study of importance, of the evolution of the republic. Irving had given thought and planning to the biography for years before he was able to put a pen to the work. As early as 1832 he had confided to some of his nearer friends his ambition to associate his name with that of Washington and to devote such literary and historical ability as he possessed to the creation of a literary monument to the Father of the Republic. The work had, of necessity, been postponed during his long sojourn in England and the later residence in Spain, but he never permitted himself to put the plan to one side. As soon as the sales of the new Putnam edition of the earlier works and of the later volumes that he had been able to add to these freed him from financial care, he began the collection of material for the great history. He had already travelled over much of the country with which the career of his hero was connected. He knew by the observations of an intelligent traveller the regions of New England, New Jersey, Western Pennsylvania, and Virginia, while with the territory of New York he had from his youth been familiar. The Hudson River, which had heretofore served as the pathway for Irving's dreams of romance, was now to be studied historically as the scene of some of the most critical of the campaigns of the Revolution. Since the date of Irving's work, later historians have had the advantage of fuller material, particularly that secured from the correspondence in the homes of Revolutionary leaders, North and South, but no later historian has found occasion for any corrections of importance, either in the details of Irving's narrative, or in his analysis of the characters of the men through whom the great contest was carried on. Irving possessed one qualification which is lacking in the make-up of not a few conscientious and able historians. His strain of romance and his power of imagination enabled him to picture to himself and to make vivid the scenes described, and the nature, the purpose, and the manner of thought of each character introduced. The reader is brought into personal association with the force and dignity of the great leader; with the assumption, the vanity, the exaggerated opinion of his powers and ability of Charles Lee; with the sturdy patriotism, the simple-hearted nature, persistence, and pluck of the pioneer fighter Israel Putnam; with the skill, leadership, and unselfishness of Philip Schuyler; with the pettiness and bumptiousness of Gates; with the grace, fascination, and loyalty of Lafayette; and with the varied attainments and brilliant qualities of that wonderful youth Alexander Hamilton. We are not simply reading descriptions, we are looking at living pictures, and the historic narrative has the quality of a vitascope.

The production of this great history constituted a fitting culmination to the literary labours of its author. When Irving penned the last word of the fifth volume of the *Washington*, he was within a few months of his death. The work on this volume had in fact been a strain upon his vitality, and there were times when he needed to exert his will power to the utmost in order to complete the task allotted to himself for the day. He said pathetically from time to time to his nephew and loyal aid Pierre and to his friend Putnam, "I do not know whether I may be spared to complete this history, but I shall do my best." In this his final work, the shaping of the fifth volume, he did his best.

It may fairly be contended for this American author, whose work dates almost from the beginning of the Republic, that his writings possess vitality and continued importance for the readers of this later century. His historical works have, as indicated, a distinctive character. They are trustworthy and dignified history, while they possess the literary charm and grace of the work of a true man of letters. For the world at large, Irving will, however, doubtless best be known by his works of imagination, and the students in the gallery in Oxford who chaffed "Diedrich Knickerbocker" as he was receiving his degree were probably right in selecting as the characteristic and abiding production of the author his *Rip Van Winkle*.

## CHAPTER V

# Bryant and the Minor Poets

## I. BRYANT

TO the old-fashioned prayers which his mother and grandmother taught him, the little boy born in Cummington,
Massachusetts, 3 November, 1794, a year before John
Keats across the sea, was wont to add (so we learn from the
Autobiographical Fragment),[1] his private supplication that he
might "receive the gift of poetic genius, and write verses that
might endure."

This inner urge and bent, witnessed so early and so long,
could not be severed, early or late, from the unfathomable
world. Bryant's was a boyhood and youth among the virginal
woods, hills, and streams, among a farmer folk and country
labours and pastimes, in a Puritan household, with a father
prominent in the state as physician and legislator, whose
independence and breadth are attested by a leaning toward
that liberalism which was to develop into the American Unitarian movement and by his enlightened devotion, as critic and
friend, to the boy's ambitions in rhyme. Private tutoring by
unpretending clergymen, a year at poverty-stricken Williams
College, law studies in an upland office, distasteful practice as
a poor country lawyer, a happy marriage with her whose
"birth was in the forest shades,"[2] death, season by season, of
those nearest and dearest, travel down among the slave-holding
states and out to the prairies of Illinois, where his brothers and
mother were for a second time pioneers, with voyages on various

[1] Godwin, *Life*, vol. I, p. 26.
[2] *Poems*, p. 82. Roslyn edition (1913), from which all poetical quotations
are cited in this chapter.

occasions to the West Indies, to Europe, and to the Levant, and fifty years as a New York editor, who with the wisdom of a statesman and the courage of a reformer made *The Evening Post* America's greatest newspaper,—all this gives us a life of many visions of forest, field, and foam, of many books in diverse tongues, of many men and cities, of many problems in his own career and in the career of that nation which he made so much his own, a life not without its own adventures, struggles, joys, and griefs. So it stands recorded, a consistent and eloquent and (fortunately) a familiar chapter in American biography, even as it passed before the visionary octogenarian back in the old home, sitting "in the early twilight," whilst

> Through the gathering shade
> He looked on the fields around him
> Where yet a child he played.[1]

One might regard the events of this lifetime either as in subtle and inevitable ways harmoniously contributory to the poet-nature that was Bryant's (if not indeed often its persistent and victorious creation), or as in the main a deflection, a check. If no other American poet has written, year measured by year, so little poetry, the poetry of no other so clearly defines at once its author's character, environment, and country; if no other American poet was apparently so much occupied with other interests than poetry, not excepting the critic, diplomat, orator, and humorist Lowell, none felt his high calling, it seems, with as priestly a consecration,—no, truly, not excepting Whitman, who protested thereon sometimes a little too much.

Bryant's public career as poet fulfilled the psalmist's three-score years and ten, if we date from *The Embargo*, an anti-Jefferson satire in juvenile heroics (1808). It began with the year of Scott's *Marmion;* it was barely completed with *Sigurd the Volsung* of William Morris; it included the lives of Byron and Shelley and most that was best in those of Tennyson, Arnold, Browning. It began the year following Joel Barlow's American epic *The Columbiad*, and the publication of *The Echo* by the Hartford Wits. Longfellow and Whittier were in the cradle, Holmes and Poe unborn. Except Freneau, there were no poets

[1] *A Lifetime.*

in the country but those imitative versifiers of an already antiquated English fashion whom Bryant was himself to characterize[1] with quiet justice in the first critical appraisal of our
"literature," the first declaration of intellectual independence,
antedating Emerson's *American Scholar* by nineteen years.
He compassed the generations of all that was once or is still
most reputed in American poetry: the generations of Paulding,
Percival, Halleck, Drake, Willis, Poe, Longfellow, Whittier,
Emerson, Lowell, Whitman, Bret Harte.

Yet he was from very early, in imagination and expression,
curiously detached from what was going on in poetry around
him. *The Embargo* is a boy's echo, significant only for precocious facility and for the twofold interest in verse and politics
that was to be lifelong. Byron's voice is audible in the Spenserian stanzas and subject matter of the Phi Beta Kappa poem
of 1821, *The Ages*[2]; the New York verses, so painfully facetious
on Rhode Island coal and a mosquito, are less after Byron than
after the town wit Halleck and his coterie. Wordsworth, at the
reading of whose *Lyrical Ballads* in 1811, "a thousand springs,"
Bryant said to Dana, "seemed to gush up at once in his heart,
and the face of Nature of a sudden to change into a strange
freshness and life," was the companion into the woods and
among the flowers who more than all others helped him to find
himself; but *Thanatopsis*, so characteristic of Bryant, was
written almost certainly some weeks before he had seen the
*Lyrical Ballads*,[3] and, even if Bryant's eminence as poet of
nature owed much to this early reinforcement, his poetry is
not Wordsworthian either in philosophy or in mood or in
artistry. Wordsworth never left the impress on Bryant's
work that the realms of gold made upon the surprised and
spellbound boy Keats. No later prophets and craftsmen,

[1] *North American Review*, July, 1818.

[2] Thomson's *Liberty* may have contributed something to the choice of theme.

[3] The time relations seem to have been as follows. Bryant's father purchased
the *Lyrical Ballads* in Boston during 1810, when the son was at college (till May,
1811); Bryant "had picked it up at home" (Godwin, *Life*, vol. 1, p. 104) to take
with him to Worthington (Dec., 1811), where it was that, as a young law student,
he first read it with such surprised delight. *Thanatopsis* had been written between
May and December, apparently in the autumn (Godwin, *Life*, vol. 1, pp. 97–99),
and if (as likely) before 3 November, then written when Bryant was still a lad of
sixteen. See Van Doren, C., *The Growth of "Thanatopsis,"* Nation, 7 October,
1915.

American, English, or continental, seem to have touched him at all.[1]

More obvious to the registrar of parallels are Bryant's literary relations to the poets he read, and read evidently with deeper susceptibility than has been realized, before 1811.[2] The reference is not alone to the well-known relation *Thanatopsis* bears to Blair's *Grave*, Porteus's *Death*,[3] Kirk White's *Time*, *Rosemary*, etc., and the whole Undertaker's Anthology so infinitely beneath the Lucretian grandeur of America's first great poem with its vision of

Dead men whose bones earth bosomed long ago.

The reference is equally to certain themes and moods and unclassified details in poems written long after *Thanatopsis*, all of which, though so characteristically Bryant's, make us feel him as much closer to the eighteenth century tradition than any of his contemporaries, even than Holmes with his deference to "the steel-bright epigrams of Pope"; so that we may appraise him much better by going forward from the moralizing, "nature" blank verse of Thomson, Cowper, Young, and Akenside, than backward from Wordsworth and Tennyson. In the eighteenth century tradition is the very preference for blank verse as the instrument for large and serious thought, and the lifelong preference itself for large and serious thought on Death, History, Destiny. The Biblical note too is of the former age. But the diction is, if anything, freer than the mature Wordsworth himself from eighteenth century poetic slang, and the peculiarities of this blank verse (to be mentioned later) have fewer cadences suggestive of Cowper than, perhaps, of the early poems of Southey, whose impression on those impressionable first years of Bryant's has apparently been overlooked.[4] With this early romanticism we may connect the sentimental element in the appeal of innocent and happy savages, whether

[1] Tennysonian blank-verse in *Sella* has been suggested—unconvincingly.

[2] See Autobiographical Fragment for a partial list.

[3] Winner of the Seaton Prize at Cambridge for 1759. *Death* may be found in *Musae Seatonianae*, Cambridge, 1808—a copy of which was apparently in Doctor Bryant's library.

[4] Compare Southey's *Inscriptions* (themselves imitated from Akenside), especially *In a Forest*, with *Inscription for the Entrance to a Wood*.

on Pitcairn's Island or in the pristine Indian summers; likewise
the two or three tales of horror and the supernatural, in which
he succeeded so poorly.  But he arrived soon enough to contribute his own influence to the nineteenth-century poetry of
nature.

He came to himself early, for one who had so many years in
which to change, if he would change or could.  The first volume,
the forty-four pages of 1821, contains most, the second, 1832, certainly contains all, of the essential Bryant, the essential as to
what he cared for in nature and human life, as to how he en-
visaged it in imagination and dwelt with it in intellect and
character, and as to how he gave it expression.  In the later years
there is more of Bryant's playful fancy, perhaps more of ethical
thinking and mood, a slight shift of emphasis, new constructions,
not new materials.  His world and his speech were already his:
there is no new revelation and no new instrument in any one of
the several succeeding issues of his verse (though there are many
new, many high poems), as there are new revelations and new
instruments in Byron, Tennyson, and Browning; indeed, Keats
in the three years between the volumes of 1817 and 1820 lived a
much longer, a more diversified life of steadily increasing vision
and voice.  It need hardly be remarked, then, that he experienced no intellectual and moral crisis,—neither from without,
as did Wordsworth when his country took up arms against
Liberty, Fraternity, and Equality and when shortly Liberty,
Fraternity, and Equality danced, like the Weird Sisters,
around the cauldron of horror; nor from within, like the ex-
patriated husband and father Byron, and the political idealist
Dante, and even the *flâneur* who wrote *The Ballad of Reading
Gaol*.

He came, likewise, early to his fame.  He was first and alone.
The little world of the lovers of good things on the North
Atlantic seaboard in those days, trained as it was in the English
and ancient classics, quickly set the young man apart; Bryant
became established, fortunately, somewhat before American
literary criticism had become self-consciously patriotic, indiscriminate, vulgar.  England, too, long so important an influence
on American judgments of American products, early accorded
him a measure of honour and thanks.  It is well known that
Washington Irving secured the English reprinting of the volume

of 1832 in the same year, with a brief criticism by way of dedication to Samuel Rogers, whose reading of the contents was the
delight of that old Maecenas and Petronius Arbiter. It has,
however, apparently not been observed that the entire contents
of the volume of 1821 were reprinted, indeed in the same order,
in *Specimens of the American Poets* (London, 1822) with a noteworthy comment[1] on the lines *Thanatopsis* that "there are
few pieces, in the works of even the very first of our living poets.
which exceed them in sublimity and compass of poetical
thought." And Bryant was spared from the beginning furor
and contempt: he was never laurelled like Byron, never fools-
capped like Keats by critics or public; his repute was always,
like himself, dignified, quiet, secure. And so the critical problem is initially simplified, in two ways: there is no story of
struggle for recognition, and the effects of that struggle on the
workman; there is no story of evolution of inner forces. Thus
the poetry of Bryant admits of treatment as one performance,
one perception and one account of the world, in a more restricted sense than is generally applicable to poetic performance,
where the unity is the unity of psychological succession in a
changing temporal order: *Don Juan* is, perhaps, implied in the
*English Bards* and *Childe Harold, Paradise Lost* in the *Nativity,
Hamlet* in *Romeo and Juliet;* but, in a humbler sphere, *Among
the Trees* and *The Flood of Years* are less implied than actually
present in *A Forest Hymn* and *Thanatopsis*. If Bryant's poems
need sometimes the reference of date, it is for external occasion
and impulse, not for artistic registration. Three periods have
been discovered for Chaucer, and four for Shakespeare; our
modest American was without "periods."

The critical problem is simple, though not necessarily
trivial or easy, in another way: this one performance was itself
of a relatively simple character. Bryant's poems stress perpetually a certain few ideas, grow perpetually out of a certain
few emotional responses, and report in a few noble imaginative
modes a certain few aspects of man and nature, with ever
recurring habits of observation, architectonics, and style. This
absence of complexity is, again, emphasized by the elemental
clarity and simplicity of those same few ideas, emotions, modes,
methods. Within his range he is complete, harmonious, and,

[1] P. 190.

in a deeper sense than above, impressively one. It is for this, perhaps, that of all American poets he makes the strongest impression of an organic style, as contrasted with an individual, a literary style, consciously elaborated, as in Poe and Whitman. It is partly for this, perhaps, that the most Puritan of our poets is also the most Greek. Bryant's limitations, then, are intimately engaged in the peculiar distinction of his work; and it is ungracious, as well as superficial, to quarrel with them.

Bryant's ideas, stated in bald prose, are elementary,— common property of simple minds. His metaphysics was predominantly that of the Old Testament: God is the Creator and His works and His purposes are good. Bryant communicated, however, little sense of the loving fatherhood and divine guidance in human affairs: perhaps once only, in *To a Waterfowl*, which originated in an intensely religious moment of young manhood.[1] His ethics stress the austerer loyalties of justice and truth rather than those of faith, hope, and charity. His politics in his poems, however analytic and specific he might be as publicist, reiterate only the ideals of political freedom and progress, with ever confident reference to the high destinies of America, that "Mother of a Mighty Race." His assurance of individual immortality for all men, which scarcely touches the problem of sin, rests not on revelation, not on a philosophy of the transcendental significance of intellect, struggle, and pain, but mainly on primitive man's desire to meet the loved and lost, the father, the sister, the wife. There is nothing subtle, complex, or tricky here; there are no philosophers, apparently, on his reading desk; no Spinoza, Plotinus, Berkeley, Hartley, who were behind Coleridge's discursive verse; no Thomas Aquinas who was the propedeutic for *The Divine Comedy*. And of any intricate psychology, or pseudo-psychology, such as delighted Browning, there is of course not a bit. There is in these ideas, as ideas, nothing that a noble pagan, say of republican Rome, might not have held to, even before the advent of Stoic and Academician. But there is a further paganism in the emphasis on the phenomena of life as life, on death as death. Man's life, as individual and type, is what it is—birth and toil in time; and death is what it is, save when he mentions a private grief—for men and empires it is a passing away in a

[1] Godwin, *Life*, vol. I, pp. 143–145.

universe of time and change. The original version of *Thanatop-sis* is more characteristic than its inconsistent introductory and concluding lines, now the oftenest quoted of all his writings. If Bryant was the Puritan in his austerity and morale, he was quite as much the Pagan in the universality of his ideas, and in his temperamental adjustment to brute fact.

On nature and man's relation to nature, one who reads without prepossession will find the American Wordsworth equally elemental. He raises his hymn in the groves, which were God's first temples,—venerable columns, these ranks of trees, reared by Him of old. And "the great miracle still goes on"; and even the "delicate forest flower" seems

> An emanation of the indwelling Life,
> A visible token of the upholding Love,
> That are the soul of this great universe.[1]

But more frequently nature is herself enough, in the simple thought that personifies and capitalizes: it is She herself that speaks to man, in his different hours, a various language. But it is only casually, as in *Among the Trees*, that he wonders if the vegetable world may not have some

> dim and faint
> . . . sense of pleasure and of pain,
> As in our dreams;

only casually, for conscious mysticism was foreign to Bryant's intellect, and the conception had yet to be scientifically investigated in the laboratories of the Hindoo botanist Bose. Here nature, as herself the Life, is simply an hypostasis of the racial imagination in which Bryant so largely shared, just like his intimate personifications of her phenomena, her flowers, her winds, and waters; it is not a philosophic idea, but a primitive instinct. "Nature's teachings" for men are simply the ideas that suggest themselves to Bryant himself (not inevitably to everyone) when he observes what goes on, or what is before him:

> The faintest streak that on a petal lies,
> May speak instruction to initiate eyes.[2]

[1] *A Forest Hymn.*          [2] *The Mystery of Flowers.*

But this apparently Wordsworthian couplet can be related to no system of thought or Wordsworthian instruction. These ideas are sometimes merely analogies, where in effect the flower (be it the gentian), or the bird (be it the waterfowl), is the first term in a simile on man's moral life; in this phase Bryant's thought of nature differs from that of Homer, the Psalmist, Jesus, or any sage or seer, Pagan or Christian, only in the appositeness, more or less, of the illustrative symbol. It implies no more a philosophy of nature than similes drawn from the action of a locomotive or a motor-boat would imply a philosophy of machinery. As a fact, Bryant's one abiding idea about nature is that she is a profound influence on the human spirit, chastening, soothing, encouraging, ennobling—how, he does not say; but the fact he knows from experience, and mankind knows it with him, and has known it from long before the morning when the sorrowful, chafed soul of Achilles walked apart by the shore of the many-sounding sea.

Every poet, like every individual, has of course his favourite, his recurrent ideas: Wordsworth, again and again, adverts to the uses of old memories as a store and treasure for one's future days, again and again he sees his life as divided into three ages; Browning again and again preaches the doctrine that it is better to aim high and fail than to aim low and succeed; Emerson that the soul must live from within. But with Bryant the recurrence is peculiarly insistent and restricted in variety.

But these ideas were involved in a temperament. The chief differences among men are not in their ideas, as ideas, but in the power of the ideas over their emotions, or in the ideas considered as the overflow of their emotions. In Bryant presumably the ideas became formulas of thought, clarified and explicit, through his feelings. A man of great reserve and poise, both in life and art, his " coldness," well established in our literary tradition by some humorous lines of Lowell and a letter of Hawthorne, is a pathetic misreading. There is no sex passion; if there was in Bryant any potentiality of the young Goethe or Byron, it was early transmuted into the quiet affections for wife and home. There is no passion for friends; without being a recluse, he never craved comradeship, like Whitman, for humanity's sake, nor, like Shelley, for affinity's sake, and was, in the lifelong fellowship with such men as the elder Dana, the literary mentor who is responsible for more of Bryant's revisions in verse than any one knows,[1] spared the shocks that usually stimulate the expression of the passion of friendship. But his feelings, for woman and friend, were deep if quiet—perhaps deeper because quiet. And the other primary feelings were equally deep: awe in the presence of the cosmic process and the movements of mankind, reverence for holiness, pity for suffering, brooding resentment against injustice, rejoicing in moral victory, patriotism, susceptibility to beauty of outline and colour and sound, with peculiar susceptibility to both charm and sublimity in natural phenomena. These emotions, in Bryant, ring out through his poetry, clear, without blur or fringe, like the Italian vowels. He had no emotional crotchets, no erratic sensibilities; among other things, he was too robust and too busy. He had the "feelings of calm power and mighty sweep" of which he himself speaks, as befitting the poet.[2]

The few aspects of man and nature he reported have, in a way, been necessarily already suggested. With senses more alert to observe details in the physiognomy and voice of nature than of man, his imagination continually sees the same general vision: the Indian, shadowy type of a departed world, accoutred with feathers and tomahawk, realized, however, in almost none of his actual customs and in none of his actual feelings save that of sorrow for tribal ruin; the warriors of freedom, especially of the American Revolution; the infinite and mysterious racial past on this earth with all its crimes, triumphs, mutations, rather than with its more ethical future which he believes in more than he visualizes, an act of his thinking rather than of his imagination; the earth itself as the sepulchre of man; and, like one great primeval landscape, the mountain, the sea, the wind, the river, the seasons, the plain, the forest that undergo small change from their reality, take on few subjective peculiarities, by virtue of an imagination that seems, as it were, to absorb rather than to create its objects,—in this more like the world of phenomena in Lucretius than, say, in Tennyson, or in the partially Lucretian Meredith, certainly than in Hugo, to whom

---

[1] See some correspondence between Bryant and Dana apropos the 1846 edition of the *Poems*, Godwin, *Life*, vol. II, p. 14 ff.

[2] *The Poet*.

nature becomes so often monstrous and grotesque. And yet Bryant's imagination has its characteristic modes of relating its objɛts. Three or four huge and impressive metaphors underlie a great part of his poetry: the past as a place, an underworld,[1] dim and tremendous, most poignantly illustrated in the poem *The Past* with its personal allusions, and most sublimely in *The Death of Slavery*, a great political hymn, with Lowell's *Commemoration Ode*, and Whitman's *When Lilacs last in the Dooryard Bloomed*, the highest poetry of solemn grandeur produced by the Civil War; death as a mysterious passage-way, whether through gate[2] or cloud,[3] with the hosts ever entering and disappearing in the Beyond; mankind conceived as one vast company, a troop, a clan; and, as suggested above, nature as a multitudinous Life.

Bryant wonderfully visualized and unified the vast scope of the racial movement and the range of natural phenomena. His "broad surveys," as they have been called, are more than surveys: they are large acts of the combining imagination, presenting the significance, not merely the catalogue. These acts take us home to the most inveterate habit of his poet-mind. As method or device they seem to suggest a simple prescription for writing poetry; superficially, after one has met them again and yet again in Bryant, one might call them easy to do, because easy to understand. The task is, however, not to make a list, but to make the right list; a list not by capricious association of ideas, but by the laws of inner harmony of meaning. Again, in Bryant the list is itself often a fine, far look beyond the immediate fact—the immediate fact with which all but the poet would rest content. *The Song of the Sower* needed no suggestion from Schiller's *Song of the Bell*, which, however, Bryant doubtless knew;[4] it highly illustrates his own natural procedure:

[1] The figure is in Kirke White's *Time*:

> "Where are conceal'd the days which have elapsed?
> Hid in the mighty cavern of *the past*,
> They rise upon us only to appal,
> By indistinct and half-glimpsed images."

This is doubtless one of the many indications of how thoroughly Bryant's early reading penetrated his subconsciousness and, with boyhood's woods and mountains, contributed to his essential make-up in maturity.

[2] *Poems*, p. 260.      [3] *Ibid.*, p. 250.      [4] See *The Death of Schiller*.

Fling wide the golden shower; we trust
The strength of armies to the dust.

The grain shall ripen for the warrior. Then he goes on: 'O
fling it wide, for all the race: for peaceful workers on sea and
land, for the wedding feast, for the various unfortunate, for the
communion, for Orient and Southland'—and we live, as we
read, wise in the basic fact of agriculture and wise in the activities of humankind. The precise idea is handled more lightly
in *The Planting of the Apple Tree*. Often the "survey"—
the word is convenient—starts from some on-moving phenomenon in nature—again an immediate fact—and proceeds by
compassing that phenomenon's whence or whither, what it has
experienced or what it will do: let one re-read his tale of *The
River*, by what haunts it flows (like, but how unlike, Tennyson's
brook); *The Unknown Way*, the spots it passes (becoming a
path symbolic of the mystery of life); *The Sea*, what it does
under God (like and unlike Byron's apostrophe); *The Winds*,
what they do on sea and land; *A Rain-Dream*, imaging the
waters of the globe. Sometimes the phenomenon is static and
calls his imagination to penetrate its secret history, or what
changes it has seen about it, as when he looks at the fountain[1]
or is among the trees.[2] Sometimes the vision rides upon or
stands beside no force in Nature, but is his own direct report,
as in *Fifty Years*, on the changes in individual lives, in history,
in inventions, especially in these States, since his class graduated
at Williams. "Broad surveys" of human affairs and of the
face of earth, so dull, routine, bombastic as far as attempted in
Thomson's *Liberty*, in Blair's *Grave*, in White's *Time*, become
in Bryant's less pretentious poems the essential triumph of a
unique imagination. The mode remained a favourite to the
end: large as in *The Flood of Years*, intimate and tender in
*A Lifetime*. No American poet, except Whitman, had an
imagination at all like Bryant's, or, indeed, except Whitman and
Emerson, as great as Bryant's.

No reminder should be needed that Bryant, like Thoreau
and Burroughs, was a naturalist with wide and accurate knowledge. He knew the way of the mist on river and mountain-
crest, all tints of sunset, the rising and the setting of the

[1] *Poems*, p. 185.  [2] *Ibid.*, p. 321.

constellations, every twig and berry and gnarled root on the forest floor, all shapes of snow on pine and shrub, the commoner insects and wild creatures, and especially the birds and the flowers; and he knew the hums and the murmurs and the boomings that rise, like a perpetual exhalation, from the breast of earth. A traveller from some other planet could take back with him no more useful account of our green home than Bryant's honest poems of nature. There is a group of his poems that details the look, habits, and habitat of single objects: *The Yellow Violet* (with an intrusive moral—but his "morals" are, contrary to traditional opinion, seldom intrusive, being part of the imaginative and emotional texture), and *Robert of Lincoln* (which is besides most fetching in its playfulness and Bryant's one success in dramatic portrayal). He was a good observer; he would never have placed, like Coleridge, a star within the nether tip of the crescent moon. There is an allied group which impart the quality of a moment in nature, as *Summer Wind:*

> It is a sultry day; the sun has drunk
> The dew that lay upon the morning grass;
> There is no rustling in the lofty elm . . .
> . . . All is silent, save the faint
> And interrupted murmur of the bee,
> Settling on the sick flowers . . . .
> . . . Why so slow?
> Gentle and voluble spirit of the air?

These, if not the most representative, are the most exquisite of all his poems.

And no reminder should be needed that he knew best the American scene, and was the first to reveal it in art. Irving, in the London edition of 1832, naturally emphasized this claim to distinction; and Emerson, many years later, at an after-dinner speech on the poet's seventieth birthday, dwelt on it with a winsome and eloquent gratitude[1] that has made all subsequent comment an impertinence.

Apart from the characteristics outlined above, Bryant had, as if a relief and release from the verities and solemnities, a love of fairyland: he had found it already, for instance, in the snow

[1] Godwin, *Life*, vol. II, p. 216 ff.

world of the *Winter Piece;* he went to it more often and eagerly
from the editorial desk and the noise and heat of the Civil War:
in *The Little People of the Snow,* in *Sella* (the underwater
maiden), and in the fragments, *A Tale of Cloudland,* and *Castles
in the Air.* Their flowing blank verse (each some hundreds of
lines), unlike his early experiments in prose narrative (which in
their wooden arrangement, dull plot, and stilted characteriza-
tions are of a piece with the American short story before Poe
and Hawthorne), tells, in simple chronological order, of one
simple type of adventure, a mortal penetrating beyond the
confines of nature—again the repetition of theme and architectonics, and one more manifestation of the primitive in
Bryant (for the fairy-tale is, as the anthropologists tell us,
among the most primitive activities of man) as dreamer and
poet.

Like Cowper and Longfellow, and so many others, Bryant
turned, in later life, to a long task of translation, in his case
Homer, as relief from sorrow. The literary interest was to see
if he might not, by closeness to the original and simplicity of
straightforward modern English, supersede the looseness and
artificial Miltonic pomp of Cowper. His translation, by detailed comparison line for line with the Greek and with the
English poet, will be found to be exactly what Bryant intended
it. By block comparison of book for book, or version for version, it will be found to be the better translation, from the point
of view of limpid and consequent story-telling—perhaps the
best in English verse. Of Arnold's four Homeric characteristics,
rapidity of movement, plainness of style, simplicity of ideas,
nobility of manner, Bryant's translation is inadequate mainly
in the first and the last, but the *Homer* is, in any case, a proof
of intellectual alertness, scholarship, and technical skill. All
his translations, many of them made before Longfellow's now
widely-recognized activities as spokesman in America for
European letters, are a witness to Bryant's knowledge of foreign
tongues and literatures, to his part in the culturization of
America, to the breadth of his taste and a certain dramatic
adaptability (for the originals that attracted him had often
not much of the specific qualities of his own verse), and to his
all but impeccable artistry.

Of his artistry this study has scarcely spoken; yet it has

been throughout implied. His qualities of thought, feeling, imagination, were communicated, were indeed only communicable, because so wrought into his diction, his rhymes, cadences, and stanzas. Indeed, there is no separating a poet's feeling, say, for a beautiful flower from his manner of expressing it—for all we know about his feeling for the flower is what he succeeds in communicating by speech. It is tautology to say that a poet treats a sublime idea sublimely—for it is the sublimity in the treatment that makes us realize the sublimity of the idea. We can at most conceive a poet's "style" as a whole; as, along with his individual world of meditation and vision, another phase of his creative power—as his creation of music. Possibly it is the deepest and most wonderful of the poet's creations, transcending its manifestation in connection with any single poem. Perhaps, for instance, Milton's greatest creative act was not *Lycidas*, or the *Sonnets*, or *Paradise Lost*, but that music we call Miltonic. Certainly this is the more true the more organic the style is; and, as said before, Bryant's style was highly organic.

An astute and sympathetic mind who might never have seen a verse of Bryant's could deduce that style from what has been said in this chapter—if what has been said has been correctly said. Such a mind would not need to be told that Bryant's diction was severe, simple, chaste, narrower in range than that of his political prose; that his rhymes were dignified, sonorous, exact and emphatic rather than subtle or allusive, and narrow in range—not from artistic poverty but because the rhyme vocabulary of the simple and serious moods is in English itself narrow, and much novelty and variety of rhyme is in our speech possible only when, like Browning, one portrays the grotesque and the eccentric, or like Shelley the fantastic, or like Butler the comic, or like Chaucer the familiar. Such a mind would deduce Bryant's most fundamental rhythm, the iambic; his most fundamental metre, the pentameter; together with his preference for stanzaic, or periodic, treatment, whether in blank verse or in rhyme, rather than for couplets; yes, together with the most characteristic cadences,—like the curves of a distant mountain range, few and clear but not monotonous; like the waves of a broad river, slow and long but not hesitant or ponderous, never delighting by subtle surprises, nor jarring by abrupt stops and shifts. Indeed, and would our critic not likewise guess, especially if recently schooled at Leipzig under Sievers, the very pitch of his voice in verse—strongest in the lower octaves—as well as the intrinsic alliteration, [1]—an alliteration as natural as breathing, in its context unobtrusive as such to the conscious ear because so involved in a diction which is itself the outgrowth of very mood and meaning? In quite different ways, Bryant is, with Poe, America's finest artist in verse. Perhaps this is, with Bryant's genuineness of manhood, a reason why Bryant was the one native contemporary that Poe thoroughly respected.

What to puzzled readers seems "characteristically Bryant's blank verse" is really the total impression of both materials and manner, manner itself including diction as well as metrics. But the metrics alone do have their peculiarities, which can, however, hardly be examined here: line endings like "and the green moss," caesuras at the end of the first and of the fourth foot, the tendency to repeat the same caesura and cadence through a succession of lines, a stanza group of five or more lines with full stop followed by a single line or so, inverted accent at the beginning of a line, and a differentiated, strong cadence at the conclusion of the whole poem which gives the effect of a completion, not of a mere stopping,—these are all contributing factors.

Yet Bryant is not one of the world's master-poets. It is not so much that he contributed little or nothing to philosophic thought or spiritual revolution, not altogether that his range was narrow, not that he never created a poem of vast and multitudinous proportions, drama, epic, or tale, not that he knew nature better than human life and human life better than human nature, not that he now and then lapsed from imaginative vision into a bit of sentiment or irrelevant fancy,—not either that there is not a single dark saying, or obscure word, construction, allusion, in all his verse, for the judicious to elucidate at a club or in a monograph. He is not one of the world's master-poets, because he was not pre-eminently endowed with intellectual intensity and imaginative concentration. The character of his whole mind was discursive, enumerative,

[1] Largely on b and frequently in idiomatic pairs, as "bees and birds," "bled or broke."

tending, when measured by the masters, to the diffuse. Thus, among other results, his report of things has given man's current speech but few quotations, of either epigrammatic criticism or haunting beauty. A book could be written on this thesis, but a paragraph must suffice. It is just as well: it is better to realize what Bryant was than to exploit what he was not.

And if he was and is a true poet, he belongs to our best traditions also as critic. He was never, to be sure, the professional guide of literary taste, like Arnold and Lowell. Apart from sensible but obvious memorial addresses on Irving, Halleck, and Cooper, his best known essay is introductory to his *Library of Poetry and Song;* it enunciates fewer keen judgments on individuals, fewer profound principles, than does Emerson's introduction to his *Parnassus,* but it does enunciate the primacy of "a luminous style" and of themes central to common man, in noble paragraphs that should not be forgotten, certainly not by any one who believes that criticism gains in authority when it is the concentrated deduction of experience. Of his services as editor of a leading metropolitan paper, through nearly two generations of crisis after crisis in the nation's life, only an historian should speak. Not even Godwin, his editorial colleague, has spoken, it seems, quite the definitive word. Why should it not be spoken? The fact is, no such man ever sat, before or since, in the editorial chair; in no one other has there been such culture, scholarship, wisdom, dignity, moral idealism. Was it all in Greeley? in Dana? What those fifty years may have meant as an influence on the American press, especially as counteracting the flamboyant and vulgar, the layman may only conjecture.

There is no space to speak of his letters beyond noting that, with all their elegance, courtesy, criticism, information, they do not belong, with Cicero's, Gray's, Cowper's, Byron's, Emerson's, Meredith's, to the literature of correspondence, because they are without zest for little details of human life (whether in others or in himself), or without informal spontaneity and flashes of insight—or without whatever it be that makes a private letter ultimately a public joy.

As a whole, Bryant's prose style has quality as well as qualities, but here a word only on its relation to the style of his poetry. Bryant more than once explicitly differentiated the functions of the two harmonies[1]; but Prescott[2] was not the only one who detected in both the same qualities of mind: obviously a man is not two different beings according to whether he is playing a violin or a cello, singing or talking. Bryant, as Dowden said of Burke, saw "the life of society in a rich, concrete, imaginative way"; and not unlike Burke he had, as politician, the poet's generalizing power. But the point here of special interest is the recurrence in his prose so often, when his prose rises to things in their significance (as apart from their mere relations), of the same imaginative procedure: there is the "broad survey," as in the account of the waters of the Mississippi[3] (themselves introduced as a simile to illustrate the fame of Homer); there are his fundamental metaphors, the grammar of his dialect, as that of the past as a place, occurring in the editorial[4] on the amendment abolishing slavery, which is besides in many details of imagery almost another version of the poem on the same theme, written, says Godwin, a little later. In a public address on the electric telegraph[5] he said:

My imagination goes down to the chambers of the middle sea, to those vast depths where repose the mystic wire on beds of coral, among forests of tangle, or on the bottom of the dim blue gulfs strewn with the bones of whales and sharks, skeletons of drowned men, and ribs and masts of foundered barks, laden with wedges of gold never to be coined, and pipes of the choicest vintages of earth never to be tasted. Through these watery solitudes, among the fountains of the great deep, the abode of perpetual silence, never visited by living human presence and beyond the sight of human eye, there are gliding to and fro, by night and by day, in light and in darkness, in calm and in tempest, currents of human thought borne by the electric pulse which obeys the bidding of man.

Is not this in imagination, mood, manner, even in the recurrent blank verse cadences, veritably as if an unpublished fragment of *A Hymn of the Sea?*

So we return to the Poet. Yet when all is said, it is the whole man that is ours and that should be ours. He is the Citizen of

---

[1] Godwin, *Prose*, vol. II, p. 22.

[2] Godwin, *Life*, vol. II, p. 36.

[3] Godwin, *Prose*, vol. II, p. 269.

[4] Godwin, *Life*, vol. II, p. 235.

[5] Godwin, *Prose*, vol. II, p. 259.

our tradition; not to us today so much for his hand in the founding of two political parties, nor for his counsels by personal letter and speech that Lincoln, the Statesman of our tradition, heard with such grave respect, nor for his civic activities in art, charity, and reform; but for that Mosaic massive head, those deep, peering, brooding eyes, those white shaggy brows, and the great beard over the old man's cloak that, in the engraving after Sarony's photograph, has been now for a generation familiar in so many homes of our land.

## II. Minor Poets

When Bryant, pioneer and patriarch, was laid away on that bright June afternoon of 1878 in the cemetery at Roslyn, Long Island, his oldest and dearest friend was still alive. Richard Henry Dana (1787–1879), one of the founders of *The North American Review*[1] and of the serious tradition in our literary criticism, is remembered, if at all, as verse-writer mainly through Bryant's praise, as Mason is remembered through Gray's. How remote the short jerky stanzas of *The Buccaneer* (1827), an ambitious tale of pirate and spectre, were from the talents and temper of the Bostonian descendant of the Puritan Anne Bradstreet, one may realize who reflects what Coleridge would have done with the spell and the uncanny, and what Byron with the crime and the movement—the two poets whom Dana was obviously emulating. But there are some good lines on the sea in *The Buccaneer*, and Dana's lyric, *The Little Beach Bird*, gets a traditional honourable mention in the manuals.

The other minor poets about Bryant lived in or near New York. James Kirke Paulding, humorist and proseman of no mean reputation,[2] and collaborator with Bryant in prose stories,[3] deserves mention here as an early representative of a conscious movement to make poetry out of American materials, convinced that

> Thrice happy he who first shall strike the lyre
> With homebred feeling, and with homebred fire.

[1] See Book II, Chap. xx.     [2] See also Book II, Chaps. i, iii, iv, and vii.
[3] *Tales of the Glauber Spa* (1832).

*The Backwoodsman* (1818), from which this conventional couplet is taken, recounts, without much plot, in sturdy heroics
more like Crabbe's realism than Goldsmith's idyllic sentiment,
the rugged life and wild surroundings of a frontiersman and
his family. It is an honest document, if not distinguished
literature.

James Gates Percival (1795–1856) typified that crude manifestation of Romanticism, the self-constituted, the self-conscious poetic genius. Similarly, he typified the poetic mood
that is without the poetic reason. The stuff of him is pre-
eminently the stuff of poetry, but unclarified, uncontrolled,
unorganized. It is often as if the personalities of Byron, Shelley,
Wordsworth, Moore, and Bryant had been merged into one
helpless hypnoidal state of metrical and emotional garrulity.
Yet every now and then an open-minded reader is surprised
by some first-hand observation, some graceful analogy, some
picturesqueness or energy, some short lyric cry; and once at
least he wrought a little gem—his simple stanzas on *Seneca
Lake*. He typified, too, a not altogether ignoble phase of
earlier American culture in his zealous acquisitiveness, both in
science (he died as state geologist of Wisconsin), and in languages (he wrote verse in Scandinavian and German, and translated from innumerable tongues). But he belongs chiefly to
the student of human nature; lonely, shy, unmarried, disappointed, poor, and dirty, he was in appearance and mode of
life a character for Dickens, in heart and soul a character for
Thackeray or George Eliot. Lowell pilloried him in an essay;
Bryant was perhaps juster in his kindlier obituary criticism in
*The Evening Post*. He was once a famous man.

Samuel Woodworth (1785–1842)[1] and George P. Morris
(1802–1864), Knickerbocker editors of literary journals[2] and
charitably remembered respectively for *The Old Oaken Bucket*
and *Woodman, Spare that Tree*, were popular song writers in the
sentimental fashion (perhaps more developed in America than
in England) that seems to have originated with Tom Moore.
Yet such songs had music, point, and refinement that sets them
far above their popular descendants—the raucous, vulgar
inanities born of vaudeville and cabaret.

Charles Fenno Hoffman (1806–1884), another Knicker-

---

[1] See Book II, Chaps. II and VI.    [2] See Book II, Chap. XX.

bocker editor[1] and a song-writer, who, says a recent critic,[2] "possessed a lyric note almost completely unknown in the America of his time,"—by which is meant a certain catchy musical lilt,—is, however, chiefly memorable for the fine ballad *Monterey:*

> We were not many, we who stood
> Before the iron sleet that day:
> Yet many a gallant spirit would
> Give half his years if but he could
> Have been with us at Monterey.

This is, or should be, a classic in a genre rare in our literature, whose poets have seldom communicated with martial fire the rapture of the strife or celebrated worthily the achievements of our arms. Bryant wrote a critical sketch for the last edition of Hoffman's poems.

Nathaniel Parker Willis, the most honoured among these literary editors of old New York,[3] began as a sentimental poetizer of Scripture for meek ladies, and then helped to establish a still existing journalistic tradition in our literature—that of the light, the pretty, the clever, the urbane negligee in prose and rhyme; while his *Lady Jane*, a story after *Don Juan* and *Fanny*, and his *Melanie*, after Byron's *Tales*, only too well illustrate the now dead but once potent influence of Byron on our minor poets, even on poets utterly unlike Byron in temperament and in mode of life.[4] Yet Willis was a true poet in a half dozen lyrics where a human form, a bit of nature, or a moral insight is registered in sincere, graceful, dignified, and, at least once (*Unseen Spirits*), noble speech. These, with his brief prose obituary notice of Poe and its tribute to Mrs. Clemm, are higher things than conventional criticism now associates with the brilliant and versatile gentleman of provincial but polished Broadway.

Joseph Rodman Drake (1795–1820) and Fitz-Greene Halleck (1790–1867) are remembered first for a romantic youthful friendship, not common in our literary history. For a time they

---

[1] See Book II, Chaps. VII and XX.

[2] Trent, W. P., in *American Literature*, p. 457.

[3] See also Book II, Chap. III.

[4] See Leonard, W. E., *Byron and Byronism in America* (Columbia Univ. Diss.), 1905.

amused themselves and the town by facile and often pointed
skits on contemporary politics, people, and events, under the
title Croaker and Co., after the manner of English wits of the
time, as Moore and the Smith brothers. Halleck is said to have
written the last four lines of Drake's *American Flag*, a lyric
full of the old-fashioned expansive and defiant Americanism,
and, with its flare of imagery and blare of sound, still sure to
stir the blood of any one but a professional critic. And it was
on Drake, dead at twenty-five, that Halleck wrote what is the
tenderest, the manliest little elegy of personal loss in American
literature, beginning with the familiar lines:

> Green be the turf above thee,
>     Friend of my better days!
> None knew thee but to love thee,
>     Nor named thee but to praise.

Yet they are remembered no less for achievements more
noteworthy than those of the other minor men in this sketch.
Drake's *Culprit Fay* is the best and in fact the one fairy story in
American verse, if we except Bryant's *Sella* and *The Little
People of the Snow*, which are indeed rather stories of mortals
in fairyland than of the tiny, tricksy creatures themselves.
Though in a sense exotic, for it roots in no folklore despite the
setting on the Hudson, *The Culprit Fay* reports quite as well as
Drayton's *Nimphidia*, its nearest analogue, the antic characteristics of the elfland of man's universal fancy. But it is most
remarkable for its reading of nature. The Culprit Fay's
adventures take him through woods, waters, and air, on to
the stars above, amid the iridescent, elusive, darting, rended,
prickly little objects of the real universe that heavy-lidded folk
seldom observe. There are also—and this before Bryant's first
volume—the American plant, bird, and insect: the chickweed
and sassafras, the whippoorwill, the katydid and woodtick.
The music, though perhaps influenced by Coleridge, sang itself
under the unconscious guidance of a delicate and independent
ear—the most striking creative act in American versification
up to that time and for some time to come. Of the obvious
faults of *The Culprit Fay* it were ungracious to speak; it was
the two days' diversion of a very young man, and published
posthumously (1835).

Halleck was the one worthy American representative of the
contemporary popular English Romanticists, Scott, Campbell,
and Byron—worthy, because something of their matter and
manner, despite occasional crude imitation, was thoroughly
natural to his vigorous feelings, to his alert though not subtle
masculine intellect, and to his sounding voice.   His Spenserians
on *Wyoming* remind one of Campbell and Byron in stanza and
phraseology.   The still popular *Marco Bozzaris* reminds one of
Byron in the enthusiasm for Greek freedom (also the inspiration of some of Bryant's early verse), and of Campbell in martial vigour, while its octosyllabics have the verve of Scott's.
In *Alnwick Castle* and several other poems grave and gay are
whimsically mixed after Byron's later manner.   Indeed Byron,
whose works Halleck subsequently edited, was his most kindred
spirit.   As early as 1819 appeared his *Fanny*, suggested by
*Beppo* and in its present form sometimes reminiscent of *Don
Juan*—

> With the wickedness out that gave salt to the true one,

as Lowell's *Fable for Critics* observed as late as 1848—a social
satire on a flashy New Yorker and his fashionable daughter,
with Byronic anti-climax and Byronic digressions on Greece,
European and American politics, bad literature and bad
statues.   But a financial failure was substituted for Byronic
*crim.-cons.*, and the bluff and hearty Halleck "was never cynical
in his satire, and Byron was"—to quote Bryant,[1] who speaks,
however, a truer word for Halleck than for Halleck's master.
*Fanny* became at once popular,[2] and remained so for a generation, stimulating to several long since forgotten imitations and
doubtless serving to foster American Byronism in its pseudo-
comic phases.   A detailed study of Halleck would reveal, as
the chief source of his genuinely individual note, his power to
phrase energetically a single moment of action or of feeling
with a certain fusion of imaginative vision and of intellectual

[1] Godwin, *Prose*, vol. I, p. 374.

[2] It was reprinted almost entire in *Specimens of the American Poets*, London,
1822, in which it is called a "sprightly little poem" and "one of the cleverest
efforts of the American Muse."   The note concludes, however, with a comment
that the English edition had not apparently had "a very extensive circulation."
Part of its American popularity was due to its purely local allusions.

criticism. Moreover, Halleck's *Poems*, including such unfor-
gotten titles as *The Field of the Grounded Arms*, *Burns*, and
*Red Jacket*, still have some literary value as a volume: the
anthologies do not exhaust him.

Thus these early minor men left us some things worth
keeping; but, nevertheless, taken all in all, they emphasize
for us today, as they never could for their contemporaries,
the relative greatness of Bryant.

# CHAPTER VI

# Fiction I

## BROWN, COOPER

THE clear victory which the first great British novelists won over popular taste did not, for some years, make them masters of the colonial public. *Pamela*, indeed, was printed as early as 1744 in Philadelphia, by Benjamin Franklin, and in the same year in New York and in Boston. But the only other novels printed in America before the Declaration of Independence seem to have been *Robinson Crusoe* (1768), *Rasselas* (1768), *The Vicar of Wakefield* (1772), *Juliet Grenville* (1774), and *The Works of Laurence Sterne M.A.* (1774). Publishers, however, were less active than importers, for diaries and library catalogues show that British editions were on many shelves. The Southern and Middle colonies may have read more novels than did New England, yet Jonathan Edwards himself, whose savage quarrel with the Northampton congregation had arisen partly over the "licentious books" [possibly *Pamela*, among others] which some of the younger members "employed to promote lascivious and obscene discourse," was later enchanted by *Sir Charles Grandison*.

Edwards did not relent in advance of the general public. After the Revolution the novel-reading habit grew, fostered by American publishers and cried out against by many moralists whose cries appeared in magazines side by side with moral tales. Nearly every grade of sophistication applied itself to the problem. It was contested that novels were lies; that they served no virtuous purpose; that they melted rigorous minds; that they crowded out better books; that they painted adventure too romantic and love too vehement, and so unfitted readers for solid reality; that, dealing with European manners, they tended to confuse and dissatisfy republican youth. In the face of such censure, native novelists appeared late and apologetically, armed for the most part with the triple plea that the tale was true, the tendency heavenward, and the scene devoutly American. Before 1800 the sweeping philippic of the older school had been forced to share the field of criticism with occasional efforts to distinguish good novels from bad. No critical game was more frequently played than that which compared Fielding and Richardson. Fielding got some robust preference, Smollett had his imitators, and Sterne fathered much "sensibility," but until Scott had definitely set a new mode for the world, the potent influence in American fiction was Richardson. The amiable ladies who produced most of these early novels commonly held, like Mrs. Rowson, that their knowledge of life had been "simply gleaned from pure nature,"[1] because they dealt with facts which had come under their own observation, but like other amateurs they saw in nature what art had assured them would be there. Nature and Richardson they found the same. Whatever bias they gave this Richardsonian universe was due to a pervading consciousness of the sex which read their novels. The result was a highly domestic world, limited in outlook, where the talk was of careless husbands, grief for dead children, the peril of many childbirths, the sentiment and the religion which enabled women to endure their sex's destiny. Over all hangs the furious menace of the seducer, who appears in such multitudes that one can defend the age only by blaming its brutality less than the pathetic example of Clarissa Harlowe.

Thus early did the American novel acquire the permanent background of neutral domestic fiction against which the notable figures stand out. A few of the early names have a shade of distinction. Mrs. Sarah Wentworth Morton (1759–1846), a "Lady of Boston," produced the first regular novel, *The Power of Sympathy* (1789). Its two volumes of stilted letters caused a scandal and were promptly suppressed, but they called forth a much better novel, *The Coquette* (1797), by Mrs. Hannah Webster Foster (1759–1840). Based upon the tragic and widely known career of Elizabeth Whitman of Hartford, it saw

[1] Preface to *Mentoria*.

thirteen editions in forty years, but it was still less popular than Mrs. Susannah Haswell Rowson's *Charlotte* (1794), one of the most popular novels ever published in America. Mrs. Rowson (1762–1824), an American only by immigration, had indeed written the novel in England (1790?), but *Charlotte Temple*, to call it by its later title, was thoroughly naturalized. It has persuaded an increasingly naïve underworld of fiction readers to buy more than a hundred editions and has built up a legend about the not too authentic tomb of Charlotte Stanley in Trinity Churchyard, New York.

A particular importance of *The Coquette* and *Charlotte Temple* was that they gave to fiction something of the saga element by stealing, in the company of facts, upon a community which winced at fiction. And this brief garment of illusion was not confined to New York and New England. In 1792–3–7 Pennsylvania saw the publication, in four volumes, of the first part of the remarkable *Modern Chivalry*. The author, Hugh Henry Brackenridge (1748–1816), son of a poor Scotch immigrant, graduate of Princeton, tutor and licensed preacher, master of an academy in Maryland, editor of *The United States Magazine* in Philadelphia (1776), chaplain in the Revolutionary army, author of patriotic tragedies and pamphlets, and lawyer and judge in Pittsburg after 1781, brought to his work a culture and experience which gave his satiric picture of American life many of the features of truth. Farrago, the hero, is a new Don Quixote, his servant Teague a witless and grotesque Sancho Panza, but the chief follies of the book are found not in them but in the public which they encounter and which would gladly make Teague hero and office-holder. No man was a more convinced democrat than Brackenridge, but he was also solid, well-read, and deeply bored by fools who canted about free men and wise majorities. Against such cant and the excesses of political ambition he directed his chief satire, but he let few current fads and affectations go unwhipped. His book had an abundant popularity, especially along the frontier which it satirized. The second part (1804–5), ostensibly the chronicle of a new Western settlement, is almost a comic history of civilization in America. It is so badly constructed, however, and so often goes over ground well trodden in the earlier part as to be generally inferior to it in interest. Here Brackenridge depos-

ited scraps of irony and censure which he had been producing since 1787, when he had set out to imitate *Hudibras.*
His prose is better than his verse, plain and simple in style, by
his own confession following that of Hume, Swift, and Fielding.
Swift was his dearest master. Very curious, if hard to follow,
are the successive revisions by which Brackenridge kept pace
with new follies.

Smollett had something to do with another novel which,
though less read than *Modern Chivalry,* deserves mention with
it, *The Algerine Captive* (1797) of Royall Tyler, poet, wit,
playwright, and jurist.[1] The first volume has some entertaining
though not subtle studies of American manners; the second, a
tale of six years' captivity in Algiers, belongs with the many
books and pamphlets called forth by the war with Tripoli.[2]
Historically important is the preface, which declared that the
American taste for novels had grown in the past seven years
from apathy to a general demand.

Apparently the time was slowly ripening to the point at
which taste begins to support those who gratify it, and it is
notable that the first American to make authorship his sole
career had already decided for fiction. Charles Brockden
Brown came of good Quaker stock long settled in Pennsylvania,
where, at Philadelphia, he was born 17 January, 1771. He was
a frail, studious child, reputed a prodigy, and encouraged by
his parents in that frantic feeding upon books which was expected, in those days, of every American boy of parts. By
the time he was sixteen he had made himself a tolerable
classical scholar, contemplated three epics—on Columbus,
Pizarro, and Cortez—and hurt his health by over-work. As
he grew older he read with a hectic, desultory sweep in every
direction open to him. With his temper and education, he
developed into a hot young philosopher in those days of revolution. He brooded over the maps of remote regions, glowed with
eager schemes for perfecting mankind, and dabbled in subterranean lore as an escape from humane Philadelphia. He
kept a journal and wrote letters heavy with self-consciousness.
Put into a law office by his family, he found that his legal studies
only confirmed him in his resolution to be a man of letters. His

[1] See also Book I, Chap. IX and Book II, Chaps. II and III.
[2] See also Book II, Chap. II.

parents and brothers, who supported him in his adventure, urged him from a path so unpromising, but Brown, though he felt the pressure of their distress, clung stoutly, if gloomily, to the pursuits of literature. He speculated, debated, and wrote for the newspapers. His first identified work, a series of papers called *The Rhapsodist*, which appeared in *The Columbian Magazine*, August–November, 1789, glorified the proud and lonely soul.

Little is known of the next few years of his life. In 1793 he seems to have gone to New York to visit his friend Dr. Elihu Hubbard Smith, formerly a medical student in Philadelphia. Removed from the scenes of his old solitude, Brown became less solitary. Smith's friends, among them S. L. Mitchill, James Kent, and William Dunlap, Brown's future biographer, who belonged to a club called the Friendly Society, forced the young misanthrope to cast part of his coat. In 1795, after another visit to New York, he began an unidentified work, apparently speculative but not a romance, to "equal in extent Caleb Williams," a book in which Brown saw "transcendant merits." In spite of the first ardour which had made him sure he could finish his task in six weeks, he lost faith in its moral utility and never got beyond fifty pages, but he had gradually given up Dr. Johnson for Godwin as his model. July, 1796, saw him cease to be even a sleeping partner in his brother's counting house. Thenceforth he was nothing but an author.

The spirit of Godwin stirred eagerly in Brown during the early days of his freedom. Toward the end of 1797 he bore witness by writing *Alcuin*, a dialogue on the rights of women which took its first principles from Mary Wollstonecraft and Godwin. On the last day of December he says he finished a romance which appears to have been *Sky-Walk*, the manuscript of which was lost before it could be published. Early in 1798 he became a contributor to the new Philadelphia *Weekly Magazine*, which contains, among the fragments which always mark Brown's trail, the first two parts of *Alcuin*, called *The Rights of Women*, and nine chapters of *Arthur Mervyn*.[1] He announced *Sky-Walk* 17 March, 1798, in a letter to the *Weekly Magazine* signed "Speratus." In this earliest public statement of his ideals of fiction Brown spoke of the need of

[1] Published in 1799, with a second part, 1800.

native romances and ascribed the "value of such works" to "their moral tendency." Only by displaying characters "of soaring passions and intellectual energy," he believed, could a novelist hope "to enchain the attention and ravish the souls of those who study and reflect." But Brown was too good a democrat to write for geniuses alone. "A contexture of facts capable of suspending the faculties of every soul in curiosity, may be joined with depth of views into human nature and all the subtleties of reasoning."

With these opinions, and his apprenticeship already served, Brown took up his residence in New York during the summer of 1798. In two ardent years, which were more social than any that had gone before, Brown did all his best work. The single month of August served to produce *Wieland*, which made a stir and is still commonly held his masterpiece. The source of its plot has been shown[1] to be, in part, the actual murder of his whole family by a religious fanatic, "Mr. J—— Y——," of Tomhannock, New York, in December, 1781. To this Brown added the mysteries of spontaneous combustion and ventriloquism to make up the "contexture of facts capable of suspending the faculties of every soul in curiosity." These were for the vulgar. The apparent scene of action is laid upon the banks of the Schuylkill; this was patriotism. But the real setting is somewhere in the feverish climate of romantic speculation, and the central interest lies in the strange, unreal creatures "of soaring passions and intellectual energy," Wieland, crushingly impelled to crime by a mysterious voice which, however, but germinates seeds of frenzy already sleeping in his nature, and Carwin, the "biloquist," a villain who sins, not as the old morality had it, because of wickedness, but because of the driving power of the spirit of evil which no man can resist and from which only the weak are immune. These were cases of speculative pathology which Brown had met in his morbid twilights, beings who had for him the reality he knew best, that of dream and passion. It is the fever in the climate which lends the book, in spite of awkward narrative, strained probabilities, and a premature solution, its shuddering power. Here at least Brown was absorbed in his subject; here at least he gave a profound unity of effect never equalled in his later works.

[1] Van Doren, C., *Early American Realism*, *Nation*, 12 Nov., 1914.

Close upon this August followed the plague in New York. Brown was then living with Dr. Smith in Pine Street, and Smith, firm in the opinion that yellow fever could not be contagious, insisted upon taking into the house a stricken young Italian. Of the three only Brown escaped death. He thus came hand-to-hand with a hard reality, and, like other men of many dreams and few experiences, was deeply impressed by it. The effect upon his work, however, of this month of pestilence may be easily overstated. Five years before, Brown's family had left Philadelphia for a time to escape the great plague of 1793, and Brown had put memories of that visitation into *The Man at Home*, in *The Weekly Magazine*, and the earliest chapters of *Arthur Mervyn*, both written before his removal to New York. Curiously enough, the Dr. Stevens of the novel, by his hospitality to Mervyn, behaves much as did the Dr. Smith of reality, but invention was before fact. And when, in December, 1798, Brown wrote *Ormond* (1799), he not only laid his scene in Philadelphia in 1793, but he borrowed a whole chapter from *The Man at Home*. What the plague had been to Brown in 1793 it remained: a chapter in the annals of his native city, mysterious, the stuff of passion, and therefore fully congenial to his temper and ideals of art. He used it with sombre and memorable detail, as a background for mental or social ills.

It is characteristic of Brown that, while two of his notable romances recall his most vivid personal experience, all four of them wear the colours of *Caleb Williams*. From Godwin, Brown had his favourite subject, virtue in distress, and his favourite set of characters, a patron and a client. Perhaps he comes nearest to his master in *Ormond*. Constantia Dudley won the passionate regard of Shelley, to whom she was the type of virtuous humanity oppressed by evil customs. She is Brown's picture of feminine perfection, learned, self-reliant, pure, priggish. Ormond is quite clearly the child of romance and revolution, a hero who is a villain, a creature of nature who is the master of many destinies, a free will which must act as the agent of inevitable malice. All this seems pure Godwin, but it has a certain spirit of youth and ardour which Godwin lacked. In *Arthur Mervyn* the hero has to undergo less than the cumulative agony of Caleb Williams, for the simple reason that

Brown worked too violently to be able to organize a scheme of circumstances all bearing upon a single victim. At least in the second part of the book, the plot frays helplessly into flying ends which no memory can hold together, and the characters and "moral tendency" of a story rich in incident suffer a sad confusion. Brown was no match for Godwin in the art of calm and deliberate narrative, partly because of his vehement methods of work, partly because he lacked Godwin's finished and consistent philosophy of life. The leaven of rationalism stirs in his work, but it does not, as with Godwin, pervade the mass.

Passion, not hard conviction, gives Brown his positive qualities. He had a power in keeping up suspense which no clumsiness could destroy. In presenting the physical emotions of danger and terror he had a kind of ghoulish force. Without the deftness to get full value from his material, he had still a sharp eye for what was picturesque or dramatic. In *Edgar Huntly*, for which Brown was considerably indebted to the memory of *Sky-Walk*, he made notable use of that pioneer life which was to bulk so large in American fiction for half a century. His preface repeats his earlier plea, as "Speratus," for native matter in native fiction. From that ideal he never swerved. The plague, Wieland's frenzy, Queen Mab in *Edgar Huntly*,— these he had studied from the facts as he knew them. That his books are not more realistic proves merely that he was a romancer interested primarily in ideas and abstruse mental states which he saw with his eyes closed. "Sir," he told prying John Davis, "good pens, thick paper, and ink well diluted, would facilitate my composition more than the prospect of the broadest expanse of clouds, water, or mountains rising above the clouds." But when Brown opened his eyes he always saw Pennsylvania. His strangest supernaturalisms, too, turn out in the end to have rested on acts of nature which science can explain. It was his characters he romanticized. He saw in man a dignity which only the days of hopeful revolution can bestow, and he was thus urged to study souls with a passion which took him past the outward facts of humanity to a certain essential truth which gives him, among his contemporaries, his special virtue.

In April, 1799, Brown began to edit *The Monthly Magazine*

in New York and so entered the decade of journalism which closed his life. He wrote, indeed, besides fragments of fiction, two other novels, *Clara Howard* (1801) and *Jane Talbot* (1801), but they lack his old vigour. In *Jane Talbot* he seemed to renounce Godwin; gradually he became subdued to humanity and lost his concern with romance. He returned to Philadelphia in 1801, where, two years later, he founded *The Literary Magazine*. The stolid orthodoxy of his prospectus makes it clear that he was no longer a philosopher of the old stamp, although he did write two acts of a tragedy for John Bernard, and, told the play would not act, burned the work and kept its ashes in a snuff-box. In November, 1804, he married Miss Elizabeth Linn of New York, and was thereafter an exemplary husband, father, and drudge, who produced pamphlets, large parts of his magazine, and practically the whole of the useful *American Register* (1807–11). The fame of his novels, of which he claimed to think little, became a legend, but new editions were not called for. In 1809 he was elected to honorary membership in the New York Historical Society, with such notables as Lindley Murray, Noah Webster, Benjamin Trumbull, Timothy Dwight, Josiah Quincy, and George Clinton. He died of consumption 19 February, 1810. In England he was well known for at least a generation. *Blackwood's* praised him with the fiery pen of John Neal; Scott borrowed from him the names of two characters in *Guy Mannering;* Godwin himself owed to *Wieland* a hint for *Mandeville*. In his native country Brown has stood, with occasional flickerings of interest, firmly fixed as a literary ancestor.

There is little to note in American fiction between the close of Brown's career and the beginning of Cooper's. An absurd romance, *The Asylum* (1811), probably by Isaac Mitchell, was popular. Tabitha Tenny (1762–1837) produced a funny if robustious anti-romance, *Female Quixotism* (1808?); Samuel Woodworth[1] mingled conventional history with conventional romance in *The Champions of Freedom* (1816), which celebrated the second war with England. By this time the humane and thrilling art of Scott had already begun to be effective in America, as in Europe. At the first, however, Scott's peculiar qualities seemed to defy rivalry.

[1] See also Book II, Chaps. II and V.

"Of native *novels*," said John Bristed in 1818, "we have no great stock, and none good; our democratic institutions placing all the people on a dead level of political equality; and the pretty equal diffusion of property throughout the country affords but little room for varieties, and contrasts of character; nor is there much scope for fiction, as the country is quite new, and all that has happened from the first settlement to the present hour, respecting it, is known to every one. There is, to be sure, some traditionary romance about the Indians; but a novel describing these miserable barbarians, their squaws, and papooses, would not be very interesting to the present race of American readers."[1]

America, that is, without aristocracy, antiquity, and a romantic border, could not have a Scott. Seldom has time contradicted a prophet so fully and so soon as when Cooper, within three years, began to show that democracy has its contrasts, that two hundred years can be called a kind of antiquity, and that the border warfare between pioneer and Indian is one of the great chapters in the world's romance.

The task weighed less upon Cooper than it might had he been from boyhood at all bookish or, when he began his career, either scholar or conscious man of letters. But, unlike Brown, he had been trained in the world. Born at Burlington, New Jersey, 15 September, 1789, the son of Judge William Cooper and Susan Fenimore, James Cooper[2] was taken in November, 1790, to Cooperstown, the raw central village of a pioneer settlement recently established by his father on Otsego Lake, New York. Here the boy saw at first hand the varied life of the border, observed its shifts and contrivances, listened to tales of its adventures, and learned to feel the mystery of the dark forest which lay beyond the cleared circle of his own life. Judge Cooper, however, was less a typical backwoodsman than a kind of warden of the New York marches, like Judge Templeton in *The Pioneers*, and he did not keep his son in the woods but sent him, first to the rector of St. Peter's in Albany, who grounded him in Latin and hatred of Puritans, and then to Yale, where he wore his college duties so lightly as to be dis-

---

[1] *The Resources of the United States*, 1818, pp. 355–6.
[2] The family name was changed to Fenimore-Cooper by act of legislature in April, 1826. Cooper soon dropped the hyphen.

missed in his third year. Thinking the navy might furnish better discipline than Yale, Judge Cooper shipped his son before the mast on a merchant vessel to learn the art of seamanship which there was then no naval academy to teach. His first ship, the *Sterling*, sailed from New York in October, 1806, for Falmouth and London, thence to Cartagena, back to London, and once more to America in September of the following year. They were chased by pirates and stopped by searching parties, incidents Cooper never forgot. In January, 1808, he was commissioned midshipman. He served for a time on the *Vesuvius*, and later in the same year was sent with a party to Lake Ontario to build the brig *Oneida* for service against the British on inland waters. He visited Niagara, commanded for a time on Lake Champlain, and in November, 1809, was ordered to the *Wasp*. In the natural course of events he would have fought in the War of 1812, but, having been married in January, 1811, to Miss Susan Augusta DeLancey, he resigned his commission the following May and gave up all hope of a naval career.

Thus at twenty-two he exchanged a stirring youth for the quiet, if happy, life of a country proprietor. He spent the next eleven years, except for a stay at Cooperstown (1814–17), in his wife's native county of Westchester, New York. There, in a manner quite casual, he began his real work. His wife challenged him to make good his boast that he could write a better story than an English novel he was reading to her. He attempted it and wrote *Precaution* (1820), which, as might have been expected from a man who, in spite of a juvenile romance and a few doggerel verses, was little trained in authorship, is a highly conventional novel. Its scene is laid in England, and no quality is more notable than stiff elegance and painful piety. Cooper was dissatisfied with his book. "Ashamed to have fallen into the track of imitation, I endeavoured to repay the wrong done to my own views, by producing a work that should be purely American, and of which love of country should be the theme."[1] He chose for his hero a spy who had served John Jay during the Revolution, according to Jay's own account, with singular purity of motive. The work was carelessly done and published at the author's risk, and yet

[1] *A Letter to his Countrymen*, 1834, p. 98.

with the appearance of *The Spy* (22 December, 1821), American fiction may be said to have come of age.

This stirring tale has been, for many readers, an important factor in the tradition which national piety and the old swelling rhetoric have built up around the Revolution. The share of historical fact in it, indeed, is not large, but the action takes place so near to great events that the characters are all invested with something of the dusky light of heroes, while the figure of Washington moves among them like an unsuspected god. Such a quality in the novel might have gone with impossible partiality for the Americans had not Cooper's wife belonged to a family which had been loyal during the struggle for independence. As it was, he made his loyalists not necessarily knaves and fools, and so secured a fairness of tone which, aside from all questions of justice, has a large effect upon the art of the narrative. It is clear the British are enemies worth fighting. Perhaps by chance, Cooper here hit upon a type of plot at which he excelled, a struggle between contending forces, not badly matched, arranged as a pursuit in which the pursued are, as a rule, favoured by author and reader. In the management of such a device Cooper's invention, which was great, worked easily, and the flights of Birch from friend and foe alike exhibit a power to carry on plots with sustained sweep which belongs only to the masters of narration. To rapid movement Cooper added the virtues of a very real setting. He knew Westchester and its sparse legends as Scott knew the Border; his topography was drawn with a firm hand. In his characters he was not uniformly successful. Accepting for women the romantic ideals of the day and writing of events in which, of necessity, ladies could play but a small part, Cooper tended to cast his heroines, as even that day remarked, into a conventional mould of helplessness and decorum. With the less sheltered classes of women he was much more truthful. Of his men, too, the gentlemen are likely to be mere heroes, though Lawton is an interesting dragoon, while those of a lower order have more marked characteristics. Essentially memorable and arresting is Harvey Birch, peddler and patriot, outwardly no hero at all and yet surpassingly heroic of soul. The skill with which Birch is presented, gaunt, weather-beaten, canny, mysterious—a skill which Brown lacked—should not make one overlook the half-supernatural spirit of patriotism which, like the daemonic impulses in Brown's characters, drives Birch to his destiny at once wrecking and honouring him. This romantic fate also condemns him to be sad and lonely, a dedicated soul who captures attention by his secrecy and holds it throughout his career by his adventures. No character in American historical fiction has been able to obscure this first great character, whose fame has outlasted every fashion for almost a century.

With *The Spy* Cooper proved his power to invent situations, conduct a plot, vivify history and landscape, and create a certain type of heroic character. His public success was instant. The novel reached a third edition the following March; it was approved on the stage; European readers accepted it with enthusiasm. Pleased, though perhaps surprised, at this reception of his work, Cooper threw himself into the new career thus offered him with characteristic energy. He removed to New York and hurried forward the composition of *The Pioneers*, which appeared in February, 1823, with Cooper's first bumptious preface. Technically this book made no advance upon *The Spy*. Cooper had but one method, improvisation, and the absence of any very definite pursuit deprives *The Pioneers*, though it has exciting moments, of general suspense. But it is important as his first trial at the realistic presentation of manners in America. Dealing as he did with the Otsego settlement where his boyhood had been spent, and with a time (1793) within his memory, he could write largely from the fact. Whatever romance there is in the story lies less in its plot, which is relatively simple, or in its characters, which are, for the most part, studied under a dry light with a good deal of caustic judgment, than in the essential wonder of a pioneer life. The novel is not as heroic as *The Spy* had been. Indian John, the last of his proud race, is old and broken, corrupted by the settlements; only his death dignifies him. Natty Bumppo, a composite from many Cooperstown memories, is nobler because he has not yielded but carries his virtues, which even in Cooper's boyhood were becoming archaic along the frontier, into the deeper forest. Natty stands as a protest, on behalf of simplicity and perfect freedom, against encroaching law and order. In *The Pioneers*, however, he is not yet of the proportions which he later assumed, and only at the end, when he withdraws

from the field of his defeat by civilization, does he make his full
appeal. Cooper may have felt that there were still possibilities
in the character, but for the present he did not try to realize
them. Instead, he undertook to surpass Scott's *Pirate* in
seamanship and produced *The Pilot*, issued in January, 1824.[1]
With this third success he practically ended his experimental
stage. Like *The Spy*, his new tale made use of a Revolutionary
setting; like *The Pioneers*, it was full of realistic detail based on
Cooper's own experience. The result was that he not only
outdid Scott in sheer narrative, but he created a new literary
type, the tale of adventure on the sea, in which, though he was
to have many followers in almost every modern language, he
remains unsurpassed for vigour and variety. Smollett had
already discovered the racy humours of seamen, but it remained
for Cooper to capture for fiction the mystery and beauty, the
shock and thrill of the sea. Experts say that his technical
knowledge was sound; what is more important, he wrote, in
*The Pilot*, a story about sailing vessels which convinces lands-
men even in days of steam. The conventional element in the
novel is its hero, John Paul Jones, secret, Byronic, always
brooding upon a dark past and a darker fate. Thoroughly
original is that worthy successor of Birch and Natty Bumppo,
Long Tom Coffin, who lives and dies by the sea which has made
him, as love of country made the spy and the forest made the
old hunter.

Cooper had now become a national figure, although critical
judgment in New England condescended to him. He founded
the Bread and Cheese Club in New York, a literary society of
which he was the moving spirit; he took a prominent part in the
reception of Lafayette in 1824; in the same year Columbia
College gave him the honorary degree of Master of Arts. He
planned a series of *Legends of the Thirteen Republics*, aimed to
celebrate each of the original states, which he gave up after the
first, *Lionel Lincoln* (1825), for all his careful research failed to
please as his earlier novels had done. During the next two
years Cooper reached probably the highest point of his career
in *The Last of the Mohicans* (February, 1826) and *The Prairie*
(May, 1827). His own interest and the persuasion of his friends
led him to continue the adventures of Natty Bumppo, and

[1] But dated 1823.

very naturally he undertook to show both the days of Natty's prime and his final fortunes. In each case Cooper projects the old hunter out of the world of remembered Otsego, into the dark forest which was giving up its secrets in 1793, or into the mighty prairies which Cooper had not seen but which stretched, in his mind's eye, for endless miles beyond the forest, another mystery and another refuge. Natty, called Hawkeye in *The Last of the Mohicans*, no longer has the hardness which marred his age in *The Pioneers*. With all his virtues of hand and head he combines a nobility of spirit which the woods have fostered in a mind never spoiled by men. He grows nobler as he grows more remote, more the poet and hero as the world in which he moves becomes more wholly his own. Chingachgook has undergone even a greater change, has got back all the cunning and pride which had been deadened in Indian John. But Hawkeye and Chingachgook are both limited by their former appearance; one must still be the canny reasoner, the other a little saddened with passing years. The purest romance of the tale lies in Uncas, the forest's youngest son, gallant, swift, courteous, a lover for whom there is no hope, the last of the Mohicans. That Uncas was idealized Cooper was ready to admit; Homer, he suggested, had his heroes. And it is clear that upon Uncas were bestowed some of the virtues which the philosophers of the age had taught the world to find in a state of nature. Still, after a century, many smile upon the state of nature who are yet able to find in Uncas the perennial appeal of youth cut off in the flower. The action and setting of the novel are on the same high plane as the characters. The forest, in which all the events take place, surrounds them with a changeless majesty that sharpens, by contrast, the restless sense of danger. Pursuit makes almost the whole plot. The pursued party moving from Fort Edward to Fort William Henry has two girls to handicap its flight and to increase the tragedy of capture. Later the girls have been captured, and sympathy passes, a thing unusual in Cooper, to the pursuing rescuers. In these tasks Hawkeye and the Mohicans are opposed by the fierce capacity of Magua, who plays villain to Uncas's hero, in moral qualities Uncas's opposite. There is never any relaxation of suspense, and the scene in which Uncas reveals himself to the Delawares is one of the most thrilling moments in fiction.

*The Prairie* has less swiftness than *The Last of the Mohicans* but more poetry. In it Natty appears again, twenty years older than in *The Pioneers*, far away on the plains beyond the Mississippi. He owns his defeat and he still grieves over the murdered forest, but he has given up anger for the peace of old age. To him it seems that all his virtues are gone. Once valiant he must now be crafty; his arms are feeble; his eyes have so far failed him that, no longer the perfect marksman, he has sunk to the calling of a trapper. There is a pathos in his resignation which would be too painful were it not merely a phase of his grave and noble wisdom. He is more than ever what Cooper called him, "a philosopher of the wilderness." The only change is that he has left the perils and delights of the forest and has been subdued to the eloquent monotony of the plains. Nowhere else has Cooper shown such sheer imaginative power as in his handling of this mighty landscape. He had never seen a prairie; indeed, it is clear that he thought of a prairie as an ocean of land and described it partly by analogy. But he managed to endow the huge empty distances he had not seen with a presence as haunting as that of the populous forest he had known in his impressionable youth. And the old trapper, though he thinks of himself as an exile, has learned the secrets of the new nature and belongs to it. It is his knowledge that makes him essential to the action, which is again made up of flight and pursuit. Once more there are girls to be rescued, from white men as well as from Indians. There is another Magua in Mahtoree, another Uncas in the virtuous Hard-Heart. The Indians ride horses and are thus more difficult to escape than the Hurons had been. The flat prairies give fewer places of concealment. But the trapper is as ready as ever with new arts, and the flight ends as romance prescribes. The final scene, the death of the trapper in the arms of his young friends, is very touching and fine, yet reticently handled. For the most part, the minor characters, the lovers and the pedant, are not new to Cooper and are not notable. The family of Ishmael Bush, the squatter, however, make up a new element. They have been forced out of civilization by its virtues, as the trapper by its vices. They have strength without nobility and activity without wisdom. Except when roused, they are as sluggish as a prairie river, and like it they appear muddy and aimless.

Ishmael Bush always conveys the impression of terrific forces lying vaguely in ambush. His wife is nearly the most memorable figure among Cooper's women. She clings to her mate and cubs with a tigerish instinct that leaves her, when she has lost son and brother and retreats in a vast silent grief, still lingering in the mind, an inarticulate prairie Hecuba.

Possibly the novel owes some of its depth of atmosphere to the fact that it was finished in France and that Cooper was thus looking back upon his subject through a mist of regret. He had sailed for Europe with his family in June, 1826, to begin a foreign residence of more than seven years which had a large effect upon his later life and work. He found his books well known and society at large disposed to make much of him. In Paris he fraternized with Scott, who enjoyed and praised his American rival. Parts of his stay were in England, Holland, Germany, Switzerland, which delighted and astonished him, and Italy, which he loved. Most of his time, however, he passed at Paris, charmed with a gayer and more brilliant society than he could have known before. He did not cease to write. In January, 1828, he repeated the success of *The Pilot* with another sea tale, *The Red Rover*, which has always held a place among the most favoured of his books. The excitement is less sustained than in *The Pilot*, but portions of the narrative, notably those dealing with storms, are tremendous. The ocean here plays as great a part as Cooper had lately assigned to the prairie. One voices the calm of nature, one its tumult; both tend to the discipline of man. In 1829 he fared better than with *Lionel Lincoln* in another historical tale of New England, *The Wept of Wish-ton-Wish*, an episode of King Philip's War. It is a powerful novel, irregular and ungenial, not only because the Puritans represented were themselves unlovely, but because Cooper had an evident dislike for them which coloured all their qualities. This was followed in the next year by *The Water-Witch*, which Cooper thought his most imaginative book. It has a spirited naval battle, but it flatly failed to localize a supernatural legend in New York harbour.

Novels were not Cooper's whole concern during his years in Europe. Unabashedly, outspokenly American, he had secured from Henry Clay the post of consul at Lyons, that he might not seem, during his travels, a man without a country.

As consul, though his position was purely nominal, he felt called upon to resent the ignorance everywhere shown by Europeans regarding his native land, and he set out upon the task of educating them to better views. Cooper was not Franklin. His *Notions of the Americans* (1828), while full of information and a rich mine of American opinion for that day, was too obviously partisan to convince those at whom it was aimed. Its proper audience was homesick Americans. He indulged, too, in some controversy at Paris over the relative cost of French and American government which pleased neither nation. Finally, he applied his art to the problem and wrote three novels "in which American opinion should be brought to bear on European facts."[1] That is, in *The Bravo* (1831), *The Heidenmauer* (1832), and *The Headsman* (1833) he meant to show by proper instances the superiority of democracy to aristocracy as regards general happiness and justice. He claimed to be writing for his countrymen alone, some of whom must have been thrilled to come across a passage like "a fairer morning never dawned upon the Alleghanies than that which illumined the Alps," but he was not sufficiently master of his material, however stout and just his opinions, to make even *The Bravo*, the best of the three, as good as his pioneer romances.

Before he returned to New York in November, 1833, he was warned by his friend S. F. B. Morse that he would be disappointed. Cooper found himself, in fact, fatally cosmopolitan in the republic he had been justifying for seven years. Always critical, he sought to qualify too sweeping praise of America precisely as he had qualified too sweeping censure in Europe. But he had not learned tact while becoming a citizen of the world, and he soon angered the public he had meant to set right. The result was the long and dreary wrangling which clouded the whole remainder of his life and has obscured his fame almost to the present day. If he had attended the dinner planned in his honour on his return, he might have found his welcome warmer than he thought it. If he had been an observer keen enough, he would have seen that the new phases of democracy which he disliked were in part a gift to the old seaboard of that very frontier of which he had been painter and annalist. But he did not see these things, and so he carried on

[1] *A Letter to his Countrymen*, p. 12.

a steady fight, almost always as right in his contentions as he was wrong-headed in his manner. From Cooperstown, generally his residence, except for a few winters in New York, to the end of his life, he lectured and scolded. His *Letter to his Countrymen* (1834), stating his position, and *The Monikins* (1835), an unbelievably dull satire, were the first fruits of his quarrel. He followed these with five books dealing with his European travels and constantly irritating to the people of both continents. He indulged in a heated altercation with his fellow townsmen over some land which they thought theirs, although it was certainly his. In 1838 he published a fictitious record, *Homeward Bound* and its sequel *Home as Found*, of the disappointment of some Americans who return from Europe and find America what Cooper had recently found it. He proclaimed his political principles in *The American Democrat* (1838). Most important of all, he declared war upon the newspapers of New York and went up and down the state suing those that had libelled him. He won most of the suits, but though he silenced his opponents he had put his fame into the hands of persons who, unable to abuse, could at least neglect him.

His solid *History of the Navy of the United States of America* (1839) turned his attention once more to naval affairs, with which he busied himself during much of his remaining career. He wrote *Lives of Distinguished American Naval Officers* (1842–5), and *Ned Myers* (1843), the life of a common sailor who had been with him on the *Sterling*. The *History* led to a furious legal battle, but generally Cooper left his quarrels behind him when he went upon the sea. As a cosmopolitan, he seemed to feel freer out of sight of land, on the public highway of the nations. His novels of this period, however, are uneven in merit. *The Two Admirals* (1842) contains one of his best naval battles; *Wing-and-Wing* (1842) ranks high among his sea tales, richly romantic and glowing with the splendours of the Mediterranean. *Mercedes of Castile* (1840) has little interest beside that essential to the first voyage of Columbus. The two parts of *Afloat and Ashore* (1844), dealing powerfully as they do with the evils of impressment, are notable chiefly for sea fights and chases. *Jack Tier* (1846–8) is a lurid piratical tale of the Mexican War; *The Crater* (1847) does poorly what *Robinson Crusoe* does supremely; *The Sea Lions* (1849) has the distinction of marking the highest point in that religious bigotry which pervades Cooper's later novels as thoroughly as the carping spirit which kept him always alert for a chance to take some fling at his countrymen.

The real triumph of his later years was that he wrote, in the very midst of his hottest litigation, *The Pathfinder* (March, 1840) and *The Deerslayer* (August, 1841). One realizes, in reading them, that the forest more than the ocean was for Cooper a romantic sanctuary, as it was for Pathfinder the true temple, full of the "holy calm of nature," the teacher of beauty, virtue, laws. Returning to these solemn woods, Cooper was subdued once more to the spirit which had attended his first great days. The fighting years through which he had passed had left him both more mellow and more critical than at first. During the same time he had gone far enough from the original character of Leather-Stocking to become aware of traits which should be brought out or explained. It was too late to make his hero entirely consistent for the series, but Cooper apparently saw the chance to fill out the general outline, and he did it with such skill that those who read the five novels in the order of events will notice relatively few discrepancies, since *The Deerslayer* prepares for nearly all that follows. In *The Pathfinder*, undertaken to show Natty in love and to combine the forest and a ship in the same tale, Cooper was at some pains to point out how Pathfinder's candour, self-reliance, justice, and fidelity had been developed by the life he had led in the forest. Leather-Stocking, indeed, does not seem more conscious of these special gifts, but Cooper does. Still there is abundant action, another flight through the woods, a storm on Lake Ontario, a siege at a blockhouse. Chingachgook, unchanged, is with Pathfinder, who varies from his earlier character in little but his love for a young girl whom he finally surrenders to a more suitable lover. His love affair threatens for a moment to domesticate Natty, but the sacrifice restores him to his old solitude.

In the final book of the series, *The Deerslayer*, Cooper performed with full success the hard task of representing the scout in the fresh morning of his youth. Love appears too in this story, but Deerslayer, unable to love a girl who has been corrupted by the settlements, turns to the forest with his best devotion. The book is the tale of his coming of age.

Already a hunter, he kills his first man and thus enters the long career which lies before him. That career, however, had already been traced by Cooper, and the distress with which Deerslayer realizes that he has human blood on his hands becomes immeasurably eloquent. It gives the figure of the man almost a new dimension; one remembers the many deaths Natty has yet to deal. In other matters he is near his later self, for he starts life with a steady philosophy which, through all the many experiences of *The Deerslayer*, keeps him to the end as simple and honourable as at the outset.

The novel is thus an epitome of the whole career of the most memorable character American fiction has given to the world. Leather-Stocking is very fully drawn; Cooper's failure to write a sixth novel, as he at one time planned, which should show Natty in the Revolution, may be taken as a sign that he felt, however unconsciously, that the picture was finished. It is hard, indeed, to see how he could have added to the scout without taking something from the spy. More important still, the virtue of patriotism, if carried to the pitch that must have been demanded for that hero in that day, would surely have been a little alien to the cool philosopher of the woods. Justice, not partisanship, is Leather-Stocking's essential trait. In him Cooper exhibited, even better than he knew, his special idea that human character can be brought to a noble proportion and perfection in the school of pure nature. Now this idea, generally current in Cooper's youth, had an effect upon the Leather-Stocking tales of the greatest moment. Because their hero, as the natural man, had too simple a soul to call for minute analysis, it was necessary for Cooper to show him moving through a long succession of events aimed to test the firmness of his virtues. There was thus produced the panorama of the American frontier which, because of Cooper's incomparable fusion of strangeness and reality, at once became and has remained the classic record of an heroic age.

He wrote more border tales before his death. *Wyandotte* (1843) deals largely with the siege of a blockhouse near the upper Susquehanna, and *The Oak-Openings* (1848), the fruit of a journey which he made to the West in 1847, is a tale of bee hunting and Indian fighting on the shores of Lake Michigan. Full of border material, too, is the trilogy of *Littlepage Manu-*

scripts, *Satanstoe* (1845), *The Chainbearer* (1846), and *The Redskins* (1846). Having tried the autobiographical method with Miles Wallingford in *Afloat and Ashore*, Cooper now repeated it through three generations of a New York family. In the last he involved himself unduly in the question of anti-rentism and produced a book both fantastic and dull; the second is better by one of Cooper's most powerful figures, the squatter Thousandacres, another Titan of the brood of Ishmael Bush; the first, if a little beneath Cooper's best work, is so only because he was somewhat rarely at his best. No other novel, by Cooper or any other, gives so firm and convincing a picture of colonial New York. Even Cooper has no more exciting struggle than that of Corny Littlepage with the icy Hudson. But the special virtue of *Satanstoe* is a quality Cooper nowhere else displays, a positive winsomeness in the way Littlepage unfolds his memories (now sweetened by many years) and his humorous crotchets in the same words. There are pages which read almost like those of some vigorous Galt or Goldsmith. Unfortunately, Cooper did not carry this vein further. His comedy *Upside Down*, produced at Burton's Theatre, New York, 18 June, 1850, was a failure, and his last novel, *The Ways of the Hour* (1851), lacks every charm of manner. With his family and a few friends he lived his latter days in honour and affection, but he held the public at a sour distance and before his death, 14 September, 1851, set his face against a reconciliation even in the future by forbidding any biography to be authorized. The published facts of his life still leave his personality less known to the general world than that of any American writer of equal rank.

This might be somewhat strange, since Cooper was lavish of intrusions into his novels, were it not that he wrote himself down, when he spoke in his own person, not only a powerful and independent man, but a scolding, angry man, and thus made his most revealing novels his least read ones. One thinks of Scott, who, when he shows himself most, wins most love. The difference further characterizes the two men. In breadth of sympathies, humanity, geniality, humour, Cooper is less than Scott. He himself, in his review of Lockhart, said that Scott's great ability lay in taking a legend or historical episode, which Scotland furnished in splendid profusion, and reproducing it with marvellous grace and tact. "This faculty of creating a *vraisemblance*, is next to that of a high invention, in a novelist." It is clear that Cooper felt his own inferiority to Scott in "creating a *vraisemblance*" and that he was always conscious of the relative barrenness of American life; it is also tolerably clear that he himself aimed at what he thought the higher quality of invention. Cooper's invention, indeed, was not without a solid basis; he is not to be neglected as an historian. No man better sums up in literature the spirit of that idealistic, irascible, pugnacious, somewhat crude, and half aristocratic older democracy which established the United States. No one fixed the current heroic traditions of his day more firmly to actual places. No one else supplied so many facts to the great legend of the frontier. Fact no less than fiction underlies the character which, for all time, Cooper gave to the defeated race of red men, who, no longer a menace as they had been to the first settlers, could now take their place in the world of the imagination, sometimes idealized, as in Uncas and Hard-Heart, but more often credibly imperfect and uncivilized. It was his technical knowledge of ships and sailors which led Cooper to write sea tales, a province of romance in which he still takes rank, among many followers, as teacher and master of them all. True, Cooper had not Scott's resources of historical learning to fall back upon when his invention flagged, any more than he had Scott's resources of good-nature when he became involved in argument; but when, as in the Leather-Stocking tales, his invention could move most freely, it did unaided what Scott, with all his subsidiary qualities, could not outdo. This is to credit Cooper with an invention almost supreme among romancers. Certainly it is difficult to explain why, with all his faults of clumsiness, prolixity, conventional characterization, and ill temper, he has been the most widely read American author, unless he is to be called one of the most impressive and original.

# CHAPTER VII

## Fiction II

### CONTEMPORARIES OF COOPER

IT is mere coincidence that Cooper was born in the year which produced *The Power of Sympathy* and that when he died *Uncle Tom's Cabin* was passing through its serial stage, and yet the limits of his life mark almost exactly the first great period of American fiction. Paulding, Thompson, Neal, Kennedy, Simms, Melville, to mention no slighter figures, outlived him, but not, as a current fashion, the type of romance which had flourished under Cooper. Although by 1851 tales of adventure had begun to seem antiquated, they had rendered a large service to the course of literature: they had removed the stigma, for the most part, from the word novel. For the brutal scrapes of eighteenth-century fiction the new romance had substituted deeds of chivalrous daring; it had supplanted blunt fleshliness by a chaste and courtly love, and had tended to cure amorous sentimentalism by placing love below valour in the scale of virtues. Familiar life, tending to sordidness, had been succeeded by remote life, generally idealized; historical detail had been brought in to teach readers who were being entertained. Cooper, like Scott, was more elevated than Fielding and Smollett, more realistic than the Gothic romancers, more humane than Godwin or Brown. The two most common charges against the older fiction, that it pleased wickedly and that it taught nothing, had broken down before the discovery, except in illiberal sects, that the novel is fitted both for honest use and for pleasure.

In Europe, at Cooper's death, a new vogue of realism had begun, but America still had little but romance. With so vast

and mysterious a hinterland free to any one who might come
to take it, novelists, like farmers, were less prompt in America
than in Europe to settle down to cultivate intensively known
fields.    There is a closer analogy, indeed, between the geo-
graphic and the imaginative frontier of the United States
than has been pointed out.    As the first advanced, thin,
straggling, back from the Atlantic, over the Alleghanies, down
the Ohio, beyond the Mississippi, across the Great Plains and
the Rockies to the Pacific, the other followed, also thin and
straggling but with an incessant purpose to find out new
territories over which the imagination could play and to claim
them for its own.    "Until now," wrote Cooper in 1828, "the
Americans have been tracing the outline of their great national
picture.    The work of filling up has just seriously commenced."
He had in mind only the physical process, but his image applies
as well to that other process in which he was the most effective
pioneer.    Two years after his death the outline of the national
picture, at least of contiguous territory, was established, and
the nation gave itself to the problem of occupation.    In fiction,
too, after the death of Cooper the main tendency for nearly a
generation was away from the conquest of new borders to the
closer cultivation, east of the Mississippi, of ground already
marked.

As late as 1825 Jared Sparks thought ten American novels
a striking output for one year, but during the second quarter
of the century Cooper had many helpers in his great task.    In
New England Neal, Miss Sedgwick, Mrs. Child, and D. P.
Thompson had already set outposts before Hawthorne came to
capture that section for classic ground.    Paulding and Hoffman
assisted Cooper in New York, and Paulding took Swedish
Delaware for himself; for Pennsylvania Bird was Brown's chief
successor; Maryland had Kennedy; Virginia, without many
native novels, began to undergo, in the hands of almost every
romancer who dealt with the founders of the republic, that
idealization which has made it, especially since the Civil War,
the most romantic of American states; South Carolina passed
into the pages of Simms; Georgia and the lower South brought
forth a school of native humorists who abounded in the truth as
well as in the fun of that border;[1] the Mississippi and the Ohio

[1] See Book II, Chap. XIX.

considerable merit as a novelist, particularly in the matter of comedy, which most of the romancers lacked. *Koningsmarke* (1823) contains some pleasant burlesquing in its stories of adventures among the Delaware Swedes. Here, as in his later works, Paulding laughed at what he called "Blood-Pudding Literature." He was too facile in lending his pen, as parodist or follower, to whatever fashion happened to be approved to do any very individual work, but *The Dutchman's Fireside* (1831), probably his masterpiece, deserves to be mentioned with Mrs. Grant's *Memoirs of an American Lady* (1809), on which it is based, and Cooper's *Satanstoe*, much its superior, as a worthy record of colonial life along the Hudson. New Jersey and Pennsylvania appear in nothing better than the minor romances of Robert Montgomery Bird (1803–54),[1] *The Hawks of Hawk Hollow* (1835), *Sheppard Lee* (1836), and *The Adventures of Robin Day* (1839), vigorous and sometimes merry tales but not of permanent merit.

To the school of his friend Irving may be assigned the urbane John Pendleton Kennedy (1795–1870). Of excellent Virginia connections, he was born and educated in Baltimore, which, like New York, made rapid progress after the Revolution, first in commerce and then in taste. Having served bloodlessly enough in the War of 1812 and been admitted to the bar, Kennedy lived as merrily as Irving in the chosen circles of his native town. With Peter Hoffman Cruse he issued *The Red Book* (1818–19),[2] a kind of Baltimore *Salmagundi* in prose and verse, and after several years devoted to law and politics made a decided success with *Swallow Barn* (1832), obviously suggested by *Bracebridge Hall* but none the less notable as a pioneer record of the genial life of a Virginia plantation. Although the story counts for little, Kennedy's easy humour and real skill at description and the indication of character make the book distinguished. His later novels, *Horse-Shoe Robinson* (1835), in which he dealt with the Revolution in the Carolinas, and *Rob of the Bowl* (1838), which has its scene laid in colonial Maryland, are nearer Cooper, with the difference that Kennedy depended, as he had done in *Swallow Barn*, on fact not invention for almost all his action as well as for his details of topography and costume. Indeed,

[1] See also Book II, Chap. II.    [2] See also Book II, Chap. III.

he founded the career of Horse-Shoe Robinson upon that of an actual partisan with such care that the man is said later to have approved the record as authentic. Decidedly Kennedy's gift was for enriching actual events with a finer grace and culture than many of the rival romancers could command. His style is clear, his methods always simple and rational. Of his miscellaneous writings *The Annals of Quodlibet* (1840) is tolerable satire, and the *Memoirs of the Life of William Wirt* (1849), substantial biography. Kennedy's range of friendship with other authors was wide; he had a full and honourable public career in city, state, and national affairs.

South of the Potomac there were relatively few novelists during Cooper's lifetime. The great tradition of Virginia was sustained by her orators and scholars rather than by her writers of fiction, but Nathaniel Beverley Tucker (1784–1851) was both scholar and novelist. His *George Balcombe* (1836) Poe thought the best novel by an American; his *Partisan Leader* (1836), primarily famous because it prophesied disunion, is clearly a notable though little known work. No other American of the time wrote with such classical restraint and pride as Tucker. No book, of any time, surpasses *The Partisan Leader* for intense, conscious Virginianism. Mention should be made of Dr. William Alexander Caruthers (1800–46), perhaps less for his genial novels, *The Cavaliers of Virginia* (1835) and *The Knights of the Horse-Shoe* (1845), than for his widely-known sketch *Climbing the Natural Bridge.*[1] The lower states best appeared in the pages of their native humorists, who seldom wrote novels. South Carolina produced the writer who, among all the American romancers of the first half century, ranks nearest Cooper for scope and actual achievement.

William Gilmore Simms has been, to a pathetic degree, the victim of attachment to his native state. It was one of his strongest passions. He loved every foot of South Carolina, he honoured its traditions and defended its institutions even when they hurt his own fame. His best work was largely devoted to an heroic account of the Revolution in the Carolinas. But, whether his birth did not admit him to the aristocracy of Charleston, or because of a traditional disrespect for native

[1] First published in *The Knickerbocker Magazine*, July, 1838.

books, South Carolina refused Simms the honour certainly due his powers. In this the whole South was negligent; Simms had to depend too largely upon the North for publishers and a public. Unfortunately, Northern readers, though hospitable to his tales from the first, were not as familiar with Southern manners and traditions as with those nearer home, and Simms had not the mastery of illusion which might have overcome this disadvantage. The solid grounds, therefore, of his romance were partly wasted upon an audience not competent to recognize them. Time must have taught South Carolina more cordiality to her best writer had not the Civil War forced all literary matters into the background for a generation. When, later, the South became eager to establish its claims to a literature, the vogue of historical romance had passed, and Simms, not yet having found the public he deserved, never has found it.

Unlike Poe, he had not the art or patience to make himself independent of general approval. Born in Charleston, 17 April, 1806, son of a merchant of Irish birth who lost both his wife and his fortune during the winter of 1807–8, Simms got but a bare schooling and was early apprenticed to a druggist. He seems, during his youth, to have been as bookish as Brockden Brown, but it was romantic poetry and history which claimed his attention, not romantic speculation. From his grandmother, with whom he lived as a boy, he heard innumerable legends of the Revolution, South Carolina's heroic age, and cherished them with a poetic and patriotic devotion. When he was eighteen he went to visit his father, who had left Charleston for the West, become friend and follower of Andrew Jackson, and finally settled on a plantation in Mississippi. The young poet was thus shown the manners of a frontier which corresponded, in many ways, to that of Cooper, and he seems, during extended travels, to have observed its rough comedy and violent melodrama with sharp eyes. But the border was not, for Simms, his first love, and he went back, against his father's advice, to the traditions and dreams of Charleston. There he was married in 1826, was admitted to the bar the next year, published the first of his many volumes of verse, and suffered the death of his young wife. Thence, in 1832, he set out to the North on a career of authorship in which necessity confirmed his training and temper by urging him to immense industry and careless work.

It is unnecessary to say more of the miscellaneous tasks of Simms than that he wrote moderate poetry to the end of his life, including three tragedies, that he edited the apocryphal plays of Shakespeare, that he produced popular histories of South Carolina and popular biographies of Marion, Captain John Smith, the Chevalier Bayard, and General Greene, and that he kept up a ceaseless flood of contributions to periodicals. His range of interest and information was large, but he commonly dealt with American, and particularly Southern, affairs. His really significant work, as a romancer, he began in 1833 with a Godwinian tale of crime, *Martin Faber*, which was so well received that he followed it in 1834 with *Guy Rivers* and in 1835 with *The Yemassee*, two romances in which almost the full extent of his powers was instantly displayed. *Guy Rivers*, a conventional piece as regards the love affair which makes a part of the plot, is a tale of deadly strife between the laws of Georgia and a fiendish bandit. A born story-teller, like Cooper, Simms was as heedless as Cooper of structure and less careful as to style, but he was too rapid to be dull and he revealed to the reading world a new adventurous frontier. In *The Yemassee* his concern for the history of South Carolina bore fruit, a moving tale of the Yemassee War of 1715. This book is to the famous Revolutionary group what *The Spy* is to the Leather-Stocking tales, a romance standing somewhat by itself at the beginning of the author's career and yet quite the equal of any of the most representative volumes. Once again Simms took hints from current romances, but when he set himself to describing the rich landscape of South Carolina or to recounting its annals he was more fully master of his material than in *Guy Rivers* and more admirable in proportion as his subject was more congenial to him. He gave his Indians the dignity and courage which, he said, they must have had at an earlier period; he invented for them a mythology. The white and black characters have somewhat less heroic dimensions, but they are done with great vigour and some realism.

His third novel having met with popular success, Simms turned to the Revolution and published *The Partisan* (1835), designed as the first volume of a trilogy which should celebrate these valorous times. He later wavered in his scheme, and, though he finally called *Mellichampe* (1836) and *Katherine Walton* (1851) the other members of his trilogy, he grouped round them four more novels that have obvious marks of kinship. *The Partisan* traces events from the fall of Charleston to Gates's defeat at Camden; the action of *Mellichampe*, which is nearly parallel to that of *Katherine Walton*, the proper sequel of *The Partisan*, takes place in the interval between Camden and the coming of Greene; *The Scout*, originally called *The Kinsmen* (1841), illustrates the period of Greene's first triumphs; *The Sword and the Distaff* (1852), later known as *Woodcraft*, furnishes a kind of comic afterpiece for the series. Simms subsequently returned to the body of his theme and produced *The Forayers* (1853) and its sequel *Eutaw* (1856) to do honour to the American successes of the year 1781.

Of these *The Scout* is perhaps the poorest, because of the large admixture of Simms's cardinal vice, horrible melodrama; *Woodcraft* is on many grounds the best, by reason of its rather close-knit plot and the high spirits with which it tells of the exploits and courtships, after the war, of Captain Porgy, the best comic character in the whole range of the older American romance. But neither of these works is quite representative of the series; neither has quite the dignity which, lacking in his sensational tales of the border, Simms always imparted to his work when he was most under the spell of the Carolina tradition. That always warmed him; indeed at times he seems drunk with history. He had a tendency to overload his tales with solid blocks of fact derived from his wide researches, forgetting, in his passionate antiquarianism, his own belief that "the chief value of history consists in its proper employment for the purposes of art," or, rather, too much thrilled by bare events to see that they needed to be coloured into fiction if they were to fit his narrative. Simms never took his art too lightly. He held that the "modern Romance is the substitute which the people of the present day offer for the ancient epic."[1] In this sense, the seven novels are his epic of the Revolution. Marion, the Agamemnon of these wars, had already become a kind of legend, thanks to the popular memory and the fantastic ardour of Weems, but it remained for Simms to

[1] Preface to *The Yemassee* (1853).

show a whole society engaged in the task which Marion did best. Simms's defect was that he relied too much upon one plot for all his tales, a partisan and a loyalist contending for the hand of the same girl, and that he repeated certain stock scenes and personages again and again. His great virtue was that he handled the actual warfare not only with interest and power but that he managed to multiply episodes with huge fecundity. He described, in a surge of rhetoric, his favourite material:

> Partisan warfare, itself, is that irregular and desultory sort of life, which is unavoidably suggestive of the deeds and feelings of chivalry—such as gave the peculiar character, and much of the charm, to the history of the middle ages. The sudden onslaught— the retreat as sudden—the midnight tramp—the moonlight *bivouack* —the swift surprise, the desperate defence—the cruel slaughter and the headlong flight—and, amid the fierce and bitter warfare, always, like a sweet star shining above the gloom, the faithful love, the constant prayer, the devoted homage and fond allegiance of the maiden heart!

The passage is almost a generalized epitome of his Revolutionary romances. It also betrays the fact that by "epic" Simms meant not Homer but Froissart. If he is more bloody, he is also more sentimental than Cooper. His women, though Nelly Floyd in *Eutaw* is strikingly pathetic and mysterious, and Matiwan in *The Yemassee* is nearly as tragic as romance can make her, are almost all fragile and colourless things, not because Southern women were, but because pseudo-chivalry prescribed. His comedy is successful only, and there not always, in the words and deeds of the gourmand Porgy. Simms is a master in the description of landscapes, from the sterile wastes of Georgia to the luxuriant swamps in which the partisans found a refuge; but he lays little emphasis on the poetry or philosophy of "nature."

In historical tales, not Cooper's forte, Simms succeeded best; he was inferior when he dealt with the border. This may have been due partly to the intrinsic superiority of the earlier frontier to that which Simms had observed. At least it shows itself chiefly in the fact that Simms grew more melodramatic, as Cooper more poetic, the farther he ventured from regions of order and law. *Richard Hurdis* (1838), *Border Beagles* (1840), *Beauchampe* (1842), and *Charlemont* (1856) are amazingly sensational. Nor was Simms happy when he abandoned native for foreign history, as in *Pelayo* (1838), *The Damsel of Darien* (1839), *Count Julian* (1845), and *Vasconselos* (1854). Even more than Cooper, he lacked judgment as to the true province of his art; like Cooper, he constantly turned aside to put his pen to service in the distracted times through which he was fated to live.

His life was singularly noble and singularly tragic. Married a second time, in 1836, to Miss Chevillette Roach, and thus master of Woodlands, a respectable plantation in his own state, he led a pleasantly feudal existence, hospitable to many guests, and helpful, as the most prosperous Southern man of letters, to nearly all the authors and journals of the South. He spent the summers in Charleston where he came to preside over a coterie of younger writers; he made not infrequent visits to New York, and was well received. Besides concerning himself unofficially with all public affairs, he served in the state legislature for the session of 1844–46. As the agitation which led to civil war grew more heated, Simms plunged into stormy apologetics for the grounds and virtues of slavery. Just on the eve of the struggle he repeated the success of *The Yemassee* with a romance of seventeenth-century Carolina, *The Cassique of Kiawah* (1859), a stirring, varied story which must be ranked with his better books. Then upon him came the disasters of war. At first he was as sure that the South would win as that the South was just. His gradual realization that it was a losing contest would have shattered him had he been of any but the strongest stuff. His house, on the line of Sherman's march, was burned in February, 1865; he witnessed the wicked burning of Columbia. When the war ended he had lost his wife, nine of his fourteen children, (two of them since 1861), many of his best friends, and the whole of his fortune, yet he managed, in a more horrid overthrow than Scott's, to drive himself to work again with courage and energy, and kept up his efforts till his death, undoubtedly hastened by his labour, on 11 June, 1870. Despite his friends and admirers, the eclipse of those last years has never been quite lifted, and the somewhat fitful republication of his romances has left him much less read than he deserves, though few competent judges will put him far below Cooper, at least as regards strength and vigour, in the type of romance in which no third American name can be associated with theirs.

West of the Alleghanies the growth of fiction during the life of Cooper was, of course, scanty. It consisted less of novels than of tales and sketches, which, produced for the most part by writers of Eastern birth dwelling for a time in the new settlements, were chiefly concerned with the representation of manners not known to the seaboard. The wittiest of these writers was Mrs. Caroline Matilda Stansbury Kirkland (1801–64), a native of New York who took advantage of a three years' stay in Michigan to produce *A New Home—Who'll Follow* (1839), a volume of keen and sprightly letters on the frontier avowedly in the manner of Miss Mitford, and a continuation, *Forest Life* (1842), which is less piquant only because it was not the first. In the later *Western Clearings* (1846) she was somewhat more regular but not so racy and natural. A more representative Western author was James Hall (1793–1868),[1] who, born in Philadelphia, went west in search of adventure, lived in Illinois and Ohio, edited an annual and a magazine, and served as interpreter between West and East much as Irving did between America and Europe. Hall's manner, indeed, is like Irving's in its leisurely, genial narrative, its abundant descriptions, and its affection for supernatural legends which could be handled smilingly. He had real powers of fidelity, the only merit he claimed, to the life he knew, but he had also a florid style and a vein of romantic sentiment which too seldom rings true. *Legends of the West* (1832), *Tales of the Border* (1834), and *The Wilderness and the War-Path* (1846) contain his best stories; he is perhaps better known, not quite justly, for such books as *Sketches of History, Life and Manners, in the West* (1835), wherein he published his wide knowledge of a section then becoming important in the national life. It is as traveller and observer, too, not as romancer, that Timothy Flint (1780–1840) has come to be remembered, though he essayed fiction as well as nearly every other type of authorship in the days when he and Hall divided the West between them as a province to be worked by their

[1] See also Book II, Chap. xx.

versatile pens. Many novels celebrated Kentucky, which, as the first Western state of the Union, had secured a primacy in romance, between the Alleghanies and the Mississippi, that it has never lost. Paulding, Simms, and Bird were chief among those who laid plots there. Bird's best novel, *Nick of the Woods* (1837), an exciting tale of border warfare in 1782, is notable for its attempt to correct Cooper's heroic drawing of the Indian and for its presentation of a type often spoken of in frontier annals, the white man who, crazed by Indian atrocities, gave his whole life to a career of ruthless vengeance.[1] The great romance of Kentucky, however, while perpetuated by no single novel or novelist, centres round the life and character of Daniel Boone, who became, by the somewhat capricious choice of tradition, a folk hero, standing among other pioneers as Leather-Stocking stands among native characters of fiction. A similar, though smaller, fame belongs to David Crockett of Tennessee, who comes somewhat closer to literature by the fact of having written an *Autobiography* (1834).

The region west of the Mississippi continued in the popular mind to be a strange land for which the reports of explorers and travellers did the work of fiction, and Cooper's *Prairie* had few followers. In 1834, however, Albert Pike (1809–91) published in his *Prose Sketches and Poems* some vivid tales of life in the South-west. That same year appeared *Calavar*, in writing which Bird had the avowed purpose of calling the attention of his public to romantic Mexico. The next year he repeated his success with *The Infidel*, another story of Cortez and the Conquest. Reading these novels with their tolerable learning in Mexican antiquities, their considerable power, and their superior sense of the pomp of great historical events, one is reminded how few romances of the period ventured beyond native borders. Whatever may be said of the poets, the novelists kept themselves almost always scrupulously at home. One set of exceptions was those who dealt with Spain and Mexico, and even with them the motive was largely, as with the contemporary historians, to honour the ancient bond between America and the European nation which had discovered it. In a more distant scene Mrs. Child laid her

[1] For the play founded on this novel, see Book II, Chap. II.

*Philothea* (1836), a gentle, ignorant romance of the Athens of Pericles, the fruit of a real desire to escape from the clang of current life. Not much more remote from any thinkable reality was George Tucker's *Voyage to the Moon* (1827), in which a sound scholar satirized terrestrial follies in the spirit which seemed to his friends like that of Swift.[1] To a slightly later date belong the two novels of William Starbuck Mayo (1812–95), *Kaloolah* (1849) and *The Berber* (1850), stories of wild adventure in Africa. The first contains a strange mixture of satire and romance in its account of a black Utopia visited by the Yankee hero Jonathan Romer.

Contemporaries suspected, what Mayo denied, that *Kaloolah* must have taken hints from *Typee*. The suspicion was natural at a time when Melville, at the height of his first fame, had not entered the long seclusion which even yet obscures the merit of that romancer who, among all Cooper's contemporaries, has suffered least from the change of fashion in romance. Herman Melville, grandson of the conservative old gentleman upon whom Holmes wrote *The Last Leaf*, and son of a merchant of New York, was born there, 1 August, 1819. The early death of his father and the loss of the family fortune having narrowed Melville's chances for higher schooling to a few months in the Albany Classical School, he turned his hand to farming for a year, shipped before the mast to Liverpool in 1837, taught school from 1837–40, and in January, 1841, sailed from New Bedford on a whaling voyage into the Pacific. Upon the experiences of that voyage his principal work is founded. The captain of the *Acushnet*, it seems, treated the crew badly, and Melville, with the companion whom he calls Toby, escaped from the ship to the Island of Nukuheva [Nukahiva] in the Marquesas and strayed into the cannibal valley Typee [Taipi], where the, savages kept Melville for four months in an "indulgent captivity." Rescued by an Australian whaler, Melville visited Tahiti and other islands of the Society group, took part in a mutiny, and once more changed ship, this time setting out for Honolulu. After some months as a clerk in Hawaii, he joined the crew of the frigate *United States* and returned by the Horn to Boston, October, 1844. "From my twenty-fifth year," he told Hawthorne, "I date my life." Why he held 1844

[1] For Tucker, see also Book II, Chap. XVII.

so important is not clear; he may then first have turned to authorship. Though he had kept no notes of his journeying, within a year he had completed his first book, *Typee*, the record of his captivity. This was followed the next year by *Omoo*,[1] which completes his island adventures. In 1849 came *Redburn*, based on his earlier voyage to Liverpool, and in 1850 *White-Jacket*, an account of life on a man-of-war.

The first two had a great vogue and aroused much wonder as to the proportion of fiction and fact which might have gone to their making. Murray published *Typee* in England in the belief that it was pure fact. There were others to rank it with Richard Henry Dana's *Two Years before the Mast* (1841) as a transcript of real events. But though little is known of Melville's actual doings in the South Seas, it is at least clear that *Typee* and *Omoo* are no more as truthful as *Two Years before the Mast* than they are as crisp and nautical as that incomparable classic of the sea. Melville must be ranked less with Dana than with George Borrow. If he knew the thin boundary between romance and reality, he was still careless of nice limits, and his work is a fusion which defies analysis. *White-Jacket*, of these four books, is probably nearest a plain record; *Redburn* has but few romantic elements. *Omoo*, as a sequel, has not the freshness of *Typee*, nor has it such unity. *Typee*, indeed, is Melville at all but his best, and must be classed with the most successful narrations of the exotic life; after seventy years, when the South Pacific seems no longer another world, the spell holds. The valley of Taipi becomes, in Melville's handling, a region of dreams and languor which stir the senses with the fragrance and colour of the landscape and the gay beauty of the brown cannibal girls. And yet Melville, thoroughly sensitive to the felicities of that life, never loses himself in it but remains the shrewd and smiling Yankee.

The charge that he had been writing romance led Melville to deserve the accusation, and he wrote *Mardi* (1849), certainly one of the strangest, maddest books ever composed by an American. As in *Typee*, two sailors escape from a tyrannical captain in the Pacific and seek their fortune on the open sea, where they finally discover the archipelago of Mardi, a para-

[1] The word is Polynesian for "rover."

dise more rich and sultry than the Marquesas, which becomes, as the story proceeds, a crazy chaos of adventure and satirical allegory. In *Mardi* for the first time appear those qualities which made a French critic call Melville "un Rabelais américain," his welter of language, his fantastic laughter, his tumultuous philosophies. He had turned, contemporaries said, from the plain though witty style of his first works to the gorgeous manner of Sir Thomas Browne; he had been infected, say later critics, with Carlylese. Whatever the process, he had surely shifted his interest from the actual to the abstruse and symbolical, and he never recovered from the dive into metaphysics which proved fatal to him as a novelist. It was, however, while on this perilous border that he produced the best of his, and one of the best of American, romances; it is the peculiar mingling of speculation and experience which lends *Moby Dick* (1851) its special power.

The time was propitious for such a book. The golden age of the whalers was drawing to a close, though no decline had yet set in, and the native imagination had been stirred by tales of deeds done on remote oceans by the most heroic Yankees of the age in the arduous calling in which New England, and especially the hard little island of Nantucket, led and taught the world. A small literature of whaling had grown up, chiefly the records of actual voyages or novels like those of Cooper in which whaling was an incident of the nautical life. But the whalers still lacked any such romantic record as the frontier had. Melville brought to the task a sound knowledge of actual whaling, much curious learning in the literature of the subject, and, above all, an imagination which worked with great power upon the facts of his own experience. Moby Dick, the strange, fierce white whale that Captain Ahab pursues with such relentless fury, was already a legend among the whalers, who knew him as "Mocha Dick."[1] It remained for Melville to lend some kind of poetic or moral significance to a struggle ordinarily conducted for no cause but profit. As he handles the story, Ahab, who has lost a leg in the jaws of the whale, is driven by a wild desire for revenge which has maddened him and which makes him identify Moby Dick with the very spirit of evil and hatred. Ahab, not Melville, is to blame if the story seems an allegory,

[1] See Reynolds, J. N., *Mocha Dick, Knickerbocker Magazine*, May, 1839.

which Melville plainly declared it was not[1]; but it contains, nevertheless, the semblance of a conflict between the ancient and scatheless forces of nature and the ineluctable enmity of man. This is the theme, but description can hardly report the extraordinary mixture in *Moby Dick* of vivid adventure, minute detail, cloudy symbolism, thrilling pictures of the sea in every mood, sly mirth and cosmic ironies, real and incredible characters, wit, speculation, humour, colour. The style is mannered but often felicitous; though the book is long, the end, after every faculty of suspense has been aroused, is swift and final. Too irregular, too bizarre, perhaps, ever to win the widest suffrage, the immense originality of *Moby Dick* must warrant the claim of its admirers that it belongs with the greatest sea romances in the whole literature of the world.

Married in 1847, Melville lived for three years in New York and then for thirteen years in a farmhouse near Pittsfield, Massachusetts. Although he did not cease to write at once, *Moby Dick* seems to have exhausted him. *Pierre* (1852) is hopelessly frantic; *Israel Potter* (1855) is not markedly original; neither are *The Piazza Tales* (1856), and *The Confidence Man* (1857). The verses which he wrote in his later years, his sole output, are in a few instances happy, but far more often jagged and harsh. Whatever the causes of his loss of power, he fretted under it and grew more metaphysical, tortured, according to Hawthorne, his good friend, by uncertainty as to a future life. That way, for Melville, was madness; his earlier works should have taught him that he was lost without a solid basis in fact. He moved restlessly about, lecturing on the South Seas during the years 1857–1860 in many cities of the United States and Canada. He visited Europe and Palestine. Finally, having returned to New York, he was appointed to a place in the Custom House in 1866, and served there for twenty years, living a private life of almost entire, though voluntary and studious, seclusion. His death, 28 September, 1891, after nearly forty silent years, removed from American literature one of its most promising and most disappointing figures. Of late his fame has shown a tendency to revive.

Another type of romance which had some vogue during the

[1] *Moby Dick*, Chap. XLV.

later years of Cooper was the religious romance, of which, though many essayed it, the chief writers were William Ware (1797–1852), and Sylvester Judd (1813–53). Ware, a clergyman and fair classical scholar, wrote three novels, *Letters from Palmyra* (1837), later called *Zenobia*, *Probus* (1838), a sequel now known as *Aurelian*, and *Julian* (1841), which, though strongly biased in favour of the creed Ware preached, and often diffuse and monotonous, had still enough force and charm to have continued to be read by those to whom all books dealing with the origins of Christianity are an equal duty and delight. Judd has not been so widely read as Ware, though generally considered a novelist of superior truth and subtlety. His first novel, *Margaret* (1845), was born of a desire to show that Unitarians could produce imaginative literature. Its special merits are its vivid fidelity to the life of rural Massachusetts just after the Revolution, its thorough, loving familiarity with the New England temper and scene, and a kind of spiritual ardour which pervades the whole book; but it is badly constructed and it runs, toward the close, into a region of misty transcendentalisms where characters and plot are lost. *Richard Edney* (1850), a companion piece with its hero a boy and its setting contemporary, suffers, either as narrative or sense, from the same theological obsession, which appears in Judd's poems as little less than pathological.

By 1851 there were, or had been, many novelists whose names could find place only in an extended account of American fiction[1]: writers of adventure stories more sensational than Simms's or of moral stories more obvious than Miss Sedgwick's and Mrs. Child's, authors for children, authors preaching causes, authors celebrating fashionable or Bohemian life in New York. Not only regular novels and romances but briefer tales multiplied. The period which could boast in Cooper but one novelist of first rank could show three such tale-tellers as Irving, Hawthorne, and Poe. The annuals and magazines met the demand for such amusement and fostered it,[2] but the novel was encouraged more than it was hurt by the new type. Prose fiction, in fact, though somewhat late in starting,

---

[1] See Northrup, C. S., *The Novelists*, in *A Manual of American Literature*, ed. Stanton, T., 1909.

[2] See Book II, Chap. xx.

had firmly established itself in the United States by the middle of the century, and Cooper, followed in Great Britain by the nautical romancers, and on the Continent by such writers about wild life as Karl Anton Postl ("Charles Sealsfield"), Friedrich Gerstäcker, and Gustave Aimard, and everywhere read, had become a world figure.

# CHAPTER VIII

# Transcendentalism

N EW ENGLAND transcendentalism was a late and local manifestation of that great movement for the liberation of humanity which, invading practically every sphere of civilized activity, swept over Europe at the end of the eighteenth and the beginning of the nineteenth century.

With the fading of the Renaissance, Europe had passed into an age of criticism, during which all it had inherited and achieved in the preceding era was subjected to the test of reason. Throughout the eighteenth century especially, the existing structure of society was subtly undermined, and when, at the end of that century, it finally collapsed, the revolution which in reality had long been in preparation took on an abrupt and miraculous appearance.

> Heaven smiles, and faiths and empires gleam
> Like wrecks of a dissolving dream,

cried Shelley, attempting to describe this remarkable period, and his lines are scarcely an exaggeration. Smiles and wrecks, these were the characteristic products of the time, blasted institutions and blossoming ideals.

What those ideals were—some of them soon to be realized, others destined to remain distant visions—is tolerably clear. Socially this revolution meant democracy, the assertion of the brotherhood and potential equality of men. Politically and religiously it meant the overthrow of feudal and ecclesiastical tyrannies and customs, and the setting up of liberal forms of government and belief as instruments for testing the new social doctrine. Philosophically it meant the contention, in the face of existing rationalisms and skepticisms, that man's practical and imaginative faculties play a part in his apprehension of the truth. In the realm of art and literature it meant the shattering of pseudo-classic rules and forms in favour of a spirit of freedom, the creation of works filled with the new passion for nature and common humanity and incarnating a fresh sense of the wonder, promise, and romance of life. In the scientific and industrial worlds it meant those fundamental and far-reaching changes which came with the constantly fuller recognition and adoption of the scientific method.

To the special student, each of these revolutionary movements has its separate history. But life, in spite of the student, is not a matter of water-tight compartments, and a first fact to be seized and held fast in any discussion of New England transcendentalism is that the new spirit which appeared in Europe a century and more ago was neither social, nor political, nor industrial, nor economic, nor literary, nor scientific, nor religious. It was all of them at once. It transcended every phase of life—though it is true, of course, that in this particular locality or at that particular time, in this individual or in that social atmosphere, it did take on this or that predominant emphasis or colour.

On this side of the Atlantic, for instance, it assumed at the outset a pre-eminently political character, and America, in her own Revolution and in the events which followed it, made an early and memorable contribution to that greater revolution of the human spirit of which the source and centre was in Europe. But America, save in the case here and there of an exceptional mind, remained largely unconscious, even as a matter of political theory, of the general significance for the world of what she had accomplished. Still less had she distilled from her democratic practice any fresh philosophy or faith. When, then, voices from abroad of those who were seeking a religion for the new order of things penetrated to a community which, religious to the core, had long been religiously starved, those voices were bound to be heard and answered. That is precisely what began happening near Boston shortly before the year 1830. The result was similar to what occurs, under like conditions, in the case of an individual.

Whoever has seen a young man of high mental and spiritual endowment lifted out of a provincial environment and placed suddenly in contact with the central intellectual and religious forces of his time, has a key to much of the transcendental movement in New England. The unsettling of traditional foundations, the ferment of thought and emotion, the aspirations, the excesses, the unleashing of dormant and unsuspected powers, all the effects, in fact, which attend such an experience in the case of the individual were reproduced on a wider scale when the spirit of revolutionary Europe descended upon a group of the finest minds of early nineteenth-century New England. The spirit of the eighteenth century had survived in the neighbourhood of Boston long after the eighteenth century was dead. And suddenly—so at least it seemed—this group of young men and women became intensely aware of that fact. The new ideas and ideals found their way to them through a score of channels and affected as many phases of New England life. But because of the predominant part which religion still played in that life and its traditions, it was within the religious world that the influence of the new spirit was immediate and marked. Transcendentalism was the religious conversion of early nineteenth-century New England. And because of the relative cultural eminence of New England, it became indirectly, in some measure, the religious conversion of America. Emerson's address, *The American Scholar*, is called our intellectual Declaration of Independence. With far more fundamental truth his little volume, *Nature*, might be called our religious Declaration of Independence.

New England transcendentalism, then, was the product of European forces brought to bear on New England character and conditions. To analyze the movement further it will be necessary to look somewhat more closely at the nature of those conditions and that character and to study in a little more detail the outside forces which were brought in contact with them.

The religious evolution of New England from the period of the Puritan theocracy to the beginning of the nineteenth century is on the whole, with a certain change of scale and retardation of movement, strikingly similar to the religious development during the same period abroad, a fact which, at the outset, renders futile any hope to estimate with exactness how far the two movements were parallel, how far the one was influenced by the other.

intense hatred of slavery. During this period, too, he became acquainted with the works of Rousseau, Godwin, and Mary Wollstonecraft, and from that time the kinship of many of his ideas with those of French Revolutionary origin can be clearly traced, though in passing through his serene and profoundly Christian mind those ideas often became scarcely recognizable.

On returning north Channing studied theology, becoming in 1803 minister of the Federal Street Society, Boston, a pulpit from which, until his death in 1842, he preached, in a spirit of singularly mingled benignity and power, sermons of constantly increasing influence that emphasized consistently the spiritual and practical as opposed to the doctrinal aspects of Christianity. Ultimately his fame even crossed the ocean, a number of his essays and reviews being translated and widely read, especially in France. The eminence he attained was due fundamentally to the gracious, almost saintly, character behind both his written and his spoken words; and it is worth remembering that all he did was accomplished in the face of a physical condition that made him essentially an invalid.

Although Channing is usually spoken of as the greatest Unitarian of his time, his sermon on *Unitarian Christianity*, preached at the ordination of Jared Sparks at Baltimore in 1819, being often called the creed of that denomination, he was, if we are to give him that name, a Unitarian of an entirely new type, and his works are full of indictments of what Emerson later called "the pale negations of Boston Unitarianism."

"Unitarianism," we find him writing, for instance, " has suffered from union with a heart-withering philosophy. . . . I fear that we must look to other schools for the thoughts which thrill us, which touch the most inward springs, and disclose to us the depths of our own souls."

Or again:

Now, religion ought to be dispensed in accommodation to this spirit and character of our age. Men desire excitement, and religion must be communicated in a more exciting form. . . . Men will not now be trifled with. . . . They want a religion which will take a strong hold upon them.

And they desire the same quality in their literature, he says elsewhere, "a poetry which pierces beneath the exterior of life to the depths of the soul."

Manifestly, as these references to changing standards in philosophy, religion, and literature make clear, a new spirit was abroad in the land, and though Channing himself had caught much of it from other and earlier sources, it is certain that German philosophy and literature, some of it directly, much more of it indirectly, was, by the third decade of the century, becoming a chief influence in its dissemination.

The impetus toward things German had come, about 1819, with the return to America from Göttingen of George Ticknor, George Bancroft, and Edward Everett, young men, all of them, of brilliant parts. The interest thus aroused was fostered by the coming to Harvard a few years later, as instructor in German, of Charles T. Follen, a political exile. From about this time, some direct knowledge of Kant, Fichte, and Schelling, of Schleiermacher, of Goethe and Schiller—of Goethe probably more than of any other German writer—gradually began to make its way into New England, while the indirect German influence was even greater, coming in part through France in the works of Madame de Staël, Cousin, and Jouffroy, but much more significantly through England, in subtle form in the poetry of Wordsworth, more openly in the writings of Coleridge,[1] and, a little later, in the essays of Carlyle.

This interest in German thought and in English romantic literature, moreover, was but the beginning of a wider literary and philosophical awakening which brought with it increasing attention to general European literature, a revitalized attitude toward the classics, and considerable exploration in the realms of Neo-Platonic philosophy and Oriental "Scriptures."

It is natural that those who began to feel the vital effect upon their own religious convictions of this new spirit in philosophy and literature should have found one another out.

---

[1] There is practically no question that of all these influences the works of Coleridge stand first in importance, and it is due to this fact that New England transcendentalism, in so far as it is a philosophy, bears a closer resemblance to the metaphysical system of Schelling (whose influence on Coleridge is well known) than to that of any other thinker.

This they had done many months before any regular gatherings were contemplated. It was not until 1836 that these were begun when on 19 September—after a still smaller preliminary conference—Ralph Waldo Emerson, Frederick Henry Hedge, Convers Francis, James Freeman Clarke, and Amos Bronson Alcott met at the house of George Ripley and formed an organization to aid an exchange of thought among those interested in the "new views" in philosophy, theology, and literature. Among those who joined the group at later meetings were Theodore Parker, Margaret Fuller, Orestes A. Brownson, Elizabeth and Sophia Peabody, Thoreau, Hawthorne, Jones Very, Christopher P. Cranch, Charles T. Follen, and William Henry Channing. For a number of years, following 1836, this group, generally referred to as the Transcendental Club, continued occasionally to come together.

Of the less familiar names among its members, several, in a fuller treatment of the subject, would deserve discussion: Hedge and Clarke, for instance, Unitarian clergymen, the former a man of wide reading and sound scholarship who did much to spread a knowledge of German philosophy, the latter a leader of his denomination and of some contemporary standing as an author; Brownson, one of the most forceful but erratic figures of the time, minister, editor, politician, and novelist—beginning life as a Presbyterian and becoming in turn Universalist, Unitarian, transcendentalist, and Roman Catholic; Very and Cranch, two of the poets of the period, the former probably the extreme mystic of the whole group, a victim for a time of religious mania, the latter a picturesque figure, painter, musician, and ventriloquist, as well as poet. Some of these men attained considerable eminence in their own time, but for the present discussion these passing comments on them must suffice.

It is characteristic of the extreme individualism of the movement that the Transcendental Club was never a really formal organization. The transcendentalists, though most of them were Unitarians, did not leave the fold and form a new church—though such an event as Emerson's withdrawal from the ministry in 1832 is symbolic of a general spiritual secession then taking place. But in spite of the absence of definite organization, there was essential unity of belief among the dissenters. This belief is as well embodied as anywhere, perhaps, in Emerson's little treatise *Nature*, a work which, appearing the same year the Club was formed, may be fittingly considered the philosophical "constitution" of transcendentalism, all the more so since the same author's better known Phi Beta Kappa Oration, *The American Scholar* (1837), and his profoundly influential *Divinity School Address* (1838) are merely applications of the doctrine of *Nature* to the realms of letters and theology.

Into any detailed discussion of what that doctrine was, into any minute exposition, in other words, of the transcendental philosophy, it is impossible here to enter. A glance, however, may be taken at a few of its central and controlling features.

The word "transcendental" in its philosophic sense goes back to Kant and the *Critique of Pure Reason*, though in New England, as elsewhere, the term lost its narrowly technical application and borrowed at the same time a new shade of meaning from the *Critique of Practical Reason*. Kant had taught that time and space are not external realities but ways in which the mind "constitutes" its world of sense. The same is true, he had contended, of cause and effect and the other categories of the mind. Furthermore, as he brought out in his second *Critique*, the ideas of God, of freedom, and of immortality are inevitable intuitions of the practical nature of man, and these intuitions, since man is essentially a practical and moral being, have therefore not a merely sentimental but a real validity. From these and other Kantian conceptions a broad generalization was made, and the word "transcendental" came to be applied, in New England, to whatever in man's mental and spiritual nature is conceived of as above experience and independent of it. Whatever transcends the experience of the senses is transcendental. Innate, original, universal, *a priori*, intuitive—these are words all of which convey a part of the thought swept under the larger meaning of the term. To the transcendentalists the name John Locke stood for the denial of innate ideas. "Sensationalism" was the prevalent description of the doctrine of his *Essay*. Transcendentalism, on the other hand, reaffirmed the soul's inherent power to grasp the truth, and upon this basis went on to erect a metaphysical structure similar in its main outlines to the leading Platonic and idealistic philosophies of the past.

According to this view of the world, the one reality is the vast spiritual background of existence, the Over-Soul, God, within which all other being is unified and from which it derives its life. Because of this indwelling of divinity, every part of the world, however small, is a microcosm, comprehending within itself, like Tennyson's flower in the crannied wall, all the laws and meaning of the whole. The soul of each individual, therefore, is identical with the soul of the world, and contains, latently, all that that larger soul contains. Thus the normal life of man is a life of continuous expansion, the making actual of the potential elements of his being. This may occur in two ways: either directly, in states which vary from the ordinary perception of truth to moments of mystical rapture in which there is a conscious influx of the divine into the human; or indirectly, through the instrumentality of nature. Nature is the embodiment of spirit in the world of sense—it is a great picture to be appreciated, a great book to be read, a great task to be performed. Through the beauty, truth, and goodness incarnate in the natural world, the individual soul comes in contact with and appropriates to itself the spirit and being of God.

From these central conceptions all the other teachings of the transcendentalists are derived: their doctrines of self-reliance and individualism, of the identity of moral and physical laws, of the essential unity of all religions, of the negative nature of evil; their spirit of complete tolerance and of absolute optimism; their defiance of tradition and disregard for all external authority.

It must not be understood, however, that metaphysics was a central interest of the transcendentalists. They were not system makers. The idealistic philosophy was to many of them more a spirit and attitude of mind than a consciously reasoned-out theory of the world, and it is as such a pervading spirit that its virtue still survives. As an explanation of the mystery of existence the transcendental philosophy makes little appeal to our own hard-headed and scientific generation; but no one, assuredly, with any measure of spiritual and poetic perception can give himself sincerely and unreservedly to one of the literary masterpieces of the transcendental school, to one of the greater essays of Emerson for example, the *Self-Reliance*, *Compensation*, *Spiritual Laws*, or *The Over-Soul*, without a consciousness, as he puts down the volume, of having passed for the time into a higher sphere of being, without a deepened conviction of the triviality, the relative unreality, of material concerns, without a sense of spaciousness, of clarity, of nobility, of power, a feeling that that much abused word "eternal" has suddenly put on a very real and concrete meaning. Against such an actual experience no mere argument can avail. Nor does the emotion thus evoked end in a vague mystical exaltation. It leaves, rather, whether the reader profit by it or not, a distinct sense of its bearing on the daily conduct of life. This spirit of uplift, together with the moral impulsion it imparts, is the heart of New England transcendentalism.

But the transcendentalists were not always at the level of their masterpieces, and from the outset two results of a movement whose essence was so intangible and ideal were practically inevitable: first, that it should be misunderstood and misinterpreted by those who viewed it from outside; and second, that it should lead to excesses among the initiated themselves which would lend colour and, in a measure, justification to its critics. So quickly, indeed, did these results appear that to the public the word "transcendental" soon came to mean, to all intents and purposes, "transcending common sense," and this use of the term gained added sanction from the difficulty of distinguishing sharply between transcendentalism and other currents of social and religious unrest then pulsing through New England. Some notion of the varieties of "dissent" and "reform" contending at that time for public attention is conveyed in Emerson's description of the Chardon Street Convention which was held in Boston in 1840:

Madmen, madwomen, men with beards, Dunkers, Muggletonians, Come-outers, Groaners, Agrarians, Seventh-day Baptists, Quakers, Abolitionists, Calvinists, Unitarians, and Philosophers.

Surely these were wild and "transcendental" times!

Of the members of the Club it was Amos Bronson Alcott,

father of Louisa May Alcott, who was particularly singled out as a target for the shafts of a jesting and unsympathetic public. The stories told of him, to be sure, were often outright inventions or gross exaggerations. But we do not need to go beyond the testimony of his daughter to discover considerable basis for the popular conception of his character. Alcott, in fact, becomes an especially significant figure as embodying in excessive degree the mystical tendency of the transcendentalists together with those extravagances and eccentricities which often accompany the mystic's habit of wrapping himself up in the clouds of his own speculation and aspiration.

Alcott was born in Connecticut in 1799. After a fragmentary education he went to Virginia planning to teach but was compelled to earn his living by peddling. For four or five years this was his chief vocation, and it is interesting to note that toward the end of this period he came in contact with North Carolina Quakers, whose religious views seem to have influenced his thinking. Following this he returned to New England and for nearly fifteen years devoted himself in the main to school-teaching, putting into practice with considerable success, especially in his last and most famous school at the Masonic Temple in Boston, radical educational theories, some of which seem to have anticipated kindergarten methods now in vogue and which earned for Alcott the title of the American Pestalozzi.

Alcott's fundamental educational conceptions were Platonic, and he exhibited an astonishing but entirely characteristic consistency in carrying out his most radical ideas. He believed in the plenary inspiration of childhood, and his method may be described as an attempt to realize in practice the thought of Wordsworth's ode on the *Intimations of Immortality*.

The publication of some of his conversations with his pupils, owing to their references to the phenomena of birth, brought adverse criticism and tended to impair the prosperity of the school. Finally, on his refusal to dismiss a coloured child whom he had received as a pupil, patronage was withdrawn and he was compelled to give up the enterprise.

After the failure of his school Alcott first tried his scheme of public "conversations," with little financial success, however. In these years, too, he showed an interest in many of the reform movements of the day, the temperance cause, woman's rights, the anti-slavery agitation. Moving with his family to Concord in 1840, he tried for a time to stick to farm work, but his taste for transcendental thought was too strong and he again began holding conversations and giving lectures. Shortly after this he removed to a farm in the town of Harvard, where, with two English friends, he instituted the community of Fruitlands.

The ideals of this miniature Utopia were extreme. The diet was strictly vegetarian, even milk and eggs being tabooed. Water was the only beverage. The "aspiring" vegetables, those which grow into the air like the fruits, were allowed, but the baser ones, like potatoes and beets, which grow downward, were forbidden. When cold weather came the experiment had proved itself, materially at least, a complete failure. This was too much for Alcott, who, losing for once his perennial serenity and turning his face to the wall, asked only to be allowed to die. He had a brave wife, however, who eventually brought him to his senses.

Following the failure of Fruitlands, the Alcotts had a long struggle against poverty first in Concord and later in Boston, Mrs. Alcott apparently being the financial mainstay of the family, her husband contributing what little he could earn from his conversations. The journal of Louisa May Alcott covering this period gives us many intimate glimpses into the life of "the pathetic family," and while the father is revealed as a man of extreme impracticality and even of unwitting selfishness, his extraordinary gentleness of temper and his unfailing optimism under adversity are not less conspicuous. When, a few years later, Miss Alcott gained literary distinction, the family was freed from financial embarrassment. The latter part of Alcott's life brought the Concord School of Philosophy and the realization of his long-cherished dream to see himself the American Plato surrounded by a group of admiring disciples.

It is singularly difficult to arrive at a just estimate of Alcott. The whole affinity of his mind was mystical, Neo-Platonic and Oriental writers being his favourite authors. The rarified nature of his subject-matter combined with a certain deficiency in power of literary expression makes his published works inadequately representative of the man, and the critic pauses between the belief that admiring contemporaries grossly over-rated the ability of an active and elevated but withal rather ordinary mind, and the opposite view that Alcott had a touch of real genius in him, a kinship in due degree with the inspired talkers of literary history. Carlyle's famous description of him gives us part of the truth:

> The good Alcott: with his long, lean face and figure, with his grey worn temples and mild radiant eyes; all bent on saving the world by a return to acorns and the golden age; he comes before one like a kind of venerable Don Quixote, whom nobody can even laugh at without loving.

But Emerson probably came nearer than anyone else to doing justice to both sides of Alcott's nature when he called his friend a "tedious archangel."

If Alcott embodied the extreme mystical and esoteric side of transcendentalism, the Brook Farm Association represents its social and experimental aspect.

George Ripley (1802–1880), the leader of this enterprise, was a graduate of Harvard and a Unitarian minister. A wide and increasing knowledge of European writers, however, gradually led his interest from theology into the sphere of social reform. He accordingly gave up his pastorate, and in 1841 he and his wife and a number of loyal friends established the Brook Farm Institute of Agriculture and Education on a farm at West Roxbury, nine miles from Boston. The association was a joint-stock company and financially it was inaugurated and conducted with considerable practical saga-city. On its theoretical side the enterprise, while the product in a general way of the speculations and example of Owen and Fourier, was not, especially at the beginning, in any precise sense an experiment in socialism. The hope of its founders was merely to make Brook Farm a self-supporting group of men and women, where all should share in the manual labour, the leisure, and the educational and cultural advantages, a place of "plain living and high thinking" where life might be lived in an atmosphere of fraternity, free from the strife and burdens of ordinary competitive society. That the attempt was far from being unsuccessful is revealed by many anecdotes which have come down showing the hearty and genuine spirit which prevailed among its members, a spirit to the happy influence of which on their later lives more than one of the survivors of the enterprise has borne witness.

The adoption in 1844, with some modifications, of the principles of Fourier seems, however, to have put an end to some of the more Arcadian features of Brook Farm; and this, together with the fact that the efforts of inexperienced farmers on a rather poor farm yielded insufficient financial return, was enough to doom the experiment to ultimate failure. The disbanding of the members was immediately occasioned by the burning in 1846 of the unfinished "phalanstery," upon which seven thousand dollars had already been expended and which was wholly uninsured.

Brook Farm, being the most tangible and visible product of this whole New England movement, has come to stand in the public mind for a perfect incarnation of the transcendental spirit. This is an error. Brook Farm was characteristic of transcendentalism in its belief that the material factors of life should be subservient to the spiritual and ideal and in its conviction that right thinking would lead toward better social conditions—in the end, indeed, to a perfect society. But it is important to notice that Ripley alone of the original members of the Transcendental Club had an active share in the enterprise and that while Emerson, Alcott, Theodore Parker, and Margaret Fuller were interested and on the whole sympathetic visitors, they were too thoroughly individualistic, too distrustful of the institutional factor in life, to be completely satisfied with the experiment. In not a few respects incidents more characteristic, in their individualism, of the transcendental spirit were Alcott's sojourn with his friends at Fruitlands and, still more so, Thoreau's experiment on the shore of Walden Pond.[1]

An achievement more intimately connected than Brook Farm with the Transcendental Club and the leading transcendentalists was *The Dial*,[2] the literary organ of the movement, the first number of which appeared in 1840 with Margaret Fuller as editor, and George Ripley as assistant editor. *The*

[1] See Book II, Chap. x.　　　　　　[2] See also Book II, Chap. xx.

*Dial* never approached financial success, and it was only through real devotion and sacrifice on the part of its editor and of Elizabeth Peabody that it was issued as long as it was. Miss Fuller resigned the editorship after two years and Emerson assumed it for a like period, after which it was discontinued.

Whatever defects *The Dial* may have had, a comparison of its pages with the dusty contemporaneous numbers of, let us say, *The North American Review* is not to its disadvantage and lends some weight to the assertion of its main contributors that they were dealing with subjects of deeper than passing interest. The journal discussed questions of theology and philosophy; it contained papers on art, music, and literature, especially German literature; translations from ancient "Oriental Scriptures"; original modern "scriptures" in the form of Alcott's *Orphic Sayings;* and finally, a good deal of verse. In this latter connection one of the most interesting features of *The Dial* to the present-day reader is the opportunity and encouragement it afforded to the literary genius of Thoreau. In addition to his and Emerson's, there were, among others, metrical contributions from Lowell, Cranch, and William Ellery Channing, the younger, the last-named one of the poets of transcendentalism, now best remembered for the single line,

If my bark sinks, 'tis to another sea.

*The Dial*, needless to say, did not satisfy the public. Dozens of parodies, especially of the *Orphic Sayings*, were forthcoming, and (in the words of Colonel Higginson)

epithets, too, were showered about as freely as imitations; the Philadelphia "Gazette," for instance, calling the editors of the new journal "zanies," "Bedlamites," and "considerably madder than the Mormons."

Alcott, on the other hand, considered its policy tame and compromising. Whatever, between these extremes, our own estimate of its intrinsic merit may be, we shall not be likely to overrate its significance in the history of American literature or the importance of the part it played in our literary emancipation. Its volumes stand as a reminder that the transcendental movement was, among other things, a literary renaissance— the enthusiasm for art and literature which appeared in New

England after the long æsthetic starvation of the Puritan ascendency being comparable in kind if not in degree to the immense artistic expansion of Western Europe after a thousand years of mediæval Christianity.

No one of the leading transcendentalists illustrates this aspect of the movement more completely than does the first editor of *The Dial*, Sarah Margaret Fuller (1810-1850).

The character of Margaret Fuller's childhood and early training is the key to much in her later career. She was brought up by a father whose stern temperament and uncompromising notions on education made him peculiarly unfitted to understand and mould the delicately sensitive nature of his daughter. Under the mental tasks he imposed upon her, her health became impaired and she was overstimulated intellectually and emotionally. All the early part of her life was a struggle against the sentimentalism and self-consciousness which her early education had engendered. As a young woman she was proud and imperious, at times overbearing, in her nature. She could use her tongue sharply and sarcastically, a quality which, combined with a high temper and a tendency to tell the truth, made her many enemies; and gradually, as she became more widely known, out of these hints that she herself supplied, there emerged in the public mind a distorted conception of her personality—a view that still lingers—which made her out a woman of insufferable vanity and masculinity, a veritable intellectual virago. Along with Alcott she became a chief butt of coarse and unsympathetic critics.

As a matter of fact, however, the unloveliest features of Margaret Fuller's personality were but the reverse sides of sterling virtues, and it is to her lasting credit that she lived to master and in the main to outgrow her early defects. The family duties devolving upon her at the death of her father, the sacrifice of long-cherished plans for foreign travel, a brief period of teaching, her work as editor of *The Dial*—these experiences gave her needed self-control and contact with practical problems, and the figure that emerges from them some years later as literary critic of *The New York Tribune* and social and philanthropic worker is an exceedingly able, sensible, and admirable woman.

From her early years, Margaret Fuller read omnivorously

(at a rate like Gibbon, Emerson once said). Her linguistic equipment was good, and there is little question that she came to know Continental literature, that of Germany especially, more fully and appreciatively than any other of the transcendentalists. Her choice as editor of *The Dial* therefore was natural. She also put her literary acquirements to use— as did Alcott his educational theories and mystical lore—by holding conversations on Greek mythology and other subjects. While these at the beginning were not free from amateurishness and a narrowly self-cultural ideal, they had deeper qualities, the promise of powers more fully revealed in her *Woman in the Nineteenth Century* (1845) and her collected *Papers on Literature and Art* (1846), which, in spite of their decidedly uneven quality, reveal her on the whole as one of the best equipped, most sympathetic and genuinely philosophical critics produced in America prior to 1850.

Following Miss Fuller's removal to New York, the realistic element in her work grew stronger, her interest in social and political questions increased, and particularly during her three years in Italy from 1847 to 1850—where she was married to the Marquis Ossoli—did her intimate contact with the struggle for Italian freedom broaden and deepen her nature. In fact her career seemed just entering on its most useful phase when it was tragically cut short by her death in the wreck off Fire Island in 1850 of the ship that was bringing her back to New York, a disaster in which her husband and child also perished.

Though her later promise was thus unfulfilled, Margaret Fuller had already accomplished much.

"It has been one great object of my life," she once declared, "to introduce here the works of those great geniuses, the flower and fruit of a higher state of development, which might give the young who are soon to constitute the state, a higher standard in thought and action than would be demanded of them by their own time. . . . I feel with satisfaction that I have done a good deal to extend the influence of the great minds of Germany and Italy among my compatriots."

She had, in truth, accomplished this, and her words are suggestive of one of the greatest achievements of the transcendental movement on its literary side.

If Margaret Fuller is the literary critic of transcendentalism, Theodore Parker (1810–1860) is its theologian and reformer. Parker was a graduate of Harvard and of the Harvard Divinity School, and held pastorates near or in Boston during the whole of his ministerial career. He carried to its extreme form the theological reaction from eighteenth-century Unitarianism begun by Channing, his South Boston sermon in 1841 on *The Transient and Permanent in Christianity* being generally considered a milestone not only in the history of transcendentalism but in the development of American theology.

Parker, though his nature was not lacking in qualities of engaging simplicity and kindliness, was a man of warlike and aggressive temperament, of indomitable energy whether in thought or action, "our Savonarola," as Emerson called him. During the earlier part of his life, much of his tremendous power of activity was expended upon books, and he became a man of immense erudition, the most widely read member of the transcendental group. His learning, however, savoured a little too much, as Lowell suggested, of an attempt to tear up the whole tree of knowledge by the roots, and he surely misconstrued his own nature when he declared "I was meant for a philosopher, and the times call for a *stump orator*." His mind was in reality more practical than metaphysical in its cast, and it was with the turning of his interest to the slavery question and especially with the arousing of all the fires of his nature at the passage of the Fugitive Slave Law that the tremendous will power and earnestness of the man came out to the full. During the years of this controversy, he interspersed an endless mass of correspondence, lectures, sermons, and addresses with deeds of conspicuous moral and physical courage. He was chairman of the executive committee of the Vigilance Committee, sheltered fugitive slaves in his own house and aided their escape in all ways possible, was indicted but never brought to trial in connection with the famous Burns Affair, and came into intimate relations with John Brown. It was the strain of labours of this sort that led to his premature death in 1860.

These anti-slavery activities of Parker came, of course, after the crest of the transcendental movement, but they are mentioned here as an illustration of that tendency in transcendentalism, already noted in connection with Brook Farm and the life of Margaret Fuller, to pass from its early sentimental and romantic stage into a phase of social or political activity. Parker's life reveals with special clearness the link between transcendentalism and the abolition movement. There is probably little likelihood of exaggerating the relation between a philosophy which taught the divinity of every human soul and the agitation for the freedom of the Southern slaves.

Although the transcendental philosophy was of course only one of many forces that led to abolitionism in New England, the connection between the two is a powerful reminder that, in spite of its underlying unity of spirit, transcendentalism was an exceedingly varied and complex movement. Even the present rapid survey of a few of its characteristic incidents and leading figures has served perhaps to emphasize that fact.

In Channing, for instance, to glance back for a moment, we perceive it as a force mellowing and humanizing the stern Calvinistic tradition and touching with emotion the prosaic rationalism of the Unitarians. In Emerson it shines forth as an unfailing sense of the unity of the soul with God and nature, a religious aspiration constantly translated into incentives toward the noble conduct of life. In Alcott we behold it at first touching education and the child, then volatilizing into clouds of Oriental mysticism. In Margaret Fuller we catch its significance as a literary renaissance, an effort for culture, for criticism, passing over at last into an effort for social betterment—which latter note is struck earlier and more resoundingly in the social Utopianism of Ripley and the other Brook Farmers. In Parker it takes on particularly the form of extreme theological radicalism, a radicalism successfully undergoing the test of practical application in the abolition movement. In Thoreau it is present—in none of the group more ethereally—as a spiritualized feeling for nature, a fine dissolvent of convention, a pervasive and contagious influence toward natural and simple living.

These considerations, together with the implication of such names as Hawthorne, Dana, Curtis, and a dozen others, show how impossible it is not only to define the nature but to fix the limits of transcendentalism. Transcendentalism was, in fact, simply the focus and energizing centre of that larger area of illumination and activity which is coextensive with the whole movement of literary and spiritual expansion that transformed New England during the second and third quarters of the nineteenth century. For purposes of historical and critical discrimination, to be sure, it is convenient, as we have done, to treat transcendentalism as a distinct and separate movement. But in reality it was not. In reality it was so blended with wider currents of spiritual change that the relation between the two can never be precisely determined. All that can be asserted with any certainty is that the fundamentally religious complexion of New England life makes it a fair presumption that the religious phase of the whole development was as nearly central and determinative as any.

It is equally difficult, as may now be seen more clearly than at the outset of our discussion, to separate the European and the American contributions to transcendentalism. That spirit of freedom, of individualism, of revolution, of romance, which was abroad throughout the Western world during this period, took on a peculiar local colour in New England. Distilled in the New England alembic, French Revolutionary dogmas, German philosophy, Oriental mysticism, assume a semblance that often makes them scarcely recognizable. Yet, however fresh the utterance, an alert sense can usually detect, if not its particular source, at least its general European kinship.

When Emerson in the opening pages of *Nature* exhorts his countrymen to come forth and live their own lives, reminding them that "the sun shines to-day also," we catch echoes of Rousseau's "Man is born free; and is everywhere in chains." When Thoreau proclaims an intention "to brag as lustily as chanticleer in the morning, standing on his roost, if only to wake my neighbours up," we feel that here is the homely New England version of Shelley's cry to the West Wind:

> Be through my lips to unawakened earth
> The trumpet of a prophecy!

When Thoreau, on another occasion, writes that he was not aware "that the capacity to hear the woodpecker had slumbered within me so long," the words have all the spontaneity of underived utterance, and yet who can deny that the peculiar turn of that expression goes back through German or we know not what other channels to Plato and still remoter Eastern sources?

This mention of the East is suggestive of all the weaknesses of transcendentalism: its tendency to neglect proximate and to refer everything to primal causes; its attempt to attain the spiritual not by subduing but by turning its back on the material; its proneness to substitute passivity and receptiveness for alertness and creative force; its traces of a paralysing pantheism and fatalism; its ineffectualness; its atrophy of will. More than a touch of each of these qualities transcendentalism indisputably has; but if this were all there were to it, we should brand it as one more vain revival of a philosophy of life long since proved futile.

But who can doubt that there is in it also something the precise opposite of all this, the strange union of which with its Oriental elements makes it precisely the unique thing it is? Who can doubt that in speaking the last word of transcendentalism we should come back from India, even from Europe, to Concord and Boston? For, at bottom, it is the strong local flavour of it all, a smell of the soil through the universal generalizations, a dash of Yankee practicality in the midst of the Oriental mysticism, a sturdy Puritan pugnacity and grasp of fact underneath its serenest and most Olympian detachments, that gives this movement its reality and grip, and rescues it in large part not only from the ineffectiveness of the East but from the sentimental, the romantic, and the anarchic excesses of many of its related European movements.

These men were no mere dreamers. Emerson resigning his pulpit rather than administer the Lord's Supper or pray when he did not feel like praying, Thoreau going to jail for a refusal to pay his taxes, Alcott closing his school sooner than dismiss a coloured pupil (yes! even Alcott planting "aspiring" vegetables), Parker risking reputation and life in the anti-slavery crusade—these are typical examples of the fact that when these men were put to the test of acting up to their principles they were not found wanting. The Puritan character was the rock on which transcendentalism was built.

How inherent in the religious development of New England that character has been may be seen by glancing at three of her foremost spiritual figures: Jonathan Edwards, Ralph Waldo Emerson, and William James (James, curiously enough, though a New Englander only by adoption, being scarcely less representative of the most recent phase of New England religious evolution than Emerson and Edwards were of two of its earlier stages). Edwards, the last great apostle of theocratic dogmatism; Emerson, the prophet of a generation of romantic aspiration; James, the pragmatic philosopher of a scientific and democratic age—how far apart, at first thought, they seem! And not merely far apart, but often hostile. Emerson gave much of his best effort to demolishing the remnants of the Calvinistic structure Edwards had done so much to fortify. James's career was one long assault on that philosophy of the Absolute which is the intellectualized counterpart of the religion of the Over-Soul. The respective attitudes of the three men toward nature well illustrate their differences. To Edwards, in spite of his feeling for natural beauty, nature is essentially evil and is consistently set over against grace, which is of God. To Emerson, God and Nature are merely two aspects of a single spirit. To James, endlessly interesting as the natural world is in its instrumental capacity, in any ultimate sense nature is merely "so much weather." And yet, under analysis, such distinctions turn out to be partly nominal and relatively superficial, for, deeper than all their differences of doctrine, there is a community of spirit among these men, a something central and controlling in them all, something which in its day was the driving force of transcendentalism, the innate idealism and individualism of the New England mind.

# CHAPTER IX

# Emerson

I T becomes more and more apparent that Emerson, judged by an international or even by a broad national standard, is the outstanding figure of American letters. Others may have surpassed him in artistic sensitiveness, or, to a criticism averse to the stricter canons of form and taste, may seem to be more original or more broadly national than he, but as a steady force in the transmutation of life into ideas and as an authority in the direction of life itself he has obtained a recognition such as no other of his countrymen can claim. And he owes this pre-eminence not only to his personal endowment of genius, but to the fact also that, as the most perfect exponent of a transient experiment in civilization, he stands for something that the world is not likely to let die.

Ralph Waldo Emerson, born in Boston, 25 May, 1803, gathered into himself the very quintessence of what has been called the Brahminism of New England, as transmitted through the Bulkeleys, the Blisses, the Moodys, and the direct paternal line. Peter Bulkeley, preferring the wilderness of Satan to Laudian conformity, founded Concord in 1636; William Emerson, his descendant in the fifth generation, was builder of the Old Manse in the same town and a sturdy preacher to the minute-men at the beginning of the Revolution; and of many other ministerial ancestors stories abound which show how deeply implanted in this stock was the pride of rebellion against traditional forms and institutions, united with a determination to force all mankind to worship God in the spirit. With William, son of him of Concord and father of our poet, the fires of zeal began to wane. Though the faithful pastor of the First Church (Unitarian) of Boston, it is recorded of him that he

entered the ministry against his will. Yet he too had his unfulfilled dream of "coming out" by establishing a church in
Washington which should require no sort of profession of faith.
He died when the future philosopher was a boy of ten, leaving
the family to shift for itself as best it could. Mrs. Emerson
cared for the material welfare of the household by taking in
boarders. The chief intellectual guidance fell to the Aunt
Mary Moody Emerson, of whom her nephew drew a portrait in
his *Lectures and Biographies.* "She gave high counsels," he
says. Indubitably she did; but a perusal of her letters and of
the extracts from her journals leaves the impression that the
pure but dislocated enthusiasms of her mind served rather to
push Emerson in the direction of his weaker inclination than to
fortify him against himself. When a balloon is tugging at its
moorings there may be need of low counsels.

In 1817, Emerson entered Harvard College, and in due
course of time graduated. Then, after teaching for a while in
his brother's school in Boston, he returned to Cambridge to
study for the ministry, and was in the autumn of 1826 licensed
to preach. Three years later he was called, first as assistant
to Henry Ware, to the Second Church of Boston. His ministra-
tion there was quietly successful, but brief. In 1832, he gave
up his charge on the ground that he could not conscientiously
celebrate the Communion, even in the symbolic form customary
among the Unitarians. He was for the moment much adrift,
his occupation gone, his health broken, his wife lost after a short
period of happiness. In this state he went abroad to travel in
Italy, France, and England. One memorable incident of the
journey must be recorded, his visit to Carlyle at Craigenputtock, with all that it entailed of friendship and influence; but
beyond that he returned with little more baggage than he took
with him. He now made his residence in Concord, living
first with his mother and then with his second wife. Thenceforth there was to be no radical change in his life, but only the
gradual widening of the circle. The house that he now bought
he continued to inhabit until it was burned down in 1872; and
then his friends, in a manner showing exemplary tact, subscribed money for rebuilding it on the same lines. For a
number of years he preached in various pulpits, and once even
considered the call to a settled charge in New Bedford, but

he could not overcome his aversion to the ritual of the Lord's Supper and to regular prayers.

Meanwhile, by the medium of lectures delivered here and there and by printed essays, he was making of himself a kind of lay preacher to the world. His method of working out the more characteristic of these discourses has long been known: he would commonly select a theme, and then ransack his notebooks for pertinent passages which could be strung together with the addition of such developing and connecting material as was necessary. But since the publication of his *Journals* it has been possible to follow him more precisely in this procedure and to see more clearly how it conforms with the inmost structure of his mind. These remarkable records were begun in early youth and continued, though at the close in the form of brief memoranda, to the end of his life. The first entry preserved (not the first written, for it is from *Blotting Book No. XVII*) dates from his junior year at college and contains notes for a prize dissertation on the Character of Socrates. Among the sentences is this:

What is God? said the disciples, and Plato replied, It is hard to learn and impossible to divulge.

And the last page of the record, in the twelfth volume, repeats what is really the same thought:

The best part of truth is certainly that which hovers in gleams and suggestions unpossessed before man. His recorded knowledge is dead and cold. But this chorus of thoughts and hopes, these dawning truths, like great stars just lifting themselves into his horizon, they are his future, and console him for the ridiculous brevity and meanness of his civic life.

There is of course much variety of matter in the *Journals*—shrewd observations on men and books, chronicles of the day's events, etc.—but through it all runs this thread of self-communion, the poetry, it might be called, of the New England conscience deprived of its concrete deity and buoying itself on gleams and suggestions of eternal beauty and holiness. Of the same stuff, not seldom indeed of the same words, are those essays of his that have deeply counted; they are but a repetition to the world of fragments of this long inner conversation.

Where they fail to reach the reader's heart, it is not because they are fundamentally disjointed, as if made up of sentences jostled together like so many mutually repellent particles; but because from the manner of his composition Emerson often missed what he might have learned from Plato's *Phaedrus* was the essence of good rhetoric, that is to say, the consciousness of his hearer's mind as well as of his own. We hear him, as it were, talking to himself, with no attempt to convince by argument or enlighten by analysis. If our dormant intuition answers to his, we are profoundly kindled and confirmed; otherwise his sentences may rattle ineffectually about our ears.

Emerson's first published work was *Nature* (1836), which contains the gist of his transcendental attitude towards the phenomenal world, as a kind of beautiful symbol of the inner spiritual life, floating dreamlike before the eye, yet, it is to be noted, having discipline as one of its lessons for the attentive soul. The most characteristic and influential of his books are the two volumes of *Essays*, issued respectively in 1841 and 1844. In the former of these are those great discourses on *Self-Reliance*, *Compensation*, and *The Over-Soul*, into which was distilled the very quintessence of the volatile and heady liquid known as Emersonianism. Other volumes followed in due course. The latter publications, however, beginning with *Letters and Social Aims* (1875), are made up mainly of gleanings from the field already harvested, and were even gathered by hands not his own.

Two of his addresses (now both included in the volume with *Nature*) deserve special notice for the attention they attracted at the time. The first of these is the oration before the Phi Beta Kappa Society of Harvard, in 1837, a high but scarcely practical appeal to the American scholar to raise himself above the dust of pedantries, even out of the routine of what is "decent, indolent, complaisant," and to reach after the inspiration of "the Divine Soul which also inspires all men." The other lecture was delivered the next year before the senior class in Divinity College, Cambridge, and held up to the prospective preacher about the same ideal as was presented to the scholar. Historical Christianity is condemned because "it is not the doctrine of the soul, but an exaggeration of the personal, the positive, the ritual. It has dwelt, it dwells, with noxious exaggeration about the *person* of Jesus." The founder of Christianity saw, indeed, "with open eye the mystery of the soul," but what as a man he saw and knew of man's divinity cannot be given to man to-day by instruction, but only on the terms of a like intuition. The Unitarians of Massachusetts had travelled far from the Calvinistic creed of the Pilgrim Fathers, but Emerson's suave displacement of the person of Jesus for the "chorus of thoughts and hopes" in any human soul, perhaps even more his implicit rejection of all rites and institutions, raised loud protest among the worshippers of the day. For the most part he answered the criticism by silence, but in a letter replying to one of the more courteous of his opponents he used these significant words:

I could not give an account of myself, if challenged. I could not possibly give you one of the "arguments" you cruelly hint at, on which any doctrine of mine stands; for I do not know what arguments are in reference to any expression of a thought.

There may be some guile in this pretence to complete intellectual innocence, but it is nevertheless a fair statement of a literary method which seeks, and obtains, its effect by throwing a direct light into the soul of the hearer and bidding him look there and acknowledge what he sees.

Of the events of these years there is not much to relate. A journey to Europe, in 1847, resulted in the only two of his books which may be said to have been composed as units: *Representative Men* (published in 1850, from a series of lectures delivered in London), which displays Emerson's great powers as an ethical critic, in the larger use of that phrase, and *English Traits* (1856), which proves that his eyes were observing the world about him with Yankee shrewdness all the while that he seemed to be gazing into transcendental clouds. Into the question of slavery and disunion which was now agitating the country, he entered slowly. It was natural that one to whom the power and meaning of institutions had little appeal and to whom liberty was the all-including virtue, should have been drawn to the side of the Abolitionists, but at first there was a philosophical aloofness in his attitude. Only after the passing

of the Fugitive Slave Law and Webster's defection were his
passions deeply engaged.   Then he spoke ringing words:

> There is infamy in the air.   I have a new experience.   I awake
> in the morning with a painful sensation, which I carry about all
> day, and which, when traced home, is the odious remembrance of
> that ignominy which has fallen on Massachusetts, which robs the
> landscape of beauty, and takes the sunshine out of every hour.

And the war came to him as a welcome relief from a situation
which had grown intolerable.

A third trip to Europe was made in 1872, when his central
will was already loosening and his faculties were losing their
edge.   It was at this time that Charles Eliot Norton talked
with Carlyle, and heard the old man, eight years older than
Emerson, expatiate on the fundamental difference in their
tempers.   And on the voyage home in the same boat, Norton,
who so fully represents the judgment of New England, had
much conversation with Emerson, and recorded his opinion
in words that, whether welcome or not, should not be forgotten:

> Emerson was the greatest talker in the ship's company.   He
> talked with all men, and yet was fresh and zealous for talk at
> night.   His serene sweetness, the pure whiteness of his soul, the
> reflection of his soul in his face, were never more apparent to me;
> but never before in intercourse with him had I been so impressed
> with the limits of his mind.   His optimistic philosophy has hardened
> into a creed, with the usual effects of a creed in closing the avenues
> of truth.   He can accept nothing as fact that tells against his
> dogma.   His optimism becomes a bigotry, and, though of a nobler
> type than the common American conceit of the preeminent excellence
> of American things as they are, has hardly less of the quality of
> fatalism.   To him this is the best of all possible worlds, and the
> best of all possible times.   He refuses to believe in disorder or
> evil. . . . But such inveterate and persistent optimism, though it
> may show only its pleasant side in such a character as Emerson's,
> is dangerous doctrine for a people.   It degenerates into fatalistic
> indifference to moral considerations, and to personal responsibilities;
> it is at the root of much of the irrational sentimentalism in our
> American politics, of much of our national disregard of honour in
> our public men, of much of our unwillingness to accept hard truths,
> and of much of the common tendency to disregard the distinctions

between right and wrong, and to excuse guilt on the plea of good intentions or good nature.[1]

For some time there had been a gradual relaxation of Emerson's hold on life. Though always an approachable man and fond of conversation, there was in him a certain lack of human warmth, of "bottom," to use his own word, which he recognized and deplored. Commenting in his *Journal* (24 May, 1864) on the burial of Hawthorne, he notes the statement of James Freeman Clarke that the novelist had "shown a sympathy with the crime in our nature," and adds: "I thought there was a tragic element in the event, that might be more fully rendered,—in the painful solitude of the man, which, I suppose, could not longer be endured, and he died of it." A touch of this romantic isolation, though never morose or "painful," there was in himself, a failure to knit himself strongly into the bonds of society. "I have felt sure of him," he says of Hawthorne in the same passage, "in his neighbourhood, and in his necessities of sympathy and intelligence,— that I could well wait his time,—his unwillingness and caprice, —and might one day conquer a friendship. . . . Now it appears that I waited too long." Eighteen years later, standing by the body of Longfellow, he was heard to say: "That gentleman was a sweet, beautiful soul, but I have entirely forgotten his name." Such forgetfulness, like a serene and hazy cloud, hovered over Emerson's brain in his closing years. A month afterwards, on 27 April, 1882, he himself faded away peacefully.

To one who examines the events of Emerson's quiet life with a view to their spiritual bearing it will appear that his most decisive act was the surrender of his pulpit in 1832. Nearly a century earlier, in 1750, the greatest of American theologians had suffered what now befell the purest of American seers; and though the manner of their parting was different (Jonathan Edwards had been unwillingly ejected, whereas Emerson left with good will on both sides), yet there is significance in the fact that the cause of separation in both cases was the administration of the Lord's Supper. Nor is there less significance in the altered attitude of the later man towards this vital question. Both in a way turned from the ritualistic

[1] *Letters of Charles Eliot Norton*, vol. 1, pp. 503 and 506.

and traditional use of the Communion, and in this showed themselves leaders of the spirit which had carried the New England Fathers across the ocean as rebels against the Laudian tyranny of institutions. Edwards had revolted against the practice of Communion as a mere act of acquiescence in the authority of religion; he was determined that only those should approach the Table who could give evidence of a true conversion, by conversion meaning a complete emotional realization of the dogma of divine Grace and election. The eucharist was not a rite by conforming with which in humility men were to be made participators in the larger religious experience of the race, but a jealously guarded privilege of the few who already knew themselves set apart from the world. He was attempting to push to its logical issue the Puritan notion of religion as a matter of individual and inward experience, and if he failed it was because life can never be rigidly logical and because the worshippers of his day were already beginning to lose their intellectual grasp on the Calvinistic creed.[1] By Emerson's time, among the Unitarians of Boston, there could be no question of ritualistic grace or absolute conversion, but his act, nevertheless, like that of Edwards, was the intrusion of unyielding consistency among those who were content to rest in habit and compromise. In his old age Emerson gave this account of his conduct to Charles Eliot Norton:

He had come to the conviction that he could not administer the Lord's Supper as a divinely appointed, sacred ordinance of religion. And, after much debate with himself, he told his people that he could henceforth conduct the service only as a memorial service, without attributing to it any deeper significance. A parish meeting was held; the parish, though most kindly affected to him, could not bring themselves to accept his view,—it would be tantamount to admitting that they were no longer Christians. He resigned his charge, but an effort was made to induce him to remain, he administering the Lord's Supper in his sense, the people receiving it in theirs. But he saw that such an arrangement was impossible, and held to his resignation.[2]

Emerson had come to the inevitable conclusion of New England individualism; he had, in a word, "come out." Ed-

[1] See also Book I, Chaps. IV and V.
[2] *Letters of Charles Eliot Norton*, vol. I, p. 509.

wards had denied the communal efficacy, so to speak, of rites, but had insisted on inner conformity with an established creed. Emerson disavowed even a conformity in faith, demanding in its stead the entire liberty of each soul to rise on its own spiritual impulse. He was perspicacious and honest enough to acknowledge to himself the danger of such a stand. "I know very well," he wrote in his journal at the time of his decision, "that it is a bad sign in a man to be too conscientious, and stick at gnats. The most desperate scoundrels have been the over-refiners. Without accommodation society is impracticable." But, he adds, he could "not go habitually to an institution which they esteem holiest with indifference and dislike"; and again, looking deeper into his heart, "This is the end of my opposition, that I am not interested in it."

Emerson's act of renunciation was not only important as determining the nature of his career, but significant also of the transition of New England from theological dogmatism to romantic liberty. Much has been written about the influences that shaped his thoughts and about the relation of his transcendentalism to German metaphysics. In his later years it is clear that the speculations of Kant and Schelling and Fichte were known to him and occasionally coloured his language, but his *Journals* prove conclusively enough that the whole stamp of his mind was taken before these sources were open to him. Indirectly, no doubt, something of the German spirit came to him pretty early through Carlyle, and a passage in his *Journal* for 13 December, 1829, shows that he was at that time already deeply engaged in the Teutonized rhapsodies of Coleridge. But it would be easy to lay too much stress even on this indirect affiliation. Long before that date, as early as his senior year in college, he is yearning "to separate the soul for sublime contemplation till it has lost the sense of circumstances," and otherwise giving implicit expression to the full circle of transcendental faith. He was in fact a product of the great romantic movement that was sweeping over the world as it listed; his ideas, so far as they came to him from books, go back mainly to the Greek philosophers and the poets and preachers of seventeenth-century England, as these were interpreted under the light of the new movement. When he declared, in *Nature*, that "the vision of genius comes by re-nouncing the too officious activity of the understanding, and giving leave and amplest privilege to the spontaneous senti-ment," he was stating in precise terms an idea familiar to Blake and to the romanticists of every land—the elevation of enthusiasm above judgment, of emotion above reason, of spontaneity above discipline, and of unlimited expansion above centripetal control. But there was another element as strongly formative of Emerson's disposition as was the current of romanticism, and that was his ancestral inheritance. Ro-mantic spontaneity moved in various directions in accordance with the field in which it worked; in an Emerson, with all the divinity of Massachusetts in his veins, it might move to repudi-ate theological dogma and deny Jehovah, but it could not get out of hearing of the question "What is God?" It could not fall into the too common confusion of spiritual aspiration with the sicklier lusts of the flesh; it could never, for all its centrifugal wandering, overstep the bounds of character. Emersonianism may be defined as romanticism rooted in Puritan divinity.

In literary form and style the privilege of spontaneous sentiment showed itself with Emerson not in that fluency which in many of his contemporaries meant mere longwinded-ness, but in the habit of waiting for the momentary inspiration to the neglect of meditated construction and regularity. He has indeed succeeded in sustaining himself to the end in three or four poems of some compass, but his noblest work in verse must be sought in those quatrains which need no context for their comprehension and might be called spiritual ejacula-tions. Matthew Arnold has quoted for approval the two familiar stanzas,

> So nigh is grandeur to our dust,
>   So near is God to man,
> When Duty whispers low, *Thou must*,
>   The youth replies, *I can*.

and,

> Though love repine and reason chafe,
>   There came a voice without reply:
> "'Tis man's perdition to be safe,
>   When for the truth he ought to die."

These quatrains are, he says, "exceptional" in Emerson. They are that, and something more: they are exceptional in literature. One would have to search far to find anything in English equal to them in their own kind. They have the cleanness and radiance of the couplets of Simonides. They may look easy, but as a matter of fact the ethical epigram is an extremely difficult *genre*, and to attain this union of gravity and simplicity requires the nicest art. Less epigrammatic in tone but even more exquisitely finished are the lines entitled *Days*, pre-eminent in his works for what may truly be called a haunting beauty:

> Daughters of Time, the hypocritic Days,
> Muffled and dumb like barefoot dervishes,
> And marching single in an endless file,
> Bring diadems and faggots in their hands.
> To each they offer gifts after his will,
> Bread, kingdoms, stars, and sky that holds them all.
> I, in my pleachèd garden, watched the pomp,
> Forgot my morning wishes, hastily
> Took a few herbs and apples, and the Day
> Turned and departed silent. I, too late,
> Under her solemn fillet saw the scorn.

And as his verse, so is his prose. Though in one sense, so far as he writes always with two or three dominant ideas in his mind, he is one of the most consistent and persistent of expositors, yet he is really himself only in those moments of inspiration when his words strike with almost irresistible force on the heart, and awake an echoing response: "This is true; this I have myself dimly felt." Sometimes the memorable paragraph or sentence is purely didactic; sometimes it is highly metaphorical, as is the case with the closing paragraph of the *Conduct of Life:*

There is no chance, and no anarchy, in the universe. All is system and gradation. Every god is there sitting in his sphere. The young mortal enters the hall of the firmament; there is he alone with them alone, they pouring on him benedictions and gifts, and beckoning him up to their thrones. On the instant, and incessantly, fall snowstorms of illusions. He fancies himself in a vast crowd which sways this way and that, and whose movement and doings he must obey: he fancies himself poor, orphaned, insignificant. The mad crowd drives hither and thither, now furiously commanding this thing to be done, now that. What is he that he should resist their will, and think or act for himself? Every moment, new changes, and new showers of deceptions, to baffle and distract him. And when, by and by, for an instant, the air clears, and the cloud lifts a little, there are the gods still sitting around him on their thrones,—they alone with him alone.

There is, it need scarcely be said, a good deal in the works of Emerson—literary criticism, characterization of men and movements, reflection on the state of society—which lies outside of this ethical category; but even in such essays his guiding ideas are felt in the background. Nor are these ideas hard to discover. The whole circle of them, ever revolving upon itself, is likely to be present, explicit or implicit, in any one of his great passages, as it is in the paragraph just cited—the clear call to self-reliance, announcing that "a man should learn to detect and watch that gleam of light which flashes across his mind from within"; the firm assurance that, through all the balanced play of circumstance, "there is a deeper fact in the soul than compensation, to wit, its own nature"; the intuition, despite all the mists of illusion, of the Over-Soul which is above us and still ourselves: "We live in succession, in division, in parts, in particles; meanwhile within man is the soul of the whole; the wise silence; the universal beauty . . .; the eternal *One*."

Emerson's philosophy is thus a kind of reconciled dualism, and a man's attitude towards it in the end will be determined by his sense of its sufficiency or insufficiency to meet the facts of experience. One of Emerson's biographers has attempted to set forth this philosophy as "a synthesis and an anticipation." It is a synthesis because in it we find, as Emerson had already found in Plato and Plotinus, a reconciliation of "the many and the one," the everlasting flux and the motionless calm at the heart of things:

An ample and generous recognition of this transiency and slipperiness both in the nature of things and in man's soul seems more and more a necessary ingredient in any estimate of the universe which shall satisfy the intellect of the coming man. But it seems equally true that the coming man who shall resolve our problems will never content himself with a universe a-tilt, a universe in cascade, so to speak; the craving for permanence in some form cannot be jauntily evaded. Is there any known mind which fore-shadows the desired combination so clearly as Emerson's? Who has felt more profoundly the evanescence and evasiveness of things? . . . Yet Emerson was quite as firm in his insistence on a single unalterable reality as in his refusal to believe that any aspect or estimate of that reality could be final.[1]

The necessity of the dualism that underlies Emerson's philosophy could scarcely be put more neatly, and the kind of synthesis, or reconciliation, in which Emerson floated is admira-bly expressed. But it is not so plain that this synthesis antici-pates the solution of the troublesome problems of life. There will be those who will ask whether the power of religion for mature minds does not depend finally on its feeling for evil. How otherwise, in fact, shall religion meet those harder ques-tions of experience when its aid is most needed? And in like manner they will say that the power of philosophy as the *dux vitae* depends on its acquaintance with the scope and difficulties of scepticism. Both religion and philosophy would seem, in such a view, to rest not only on a statement of the dualism of good and evil, knowledge and ignorance, but on a realization of the full meaning and gravity, practical and intellectual, of this dualism. Now Emerson certainly recognizes the dualism of experience, but it is a fair question whether he realizes its full meaning and seriousness. He accepts it a trifle too jauntily, is reconciled to its existence with no apparent pang, is sometimes too ready to wave aside its consequences, as if a statement of the fact were an escape from its terrible perplexities. Carlyle meant something of the sort when he worried over Emerson's inability to see the hand of the devil in human life. Hence it is that Emerson often loses value for his admirers in proportion to their maturity and experience. He is above all the poet of religion and philosophy for the young; whereas men, as they grow older, are inclined to turn from him, in their more serious moods, to those sages who have supple-mented insight with a firm grasp of the darker facts of human nature. That is undoubtedly true; nevertheless, as time passes, the deficiencies of this brief period of New England, of which

[1] O. W. Firkins, *Ralph Waldo Emerson*, p. 364.

Emerson was the perfect spokesman, may well be more and more condoned for its rarity and beauty. One of the wings of the spirit is hope, and nowhere is there to be found a purer hope than in the books of our New England sage; rather, it might be said that he went beyond hope to the assurance of present happiness. The world had never before seen anything quite of this kind, and may not see its like again.

# INDEX

# THE CAMBRIDGE HISTORY

## OF

# AMERICAN LITERATURE

Volume II

Early National Literature: Part II
Later National Literature: Part I

# The Cambridge History

of

# American Literature

Edited by

William Peterfield Trent

John Erskine

Stuart P. Sherman

Carl Van Doren

In Three Volumes

★  ★

Early National Literature: Part II
Later National Literature: Part I

New York: The Macmillan Company

Cambridge, England : at the University Press

# PREFACE

*T*HE *Cambridge History of American Literature* was originally planned to appear in two volumes, but the abundance of the material submitted and the importance of having the biography comprehensive and practically complete, made it necessary for the publishers to extend the work to four.

In the later volumes, the editors have found increasing difficulty in connection with the problem of how far to include living writers, some of whom could not be omitted without making the record obviously inaccurate. We have felt justified in dealing with certain contemporaries who before 1900 had written notable books and who have exerted important influence in our literary history, even when, as for example in the case of Professor Brander Matthews, these writers have, as contributors, been associated with the present work to the advantage of the readers and to our own satisfaction.

THE EDITORS.

May 1, 1918.

# CONTENTS

*BOOK II (Continued)*

EARLY NATIONAL LITERATURE: PART II

## CHAPTER X

### THOREAU

By Archibald MacMechan, Ph.D., F.R.S.C., George Munro Professor of the English Language and Literature in Dalhousie University.

PAGE

## CHAPTER XI

### HAWTHORNE

By John Erskine, Ph.D., Professor of English in Columbia University.

## CHAPTER XII

### LONGFELLOW

By William Peterfield Trent, M.A., LL.D., Professor of English Literature in Columbia University.

## CHAPTER XIII

### WHITTIER

By William Morton Payne, LL.D.

# Contents

# CHAPTER XVIII

## PRESCOTT AND MOTLEY

By RUTH PUTNAM.

# CHAPTER XIX

## EARLY HUMORISTS

By WILL D. HOWE, Ph.D., Professor of English in Indiana University.

# CHAPTER XX

## MAGAZINES, ANNUALS, AND GIFT-BOOKS, 1783–1850

By WILLIAM B. CAIRNS, Ph.D., Associate Professor of American Literature in the University of Wisconsin.

# CHAPTER XXI

## NEWSPAPERS, 1775–1860

By FRANK W. SCOTT, Ph.D., Assistant Professor of English in the University of Illinois.

# Contents

## CHAPTER XXII

### DIVINES AND MORALISTS, 1783-1860

By SAMUEL LEE WOLFF, Ph.D., Instructor in English, Extension Teaching, Columbia University.

## CHAPTER XXIII

### WRITERS OF FAMILIAR VERSE

By BRANDER MATTHEWS, D.C.L., Litt.D., LL.D., Professor of Dramatic Literature in Columbia University.

## CHAPTER XXIV

### LOWELL

By ASHLEY H. THORNDIKE, Ph.D., L.H.D., Professor of English in Columbia University.

## BOOK III

## LATER NATIONAL LITERATURE: PART I

## CHAPTER I

### WHITMAN

By EMORY HOLLOWAY, A.M., Assistant Professor of English in Adelphi College.

# Contents

# Book II (Continued)

## CHAPTER X

## Thoreau

THE life of a village community is not seldom enriched by the inclusion of a rebel, an original who refuses obstinately to conform to type, and succeeds in following out his idea, in contrast to the humdrum routine of his fellows. When the community happens to be Concord, the picturesque and historic village where the Revolution began, the Weimar of American literature, and when the rebel happens to be an American faun, the conjunction must result in no ordinary enrichment. There on 12 July, 1817, just after the second war with Britain, David Henry Thoreau was born to a small farmer and artisan who kept a shop and painted signs. The French-looking surname came by way of the Channel Islands, for the author's grandfather was born in Jersey, and, in spite of his British origin, had served as a sailor in a Continental privateer. Thoreau passed his life in the village of his birth, and now his name is indissolubly associated with it.

For a generation which plumes itself upon its "breadth," no slight effort is needed to picture the life of a typical New England village before the Transcendental movement had broken up the hard old Puritanic crust. It was a rigid and limited life made up of work, thrift, duty, and meetings. Caricatured and ridiculed though it be, that old stern life moulded men and women of the toughest moral and intellectual fibre. Puritanism was an intellectual creed, and led directly to the cultivation of the intellect. The minister and the schoolmaster were twin ruling powers. None questioned the value of education; it was almost a fetish. So as a child in a Puritan community, Henry Thoreau followed the regular routine of the common school until he was ripe for the university.

Thoreau became a man of letters, but he was also a wild man, a faun; he became Emerson's man, and—although it is rather difficult to fit into the picture—he was a Harvard man. He went up at sixteen and took his degree at twenty. His portrait at this time shows a smooth, grave face dominated by a Roman nose and overhung by a bush of fine brown hair. What benefit he derived from his college years is a matter both of record and of inference. "What I was learning in college was chiefly, I think, to express myself," he writes five years after leaving Harvard. Perhaps the most significant memorial of his college career is the Latin letter he wrote to his sister Helen, in 1840. It gave him pleasure to use the language of Virgil and Cicero, for one of the many paradoxes in Thoreau's life was the union of true American contempt for tradition with an unaffected love of the classics. After a diatribe against the narrow religiosity of New England, he draws breath to praise "the Ionian father of the rest," with the enthusiasm of Keats.

There are few books which deserve to be remembered in our wisest hours, but the Iliad is brightest in the serenest days, and embodies still all the sunlight that fell in Asia Minor. No modern joy or ecstasy of ours can lower its height, or dim its lustre, but there it lies in the east of literature, as it were the earliest and latest production of the mind.

From the wildwood simplicity of Walden, he startles the reader with deliverances which might have come from the Bodleian.

Those who have not learned to read the ancient classics in the language in which they were written must have a very imperfect knowledge of the history of the human race. . . . Homer has never been printed in English, nor Æschylus, nor Virgil even,—works as refined, as solidly done, as beautiful almost as the morning itself; for later writers, say what we will of their genius, have rarely if ever equalled the elaborate beauty and finish and the lifelong and heroic literary labours of the ancients.

Thoreau translated the *Prometheus Vinctus* and tried his hand at Pindar. His pages are sown with classical allusions and quotations. The sunset at Cape Cod brings a line of Homer into his memory "with a rush," as the shining torch of the sun falls into the ocean. He has words of just appreciation for Anacreon. His odes

charm us by their serenity and freedom from exaggeration and passion, and by a certain flower-like beauty, which does not propose itself, but must be approached and studied like a natural object.

Such genuine admiration for Greek genius is rare at any time, and certainly not many American hands could have been busy translating Æschylus, Pindar, and Anacreon in the hurried forties and fifties of the nineteenth century. This large and solid academic basis for Thoreau's culture is not generally observed. His devotion to the Greeks rings truer than his various utterances on Indian literature and philosophy. Besides, he was well seen in the English classics from Chaucer downwards. A few pages of *A Week* yield quotations from Emerson, Ovid, Quarles, Channing, *Relations des Jesuits*, Gower, Lydgate, Virgil, Tennyson, Percy's *Reliques*, Byron, Milton, Shakespeare, Spenser, Simonides. As Lowell remarks, "His literature was extensive and recondite." The truth is, Thoreau was a man of letters, whose great ambition was to study and to write books.

During and after his college career, Thoreau taught school, like the hero of *Elsie Venner*. He is quite frank about this episode. "As I did not teach for the good of my fellow-men, but simply for a livelihood, this was a failure." Brief as was his apprenticeship to the schoolmaster trade, one might possibly conjecture that it left some mark upon him. The many citations of recondite literature do not escape the suspicion of parade and pedantry. There is a certain gusto with which he inserts the botanical name of a plant after the picturesque vernacular, and distinguishes between *Rana palustris* and *Rana pipiens*. In general, the tone he adopts towards the world is that of the pedagogue dealing habitually with inferior minds.

After his college days comes an episode which his biographers seem inclined to slur over, perhaps from a false sense of the dignity of biography, and that is the two years, from 25 April.

1841, to May, 1843, which Thoreau spent under Emerson's roof. By the time Thoreau left Harvard, Emerson had become a power in the spiritual life of America. His brief career as a Unitarian minister was already far behind him; he had made his pilgrimage to Europe; he had penetrated the wilds of Scotland to Craigenputtock because one Thomas Carlyle, another unrecognized genius, lived there. He had given in Boston those lectures on *Great Men* and *The Philosophy of History* which foreshadow the great address commonly called the declaration of independence for American literature.[1] He had brought out his Scottish friend's odd book, *Sartor Resartus*, a publication which accelerated the Transcendental movement. Emerson discovered the youth Thoreau as a true poet, and communicated the discovery in a letter to Carlyle. Thoreau became a member of Emerson's household, apparently as general "help," a relationship which all Americans will understand but which will be the despair of Europeans.

> The most practical and handy person in all matters of every day life, a good mechanic and gardener, methodical in his habits, observant and kindly in the domestic world,

is the character Emerson gives him. There must have been a cash nexus, but the essence of the relationship was the tie uniting master and pupil, sage and disciple. This long and close association with the great literary force of that time had no slight effect in moulding Thoreau's character and determining his bent.

> His biographer, who knew him personally, says that he imitated Emerson's tones and manners so that it was annoying to listen to him.

The imitation of Emerson in Thoreau's writing is equally apparent. Lowell saw and condemned it in his criticism of *A Week*. In prose there is the sentence which reads like an oracle. It may be the profoundest wisdom, or it may be the merest matter of moonshine. When Thoreau writes "Ancient history has an air of antiquity," or, "Give me a sentence which no intelligence can understand," the critic can only fall

[1] See Book II, Chap. IX.

back on the Gilbertian comment upon the young man who "expresses himself in terms too deep for me." The imitation of Emerson's poetry is even more marked and results in what Lowell calls Thoreau's "worsification." He had no candid friend to tell him what Dryden told "Cousin Swift." There was, on the other hand, no little benefit in mere contact with such a personality as Emerson, much more in continual and close intercourse with him. The stimulus to thought must have been most potent, and Emerson's influence could not but stiffen Thoreau in his natural independence and confirm him in his design of living his own life.

The village rebel who will not conform rebels first against the local religion. It is the obvious thing to rebel against. What Thoreau dissented from was New England Puritanism, as is plainly shown in "Sunday" of *A Week*. The atmosphere of that lost religion hangs about the letter of his roommate at Harvard, who became a minister in due course. One thinks of the letters young Mr. Tennyson of Trinity was exchanging with other Cambridge "Apostles" about the same time. The salutation is "Friend Thoreau," which seems to have been the accepted convention at the time. Perhaps the most significant sentence in it runs:

I hear that you are comfortably located in your native town, as the guardian of its children, in the immediate vicinity, I suppose, of one of our most distinguished apostles of the future, R. W. Emerson, and situated under the ministry of our old friend Reverend Barzillai Frost, to whom please make my remembrances.

It does not appear that Thoreau after reaching manhood was ever "situated under the ministry" of the Reverend Barzillai Frost. In "Civil Disobedience," he writes:

Some years ago, the State met me on behalf of the Church and commanded me to pay a certain sum toward the support of a clergyman, whose preaching my father attended, but never I myself. "Pay" it said, "or be locked up in jail." I declined to pay. But unfortunately, another man saw fit to pay it.

The recusant even rendered the authorities a reason in writing for his recusancy.

Know all men by these presents that I Henry Thoreau do not wish to be regarded as a member of any incorporated society which I have not joined.

Opposition to the State followed naturally on opposition to the Church. To his honour, Thoreau took a stand against slavery when it was anything but popular to do so, even in the State of Massachusetts. In all his words on this theme there is a fire not to be found elsewhere. What roused him was the spectacle of fugitive slaves escaping to the free North, and, through the action of Northern courts, dragged back into slavery. The State was clearly in the wrong; Thoreau, in his own phrase, "declared war on the State," by refusing to pay his poll-tax. He believed that such passive resistance by a number of taxpayers would bring about the abolition of slavery. He was therefore quite consistent with himself when he stood forth from the crowd as the champion of John Brown in his history-making raid on Harper's Ferry. Public opinion, North and South, condemned the raid as the outrage of a fanatic attempting to kindle a servile war. Thoreau was of the remnant who saw its true bearing.

It was in the first year of his Walden hermitage that Thoreau was arrested and lodged in jail for refusing to pay his poll-tax. He tells how he was going to the cobbler's, with a shoe to be mended, when the Law laid hold of him, how he spent the evening very pleasantly with the other inmates of the lock-up, how he was released next morning, and immediately started off with a berry-picking party. This "grand refusal" struck the imagination of Stevenson, who considers it the most significant act of Thoreau, and more important than his retreat in Walden. A parallel might be found in Stevenson's account of his brief incarceration in a French prison in the epilogue to *An Inland Voyage*. Again, some friend paid Thoreau's poll-tax for him, but he never wavered in his reasoned policy of passive resistance to an unjust, slavery-supporting State. At the same time, he never refused to pay the highway tax, because, "I am as desirous of being a good neighbour as I am of being a bad subject." "I simply wish," he continues, "to refuse allegiance to the State, to withdraw and stand aloof from it effectually."

His next step was a more remote withdrawal, an attempt to stand aloof from his kind. It was an attempt to live by himself and to himself, in fact, to turn modern hermit. Apparently the idea had long been germinating in his mind. On that far-off Harvard commencement of 1837, he took part in a "conference," an obsolete academic exercise resembling a medieval "disputation." He took one side of an argument and a fellow-student, afterwards a judge, maintained the opposite. The subject debated was "The Commercial Spirit." In his set speech, the grave, shock-headed graduate from Concord suggested that

the order of things should be somewhat reversed; the seventh should be man's day of toil, wherein to earn his living by the sweat of his brow; and the other six his Sabbath of the affections and the soul—in which to range this widespread garden, and drink in the soft influences and sublime revelations of Nature.

The young collegian's division of time may have provoked a smile, but the day was to come when he was to make the actual experiment. Thoreau had turned against the Church, he had turned against the State, and now he turned against organized society. He perceived that man was bound to the wheel of circumstance, he was the passive, unquestioning slave of a vain and sordid routine. One man at least would wrench himself free from the mill at which he saw his fellows ceaselessly toiling. He would carry out his boyhood's dream, and, by reorganization of his life, obtain freedom for the things that matter. By making life more simple, he would cheat circumstance and really begin to live.

I dream of looking abroad summer and winter, with free gaze from some mountainside, while my eyes revolve in an Egyptian slime of health—I to be nature looking into nature with such easy sympathy as the blue-eyed grass in the meadow looks in the face of the sky. From such recess, I would put forth sublime thoughts daily, as the plant puts forth leaves.

It only remained to choose his "recess."

Apparently the suggestion as to the particular recess came from his friend, Channing, who writes,

I see nothing for you in this earth but that field which I once christened "Briars"; go out upon that, build yourself a hut, and there begin the grand process of devouring yourself alive.

Thoreau was a natural ascetic.  He ate little flesh meat, but subsisted almost entirely on vegetable food; he drank nothing but water; he never married.   He refers in a letter to a nameless lady who wished to marry *him*, and he calls the inverted courtship "tragic."   In the Age of Faith he would have fled to the wilderness for the same reason that he built his hut by Walden pond, in order to save his soul.   Salvation for him meant escape from endless labour for the acquisition of useless things.   By another paradox of his career, he freed himself from New England thrift by being still more thrifty.   By denying himself and faring more scantily than his neighbours, he secured leisure for pursuits they could not comprehend. Thoreau is a prophet of the simple life, perhaps the first in America.   He uses the very term.

I do believe in simplicity.   When the mathematician would solve a difficult problem, he first frees the equation from all encumbrances, and reduces it to its simplest terms.   So simplify the problem of life, distinguish the necessary and the real.

He was preaching to his friend Blake what he had already practised.   He had felled the pines with his borrowed axe, and dug his cellar, and built his

tight shingled and plastered house, ten feet wide by fifteen long, and eight feet posts, with a garret and a closet, a large window on each side, two trap-doors, one door at the end, and a brick fireplace opposite.

It was a little smaller than the room he occupied at Harvard. The materials cost less than twenty-nine dollars; and by cultivating beans and other vegetables he was able to support himself at an annual expense of a little more than eight dollars. This was removing the encumbrances from the equation, with a vengeance, but Thoreau could make a "dinner" of berries. The experiment lasted from March, 1845, until September, 1847, and then having satisfied himself that the thing could be done, he gave it up.

Two years later, Thoreau published his first book, *A Week on the Concord and Merrimack Rivers*. The actual voyage was performed by the two brothers Henry and John in the late summer of 1839 in a boat of their own making, "painted green below with a border of blue, with reference to the two elements in which it was to spend its existence." During his Walden retirement, Thoreau worked over the original record of his pleasant outing, expanding it greatly by the inclusion of very various material, and had it published at his own risk by Monroe in 1849. It was the year of the Argonauts, of the gold-rush to California, and such literary treasure as the odd book contained was not much regarded. Though favourably reviewed by Ripley and by Lowell, it did not please the public, and over seven hundred copies out of an impression of one thousand were thrown back on the author's hands. It is another of the paradoxes of Thoreau's career that since his death, this failure has been edited with almost benedictine care.

Lowell's praise of *A Week* can hardly be termed excessive. After dwelling on its weak points, its lack of unity, its imitation of Emerson, its dolorous verse, he continues,

the prose work is done conscientiously and neatly. The style is compact and the language has an antique purity like wine grown colourless with age.

The truth is that Thoreau with all his genuine appreciation of the classics never learned their lessons of proportion, restraint, "nothing too much." Nor was the example of his master Emerson likely to correct his own tendency to formlessness. The principle of selection is absent. The week's excursion is only an excuse for including Emersonian essays on friendship and chastity, or dissertations on the Laws of Menu, or translations of Anacreon, till the reader asks resentfully what they are doing in this dory-modelled *galère*, painted green below with a border of blue, on the Merrimack and Concord, lucid streams. If he had possessed the artistic instinct of Stevenson, or had undergone Stevenson's rigid self-imposed discipline in the writer's craft, he might have made *A Week* as complete a little masterpiece as *An Inland Voyage*. *A Week* fails on account of its scattering aim. It is neither a record of a week's excursion, nor a book of essays, but a jumble of the two. Thoreau's American contempt for tradition accounts for the artistic failure.

Where Thoreau is not the transcendental essayist, but the first-hand observer of nature, he is delightful. When discoursing on such a theme as the common sunfish, the reader wishes he would never end.

The breams are so careful of their charge that you may stand close by in the water and examine them at your leisure. I have stood over them half an hour at a time, and stroked them familiarly without frightening them, suffering them to nibble my fingers harmlessly, and seen them erect their dorsal fins in anger when my hand approached their ova, and have even gently taken them out of the water with my hand. . . . As you stand thus stooping over the bream in its nest, the edges of the dorsal and caudal fins have a singular dusty golden reflection, and its eyes, which stand out from its head, are transparent and colourless. Seen in its native element, it is a very beautiful and compact fish, perfect in all its parts, and looks like a brilliant coin fresh from the mint.

If the whole book had been of this texture, it would be a classic. Another element in the book which Thoreau valued slightly— those incidental glimpses of a vanished America—will be prized by later generations. His accounts of the mountain people he discovered, of the girl combing her black hair, of his surly host, Rice, and his strange inn, of the old farmer praying in the dim morning pasture, of the canal boatmen, of the lockmen's house, and the small-voiced but sincere hospitality of the Yankee housewife offering the obsolete refreshment of "molasses and ginger," read like pages Irving forgot to put into *The Sketch Book*. These things are seen with the naturalist's clear grave eyes and recorded in plain words with no attempt at oracular profundity. For the sake of more such true pictures of reality, how gladly would the modern reader forego the disquisitions on Persius and Ossian.

The next year, 1850, Thoreau and his friend Channing made a brief raid across the border into Quebec, though the record of his experience was not published until 1866, with the title *A Yankee in Canada*. Stevenson found the book dull.

Still, it has an interest of its own for the light it sheds on Thoreau's peculiar temperament, and particularly on his robust Americanism, a sentiment based on traditional dislike of Britain and on contempt for monarchy as an effete institution. Patriotism is a curious passion. It does not seem possible to love one's own country except by hating some other country. Emerson defines Thoreau almost in these terms:

No truer American existed than Thoreau. His preference of his country and condition was genuine, and his aversation from English and European manners and tastes almost reached contempt.

With no great love for the institutions of his own land, he showed his instinctive preference for them during his one brief sojourn under an alien flag. His attitude throughout is one of consistent patronage to all he sees and hears. The red-coats in the citadel at Quebec have the manhood drilled out of them. Britain, he believes, is "red in the knuckles" with holding on to the Canadas, and must soon relax her grasp. Towards the great mystery of historical Christianity, he is equally contemptuous. The devout worshippers in the Cathedral at Montreal, absorbed in prayer and regardless of gazing strangers, suggest the parallel of his fellow Yankees going to meeting on a week-day, after the cattle-fair. The Sisters of Charity whom he saw in the street looked as if they had cried their eyes out, "insulting the daylight with their presence." That the soldier and the religious had something valuable to which he was a stranger, never occurred to him. In other words, he was blind to the romance of war and the poetry of faith. Even the natural courtesy of the *habitants* seems to him mere servility. For the American of Thoreau's generation, history began with the musketry of the embattled farmers at Concord bridge. Before that day, there was only a dark welter of wicked kings and mad tories. These limitations prevented him from realizing, as Parkman did, the epic struggle which ended on the Plains of Abraham. He indeed transcribes the inscription on the monument to Wolfe and Montcalm, but the splendour and pathos of their fate leave him unmoved. Still, this rigid and narrow provincialism gives salt to his books and explains his revolt against convention.

It was his Americanism which drove Thoreau to realize himself in his own way.

In 1854, Thoreau published the book by which he will always be best known, *Walden, or Life in the Woods*. It is by far the deepest, richest, and most closely jointed of his books. It shows Thoreau at his best, and contains all that he had to say to the world. In fact, he is a man of one book, and that book is *Walden*. In plan, it is open to the same objection as *A Week*, and might almost plead guilty to the charge of obtaining a hearing under false pretences. "Life in the woods" suggests the atmosphere of *As You Like It* and the Robin Hood ballads, but not moralizings on economy and the duty of being yourself. The reader who takes up the book with the idea that he is going to enjoy another *Robinson Crusoe* will not be pleased to find that every now and then he will have to listen to a lay sermon, or a lyceum lecture.

Still it is the adventurous, *Robinson Crusoe* part that is imperishable. How a man resolved to live in a new way, how he borrowed an axe and began felling pines on the ground that sloped southward to a wonderful pond, how he trimmed his rafters, dug his cellar, bought an Irish labourer's shanty, transported the materials to a new site and raised the frame, appeal to the open-air instinct of every man. Even how he maintained the fire on the hearth, and grubbed out the fat pine roots to feed it, are matters of absorbing interest. His struggle with the weeds and poor soil of the two-acre patch on which he raised his beans and potatoes, every item of his various accounts, his food, his daily routine, his house-cleaning, have the fascination of a narrative by Defoe. The reader follows the solitary in his swim across the lake, or through the wood to the village, or about the hut, or along the rows of beans, with a zest he can hardly explain to himself. The reason is that Henry Thoreau in Walden wood is the same as the mariner of York on the Island of Desolation; he represents once more the struggle of primitive man to obtain food and shelter, in fact the epic of civilization. The interest of the theme is perennial.

*Walden* is also the memorial of an American faun, of a wild man who lived in the woods, who carried an umbrella like Robinson Crusoe, to weatherfend his head, and used a microscope to study insects with. About the same time, just after leaving Harvard, Thoreau found his first arrowhead and began his first journal, and the two streams of tendency ran side by side in his nature till the end.   Intercourse with nature was even more necessary to Thoreau than intercourse with books.   Intercourse with human beings he thought he did not need, but he was always tramping off to the village for a chat. He was not a real solitary, for visitors were always coming to view the progress of the odd experiment in living.   Still Thoreau differed widely from the ordinary gregarious man in that he could manage to be alone for long periods with the woods and the sky.   A friend called him a poet-naturalist; but the description is not exact.   He hardly views nature as a poet, and he is surpassed by not a few observers of nature, who have had the stimulus of Darwin.   The merely pictorial in nature does not much interest him, probably because he had seen no pictures.   To Thoreau nature is no divinity as she is to Wordsworth; she is simply the pleasantest of companions, or rather the pleasantest environment for a natural man.   In a house, in a town, he is like a creature caged.   It is characteristic that after swimming across the lake, he would sit in his doorway all morning, "in a wise passiveness," as Wordsworth would term it.   So wild creatures live in the wild, when not hunger-driven.   The wild things found him to be of their own kind; a mouse made friends with him, a hen partridge led her brood about his hut, he could take a fish out of the water in his hand. Thoreau is perhaps the first to suggest the pleasure of hunting animals without a gun, of learning about them without any desire to kill.   He was not influenced by Darwin, or such a conception as the struggle for existence.   Nature to him was not red in tooth and claw with ravin; it was a gentle, friendly, peaceful alternative to the mean greed and futile toil of man. The atmosphere of Walden is always serene and free from cloud or storm.   Rain and winter come in their season; but they never seem to touch him; the rain does not wet, and the winter does not chill.   There may be a thousand nooks in New England more beautiful than Walden, but they remain unknown, while the pine-clad slope which this strange being discovered and haunted for two years is charted as a permanent addition to the world-wide map of Romance.

Thoreau has two styles, the oracular and the simple; and

in *Walden* the simple prevails. Like the water of the pond, it is clear, colourless and wholesome. Thoreau is a careful writer, with an instinct for the right word which was developed and strengthened by a lifelong devotion to the best books. His love of the classics must have tended to purify his style and increase its natural dignity. *Walden* is generally free from oracular phrases and grotesque locutions like "eyes revolve in an Egyptian slime of health." It must always retain the deep unfailing value of all autobiography, personal memoirs, "confessions." The record of a life will never fail of an audience. When a man declares, "Thus I did, thus I thought, thus I felt," other men are always eager to attend his tale.

The Walden experiment was not unlike the other Transcendental experiment of Brook Farm. Both were declarations of independence; both were attempts to place life on a new basis; both broke down. The Greek dog-sage in his tub, the English Quaker in his suit of leather, the Yankee land-surveyor in his wooden hut are three object lessons to the world of the ancient truth that "a man's life consisteth not in the abundance of the things that he possesseth." The Walden experiment is open to all the criticism of Lowell: "it presupposed all the complicated civilization which it theoretically abjured." Even for Thoreau it was not a success. In the first year, his Homer lay open on the table, but he was so busy that he could only read it by snatches; in the second year, he was forced to set up a prosaic stove in the place of the romantic fire-place. Thoreau's ideal of a world of book men, or contemplatives, is a dream. Still, the experience of the ascetic always shames the grossness of the worldly wiseman. If a man can live for a year for eight dollars, we certainly spend too much on things we could do without. Thoreau's experiment will always have its appeal to hot, ambitious spirits on their first awakening to the intricacy of life. The hero of *Locksley Hall* longs to escape from civilization to summer isles of Eden. At least one American man of letters has followed Thoreau's example by going into retreat.

After living in his hut for two years, Thoreau supported himself for three more by cultivating his garden, like Candide. Thus he obtained the freedoms he desired, the leisure to think, and to read, and to write, and to be himself. Then he went back to his land-surveying, his communing with the spirits of the wild, and the compilation of his voluminous journals. From the latter, several volumes have been quarried for the definitive edition of his works. They must always be of more interest to the admirer of Thoreau and the student of literature than to the general reader.

Then came the break-down of his health. It was the irony of fate that the man who lived according to nature, who obeyed the dictates of spare temperance, who never seemed to tire, should die of tuberculosis, the scourge of civilized life. His latest portrait, a daguerreotype taken in New Bedford, seven months before his death, shows a hairy, innocent, pathetic face; the eyes have the mute appeal of the consumptive. In 1861, the stricken man made a trip to the West, in the vain hope of restoration to health by change of air. He died in his birth-place, Concord, on 2 May, 1862, in the second year of the Civil War. He has been blamed for expressing his sense of detachment from that terrible conflict, but if, like Mercutio, he cries, "A plague on both your houses!" it must be remembered that, like Mercutio, he was a dying man. His last letter, dictated to his sister, concludes, "I am enjoying existence as much as ever, and regret nothing."

Emerson has written an appreciation of Thoreau with intimate knowledge and tender humanity. To that estimate, little can be added, or taken away. Lowell and Stevenson have appraised his character and his work, none too gently. Of himself he said, "I am a mystic, a Transcendentalist, and a natural philosopher."

## CHAPTER XI

# Hawthorne

THE romances of Hawthorne can hardly be understood apart from the current of Transcendentalism in which his genius was formed. Most foreigners and many of his countrymen have thought of him as an affectionate student of the New England past, in a small way comparable to Scott with his love of Border history, and especially they have thought of him as a kind of portrait painter, who magically resharpened for us the already fading lineaments of Puritanism. Reflection might suggest, however, that the portrait he restored bears an unlucky resemblance in its sombreness and its unloveliness to the portrait of Edward Randolph in the *Twice Told Tales*, and a little further thought would perhaps convince us that Hawthorne usually treats Puritanism, not as the central theme in his canvas, but as a dark background for the ideas and for the experiences which more deeply concern him. Those ideas and experiences have little to do with Puritanism except by contrast; they were partly furnished to his imagination by the enthusiastic but uncritical thinkers among his acquaintance who kindled rapturously at Alcott's conversations or basked in the indefiniteness of Emerson's lectures, and partly they were furnished by his own contact with Alcott and Emerson and with their writings. Like them, he was less a Puritan than a lover of the present, and if he seemed often to deal with things long past, it was only because he had the faculty, more than other men, of recognizing in the present whatever had served its purpose or was worn out or dead.

But if as a Transcendentalist he stood aloof from Puritanism, his temperament forced him to stand aloof also from the other

Transcendentalists. Although their philosophy, as they liked to say, was a "questioning" of life, he differed from them all in being a true skeptic. To be quite precise, let us say that he drew the inspiration of his romances not so much from their ideas as from the neglected but inevitable conclusions of their ideas. Alcott and Emerson uttered between them a set of doctrines so full of apparent contradictions as to seem almost double-faced. They preached the sacredness of fact as against the authority of tradition; they made much of physical heredity, of evolution, of fate; they pointed out the inadequacy of any moral scheme to comprehend all the surprises of nature; yet being inveterate optimists, both of them, and both at certain moments curiously mystical, and both enjoying an outward orthodoxy of manners and culture, they soothed their hearers and seemed less dangerous than they were. Their sincerity, of course, was unquestionable, but they obscured even to themselves the startling conclusions of their own surmises, and having shaken their moral world to its foundation, they allowed the structure to settle again, and all this in such a glamour of temperamental cheerfulness that those who felt only the eloquence of their mood could depart conscious of spiritual uplift, and none but the few who attended to the implications of their specific ideas went away troubled. How few these critics were is attested by the lonely position in which their spokesman, Hawthorne, seems to stand. He was no mystic; what attracted him in Transcendentalism was its free inquiry, its radicalism, its contact with actual life. In his stories, therefore, he was a philosophical experimenter, in whose method was no room for optimism nor for prepossessions of any kind; he had recourse to life in order to try out the efficacy or the consequences of Transcendental ideas, and if the result was hardly what he expected, he still pursued the hypothesis to the bitter end. He was really the questioner, the detached observer, that other Transcendentalists thought they were. The soul, Emerson had said, "accepts whatever befalls, as part of its lesson. It is a watcher more than a doer, and it is a doer only that it may the better watch." The description is truer of Hawthorne's soul than of Emerson's. In accepting whatever befalls, Emerson was convinced, as he says in the essay on *Circles*, that there is a saccharine principle in all things; small wonder that Hawthorne seems an alien among such cheerful sages. When Emerson says that either love or crime leads all souls to the good, that there is no straight line in nature, that evil in the end will bless, Hawthorne examines the doctrine somewhat dubiously in Hepzibah and Clifford Pyncheon and in Donatello; and when the cheerful philosopher tells us to trust ourselves, to follow our own nature, to live from the Devil if we are the Devil's children, Hawthorne projects the advice experimentally in *The Scarlet Letter* and in *The Blithedale Romance.*

Those who classify Hawthorne in a loose way as the romancer of Puritanism sometimes speak of him also as a psychologist. The term needs defining. To him, as to other Transcendentalists, the fortune of a human soul was the most critical of experiences, comparatively negligible were the doings of society as a whole or the outward panorama of events and scenes. If to be thus interested in the soul is to be a psychologist, then Hawthorne was one, as to some extent are all who write of human nature. But if the term denotes attention to motives and to fine mental processes, to the anatomy, as it were, of character, then Hawthorne was no such psychologist as, let us say, Henry James or George Meredith. It is important to realize how broad and general his ideas and his art were, how completely he avoided the special and the minute. He studied no subtle character, nor any character subtly. He was a moralist rather than a psychologist. Were it not sufficiently evident in the stories themselves, the notes preserved in his journals would show that his imagination was engaged first by a moral idea, which he afterwards incorporated in plot and in persons. When he is most successful the plot seems actually to occur, and the persons really live; when his imagination fails him, the incidents seem allegorical and the figures become shadowy; but in either case the abstract idea from which he started is likely to be clear enough, and his own personality will probably be felt as standing outside the story, looking on. Since he is neither novelist nor preacher, but only an investigator of moral ideas, it is equally beside the mark to expect of him Balzac's sense of the social panorama, or Bunyan's certitude of faith.

A writer who pictures life chiefly in order to project abstract ideas is not likely to reveal in his art more of himself than his general disposition. Hawthorne's biography makes rich and human reading, for he was an admirable man in all ways and his private life was in the best sense fortunate; if at first he endured poverty, he earned success later, and even in the obscure years he had the admiration of loyal friends. But only in a few instances does his biography aid directly in the understanding of his works, and then for the most part by explaining his contact with Transcendental ideas. Of the non-literary events in his life it is enough to say that he was born in Salem, Massachusetts, 4 July, 1804, of an old New England family; that after his father's death he was educated by his mother's brothers, and in 1825 he was graduated from Bowdoin College; that among his classmates he made three lifelong friends—Longfellow, the poet, Franklin Pierce, later President of the United States, and Horatio Bridge, who first appreciated his genius; that chiefly through Bridge's thoughtfulness he was made weigher and gauger at the Boston Custom House, 1839–1841, and surveyor at the Salem Custom House, 1846–1850; that President Pierce appointed him to the consulship of Liverpool, 1853–1857; that he lived in Italy for two years, 1857–1859, and that while travelling for his health, attended by Pierce, he died at Plymouth, New Hampshire, 18 May, 1864.

The facts of his literary record are hardly more numerous, but they invite more comment. His college letters to his mother and his sisters show how early he mastered his superb style. Indeed, they are much better written than his first published story, *Fanshawe* (1828), which was probably composed, in part at least, during his college days. From 1825 to 1837 he lived at home in Salem, laboriously perfecting his short stories and sketches, and publishing them anonymously or under assumed names, chiefly in Goodrich's annual, *The Token*, and in *The New England Magazine*. He gives an idealized account of this period in his sketches *The Devil in Manuscript* and *The Journal of a Solitary Man*. In 1837, again through Bridge's good offices, a publisher was found for the *Twice Told Tales* (enlarged edition in two volumes, 1842). With this practical beginning of his reputation coincided his first acquaintance with the Peabody family. In all the biographies his love for Sophia Peabody has naturally filled a large place, but no sufficient estimate has perhaps been made of the intellectual enrichment his love brought him. It was through the Peabodys that he became really alive to the philosophical currents of his time. Transcendentalism had, of course, enfolded him, as it had the average New Englander, in its general atmosphere, and its temper is felt in some of his earliest writings, but it can hardly be said to have possessed his thought as it did later, and he had been in personal contact with none of the leaders. The Peabodys, however, were on intimate terms with Emerson, the young rhapsodist of *Nature*, whose recent triumph in *The American Scholar* had more recently been rendered equivocal by his *Divinity School Address;* and Alcott, Emerson's inspirer, they knew still better, for Elizabeth and to some extent Sophia had assisted at his Temple school in Boston, and Elizabeth had published in her *Records of a School* (1835) verbatim reports of Alcott's conversations with his pupils. When *The Dial* was founded in 1840, Elizabeth Peabody, who by that time had organized a remarkable book store, became its publisher. It was not extraordinary, therefore, that Hawthorne was drawn, though with some mental qualms, into the full tide of Transcendentalism, nor that upon the termination of his service in the Boston Custom House, in 1841, he joined the Brook Farm venture,[1] in the hope of establishing a home there. His note-books tell us the most interesting aspects of this passage in his life. At the end of a year and a half, completely disillusioned with the community experiment, he married and settled at Concord, in the Old Manse, where for neighbours he had Emerson, Alcott, and Thoreau, all busy with *The Dial*, and where Thoreau was shortly to undertake his Walden solitude. In Concord most of the stories were written which Hawthorne published in 1846 as *Mosses from an Old Manse*. A still later collection, *The Snow Image* (1852), gathered up practically all of the remaining sketches which he cared to preserve. His longer romances show a tendency to rework or develop this earlier material, or to draw upon actual scenes and events for their narrative fabric; the controlling problems, however, which the romances deal with are more obviously than in the shorter stories suggested

[1] See Book II, Chap. viii.

by Transcendental ideas. *The Scarlet Letter* (1850) is developed from a brief description in *Endicott and the Red Cross*, one of the *Twice Told Tales*. In *The House of the Seven Gables* (1851), Hawthorne makes use of such a curse as was pronounced on his own ancestor, John Hawthorne, or Hathorne, a severe magistrate in witchcraft times. In *The Blithedale Romance* (1852) it is hard not to identify Hawthorne's Brook Farm experience, though he warned us against the temptation. The outward details of *The Marble Faun* (1860) are clearly the observations of his two years in Italy.

Besides the short stories and the romances, Hawthorne wrote several important books for children—the series called *Grandfather's Chair* (1841–1842) and the two *Wonderbooks* (1852–1853). He also edited his friend Bridge's *Journal of an African Cruiser* (1845), wrote a campaign life of his friend Pierce (1852), and published some of his notes on England under the title of *Our Old Home* (1863).

If it is just to see in the early writings a picture of his native temper before he was consciously engaged with Transcendental doctrines, it is also true that from the first his mind was of another order than Alcott's or Emerson's, and that though he might be interested in the same ideas, he would treat them very differently. Most philosophers can be classed roughly among those who conceive of the ideal ends of life as already existing in heaven, in some order or pattern which may be imitated on earth, or among those who think of the ideal as of something which does not yet exist, but which is implicit in the universe, and toward which the universe evolves. A philosopher of the first or Platonic type, if he notices facts at all, is likely to be disconcerted by them, since they rarely conform to his ideal or serve to authorize it; his comfort is in rising superior to actual life—that is, in ignoring it. Alcott was an almost pure example of this type. The other kind of philosopher is likely to entertain a respect amounting almost to reverence for any concrete existing condition, because as two points determine a straight line, so a recent moment observed against the past gives indication of the order to come. Emerson was partly, like Alcott, a Platonist, but he had also a profound and inconsistent disposition toward this other way of thought; having two points of view at once, therefore, he is

not only perplexing at times, but really contradictory, and it
is not strange that he should have proved in one aspect of his
genius inspiring to Maeterlinck and in the other aspect acceptable to Nietzsche.  Hawthorne belonged altogether to the
second type of thinker.  Concerned primarily with the actual
world before him, he found a natural use for the past in the
explanation it might give of the present, but the present was
to him just as naturally the more important moment, and most
interesting of all was the occasional hint or prophecy of that
to which time through its past and present changes might be
tending.  He was a radical, therefore, but he saw clearly that
this particular present will soon be no more sacred than any
other moment of the past, and that to devote oneself to any
cause as though it were a final remedy of circumstances, promising rest thereafter, is merely to postpone stagnation for a
while.  With this insight he could not readily give his faith
to any reform or reformer; even the crusade for abolition and
the war for the Union left him cold, for he wisely doubted
whether measures conceived in the root-and-branch spirit
might not raise more evils in the state than they were intended
to cure.  True reform, the only kind that could enlist his
sympathy, must work hand in hand with nature's slowly
evolving but inevitable order, and so long as that order can
be but partially or infrequently discerned, it is best to do
nothing violent, nothing headlong.  Even when we discern
the order, from time to time, we should become humble, observing how little it resembles our own morality, our own
dreams of perfection.

It needs no fine perception to discover these principles or
attitudes in Hawthorne, for they are displayed quite simply
on the surface of his early stories.  The significance he attached to the present world, whatever it might be, can be
seen in the important group of essay sketches such as *A Rill
from the Town Pump*, *David Swan*, *Sights from a Steeple*, and
*Main Street*.  Some resemblance has been found between this
department of his work and the essays of Addison and of
Irving, and certainly Addison's cheerfulness is here, and often
something more than Irving's fancy.  But neither *The Spectator* nor *The Sketch Book* would suggest that Addison or Irving
was in the habit of keeping a diary; whereas Hawthorne's

simple studies, of the group just referred to, are in form nothing more than episodes in a journal. The fact is of some consequence in understanding his genius. When the American and European notebooks were finally included in the complete editions of his writings, they took their place, not as an appendix or illustration of more perfect things, but on equal terms with his other works; for the journal manner was suited to his realistic, unprejudiced search into the world about him, and his lifelong preoccupation with his diary was not, as with most novelists, for the sake of books to be written later, but was itself the satisfaction of a primary literary interest. Like the journals, the essay sketches take the scene as they find it, extract from it all that observation can, and then discard it, having proved no point and exhibited no characters in continuous interplay, but having uncovered possibilities, hints, causes, coincidences. In the simpler essays Hawthorne observed these possibilities and coincidences in a kind of stationary cross-section, and left them undeveloped; but in more elaborate stories he played with the ironic contrasts between the order which we foresee in life and the order which time brings to pass. Emerson often came out of his mysticism and contemplated the "beautiful necessity," the inevitable consequence of things, to which man must submit himself before he has either happiness or power. Hawthorne was inclined to stress rather man's inability to submit himself to this necessity, since he seldom guesses correctly what it would be. *Mr. Higginbotham's Catastrophe* is a lighter treatment of this theme of consequences; *Edward Fane's Rosebud* and *The Wives of the Dead* are in a darker tone. Or sometimes Hawthorne would turn the irony in another direction, by emphasizing the incredible swiftness with which the present becomes the past, and the insidiousness with which antiquity begins to show its symptoms even in what seems youthful and emancipated. *The May-pole of Merry Mount* brings this idea home, less in the overthrow of the maskers at Merry Mount than in the expressed faith of the stern Puritan leader that the troubles of life come soon and unexpectedly—a confession which somehow brings a chill over his own righteous success. A still better illustration is *Endicott and the Red Cross*, which shows the Puritans, who crossed the ocean for freedom of conscience and who in the moment of the story proclaim themselves champions of religious liberty, as having nevertheless instituted already the pillory and the stocks for those who disagree with them.

The Transcendental ideas which chiefly occupied Hawthorne's thought in the long romances were the doctrines of self-reliance, of compensation, and of what Emerson expressed in his essay on *Circles*. The ideal of self-reliance was that a man should live according to his own nature, by listening to the dictates of the over-soul as revealed in his impulses; to this end he should keep himself free of the imprisoning past, and of conventional society, which embodies the past. To Alcott or to Emerson this doctrine was so obviously sound that they stated it with every emphasis of rhetoric and with no qualifications. "Whoso would be a man must be a non-conformist." Hawthorne doubtless felt the truth of the doctrine as keenly as any one, but he was alive also to the unsocial results which might follow a narrow practice of it. A man consciously and entirely free of the past and on his guard against it might indeed possess his soul, but he might also miss the essence of culture, and having renounced the finer instruments of the art of life, he might so isolate himself from his fellows as to become ineffective in his noblest virtues. Since nature is unfolding a necessary order in and around us, an order which we apprehend with difficulty, the great danger of asserting ourselves is that we may thereby place ourselves outside of our true development, and never return to it. This danger of stepping out of the order, of doing violence to our proper destiny, gave Hawthorne the theme of such stories as *Wakefield*, *The Prophetic Pictures*, and *Rappaccini's Daughter*. The doctrine of compensation, in one form or another, was peculiarly dear to Transcendental optimism. Every action carries its reward or punishment with it. The thief is punished, though the police never find him, for the price of theft is loss of innocence, fear of arrest, suspicion of other men. What compensation is destined for the victim of the thief, optimistic Transcendentalism preferred not to investigate, but it was into just such a neglected area of morals that Hawthorne liked to push his inquiry. His observations brought him into a certain agreement with the doctrine; because a natural order constantly unfolds in the world, he believed in the efficacy of mere time to break down conventions and to reveal a nobler law, and in his historical scenes—*Howe's Masquerade*, for example, or *The Gray Champion*—he liked to show a fossilized past at the moment when it is shattered. He could believe that life does so far make restitution, but in daily life he could find no compensation for the injuries suffered by the innocent, nor could he persuade himself that a noble bearing of wrongs will necessarily lead to spiritual profit. Indeed, though Emerson's sunny temperament had spread its glamour over his discussion of this theory, to Hawthorne the theory seemed, so far as it was true, one of the darkest and most perplexing. Still less could he agree with Emerson's exaggeration of the same doctrine in *Circles*. Optimism here, taking the bit in its teeth, contended that as there is in experience no such thing as a straight line, so there is practically no such thing as evil—a prophetic application, it would seem, of Riemannian geometry to morals; that what seems hopelessly bad will in the end be found to contain the good principle; and, quite illogically, that what seems to be good will actually prove to be so.

> In vain produced, all rays return;
> Evil will bless and ice will burn.

In a famous passage in *Circles*, Emerson acknowledges the awkwardness of this position, and explains that his temperament dictates it. Hawthorne could not undertake any such cheerfulness, but he was profoundly concerned with the moral phenomena by which Emerson may have justified his faith. Here springs that paradox of experience, that mystery of sin, the question as to what sin is, which threw its shadow over three at least of the four romances. Since we rarely discern our true destiny, the human being who steps out of what seems the moral order may really have chanced upon a sounder morality; through what appears to be sin, therefore, may sometimes come the regeneration of a soul—not through repentance, be it observed, but through sincere adherence to the sin. Conversely, though a man should devote himself to the highest ideal he is aware of, if that ideal does not lie in the true order of nature, his devotion may bring him to an evil end. These possibilities, together with the implications of self-reliance and compensation, furnish the moral problems of Hawthorne's romances.

Hester Prynne, for example, in *The Scarlet Letter*, illustrates self-reliance in a way that some Emersonians may have found not altogether comfortable. Since her love for Dimmesdale was the one sincere passion of her life, she obeyed it utterly, though a conventional judgment would have said that she was stepping out of the moral order. There is nothing in the story to suggest condemnation of her or of the minister in their sin; the only blame attaches to Dimmesdale's cowardice, his lack of self-reliance, his unreadiness to make public acknowledgment of his love. The passion itself, as the two lovers still agree at the close of their hard experience, was sacred, and never caused them repentance. The doctrine of compensation is illustrated in Chillingworth, who, having determined on a fiendish revenge, becomes himself a fiend. There is a kind of comment on Emerson's cheerful doctrine in the fact that this gloomy soul, marked for perdition, is a firm believer in compensation; he wronged Hester's youth by marrying her, and therefore he bears her no ill will for wronging him, but he argues that since the minister had never received a justifying harm at his hands, the secret lover should therefore be punished by the injured husband. As Chillingworth discusses the matter with Hester, compensation seems to be at one moment sheer fatalism, at another moment a primitive exacting of an eye for an eye, but never does it come to a happy issue. The optimistic turn in the doctrine is illustrated by Hester—or perhaps it is better to say that she illustrates the optimism of *Circles*. She has sinned, but the sin leads her straightway to a larger life. Like Adam and Eve driven out of Paradise, she finds she has a career at last. Social ostracism first gives her leisure for meditation and a just angle from which to attack social problems, and then it permits her to enter upon a life of mercy and good works which would have been closed to a conventional woman. Hawthorne had described the original wearer of the scarlet letter in *Endicott and the Red Cross* as a woman who braved her shame by embroidering the guilty "A" into an elaborate and beautiful emblem; so in the romance he lets the sin elaborate itself, so far as Hester's nature is concerned, into nothing but beauty. She becomes more loving, more sympathetic, more tender; and intellectually she becomes emancipated from the narrowness of her age, so that even now she seems prophetic of what the noblest women may be. Thoughts were her companions which, says Hawthorne, would have been held more dangerous than the sin of the scarlet letter, had they been seen knocking at her door. She saw how completely the social scheme must be altered before woman can enjoy a true equality with man, and she suspected the losses in the best of manhood and womanhood which might be the incidental or temporary price of the belated justice.

The greatness of *The Scarlet Letter*, on repeated readings, seems to lie in this social interest, this inexorable study of the world as it is, which distinguishes Hawthorne from other Transcendentalists. The Puritan environment is represented as already dying, young as it was in the new world; at the outset of the story Hawthorne shows us that these courageous founders of religious liberty in the wilderness felt the necessity at once of building a prison and of setting up a pillory. The ideals which a little while before were an inner light for the community, carrying inevitable conviction, were now stiffened into convention and leaned upon force. In making the point that Hawthorne was no special admirer of Puritanism, we must add that neither was he a special critic of it; he used the Puritan moment in our history merely to illustrate the truth of all moments, that society conventionalizes its ideals and becomes cruel, and that time, which annihilates one set of conventions, substitutes another. But some specific criticism of Puritan New England, of New England in his own day, may be discerned in the fortunes of Hester, and may be still more clearly felt in Zenobia and in Miriam, the later heroines; these are all represented as physically beautiful, and as in some way estranged from life, and we wonder whether it was not their beauty rather than their conduct that alienated them from their environment. What career has a beautiful woman in New England?—Hawthorne seems to ask, and he seems to imply that if she is conventional she may live down the handicap of beauty, but meantime she is dangerous to others and to herself. The danger to herself is indicated by the fact that Hester, Zenobia, and probably Miriam, were all married for their beauty, when they were very young, to men who could not appreciate their greatness of soul, and whom therefore they were forced to divorce or to desert.

*The House of the Seven Gables* is so quiet a story that Hawthorne's characteristic criticism of self-reliance or of compensation is not at first disturbing, but in none of his books does he take more essential issue with Alcott and Emerson. On the surface of the romance lies the theme of long-delayed retribution—the curse of old Maule falling on each generation of the usurping Pyncheons. But what punishment does after all overtake the thoroughly bad man who allows his innocent cousin to rest in jail for years? He dies of apoplexy, as he would have died had he been the innocent cousin. And what happens to his victims? It is easy to guess how Emerson might have treated Clifford and Hepzibah; the innocence of the imprisoned brother would somehow have been its own reward, and the loyalty of the devoted sister, waiting for his release, would have ennobled her character. But confinement in prison is not likely to sweeten even innocence; Hawthorne shows Clifford on his return to the old house a broken man, irritable and unappreciative. Hepzibah's long waiting proved for her a solitude almost as complete as prison confinement; Hawthorne shows her as a shrivelled old maid, angular and grim, with hardly a grace remaining. He had no more wish than Emerson would have had to decry the ethical beauty of her patient loyalty, but he could not help seeing that she, like Clifford, was the victim of gross wrong, and that it is disastrous to be even an innocent victim. Similarly he insists on a precise account of self-reliance in Holgrave, the descendant of old Maule. Emerson himself could not have portrayed a more thorough-going critic of the past.

"Shall we never, never get rid of this Past?" asks Holgrave. "It lies upon the Present like a giant's dead body. In fact, the case is just as if a young giant were compelled to waste all his strength in carrying about the corpse of the old giant, his grandfather, who died a long while ago, and only needs to be decently buried. . . . A dead man, if he happen to have made a will, disposes of wealth no longer his own; or, if he die intestate, it is distributed in accordance with the notions of men much longer dead than he. A dead man sits on all our judgment-seats; and living judges do but search out and repeat his decisions. We read in dead men's books! We laugh at dead men's jokes, and cry at dead men's pathos! We are sick of dead men's diseases, physical and moral, and die of the same remedies with which dead doctors killed their patients! We worship the living Deity according to dead men's forms and creeds. Whatever we seek to do, of our own free motion, a dead man's icy hand obstructs us! Turn our eyes to what point we may, a dead man's white, immitigable face encounters them, and freezes our very heart! And we must be dead ourselves before we can begin to have our proper influence on our own world, which will then be no longer our world, but the world of another generation, with which we shall have no shadow of a right to interfere."

How far Hawthorne agrees with Holgrave we cannot tell, but there is no doubt what sort of character he thought would result from a sincere practice of such philosophy. Holgrave is free of the past, and thereby he is practically free of the present too; his honesty and his emancipation attract the reader, yet he has little or no influence. Few men really wish to detach themselves so far. Even Phœbe, the young girl whom he marries, who has the natural freshness of innocence, seems curiously social in comparison with this conscientious rover whose one dread is that he may take root somewhere.

Hawthorne showed an increasing disposition to discuss these philosophical questions in frank comment outside the plot of his romances. Hollingsworth, in *The Blithedale Romance*, illustrates his fear of tampering with the natural order of things, especially by organized reform; and Zenobia illustrates his reflections on self-reliance, especially where woman is concerned. Hollingsworth was a determined social reformer; he wished to reform criminals through an appeal to their higher instincts. Hawthorne observed that such philanthropy, admirable in its intention, often proceeded on slight knowledge of the facts. "He ought to have commenced his investigation of the subject by perpetrating some huge sin in his proper person, and examining the condition of his higher instincts afterwards." As a matter of fact, Hollingsworth does ruin two lives, Zenobia's and Priscilla's, in the selfish pursuit of his philanthropic ideal, and, if he had chosen, might well have furnished the state of his own heart for examination. Hawthorne comments again, making his familiar point that a good ideal brings a man to a good end only if it does not lead him out of the natural sympathies of life:

The moral which presents itself to my reflections, as drawn from Hollingsworth's character and errors, is simply this—that, admitting what is called philanthropy, when adopted as a profession, to be often useful by its energetic impulse to society at large, it is perilous to the individual whose ruling passion, in one exclusive channel, it thus becomes. It ruins, or is fearfully apt to ruin, the heart, the rich juices of which God never meant should be pressed violently out and distilled into alcoholic liquor by an unnatural process, but should render life sweet, bland, and gently beneficent, and insensibly influence other hearts and other lives to the same blessed end.

Zenobia is a modern and conscious Hester—or rather, her experience is the reverse of Hester's, for she is a woman naturally emancipated who is ruined by disappointed love. It is this difference in their problems that makes her seem less noble than Hester, less tragic than pitiful. But in portraying her, Hawthorne raises more especially the question he had suggested in *The Scarlet Letter:* is not such a woman, so beautiful and so intellectual, an exotic creature in our society? Here is the modern woman whom Hester dreamed of, but the old misfortune still overtakes her; like Hester, she has married one who could not appreciate her, but she has never found the lover who should have been her mate, and she has no true companionship with other women. She seems to be a foreigner, and in the New England thought of Hawthorne's time foreigners had the right to be, like Zenobia, physically beautiful.

*The Marble Faun* repeats in Miriam the problem of Hester and of Zenobia, and in Hilda, the simple Puritan girl who finds peace in the Roman Catholic confessional, the story illustrates beautifully Hawthorne's faith that some of our most unconventional impulses lead us to a practical morality. But the philosophy of the book centres in Donatello, that wonderful creature who begins life with the animal-like innocence which radical thought seems often to desire for man, and who develops an immortal soul by committing an impulsive murder. The doctrine of *Circles* has its most elaborate illustration here; here is the evolution of good out of sin—not out of repentance for sin. But if the doctrine is sound, our theology needs thorough revision, and Hawthorne suggests the logical change in our conception of sin:

Is sin then—which we deem such a dreadful blackness in the universe—is it, like sorrow, merely an element of human education, through which we struggle to a higher and purer state than we could otherwise have attained? Did Adam fall that we might ultimately rise to a far higher Paradise than his?

These problems, suggested by the Transcendental philosophy, occupied Hawthorne to the last. It was not in his disposition to suggest answers to them. His distinction in American literature is the extent to which he projected them experimentally into life, and the sincerity with which he modified them to conform to stubborn and perplexing facts.

# CHAPTER XII

# Longfellow

HENRY WADSWORTH LONGFELLOW was born in Portland, Maine, 27 February, 1807. In view of what America as a whole then was and of what he was destined to accomplish for the literature of the country, it is difficult to see how he could have been more fortunately circumstanced with respect to stock and environment. Both the Longfellows and his mother's people, the Wadsworths, were well-to-do, and they represented the best New England, particularly Massachusetts, traditions, which, with the spread of Unitarianism, were losing some of their rigidity. Thus the child experienced little that was specially straitening, and he received a training well adapted to bring out the talents that soon manifested themselves. His native town furnished the influence of the sea and sea-faring men; the virgin District soon to be the State of Maine, afforded other impressive features of nature; and the frontier situation, even if it could not make strenuous a constitutionally gentle and refined disposition, at least inculcated feelings of sympathy with a pioneer, rugged, prevailingly practical population, which were to be of great use to a poet who in after years could point to his successful fulfilment of the threefold function of transmitter of Old World culture to the New, shaper into verse of aboriginal, colonial, and Revolutionary material, both legendary and historical, and lyric interpreter of the simple thoughts and feelings of an unsophisticated people. His career was well foreshadowed when he published anonymously at the age of thirteen, in a local newspaper, a Revolutionary battle-lyric.

After a good schooling and an introduction to the best reading old and new, including Irving's *Sketch Book*, Longfellow, in the autumn of 1822, entered Bowdoin College as a sophomore, having Nathaniel Hawthorne as a classmate. Here, as at home, he continued to come under unpretentious, wholesome influences, to which were added those of rural seclusion. Before he graduated in 1825, he was writing verse rather copiously, and some of it was published in a literary journal just founded in Boston. As is not surprising, it was overpraised by a provincial public, but for a wonder, in view of the vogue of Byron, it was not stormily romantic. His success gave point to his plans for leading a literary life, but his more experienced father held out for the law, although he was willing to give his son a year of grace to be spent in less uncongenial studies at Harvard. This plan was abandoned because it was found feasible for Longfellow to fit himself to become the first incumbent of a chair of modern languages to be established at Bowdoin.

Travel and study in Europe were essential to such a design, and the middle of June, 1826, saw the youth of nineteen beginning at Havre a European sojourn of a little more than three years. Temperament and immaturity, combined doubtless with a shrewd perception of the fact that great erudition was not a prerequisite to successful language-teaching in Maine, made it natural that Longfellow should become rather a sentimental pilgrim than a delving student or a philosophical observer, and that he should make but slight use of Ticknor's recommendation of Göttingen as a centre and source of the exact scholarship so much needed in America. German sentiment and romance were later to mean much to the poet; but Latin colour and picturesqueness meant more to the young traveller. France, Spain, where he met Irving, and Italy, from whose greatest writer his mature and declining years derived their chief solace, were in turn visited, their manners noted, their literatures studied, their languages in more than polite measure mastered. Then several months were given to Germany, including a little studying at Göttingen, and in August, 1829, the neophyte professor was back in America ready to take up the duties of his chair.

Those duties occupied him until his second visit to Europe, which took place nearly six years later. He was a conscientious and successful teacher and compiler of text-books, he lectured on literary history, he wrote for *The North American*

*Review* essays flavoured with scholarship, he gave a pledge to society by taking to himself, in 1831, a wife, Mary Storer Potter, of Portland. Except for some verse translations from the Spanish and certain traces of the poet to be discovered in a series of travel-sketches, which appeared in a volume entitled *Outre-Mer: a Pilgrimage beyond the Sea* (1835), one might have been justified in supposing that without doubt the undergraduate whose heart was set on "future eminence in literature" would end his life as a distinguished academic personage, not as the most popular poet of his generation. His fate seemed sealed with his acceptance of the Smith Chair of Modern Languages at Harvard, in succession to Ticknor, and with his departure for Europe in April, 1835, in order that by study of the northern literatures he might the better qualify himself for his important post.

His second period of training in Europe, although shorter, rendered Longfellow a greater service than his first. As he was more mature, his genius was better prepared to receive a definitive bent, and his experiences determined that that bent should take an emotional rather than an emphatically intellectual direction. After a short visit to England he spent some months in Sweden and Denmark studying their literatures with results obvious to the reader of his later poetry. Then he went to Holland, where his wife fell ill and died in the autumn. This meant that the ensuing winter at Heidelberg saw no notable progress made by the young professor in his German studies, but did see a deep absorption of the spirit of German romanticism by the young widower and the future poet. The sentimental prose romance *Hyperion* and the collection of poems entitled *Voices of the Night*, both published in 1839, show what bereavement and the new environment, physical as well as mental and spiritual, had brought to the man entering his fourth decade. We track the footsteps of the naïve hero of *Hyperion* with less confiding delight than our grandfathers and grandmothers probably experienced, but then we are less sentimental and more widely travelled than they were, facts which of course do not warrant us in arrogating to ourselves a taste necessarily superior to theirs. *Hyperion* doubtless meant more to the author and his countrymen than a scholarly monograph would have meant, for what

America needed just then, apparently, was some one who, like Longfellow, could carry on the work begun by Irving of interpreting the Old World to the New. The younger man was not only better endowed with the faculty of specific poetic utterance, but he was naturally more fully qualified than his predecessor to gratify the taste of a generation that was beginning to be affected by the work of the newer English romantic poets. Thus we are not surprised to find the Smith Professor writing poems on European subjects instead of grammars and histories of literature, and editing in place of textbooks a small collection of poems entitled *The Waif* (1843), a similar volume, *The Estray* (1847), and the comprehensive and useful *Poets and Poetry of Europe* (1845). Even the thirty-one volumes of the much later *Poems of Places* (1876–1879) with which Longfellow's name is more or less associated, bear witness to the influence of the teacher-poet's second sojourn in Europe both upon him and upon American culture.

But the greatest influence of that sojourn, exhibited after he took up his duties at Harvard in December, 1836, is to be seen in the simple, wholesomely emotional, and unblushingly didactic poems with which Longfellow now began to win the hearts of his provincial readers. *The Psalm of Life* is perhaps the best known and the best chosen example of these "household poems," shall we call them? With its companion pieces *The Reaper and the Flowers, The Light of Stars,* and *Footsteps of Angels*, it is undoubtedly amenable to some of the harsh criticism it has received from those persons who seem to imagine that taste thrives only on its own exigency. But it is hard to see how verses of subtler quality would have so sung themselves through the length and breadth of young America, or could have laid so broad and deep a foundation for the fame of the most heartily loved poet of his generation.

Long before that poet had reached the zenith of his reputation the professor had grown weary of his chair. At first he worked hard enough to justify weariness, particularly at the uncongenial task of supervising the instruction in the elementary language courses given by his assistants; but gradually, whatever enthusiasm he may have had for a scholarly, academic career wore itself out, and toward the end of his eighteen years of service—he resigned in 1854—he was almost querulous in his attitude toward a calling without the aid of which he would probably have remained a somewhat local and minor writer, his disposition scarcely prompting him to draw inspiration from Transcendentalism or the anti-slavery movement, and his genius not qualifying him to probe the heart or to wander in shadowland.

Whatever its irksomeness, however, his position at Harvard brought with it compensations. He soon secured a congenial habitat—the now famous Craigie House—he gathered about him a group of sympathetic friends, he became a distinguished figure in the most cultured community in America, the Cambridge of Lowell's essay and of Colonel Higginson's books, he added to his happiness and his income by a second marriage— to Miss Frances Elizabeth Appleton in 1843—and he found time and incentive to write whatever he had in his mind and heart to say. Reading his letters and his diaries, putting together the biographical details furnished by others, and constructing as best one can the man's life and spirit from his writings, one is forced to the conclusion that except for a single great tragedy—the accidental burning to death of his wife in 1861—Longfellow's is one of the most serenely fortunate careers ever led by a man of letters. Some of his critics have wished that it might have been otherwise, apparently supposing that, if he had been more unfortunate, his poetry would have been more to their liking. It is not, however, on record that any critic has deliberately wooed infelicity in order to qualify himself for a fuller enjoyment of Longfellow's placid verses.

In 1842 a third visit was made to Europe, this time a short one for the sake of health. It was preceded by the *Ballads and Other Poems* (1841), and followed by the *Poems on Slavery* (1842). These justly enhanced his reputation, but the meritorious anti-slavery verses proved no prelude to active participation in the great conflict that was leading up to the Civil War. The prior volume with such pieces as *The Village Blacksmith*, *God's Acre*, *Maidenhood*, and the egregiously anabatic *Excelsior*, strengthened his hold upon the popular heart, and in the successful ballads proper, such as *The Wreck of the Hesperus* and *The Skeleton in Armor*, it gave him, in addition, some incentive to address his readers in narrative verse, the form of poetry in which, during his middle period, he made himself easily the chief American master. Neither in these earlier volumes, to which may be added *The Belfry of Bruges and Other Poems* (1846), nor in *Evangeline* (1847) and succeeding tales in verse, did Longfellow show himself to be a consummate metrical and verbal artist of the highest order or a poet of sustained imaginative flight; nor was he, in compensation, one of those writers who produce a strong effect through their subtle knowledge of human character or their exceptional ability to describe and interpret nature or their profound understanding of a country or a period. Yet even in these particulars he was capable of exhibiting distinguished merit—witness his command of the simpler rhythms, his wide-reaching metrical experimentation, his feeling for the sea, his sympathetic attitude toward the Middle Ages displayed in *The Golden Legend* (1851), his presentation of the larger natural features of America in *Evangeline*—and in his lyrical appeal, especially through his semi-didactic poems of reflection and sentiment, as well as in his general narrative power, he was during his life, and he still remains, unapproached by any other American poet.

The years immediately preceding his second marriage in 1843 were partly devoted to the composition of a poetical drama in three acts, *The Spanish Student*, which was published serially in 1842, and the next year was issued in book form. It is generally and justly regarded as a failure, since Longfellow exhibited neither in it nor in later poems cast in similar form —*The New England Tragedies* (1868), *Judas Maccabaeus* (1872), and *Michael Angelo* (1883),—the slightest trace of dramatic genius. A poet of literary derivation, so to phrase it, inspired by his own wide reading, and a useful transmitter of culture he could not help being from first to last, and his growing reputation naturally prompted him to undertake elaborate works in a form of art practised by preceding poets in every age. His countrymen were not exigent critics, and were inclined to resent it when he was accused, as by Poe and by Margaret Fuller, of unoriginality; latter-day readers are likely to skim, or else altogether to neglect the dramas that are protected from complete oblivion by the venerated and still venerable name. If they desire any justification for their conduct, such prudent readers may ejaculate "*habent sua fata libelli,*" or may recall the facts that Dr. Samuel Johnson wrote *Irene* and William Wordsworth, *The Borderers*.

In all probability, neither of these ominous dramatic productions was in Longfellow's mind when he was writing *The Spanish Student*, or planning his presumptive masterpiece, *Christus: A Mystery*, which finally saw the light in 1872, more than twenty years after the first appearance of its second part, *The Golden Legend*, one of the most attractive and yet one of the least widely read of its author's books. Poems Swedish and German, ominous in no bad sense, were in his mind when he wrote his sentimental idyllic narrative in hexameters, *Evangeline*, not perhaps the best of his longer poems, but certainly the most popular both at home and abroad. Hawthorne, from whom Longfellow secured the theme of the Acadian maiden's vain search for her lover, might have made more of the pathetic story, but he would have done it for fewer readers. Other writers might have improved the local colour of the poem, still others might have laboured more heroically to keep the hexameters from making forays across the borders of prose, but it may be doubted whether any contemporary could have written, on the whole, a better *Evangeline*, at least one more suited to the taste of the period. Few of his contemporaries, however, have left behind a more negligible prose romance than the story of an impossible New England village which Longfellow published in 1849 under the title *Kavanagh; A Tale*.

The end of the fifties saw the culmination of his genius in the appearance of *The Courtship of Miles Standish and Other Poems* (1858). This narrative poem, another experiment in hexameters, seems to surpass Longfellow's other successful achievements in the same category because it is more racy of New England, fuller of humour, superior in movement and in characterization. It is less popular than *Evangeline*, partly no doubt because it is less sweet, and it seems to have made less impression than its predecessor the Indian epic *Hiawatha* (1855)—another metrical experiment, this time in rhymeless trochaic tetrameters—partly because it is less ambitious and exotic. The popularity of *Hiawatha* is not undeserved, however, since novelty and quaintness may well be set over against facility and factitiousness, and since, being in a certain sense

American, the poem may justly make more of a local appeal than such a work as *The Golden Legend* based on *Der Arme Heinrich*. Yet it may be doubted whether either *Hiawatha* or *Miles Standish* did as much to establish Longfellow as the most admired poet of his time as some of the unpretentious poems contained in the collection entitled *The Seaside and the Fireside* (1850), such poems, for example, as the tender *Resignation*, to say nothing of the patriotic close of *The Building of the Ship*.

From the date of the tragic accident to his wife—July, 1861—to his death 24 March, 1882, at his home in Cambridge, Longfellow's life takes on dignity without losing its quiet charm, and his genius—shall we say, mellows, or slowly abates in energy? There was no marked falling off in the number of published volumes, in the range of his interests, in his hold upon his intimate friends, such as Charles Eliot Norton and James Russell Lowell, in his endeavours, conscious and unconscious, to deserve the affectionate gratitude of his countrymen. Even in the South, for a time rent away from the rest of the country politically, and for a longer period estranged in sentiment, his was a Northern name not anathema to the rising generation, and in Great Britain he rivalled in popularity Tennyson himself. But, as might have been expected, these years saw the production of little, except for some excellent sonnets, that adds permanently to his fame as a poet.

True, he added considerably to the mass of his narrative poetry by the three series of *Tales of a Wayside Inn*, the first of which appeared under its own name in 1863, the second and third of which were included respectively in *Three Books of Song* (1872—along with *Judas Maccabaeus*), and in *Aftermath* (1874), but save for the spirited *Paul Revere's Ride* and the *Saga of King Olaf*, of the first series, these tales in verse have made only a mild impression. This is about all that may justly be said with regard to the twelve poems collected in *Flower-de-luce* (1867); it is more than should be said of *The New England Tragedies*, the third part of *Christus*, consisting of *John Endicott* and *Giles Cory of the Salem Farms*. These, with the first part of the ambitious trilogy, *The Divine Tragedy* (1871), constitute what may best be ambiguously denominated "efforts." Longfellow was more fortunately employed when he put himself in the company of Cowper and Bryant, and sought solace for his private woes in an extensive piece of poetical translation. Perhaps his true genius as a translator, seen early in the *Coplas de Manrique* (1833), is better exemplified in his numerous renderings of lyrics, particularly, as in Uhland's *The Castle by the Sea*, from the German, than in the faithful, meritorious version of *The Divine Comedy*, which appeared in three volumes between 1867 and 1870; but, despite a certain lack of metrical charm resulting from the facile character of the rhymeless lines printed in threes, the version of the masterpiece to which Longfellow gave so many years of love and study seems worthy of his pains and of the praise it has received from other admirers of Dante.

After the appearance of the translation of Dante and of the *Christus*, two works *de longue haleine* which show that the retired professor of nearly twenty years' standing was not open to the charge of idleness, Longfellow had still about a decade to live and to continue his writing. Some of the titles of his collections of verse have been already given; others are *The Masque of Pandora, and Other Poems* (1875), *Kéramos; and Other Poems* (1878), *Ultima Thule* (1880), and *In the Harbor* (1882—posthumous). The first of these volumes contained one of the most dignified and impressive of all his poems, one of the best occasional poems in American literature, the *Morituri Salutamus*, written for the semi-centennial of the poet's class at Bowdoin. It also contained *A Book of Sonnets*, fourteen in all, considerably extended in number in later editions of the poetical works. Some notable sonnets had been published with the translation of Dante, and to these Longfellow's later achievements in the same form are worthy pendants. High praise has been given to them by many critically minded readers of a later generation, who have wished, in default of admiration for Longfellow's earlier work, to combine patriotism with acumen in their praise of a poet whose reputation seemed to require rather delicate handling. Both the sonnets and their American encomiasts are fortunately unamenable to comments lacking in amiability, although it is open to doubt whether even such a pathetic sonnet as *The Cross of Snow*, written at the close of the poet's life in memory of his unfortunate second wife, will ever mean to the great public what *The Bridge* and *The Day is Done* have meant. It is perhaps more to the purpose to express satisfaction that the poet was capable of making the double appeal—to the reader who thinks he knows what to think and to the reader who knows he knows how to feel.

It may be gathered from this brief survey of a long life and a productive career that Longfellow's reputation, in the opinion of the present writer, was amply deserved in the poet's day, and rested in the main on his gifts as a story-teller in verse, on his power to transplant to American literature some of the colour and melody and romantic charm of the complex European literatures he had studied, and, more especially, on his skill in expressing in comparatively artless lyrics of sentiment and reflection homely and wholesome thoughts and feelings which he shared with his countrymen of all classes throughout a broad land the occupation of which proceeded apace during his own span of years. Whatever he accomplished beyond this as teacher and editor and writer of prose, and as self-conscious poet seeking success in the more elaborate traditional forms of his art, is worthy, to say the least, of as much praise as the similar work of his predecessors, contemporaries, and successors among American poets, and is not clearly doomed to a speedier death than the elaborate productions of his contemporaries and successors among the British poets. His place is not with the few eminent poets of the world, or even of his century, as the admiration of the mass of his countrymen and the critical lucubrations of some of them might be held to imply; but it is, legitimately and permanently, in the forefront of the small band of important writers in verse and in prose who during the first century of the republic's existence laid firmly and upon more or less democratic lines the foundations of a native literature.

## CHAPTER XIII

# Whittier

IT was in 1638, when the great Puritan emigration to Massachusetts was beginning to slacken, that Thomas Whittier, a youth of eighteen, possibly of Huguenot extraction, landed in New England and made a home for himself on the shores of the Merrimac River. The substantial oak farmhouse which, late in life, he erected for his large family near Haverhill, is still standing. Descended from him in the fourth generation, John Greenleaf Whittier, the poet, was born in this house, 17 December, 1807. This is the homestead described with minute and loving fidelity in *Snow-Bound*, and it is typical of the many thousands of its sort that dotted the New England country-side, rearing in the old Puritan tradition a sturdy pioneer stock that was to blossom later in the fine flower of political and ethical passion, of statesmanship and oratory and letters. Though Whittier's family tree was originally Puritan, a Quaker scion was grafted upon it in the second American generation, when Joseph Whittier, the youngest son of the pioneer, married Mary Peaslee, whose father had been an associate and disciple of George Fox. The descendants in this line remained faithful to the doctrines of the Society of Friends, and the poet, although he persisted in the characteristic and quaint (although ungrammatical) use of the second person singular pronoun in address, found the principle of non-resistance something of a strain in the days when his fondest hopes were bound up in the holy cause for which his friends were bearing arms and laying down their lives upon the battle-field.

> The levelled gun, the battle brand
> > We may not take,
> But, calmly loyal, we can stand
> And suffer for our suffering land
> > For conscience' sake.

The temperament of the New England Quaker was not unlike that of the New England Puritan. The one could be as cantankerous as the other, on occasion, but when the early Puritan intolerance of the sect had been smoothed away, the Quaker was found to be a man whose ideals were essentially those of the founders of Massachusetts, contributing to those ideals his own element of kindly sympathy, his own insistence upon the dignity of the individual, and his own uncompromising spirit of democracy. These traits were permanently stamped upon Whittier's character, and all rested upon a foundation of unshakable faith in the spiritual order of the world. Christianity has perhaps never assumed a purer or lovelier guise than it took in the lives of those New England Quakers of whom Whittier was the type.

The life of the household in which the poet grew to manhood is reproduced in *Snow-Bound* with a fidelity which makes of that poem, for its truthfulness and sincerity, one of the imperishable things in American literature—a document whose significance is becoming fully apparent only now that the phase of life it describes has all but vanished from American life, whether in New England or elsewhere. The home which *Snow-Bound* describes was a comfortable one, as New England farmsteads went, and, in poetical retrospect, its gracious human aspects are raised to a prominence which somewhat obscures the hard facts of the daily life of the household. It was a life of toil, with meagre opportunities for recreation, and the young Whittier did not have the constitution needed for its requirements. The physical disabilities under which he laboured all his life were doubtless traceable to the hardships of these early years on the farm.

Whittier had but little education of the formal sort. There were sessions of the district school for a few weeks every year, and these he attended off and on. In his twentieth year, an academy was opened in Haverhill, and in this institution he

was enrolled as a student for two terms, earning the money to
pay for his tuition. Meanwhile, he had been acquiring the
best kind of education by devouring every book that he could
lay his hands on, including the few on the family shelf—mostly
the writings of pious Quakers—and

> The Bible towering o'er the rest,
> Of all other books the best.

One evening the district school teacher, Joshua Coffin, brought
to the house a volume of Burns, and read from it to the family.
This reading was a revelation to the boy of fourteen, who
eagerly sought permission to keep the book for a while. The
Scotch poet aroused in him the poetical stirrings which were
to occupy his mind from that time on, and marked an epoch
in the intellectual development of his boyhood. It was Burns,
as he confessed many years later, who made him see

> through all familiar things
> The romance underlying;
> The joys and griefs that plume the wings
> Of Fancy skyward flying,

and so shaped his imaginings that he became, in a more exact
sense than is usually connoted by such literary analogies, the
Burns of his own New England country.

From this time on, Whittier was an industrious scribbler
of rhymes. Most of them have been lost, but enough remain
to reveal a promise which may perhaps be characterized as
similar to that of the *Poems by Two Brothers*, or the *Poems by
Victor and Cazire*. The first of his verses to appear in print
were sent, unknown to the author, by his sister Mary to *The
Free Press*, a weekly paper just established by William Lloyd
Garrison in Newburyport. The boy's surprise was great
when he read his own composition in an issue of the paper
that was delivered at the Whittier farm in the summer of 1826.
Other pieces followed, and one day shortly afterward, Garrison
made a journey to the farm for the purpose of hunting up his
promising contributor. He found Whittier at work in the
field, urged the poet's father to send him to the academy, and
thus began what was to be the life-long friendship of these

two remarkable personalities. During the next two years Whittier published in the Haverhill *Gazette* nearly one hundred poems, besides prose articles on *Burns, War,* and *Temperance.* In 1828, a volume to be entitled *The Poems of Adrian* was projected, but this venture was abandoned. In the summer of that year his schooldays came to an end, and he began to look about for a means of earning his living. An offer was made him of the editorship of *The Philanthropist,* a paper devoted to the cause of what is called "temperance" in the current perverted sense of that term, but this offer he declined in a letter containing this significant confession: "I would rather have the memory of a Howard, a Wilberforce, and a Clarkson than the undying fame of Byron." By this time, he had acquired a considerable local reputation as a young writer of promise, and various modest openings already lay in his path.

During the next four years of his life (1828–32), Whittier was the editor of papers in Boston and Haverhill, and of *The New England Review,* in Hartford, Connecticut, besides contributing to many others. He became a partisan of Clay and the protective system, and looked askance at Jackson, "the blood-thirsty old man at the head of our government." The death of the elder Whittier in 1830 kept him for some time in Haverhill for the settlement of the family affairs. His interest in politics became more and more pronounced, and he thought seriously of standing for an election to Congress in 1832 but gave up the idea because he would, at the time of the election, be a few weeks short of the legal age requirement. When he identified himself, the next year, with the unpopular cause of the abolitionists, he gave up all hopes of political advancement.

Whittier's first published book was entitled *Legends of New England, in Prose and Verse.* It appeared in 1831, and was followed in 1832 by a pamphlet containing *Moll Pitcher.* Both these publications he afterwards did his best to suppress. Reform still appealed to him even more than poetry, and he wrote upon one occasion: "I set a higher value on my name as appended to the Antislavery Declaration of 1833 than on the title-page of any book." This Declaration was issued by the Convention held in Philadelphia, in 1833, to which Whittier was a delegate. In taking this momentous decision, he builded better than he knew, for the poet in him was aroused, and the *Voices of Freedom* which from that time flowed from his pen were the utterances of a deeply-stirred soul, as different as possible from the imitative exercises which had hitherto engaged him.

The incidents of Whittier's life during the following few years may be briefly summarized. In 1835 he served a term in the Massachusetts Legislature. In 1836, the Haverhill homestead was sold, and he bought in Amesbury, a few miles down the Merrimac, the cottage which was to be his home for the rest of his life. He occupied various editorial positions, which, together with activities in connection with the abolitionist agitation, kept him moving about until 1840, when he found his health badly broken and returned to Amesbury, there to remain for the greater part of the half-century that was still vouchsafed to him. In his abolitionist activities he proved his mettle, often suffering indignities at the hands of mobs and being on several occasions in no small physical peril. His shrewd and persuasive political activities made him a force to be reckoned with, and he kept in close touch with the leaders and movements of the time, allying himself with the Liberty Party of 1840, which, like the scriptural mustard seed, was destined to wax into so great a tree.

In 1836, Whittier published *Mogg Megone*, and, in the following year, a collection of his miscellaneous poems. In 1849, a comprehensive collection of his poems appeared, followed a year later by *Songs of Labor and Other Poems*. The first English edition of his collected poems also appeared in 1850. These volumes included all that he thought worth preserving of the work of twenty years. In 1857, the "blue and gold" collected edition of the poems was published in Boston. From this time onward small volumes of new poems appeared at intervals of about two years down to the year of the author's death, *At Sundown*, the last of the series, bearing the date of that very year (1892). Of special significance are the idyl entitled *Snow-Bound* (1866) and the cycle called *The Tent on the Beach* (1867). These two volumes marked a broadening of Whittier's fame, a higher recognition of his standing as an artist, and a noticeable measure of release from the financial difficulties under which he long had struggled. For the rest, the ballads, lyrics, and occasional pieces which made him most famous are scattered somewhat indiscriminately through the score or more of his volumes. For upwards of half a century verse flowed profusely from his pen, and his career did not fall into the distinctive periods that it is the task and the delight of the critic to define and to characterize in the work of many other poets.

From 1840 onward Whittier made Amesbury his home, although he allowed himself many protracted visits to friends and relatives, to Danvers and Newburyport, to the waters and mountains of New Hampshire, to Maine and the Isles of Shoals. From 1847 to 1860 he was associated, at long distance, with *The National Era*, a weekly paper published at Washington, and best remembered as the periodical in which *Uncle Tom's Cabin* was first given to the world. This paper was the chief medium for his expression until the establishment of *The Atlantic Monthly* in 1857, in whose pages a large part of his later work appeared. His seventieth birthday, in 1877, was made the occasion of a celebration more elaborate than had before been the reward of any American poet. He attended the Boston dinner then given in his honour, feeling

> Like him who in the old Arabian joke
> A beggar slept and crownéd Caliph woke.

His eightieth birthday was also celebrated, bringing to him a striking memorial signed by all the members of the Supreme Court bench, nearly all the members of both houses of Congress, and many private citizens of the highest distinction, making it clear that the nation held him in love and veneration as one of its greatest spiritual assets. He was visiting at the house of a friend, a few miles from Amesbury just over the New Hampshire border, when a cerebral hemorrhage brought him to a peaceful death, 7 September, 1892. "Love to all the world," were the words that played upon his lips just before the end.

In the classification of Whittier's work, the narrative poems are the first to call for consideration. "Of all our poets he is the most natural balladist," says E. C. Stedman, and throughout his entire life he was always ready to turn from the strenuous exactions of the causes which claimed his most ardent sympathies to the delightful relaxation of story-telling. From childhood he was steeped in the legendry of New England, its tales of Indian raids, of Quaker persecutions, of picturesque pioneers, and of romantic adventure; while the wide reading which made Whittier in later life a cultivated man fed his narrative faculty with old-world themes, ranging all the way from the Norse to the Oriental. The grim tragic economy of the folk-ballad, as it sprang from the heart of the people in England, Denmark, or Germany, never imparted its secret to him, although in *The Sisters* he came near to plucking the heart out of that mystery; but the ballad was to him the occasion for a rambling narration, diffuse in its unfolding and unrestrained in its form, often with decorative illustrations drawn from quite unexpected sources, and usually shaped to the point of a rather obtrusive moral. Such pieces as *Maud Muller* and *Barclay of Ury* would doubtless have been better poems without the moralizing tags which conclude them, but probably they would also have been less popular. Whittier's public expected a certain element of sermonizing in his verse and the America of his time paid scant heed to the cry that "art for art's sake" should be the guiding principle of poetic practice. The best of Whittier's ballads, nevertheless, are comparatively unburdened with didacticism. Among these may be mentioned *Pentucket*, with its memories of old-time Indian raids along the Merrimac; *Cassandra Southwick*, a tale of the Quaker persecutions; *The Angels of Buena Vista*, an echo from the battle-fields of the Mexican War; *The Garrison of Cape Ann*, which tells how the New Englander of old vanquished the powers of darkness; *Skipper Ireson's Ride*, a spirited song of the vengeance wrought by the women of Marblehead upon a sea-captain thought to have abandoned the crew of a sinking ship; *Mabel Martin*, an idyl of the days of witchcraft, and *Amy Wentworth*, a dainty romance of the old colonial time. Upon these ballads, and many others, New England childhood has been nurtured for a century, gaining from them its special sense of a heritage of no mean spiritual content, rich also in picturesque associations and romantic memories.

The high-water mark of Whittier's artistic achievement was undoubtedly reached in the years that gave birth to *Snow-*

*Bound* and *The Tent on the Beach*.  The latter and less important of these two works is a cycle of narratives in verse, linked together in the fashion of Longfellow's *Tales of a Wayside Inn*.  The company are three in number, "Fields the lettered magnate and Taylor the free cosmopolite" being foregathered on Salisbury Beach with Whittier, who thus describes himself:

> And one there was, a dreamer born,
>    Who, with a mission to fulfil,
> Had left the Muses' haunts to turn
>    The crank of an opinion-mill,
> Making his rustic reed of song
> A weapon in the war with wrong.

The poems which make up the cycle fall into the general class of Whittier's narrative verse; the thousand lines of octosyllabic rhyme which are entitled *Snow-Bound* are almost in a class by themselves.  This idyllic description of the Whittier household shut in for a week by

> The chill embargo of the snow,

which bids us

> pause to view
> These Flemish pictures of old days,

is not only a poem but a social document of the highest value. In the words of T. W. Higginson,

Here we have absolutely photographed the Puritan Colonial interior, as it existed till within the memory of old men still living. No other book, no other picture preserves it to us; all other books, all other pictures combined, leave us still ignorant of the atmosphere which this one page re-creates for us; it is more imperishable than any interior painted by Gerard Douw.

It has been said of Whittier that he could never be concise— and a diffuse style is undoubtedly one of the greatest artistic defects of the body of his verse—but the criticism falls flat in the presence of the lines which describe the fireplace on that winter evening.

This poem has often been compared with *The Cotter's Saturday Night* and it means to the American all and more than Burns's famous poem means to the Scotsman. There is also much aptitude in a comparison with Crabbe, but it has qualities of wistful sentiment and tender reminiscence that are not to be found in the poet of *The Village* and *The Borough*. Akin to *Snow-Bound*, and to be mentioned as offering a foretaste of its subtle charm, is the short poem *The Barefoot Boy*, dated some ten years earlier, and cast in the same mould of retrospective yearning for the happy and wholesome days of childhood.

The most considerable section of Whittier's verse in point of volume is that in which the poet voices the burning indignation fanned in his breast by the curse of negro slavery in America. His fellow-poets—Holmes, Longfellow, Lowell, and Emerson—were all enlisted in the warfare against this monstrous evil, and did yeoman service in the cause of freedom, but Whittier alone gave himself heart and soul to the crusade, from early manhood until the cause was won, from the time of his first association with Garrison to the time when his jubilant *Laus Deo* acclaimed the writing into the fundamental law of the republic of the ban upon slavery throughout the extent of its domain. Every step in the history of the conflict, which is the history of the United States for the period of a full generation, was seized upon by Whittier as a pretext for poetical expression—the terrorizing of the pioneer abolitionists, the war which the annexation of Texas made inevitable, the efforts of Clay and Webster to heal the wounds of dissension by compromise, the outrage of the Fugitive Slave Law, the struggle for freedom in the Territory of Kansas, the growth of the modern Republican party, and the holocaust of the Civil War. The majority of the poems occasioned by these themes are too entirely of and for the moment to have any lasting value, but their immediate effect was potent in strengthening the mighty moral resolve of the nation, and they made Whittier perhaps the best beloved of contemporary American poets. When this mass of work is sifted by criticism, only a few pieces seem to preserve much of the fire which made them so effective at the time of their publication. We may still be stirred by the stanzas of *Le Marais du Cygne* and the marching-song of *The Kansas Emigrants:*

> We cross the prairies as of old
> The pilgrims crossed the sea,
> To make the West, as they the East,
> The homestead of the free!

The ballad of *Barbara Frietchie* still has power to thrill its readers, and the terrible *Ichabod*, occasioned by Webster's willingness to make terms with the abhorred evil of slavery, has lost little or none of its original force. "It is a fearful thing," says Swinburne, paraphrasing the Scriptures in praise of Victor Hugo, "for a malefactor to fall into the hands of an ever-living poet." And nowhere in the *Châtiments* of the French poet is there to be found a greater finality of condemnation than that with which Whittier stamped the subject of this truly great poem.

It will have been observed that many of the pieces already mentioned belong to the class of occasional or personal compositions. This class constitutes a large fraction of the total of Whittier's work. The long list of his friendly tributes and poems written for occasions includes many that are merely trivial or without any special appeal to readers for whom the incidents or personalities commemorated have no longer any meaning. Whittier had neither the wit nor the erudition that have preserved many of the occasional pieces of Holmes and Lowell from decay. The tributes to Garrison, Sumner, and a few others still stand out as significant from this mass of metrical exercises, and when a great occasion inspired Whittier to song, the result was likely to be memorable, as in the verses which celebrate the Emancipation Proclamation, the Thirteenth Amendment to the Federal Constitution, the Chicago Fire of 1871, and the Centennial Exhibition of 1876.

The deep and sincere religious feeling of the *Centennial Hymn* is characteristic of the entire body of Whittier's verse, and not merely of the poems specifically religious in their subject-matter. His consciousness was shot through with a sense of the divine. and the essential spirituality of his thought suffuses his expression like the sunlight in cloud-banked western skies. But his religious faith was far from being of the dogmatic type. "I regard Christianity as a life rather than as a creed," he once said, and the whole of his writing exemplifies the statement. He found in the doctrines of the Society of Friends exactly the framework which his nature needed, saying that "after a candid and kindly survey" of all the other creeds, "I turn to my own Society, thankful to the Divine Providence which placed me where I am; and with an unshaken faith in the one distinctive doctrine of Quakerism —the Light Within—the immanence of the Divine Spirit in Christianity." In this doctrine, he says elsewhere, "will yet be found the stronghold of Christendom, the sure, safe place from superstition on the one hand and scientific doubt on the other." The perfect expression of this simple and serene faith is found in *The Eternal Goodness*, and still again in the very last of all his poems. The sunset song of Tennyson's soul, just before "crossing the bar" that divides the harbour of Time from the ocean of Eternity, illustrates no better than do these final lines of Whittier the matchless beauty that may crown the simplest modes of expression, if only they are based upon perfect faith and perfect sincerity.

While Whittier was primarily a poet, his activities as a reformer and philanthropist, and his editorial work in connection with the many papers that claimed his services, made him an important writer of prose. The amount of his prose writing is very great, and, although the larger part of it is too ephemeral to have any place in the history of American literature, the part which has been thought worthy of inclusion in the standard edition of his collected works fills three of the seven volumes. Much of this writing is controversial in character, like the early tract on *Justice and Expediency*, but the greater part of it belongs to the permanent literature of New England history and thought. The most important titles are *The Stranger in Lowell, The Supernaturalism of New England, Leaves from Margaret Smith's Journal in the Province of Massachusetts Bay*, and *Literary Recreations and Miscellanies*. The story of Margaret Smith is almost a work of fiction. It recounts the imagined observations of a young woman who comes from England on a visit to the Bay Colony in its early days. She meets the chief worthies of the time, describes the landscape and the crude pioneer life, and writes of witch-hunting, Quaker-baiting, and Indian warfare. G. R. Carpenter says of this work that "no single modern volume could be found which has so penetrated the secret of colonial times in Massachusetts, for it is almost line by line a transcript and imaginative interpretation of old letters, journals, and memoirs." Its Quaker authorship, moreover, gives it just the detachment needed to save it from the danger of accepting too unreservedly the view of New England colonial life that the leaders of the Puritan theocracy so zealously sought to perpetuate.

In the history of English literature in the larger sense, Whittier is probably no more than a poet of the third rank. His native endowment was rich, but it was supplemented by neither the technical training nor the discipline required for the development of the artist. He was extremely careless about his rhymes—"good Yankee rhymes, but out of New England they would be cashiered," he once said of them. The construction of his stanzas was diffuse and often slovenly. The organ voice and the lyric cry were not, except at rare moments, his to command. But no American who lived in the shadow of slavery and internecine strife, none who grew to manhood in the generation succeeding those epic days, would dream of measuring his love and veneration for Whittier by the scale of absolute art. Whittier's verse is so inwrought with the nation's passion during that period of heightened consciousness that preserved the Union and redeemed it from the curse of slavery that it cannot be coldly and critically considered by any one who has had a vital sense of the agonies and exaltations of that critical time. To such, the invocation of Stedman's *Ad Vatem* will always be a truer expression of their feeling than any critical judgment, for they can never forget their debt to him for

> righteous anger, burning scorn
> Of the oppressor, love to humankind,
> Sweet fealty to country and to home,
> Peace, stainless purity, high thoughts of heaven,
> And the clear, natural music of [his] song.

Fifty years ago, the verdict of thoughtful Americans acclaimed Whittier as the foremost American poet, with the possible exception of Longfellow, and while now there would be more dissentients from that judgment than there were then, his fame still rests upon a very solid basis of acceptance and esteem. And especially to those who have sprung from the soil of New England, he will always be the incomparable poet of their childhood home, of its landscape, its legendry, and the spiritual essence of its history.

# CHAPTER XIV

# Poe

T HE saddest and the strangest figure in American literary history is that of Edgar Allan Poe. Few writers have lived a life so full of struggle and disappointment, and none have lived and died more completely out of sympathy with their times. His life has been made the subject of minute and prolonged investigation, yet there are still periods in his history that have not been satisfactorily cleared up. And the widest differences of opinion have existed as to his place and his achievements. But there are few today who will not readily concede to him a place among the foremost writers of America, whether in prose or in verse, and there are not wanting those who account him one of the two or three writers of indisputable genius that America has produced.

Poe was born at Boston, 19 January, 1809, the son of actor parents of small means and of romantic proclivities. Before the end of his third year he was left an orphan, his mother dying in wretched poverty at Richmond, Virginia, 8 December, 1811, and his father a few weeks later, if we may believe the poet's own statement. He was promptly taken under the protection of a prosperous tobacco exporter of Richmond, John Allan, in whose family he lived, ostensibly as an adopted child, until 1827. In his sixth year he attended for a short time the school of William Ewing in Richmond. In the summer of 1815 he went with his foster-father to England, and for the next five years, with the exception of a few months spent in Scotland shortly after reaching England, he lived in London, attending first a boarding school kept by the Misses Dubourg in Sloane Street, and later the academy of the Rev. John Bransby in Stoke Newington. He impressed Bransby as a "quick and clever boy," though embarrassed by "an extravagant amount of pocket-money"; and John Allan wrote of him in 1818 that he was "a fine boy" and read "Latin pretty sharply." In 1816 Allan described him as "thin as a razor," but in 1819 he wrote that he was "growing wonderfully."

On his return to Richmond in the summer of 1820, Poe entered an academy kept, first, by Joseph H. Clarke and, later, by William Burke, under whom he continued his work in the languages, earning the admiration of his fellows by his readiness at "capping verses" from the Latin and by his skill in declamation. He also wrote verses of his own, and it is said that a sheaf of his juvenilia was collected in 1822 or 1823 in the hope that they might be published in volume form. But before the end of 1824 he had somehow broken with his foster-father, and the breach between the two was never to be entirely healed. "The boy possesses not a spark of affection for us," wrote John Allan in November, 1824, "not a particle of gratitude for all my care and kindness towards him. . . . I fear his associates have led him to adopt a line of thinking and acting very contrary to what he possessed when in England." The immediate cause of the breach we do not know; but a parting of the ways between the two, who were radically dissimilar in tastes and ideals, was inevitable sooner or later.

The year 1826 Poe spent as a student at the University of Virginia. Here he made a creditable record in his classes, winning honourable mention in Latin and French; and he at no time fell under the censure of his instructors. At the end of the year, however, because of his having accumulated gambling debts of some twenty-five hundred dollars, he was withdrawn from college; and with the beginning of the next year he was placed by his adoptive father in his counting-house in Richmond, in the hope that he might develop a taste for a business career. But he had small leaning that way; besides, he had been disappointed in a love-affair, having become engaged before going to college to Miss Sarah Elmira Royster, of Richmond, who, in consequence of a misunderstanding, had jilted him in his absence and had betrothed herself to another. Smarting under this disappointment and completely out of sympathy with the life marked out for him by his foster-father, Poe now determined to run away; and at some time in March, 1827, he left Richmond for parts unknown. In May he appeared at Boston, and there, 26 May, he was mustered into the army of the United States. The next two years he served as a soldier in barracks, being stationed first at Boston, then at Charleston, South Carolina, and finally at Fortress Monroe. In the spring or summer of 1827 he brought out at Boston his first volume of poems, *Tamerlane and Other Poems*, a collection of ten fugitive pieces, all brief save one, and all plainly imitative either of Byron or of Moore.

In February, 1829, Mrs. Allan died, and in April Poe was discharged from the army, a substitute having been provided, and efforts were made to obtain for him an appointment to West Point. Some time intervened, however, before an appointment could be procured, and it was not until July, 1830, that he was admitted to the Academy. In the preceding December he had published at Baltimore a second volume of poems, made up largely of his earlier pieces revised, but containing his long poem *Al Aaraaf*, the most ambitious and the most promising of his earlier productions. At West Point he took high rank in his classes; but in October, 1830, John Allan had married a second time, and Poe, concluding that there was no longer any prospect of succeeding to a fortune, determined with the beginning of the new year to bring about his dismissal from the Academy. He adopted the very effective means of absenting himself from roll calls and from classes, was court-martialled in consequence, and 6 March, 1831, was formally expelled. In April a third volume of his poems appeared, containing some of the best work that he ever did, but in a state much inferior to that in which he ultimately left it.

During the ensuing four years Poe seems to have made his home in Baltimore, though it is impossible to trace his history with complete certainty throughout this period. Much of his time, no doubt, was given to his prose tales, five of which appeared in the Philadelphia *Saturday Courier*, in 1832,[1] and a sixth—for which he won a prize of a hundred dollars—in the Baltimore *Saturday Visiter* in October, 1833; and he also worked at intervals during these years on a play, *Politian*, which, though published in part, was never completed. That

[1] These stories were originally submitted in competition for a prize—won, as it happens, by Delia Bacon.

he lived in poverty and in much obscurity is evident from the reminiscences of John Pendleton Kennedy, the novelist,[1] who had been one of the judges in the *Visiter's* contest in 1833 and who now proved his most helpful friend.

In the summer of 1835, Poe went to Richmond to assist in the editing of *The Southern Literary Messenger*, and before the end of the year he had been promoted to be editor-in-chief of that magazine. He was now fairly launched on his career as man of letters. In the columns of the *Messenger* he republished, with slight revisions, the tales that had already appeared, and in addition a number of new tales and poems, together with a long line of book reviews, which promptly won for the *Messenger* a popularity such as no other Southern magazine has ever enjoyed. In May, 1836, relying on his suddenly acquired prosperity, he married. His wife was Virginia Clemm,[2] a child of thirteen and the daughter of a paternal aunt, in whose home he had lived for a time in Baltimore. In the fall he was absent from his post for several weeks in consequence of illness brought on by excessive indulgence in drink; and though on his recovery he returned to his duties with his accustomed vigour, he was unable to satisfy his employer as to his stability of habit; and with the initial number of the *Messenger* for 1837 his resignation as editor was formally announced.

From Richmond he went to New York, where he hoped to find employment with *The New York Review*. In October, 1837, he was in Richmond again, posing as editor still of the *Messenger*, though we cannot be certain that he contributed anything to its columns at this time. At the end of the year he was again in New York; and in the following summer he moved to Philadelphia. In July he published at New York, in book form, the longest of his tales, *The Narrative of Arthur Gordon Pym*.

The next six years (1838–1844) he spent in Philadelphia. During the first year he was engaged largely in hack-writing, busying himself with a work on conchology (published in

[1] Tuckerman, *Life of Kennedy*, pp. 373 f.
[2] A license for marriage to Virginia Clemm was procured at Baltimore in September, 1835, but it has not been established that there was a wedding at that time.

1839) among other things, though he also composed at this time some of the best of his tales. In May, 1839, he became associate editor of *Burton's Gentleman's Magazine*, but a year later he quarrelled with Burton and lost his place. From April, 1841, to May, 1842, he edited *Graham's Magazine*. And in 1843 he had for a while some tacit connection with a Philadelphia weekly, *The Saturday Museum*. In *Burton's* and in *Graham's* he published a number of the ablest of his book-reviews and some of the most striking of his tales. At the end of 1839 he brought out at Philadelphia a collection of his tales, in two volumes; and in 1843 a further edition of his tales was projected, of which, however, only one fascicle, containing but two of his stories, was published. In the same year he won a prize of a hundred dollars for his story *The Gold Bug*. But at no time during these years was his income from his writings or from his editorial labours sufficient to enable him to live in comfort. During his later years in Philadelphia, moreover, his weakness for drink had grown on him, and he had as a result lost many of his friends; his wife, too, frail from childhood, had become an invalid in 1841 or in 1842; and so, early in 1844, the poet concluded to seek a new field.

In April, 1844, he moved with his family to New York; and there, either in the city or at Fordham, a few miles out, he lived during the remaining five years allotted to him. The year 1844 was uneventful, but the year 1845 proved to be the pivotal year of his history. At the end of January appeared in the New York *Evening Mirror*, on which he had held a minor editorial position for several months, *The Raven;* and he became at once the most talked of man of letters in America. In the summer he published a new volume of his tales, and in the fall, a collected edition of his poems, *The Raven and Other Poems*. Early in the year he became assistant editor of *The Broadway Journal;* in July he became sole editor, and in October editor and proprietor of this paper; and thus was enabled to realize an ambition that he had cherished for more than a decade, to edit a paper of his own. But owing to financial embarrassments arising from various causes, he was compelled to give up this paper at the end of the year. During the first half of 1846 he was ill, so he himself claimed, for several months. In the middle of the year (May to October) he published, in Godey's *Lady's Book*, his *Literati*, a series of bio-graphical-critical papers dealing with the chief living writers of Gotham; and the year was further made memorable by the controversy with Thomas Dunn English engendered by the publication of the *Literati*, and by a scandal growing out of his friendship with the poetess, Mrs. F. S. Osgood. Early in 1847 the poet's wife died, and throughout the year, as indeed during the preceding year, the family suffered keenly from the pinch of poverty. The year 1848 saw the culmination of two unhappy love-affairs—first, with Mrs. Shew, who had nursed the poet through a spell of illness following the death of his wife, and then with Mrs. Whitman, the Rhode Island poetess; and this year also witnessed the publication of his *Eureka*, a philosophical disquisition on the origin and composition of the universe.

The year 1849 opened auspiciously for the poet; during the first half he wrote at least one new tale, and several new poems, including the lines *For Annie*, *Eldorado*, a revised and much enlarged version of *The Bells*, and the last of his poems, *Annabel Lee*. In the summer of 1849 he went to Richmond, where he renewed his addresses to the sweetheart of his boyhood, Miss Royster, now the widow Mrs. Shelton and wealthy, and they became engaged for a second time. Late in September Poe left Richmond for the North, intending to bring his mother-in-law, who remained loyal to him throughout the years, to the South for the marriage; but at Baltimore he was induced to break a temperance pledge that he had made in the summer, and as a result he fell into excesses from the effects of which he died 7 October, 1849. He lies buried in the churchyard of Westminster Presbyterian Church, Baltimore.

Such are the leading facts that have been established concerning Poe's life. But despite the labours of his biographers —and no American writer has had more and abler biographers —there are still certain periods of his life for which our knowledge is exceedingly meagre and unsatisfactory. We have, for instance, no specific knowledge as to how or where he spent the two months intervening between his departure from Richmond in March, 1827, and his mustering into the army at the end of May. We are likewise ignorant both as to his whereabouts and as to his activities during the year immediately preceding his winning of the *Visiter's* prize in October, 1833; and the entire period from 1831 to 1835 is obscure. He sinks out of sight again for six months in the middle of 1837. And a hiatus of several months also occurs in his history during the first half of the year 1846. For this obscurity Poe is himself mainly responsible. He took pleasure in mystifying his public about himself; and in a few instances he deliberately misstated the facts.[1]

As to Poe's character and personality the most divergent views have been expressed. According to Griswold, whom he chose as his literary executor, Poe was a "naturally unamiable character," arrogant, "irascible, envious," without "moral susceptibility" or sense of gratitude, and exhibiting "scarcely any virtue in either his life or his writings." According to the Richmond editor, John M. Daniel, who saw him frequently during the summer of 1849, he was sour of nature, capricious, selfish, a misanthrope, possessing "little moral sense." In the view of Lowell's friend, C. F. Briggs, with whom he was associated for several months in 1845 as co-editor of the *Broadway Journal*, he was "badly made up," a "characterless character," and "utterly deficient of high motive." And Horace Greeley was disturbed lest Mrs. Whitman should marry him, giving it as his opinion that such a union would be a "terrible conjunction." To N. P. Willis, on the other hand, who perhaps knew him better than any other outside of his immediate family during his last half-dozen years, there appeared, during several months of close association with him in 1844–1845, "but one presentment of the man,—a quiet, patient, industrious, and most gentlemanly person, commanding the utmost respect and good feeling by his unvarying deportment and ability"; and in subsequent years he saw, so he declares, nothing of the arrogance, vanity, and depravity of heart "that were commonly attributed to him." And George R. Graham, editor of the magazine that bore his name, testifies that, when he knew him best (in the first half of the forties), "he had the docility and kind-heartedness of a child," and that "no man was more quickly touched by a kindness, none more prompt to make return for an injury," and, further, that he was "the soul

[1] See, in particular, in this connection, an autobiographical memorandum sent to Griswold in 1841 (*Works of Poe*, ed. Harrison, Vol. I, pp. 344–346), in which most of the dates are inaccurately given, and in which we have one of several apocryphal accounts of a voyage to Europe in 1827.

of honour in all his transactions." Kennedy notes that he was "irregular, eccentric, and querulous," but adds—as if in set rejoinder to Griswold's charge that he was incapable of gratitude for service done—that "he always remembered my kindness with gratitude." As time has passed and we have come to know more about Poe's life, it has become more and more evident that the view of his character held by Griswold and those who sided with him was unduly harsh,[1] though it remains clear, nevertheless, that Poe was not without regrettable traits and serious weaknesses. It is plain, first of all, that he was abnormally proud and sensitive and impulsive; it is equally plain that he was thoroughly undignified and ungenerous in his attacks on certain of his contemporaries who had aroused his envy or incurred his dislike. We have already noted that he was not invariably accurate of statement, especially in matters pertaining peculiarly to himself; we know, too, that he was an incessant borrower, and that he neglected in some instances to make good his borrowings at the appointed time,—though there is no conclusive evidence of dishonesty of intent on his part. And all the world knows that he sometimes drank to excess. But it is also clear—contrary to the popular assumption—that Poe was not a confirmed inebriate: the volume and the quality of his writings sufficiently demonstrate this; and it is not to be denied that he made repeated and manful efforts to shake off the tyranny of drink. Nor can we read his letters —in which we see the true Poe more plainly than elsewhere— without being convinced that he also possessed amiable traits and noble impulses. In any estimate of his character, moreover, it is but just to take into account—as, indeed, most of his recent biographers have done—the influences exerted on his character by heredity and by his early environment[2]; and it should also be borne in mind that he suffered during most of his later career from serious physical infirmities.[3]

[1] It is due to Griswold, however, to say that his account of Poe's life, though inaccurate at many points and jaundiced throughout, is more to be relied on than is now commonly assumed. For exposing most of Griswold's inaccuracies we are indebted to Poe's English biographer, the late John H. Ingram.

[2] His father before him was highly impulsive and was over-fond of drink, and his foster-father was not only given to wine-bibbing but was an arch-hypocrite besides.

[3] The clash of opinion with respect to Poe's character appears to be due

It was as critic that Poe first attracted widespread attention. As editor of the *Messenger* and *Burton's* and *Graham's* his chief function was that of book-reviewer; and much of the work that he did for other periodicals was of the nature of book-reviews and gossip about books and authors. The bulk of his work in this field is journalistic in style and of ephemeral interest, much of it being the merest hack-writing; but there remains a small body of critical matter that possesses genuine worth and distinction, and that entitles Poe to an honourable place among the literary critics of America.[1] Assuredly no other American critic of his day, save Lowell, may take rank above him. This residue of good work comprises a score of masterly book-reviews, including the memorable notices of Longfellow's *Ballads*, Hawthorne's *Twice-Told Tales*, and Dickens's *Barnaby Rudge;* some half-dozen essays in the theory of criticism, of which the earliest is his *Letter to B——*, and the most significant is his *Poetic Principle;* and a series of *obiter dicta*, collected under the title *Marginalia*, which have justly been held to contain much of his best work as critic.[2]

His most distinctive gifts as critic were clearness of intellect and a faculty for analysis. Few Americans of his time had finer intellectual endowments. He also had the poet's "faculty of ideality," on which he laid great stress in his judgments of others. And he was the most independent and fearless of critics, disdaining not to attack either high or low. He had not read very widely; but he knew his Milton well, and probably his Shakespeare and his Pope, and he was familiar

---

mainly, as Willis suggested, to the fact that most of the contemporary judgments adverse to him were based on his conduct during his spells of inebriation, at which times (as he pathetically admitted more than once) he was largely irresponsible. Most of these estimates, too, are based, naturally, on the poet's later years, after both body and mind had become enfeebled. Poe himself urged, in partial explanation of his irregularities in his later years, the plea of insanity; and there is reason to believe that he was at one time addicted to the use of opium.

[1] "Poe's critical writing was so much superior to the best of what had preceded it," remarks William Morton Payne (*American Literary Criticism*, 1904, p. 14), "that one might almost be pardoned for saying that this department of our literature began when, in 1835, *The Southern Literary Messenger* engaged his services."

[2] F. C. Prescott, *Selections from the Critical Writings of Edgar Allan Poe*, p. xix; J. M. Robertson, *New Essays towards a Critical Method*, p. 117.

with the chief Romantic poets of the age immediately preceding his own; while as editor and magazinist he kept in close touch with contemporary literature. On the other hand, he was prone to exaggerate technical blemishes and to underestimate ethical and philosophical significance. And his taste was not always impeccable. By his contemporaries he was thought of as inexcusably harsh in his criticisms: by one of them he is dubbed the "tomahawk man," by another the "broad-axe man"; and Lowell remarks, in his sketch of him, that he seemed "sometimes to mistake his phial of prussic-acid for his inkstand." What is more to his discredit, he stooped now and then to log-rolling both on his own account and on behalf of his friends, and his unfavourable judgments appear to have been actuated in some instances by animus and jealousy. But most of his critical judgments have been sustained by time. And despite the arrogance charged against him by Griswold and others, it is to be set down to his credit that he ungrudgingly conceded to Longfellow and Lowell the primacy among the American poets of his time and that he generously proclaimed Hawthorne to be without a peer in his peculiar field. His chief hobbies as critic were originality—and, *per contra*, imitation and plagiarism—"unity or totality of effect," consistency and "keeping," verisimilitude, "the heresy of the didactic," provinciality, metrical imperfections of whatever sort, and verbal inaccuracies and infelicities; some of which hobbies—as plagiarism—he rode over-hard. But his influence in an age when wholesale adulation was the rule, and when art counted for but little, was naturally wholesome.

Among the best known of his critical *dicta* is his characterization of the short story in his notice of Hawthorne's *Twice-Told Tales* (1842). Probably no other passage in American literary criticism has been quoted so often as the following extract from this review:

A skilful literary artist has constructed a tale. If wise, he has not fashioned his thoughts to accommodate his incidents; but having conceived, with deliberate care, a certain unique or single *effect* to be wrought out, he then invents such incidents—he then combines such events as may best aid him in establishing this precon-

ceived effect.   If his very initial sentence tend not to the outbring-
ing of this effect, then he has failed in his first step.   In the whole
composition there should be no word written, of which the tendency, direct or indirect, is not to the one pre-established design.
And by such means, with such care and skill, a picture is at length
painted which leaves in the mind of him who contemplates it with
a kindred art, a sense of the fullest satisfaction.   The idea of the
tale has been presented unblemished, because undisturbed; and
this is an end unattainable by the novel.[1]

Scarcely less famous are some of his deliverances on the meaning and the province and aims of poetry.   Poetry he defined
as the "rhythmical creation of beauty," holding with Coleridge, his chief master as critic, that its "immediate object"
is "pleasure, not truth"; and that "with the intellect or with
the conscience it has only collateral relations."   "Poetry and
passion" he held to be "discordant."   And humour, also, he
believed to be "antagonistical to that which is the soul of the
muse proper."   Sadness he declared to be the most poetic of
moods; and "indefinitiveness" one of the chief essentials of
lyric excellence.   A long poem he held, with Bryant, to be
a "contradiction in terms."

Poe's critical doctrines find their best exemplification in his
own poems.   He is, first of all, a poet of beauty, paying little
heed to morality or to the life of his fellow-men.   He is, in the
second place, a master-craftsman, who has produced a dozen
poems of a melody incomparable so far as the western world
is concerned; and he has achieved an all but flawless construction of the whole in such poems as *The Raven, The Haunted
Palace,* and *The Conqueror Worm;* while in *The Bells* he has
performed a feat in onomatopœia quite unapproached before
or since in the English language.   He is, moreover, one of the
most original of poets.   And the best of his verse exhibits a
spontaneity and finish and perfection of phrase, as well as,
at times, a vividness of imagery, that it is difficult to match
elsewhere in American poetry.

But his poems of extraordinary worth are exceedingly few
—scarcely above a score at most—in which must be included
the earlier lines *To Helen, Israfel, The City in the Sea, The Sleeper,*

[1] *Works of Poe,* ed. Harrison, Vol. XI, p. 108.

*The Haunted Palace, Dream-Land, The Raven, Ulalume, For Annie,* and *Annabel Lee.* And most of his earlier verses are manifestly imitative, Byron and Moore and Coleridge and Shelley being his chief models; while much of his earlier work, including all of the volume of 1827, and some of his latest— notably the verses addressed to Mrs. Osgood and Mrs. Shew and Mrs. Lewis—are either fragmentary and "incondite" or mere "verses," or both. It has been justly said that "there is almost no poet between whose best and worst verse there is a wider disparity."[1] His range, too, is narrower than that of any other American poet of front rank. Consistently with one of his theories already adverted to, he wrote no long poem, save the juvenile *Tamerlane* and *Al Aaraaf,* both of them extremely crude performances (though *Al Aaraaf* contains excellent passages and played a large part in his development as poet), and an abortive play, *Politian,* which he never saw fit to publish in its entirety; so that he lives as poet solely by reason of his lyrics. And within the realm of the lyric he confined himself to the narrowest range of ideas. Nature he employed merely as ornament or as symbol or to fill in the background; and nowhere in his poems does he deal with the life about him, except in so far as he writes of friends and kindred. His most constant theme—if we exclude the poet himself, for few writers have so constantly reflected themselves in their work—is either the death of a beautiful woman and the grief occasioned thereby, or the realm of shades—the spirit-world —a subject to which he was strongly attracted, especially in his middle years. Hence, although most European critics have accorded him first place among American poets, most American critics have hesitated to accept their verdict.

Much of the excellence of his best poems arises from the never-ending revisions to which he subjected them. *The Raven,* for example, exists in upwards of a dozen variant forms, and some of his earlier verses were so radically altered as to be scarcely recognizable in their final recast. His melody, especially in his later poems, grows in large measure out of his all but unexampled use of parallelism and of the refrain.[2] Not a little of his charm, moreover, both in his earlier and in

---

[1] J. M. Robertson, *New Essays,* p. 76.
[2] C. A. Smith, *Repetition and Parallelism in English Verse,* pp. 44 f.

his later work, results from his use of symbolism. It is idle to complain that his best verses—as *Israfel* or *The Haunted Palace* —are superficial; and it is futile to contend that such poems as *Annabel Lee* or the sonnet *To My Mother* are not sincere, or that his poems, one and all, lack spontaneity. But it is not to be denied that some of his best-known poems—as *Lenore* and *The Raven*—exhibit too much of artifice; that *The Conqueror Worm* and passages in still other poems approach too near to the melodramatic; and that, with many readers, his verses must suffer by reason of their sombreness of tone.

Poe's tales, which exceed in number his fully authenticated poems, have been held by some of the most judicious of his critics to constitute his chief claim to our attention.[1] There are those who will not subscribe to this view, but it is plain that he was the most important figure in the history of the short story during his half-century. Hawthorne alone may be thought of as vying with him for this distinction; but although the New Englander is infinitely Poe's superior in some respects—as in the creation of character and in wholesomeness and sanity—he must yield place to him in the creation of incident, in the construction of plot, and in the depicting of an intensely vivid situation. Whether or not we allow Poe the distinction of having invented the short story will depend on our interpretation of terms; but at least he invented the detective story, and more than any other he gave to the short story its vogue in America.

Like his poems, his tales are notably unequal. Some of his earlier efforts—especially his satirical and humorous extravaganzas, as *Lionizing* and *Bon-Bon*—are properly to be characterized as rubbish; and he was capable in his later years of descending to such inferior work as *The Sphinx*, *Mellonta Tauta*, and *X-ing a Paragrab*. One feels, indeed, that Lowell's famous characterization of him:

Three fifths of him genius and two fifths sheer fudge,

applies with entire justice to him as a maker of short stories. The best of his narrative work is to be found in his analytical

[1] E. C. Stedman in the Stedman-Woodberry edition of Poe, Vol. x, p. xiii; and Robertson, *l. c.*, p. 75.

tales, as *The Gold Bug* or *The Descent into the Maelstrom*, in certain stories in which he combines his analytical gift with the imaginative and inventive gift, as *The Cask of Amontillado* and *William Wilson*, or in certain studies of the pure imagination, as *The Fall of the House of Usher* and *The Masque of the Red Death*.    In all of these he displays a skill of construction and of condensation surpassed by few if any other workers in his field.    In some—as in *The Masque of the Red Death*, or in *Eleonora*, or in his landscape studies—he shows himself a master of English style; and in two of his briefer studies—*Shadow* and *Silence*—he approaches the eloquence and splendour of De Quincey.

His main limitations as a writer of the short story are to be found in the feebleness and flimsiness of his poorer work; in his all but complete lack of healthy humour; in his incapacity to create or to depict character; in his morbidness of mood and grotesqueness of situation.[1]    He suffers also in comparison with other leading short-story writers of America and England in consequence of his disdain of the ethical in art (though neither his tales nor his poems are entirely lacking in ethical value); he suffers, again, in comparison with certain present-day masters of the short story in consequence of his lack of variety in theme and form; and he was never expert in the management of dialogue.

By reason of his fondness for the terrible and for the *outré*, he is to be classed with the Gothic romancers: he makes constant use of Gothic machinery, of apparitions, cataleptic attacks, premature burial, and life after death.    In several of his stories—as also in his long poems, *Tamerlane* and *Al Aaraaf* —he follows in the steps of the Orientalists.    On the other hand, in some of his tales of incident he achieves a realism and a minuteness of detail that betray unmistakably the influence of Defoe.    And it is easy to demonstrate an indebtedness to divers

---

[1] His friend, P. P. Cooke, wrote of him in 1847: "For my individual part, having the seventy or more tales, analytic, mystic, grotesque, arabesque, always wonderful, often great, which his industry and fertility have already given us, I would like to read one cheerful book made by his *invention*, with little or no aid from its twin brother *imagination*, . . . a book full of homely doings, of successful toils, of ingenious shifts and contrivances, of ruddy firesides—a book healthy and happy throughout" (*Southern Literary Messenger*, January, 1848, p. 37).

of his contemporaries, as James and Bulwer and Disraeli and Macaulay. It has been proved also that he knew the German romancer, E. T. A. Hoffmann, if not in the original, at least in translation, and that he caught his manner and appropriated his themes.[1] For the rest, he drew for his materials largely on the magazines and newspapers of his day, finding in a famous newspaper sensation of the forties the suggestion of his *Mystery of Marie Rogêt* (as he had found in another sensation, of the twenties, the plot of his *Politian*), and taking advantage of certain contemporary fads in his myth-making about mesmerism, ballooning, premature burial, and the like; and he boldly pilfered from government reports, scientific treatises, and works of reference such material as he found serviceable in some of his tales of adventure. Hence his originality may be said to consist rather in combination and adaptation than in more obviously inventive exercises of the fancy.

Poe's influence has been far-reaching. As poet, he has had many imitators both in his own country and abroad, but especially in France and England.[2] As romancer he has probably wielded a larger influence than any English writer since Scott. And as critic it is doubtful whether any other of his countrymen has contributed so much toward keeping the balance right between art-for-art's-sake and didacticism. His fame abroad is admittedly larger than that of any other American writer, and his vogue has been steadily growing among his own people.

[1] Palmer Cobb, *The Influence of E. T. A. Hoffmann on the Tales of Edgar Allan Poe.* Woodberry, *Life of Poe*, vol. I, pp. 379–381, and *passim*.

[2] In the view of Edmund Gosse, "there is hardly one [of the later English poets] whose verse-music does not show traces of Poe's influence" (*Questions at Issue*, p. 90). On Poe's influence and vogue in France, see L. P. Betz, *Edgar Poe in der franzoesischen Litteratur: Studien zur vergleichenden Litteraturgeschichte der neueren Zeit* (1902), pp. 16–82; C. H. Page in *The* [New York] *Nation* for 14 January, 1909; and G. D. Morris, *Fenimore Cooper et Edgar Poe*, pp. 67 f. (Paris, 1912).

# CHAPTER XV

# Publicists and Orators, 1800–1850

I N America, political theory and political philosophy have always been closely associated with practical politics and with the problems of very immediate interest. The cogent and effective theory of the American Revolution was distinctly part of a determined effort to reach results in civil organization. And so too in the first half of the nineteenth century, a period by no means without its contribution to the philosophy of the state, most of the political theory appeared in speeches and pamphlets directed to the accomplishment of a present and very concrete purpose. The Americans have been charged with incapacity for sustained theorizing, or for prolonged logical discussion; and yet one may safely say that no other people of modern times have so widely used political theory or so generally discussed practical affairs on a theoretical basis. The whole nature of our institutions has prompted men to indulge in argument which was legalistic and was often tinctured with philosophy. Even the unlearned could not speak and think of democracy and its hopes without indulging in visions; they could not discuss the presence of slavery without touching the border of the deepest problems of social order; they could not speak of union or states' rights without entering at least the outer portal of philosophic argument. But we need not look for detached theoretical treatises; the statesman, the politician, and the jurist were busily using such learning as they had and such aptitude for theory as they possessed in the concrete and difficult problems which were begotten by democracy in a country which, to use Calhoun's words, was "rapidly—I was about to say fearfully —growing." Calhoun himself, a philosopher of real distinction, probably never claimed a higher rôle than that of statesman; and though he published two treatises which belong in the field of political theory, they were produced because of an immediate tangible condition and they were partly vitiated for permanent service because of their defence of a decaying institution which dimmed his own outlook on the world.

The first few decades of the century, if they produced no notable pieces of abstract political theory, gave alluring opportunity for oratory and offered also an unusual field for the jurist. The orator had big themes—democracy, slavery, free labour, expansion, states' rights, nationalism, as well as the well-worn subjects of banks and tariffs and lands and commerce. The jurist was called to the novel task of construing constitutions, of passing on the fundamental law of a federal republic, and more—the task of developing and adjusting a system of private law suited to the needs of a new people and a new country. In both of these fields of action and of thought the Americans did much; in oratory appeared Webster, Clay, Calhoun, Randolph, Choate, Benton, and John Quincy Adams, and others only less worthy of note; in jurisprudence, Marshall and Kent and Story and Wheaton, by judicial opinion or by written text, laid the foundations of American public and private law and ably performed a creative task such as rarely, if ever, before fell to the lot of the jurist.

Much of the oratory of the time was of a kind which appeals but little to the reader of the present day. The speeches that have come down to us are often diffuse and occasionally florid. Nothing else could be expected from the leaders of a nation which was full of eager life and was assured of its own high destiny, a nation in which a man to be a popular leader must have power in appealing to the multitude, uncritical in its attitude toward literary form, provided the speaker himself have vitality, assurance, and a plentiful store of winged words. This, it is true, is not altogether just, for Webster's diction was on the whole restrained and strong; Calhoun rarely declaimed; Clay and Benton and Adams were always earnest and did not merely toy with words; Everett's orations, polished and academic, never descended into the lower realms of commonplace word-juggling for applause. And yet it is probably right to say that most of the speaking of the time was affected by the fact that orators were appealing to a wide constituency, to a people engaged in very practical tasks, but self-confident, buoyant, and withal emotional or at least idealistic.

The jurists of the time may here be considered first, although, as already said, it is not possible to disassociate the greatest among them from the problems which enlisted the enthusiasm and interest of the orator and political leader. If one turns, for example, to the decisions which John Marshall (1755-1835) gave as chief justice, one at once thinks of the work of Calhoun and other great particularists, who in the field of active politics put forth theories totally at variance with those coming from the Court. It is, therefore, quite impossible to detach Marshall from the most important movements of his time; for his words lose significance unless we see that they marked out lines of social and political progress and profoundly affected the character and career of the nation. And thus too, if the establishment of a widely accepted system of jurisprudence is necessary for the building up of a common industrial and social life for the nation at large, the work of Joseph Story, James Kent, and others, cannot be assigned to any narrow field of technical jurisprudence of interest to the professional lawyer alone.

The appointment of Marshall to the chief justiceship (January, 1801) was of great significance, for in the course of a few years he showed the importance of the Federal judiciary and the great authority of his office. For thirty-four years he presided over the Court and gave out a series of decisions which fixed permanently the principles of constitutional construction. His task was in some respects more that of the statesman than the lawyer; he was called upon to consider public questions of far-reaching importance and to lay down principles which he must gather from the nature of the United States, which was itself, in its composite organization, an experiment, a new form of political order. He was the first judge in history on whom fell the duty of interpreting and expounding the fundamental basis of the state; for, though the Supreme Court had been in existence twelve years before Marshall took his seat on the bench, not much had been done to prepare the way or to throw light on the solution of perplexing problems which Marshall had to solve. Ordinary legal learning and, above all, learning in the domain of ordinary private law could not avail him much; indeed one may question whether, had his mind been stored with vast legal lore, he could have entered on his work without falling into traps of pedantry or finding himself clogged by precedent and technicality. He brought to his great undertaking considerable experience in public affairs, an interest and a viewpoint arising from practical participation in government, and no small amount of learning in international and municipal law and in what we should now call political science.

The layman reading Marshall's decisions will be struck by the fact that he did not balance an opinion on a long line of precedents or seek refuge behind the thoughts and words of others. Few references to authority are to be found, and in some of his greatest cases there is not a single citation of precedent. He begins with simple statements, founded, one is led to think, in common sense, and then, with a careful but not overwrought analysis, he leads one forward to his conclusions, always with a directness and a simplicity which are characteristic of strong mental grasp but conceal the cleverness with which the road has been chosen or the arguments exposed. By his very statement of the issues involved in a case he could quietly disclose to the litigants against whom he was ruling the far-reaching and perhaps destructive consequences of their own contentions. And, as we have said, he did this, as he must needs do it in constitutional decisions, not by an elaborate dissecting of precedent and legal authority, but by a calm outlook upon the field and a searching analysis of the elements involved in the discussion. In his most important cases he appears to rise far above the details of the immediate controversy, one might almost say above the merits of the particular case, and to have his eye on the big principles affecting the future growth of the nation. And thus he created American constitutional law; at least, not to exaggerate, he marked out the broad lines of constitutional construction and fashioned the fundamental principles on which union and government might rest.

To select his opinions for separate comment, or to choose those most noteworthy, is not an easy task. Probably *Marbury vs. Madison* is the most famous, because in that decision the Supreme Court exercised, for the first time, the power to declare an act of Congress unconstitutional. The principle on which Marshall gave the decision had been stated several times before, for the state courts had announced it when declaring statutes void and, among others, Hamilton had clearly set forth the doctrine in *The Federalist.* Moreover, modern scholars are not altogether content with the method of approach which Marshall followed in reaching his conclusion that a court had the right to declare a law void. Withal, however, the case is of signal importance and there would be considerable difficulty in presenting the power of the court with more simplicity and cogency.

In the decade after the War of 1812, Marshall rendered a series of opinions of the first importance. Thoroughly permeated with the conviction that the states of the Union must be kept within their proper bounds, he gave to the task of interpreting the Constitution and maintaining the authority of the national government his greatest power. Possibly his ablest decision, certainly the one most elaborately wrought out, is *Cohens vs. Virginia,* in which the question arose as to the right of the Supreme Court to exercise its appellate jurisdiction over the judgment of a state court involving the validity of state legislation. The contention of the counsel for the state struck at the very root of the judicial system of the Union, with its authority to review state decisions which involved the binding effect of the Federal Constitution and laws: and so to the discussion of this fundamental question Marshall brought his heaviest artillery. In a series of powerful paragraphs he proclaimed the principle of nationalism and the existence of a real union resting on the will and determination of the people:

"That the United States," he said, "form, for many, and for most important purposes, a single nation, has not yet been denied. In war, we are one people. In making peace, we are one people. In all commercial regulations, we are one and the same people. In many other respects, the American people are one; and the government which is alone capable of controlling and managing their interests in all these respects, is the government of the Union. It is their government, and in that character they have no other. America has chosen to be, in many respects, and to many purposes, a nation; and for all these purposes, her government is complete; to all these objects, it is competent."

These words give us some idea of the simplicity of the style, the evidence of power and confidence, the eloquence which can raise a judicial opinion into the realm of literature. This decision, emphatically maintaining the appellate authority of the Court and the supremacy of the national law when the law is consonant with the Constitution, left no further ground for legal discussion, though the men of Virginia, fretting under the authority of the Court, poured out their wrath in many words.[1]

In other decisions of vast influence on developing America, Marshall announced his doctrine of nationalism and marked out the limits of state competence. One of these, the case of *McCulloch vs. Maryland*, gave with renewed elaboration the doctrine of implied powers in the hands of the national government and laid down principles limiting the rights of the states. Here too Marshall examined the character of the Union and the scope of governmental authority under the Constitution, and did so with remarkable clearness. In the well-known case of *Dartmouth College vs. Woodward*, Marshall declared that a charter of a private corporation was a contract, inviolable by state authority. This decision is probably more sharply criticized by the modern lawyer than any other, and yet it is still standing and has stood for a century, the bulwark of the corporations, saving them at least from unreasonable and purely gratuitous attacks upon their privileges and property. A third case, *Gibbons vs. Ogden*, proclaiming in broad terms the extent of Federal power over interstate commerce, served as the foundation on which later decisions rested and at least suggested the legal foundation for the great development of nation-wide commerce. Thus, it will be seen, his work was of significance not alone because it furnished theories and principles of national organization and helped in determining the character of the Union, but also because, in passing on questions of state competence, his vision was sufficiently wide and

[1] See William E. Dodd, *Chief Justice Marshall and Virginia*, in *American Historical Review*, XII (1907), 776–787.

far-reaching to comprehend the need for secure industrial growth.

Though Marshall's best-known decisions were in the field of constitutional law, where he was easily master, his work was by no means confined to that subject, for many problems besides those involving constitutional construction came before the court. During his term as chief justice he rendered over five hundred opinions, dealing with almost every one of the main divisions of modern jurisprudence. But he did even more; he placed the Court itself in a position of authority and influence, dignified and made potent the whole Federal judicial system, and thus helped to build up that respect for the Federal courts which has been of such tremendous importance in the development of American life. This in fact was no easy task; the Supreme Court itself was often fiercely attacked; it often went counter to the intense prejudice of parties, states, and sections. But by virtue of his own integrity and inherent power he compelled respect and overcame prejudice.

In the general field of constitutional law, Joseph Story (1779–1845) must be placed next to Marshall, though he did much less than the great chief justice of a purely constructive or creative character. His work as associate justice on the Supreme Bench was important, but his most substantial contribution was his *Commentaries on the Constitution*, which appeared in 1833 and long remained the only extensive and authoritative treatise on the subject. It passed through various editions, the best known, the fourth, containing copious annotations by Thomas M. Cooley, a distinguished publicist of a later generation. Thus for fifty years after its first appearance it furnished students of the law with the principles which Marshall and Story himself had done so much to establish by their decisions, and it doubtless had great influence on the thinking of bench and bar for two generations at least. It would be difficult to overestimate the importance of such volumes in the days when the critical case system was not used by beginners, when texts were comparatively few, and when practising attorneys and judges were not provided with long series of reports, in days also when the layman was interested in problems concerning the nature of the Union and the powers of government.

If Story's name is associated in our minds with that of

Marshall, because Story's *Commentaries* carried forward the Marshall tradition, we may also justly associate him with James Kent (1763–1847). Both were judges, both also teachers and writers, and by their published works on various fields of American law they gave it coherence, stability, and strength. Though Marshall has undimmed honour as the founder of constitutional law, we look to these two men as the chief influences in building up other branches of American jurisprudence.

They began their work when there was practically nothing written on American law, and when there was a feeling of opposition to the English common law, even as it was presented in Coke and Blackstone. The times were critical, and the work of these two men in laying the foundations of American law, in seizing upon the principles of the common law and adapting them to American conditions, and in building up, in general, a coherent and usable system was of great importance. A competent author, attributing much to the influence of these men, asserts that the achievements of the seventy-five years before the Civil War compare favourably with those of any period of growth and adjustment in legal history, and declares that the "closest analogy, both in the time taken and the amount and character of the work accomplished, is the classical period in England—the age of Coke."[1] Kent's *Commentaries on American Law* (1826–1830) was of very great effect; it was long read by students of the law and occupied a place of distinction by the side of Blackstone's famous work. Story, in addition to his work as a teacher of law in Harvard and to his duties on the bench of the Federal Supreme Court, wrote a number of volumes which did perhaps even more than those of Kent to standardize and shape the law. His *Conflict of Laws* and *Equity Jurisprudence* were of transcendent value, restating and formulating in convenient form the judge-made law of the past and making it adaptable to American conditions. Of the former treatise it has even been said that "It forthwith systematized, one might almost say, created, a whole branch of the law of England." Kent's decisions, when he was chancellor of New York, fashioned and made applicable in America the principles of equity, and

[1] Roscoe Pound, *The Place of Judge Story in the Making of American Law. Proceedings of the Cambridge Historical Society*, vol. VII (1914), p. 39.

Story's treatise on the same subject had as much or even greater influence in establishing and maintaining the system of equity jurisprudence.

What two men could do in expounding the law, making it intelligible and effective, and showing the strength and reasonableness of fundamental principles, in short, what could be done in fashioning the main lines of a growing jurisprudence for a rapidly growing country, these two men accomplished. The layman commonly thinks of the law as fixed, or as developing only by the addition of statutes passed by some legislative body, but the truth is that law grows, and the common law above all, as questions and problems arise; judges on the bench and writers of text-books who do more than merely chronicle decisions, have great opportunity to direct the law into new channels and to determine the course of its development. Such power and influence naturally belonged in unusual measure to Kent and Story, because of their learning, because they taught and wrote as well as gave opinions from the bench, and above all because the period in which they worked was a formative period in the early life of a nation, during which law, like everything else, had to find expression and formulation.

To the list of jurists deserving special mention must be added Henry Wheaton (1785-1848). His early important work was that of reporter of the Supreme Court; but in 1827 he was appointed *chargé d'affaires* to Denmark, and a few years later minister to the court of Prussia. His diplomatic experience was doubtless of much service to him in his career as a publicist. In 1836 appeared the work by which he is chiefly known, the *Elements of International Law*. It passed through various editions, was translated into foreign languages, and is justly considered one of the most valuable contributions to the science of international law made during the nineteenth century.

With the possible exception of Marshall and Webster,[1] John C. Calhoun (1782-1850) was the most important statesman and writer on public affairs in the forty years preceding 1850. A South Carolinian, he belonged by birth, not to the lowland planter class, but to the men of the up-country. At an early day his father purchased a slave, not a usual possession for an up-country man, and when John Calhoun grew to manhood

[1] For whom see Book II, Chap. XVI.

he married a distant cousin of social standing and with some means, and thus the young man was connected with the social aristocracy and the slave-owning interests of the state. These simple facts stand out prominently in any effort to understand him in his development, because he became the learned and devoted advocate of the slave interests and defended, with his logic and his power in debate, the economical and social régime of the South. In 1811 he entered Congress, and was at once one of the leaders among the new young men, who were out of patience with the dallying methods of the older Jeffersonian politicians. For some years he was an ardent nationalist; possibly it is too much to say that he committed himself by votes or speeches to an interpretation of the Constitution radically opposed to state sovereignty; but in these earlier days we find in his spirit no traces of sectionalism or of any narrow particularism. In the latter part of the decade between 1820 and 1830, overcome by the unrest in his state and moved, it would seem, by its economic difficulties, he succumbed to the pressure of his surroundings and became the leader in formulating doctrines which South Carolina put forth to the world to defend itself against the tariff—shrewdly reasoned and highly elaborated doctrines of state sovereignty, the basis of nullification and secession.

Though other Southern states were at first by no means in agreement with South Carolina, when she presented to the world the theories which Calhoun so neatly phrased and so ably defended, he came to be, as the days went by, the leader of his section as well as the idol of his state. Sometimes he was a leader so far in advance that Southern people scarcely knew that they were slowly following his footsteps. More and more the South was identified with slavery; and more and more the people took their cue from Calhoun. He did not pose as a friend of disruption, and probably was a sincere friend of the Union; but the Union, he insisted with increasing fervour, must be a Union respecting the rights of the states, a Union which would hold together only if its government respected the varying conditions and the different interests of states and, indeed, of sections. He thus became the chief defender of two things or two ideas, slavery and particularism, to which the developing character of the nineteenth century was utterly opposed; slavery here and everywhere was doomed to be beaten down by the tide of humanitarianism, while localism, and sectionalism, and all other tendencies to exclusiveness and segregation, were at variance with those great forces of aggregation and of nation-building which were manifest in the whole civilized world. Calhoun's great talents were actually devoted to elaboration and vehement promulgation of theories to the effect that the American Union was a clever political system devised for the express purpose of protecting peculiar local interests against external attack; and the chief local interest was the "peculiar institution" of the South!

Calhoun's important contributions to the theory of American government began in 1828 in connection with the agitation in South Carolina about the tariff question. From that time on, his attention was largely devoted to inculcating the doctrine that the state had the right under the Constitution to protect its local interest against national aggression. His task was, and needed to be, in the presence of the growing power of the North, to develop principles for the protection of the minority, and in his quest for these doctrines he worked out a notable series of constitutional principles and philosophical theories.

Between 1828 and 1833 he developed his theories in defence of nullification by a single state. The basis of the right is of course the sovereignty of the state, and Calhoun insisted on indivisibility of sovereignty. "I maintain," he said, "that sovereignty is in its nature indivisible. It is the supreme power in a state, and we might just as well speak of half a square, or half of a triangle, as half a sovereignty." Probably it is not quite evident that one cannot justly speak of half a square; but without cavilling at his illustration we may see that in these words he swept aside statements which had been common before this time, to the effect that states, coming into the Union, surrendered a portion of their sovereignty and retained the remainder. Beneath his whole reasoning, therefore, lay the principles of what we may call organic philosophy, the recognition of the vital character of the body politic, though, of course, in this case, the body politic was the commonwealth, not the nation. He also believed that mere agreement could not establish law or political unity. This notion, at variance with the older one that men by consent could form themselves, artificially as it were, into a new entity, was beginning to take its hold on the philosophic world, and it was Calhoun's appreciation of this notion and his use of it in concrete political controversy which constitutes one of his signal contributions to the history of political theory.

He did not, in these early days, dwell on the right of secession. In fact he did not wish, especially then, to emphasize that right; he relied, rather, on the right of nullification, that is, on the power of any state to declare, not through its legislature but through a convention representing the sovereignty of the state, that a federal law is void and must not be enforced within the state. Nullification, in fact, was put forth as a device whereby the state might be preserved, with its authority untouched, without having to resort to secession from the Union. It was, therefore, as he conceived it, conservative in a twofold sense: it conserved the right of the individual state, and it saved the Union; for, without nullification, secession was the only remedy for wrong. To preserve the appearance of constitutional method, he insisted that when a law was nullified the judgment of all the states should be sought, and they, by a three-fourths vote, might declare that the disputed power belonged to the national government. It is quite unnecessary to assert that Calhoun was insincere in announcing this method of passing on controverted points; the protection of the minority and the real desirability of maintaining the Union were cogent in his mind; the Union was too much of a reality for him to think easily of its being altogether at the beck and nod of a single state. It is plain, however, that one more than one-fourth of the states could, by his plan, pronounce a measure void; and, moreover, if three-fourths declared it constitutional, such declaration could not deter a state, all-powerful in its sovereignty, from seceding. A resort to nullification was, in Calhoun's mind, a means of determining whether the states supported the government, which was only their agent, and, if they did support it, then and only then might secession be resorted to. Secession, in other words, though theoretically within the competence of any state, would not as a rule be justified simply because of the action of the central government, for the government was the agent of the states; until the principals acted, the individual state should content itself with nullification.

At the very outset, as we have seen, Calhoun announced principles calculated to defend the minority. His later and more elaborate treatises, notably his *Disquisition on Government* and his *Discourse on the Constitution and Government of the United States*, pushed to the end his theories as to the constitutional guarantees of minority. Here we find a very able discussion of constitutional principles so cogently expressed that they challenge one's admiration if they do not carry conviction. Intent upon disproving the notion that a mere majority of individuals, mere numbers, can decide upon rights or impose decisions on others, he insists that each interest or portion of the community must have a negative, and thus only when there is concurrence of the elements can there be the right to exercise power; where this principle of negation and concurrence does not exist, government rests on force; where they do exist, there is constitutionalism; a majority may be tyrannical, and therefore an unrestrained majority is inconsistent with constitutional liberty. It would be hard to deny that our constitutional system rests in part on the belief that majorities have not all power over the individual; but Calhoun's theory was different from this: interests, individual communities, must have, through the negative, the power of self-defence—and this meant, in reality, the South as a section and slavery as an interest. Through his whole career from 1828 till his death in 1850 there appears consistently this right of a minority to protect itself.

One other word must be said of Calhoun's work; for he did much more than outline the principles of state sovereignty. In the thirties, when the South began to defend slavery as never before, Calhoun stepped forward as a leader; and henceforward he was prepared to defend slavery as an institution and to use his theories concerning the Union to safeguard the institution at every turn. Here was the unnatural union: constitutional theory skilfully adapted to warding off intrusion was wedded to an economic, social, and moral condition of society. This union was all the more significant because slavery, though defended by theories of localism, was in need of recognition and of protection by national law: it needed in fact to expand, if it were to hold its own; and thus Calhoun's doctrine of the individual rights of the individual states must so be turned, by infinitely cautious curves of logic, as to justify the protection of slaves on the high seas, the existence of slavery in the District of Columbia, national guardianship of slavery in the national domain, the denunciation of free speech on the subject at the North. No one save a giant among clever logicians and a devotee among enthusiasts could have played the rôle with success. His arguments and assertions are cogent and philosophical, keen, yet exhibiting a certain breadth and firmness of grasp. He early recognized the danger of a moral agitation against slavery; he did not say that the Union could not exist half slave and half free; but he did announce (1837) that "Abolition and the Union cannot co-exist"; the fell spirit of abolitionism, based as it was, or pretended to be, on moral grounds, was irreconcilable with the safety of slaves. To meet the attack of moral crusaders, he laid down the philosophy of slaveholding and above all its value in America:

I hold that in the present state of civilization, where two races of different origin, and distinguished by colour, and other physical differences, as well as intellectual, are brought together, the relation now existing in the slaveholding states between the two, is, instead of an evil, a good—a positive good.

He also declared—what may perhaps appear today to be a gruesome fact, or at least something near the fact—that, as social and political equality between the races was impossible, "to change the present condition of the African race . . . would be but to change the form of slavery." If the black race must exist among us deprived of social equality, political rights, and, largely, of industrial opportunity, have the former slaves become freemen or have they passed into a new form of servitude?

Calhoun's written treatises on government and the rights of the South do not differ essentially from his spoken words on the same subjects. They are often metaphysical and subtle; but his doctrines rested on certain philosophical conceptions; and in presenting his theories he used language that

was calm and clear, as clear at least as the nature of his delicately wrought system might well allow.   In his speeches, he
rarely, if ever, sought to stir his audience by mere flights of
eloquence; he spoke, rather, as a man with his back to the
wall, striking hard blows, seeking to defend himself and his
section, unconsciously appealing to the emotions, if appealing
at all, because his own position was not free from pathos; for
here was a great man defending a losing cause and heroically
beating back the forces that were hourly gaining in numbers
and strength.   Even when discussing subjects which now
appear of bygone interest, he commonly struck at fundamentals
and at principles with such force and precision that many of
his words still have vitality; and much that he said will long
retain interest for the academic student of politics.   With the
possible exception of Hamilton there is no other politician in
our history whose writings today—decades after the disappearance of the subjects discussed—contain so much deserving
attention and challenging respect even from the unbeliever.
History offers few examples of such leadership, such success
in mapping out for some millions of people a course of conduct
and the ideas and beliefs on which conduct rests.

We have spoken of Calhoun as the great Southerner who
presented with logical power the doctrines on which the South
came to rest its case in defence of slavery.   There were, however, others almost as able and gifted who wrote and spoke
on similar lines.   In the early years of the century, the Southerners were on the whole nationalistic in sentiment; opposition
to national authority came from the North-east; but after the
War of 1812 the conditions changed; the South, partly doubtless because it felt economic distress, began to complain.   The
first formidable protest came from Virginia and was directed
against the Federal Court and its great chief justice, himself a
Virginian, who was declared to be interpreting the Constitution in violation of states' rights and to be intent on building
up a consolidated government, or as we should now say a
unitary state.   Jefferson, thoroughly disliking Marshall and
all his works, was in or behind these attacks, but the great
protagonists were Judge Spencer Roane (1762–1822) and John
Taylor (1750–1824) of Caroline.   Roane's argument was chiefly
directed against the assumed right of final review of constitu-

tional questions by the Federal Court in cases involving the validity of state legislation. Taylor in a number of very able books and pamphlets discussed the same subject; but he treated also the nature of the Union in a manner so critical and acute that, more nearly than any one else, he foreshadowed Calhoun and suggested the clear undimmed features of state sovereignty. Naturally we cannot omit from this list of Southern advocates Robert Y. Hayne (1791–1839), who was Webster's opponent in the "great debate" of 1830; for he made a deep impression and presented Calhoun's theories with eloquence and vigour.

Among the men of Congress who indulged in far-flung speech and whom we shall have to class as orators, John Randolph (1773–1833) of Roanoke claims our first attention. Totally without the qualities for party leadership, unable to retain the devotion or following of friends, unable to handle a big constitutional question with confident learning and logic, unable to develop theories and to win people by the force of his argument or the steady adherence to a cause and a principle, he nevertheless played a conspicuous rôle during the first quarter of the nineteenth century, and, if we judge now only by the records of his speeches, he was gifted with a power of expression, a cutting brilliant invective and devilish cleverness in criticism and attack, such as few speakers have ever possessed. He was essentially a busy fault-finder, an active, alert, denunciatory enemy, at his best—or perhaps we should say, his worst—when dealing out taunts and pouring out the vial of his wrath on the less gifted but more wise. It should also be said of him that by his vehement defence of the slavery interest, though he professed opposition to slavery in itself, and by his attack on the growing power of the Federal government, he prepared the way for the later arguments and positions of Calhoun, the real leader of the South. One passage will illustrate almost as well as many the character of his declamation:

"We are the eel," he said of the South, "that is being flayed, while the cookmaid pats us on the head and cries, with the clown in King Lear, 'Down, wantons, down! . . .' If, under a power to regulate trade, you prevent exportation; if, with the most approved spring lancets, you draw the last drop of blood from our veins; if, *secundum artem*, you draw the last shilling from our pockets, what

are the checks of the Constitution to us?  A fig for the Constitution!  When the scorpion's sting is probing us to the quick, shall
we stop to chop logic?  Shall we get some learned and cunning
clerk to say whether the power to do this is to be found in the Constitution, and then, if he, from whatever motive, shall maintain
the affirmative, shall we, like the animal whose fleece forms so
material a portion of this bill [tariff, 1824], quietly lie down and be
shorn?''

Randolph's idiosyncrasies have been variously accounted
for.  He said himself that his unprosperous life was the fruit
of an ungovernable temper; but his temper and his violent
vagaries were such evidences of a morbid mind that there
is temptation simply to consider him mentally unbalanced if
not insane.  His very maddening skill with words recalls the
adage about children and edged tools, for it seems a pity
that one so unsedate should have had such weapons of offence
in his arsenal.

From scarcely any point of view can the orations of Henry
Clay (1777-1852) be classed as literature of the same grade and
importance as those of Webster and Calhoun.  And yet just why
one should say this is not quite clear even to oneself.  The
conclusion, if it be just, rests on the fact that today his speeches
seem unprofitable and to be wanting in carrying power and effect.  If in order to be classed as literature orations must either
be marked by beauty of language and peculiar felicity of word
and phrase, or contain, though without distinction of language,
a profound and philosophic discussion of matters of lasting
human interest, then Clay's speeches can scarcely deserve a
high place in literature.  But if Clay's words do not now move
us deeply, they did move and captivate the men to whom he
spoke, and that is the aim of oratory.  He was more nearly
the great popular orator of his time than was any other; in
power over a general audience and in ability to touch the chord
of human sympathy, no one was quite his equal, at least in
the field of politics.  This is much to say of an orator in a
generation of free oratory, when men were not hesitant in the
use of burning words or hindered by sophisticated self-restraint.
No one else had the gracious manner, the voice and the presence, or those nameless qualities of personal charm, which
are powerful and dominant in all the relations of life.  If he

could not win men by his logic or his facts, he could win and hold them simply because of himself. Randolph could arouse the interest of the crowd and amaze his audience by the brilliance of his epigrams; Rufus Choate could pour out strains of sonorous sentences which might for the time dazzle his admirers and confound his adversaries; Everett was able, with admirable grace and with decorous regard for niceties of expression, to utter polished periods which were almost too elegant to be convincing. But Clay conquered because he made friends and held them to himself; he enlisted their sympathies; with gracious persuasiveness he appealed to the hearts and the simple emotions of the crowd before him.

From the time when he became Speaker in 1811 and helped to bring on the war with England, to and through the compromise of 1850, Clay was intimately connected with all the great political movements of his day. The recognition of the South American republics, the tariff, the bank, the public lands, the distribution of the surplus revenue, the slavery question in all its phases, expansion, and the Mexican War can scarce be studied better than in the story of his life. Despite this fact or because of it, despite the fact that his life was in unusual degree the public life of a generation or more, it is perhaps not unjust to think of his speeches as occasional and of his work as that of an opportunist—a fairly consistent opportunist, it must be said, for he did not always trim his sails for popular favour, but represented instinctively and honestly, on the whole, certain human impulses of the people, and above all those elements of nationalism, conservatism, and democracy which were inherent in the strangely mingled Whig party of which he was the founder and guide. Though Jackson was for a time more popular and more successful, and though Webster's eloquence appealed more to the New Englander and to the book-read classes, Clay held for decades the devotion of large portions of the people and peculiarly embodied the sense and sensibility of the nation at large. It is only when one understands the intricacies of political controversy, the sentiments of Jacksonian democracy in the West, all the entanglements of banks, and tariffs, and roads, and slavery, that we can account for Clay's failure to attain the presidency, which he so ardently desired.

The thing which lifts him into a place of undoubted significance in the course of American history is this: he embodied the spirit of developing nationalism and gave it constant expression. As Jackson, though a nationalist, represented the attitude of domineering individualism so characteristic of the untutored frontier, Clay in a wider and a deeper way appealed to the lofty sentiments of the whole people. It is not a question now of broad interpretation of the Constitution, or of any theory of governmental authority, or of any opposition to states' rights, or of anything that was legalistic or even argumentative in character; it is a question of the spirit which made America a nation, the sense of national existence, of power, of bigness, of duty, in a word, of reality. Without this sense, without this feeling in the hearts of Americans, the Union could not have resisted the corroding influence of slavery and could not have made itself, by a mighty effort, the huge, self-conscious, personal being that it is today. Of course, this was the work of others also; it was the natural product of modern life and culture; it rested on the elaborate argumentation of Webster and Marshall; but Clay by the spell of an attractive presence, by personal charm, and by the lure of a fervid eloquence awakened and developed this sentiment and made it irresistibly strong.

Perhaps the student of American literature might justly pass by the work of John Quincy Adams (1767–1848), on the ground that it possesses nothing of real literary merit and deserves no special distinction; he was not a great orator, if one judge by grace of expression and by power of public appeal, and he was not a writer gifted with special originality or charm of style. He was, however, for fifty years and more a prominent figure in public life—foreign minister, senator, secretary of state, president, representative in Congress; he prepared able state papers; for nearly twenty years and at an age when most men enjoy retirement from active service, he played a conspicuous rôle in Congress, speaking in behalf of free speech and the right of petition and defending the cause of free labour against the demands of slavery; he left for the use of succeeding generations a diary of his life, a source of comfort to the historical investigator and a pleasure to the lay reader of history, a diary astonishingly full and minute, filled with reflections and with stern and caustic comments on men and events. The years after his presidency, when he was a representative in Congress, have given his name a peculiar lustre, for he laboured there boldly and almost alone.

He was too intense in his devotion to what he thought right, too unbending, too severe, too outspoken, too blunt perhaps, to be a political leader or a popular idol, but that he had power is plain, for by dint of fearless speech he won the well-earned title of "old man eloquent,"—and eloquent he undoubtedly was, when he rose to his height in defence of principles he believed just and sacred. Without descending into vulgar abuse, he could indulge in scathing attack, while his wide learning and experience in public affairs gave him advantage over most of his adversaries.

From even a hurried sketch of this period we cannot omit to mention the names of a few other men who were well known in this time and deserve to be known now. Albert Gallatin (1761–1849), one of the ablest and most learned of American statesmen, served his country in Congress, as foreign minister, and as secretary of the treasury; he was an administrator rather than a publicist or orator, but some of his pamphlets and reports were of marked ability. Roger Brooke Taney (1777–1864), secretary of the treasury under Jackson, and chief justice of the United States from 1836 to 1864, was a learned jurist, whose fame was clouded for the later part of his life by his opinion in the Dred Scott case. Josiah Quincy (1772–1864), an orator of no mean power, represented during the earlier part of his life the narrow New England Federalism which was so bitterly opposed to the politics of Jefferson and Madison. Edward Everett (1794–1865) occupied various public positions—member of Congress, governor of Massachusetts, minister to England, president of Harvard College. Although long active in political affairs he won chief destinction by lectures on literary subjects and by orations of an occasional character. In no other speeches of his generation, probably in no others in our whole history, do we find the same precision and elegance or equal refinement, ease, and grace; in no others are there such marks of real distinction in expression.

More than a word should be given to Thomas H. Benton (1782–1858), if the real importance of his work be given proper recognition; but we must content ourselves with a brief statement. For over thirty years, from the time of the Missouri Compromise until almost the outbreak of the Civil War, he was prominent in public life, an active, untiring representative of the active, untiring West. No man, not even Clay or Jackson or Lincoln, better typified the young, self-confident Western democracy; he represented the West of his day not only in the measures he advocated and the principles he followed, but in his very manner of speech—earnest, assured, buoyant, boastful, idealistic. If one would know America and its differences, how training and environment have affected oratory as well as views of public policy, one could get no better lesson than by comparing the full-blooded oratory of Benton with the acrid speech of Josiah Quincy or the polite eloquence of Everett. After Benton's retirement from Congress, he prepared and published his *Thirty Years' View*, a political history of the decades between 1820 and 1850 written from the viewpoint of an actor in the scenes described, with copious extracts from his own speeches and without special care to diminish the importance of his own influence. After this, though he was now past threescore and ten, he prepared his *Abridgment of the Debates of Congress from 1787 to 1856*, the last sentences of which he is said to have dictated in whispers from his deathbed.

Though only the most noteworthy persons have been spoken of in this chapter, enough has been said to indicate that in the first fifty years of the nineteenth century there was much good oratory and a large amount of able writing on subjects of political interest. As we look back on those decades, the years seem to be hurrying past with great rapidity, changing the primitive United States in the span of a single lifetime from a row of scattered republics scarcely realizing national existence into a great empire stretching across the continent. And in those hurrying years, all sorts of questions arose to be vehemently and earnestly discussed before an increasing number of eager hearers who felt that their destiny was in their own hands. These crowding problems full of intense human meaning; this developing democracy with all its trials, hopes, and determinations; this people, beset with slavery and boasting its freedom, bent upon the big job of taking possession of a continent and turning wilderness into farms and villages—these form the background of the oratory and the public tasks of the day. If no single piece of the very highest value in literature came out of the mêlée, we cannot wonder. And yet in the restless years there were men to be classed well up among the world's orators—for their themes were inspiring and a multitude was ready to hang upon their words. And in addition to all this product of earnest political strife and fervid declamation, is the fact, surprising, almost disconcerting, that the years produced jurists and publicists of erudition who quietly and methodically, amid all the hurry and change, framed the basic laws for a new nation, or, grasping essentials of older systems, gave them new life and form.

# CHAPTER XVI

# Webster

WE may take it for granted that Webster knew well how large a place he would fill in the history of his time. He was singularly free from small vanities and petty conceit but he was too great a man not to be conscious of his own intellectual power or of the part which he had played in his day and generation. His feeling about himself comes out in the famous passage of the Seventh of March speech when he asked: "What States are to secede? What is to remain American? What am I to be?" A remarkable question that last one! With the exception of Washington and Lincoln, who in our history could have solemnly put it forth in a public speech without being laughed at and ridiculed? Yet Webster uttered the words in a speech in the Senate, and a political opponent said that the tone of that question made him shudder as if some dire calamity were at hand. Laughter and ridicule fled before this naked assertion of a personality, and men not only shrank from the visions which it conjured up but accepted it as very solemn and entirely natural. The power of the orator was one reason, no doubt, for the impression, but the greatness of the man himself was the controlling cause.

Yet despite this just sense of his place in the history of his time and of his own greatness, Webster would have been profoundly surprised to find himself included as a marked figure in the history of our literature.[1] Except for a fragment of an autobiography and some private letters he never wrote anything in the literary sense. In his day public men did not turn to the newspaper or the magazine for an opportunity to express their views upon public questions. The age of pamphlets, so

[1] There are used here, with modifications, two or three passages from an address delivered by the writer at the unveiling of the Webster monument in Washington, 14 January, 1900.

much used by the framers of the Constitution and the founders of our government, had passed away. That of the magazine and the review had not arrived. Men in public life trusted to their speeches in Parliament or Congress or before the people, almost as in the days of Fox and Pitt, to make their arguments and opinions known, and they would have thought any other course hardly consistent with their dignity. Moreover, Webster did not give his leisure, as many statesmen have done, to writing memoirs or history or to the discussion in book form of some question which interested him. The reason was simple. When Webster was not in office or when he had an interval between the sessions of Congress, he gave his time to the practice of his profession, and great cases before the courts absorbed all his energy.[1]

[1] Daniel Webster was born in Salisbury [now Franklin], New Hampshire, 18 January, 1782, of pioneer stock. A frail child, and therefore spared the hard work of his father's farm, he was sent to Phillips Exeter Academy and to Dartmouth College, from which he graduated in 1801. He taught school as a makeshift, studied law, and was admitted to the bar in 1805. He practised first at Boscawen and then at Portsmouth, where he rapidly rose to prominence both as lawyer and public speaker. In 1813 he was sent to the House of Representatives as a Federalist member from Massachusetts, and thus came in close contact with Clay, then speaker, and Calhoun. Within a year Webster was a marked man in Congress. After four years, during which he struck many heavy blows at the administration, he resumed the practice of law. The great cases which he argued—the Dartmouth College Case, *M'Culloch v. Maryland, Gibbons v. Ogden, Ogden v. Saunders*—brought him into the first rank of American lawyers by the time he was forty. Meanwhile his reputation as the greatest American orator was built up by his oration at Plymouth in 1820, the Bunker Hill oration of 1825, and the speech in which he commemorated Adams and Jefferson in 1826. He returned to the House of Representatives in 1823 and in 1827 entered the Senate, in which he served till 1841.

Ever since 1800 Webster had been the exponent of a doctrine of nationalism which now made him the chief defender of the idea of union. His debate with Hayne of South Carolina in 1830, commonly called "The Great Debate," is a classic statement of the doctrine and the idea. For twenty years Webster was the voice of New England. He failed of election as President, but he had a notable, if brief, career as secretary of state under Harrison and Tyler, 1841–43, during which he concluded with Great Britain the important Webster-Ashburton Treaty. Once more in the Senate after 1845, Webster opposed the annexation of Texas and the Mexican War. As the struggle over slavery grew more violent he turned to the side of Clay and in the famous "Seventh of March Speech" defended Clay's Compromise Bill, with the result that he was bitterly denounced in the North as a renegade. The same year he became secretary of state again. He died under a kind of cloud, 24 October, 1852, but there can be little doubt that he, more than any other one man, contributed to the growth of that sentiment of union which sustained the national idea during the Civil War.—THE EDITORS.

He loved literature undoubtedly. He had been educated, both at school and at college, upon the old classical system, and it is obvious that he always retained his knowledge of Latin: in fact, he was a good Latin scholar. There is no evidence that he was a good Greek scholar or even kept up the Greek of his youth. He knew the history of Greece and Rome and much of modern history, but he was not a student of history, and this he realized. It is also apparent that he was fond of pure literature, and he never forgot at least the eighteenth century poets who were the standard poets of his youth. The story of his dispute with Rufus Choate over a quotation illustrates not his knowledge of Pope, which is unimportant, but his love of literature, which is significant. At a most exciting moment in the trial of a case very famous in its day, Webster was observed to write a few words upon a slip of paper and pass it to Choate. The spectators thought something very vital to the case was going on, but what Webster wrote was this:

> Lo! where Mæotis sleeps and softly flows
> The freezing Tanais through a waste of snows.

Choate wrote "wrong" on the slip and then:

> Lo! where Mæotis sleeps and *hardly* flows
> The freezing Tanais through a waste of snows.

Webster wrote "right" against his version and offered a bet. The volume of Pope containing *The Dunciad* was sent for, and it appeared that Choate was right. Webster wrote the words "Spurious Edition" on the book, and the consultation between the two great lawyers ended.

The fact, however, that in Johnson's phrase he had literature and loved it, although it tells us of the man, would not give him a place in literary history. Yet he has that place and his right to it rests and must rest upon his speeches, for speeches and addresses are all that Webster has left to us to prove his literary quality, and it very rarely happens that a literary reputation can be based upon speeches actually spoken and delivered. The reason for this rarity of speeches which give a title to a place in literature lies, if we pause to reflect upon it, in the very nature of the speech itself.

Charles Fox was the author of the famous aphorism that "no good speech ever read well." This is a declaration in epigrammatic form that the speech which is prepared like an essay and then read or recited, which, in other words, is primarily literature and not oratory, is not a thoroughly good speech, and of the soundness of the doctrine there can hardly be a doubt. But the theory, however valid, is not without its dangers. Charles Fox lived up to his own principle. He was, it may well be thought, the greatest of English orators at the moment of speech, but he is little read and seldom quoted now. What he actually said has faded from the minds of men despite its enchanting, its enormous effect at the moment. On the other hand, the speech which is literature before it is spoken is ineffective or only partially effective at the moment, and if it is read afterwards, however much we may enjoy the essay, we never mistake it for the genuine eloquence of the spoken word.

Macaulay is an example of this latter class, as Fox is of the former. Macaulay's speeches are essays, eloquent and rhetorical, but still essays—literature, and not speeches. He was listened to with interest and delight, but he was not a parliamentary debater or speaker of the first order. The highest oratory, therefore, must combine in exact balance the living force and freshness of the spoken word with the literary qualities which alone ensure endurance. The best examples of this perfection are to be found in the world of imagination, in the two speeches of Brutus and Mark Antony following the death of Cæsar. They are speeches and nothing else— one cool, stately, reasonable; the other a passionate, revolutionary appeal, hot from the heart and pouring from the lips with unpremeditated art, and yet they both have the literary quality, absolutely supreme in this instance, because Shakespeare wrote them.

It is not the preparation or even the writing out beforehand which makes a speech into an essay, for these things can both be done without detracting from the spontaneity, without dulling the sound of the voice which the wholly great speech must have, even on the printed page. The speech loses when the literary quality becomes predominant, and absolute success as high as it is rare comes only from the nice balance of the two essential ingredients. This balance and combination are found in Demosthenes and Isocrates, although one may venture to think that those two great masters, as they have come down to us, lean, if at all, too much to the literary side. In Cicero, although in matter and manner the best judges would rank him below the Greek masters, the combination is quite perfect. One of his most famous speeches, it is said, was never delivered at all, and none the less it is a speech and nothing else, instinct with life and yet with the impalpable literary feeling all through it, the perfect production of a very beautiful and subtle art. Among English orators Burke undoubtedly comes nearest to a complete union of the two qualities, and while the words of Fox and Pitt are unread and unquoted, except by historians, Burke's gorgeous sentences are recited and repeated and his philosophic discussion of great general principles are studied and admired by successive generations. Yet there is no doubt that Burke erred somewhat on the literary side, and we find the proof of this in the fact that he often spoke to empty benches, and that Goldsmith could say of him:

> Too deep for his hearers still went on refining,
> And thought of convincing while they thought of dining.

Burke was a literary man as well as an orator and a statesman; Webster, as has just been said, was not a literary man at all. He was an orator pure and simple; his speeches, good, bad, or indifferent, are speeches—never essays or anything but speeches—and yet upon all alike is the literary touch. In all, certainly in all the great speeches, is the fine literary quality, always felt, never seen, ever present, never obtrusive. He had the combination of Shakespeare's Brutus or Antony, of Demosthenes or Cicero, and when he rose to his greatest heights he reached a place beyond the fear of rivalry. The practical proof and exhibition of this fact is apparent if we turn to any serious and large debate in Congress, for there we shall find Webster quoted, as he is in every session, twenty times as often as any other public man in our history. He said many profound, many luminous, many suggestive things;

he was an authority on many policies and on the interpretation of the Constitution.  But there have been others of whom all this might be said—there were kings before Agamemnon—but they are rarely quoted, while Webster is quoted constantly. He had strong competitors in his own day and in his own field, able, acute, and brilliant men.  He rose superior to them, it appears, in his lifetime; and now that they are all dead Webster's words are familiar to hundreds while his rivals are little more than names.  So far as familiarity in the mouths of men goes, it is Eclipse first and the rest nowhere.  That which has made this possible is his rare combination of speech and literature; it is the literary quality, the literary savour which keeps what Webster said fresh, strong, and living. When we open the volumes of his speeches it is not like unrolling the wrappings of an Egyptian mummy, to find within a dry and shrivelled form, a faint perfume alone surviving faintly to recall the vanished days, as when

Some queen, long dead, was young.

Rather it is like the opening of Charlemagne's tomb, when his imperial successor started back before the enthroned figure of the great emperor looking out upon him, instinct with life under the red glare of the torches.

Let us apply another and surer test.  How many speeches to a jury in a criminal trial possessing neither political nor public interest survive in fresh remembrance seventy years after their delivery?  One can hardly think of jury speeches of any kind which stand this ordeal except, in a limited way, some few of Erskine's, and those all have the advantages of historical significance, dealing as they do with constitutional and political questions of great moment.  But there is one of Webster's speeches to a jury which lives to-day, and no more crucial test could be applied than the accomplishment of such a feat. The White murder case was simply a criminal trial, without a vestige of historical, political, or general public interest. Yet Webster's speech for the prosecution has been read and recited until well-nigh hackneyed.  It is in readers and manuals. and is still declaimed by schoolboys.  Some of its phrases are familiar quotations and have passed into general speech.  Let us recall a single passage:

He has done the murder. No eye has seen him; no ear has heard him. The secret is his own, and it is safe.

Ah, gentlemen, that was a dreadful mistake. Such a secret can be safe nowhere. The whole creation of God has neither nook nor corner where the guilty can bestow it and say it is safe. . . . A thousand eyes turn at once to explore every man, everything, every circumstance connected with the time and place; a thousand ears catch every whisper; a thousand excited minds intensely dwell on the scene, shedding all their light, and ready to kindle the slightest circumstance into a blaze of discovery. Meantime the guilty soul can not keep its own secret. It is false to itself; or, rather, it feels an irresistible impulse of conscience to be true to itself. It labours under its guilty possession, and knows not what to do with it. The human heart was not made for the residence of such an inhabitant. It finds itself preyed on by a torment which it dares not acknowledge to God or man. A vulture is devouring it, and it can ask no sympathy or assistance either from heaven or earth. The secret which the murderer possesses soon comes to possess him, and, like the evil spirits of which we read, it overcomes him and leads him whithersoever it will. He feels it beating at his heart, rising to his throat, and demanding disclosure. He thinks the whole world sees it in his face, reads it in his eyes, and almost hears its workings in the very silence of his thoughts. It has become his master. It betrays his discretion, it breaks down his courage, it conquers his prudence. When suspicions from without begin to embarrass him and the net of circumstance to entangle him, the fatal secret struggles with still greater violence to burst forth. It must be confessed; it will be confessed. There is no refuge from confession but suicide, and suicide is confession.

Those are words spoken to men, not written for them. It is a speech and nothing else, and yet we feel all through it the literary value and quality which make it imperishable. If now we go back to Webster's earlier days we can trace throughout his speeches, once he had escaped from the flowers of eloquence which burdened his youth, the literary touch appearing with increasing frequency until it came continually, quite naturally and without effort. As the sureness of the literary touch increased, so did the taste become refined until it was finally almost unerring.

The *Discourse*, as he called it, delivered at Plymouth in 1820 upon the two hundredth anniversary of the landing of the Pilgrims, was the first of the great occasional addresses which gave so much fame to Webster as an orator, wholly apart from that which he achieved in Congress or in the courts. It was evidently prepared with extreme care and has less of the effect of words actually spoken than his later work of the same character. The perfect combination of the literary quality with the spoken word, to which he afterwards attained, has not yet been reached. The Plymouth *Discourse* shows his wide knowledge of history, and the historical illustrations are given with an easy mastery of his subject and with a conciseness that saves him from the rambling digression which is at once the temptation and the danger of the historical parallel. There are also many passages which contain, in the manner of Burke, philosophical considerations of the science of government and which deal with the general principles affecting social and political problems. The history and philosophy are all eminently appropriate to his subject and to an address of that character. They give it weight, seriousness, and the permanence which lasts far beyond the moment of speech. The manner in which they are used and introduced is distinctly literary. But we also find in this address something more, the purely literary quality in the style and in the thought.

It is this literary quality which concerns us here, and to appreciate it we must mark the distinction, often a very narrow one, between the rhetorical and the literary. Rhetoric is of course in its place a branch of literature, but it may be of the utmost excellence and yet lack the highest literary quality. Rhetoric is out of place in purely literary work which is not dramatic in character. Yet curiously enough it is not misplaced in poetry. Rhetorical verse, although not the highest kind of poetry, may yet be in its own sphere very admirable indeed.

> You have the Pyrrhic dance as yet,
>   Where is the Pyrrhic phalanx gone?
> Of two such lessons, why forget
>   The nobler and the manlier one?
> You have the letters Cadmus gave—
> Think ye he meant them for a slave?

That is rhetorical poetry and it is very fine of its kind, very splendid even. Byron was a great master of rhetorical verse,

often too much so for his own good, but none the less the rhetoric is not out of place. On the other hand, to put rhetoric, except in dramatic passages, into literary prose is almost as bad as to write metred prose, of which Dickens was guilty in the description of the death of Little Nell. But when we come to giving the literary touch to rhetoric the exact reverse is the case. The rhetoric is at once lifted up and illuminated. The only objection is that the art is as rare as it is difficult, to be found in only a few great masters of speech in human history. It was precisely in this rare and difficult art that Webster excelled. His rhetoric was always unimpeachable, but his peculiar power lay in the fact that he was able to give to it with ever-increasing ease the imperishable literary quality.

We detect the first gleams of this beautiful art in the Plymouth oration. It is not necessary to take as an example the celebrated passage about the slave trade, where the rhetoric predominates; less familiar sentences prove the point. He is speaking of Rome:

Although the time might come, when darkness should settle on all her hills; when foreign or domestic violence should overturn her altars and her temples; when ignorance and despotism should fill the places where Laws, and Arts and Liberty had flourished; when the feet of barbarism should trample on the tombs of her consuls and the walls of her Senate-house and forum echo only to the voice of savage triumph.

A little farther on, speaking of the human love of home and birth-place, a well-worn theme, he says:

When the heart has laid down what it loved most, then it is desirous of laying itself down. No sculptured marble, no enduring monument, no honourable inscription, no ever burning taper that would drive away the darkness of the tomb, can soften our sense of the reality of death, and hallow to our feelings the ground which is to cover us, like the consciousness that we shall sleep, dust to dust, with the objects of our affections.

The thought in these passages is simple, oft-recurrent, entirely familiar, expressed by many other orators with great effect and received by genuinely moved audiences with much applause. The first time one looks upon them, if one could extricate them from the limbo of forgotten speeches, they might sound as well as Webster's words. But listen to them again, read them, and it will be found that Webster's sentences have a quality which all the others lack. Literature is interwoven with Webster's rhetoric, and it is this that preserves what he said from the forgetfulness which has overwhelmed others who in public speech have said the same things but just a little differently and without the magic literary touch.

Let us take one more example from his early days. In 1826, speaking in the House upon the Monroe Doctrine, Webster said:

I look on the message of December, 1823, as forming a bright page in our history. I will neither help to erase it or tear it out; nor shall it be by any act of mine blurred or blotted. It did honor to the sagacity of the government and I will not diminish that honor. It elevated the hopes and gratified the patriotism of the people. Over those hopes I will not bring a mildew; nor will I put that gratified patriotism to shame.

Rhetorically this passage is all that could be desired. The sentences are short, effective, possessing both balance and precision. But when we come to the last we find the literary touch. It is only one word, "mildew," but that single word is imaginative and strikes us at once. Leave it out and change the sentence slightly; the rhetoric remains excellent as before, but the whole effect is altered.

Let us take one or two other familiar passages from the later speeches when the style was perfected and when the literary quality had become a second nature. As Webster stood one summer morning on the ramparts of Quebec, and heard the sound of drums and saw the English troops on parade, the thought of England's vast world empire came strongly to his mind. The thought was very natural under the circumstances, not at all remarkable nor in the least original. Some years later, in a speech in the Senate, he put his thought into words, and this, as everyone knows, is the way he did it:

A power which has dotted over the surface of the whole globe with her possessions and military posts, whose morning drumbeat, following the sun and keeping company with the hours, circles the earth with one continuous and unbroken strain of the martial airs of England.

The sentence has followed the drumbeat round the world and has been repeated in England and in the antipodes by men who never heard of Webster and probably did not know that this splendid description of the British Empire was due to an American. It is not the thought which has carried these words so far through time and space. It is the beauty of the imagery and the magic of the style. Let me take one more very simple example of the quality which distinguishes Webster's speeches above those of others, which makes his words and serious thoughts live on when others, equally weighty and serious, perhaps, sleep or die. In his first Bunker Hill oration he apostrophized the monument, just as anyone else might have tried to do, and this is what he said:

Let it rise, let it rise till it meet the sun in his coming; let the earliest light of morning gild it, and parting day linger and play on its summit.

Here the thought is nothing, the style everything. No one can repeat those words and be deaf to their music or insensible to the rhythm and beauty of the prose with the Saxon words relieved just sufficiently by the Latin derivatives. The ease with which it is done may be due to training, but the ability to do it comes from natural gifts which, as Goethe says, "we value more as we get older because they can not be stuck on." Possibly to some people it may seem very simple to utter such a sentence. One can only repeat what Scott says somewhere about Swift's style, perhaps the purest and strongest we have in the language. "Swift's style," said Scott, "seems so simple that one would think any child might write as he does, and yet if we try we find to our despair that it is impossible."

It is not easy to say how much Webster's literary art was due to intentional cultivation and how far it was purely instinctive. Undoubtedly he had a natural gift as certainly as he had an ear for the arrangement and cadence of words; but we know that he cared for style and had strong preferences in the choice of the words he used to express his thought. We have the right to infer, therefore, that he was quite aware of the art which he practised so admirably. The highly conscious art which we see in Sterne, or in Walter Pater in our own time, to take two examples at random, and which is so effective in its results, is not apparent in Webster. He would probably not have been one of the greatest of orators if it had been, for then the writer would have absorbed the speaker. We are conscious of his art, although he does not seem to be conscious of it himself. Yet, however much we may speculate as to the proportions of intentional art and of unaided natural gifts in the style of all he said, there can be no question that he possessed and had mastered the rare combination which confers the lasting quality of literature upon the speech without losing the living force of the written word. It is this most rare achievement which gives to Webster, who never wrote book or essay or verse, his uncontested place in the history of American literature.

# CHAPTER XVII

# Writers on American History, 1783--1850[1]

THE Revolutionary War gave our historians new motives for writing. A glorious struggle was to be described; the states, just raised out of the rank of colonies, began to demand the preservation of their earliest history; and the nation, inspired by great hopes for the future, felt that it must have loyal men to prepare the record of common growth and common achievement. The men who responded to these impulses were, perhaps, less cultured than the best of the old historians. It was long before there appeared among them one who could be ranked with Hutchinson, though some of them wrote well and displayed great industry. The stream was wider than formerly, but it was not so deep.

Of those who wrote about the Revolution, in one phase or another, the best were the Rev. William Gordon, Dr. David Ramsay, William Henry Drayton, General William Moultrie, John Marshall, and William Wirt. Less scholarly but more widely influential were Mrs. Mercy Warren and "Parson" Weems.

Gordon, who was born in England, preached at Roxbury, Massachusetts, from 1770 to 1786. He was an active Whig, and after his return to England he wrote in four volumes a history of the Revolution (1788), which was widely read by the English, and in America was honoured with a pirated edition and long extracts in the newspapers. We now know that Gordon copied freely from *The Annual Register*, of which the parts dealing with America were at that time written by Edmund Burke. It is even charged that Gordon tempered his

---

[1] For a more extended treatment of the historians of the period, see the author's *Middle Group of American Historians* (1917).

narrative to please the feelings of his friends in England.  His book is but slightly esteemed.  Dr. Ramsay (1749–1815), of South Carolina, though educated to be a physician, was more a politician and *littérateur* than a scientist.  His *History of the Revolution of South Carolina* (1785) and *History of the American Revolution* (1789) were well received by an uncritical generation.  It remained for a later age to discover that the second of these books, long accepted as an original work, was largely drawn from *The Annual Register*.  Drayton and Moultrie were prominent South Carolinians, one a political and the other a military defender of the Whig cause.  Each wrote an excellent account of what he had seen in his own state.  Marshall[1] and Wirt[2] were Virginia lawyers who thought it their duty to portray the lives of two great men of the Revolution. From the first we have the *Life of Washington* (1804–07) in five volumes, a heavy book without literary style and smacking of Federalist opinions.  It displeased the followers of Jefferson but had a wide circulation among those who did not agree with the great Republican leader.  For posterity it has value chiefly as a solid source of information.  Wirt's *Life of Patrick Henry* (1817) is much unlike Marshall's book.  It was well written—Wirt had a polished style—but it was a hasty and inadequate picture of a most important life.  A better but less readable biography was William Tudor's *Life of James Otis* (1823).

Mrs. Mercy Otis Warren (1728–1814),[3] a sister of James Otis, was the wife of James Warren of Boston.  Her three-volume *History of the American Revolution* (1805), a loosely written book which contained many biographical sketches, was popular and for a long time furnished the average New Englander his knowledge of the Revolution.  Five years earlier had appeared the most successful historical book of the day, Weems's *Life of Washington*.  The author was a versatile man, who could be buffoon, fiddler, parson, or hawker of his book as occasion demanded.  He had not known Washington, but he created the impression that he wrote from personal knowledge by announcing himself as "formerly Rector of Mt. Vernon Parish."  The book was a romance, interlarded with pious

---

[1] See also Book II, Chap. xv.       [2] See also Book II, Chaps. i and iii.
[3] See also Book I, Chap. ix, and Book II. Chap. ii.

stories. It was slightly esteemed by educated men of the day but was acceptable to the unsophisticated. Except as a curiosity, it is beneath contempt or criticism.

Of the state histories that appeared in this period a few are worthy of mention. Jeremy Belknap (1744–98) wrote a *History of New Hampshire* (three volumes, 1784–92), which is of the first rank in our historical compositions. Had its theme been more extended, it would have become a household memory in the country. Benjamin Trumbull's (1735–1820) *History of Connecticut* (2 vols., 1818) and Robert Proud's (1728–1813) *History of Pennsylvania* (2 vols., 1797–98) were of scholarly standards but heavy in style. George Richards Minot (1758–1802), a brilliant Massachusetts lawyer, wrote a *History of the Insurrection in Massachusetts* (1788), dealing with Shays' Rebellion, and followed it by a continuation of Hutchinson's *History of Massachusetts* (2 vols., 1798–1803). The books were well written and have maintained their credit. Here should be mentioned Henry M. Brackenridge's (1786–1871) *History of the Western Insurrection* (1817), a fair-minded narrative of the Whisky Insurrection, which was very popular and ran through several editions. Three Southern books which may here be spoken of are hardly up to the standard of the state histories. Dr. Ramsay's *History of South Carolina* (2 vols., 1809) was not equal to his work on the Revolution. John D. Burk (d. 1808) wrote a less valuable work in his *History of Virginia* (3 vols., 1804–05).[1] He was an ardent Republican who rhapsodized on liberty. Dr. Hugh Williamson (1735–1819), who wrote a *History of North Carolina* (2 vols., 1812), was a Pennsylvanian by birth, clergyman and physician by education, merchant and politician by necessity. He lived a while in Edenton, North Carolina, was elected a member of the Continental Congress, and served in the Constitutional Convention. In 1793 he removed to New York, where he acquired a high reputation for learning. His history, however, was thin and disappointing.

These men worked under the disadvantage that they were writing at a time when the minds of the people were absorbed with the struggle for national existence. Ebenezer Hazard, in 1779, described the situation as follows:

---

[1] After his death the book was continued in a fourth volume.

The war and the numerous avocations consequent upon it, have thrown every man's mind into such an unsettled and confused state that but few can think steadily upon any subject. They hear of useful designs, they give you all the encouragement which can be derived from the warmest approbation of your plan, they will even promise you assistance. Politics intrude,—kick you and your designs out of their heads; and when you appear again, why they really forgot that the matter had been mentioned to them. I have been repeatedly served so with reference to my collection.[1]

After the war came the years of constitution-making, and then a long period during which foreign affairs occupied most minds exclusively. It was a time, also, when unusual business opportunities enthralled the best intellects in the country. Thus there were few competent persons to whom the quiet task of writing history made appeal. It is not strange that Hazard had few people to encourage him.

Our post-Revolutionary period has been compared with the years following the French Revolution, in which there was a notable outburst of literary activity. The contrast is unfair. The French Revolution came upon an old and well-developed society, kept down by outworn social ideals, and when it had passed the shackles were broken. In the United States an immature society was relieved of the power that had hitherto done no more than impose irritating checks on its development. This wilful young people were given an opportunity to do as they pleased. They had no rich culture waiting to fill a new era with its splendour. They were fighting their way up from the bottom, and the process was necessarily slow.

A third group of historians was those who undertook to write general histories of the United States. They were inspired with the spirit of nationality, whatever their views of the new Union. They wished to depict the relations of the colonies to one another and their struggle against Britain's policy of strict control. The first histories presenting a general account of the colonies came from England, where as early as 1708 John Oldmixon, in his *British Empire in America*, made a sorry attempt to treat English America as a whole. In 1780 George Chalmers published his *Political Annals of the*

[1] "The Belknap Papers," *Mass. Hist. Soc. Col.*, 5th Ser., vol. II, p. 12.

*Present United Colonies*, followed in 1782 by another work called *Introduction to the History of the Revolt of the American Colonies*. Chalmers was an able writer and gave at least continuity to his subject. He was, however, strongly British in sympathy, and his work was not esteemed in the United States. It stimulated more than one American to write what he considered a true history of the rise and progress of the Revolutionary struggle.

Of the Americans who undertook to do the same thing, and to do it in a spirit more friendly to the cause of America, the first man worthy of notice here was the Rev. Abiel Holmes (1763–1837), whose *American Annals* (2 vols., 1805) represented much accurate and careful work. It marked the author as a man of scientific mind, worthy of equal respect with his son, the delightful Autocrat. The next to take up the task was Benjamin Trumbull, whose history of Connecticut has already been mentioned. He planned to write a history of the United States in three volumes and prepared for it by collecting many documents. The first and only volume, published in 1810, carried the narrative to the year 1765. Accuracy of statement and a spiritless style are the chief characteristics of the work.

Somewhat later came Timothy Pitkin's (1766–1847) *Political and Civil History of the United States* (2 vols., 1828). The author was a man of great industry and painstaking care. He had a fancy for statistical knowledge, and wrote also a valuable *Statistical View of the Commerce of the United States* (1817). His political history has the merits and the demerits to be expected in a statistician. Although it is marked by accuracy and a just sense of industrial development, its style is disjointed and difficult. Pitkin strove for fairness, but he saw the history of the country as a man of New England would see it. His own section bulked large in his treatment, and he did not get the point of view of the rest of the Union.

Twenty-one years after Pitkin's book was published, New England found a still abler and more satisfying historian in Richard Hildreth (1807–65), who in 1849 gave to the world the first three volumes of his *History of the United States;* three more appeared in 1852. The six volumes cover the years 1492 to 1821. For the lover of entertaining literature the book is a failure, but for one who enjoys a solid presentation of facts it has merit. Few other men have written down so many statements of fact in so small a compass with such great reliability. In the preface Hildreth said that he wished to describe the fathers of the nation as they were,

unbedaubed with patriotic rouge, wrapped up in no fine-spun cloaks of excuses and apologies, without stilts, buskins, tinsel, or bedizzenment, in their own proper persons, often rude, hard, narrow, superstitious and mistaken, but always earnest, downright, manly, and sincere. The result of their labours is eulogy enough; their best apology is to tell the story as it was.

There can be no doubt that the author tried in all honesty to carry out his purpose. "We encounter [in Hildreth]," said *The Edinburgh Review*, "the muse of American history descended from her stump, and recounting her narrative in a key adapted to our own ears."

An historian who did not liberate himself entirely from patriotic bias was John Gorham Palfrey (1798–1881). Although he falls slightly without the limits of time assigned to this chapter, he was by nature and purpose a member of what has been called the "filio-pietistic" group. Bred a Unitarian minister, and pastor for a time of Brattle Square Church, Boston, he served as Dexter Professor of Sacred Literature in Harvard University (1830–39). From 1836 to 1843 he was editor of *The North American Review*. He held several political offices in his State, and was a member of Congress in 1847–49. From 1861 to 1867 he was postmaster of Boston. He wrote many tracts, religious, political, and historical. Nevertheless, he kept true to his love for the history of New England. In 1858–64 he brought out in three volumes a *History of New England during the Stuart Dynasty*. It won instant recognition and the author followed up his success with two more volumes, *History of New England from the Revolution of the 17th Century to the Revolution of the 18th* (1875–90). The two parts were later shorn of their most irrelevant passages and issued as a *Compendious History of New England* in four handy volumes. So far as the mere statement of facts goes, it is safe to say that Palfrey has given us a complete and sufficient history of colonial New England. He has not been careless or slothful. But to Palfrey all that New Englanders did and thought was good. He did not question the spirit of Puritanism, and he did not find its narrowness unpleasant; he accepted it as a thing of course. He was the last of the complacent defenders of the old régime in the land of Bradford and Winthrop. Before he had retired from the scene Charles Francis Adams's severe blows were beginning to tell.

Over against these books from the North we must place a Southern history, the existence of which was due to the belief that the South had not received fair consideration at the hands of men who knew little about its life and natural environment. Such a book was George Tucker's (1775–1861) *History of the United States* (4 vols., 1856–58), which carried the story of the national development to the year 1841. The author was a lawyer in Virginia, a well-known and voluminous writer on political subjects. His *History* was not an extreme Republican book, as some have thought. It represented the ideas which one would expect from a conservative Virginian of the old school; it was well written, but not brilliant. Had it been offered to a section more accustomed to reading history, it would have been recognized as a standard book of its kind; as it is, it is known chiefly for the impression it made on those who held views it was intended to counteract. Tucker[1] wrote also a *Life of Thomas Jefferson* (2 vols., 1837), probably the best of the early lives of this statesman.

The last of the general historians who fall within this chapter's limits is George Bancroft, who, during his lifetime, held a larger place in the minds of his countrymen than any other historian who has lived in the United States. This he did partly because of his literary worth, partly because of his political activity, and partly because of his social prominence. President Arthur once said that the President is "permitted to accept the invitations of members of the cabinet, supreme court judges, and—Mr. George Bancroft."

Bancroft was born in Massachusetts in 1800 and died in Washington in 1891. Having graduated from Harvard in 1817, he went to Göttingen on funds subscribed by Harvard and its friends. Back in America in 1822 with a doctor's degree, he settled for a year at Harvard as tutor in Greek. He brought

[1] See also Book II, Chap. VII.

home from Europe many affectations of manner and such marked eccentricities that his influence at Harvard was under-mined; at the end of a year he left, to become, with Joseph G. Cogswell, proprietor of a boys' school at Northampton, Massa-chusetts. As a schoolmaster Bancroft was a failure, and he retired from the school in 1831. Meanwhile, he had begun to write. School-books, translations, and articles for *The North American Review* came out in rapid succession. By 1831 he had established the literary habit and had the reputa-tion of being a ready and effective writer.

At this time Bancroft had begun to support the Democratic party. He was accused of doing it to obtain Federal office, but the charge was not substantiated. He was ever a de-fender of the doctrine of equality held by Jefferson, Jack-son, and Lincoln. In America he saw organized democracy which was to make humanity happy: to write its history be-came his hope. In 1834 appeared the first volume of his *History of the United States from the Discovery of the American Continent*. At the time neither Hildreth nor Tucker had written, and only Pitkin, Holmes, and Trumbull had under-taken a task like his. They were all didactic. Bancroft produced a work of a different character. There was a lofty and sonorous sense of detachment in his sentences. To the present age they seem sheer affectation; but to the men who had been reading the bald statements of fact hitherto offered as history, they seemed admirable. Edward Everett read the first volume through in twenty-four hours and wrote:

I think you have written a Work which will last while the memory of America lasts; and which will instantly take its place among the classics of our language. It is full of learning, informa-tion, common sense, and philosophy; full of taste and eloquence; full of life and power. You give us not wretched paste-board men; not a sort of chronological table, with the dates written out at length, after the manner of most historians;—but you give us real, individual, living, men and women, with their passions, inter-ests, and peculiarities.

Theodore Parker wrote: "I think you are likely to make, what I long since told you I looked for from *you*, the most noble and splendid piece of historical composition, not only in English, but in any tongue." Emerson said of the *History:* "It is noble matter, and I am heartily glad to have it nobly treated." Bancroft is less than a quarter of a century dead, and these beautiful laurels are already withered. A new age has accepted other standards than his.

Bancroft, our first historian who had studied in Germany, was well known at home and abroad as a hard student and a man of great learning. The abundant foot-notes in the first volumes of his history show how freely he used the sources in foreign languages. His experience in Germany led him to admire German scholarship in all its phases. At Göttingen he studied under Heeren, who was stressing the unity of history. In the preface of his first volume, Bancroft wrote: "The United States of America constitute an essential portion of a great political system, embracing all the political nations of the earth." He did not, however, try to work out this theory in his volume, but told, like others, the story of voyages, settlements, colonies, and the common struggle for freedom.

His progress was leisurely. The second volume appeared three years after the first, the third in 1840. The fourth and fifth were published in 1852. The sixth came in 1854, the seventh in 1858, the eighth in 1860, the ninth in 1866, and the tenth in 1874. During these years his literary work was interrupted by political service. He was secretary of the navy from 1845 to 1846, minister to Great Britain from 1846 to 1849, and minister to Germany from 1867 to 1874. The tenth volume carried the work to the end of the Revolution; but in 1882 came two additional volumes with the title *History of the Formation of the Constitution of the United States.* Hildreth wrote more rapidly, and his *History,* nearly as long as Bancroft's, seems to have been written in six years.

Another group of men, by collecting materials, compiling, and editing, rendered marked service to history in the first half of the nineteenth century. Beginning to collect for their own comfort they laid the foundations of great collections which have endured and grown and are now indispensable. The men who did this work are not to be forgotten; they were as truly servants of the historic muse as those who held her stylus.

Of the efforts of Prince and Hutchinson as early collectors of documents mention has already been made.[1] After the Revolution the first activity of that kind was due to the interest of Ebenezer Hazard (1744–1817) and Jeremy Belknap. Born the same year, they both graduated from college in 1762. Becoming fast friends, they left to posterity a correspondence which gives us our best glimpse of the conditions under which historical writing went forward in the two decades after the war.

Hazard first of the two began to collect documents. In 1777 he was appointed surveyor of post-roads and in 1782 postmaster-general. As surveyor he travelled over many parts of the country. He thus had opportunity to copy historical documents, and formed the design of publishing a documentary history of the Revolution. He rightly thought it a proper time to make collections of papers which otherwise would be lost. Congress gave him permission to take copies of such papers as were in its hands, free of expense of copying, and voted one thousand pounds for his expenses in securing copies elsewhere. This particular scheme was not realized, and there is no evidence that Hazard used the money voted. Dismissed from the office of postmaster-general in 1789 to make room for a politician, he soon afterwards announced a work with the title *Historical Collections, State Papers, and Other Authentic Documents;* and in 1792 the first volume was published. It contained papers, many of them very rare, relating to the American colonies before 1660. In 1794 came Volume II, most of it given up to the records of the New England Confederation. The two volumes did not pay expenses, and the editor, absorbed in business, lost interest in their continuation. Judged by what he published merely, Hazard had only a moderate influence on history in the United States. It is as the first collector and editor of documents after the Revolution that we must estimate him. He had the notion, shared by Sparks and Force in a later period, that it is possible to present the history of a people in a collection of documents. It was his failure to satisfy the general reader with such a collection that caused Hazard's publication to remain unsold, and to be a source of discouragement to its compiler.

[1] See Book I, Chap. II.

Hazard influenced the work of Belknap, who, as a minister in Dover, New Hampshire, from 1767 to 1778, early became interested in the history of the colony and began to collect documents relating to it. In this task he was aided by Governor Benning Wentworth. Though Belknap had doubts about the propriety of a minister's dabbling in history, the inclination was too strong to be resisted; and receiving encouragement from his friends, he proceeded as he had begun. In 1784 he published the first volume of his *History of New Hampshire*. Financially it was as great a failure as Hazard's *Collections*. It was many years before he sold enough copies to pay the printer, but, unlike Hazard, Belknap was not discouraged. Having resigned his parish at Dover, after a disagreeable wrangle over his salary, in the following year he accepted a call to the church in Federal Street, Boston. From this time history became a chief phase of his activity. He was in the midst of a congenial group of educated men, and one literary demand after another was made on him. The editors of magazines appealed to him for articles; whatever co-operative work of history was projected—and there were several—he was sought for the enterprise. In 1792 he published Volumes II and III of his *History of New Hampshire*. The sales were large enough to wipe out the debts incurred by the first volume.

To *The Columbian Magazine* of Philadelphia he contributed from time to time a number of very well prepared biographical sketches of persons associated with the early history of America; and in 1794 they appeared in Volume I of an *American Biography*. Other sketches came out in a second volume (1798). A third was planned, but the author died before it could be written. These sketches were based on the best sources then available and were written in the author's best style. For the same magazine Belknap also wrote a series of satirical letters dealing with the early history of New England. They were published in a separate volume called *The Foresters* (1792), enlarged in an edition of 1796. Belknap died suddenly, in the midst of literary schemes, in 1798. He was the best American historian of his day, and the most zealous in preserving historical memorials.

Probably Belknap's greatest service was his efforts in founding the Massachusetts Historical Society. While he had valuable aid from other men, he was the force that brought these others together; and until the time of his death he was the leader in the actual work of the society. Belknap himself said that he got the idea from John Pintard of New York. The project was launched in 1791, in accordance with plans prepared by Belknap. The membership was limited to thirty corresponding and thirty resident members, only ten of the latter being elected at first. The object was to collect, preserve, and publish historical materials. As long as he lived Belknap was a most active member, visiting nearby towns for document, supervising the publications, and finally leaving the Society his own manuscripts.

One of the friends of Belknap and Hazard—and a connection of Hazard's by marriage—was Jedidiah Morse (1761–1826), minister at Charlestown, Massachusetts. He was the author of the first American geography (1789), a book containing much more than mere geographical description. To gather the accounts of natural resources, means of communication, and statistics the author made many journeys. He also collected facts for his *Annals of the American Revolution* (1824), a compilation which posterity does not esteem highly. But it served its day, and was for a time widely read. Morse was probably indebted to Hazard and Belknap for the impetus that set him to writing. The latter complained that it was only Morse who could make money out of what he wrote.

When Morse published his thin work, two other men, Jared Sparks and Peter Force, were planning much greater enterprises. One was a New England man, a Harvard graduate, a minister of accepted standing, and a member of the most select literary circle of Boston. The other was a self-taught printer's boy who became publisher and editor, with a passion for collecting. Each served well the cause of historical research.

Jared Sparks was born at Willington, Connecticut, in 1789. His youth was clouded by misfortune, but his intellectual ability brought him into notice, and friends sent him to college. He took a high rank at Harvard, where he was looked upon as a man of great promise. A residence of four years in the South as a Unitarian minister in Baltimore gave Sparks a national feeling and probably stimulated his interest in national history.

In 1823 he returned to Boston to be the editor of *The North American Review*.   This journal was then languishing under the editorship of Edward Everett, but Sparks secured control and placed it on a sound basis.   In 1830, when he sold his last remaining share in the enterprise, he had received $19,000 besides an annual salary of $2200.

Sparks gave up the *Review* to devote himself to history. As early as 1824 he formed a plan to produce a complete edition of Washington's writings.   He intended to write history that paid and did not think it discreditable to have an eye on the popular demand.   In 1826 and 1827 he made journeys through the original thirteen states collecting materials from unpublished documents.    In 1828 and 1829 he visited Europe and was given access to the British and French archives.   By this time he was full of enthusiasm.   "I have got a passion for Revolutionary history," he said, "and the more I look into it the more I am convinced that no complete history of the American Revolution has been written." At this time he was full of schemes, each connected with the Revolution, and several works came out of them.   But always in the back of his mind lay the plan of a great documentary history of the Revolution. While preparing the edition of Washington he learned from President John Quincy Adams that in 1818 Congress had appropriated money to publish the foreign correspondence of the Continental Congress during the Revolution.   Adams was then too busy to give the matter his attention, and nothing was done about it.   Sparks caught at the suggestion that he should take it up, and he made an agreement with Secretary Clay by which he was to print and sell to Congress one thousand copies of this correspondence at $2.12½ a copy and to have $400 a volume for copying and editing.   The work was done in eighteen months and for the entire set of twelve volumes the editor received $30,300.   As his chief expense was for printing and translations, his net earnings must have been considerable.   In the following year (1830), he proposed to Secretary Van Buren that the work be continued through the period of the Continental Congress.   Van Buren agreed, and Congress passed the necessary act, but at the last moment the new secretary of state, Edward Livingston, made the contract with Frank P. Blair.   Livingston blandly admitted that Sparks should have had the appointment but said that Blair's selection was demanded by the politicians.

The writings of Washington now occupied Sparks's time, but before they began to appear he brought out *The Life of Gouverneur Morris* (1832), in three volumes. In 1834 appeared Volume II of *The Life and Writings of George Washington*, and the rest of the twelve volumes followed regularly until the series was complete in 1837. The last to appear was the biography, the first volume in the set. The general verdict of the day was that it was a work worthy of the exalted subject. From 1836 to 1840 was published *The Works of Benjamin Franklin*, in ten volumes, and between 1834 and 1838 came the first series, and between 1844 and 1847 the second series, of *The Library of American Biography*, in all twenty-five volumes. In 1853 he issued *The Correspondence of the American Revolution*, a series of letters to Washington in four volumes.

Sparks's letters are full of his greater plan, and he recurred to the idea again and again until he was an old man, but he did not carry out his purpose. In fact, Sparks suffered an eclipse about 1840. After that date he did little besides editing the second series of the *American Biography* and writing several pamphlets and addresses. From 1838 to 1849 he was professor of history at Harvard, but the conditions were such that he had more than half his time for writing. From 1849 to 1853 he was Harvard's president, retiring to do literary work. It is hard to explain the paucity of results during these last years without assuming that he had lost his zeal after the achievement of his first great work, the Washington cycle. He died in 1866.

As a historian Sparks is to be measured by the *American Biography*, the best work of the kind then prepared. Even here his chief service was as an editor; for he wrote comparatively few of the individual sketches. Those he did write, however, were well done. His greatest editorial achievement was the *Washington*, an epoch-making work. It set a new standard of scholarship, founded upon accurate and broad knowledge, for American students of history. Edward Everett spoke truly when he said of it in *The North American Review:* "The American press has produced no work of higher value."

But Sparks had serious faults. In 1833 he sent Judge Story a specimen volume of his work accompanied by manuscript copies of the letters in it. Story could thus see in what respects liberties had been taken with the texts. He said in reply:

> There is not an instance in which you have failed to give the identical sense with more accuracy and clearness [than in the original]. You have done exactly what I think Washington would have desired you to do, if he were living. I cannot, therefore, in any manner object to it on my own account.

But he added that he feared the critics would take objections to the changes of literary form. Had the hint been taken, Sparks's reputation as an editor would be higher.

The editor's Nemesis at length overtook him. In 1847 appeared the *Life and Correspondence of Joseph Reed*, containing many letters from Washington to Reed, his secretary. The editor had printed them as they were sent by the author. The public now had two copies of certain letters, one published by Sparks and one by Reed. Sharp eyes soon discovered discrepancies, and Sparks was charged in the press with correcting, embellishing, and altering to suit his own purposes letters which should have been reproduced literally. In 1851 Lord Mahon's *History of England* reached its sixth volume, in which an appendix repeated the charges. Then followed a long controversy in which Sparks was put to his mettle to defend himself. It is known that Washington in his old age corrected many of his letters which he had kept in letter books. Sparks sought excuse in saying that this indicated that Washington wished all his letters revised, and that he had merely done what Washington himself would have done. Needless to say, this excuse did not satisfy the critics. The controversy probably served a good turn to scholarship. Coming in connection with the first great work of editing in the field of American history, it attracted wide attention, and fixed in the minds of scholars the necessity of accurate reproduction of documents. It should be said for Sparks that many others of his time thought that an editor ought to correct the letters he reproduced. Exact reproduction, however, had become the rule with the best editors.

when the material for the fourth volume was submitted, he refused to approve it in any part. To Force he said: "I do not believe in your work, sir! It is of no use to anybody. I never read a page of it and never expect to." Neither he nor his successor, Lewis Cass, could be induced to change this decision, and *The American Archives* came to an end with Volume III of the fifth series, nine volumes in all having been issued.

In 1832 Force thought the series would contain not more than five volumes, eleven years later it was limited to twenty, but when nine had been published the story of the Revolution had been carried only to the end of 1776. At this rate it would have taken over thirty volumes to bring the story to the treaty of peace; and if it had been limited to twenty it must have been left incomplete. One other fact may have aroused Marcy's disapprobation. By 1855 each Congress had formed the habit of ordering copies of the work for its own members not previously in the House, a species of graft unlikely to be terminated by Congress itself. On the other hand, it is undeniable that Marcy did not appreciate Force's work and that he was illiberal, if not narrow-minded.

Early in the series Force adopted the following division of the matter bearing on the period any given volume was to cover: (1) The proceedings, papers, and correspondence of the Continental Congress; (2) The proceedings, papers, and correspondence of the assemblies, conventions, and councils of safety of the several states; (3) The proceedings, papers, and correspondence of the British Government and of the officers acting under it in our Revolution; (4) Miscellaneous letters and papers relating to the Revolution. This material was presented with accuracy and completeness, but poorly arranged, and with very few editorial notes. The indexes in the fourth series were inadequate, but the deficiency was remedied in the fifth.

After the rejection of his work Force continued in Washington, completing his collections and putting them into shape for publication, if fortune should bring the opportunity. The outbreak of the war removed the last hope of this kind. In 1867 he was too old to complete his task, and sold his library to the Government for $100,000. It contained 22,529 printed volumes, about 40,000 pamphlets, some valuable newspaper files, and enough transcripts to make 129 bound volumes. The collection was placed in the Library of Congress, where Force's manuscripts remain unpublished. In 1879 Congress called for a report on the value of the collection, and received a lucid statement from the Librarian of Congress. No practical results followed.[1]

Aside from the *Archives* Force is best remembered for four volumes of *Tracts* published from 1836 to 1846. They were mostly reprints of rare pamphlets relating to the earliest period of American history, and their publication was accomplished with financial sacrifices. "Whenever I found a little more money in my purse than I absolutely needed," he said, "I printed a volume of *Tracts*." Several pamphlets of his own composition were also published, none of them of much importance. They serve to show us how little of an author he was.

Bancroft and Sparks collected documents, and Sparks published documents, but each was an historian first of all. Force collected documents and published them, without a thought of editing or interpreting them. If his great work had been more discreetly conducted, it might have weathered the storm of popular criticism. But Force was not discreet. In all the confusion around him he never relaxed an inch in his plan of making a complete and all-inclusive collection.

Force has had no successor, probably because his example raised up such a large school of local collectors and compilers that there has been no room for one vast treasure. The work he did not do has been carried on by many workers and has resulted in many restricted collections. Force played a large part in awakening the interest of this group; and in doing so he contributed much to the progress of American historical scholarship in the last fifty years, its latest and most fruitful period.

[1] For a discussion of the value of Force's collection see Bassett, *Middle Group of American Historians*, p. 298.

# CHAPTER XVIII

# Prescott and Motley

## I. PRESCOTT

TO write, his first resolve; to select a topic, his second—herein lies a cardinal difference between William Hickling Prescott (1796–1859) and the typical research student who only at last commits the results of his labours to paper. Not that Prescott plunged into his task without preparation. His self-training was long and minute, but the methods were so exceptional as to be well worth noting in some detail.

Prescott's choice of a career was hampered at the outset by defective eyesight and fragile health. A seemingly trivial incident had left a permanent mark upon his life. When he was a junior at Harvard, a crust of bread thrown by one of a careless group of skylarking students hit Prescott in the very disk of the left eye, the blow being so sudden that the lid did not have time to protect its charge. The victim's whole system received a nervous shock. Later it was discovered that the one eye was destroyed and that the sight of the other could be preserved only by assiduous watchfulness. Prescott was able, however, to complete his college course, and maintained his standing so well that he received the appointment as Latin poet at Commencement and amidst applause delivered his hexameters *Ad Spem*. That was in August, 1814. He had all that a young Bostonian of a century ago could wish for, except health. He was handsome, with good and sound inheritance, cultivated surroundings, sympathetic and congenial parents and well-to-do family circumstances, and he was as well equipped for intellectual life as Harvard could make him. But ill-health barred the way to active life. All the capacity for work, for the steady occupation that enriched forty years of quiet student pursuits, had to be resolutely wooed. What was won needed careful husbanding to ensure the maximum return for the minimum nerve expenditure. But, shackled by physical limitations as he was, Prescott was fortunate in not being a prisoner of poverty. His was a case where an assured income made the labour he delighted in physic pain and then grow profitable in its turn. Far from the harvest he wanted, he was able to gather expensive source material without financial limitations.

Seven years after graduation, Prescott was still on the eve of setting himself to serious work within his capacity. By that date he had been married a year to Susan Amory, found in the circle of cultivated, prosperous Bostonians in which the Prescotts moved, and he was wonderfully fortunate in his wife. She was a splendid comrade for her husband in the sheltered life that had to be his lot. Prescott's early ventures at travelling, while they gave him a little experience of life in the Azores and slight glimpses of England and Paris, proved conclusively that changes exposed him to the risk of incapacitating suffering, though with favourable conditions he might exert himself to good effect. Thus it was, in 1821, that he decided to take up his pen as an occupation. Very deliberately he proceeded to examine the tools of expression that were ready to his hand. He found them very defective. He had no well-based accurate knowledge of English, let alone modern languages. Accordingly, on 30 October, 1821, he planned a preliminary course to lay accurate foundations for a literary career. Blair's *Rhetoric*, Lindley Murray, the introductory chapter of Johnson's *Dictionary* were studied as though the student were a small schoolboy instead of a Harvard graduate of seven years standing. At the same time he ploughed through a long course of English literature. Ascham, Bacon, Browne, Raleigh, and Milton, besides the sermons of eminent divines, were read to him in chronological series, while he used his own sight for an hour of Latin daily. At the end of the year he felt he had broken ground only. A temporary improvement in his eye enabled him to plunge into French authors from Froissart to Chateaubriand, still devoting a part of eacn day to hearing English drama from Heywood to Dryden. With his friend Ticknor, Prescott kept up a third line of English reading, connected with Scandinavian and Teutonic themes and compositions. In 1823, Sismondi's *Littérature du Midi* prepared him for Italian letters, which he proceeded to explore systematically and intelligently. Two articles in *The North American Review* contained his impressions on this field; they were written *con amore*, as the change from French to Italian had been to him especially stimulating and refreshing. The latter language was far more to his taste than the former. German was his next desire, but it had to be abandoned as too difficult for his partial eyesight. Then, through Ticknor's interest in things Spanish, Prescott turned to that language as his next venture. Once embarked, he sailed on in Spanish interests until his death, although he was not attracted immediately. "I am battling with the Spanish," he wrote to Bancroft in 1824, "but I have not the heart for it that I had for the Italian. I doubt whether there are many valuable things that the key of knowledge will unlock in that language." Still he continued to play with the key for a long time until, out of a list of subjects for a book, he made his choice. "What new and interesting topics may be admitted—not forced into— the reign of Ferdinand and Isabella?" he noted in 1825. In 1847 he endorsed the entry, "A fortunate choice."

The whole sweep of events taking place on the Peninsula seems to have flashed before his vision: the constitutions of Castile and of Aragon, of the Moorish dynasties, the causes of their decay and dissolution, the Inquisition, the conquest of Granada, the discoveries in the unknown West, monarchical power *versus* aristocracy; and he saw their relation to the whole world. Prescott had assimilated literary expression in its best forms in order to fit himself to express something in his turn; when that something had crystallized into definite form, it was as a narrator that he entered on his task of giving it a proper treatment. He began to see his story in episodes for the framing of which he had already provided the material.

A tentative bibliography was despatched to Edward Everett, United States Minister at Madrid, on 29 January, 1826. To Everett's natural suggestion that Prescott would be wise to come to Spain and look over the ground for himself, the latter answered in some detail that his one chance of success was to work even with limited resources at home rather than to jeopardize his future by groping with half sight in archives abroad. The explanation, written by his own hand, brought on an access of misery to his eye, and he recovered lost ground very slowly.

Under fresh limitations, but now with his scene firmly set, he began a systematic course of international and legal history, in addition to a general survey of Spain, geographically, economically, ecclesiastically, and civilly, especially with reference to fifteenth-century conditions. This necessitated the consultation of several hundred volumes in working days of about four hours each, with actual reading power of an hour a day at best, a few minutes or nothing, at worst. The imported sources arrived, but the author lingered on at the threshold before plunging into Spanish details. He recurred to Montesquieu's *Ésprit des lois*, to Voltaire, and to other philosophical considerations of history and human conditions; he heard governmental, theological, and chivalric works, many biographies and the classics, the last now in translation that they might be read aloud. Much of this was, of course, mere intellectual pabulum, never to be concretely adapted to his expressed results. By this time he had acquired a capacity of holding firmly in his mind the portions he saw he could use, while putting aside the non-essential. Such methods have rarely been applied so deliberately and consciously by an historical writer.

Having decided that he would use secondary material when a phase of his subject had been adequately treated by French or Spanish writers, Prescott began original work by mastering the chronicles of Andres Bernaldez as a first-hand source. Luckily the secretary devoted to his service was an able young Harvard graduate, a Mr. English, capable of supplementing the author's eyes, and sympathetic with his methods. The copy of Bernaldez obtained was in manuscript of no easy style.

The actual composition of *Ferdinand and Isabella* began in 1829, after eight years of preliminary reading, both general and special, at large and with the goal in mind. When it came to the literary form of the narrative, Prescott followed

Mably as a guide, having read his *Étude de l'histoire* ten times. He would think out a chapter on the same structural plan as for a romance or a drama, letting the events develop towards some obvious point or conclusion. Count d'Haussonville thinks this tendency to group transactions artistically a defect in historical narration, but other critics are more lenient, finding the result very readable. For six years the author worked on. Everything pertinent to his subject, and accessible at that time, that could be taken out of Spain, was imported in original or in transcript and digested very slowly. Prescott worked his direct quotations into his text, as a rule, instead of giving excerpts thrown or jerked into the narrative. At the same time, his references are precise and accurate. When the three volumes were concluded, the author again reaped an advantage from his full purse. No typewriting was available to break the fall from handwriting to the pitiless printed page, and to read handwriting was forbidden to Prescott. Feeling the need of meeting his copy face to face, he had four copies printed in large type on one side of the page. Then he was able to go over the whole, little by little, with his own sight. Submitted to the criticism of various friends, the book excited only delighted approval and stimulating comment, encouraging the author to have 1250 copies printed at his own expense by the American Stationers' Company (1836–37). Such a success America had never before seen or heard of. The edition was exhausted in five weeks. It was not surprising that the American reviews were favourable. There was no one capable of passing upon the sources. That the style was easy and the story illuminating was sufficient to make people gratefully acknowledge the introduction to Spanish history at a moment when Spanish eyes were turned anxiously towards the west. But in England there were at least two scholars who knew the subject and could pass a competent opinion on the American's work: Don Pascual de Gayangos, Spaniard and archivist in London, and Richard Ford, author of a handbook on Spain. Both accepted the new book with some puzzled queries as to how it could emanate from America. Basil Hall and Mrs. Trollope had given forth their impressions of the United States, and their readers were not prepared for scholarly yet graceful and novel historical work.

Yet such was the rating of *Ferdinand and Isabella* pronounced by these competent specialists in Spanish lore. One sympathetic and appreciative review came from the hand of Count de Circourt, a man described by Lamartine as "a living chest of human knowledge," which gave the unknown and modest American immense satisfaction. He was actually received at once into the international circle of authoritative scholarship. Hallam, Guizot, Milman, Sismondi, Thierry, were among those to give Prescott not condescending but cordial welcome as one of their own rank. Such an authority as C. P. Gooch states in 1913 that the work published in 1837 has not been superseded to this day. Research has brought, indeed, masses of documents to light that Prescott never heard of. Critics differ from him in conclusions—strange if they did not. Yet there is more serious difference of opinion between Vignaud and Harrisse, both writing on Columbus in the twentieth century, than between Prescott and Justin Winsor, in the first and second halves of the nineteenth.

Stimulated by the prompt recognition accorded to him, Prescott turned to his next venture, *The Conquest of Mexico*. It is characteristic of his methods that his first step towards beginning the narration in which one figure, Hernando Cortes, was to hold the centre of the stage, was the examination of certain celebrated biographical records of exploits—Voltaire's *Charles XII*, Livy's *Hannibal*, Irving's *Columbus*. His criticism of the last is that the interest flags at the end. That is just what can be said of his own *Mexico*, finished in 1844. Where the glow of achievement is ahead of his hero, the narrative marches and carries the reader on. Or is it that Bernal Diaz carries the story triumphantly up to the Aztec city? Prescott's method of assimilating his authority, instead of giving excerpts, was used to good purpose here, and his paraphrases are very vivid. For instance, in describing the Spanish army as it came in sight of the lake-city: "A scene so new and wonderful filled their rude hearts with amazement. It seemed like enchantment and they could find nothing to compare it with but the magic pictures in Amadis de Gaula." This is a clever turn to the simple statement by the chronicler of the Spaniards' first impressions of the Aztec city. Bernal Diaz, the veteran soldier, unskilled in letters, moved to set down his recollections of the great events in which he had participated half a century back, because Gomara's official history gave Cortes undue, and his comrades insufficient, credit for the Conquest, was a delightful guide to follow. His untaught phrases are alive and Prescott makes them more so. While later judgment discounts some of the conquistadore's statements, it cannot deny the fact that it was these glowing descriptions that affected the European imagination of the sixteenth century. For the ultimate rating of the veracity of the complaisant adventurer archæology has brought its later contribution, and of that science Prescott was ignorant, as was the rest of the world when he wrote. He almost relinquished the idea of his *Mexico* on hearing that Washington Irving had a similar scheme in mind. This would have been a real loss, as Irving's gentle raking over of unknown ground could not have produced as good fruit as Prescott's digging certainly did. Both *The Conquest of Mexico* and *The Conquest of Peru* were important works in the development of American literature and the American attitude towards knowledge. Neither the reputation nor the libraries of New England could have spared them.

The courtesy that Irving showed to a younger aspirant in his field was repeated by Prescott himself towards Motley, the latter ready to abandon his *Rise of the Dutch Republic* for fear lest Prescott's *Philip II* would fill the whole field adequately. There was a division of labour, again lucky, as Prescott's biography would have been a meagre substitute for the glowing partisan book. Count d'Haussonville ranks the incomplete *Philip II* as Prescott's best work. That is a dictum hard to accept. The author's attitude towards his central figure is less slashing than Motley's, less appreciative than Martin Hume's. In so much it may be called just, but there is a certain meagreness in the treatment. Robertson seems to have affected his style, although his work on that author's *Charles V* was not done until two volumes of *Philip II* had seen the light in 1855.

Between *Peru* and *Philip II* Prescott made a journey to England, where he was wonderfully received and fêted during his four months' visit. Oxford gave him a doctorate. In 1845 the French Institute and the Royal Society of Berlin, and in 1847 two learned societies of England, had made him a member, so that his status as a scholar was perfectly assured, and his own charm gained him permanent friendship after formal courtesy had made connecting links. During the remainder of his life, noted English scholars and statesmen kept up a correspondence with him. Perhaps the friendship accorded to him by Alexander von Humboldt on account of *Mexico* and *Peru* was one of the most grateful of the many won by the real merit of his literary labours. Fortunately he never lost the powers of enjoyment or of active occupation as death came very suddenly in 1859.

Prescott has been called a great amateur in the historical field, and in one sense, the term applies. Born only a year after Leopold Ranke, Prescott missed the influence spread abroad, eventually far beyond German university circles, by the great German scholar. The very vocabulary now used had not come into being. Prescott made his own standards. Nor did he have the incidental training that has been the strength of many an historian. Not trained in the methods of the École des Chartes, nor in the precise legal knowledge of jurisprudence, like Maitland, nor in active political service for his own state, nor in a school of philosophy, still less in the academic methods of research, Prescott simply assimilated language first and then events, and painted pictures of the past by a skilful union of the two. His style is a fine instrument of expression. His language plays him no tricks. He holds it in his own control, firmly, like a well-wrought, highly-tempered tool. His own temperament manifests itself very little in his writing. Nor is there any echo of contemporary politics in his treatment of the past. He is as aloof from the events passing in the United States as from those that he depicts. Possibly this is due to the peculiar state of affairs in those ante-bellum decades of the nineteenth century. He was a Bostonian who hated strife and felt that agitation was disagreeable. Thus nothing of his personal opinions and experience peeps out from between his lines as do those of Bancroft, Motley, and a score of French and Netherland writers whose pages are coloured by their attitude towards their immediate present. Perhaps had Prescott survived the outbreak of the Civil War his sentiments would have changed.

Those of many compromisers did. But he passed from the scene before the outbreak, and thus is crystallized as a figure detached from strife, a non-partisan, hard-working yet leisurely historian, sheltered from the hard things of life, almost untouched by his generation, endowed with the best New England could give to a few of her sons, and with the type of New England conscience that led him to use the talents he had but which also permitted him to hold aloof from his country's troubles as from something almost unclean.

Yet how many of his fellow-countrymen found his work grateful can be seen from the number of his books that were scattered over the land. Since 1837, editions of his books have appeared at frequent intervals. Exact figures seem difficult to obtain, but many thousand copies have been sold, while several editions of translations have appeared in Spain, in France, in Italy, in Germany, and in Holland.

## II. Motley

John Lothrop Motley (1814–77) was like Prescott in being a son of Massachusetts and born with a silver spoon of pure Boston metal in his mouth. In each case New England gave to her child a heritage of sturdy character, of convinced opinions of the Channing school, of the finest lineage she had woven from British material; to birth-right she added the best quality of education that had thus far been evolved on her soil. Of this late post-colonial education it can be said that, full of short-comings as it was, it usually had this characteristic—its disciples were inspired with a desire for more. To each of these Bostonians fate granted the boon of remarkable personal beauty. These endowments fell, however, upon characters of somewhat different tendencies, while their lives took them over different courses. Prescott was a prisoner within the bounds of congenial private life, his professional activity limited to the area of his own book-room filled with the imported source-material which he could not go to seek; while Motley made his own researches, touched the past with his own fingers, so close did he come to the documents, and had, in addition, the stimulus of world contact, of hearing statesmen's voices, of activities of which Prescott was wholly ignorant. Moreover, Prescott died in 1859, just too soon to fling off the shackles of repression which choked the free speech of Americans of his temperament before the Civil War. On the other hand, Motley, in every line of his later work on the sixteenth and seventeenth centuries, shows the exhilarating effect produced by the casting of the die and the ending of the compromise restraint. Born the very year Prescott finished his Harvard course, Motley was two-thirds of a generation behind the elder historian. Thus, though the immediate environment of the two Bostonians was the same, the storm brewing beyond the confines of Massachusetts had burst and had forced her conservative citizens out of their aloofness, and the Commonwealth was involved in a close bond with the other units of the Union, while Motley and his labours were still in a stage to be affected, as Prescott and his work never were, by contemporaneous politics.

From his early childhood, Motley was overflowing with expression. He was possessed to act out what he read; he made miniature theatres; he declaimed in season and out. His zeal for dramatic effect was in his blood—even though he did not evince the slightest histrionic ability or tendency. That is, he could not possibly have been an actor. It was literary expression that attracted him. He was so precocious that it would not have been surprising had his promise died out. Luckily, the colonial energy of the race was also in his blood and a New England strain well woven into the woof of his conscience so that his abilities found enduring record when, at last, he developed the powers of industry. His Harvard career was begun at the age of thirteen and completed at seventeen—an age young even for the time—and it is not surprising that his election to Phi Beta Kappa was gained only by stretching a point in his favour and including one more than the sixteen men legitimately chosen as the maximum number to be taken from each class. His class work did not give him high rank—indeed, he was rusticated for negligence—but his personality was so charming and his kind of cultivated human interest so convincing, that he could not be passed over. His facility in grasping the gist of a book was marvellous, but as it did not presage minute and accurate research, there was natural astonishment among his contemporaries over the industry evinced by his later work.

Harvard was followed by two years of study at Göttingen and Berlin and of foreign travel. George Bancroft, then fresh from his own German experience, had been a teacher in Motley's school at Northampton. Probably it was due to his influence that German was taught, as it was not a usual subject in the school curricula of the twenties. The young student was thus partially prepared for his plunge into Hanoverian university life and did not lose his first months in struggling over linguistic elements. Perhaps the most interesting contribution to his training given by the Göttingen episode was his acquaintance and intimate association with Count Bismarck, the foundations of a life-long friendship. The American had an exceptional opportunity to know a contemporary from an environment totally different from his own by heritage and tendency. Later, he had the still rarer chance of glimpses at the inside happenings or intentions of Prussian politics. He saw a master mind in the making and in the doing, as few of his generation could. The friendship has, moreover, permitted posterity some peeps at the Iron Chancellor in his moments of relaxation, a few of his intimate letters to the American having been published among those of Motley. Most delightful are the young student's own letters home during his *Wanderjahre*. He worked hard, indeed, at law in both universities, but it was the glimpses of Europe and the human side of its life, both past and present, that were the really vital part of the educational results for the young American. Intellectual Germany was still palpitating with the influence of Goethe, whom he was just too late to see, and he was deeply impressed by the atmosphere. He met scholars, such as Tieck, then at work on his translation of Shakespeare, and he learned what minute research could be. At the same time Motley retained an impressionistic attitude towards history which was wholly un-German. He always saw the past instinct with life. He is constantly reconstructing. "If you will allow me to mount my hobby, as Tristram Shandy would say," he writes from Rome in 1834, "and call fancy to the aid of history, the scene will be different, at least more lively." Thus he and his imagination travelled together, congenial companions.

When the wanderer returned to Boston he continued his preparation for law, but it never became his serious profession. He had to write, and his first venture was a novel called *Morton's Hope*. Published anonymously, it fell flat. Nor did it deserve success, although, at first view, the writer seems to have had both the training and the qualifications for a romancer. Foreign travel and study had widened his vision; he had really studied languages on the basis of a good preliminary education; and he had a fertile and graphic imagination. Moreover, at the time of writing, he was fairly bubbling over with personal happiness. The novel appeared in 1839, two years after his marriage to the sister of Park Benjamin, an intimate friend of Motley, while another intimate friend, Joseph Lewis Stackpole, married Mrs. Motley's sister. A close circle of friends was thus formed—affectionate yet all critical of each other. Mary Benjamin Motley seems, from all testimony, to have been a very rare person, whose comradeship with her husband was singularly perfect throughout her life. But despite such good auspices, *Morton's Hope* failed. The critics scarcely noticed the book, although one did admit that it must have been "written by a person of uncommon resources of mind and scholarship." As a work of art the story deserved oblivion. It is full of chronological anachronisms, the diction is bombastic and strained, the composition is faulty. The one interest in the book is that there are certain autobiographical suggestions in the reflections and self-contemplations of the hero. There is an underlying thread of aspirations, "disguised," says Dr. Holmes, "under a series of incidents, which are flung together with no more regard to the unities than a pack of cards."

The failure of his first venture did not deter Motley from making another trial in the same direction. His second novel *Merry Mount*, not published until 1849, was semi-historic in character. The scene is laid in Massachusetts in 1628—"in that crepuscular period which immediately preceded the rise of the Massachusetts Colony and possesses more of the elements of romance than any subsequent epoch," writes the author in his preface. The book plays with theological revolt and separatist movements, and introduces adventurers of somewhat dime-novel calibre to shock Puritan sentiments and to impress Indians by aristocratic hauteur.

But with all his knowledge of fundamental facts and of local colour, the author failed to command attention. *Merry Mount* is not bad, but it is dull. The characters do not carry the slightest conviction. They are simple bundles of attributes, and some of the bundles have a sensational taint. Contemporary reviews did not slight the book. *The North American Review* actually devoted seventeen pages to an abstract of the tale, in order to prove that the early settlement of New England was not a good field for fiction: "Later events only make the period interesting," "The conditions are too hard," "Romantic elements are lacking." The reviewer concludes with saying that he has been agreeably disappointed, on the whole, but he does not consider the romance a fair specimen of what the writer can achieve. [1]

Between the production of the two novels, Motley had had fresh experiences. In 1841 he was appointed secretary to the legation at St. Petersburg and spent some months in the Russian capital, long enough to be convinced that he did not wish to have his wife and children join him. So he resigned his post before his year was out. Once again in America, he began to give utterance to his opinions on political events, the failure of Henry Clay to secure the presidential nomination having roused him to mournful expressions of his conviction that all that was fine in American public life had been overpowered by mediocrity if not by evil. He had a little taste of public life himself; he served in the Massachusetts legislature for one term (1849). The one measure he seems to have worked for was an endowment of higher education at the expense of the common schools. "Failure was inevitable," says George S. Boutwell, a fellow legislator. "Neither Webster nor Choate could have carried the bill." Motley had written a report as Chairman of the Committee on Education, thinking that he had achieved a fine document, and was much surprised at the unanimity of its condemnation. He had no more desire for Massachusetts political life. By this date, Motley was thirty-five, no longer a youth, yet all his failures seem those of immaturity. It sometimes happens when a boy is precocious that the reputation of being in advance of his years lingers about him after the time when a man of

[1] *North American Review*, January, 1849.

more normal powers makes his public appearance. But Motley began to show himself in another light than that of romancer or legislator; his essays were proving that he could conquer some of the glaring faults of his style and write on sober themes. His articles on Peter the Great, on Balzac, and on Talvi's *Geschichte der Colonisation von New England* were scholarly and original. He had no desire, however, to dissipate his store of energy in ephemeral reviews. Before the publication of his half-historical *Merry Mount* he had selected the theme of the contest between the Netherlands and Spain for an extensive work, had been checked momentarily by the news of Prescott's projected *Philip II*, had been spurred on by the kindly words of the elder American, and had then devoted himself to going to the foundations of the story of the events. He says in reference to hearing of Prescott's work:

> It seemed to me that I had nothing to do but to renounce authorship. For I had not at first made up my mind to write a history and then cast about to take up a subject. My subject had taken me up, drawn me on, and absorbed me into itself. It was necessary for me, it seemed, to write the book I had been thinking much of, even if it were destined to fall dead from the press, and I had no inclination or interest to write any other.

Thus Prescott's courtesy did as much service to Motley as Washington Irving's did to the author of *The Conquest of Mexico*. To the world, too, it would have been a loss had *The Rise of the Dutch Republic* never come to light. It was indeed a work of love. Motley gave up every other thought and worked to one end only. He made no such preliminary preparation as did Prescott. Yet in a way, his whole career had been leading up to it. He had burned to express himself. He planted source-material in his mind, and the story flowered from it, naturally. For nearly ten years he plodded on, at first in Boston and then in archives abroad, in Berlin, Dresden, The Hague, and Brussels. He bathed in local colour. In 1855 he had his three volumes ready for the printer. Then came a difficulty. No publisher would look at the formidable mass of manuscript with the slightest interest. No one would believe in the chances of returns from such an expensive undertaking as its publication. Like his compatriot, Motley was obliged to take his own risks, and *The Rise of the Dutch Republic* was published at the author's expense by John Chapman in London, and by Harpers in New York. The sale of fifteen thousand copies in two years proved the fallibility of human judgment. The reviews were not, however, as uniformly favourable as in Prescott's case. *The Saturday Review*[1] brought heavy artillery to bear on the ambitious American in the same number with a censorious attack upon Browning's *Men and Women* and three columns upon the lack of interest in Miss Yonge's unpretentious domestic tale, *The Daisy Chain*. The *Review's* slashing denunciation of his flashy chapter headings was peculiarly annoying to Motley, because he had disapproved of their adoption. He comments upon this in a letter to his father, in connection with the remark that every book notice had condemned them unequivocally. *The Literary Gazette*[2] found virtues in the volumes, but added: "The book is far too ponderous both in matter and style to be popular," and commiserated Motley because his literary skill fell so far short of his diligence and learning that other writers would enter into the fruits of his labours and write more popular histories out of his store. The sequence of the prophecy proved singularly true. Motley's *Rise of the Dutch Republic* has been quarried and retold in every conceivable form. One has only to glance along the shelves in the Library of Congress to see how many books are based on Motley, with due credit to him, while many more volumes, serious and romantic, less frankly owe their being to his pages. At the same time, this use of fragments has not been due to the unpopular character of the full work, as is proved by the continued sales of the three volumes.

As a compensation for the *Saturday's* strictures on his work, *The Westminster Review* for the month following (April, 1856), had as its leading article a comprehensive paper by J. A. Froude which did full justice to the unknown American writer.

A history as complete as industry and genius can make it now lies before us of the first twenty years of the Revolt of the United Provinces. . . . It has been the result of many years of silent,

[1] 23 March, 1856.

[2] 19 April, 1856.

thoughtful, unobtrusive labour, and unless we are strangely mistaken, unless we are ourselves altogether unfit for this office of criticising which we have undertaken, the book is one which will take its place among the finest histories in this or in any language. . . . All the essentials of a great writer Mr. Motley eminently possesses. His mind is broad, his industry unwearied.

Froude did not like Motley's estimate of Queen Elizabeth, adding: "It is ungracious, however, even to find so slight a fault with these admirable volumes." This gentle animadversion is amusing, because all the eminent authorities on the period treated do just what Froude does. They like the way Motley has navigated the whole sea of difficulties but think he has lost his way on their private pools. In Holland and Belgium at the time of the appearance of *The Rise of the Dutch Republic* there were, among other scholars, three eminent archivists and one rising historian: Groen van Prinsterer, Bakhuysen van der Brink, and Professor Fruin in Holland, and Gachard in Brussels. They all received the book with pleasure as well as with profound surprise that any foreigner had cast his plummet down their deeps with so much assiduity. Mingled with their real and cordial approval there was a reserve on the part of each regarding the treatment of his own particular thesis. Groen thought that Motley did not really feel the Protestant impulse in all that happened; Bakhuysen considered that he did not understand phases of the relations with Germany; Gachard, himself less fervent in his opinions than the Hollanders, criticized Motley's partisanship; while Fruin, the first man to hold a chair at Leyden University exclusively devoted to "Vaderlandsche Geschiedenis," criticized the whole work on a larger and more ample scale. He thought that the author did not grasp fully the actual development of the congeries of provinces, found many weak spots in the generalizations, and held that, closely as Motley had followed original authorities, he had erred seriously in not testing the exact weight and authenticity of the witnesses whom he had summoned to help him tell his tale.

The English original excited immediate interest in Holland, but the most exhaustive reviews were reserved until the Dutch version appeared in 1859, made by no less an authority than

Bakhuysen himself, who said: "Motley's work seems to me to make such an excellent foundation for the history of the growth of the Commonwealth of the United Netherlands that it seems almost a duty to bring forth one's own possessions in order to rear up a structure on this foundation." Fruin repeated the words at the beginning of his review. He added a cordial appreciation of the industry and conscientiousness of the American.

We have discovered no unused source. . . . I take it for granted that everyone has read the work of the American. . . . It would be a scandal if our countrymen neglected to read what the foreigner counted of sufficient importance to discuss. . . . Motley shines in narrative [*Hij is een bekwam stylist*] but he is less fortunate in his explanations of cause and effect. What the witnesses whom he summons testify, he narrates better than they can tell, but he fails to weigh their personality and trustworthiness with sufficient accuracy. The "how" is good, the "why" defective. He is far behind Ranke in his comprehension of the beginnings of the revolt.

Then the Dutch historian proceeded to write one of the most valuable articles that ever came from his pen, *Het voorspel van den tachtigjarigen oorlog*. Herein he carefully reviewed the ground with exact references to his authorities and gave a less passionate and less biassed picture than Motley of Philip's relations to the Netherlands and to the thread of events that preceded the final outbreak. Motley could not complain of lack of appreciation in the Netherlands, and had reason to flatter himself that his work was a spur to the Netherlanders to look to their own dykes and consider carefully what was true among their writers of the sixteenth century and what needed to be winnowed. Besides, there was an interest aroused in the texts, and several valuable works, used by Motley in manuscript, were printed within a few years after the publication of his work. Now nearly everything important is in print, and the stimulus to the incessant output during the last half century was certainly largely due to the American.

Scarcely taking breath after the publication of this first great effort, the author plunged into the sequel and brought out two volumes of *The United Netherlands* in 1860. This time neither publisher nor public was shy. The English reviews were very favourable, on the whole; even *The Saturday Review*[1] was almost commendatory though it did not find the style satisfactory. Perhaps the most severe stricture was that the figurative language was uncultivated in tone, but the general attitude of the censor is quite different from that taken four years previous. *The Westminster Review* was more lavish in its praise. *The Edinburgh Review* was a trifle patronizing, but still Motley was given credit.

The American reviews had no reservations in their praise of both works. It is a trifle amusing to note the conclusion of the comments—a long and serious article—on *The Rise of the Dutch Republic* in the *North American:* "upon the whole it seems to us that the first William was a greater man than his great-grandson and namesake." This sounds as though, indeed, the elder Prince of Orange had needed an introduction to the American public in 1856.

In Holland the second book received the same greeting as did the first, a greeting marked by pride and pleasure that a stranger had devoted so much of his life to their affairs, tempered by some careful and discriminating criticism. Professor Fruin wrote: "We have delayed too long in noticing this important work. No one can put down the book until it is finished. Through the beautiful style, the vivid narrative, the artistic descriptions, this work shines out above the works on history in our own language." Fruin took Motley's notes and verified every reference: "Even where we differ from his opinion, we must do honour to his good faith, to his keen perception, to his industrious and accurate investigation." The review was another of Fruin's fine essays on Dutch history. Fruin once more criticized Motley's failure to differentiate the values of his authorities and considered him often tempted to expand a phase simply because he had a rich store of material bearing upon it, but without due regard to the need of that phase in the narrative. Letters between Leicester and his officers led him on to tell a detailed story of petty English quarrels which would have been more suitable for a separate publication. That Motley's vivid imagination inspired him with interlinear visions, hardly substantiated by a strict construction of the text, was gently intimated by Fruin with one

[1] January, 1861.

or two striking examples. Undoubtedly this is the same imagination that led the tourist to people the Rome before his eye with actors once within her walls. Life was, indeed, breathed into skeleton facts—some new joints being supplied —and life, too, into years of discussion as to the eternal verity of Motley's conception. One item in *The Rise of the Dutch Republic* gave Fruin especial concern. That was the use of the term "William the Silent." He wished that the American had lent his weight towards eliminating the unsuitable adjective from the historical vocabulary. Criticism such as this of Fruin's was the highest compliment that could have been paid to Motley.

The spring of 1861, momentous in the history of the United States, found Motley still in London. He had been abroad at work in the archives ever since the winter of 1856–57, which he had spent in Boston. The first public news of the imminent Civil War must have come to him on Monday, 29 April. That was the day when the Earl of Malmesbury opened the session in the House of Lords with the assumption that "Almost all your Lordships must have read the account that arrived this morning from America, and must have learned with pain as well as astonishment that civil war has broken out." Humanely rejoicing that no blood had been shed, the Earl proceeded to ask what the noble Lords were going to do towards settling this most unnatural quarrel. Lord Woodhouse replied that, after mature deliberation, the Government had decided that advice on internal matters would be intrusive unless solicited. From that Monday on, the London *Times* gave much space to comments on the terrible anachronism of war in general, on the horror of seeing thirty million Anglo-Saxons slaying each other like the Indians whom they had displaced, etc., etc. All civil wars known to history were reviewed. In each of these, asserted the *Times*, a vital principle had been at stake. Each had been justified by the crying needs of religion or civil liberty. But in the United States, no principle was involved. Day after day this statement was reiterated in varying forms. Admitting that, on the whole, they inclined rather to the Northern cause, they still declared that, nevertheless, the actual issue between the two sections was a mere shadow.

It is curious how long the idea of the causelessness of the strife prevailed in Europe. As late as April, 1863, Bismarck wrote to Motley in a familiar letter: "Do you all know exactly why you are waging furious war with each other? Certainly all do not know, but they kill each other *con amore*, that is the way the business comes to them. Your battles are bloody; ours are wordy." This query was, perhaps, half humorous, but the *Times* was in dead earnest in its opinion that the war was unjustifiable. It went further, after a little, and declared that the spirit of George III had passed into Seward and that his reluctance to let the South go its own way was couched in language quite as tyrannical as that of the British monarch to his colonies when they desired "secession."

Under the stimulus of these daily reiterations, Motley wrote two long letters, to which the *Times* gave prominent space, on *The Causes of the Civil War*. They appeared on Thursday, 23 May, and Friday, 24 May, and were reprinted in New York within a few weeks. The line of argument followed was that the United States was no confederacy from which a part could be lopped and both parts continue to live. A confederation of sovereign bodies had been tested and found wanting; then a more perfect government had been formed by the people themselves, at large, not in states as units. The government to which the Constitution of the United States gave birth was different in kind from its predecessor. It could not be divided any more than Scotland could be severed from the British Empire. It was a plea for the sacredness of the Union as an organic, vitalized whole. The tariff, as an irritating cause of division, was discussed, while slavery was touched on very lightly.

The Queen's Proclamation of Neutrality had already checked the press in its references to President Davis as precisely on a par with President Lincoln, and Motley's words were allowed to be worth noting, as coming from one already recognized as an historian of European reputation. For a time, at least, the English newspapers changed their tone, while in America there was warm appreciation of Motley's statement of the case.

Shortly after this incident, Motley returned home and was in Boston when the first Massachusetts regiments left their camp at Brook Farm (singularly peaceful spot for a training ground!) and marched off to war. He regretted that his forty-seven years disqualified him from enlisting without previous training, but he was stirred to the depths of his being by the emotion of the summer months of 1861. That emotion, carried abroad, kept him a fervent American during his years of foreign residence. John Bigelow considers that he was denationalized, but he was not. He only tried to hold fast to ideals crystallized at a moment of high pressure. He did not feel the meaner elements that obtruded themselves during the long-drawn-out contest.

Although he did not enlist, he was summoned to do other work for the republic, and accepted the mission to Austria, where, it was felt, the sentiment he had shown in his London letters would be serviceable. His own historical work was put aside for the six years in which he lived at Vienna, up-holding the dignity of the United States. A cultivated, polished, high-minded American official was a great asset to the United States at that juncture, when there was a disposition abroad to count the Northerners as commercial sordid folk. Here was a Yankee of the Yankees as a living witness that the name was not counted as a term of reproach by those who bore it.

His office was no sinecure. In addition to the complications arising from the war, there were others connected with Maximilian's expedition to Mexico, in which he showed good judgment. The unexpected elevation of Andrew Johnson to the presidency in 1865 brought a new element to be reckoned with. It chanced that, just at a moment when Johnson was feeling very sore about the defection of Republicans from his support, a letter came to him from Paris accusing various official Americans abroad of malignant criticism towards the administration. A passage about Motley was as follows: "Mr. Motley does not pretend to conceal his 'disgust' as he terms it elegantly, at your whole conduct. He tells every traveller that Sumner is wholly justified and that you have deserted your principles in common with Mr. Seward, who, he says, is hopelessly degraded." Under the influence of his general feeling of distrust and suspicion, the president told Seward to send a formal query to each person mentioned, asking the truth of the accusation against them. Later Seward told John Bigelow that no one resented the query, drawn up by a clerk and signed by himself as secretary of state, except Motley. In all other cases, it was taken as it was meant, a simple matter of office routine. Probably, had the President not been over-sensitive about the attitude of his subordinates, the accusing document would have been put in the waste-paper basket. No one knew the "George McCrackin" from whom it purported to come. Motley, however, did not take it as a formula. Such a question addressed to him seemed an insult, and he lost no time in replying, perhaps only less hotly than he felt, offering his resignation at the end of his denial of the charge that he had maligned the new administration. The secretary of state would have taken no notice of a resignation offered under a momentary smart, but when Johnson said "Let him go," Seward did not try to stay his hand. According to the story Seward told John Bigelow in 1869, it would seem a fair conclusion that the minister was too hot and the secretary too cold and too indifferent, when an effort on his part to interpose would have been natural under the circumstances. The result was that Motley left Vienna with a very sharp wound to his self-respect.

Luckily for the ex-diplomat, the seventeenth century was waiting till he should be released from the claims of the nineteenth, and he plunged at once into the next period of his Netherland story. *The History of the United Netherlands* was concluded by two more volumes issued in 1868. A continuation centred about John of Barneveld was finally published in 1874. Motley returned from Vienna to Boston and was settled there at the time of Grant's first campaign, into which he entered with much interest. At the suggestion of Sumner, he was honoured by Grant with the appointment to the Court of St. James, the highest diplomatic post in his gift. That was pleasant after the Vienna incident. Unfortunately, Grant identified him with Sumner, and when a breach came between the president and the senator from Massachusetts, the former found a pretext to recall Motley, and again a secretary of state failed to protect the minister. Moreover, the explanatory letter written by Hamilton Fish was not phrased in a manner to soothe the diplomat's feelings, so that the incident ended with added discomfiture for Motley. Again work was the refuge from the annoyances to which he had been subjected, but they were not forgotten. It is rather curious to note how the author's unpleasant experience colours the story of the relations between Maurice of Nassau and John of Barneveld. The inability of the soldier, acting as statesman, to understand the diplomat is dwelt on in a fashion to show that General Grant was in the historian's thoughts when he wrote of Count Maurice. Indeed, *John of Barneveld* is a reflection of autobiography almost as much as *Morton's Hope*. Every point having to do with the ambitions of the individual province and the needs of the United Netherlands is coloured by the crisis through which the United States had just passed. Sometimes the implied parallel is apt, sometimes both strained and forced. It was Motley's tendency, in general, to indulge in comparisons and metaphor that once more troubled *The Saturday Review*.[1] The carping critic evidently thought that all the expressions to which he objected were American. He did not realize that any worker in sixteenth century historical sources is living in the midst of just such language as was found objectionable. Sober documents are permeated with idioms not to be counted Americanisms; the letters of Elizabethan statesmen overflow with quaint twists and turns. Thus Motley's natural tendency in this direction was constantly fed during his researches into contemporary material. It was natural for him, writing from Vienna during a terrible drought, to declare that there was nothing green in Austria but the Archduke Maximilian, dreaming of an American empire (1863). It was phrases like that in history which shocked the reviewer. Other reviews in Great Britain and America were almost unanimous in their high praise for *John of Barneveld*. *The Edinburgh Review* said: "We can hardly give too much praise to the subtle alchemy of the brain which has enabled him [Motley] to produce out of dull, crabbed, and often illegible State-papers, the vivid, graphic, and sparkling narrative which he has given to the world."

In the Netherlands, the book was viewed from a different standpoint. The period treated was one marked by the bitterest kind of theological disputes. Motley thought he could

[1] 2 May, 1874.

discuss these impartially, but his attempt only brought down upon his head a flood of pained criticism from the heirs to both sides of the controversy,—no dead question in Holland. The old archivist, Groen van Prinsterer, fervent Calvinist as he was, declared that only an Arminian, such as an American Unitarian was, could be so antagonistic to the principles of the Reformation espoused by Maurice. (Perhaps Groen did not believe that Maurice had once declared that he did not know whether Predestination was green or blue!) Motley had become the ardent apologist of Barneveld and latitudinarian doctrine, the orthodox Hollanders felt, and a battle was started that raged for years. Groen devoted a whole book to the topic. At the same time, Dutch scholars paid warm tributes to the American's conscientious use of sources, though they might not accept his interpretation. No one accused him of neglecting what was obtainable. They only thought "He cannot understand." By that time the handsome American with his air of distinction was a well-known figure in The Hague. In 1871, the Queen of the Netherlands offered him a house in the Dutch capital, where he spent part of the years when he was working at *John of Barneveld*.

The death of Mrs. Motley in 1874 was a blow from which her husband never recovered, although he tried to resume his work and complete the story of the Eighty Years' War. The sub-title of the Barneveld volumes had been *A View of the Primary Causes and Movements of the Thirty Years' War.* But Motley was never to take the public with him beyond that view. His own death came in 1877, and he was buried in England.

What is the judgment of posterity upon the work into which Motley poured so much vigorous painstaking effort? This much can be said: he was first a brilliant searchlight, sweeping over an unknown field, and then an able draughtsman in describing the scene. Every new generation claims to have a light in its own hand which enables it to judge the past with greater accuracy than its predecessors. Scholars of today in Holland, Blok, Japikse, Colenbrander, all consider that the American failed to treat Netherland history on scientific lines. He did not understand Europe at large, he did not understand the Church. In his hands Philip II was treated too severely, as was Maurice in his conflict with Barneveld. There was a lack of perspective in his every estimate. Not only that, but in making one period so dominant, he dislocated the perspective of the whole history of the Netherlands. For the last thirty years scholars in Belgium as well as Holland have been working over the ground, bringing small dark places into sober light, shading down other points too highly illuminated. A fair result will be reached at last. But the great light was a pleasant thing.

# CHAPTER XIX

# Early Humorists

ALTHOUGH American literature was, even at the beginning, not without its humour, much of the early writing which seems to us whimsical and amusing may have had no humorous appeal for contemporary readers. From an early period, however, we can discern symptoms of the two kinds of humour which were to be represented by American writers: the one following closely English models, especially Addison, Steele, Defoe, and Goldsmith in the eighteenth century, and Lamb, Hood, Jerrold, and Dickens in the nineteenth century; the other springing from American soil and the new conditions of American life, and assuming a character as new to the world as the country that produced it. Franklin,[1] Irving,[2] Holmes[3] belong to what we may call the classical tradition; the present chapter is concerned with those aspects of American humour which are more essentially native, at least in form and tone.

The great period of American humorous writing has been the last three quarters of the nineteenth century. For all the preceding periods a very brief sketch must here suffice. In the seventeenth century the conditions of colonial life were not propitious to any sort of writing, humorous or other. To secure the means of a livelihood was a practical problem which left little time for the cultivation of the more genial side of life. In bleak surroundings where there was little physical comfort, and under the gloom of Puritanism, most writers were practical and serious. But there are a few exceptions. *New England's Annoyances* (1630),[4] a piece of anonymous

---

[1] See Book I, Chap. VI.    [2] See Book II, Chap. IV.
[3] See Book II, Chap. XXIII.    [4] See Bibliography to Book I, Chap. IX.

doggerel, shows that even the Puritans could smile as they regarded some of their discomforts. Nathaniel Ward[1] wrote *The Simple Cobler of Aggawam in America* (1647), which Moses Coit Tyler called "the most eccentric and amusing book that was produced in America during the colonial period," although Ward insisted that it should be accepted as a trust-worthy account of the spiritual state of New England. John Josselyn, who wrote *New England's Rareties* (1672), declared that most of what he wrote was true; he admits that some things which he recorded he had heard but not seen: for example, that "Indians commonly carry on their discussions in perfect hexameter verse, extempore," and that "in New England there is a species of frog which chirps in the spring like swallows and croaks like toads in autumn, some of which when they sit upon their breech are a foot high, while up in the country they are as big as a child of a year old."

In the eighteenth century humour assumed a more im-portant place in American literature, being represented less by naïve recitals of incongruous situations and incidents and more by a conscious recognition of the incongruity. The narratives of William Byrd (1674–1744),[2] perhaps the wittiest and most accomplished Virginian of the colonial time, are remarkable for their civil geniality amid rude circumstances, and for their touches of cultivated irony. Madam Sarah Kemble Knight (1666–1727),[3] in her diary written in the pauses of her horseback journeys between Boston and New York in 1704 and 1705, recorded in a most amusing manner the humours of the rough roads, the perilous crossing of rivers, the intolerable inns, and the coarse speech of the inland rustics. John Seccomb (1708–93) wrote a piece of verse called *Father Abbey's Will* (1732) facetiously describing the estate of Matthew Abdy, sweeper, bed-maker, and bottle-washer to Harvard College. These lines found their way into *The Gentleman's Magazine*. Joseph Green,[4] who became well known for his puns, has left us some mischievous lines on *Doctor Byles's Cat* (1733). The popular impression of Green is embodied in an epitaph which was written for him by one of his friends:

[1] See also Book I, Chap. III.       [2] See also Book I, Chap. I.
[3] *Ibid.*       [4] See also Book I, Chap. IX.

Siste, Viator, Here lies one
Whose life was whim, whose soul was pun,
And if you go too near his hearse,
He'll joke you both in prose and verse.

These few specimens show, if they show nothing more, that other spirits than Cotton Mather and Jonathan Edwards were alive in America in the eighteenth century.

The Revolution produced its humour chiefly in the form of political satire; the principal names are Francis Hopkinson, John Trumbull, Joel Barlow, Philip Freneau.[1] The first two were perhaps most important in this connection. Hopkinson's *Battle of the Kegs* was as good for the American cause as the winning of a real battle. In the grim year of 1778, this poem went into every American camp, cheered the patriots, and provoked hearty laughter at the awkwardness and stupidity of the enemy. And Trumbull in *McFingal* produced a Hudibrastic epic whose anger and irresistible logic reflected ingeniously the temper of a colony of sturdy militiamen that had taken upon themselves the task of offering opposition to the mother country—a task in itself not without its incongruous aspect.

During the period that followed the Revolution the colonists doubtless told their stories of war and sea, "swapped yarns," and recounted deeds of adventure along the frontier, but little has remained to show the character of the writing and to enable us to know what impression it made upon the time. There was not a little humorous political and satirical verse. Certain writers, like William Austin, Irving, Paulding, Drake, Halleck, Sands, Verplanck, brought into American literature an estimable sort of humour, but little was produced by any of them that had an emphatically native quality.

About the time of Andrew Jackson, along with the birth of popular national self-consciousness, the emergence of the frontier as a social entity in the nation's imagination, and the rise to power of the newspaper (for almost without exception the professional American humorists have been newspapermen), the kind of humour that we think of as American took

[1] For these four poets see Book I, Chap. IX.

on new life. It first found voice in New England, the section which was eventually to shudder at the tide of boisterous, outlandish mirth that set in from the new South and the newer West, along and beyond that "highway of humour," the Mississippi.

First in point of time among the new humorists came Seba Smith (1792–1868), whose *Letters of Major Jack Downing* appeared in 1830. Almost immediately after his graduation from Bowdoin College in 1818, Smith began to contribute a series of political articles in the New England dialect to the papers of Portland, Maine. These illustrated fairly well the peculiarities of New England speech and manners, and doubtless had a great influence in encouraging similar sketches in other parts of the country. Smith was in several ways a pioneer. He led the way for *The Biglow Papers* and all those writings which have exploited back-country New England speech and character. He anticipated, in the person of Jack Downing, confidant of Jackson, David Ross Locke's Petroleum V. Nasby, confidant of Andrew Johnson. He was the first in America, as Finley Peter Dunne, with his Mr. Dooley, is the latest, to create a homely character and through him to make shrewd comments on politics and life. Charles Augustus Davis (1795–1867) of New York created a pseudo Jack Downing (often confused with Smith's) who was intimate with Van Buren and the National Bank in the thirties and with Lincoln in the sixties. In 1835, only two years after Smith's first collected volume appeared, Judge Thomas Chandler Haliburton, a prolific Nova Scotian, began the series of short sketches from which emerged one of the most famous of the early Yankee characters, Sam Slick the Clockmaker.

It must suffice barely to mention a number of the earlier volumes of American humour which attained popularity but which today are known only to the student. David Crockett's *Autobiography* (1834) may not belong here, though it is certainly one of the raciest of all the books in its kind. *Crayon Sketches* (1833), by William Cox (d. 1851), an English journalist working in New York, consists of a series of amusing essays contributed to *The New York Mirror*, satirizing the literary infirmities of the times and hitting off well-known actors. Especially popular were the sketches of

himself and the burlesque biography of the old city constable, Jacob Hays. *The Life and Adventures of Dr. Didimus
Duckworth, A. N. Q. to which is added the History of a Steam
Doctor* (1833), is a mock-heroic biography of a spoiled child,
in the style of broadest farce; *The Perils of Pearl Street* (1834)
tells of the fortunes and misfortunes of a country lad who
comes to New York in search of wealth. Both were written
by Asa Green (d. 1837), a New England physician, who moved
to New York and established himself as bookseller. A clever
book, hustling with action, is *Novellettes of a Traveller, or, Odds
and Ends from the Knapsack of Thomas Singularity, Journeyman Printer* (1834), which was written by Henry Junius Nott
(1797–1837), of South Carolina, distinguished at the bar for
his learning and afterwards as professor of *belles-lettres*. The
*Ollapodiana Papers*, in the style of a more boisterous Lamb,
were contributed to *The Knickerbocker Magazine*[1] by Willis
Gaylord Clark (1810–41), whose twin brother, Lewis Gaylord Clark (d. 1873), for a long time editor of the *Knickerbocker*,
was an accomplished journalist and humorist of the chatting
sort. *The Motley Book* (1838) was a collection of original
sketches and tales by Cornelius Mathews (1817–89), a versatile poet, dramatist, and journalist who was very prolific
during the forties and whose *Career of Puffer Hopkins* (1841)
is one of the most interesting of minor American political
satires. The sprightly and observant *Sketches of Paris*
(1838), by John Sanderson (1783–1844), were made a good
deal of in London and Paris for a decade or so after their first
appearance. George P. Morris (1802–64),[2] one of the founders
of *The New York Mirror*, collected in 1838 a volume of his
sketches of New York life; the leading one, called *The Little
Frenchman and his Water Lots*, is a pathetic but graphic account
of a little French merchant duped by a Manhattan real estate
dealer. The *Annals of Quodlibet, a Political Satire by Solomon
Secondthought, Schoolmaster* (1840), by John Pendleton Kennedy, has been treated elsewhere in this history.[3] The influence of Dickens is potent in *Charcoal Sketches or Scenes in
a Metropolis* (1840), by Joseph Clay Neal (1807–47), whose

---

[1] See also Book II. Chaps. III and XX.
[2] See also Book II, Chap. V.
[3] See Book II, Chap. VII.

work was seen through the press in England by Dickens himself.

Of more importance in these times was *Georgia Scenes* (1835), a series of inimitable and clear-cut pictures of the rude life of the South-east, by Augustus Baldwin Longstreet (1790–1870). Longstreet, who was the son of a prominent inventor, graduated at Yale, and won distinction as lawyer, judge, newspaper editor, Methodist minister, and president of Emory College. His realistic descriptions of country parties, debating societies, horse-trades, fox-hunts, shooting-matches, brutal fights, and the adventures of his hero, the practical joker Ned Brace, insured a fruitful career to humour in the South, which before the Civil War enlisted at least a dozen considerable names in its ranks. From Georgia also came *Major Jones's Courtship* (1840), intimate and comic letters by William Tappan Thompson (1812–82), who had an interesting career as editor and soldier in Ohio, Pennsylvania, Florida, Maryland, and Georgia. One of the best of early Southern humorists was an Alabama editor, Johnson J. Hooper (1815–62), whose *Adventures of Captain Simon Suggs* (1846) was admired by Thackeray. Captain Suggs is an amusing rascal, who lives by his wits and who is presented with rare irony by an author who had perhaps the most delicate touch of his time and section. Charles Henry Smith, "Bill Arp so-called" (1826–1903), wrote from Georgia a series of letters, beginning with the mildly defiant "Bill Arp to Abe Linkhorn," which marked him as a brave and sensitive voice for the Confederacy. After the war Bill Arp was the first to smile and relieve the gloom. A trifle later, and farther north, appeared the letters of Moses Adams, in real life George W. Bagby (1828–83), of Virginia, editor of *The Southern Literary Messenger* and other periodicals and among the earliest to master negro psychology and dialect in literature. Tennessee is represented in this period by George Washington Harris, "Sut Lovengood" (1814–69); and Kentucky by George Denison Prentice (1802–70), who came from Connecticut in 1830 and made *The Louisville Journal* a powerful Whig organ as well as a repository for the widely quoted epigrammatic paragraphs which he collected in 1859 as *Prenticeana*.

Perhaps the most significant volume of humour by a Southerner before the Civil War was *The Flush Times of Alabama and Mississippi* (1853), by Joseph Glover Baldwin (1815–64), who was born in Virginia, practised law in Alabama, and spent the late years of his life in California. Like Lincoln, as a lawyer he had learned much from riding the circuit, and traced in his book the evolution of a country barrister with considerable skill and imagination. Although chiefly concerned with the Flush-time bar, Baldwin described as well most of the sharpers, boasters, liars, spread-eagle orators, the types of honesty and dishonesty, efficiency and inefficiency, in the newly rich and rapidly filling South. Unlike some of the books of his time, this one does not degenerate into mere horse-play or farce. We may still find interest in the characters of Simon Suggs, Jr., Esquire, and Ovid Bolus, the former a good trader and the mean boy of the school, the latter a great spendthrift and liar although handsome and possessed of a generous and winning manner.

In the North and West meanwhile, humorous books were growing steadily in number and importance. During the late forties Mrs. Frances Miriam Whitcher (1811–52) wrote for several journals a series of articles purporting to come from the pen of the Widow Bedott, "an egregiously wise and respectable and broadly humorous matron." Such was the demand for her writings that after her death two collections were published, *The Widow Bedott Papers* (1855) and *Widow Sprigg, Mary Elmer, and Other Sketches* (1867). Her humour is spirited but often obvious. Frederick Swartout Cozzens (1818–69), a New York wine merchant with literature as a hobby, cultivated a pleasant vein of mild, dry humour which produced *The Sparrowgrass Papers* (1856), describing the experiences of a New York cockney who retires to Yonkers to live. *The Travels, Voyages, and Adventures of Gilbert Go-Ahead* (1856), recording the deeds of a shrewd clock-selling Yankee in different parts of the world, was probably by the most prodigious literary hack of his day, Samuel Griswold Goodrich (1793–1860), "Peter Parley." A widely travelled New York naval officer, Henry Augustus Wise (1819–69), wrote several extravagant volumes of sea exploits, of which *Tales for the Marines* (1855) was probably best known. Thomas Bangs Thorpe (1815–78), a Massachusetts man who went as a journalist to Louisiana and became known as the author of highly coloured tales of the South-west, adopted the name of "Tom Owen, the Bee-Hunter," an eccentric person who had picturesque adventures on the frontier. Two other men, Samuel A. Hammett (1816–65) of Connecticut and John Ludlum McConnel (1826–62) of Illinois, travelled in the West and South-west and described their experiences in racy volumes.

Mrs. Partington, the American Mrs. Malaprop, was created by Benjamin Penhallow Shillaber (1814–90) of *The Boston Post* and forms the central figure in at least three books, *Life and Sayings of Mrs. Partington* (1854), *Partingtonian Patchwork* (1873), and *Ike and his Friends* (1879). Her character and manner of expression may be seen in her chance remarks:

I am not so young as I was once, and I don't believe I shall ever be, if I live to the age of Samson, which, heaven knows as well as I do, I don't want to, for I wouldn't be a centurion or an octagon and survive my factories and become idiomatic by any means. But then there is no knowing how a thing will turn out until it takes place, and we shall come to an end some day, though we may never live to see it.

Her benevolent face, her use of catnip tea, her faith in the almanac, her domestic virtue, and her knowledge of the most significant facts in the life of every person in the village immediately made a large circle of readers recognize the lifelike portrayal of a person known in every American community. It is interesting to observe that her nephew Ike and his experience with the dog and cat and with "spirits" is a striking prototype of Tom Sawyer in his relationship to his Aunt Polly.

Three New York writers of broad burlesque in both prose and verse may be mentioned together. There appeared in *The New York Herald* a series of satirical lyrics in the assumed character of an Irish private in the Union Army who rapidly became famous. These were written by Charles Graham Halpine (1829–68), a versatile Irish journalist and poet who had been with General Hunter in South Carolina, and were published subsequently in two volumes as *Life and Adventures, Songs, Services and Speeches of Private Miles O'Reilly* (1864). The best of this collection is the amusing account of the visit of the hero to the President, the members of the Cabinet, and foreign ministers at the White House. Mortimer Thompson (1832–75), actor, salesman, journalist, rhymester, was one of the most spirited of mid-century humorists, though his work is little more than (to use his own phrase) "a series of unpremeditated extravagances." He indulged in impudent prefaces, incredible titles, fantastic illustrations, and breathless satire upon every current popular enthusiasm. He went to Niagara and wrote back contemptuous letters to *The New York Tribune*. His *Plu-Ri-Bus-Tah* (1856) burlesqued *Hiawatha* in meter and the American eagle in attitude. His pseudonym was characteristically "Q. C. Philander Doesticks, P.B." In their day *The Orpheus C. Kerr*[1] *Papers* (1862–68) had a great vogue. They furnished sharp satire upon civil and military affairs in the darker days of the war. Lincoln read with great satisfaction their burlesque of the unescapable office-seeker of the time. The lampooning seems rather reckless today and the characterization overbroad. Newell was also a writer of serious and burlesque poems; he was well read, a clever wag, and an effective parodist.

George Horatio Derby (1823–61) has been called the real father of the new school of humour which began to flourish toward the middle of the nineteenth century. His sketches, with the signature "John Phœnix," began to appear about 1850, and were afterwards collected in two volumes, *Phœnixiana* (1855) and *Squibob Papers* (1859). Derby had graduated from West Point, had served in the Mexican War, and, as an engineer, had been engaged in surveying in the West and South. As a means of relaxation from his strenuous and exacting work, he set about writing down in humorous fashion his observations upon the life about him. In his books are to be found most of the elements used by humorists of more recent times. He delighted in the use of big words, high-sounding phrases and figures of speech, and euphemistic statements. We quote a short example:

This resplendent luminary, like a youth on the Fourth of July, has its first quarter; like a ruined spendthrift, its last quarter; and like an omnibus, is occasionally full and new. The evenings in which it appears between these last stages are beautifully illumined by its clear, mellow light.

[1] Orpheus C. Kerr = Office Seeker.

As a Western humorist, the first to introduce the spirit of the Pacific Coast into humorous literature, he influenced his admirer, Mark Twain, and as a writer of easy, fertile monologue he anticipated "Josh Billings," and "Artemus Ward," two of his most famous successors.

For the present discussion there remain three men who, in the history of American humour, stand out more prominently than all others from colonial days to Mark Twain: Henry Wheeler Shaw, "Josh Billings" (1818–85); David Ross Locke, "Petroleum V. Nasby" (1833–88); and Charles Farrar Browne, "Artemus Ward" (1834–67).

The first of these, a child of Massachusetts, wandered out to Ohio and finally settled as an auctioneer in New York State, where he began to contribute to various newspapers and magazines. His early writings attracted no attention until, in 1860, he changed his spelling in the *Essa on the Muel*, and then he achieved a popularity which never failed him. As a lecturer and as a witty philosopher he was not surpassed in his day. He is the comic essayist of America rather than her comic story-teller. His humour and his only strength lie in his use of the aphorism which is old but which he brings forth with as much sententiousness as if it were new. "With me everything must be put in two or three lines," he once said. He was not one to write humorously merely to amuse. He took delight in ridiculing humbug, quackery, and falsity of all kinds. His burlesque *Farmers' Allminax* (1870–80) were exceedingly popular.

Locke was born in New York State and became in turn journeyman printer, reporter, and editor in an Ohio town only a few miles west of Cleveland and Artemus Ward, whom indeed Locke began by imitating. In 1861 he began a series of letters in his paper over the signature "Petroleum V. Nasby." These letters were supposed to come from a pastor of the New Dispensation with "Copperhead" sympathies. Shortly afterwards "Nasby" settled in "Confedrit X Roads," Kentucky, where he drank whiskey, and preached to negro-hating Democrats of the type of "Deekin Pogram." After the war he received a commission as postmaster from Andrew Johnson. "Nasby" is a type of the backwoods preacher, reformer, workingman, postmaster, and chronic office-seeker, remarkable for his unswerving fidelity to the simple principles of personal and political selfishness. To him the luxuries of life are a place under the government, a glass of whiskey, a clean shirt, and a dollar bill. No writer ever achieved popularity more quickly. The letters were published in all the Northern papers, were as eagerly expected as news of the battles, and universally read by the Federal soldiers. "Nasby" was not only a humorist but he was a great force in carrying on the reconstructive measures of the Republican party after the war by his laughable but coarse and merciless pictures of the lowest elements in the Western States that had been opposed to the policy of equal justice.

Of all the humorists mentioned in this chapter "Artemus Ward" alone was known beyond the seas. He was born in Maine, travelled as a wandering printer in the South and West, and really began his career in 1857 when he was called to the local editorship of *The Cleveland Plain Dealer*. To this paper he began to contribute articles purporting to describe the experiences of Artemus Ward, an itinerant showman. He began to lecture in 1861 and had an unprecedented success on the platform in this country and in England, where he was a noted contributor to *Punch* and where he died. He had many and varied experiences and in them all saw nothing but humanity. He wrote of people and of their doings, not unkindly or profanely, but always as a moralist, waging warfare with abounding good humour upon all things that were merely sentimental and insincere and doing good service by exposing them in vivid caricatures. Although it was his genius for misspelling that first attracted attention — he was the first of the misspellers — his plaintive personality proved more attractive still, and may prove permanently so.

Derby, Shaw, Locke, and Browne carried to an extreme numerous tricks already invented by earlier American humorists, particularly the tricks of gigantic exaggeration and calm-faced mendacity, but they are plainly in the main channel of American humour, which had its origin in the first comments of settlers upon the conditions of the frontier, long drew its principal inspiration from the differences between that frontier and the more settled and compact regions of the country, and reached its highest development in Mark Twain, in his youth a child of the American frontier, admirer and imitator of Derby and Browne, and eventually a man of the world and one of its greatest humorists.

# CHAPTER XX

# Magazines, Annuals, and Gift-books, 1783–1850

## I. Magazines

O F the short-lived literary journals that were founded before and during the American Revolution, none appears to have survived the closing years of that struggle. Hardly had peace been declared, however, before new magazines were undertaken, and throughout the years covered by this chapter much of the literary history of America is bound up with a history of its periodicals. A complete account of American magazines during the early part of this period would be to a great extent a story of literary Chauvinism, of absurd literary ambition on the part of individuals and of communities, of misplaced faith in the literary tastes and interests of the people. The many failures are reminders of the unattained intellectual ambitions of the nation; a few commercially prosperous magazines furnish an index to the taste of the average reader; and a few show the best that was being thought and written. In a brief presentation only the most general tendencies can be considered and a few magazines cited as examples of important types. For convenience the period may be divided roughly into two sub-periods, one extending from the close of the Revolution to the close of the War of 1812, the other from 1815 to 1850.[1]

[1] In this treatment it will be unnecessary to draw any sharp line between "literary" magazines and those that were largely religious or scientific. The distinction between magazines and newspapers is more troublesome. By agreement with the author of the following chapter literary weeklies, except in one or two cases to be noted, will be considered as newspapers rather than as magazines.

During the period between the first and the second wars with Great Britain Americans were unduly sensitive over the lack of a national literature, and absurdly determined that such a literature should at once be produced. A considerable number of magazines were projected with the deliberate purpose of improving literary conditions, and of avoiding the taunts that crystallized in Sydney Smith's notorious question. The feeling of patriotism is reflected in such titles as *The Columbian Magazine*, *The American Magazine*, *The American Museum*, *The American Apollo*, *The Monthly Magazine and American Review*, *The United States Magazine*, *The American Universal Magazine*, *The American Moral and Sentimental Magazine*, *The National Magazine*—all of which were used before 1800. The rapid growth of periodicals was encouraged by the liberality of the post office. While under the Act of 1793 the postage on a single-sheet letter varied from eight to twenty-five cents according to distance, the postage on magazines was one and one-half cents a sheet for distances up to one hundred miles, and two and one-half cents per sheet for all greater distances— a rate but slightly higher than that charged for newspapers.

The chief centres of publication during the early period were Philadelphia, Boston, and New York, but almost every city which boasted a group of men with literary interests undertook at some time or other its literary magazine. Even Lexington, Kentucky, in what was then the extreme West, maintained as early as 1803 *The Medley*, by no means the least creditable of these ventures.

In this early time the different types of periodical were not sharply differentiated, yet it is possible to distinguish a few heavy and ambitious reviews, modelled on the British quarterlies, several literary miscellanies, which followed as nearly as might be the traditions of *The London Magazine* and *The Gentleman's Magazine*, and the more popular "Museums" and "Instructors" which contained interesting anecdotes and information gathered from all sources. Most of the more serious magazines gave summaries of current events. Few, if any, confined themselves to original articles, and some reprinted serially English works of a much earlier day. Such titles as *The American Museum, or Repository of Ancient and Modern Fugitive Pieces, Prose and Poetical* (Philadelphia,

1787), *The Universal Asylum and Columbian Magazine*
(Philadelphia, 1790), *The Omnium Gatherum* (Boston, 1809)
are significant. *Salmagundi* (New York, 1807) written by
Washington Irving, William Irving, and James K. Paulding,
was the only notable periodical essay which was published independently. As a rule the many imitators of *The Spectator*
contributed their effusions to some newspaper or magazine.

No literary periodical established before 1800 deserves
individual consideration. *The Literary Magazine and American Register* (Philadelphia, 1803–1807) was a serious and creditable work, containing reviews and miscellaneous contributions
in prose and verse, but it is better remembered because of its
editor, Charles Brockden Brown,[1] than because of its intrinsic
merits. A more important Philadelphia periodical was *The
Port Folio*, during the editorship of Joseph Dennie.[2] Dennie,
who signed himself "Oliver Oldschool," and accepted com-
placently the nickname of the "American Addison," was a conservative in letters, though he welcomed some of the earlier
work of the romantic school in England. During his editorship *The Port Folio* was devoted to what at the time was called
"elegant literature"; and though to a taste less influenced by
eighteenth-century standards it seems formal and sentimental,
it exerted a strong influence for good during a critical period
of American literature. Among the contributors were Charles
Brockden Brown and John Quincy Adams.

The most important of the Boston magazines before 1815
was *The Monthly Anthology*.[3] This was established in 1803
by one Phineas Adams, but after six months it passed into
the control of The Anthology Club, founded by the Rev.
William Emerson, which conducted it until it was abandoned
in 1811. The Anthology Club included at various times
from seven to sixteen Boston gentlemen of literary interests,
and a few honorary non-resident members. Each member

---

[1] See also Book II, Chap. VI.

[2] *The Port Folio* was founded in 1801 as a weekly newspaper. In 1806 it
changed its form and took on most of the characteristics of a magazine, though
it was still published weekly; in 1809 it became a monthly. Dennie died in 1812.
*The Port Folio* continued until 1827. For Dennie, see also Book II, Chap. III.

[3] The original title was *The Monthly Anthology and Magazine of Polite Literature*. With the change of proprietorship the sub-title became *The Massachusetts
Magazine*, and a little later *The Boston Review*.

was expected to contribute to the magazine. Books were assigned for review, manuscripts were accepted or rejected, and the policy of the magazine was determined by vote at the weekly meetings of the Club. *The Monthly Anthology* is notable for the high quality of some of its articles, and as the best example of a magazine which was actually edited "by a society of gentlemen" purely for the love of literature. It should also be remembered as, in a way, the forerunner of *The North American Review.*

In the years immediately following the close of the War of 1812 national life received a new impulse. The desire for a national literature was undiminished, though it was perhaps becoming more intelligent. Within a few years Americans were gratified by finding that in Irving and Cooper they had at least two authors who were highly appreciated abroad, and before 1850 many of the more distinguished writers of the century had established their reputations. With a real gain in literary prestige came an improvement in the tone and sanity of periodical literature, though to the close of the period far too many magazines were absurd in their pretensions and given to an excess of literary patriotism.

The return of peace soon brought another large crop of new periodicals. Boston, New York, and Philadelphia still led, of course, in the number of these ventures, but every town of literary pretensions tried to maintain a magazine. The South had its fair share; and in the region west of the Alleghanies there was a surprisingly large number. Cincinnati and Lexington were the most important publishing centres in this region, but several less famous towns in the Ohio Valley had their literary periodicals at an early date. By 1831 James Hall[1] was publishing *The Illinois Monthly Magazine* at Vandalia, and before 1850 Chicago and other cities in the central West had followed the prevailing fashion.

The different types of periodicals were a little more sharply distinguished than in the preceding period. There were several serious reviews, of which *The North American Review* was the most important, and *The American Quarterly Review* (Philadelphia, 1827-37) was perhaps the heaviest. There was a multitude of general literary magazines, con-

[1] See also Book II, Chap. VII.

taining fiction, essays, poetry, scientific and historical articles, and reviews. Magazines especially for ladies made their appearance, and one, *Godey's Lady's Book*, attained great vogue. It should also be remembered that this was a prosperous time for the popular literary weeklies, such as Willis's *Mirror* and *Home Journal*, which published the same class of contributions as the lighter literary and the ladies' magazines, but which are excluded from the scope of this chapter. In Philadelphia and Boston were published a number of periodicals that aimed at instruction, some of them reprinting classical works of English literature in large instalments, others giving in popular form miscellaneous information derived from encyclopædias and similar sources. Theological controversies, especially those over the Unitarian schism in New England, called forth a number of religious periodicals that are of importance to the student of American literature. There are also journals devoted to temperance and kindred reforms, and others too nondescript to classify.

The most important of the more serious periodicals was *The North American Review*, founded at Boston in 1815. The first editor, William Tudor, and several of the early contributors had been members of the Anthology Club. Tudor in later reminiscences gave as the reasons for establishing the magazine a desire to emancipate America from undue subservience to England in literary matters, and to neutralize the effects of the French Revolution on American political thought. But the *Review* was less flamboyant and absurd in its patriotism than many of its contemporaries, and to this fact may have been due its success. As first established it was a bi-monthly and published poetry, fiction, and other miscellaneous contributions, but in 1818 it became a quarterly and restricted the nature of its contents. The list of early contributors includes the names of Edward T. Channing, Richard Henry Dana, Jared Sparks, Edward Everett, Alexander H. Everett, John Adams, William Cullen Bryant, Gulian C. Verplanck, George Ticknor, Daniel Webster, Nathaniel Bowditch, George Bancroft, Caleb Cushing, Lewis Cass, and many more of the Americans best known in literary and political life. Like most such enterprises it was financially unprofitable at first, and it was never highly remunerative; but its literary importance was soon recognized abroad as well as at home. Until the founding of *The Atlantic Monthly* in 1857 it was the most valuable organ of the best conservative thought in New England; and it continued its traditions until 1878, when it suffered a change of management and of habitat, and to some extent of ideals.

Although the greater New England writers of the nineteenth century were well started on their careers by 1850, Boston succeeded in maintaining no general literary magazines of the first rank before *The Atlantic Monthly*. Several were begun with brilliant prospects and distinguished lists of contributors, but, sometimes for unexplained reasons, each in turn failed. Among those best remembered are *The United States Literary Gazette* (1825–27), to which Longfellow was a frequent contributor, *The New England Magazine* (Boston 1831–35), in which Holmes published two papers to which he gave the name "The Autocrat of the Breakfast Table," and Lowell's *Pioneer*. This last ran for but three issues in 1843, and left the promoters heavily in debt, though its list of contributors contained such names as those of Poe and Hawthorne. *The North American Review* furnished an opportunity for the publication of serious essays, but much of the lighter work of Longfellow, Hawthorne, Whittier, Lowell, and their contemporaries was contributed to the magazines of New York and Philadelphia. In what might be called informational periodicals Boston continued strong. Interest in one of the least of these, *The Magazine of Useful and Entertaining Knowledge*, has been preserved by the fact that Hawthorne was for a time the editor. *Littell's Living Age*, the best of the reprints from foreign journals, was begun in 1844.

The most picturesque of the Boston periodicals of the time was *The Dial*, published quarterly by a group of New England Transcendentalists from 1840 to 1844. Such an organ of the new thought had long been talked of, and as early as 1835 Emerson had proposed to Carlyle that the latter come to America and act as editor. It was not until July, 1840, however, that the first number of *The Dial* appeared, with Margaret Fuller as editor, and Emerson, Alcott, and Thoreau among the contributors. The magazine was never financially successful, the smallness of its subscription list being indicated by the rarity of complete sets today. Margaret Fuller, after serving gratuitously for two years, reluctantly resigned the editorship, and Emerson as reluctantly took it up, noting in his diary: "I wish it to live, but I do not wish to be its life. Neither do I like to put it into the hands of the Humanity and Reform Men, because they trample on letters and poetry; nor in the hands of the scholars, for they are dead and dry." After spending much time and some money Emerson too felt forced to abandon the undertaking, and *The Dial* came to an end with the close of the fourth volume. Among contributors other than those already noted were C. P. Cranch, George Ripley, William H. Channing, William Ellery Channing, Theodore Parker, James Freeman Clarke, James Russell Lowell, Charles A. Dana, and Jones Very. In its own day *The Dial* was regarded reverently by a few, but by the great mass of readers it was ignored or taken as a joke. A later generation still finds many things in its pages amusing but has come to recognize it as the best single exponent of New England Transcendentalism, and of the peculiar aspects of culture that accompanied that movement.[1]

Although *The Dial* was unique, several earlier and later Boston magazines appealed to much the same constituency. In 1838 the Reverend Orestes A. Brownson began to issue *The Boston Quarterly Review*, and the next year he urged the Transcendentalists to contribute to his journal rather than to found *The Dial*. After five years *The Boston Quarterly Review* was merged with *The Democratic Review* of New York. A more important periodical was *Brownson's Quarterly Review*, founded in 1844 after the editor had been converted to the Roman Catholic faith. An immediate successor of *The Dial* was *The Harbinger*, established in 1845 by the members of the Brook Farm community as an organ of Fourierism. From 1847 to 1850 the Reverend Theodore Parker, one of the most virile of the Transcendental group, conducted *The Massachusetts Quarterly Review*, which he humorously characterized as "*The Dial* with a beard."

One of the earliest of the popular New York magazines to attain permanency was *The Knickerbocker*.[2] This first

[1] See also Book II, Chap. VIII.
[2] Owing to some whim of Hoffman, the first editor, the spelling adopted for the earlier issues was Knickerbacker.

appeared 1 January, 1833, with Charles Fenno Hoffman[1] as editor. Bryant, Paulding, and Sands contributed to the first number. Hoffman was soon succeeded in the editorship by Timothy Flint[2] and Samuel Daly Langtree, and in April, 1834, the magazine passed into the control of Lewis Gaylord Clark,[3] who continued in the editorship until *The Knickerbocker* was abandoned in 1859. Clark's own writings in the "Editor's Table" department show little of the literary skill, taste, and knowledge which have characterized similar work by other editors of American magazines, but in spite of his apparent deficiencies he secured for many years the co-operation of the best writers of the country, and conducted what was in many ways the best general literary magazine. *The Knickerbocker Gallery*, an elaborate gift book published for the benefit of the editor in 1855, and made up of brief poems and essays donated by contributors to the magazine, contained pieces by Washington Irving, William Cullen Bryant, Henry Wadsworth Longfellow, Oliver Wendell Holmes, James Russell Lowell, N. P. Willis, Fitz-Greene Halleck, Donald Grant Mitchell, George H. Boker, Bayard Taylor, T. W. Parsons, Epes Sargent, J. G. Saxe, James T. Fields, Charles Godfrey Leland, George William Curtis, Park Benjamin, Rufus W. Griswold, Richard Henry Stoddard, C. F. Briggs, and many more; and among other contributors of the early time were Miss Sedgwick, James Gates Percival, Richard Henry Wilde, Mrs. Sigourney, William Gilmore Simms, J. G. Whittier, Horace Greeley, and James Fenimore Cooper. The importance of *The Knickerbocker Magazine* may be judged by this list of names; yet in dignity of tone and especially in the quality of its humour it was somewhat below the standard of several of its successors.

New York, like Boston, saw many ambitious attempts at literary periodicals. Only the special student of bibliography and literary biography will follow in detail the amalgamations and kaleidoscopic changes of such ventures as *The Atlantic Magazine*, *The New York Review and Athenæum Magazine*, and *The New York Literary Gazette*, even though the names of Bryant and Sands appear among the editors, and Halleck,

---

[1] See Book II, Chaps. V and VII.    [2] See also Book II, Chap. VII.
[3] See also Book II, Chaps. III and XIX.

Dana, Willis, Longfellow, and Bancroft among the contributors. Of somewhat longer continuance and greater importance was *The Democratic Review*, already mentioned as having absorbed *The Boston Quarterly Review*. In 1850, at the very close of the period, *Harper's Magazine* was established in New York, and at once took high rank.

Godey's Lady's Book, long the most popular of a class of magazines that has flourished in Philadelphia, was founded by Louis A. Godey in 1830, though not until after Mrs. Sarah J. Hale assumed the editorship in 1837 did it attain its greatest vogue. The success of the *Lady's Book* was largely due to its coloured fashion plates and a quantity of light and sentimental poetry and fiction, but its financial success enabled it to make seductive offers to distinguished writers, and it secured occasional contributions from Poe, Longfellow, Holmes, and others.

A later Philadelphia magazine was *Graham's*, established in 1841 by the union of *The Casket*, which had formerly been owned by George R. Graham and Charles J. Peterson, and *Burton's Gentleman's Magazine*, a monthly now remembered chiefly because Poe was for a time associate editor. Poe retained for something over a year a similar position on the new *Graham's Magazine*, and among his successors was the Rev. Rufus W. Griswold. The magazine achieved great popularity, and is said for a time to have brought its owner large financial returns. According to a somewhat dubious tradition its decline began when Graham published a harshly unfavourable review of *Uncle Tom's Cabin*. Among the contributors to *Graham's* in its best days were Cooper, Longfellow, Lowell, Hawthorne, and Simms.

Most of the Southern magazines were still conducted in a spirit of patriotism and local literary pride, rather than as paying business ventures. The most famous of these, *The Southern Literary Messenger*, was founded at Richmond in 1834. It was at first a semi-monthly, but soon changed to a monthly, though its appearance seems to have been at times somewhat irregular. Poe began to contribute to the *Messenger* in 1835, and later in the same year became editor. His tales and poems, and particularly his reviews, which were more independent in tone than had been common in America, added greatly to the fame of the magazine, but his editorship ceased with the beginning of the year 1837. Among later editors were Benjamin Blake Minor, who was both editor and proprietor from 1843 to 1847, and who later wrote a reminiscent history of the magazine; and John R. Thompson, who was Minor's immediate successor. Though it was distinctly Southern in tone the *Messenger* numbered among its contributors many distinguished Northerners—more, probably, than any other Southern magazine.

The rapid development of a distinctive Western literature and of Western periodicals is partly explained by the comparative isolation of the country west of the Alleghanies. In the early years of the century settlers in the Ohio and Mississippi valleys found difficulty in obtaining Eastern magazines regularly and promptly, and set about supplying their own needs. In this they were, of course, greatly encouraged by their local patriotism. *The Western Review and Miscellaneous Magazine* (Lexington, 1819–21), *The Western Monthly Review* (Cincinnati, 1827–30), *The Western Monthly Magazine* (Cincinnati, 1833–37), and other contemporary and later magazines were serious, well-considered, and, for the time and place, highly creditable; but as difficulties of communication were overcome they lost much of their significance, and Western authors exerted their greatest influence on American letters not through their local journals but by their contributions to the more cosmopolitan magazines of the seaboard cities.

To the very end of the period the publication of magazines continued to be a precarious and usually an unsuccessful undertaking. Few of the journals mentioned in the preceding pages were alive in 1850, and of these a much smaller number survived the Civil War. Indeed, of the more important literary periodicals founded before 1850, but one, *The North American Review*, was so firmly established that it lasted through the century. *Harper's*, the earliest of the literary magazines of high grade familiar today, was founded in 1850; and Boston waited seven years longer for the *Atlantic*. The short life and the financial difficulties of the earlier ventures must not always, however, be interpreted as signs of literary mediocrity, or of deficient appreciation on the part of American readers. At times such journals as the *Knicker-*

*bocker* and *Graham's,* and even others less successful, boasted lists of contributors quite as distinguished as those which most later magazines have been able to show.    It is true that in the last sixty years there has been great development in the arts of magazine editorship and of magazine authorship—the writing of articles especially adapted for publication in a periodical.    But in the same time have come improvement and cheapening of the processes of printing and of illustration, and the development of advertising.    Indeed, it is probable that it is chiefly in the mechanical and business rather than in the editorial departments that the better early magazines are at a disadvantage as compared with those of a later time.

Futile as the early experiments seemed, and slight as was the reward that they brought their editors and publishers, they did good service in their day.    By offering a ready means for the publication of literary attempts and for the exchange of ideas on literary matters they did much to clear the literary atmosphere and to make American men of letters sane and self-respecting.    Today the student of the taste and the ideals of that time finds in their files his most valuable sources of material.

## II.   ANNUALS AND GIFT-BOOKS

The publications described as literary annuals and gift-books varied in many respects but they agreed in being intended not primarily to be read but to be given away.    They were "Keepsakes," and "Souvenirs," and "Forget-me-nots," and "Tokens."    Many of them bore as sub-titles such phrases as "A gift for the holidays," or "A Christmas, New Year's and birthday present."    Almost or quite all of those published in America were literary miscellanies, the contents being original, or, in case of some of the cheaper volumes, "selected." A few, such as *The Odd-Fellows' Offering* and *The Masonic Token* were intended primarily for the members of certain organizations—there were religious annuals and temperance annuals, an anti-slavery annual, and even a "Knownothing Token"; but most such books made a general appeal to those who wished to bestow an "elegant" offering indicative of "refined" sentiment.    They varied in size and elaborateness from large paper volumes selling for twelve dollars each to diminutive and inexpensive souvenirs which a Sunday-school teacher might present to members of her class. The bindings of the best were in leather, elaborately tooled and sometimes inlaid with mother-of-pearl, or in richly watered silk. The "embellishments," as the pictures were commonly called, were most frequently engravings on steel, though there were many coloured plates, some coloured by hand.

The annual proper was supposed to be published from year to year, though many never made a second appearance. The year was frequently made a part of the title, as *The Gift of Friendship, a Token of Remembrance for 1848*, though sometimes the date appeared only at the foot of the title-page, or on the binding. The entire absence of a date was indicative of a desire to make unsold remainders available for the next year's market, or of still more questionable practices on the part of the publishers. Among these practices was that of reprinting an old annual with a new name, sometimes with change of plates and of leading article; or that of bestowing on an inferior work a name that had been made popular by another publisher. These devious procedures bring despair to bibliographers today, and they may originally have been one reason why the whole tribe of annuals fell into something of disrepute. A few of the annuals were in reality bound volumes of popular magazines with date-lines and other indications of periodical publication removed. The gift-books which are here considered resembled the annuals in form and purpose, but were avowedly not members of a series.

The annuals came as a late accompaniment of the wave of sentimentality in literature and art that swept over England and America during the early years of the nineteenth century. The fashion of issuing them is said to have started in Germany, whence it spread to England and a little later to America. *The Atlantic Souvenir* of 1826 was the first of the American annuals proper, though before that time there had been a few illustrated miscellanies which might be classed as gift-books. The number increased rapidly until, according to Mr. Faxon's excellent bibliography, "from 1846 to 1852 an average of sixty appeared each year." By the beginning of the Civil War the day of the annuals was over, though the list of holiday books has each year contained a few miscellanies intended chiefly as gifts.

A student's first impressions of the annuals are usually gained from the "embellishments." In respect of illustrations the American annuals rarely equalled the best of their English prototypes, yet the publishers enlisted the services of the foremost American engravers. John Cheney seems to have developed his talent in connection with his work for *The Token*, and he also executed plates for many other annuals. John Sartain and Alexander H. Ritchie were among the most prolific and successful of the workers in mezzotint. Publishers of the cheaper annuals employed cruder engravers, or used old plates, often so worn as to be almost worthless. It is in the subjects of the pictures rather than in the workmanship of the engravers that the sentimental character of the annuals reveals itself. Many of these were taken from British paintings, others were by American artists; they were likely to be female figures and faces, romantic landscapes, or pictures hinting at pathetic or chastely amorous tales. In an annual taken at random, *Leaflets of Memory* for 1845, the illustrations are entitled "Julia," "Was it for this?" "We part no more," "The heart's best dream," "The Christian slave," "The past and present," "The rose of the ruin," "The Grecian maid," "Myrrha." Pictures designed for fine editions of standard authors were often introduced with change of name, and not infrequently the process of illustration was reversed, and poems or tales were written to fit the renamed plate.

It is not strange that volumes which are so palpably indicative of the commercial side of publishing, and that appealed to a constituency often more "elegant" and "refined" than intellectual, should be treated in later years with scant respect. Charles Lamb, Thackeray, and George Eliot all indulged in humour at the expense of the annuals and their admirers, and in America Miss Agnes Repplier and others who have given them passing notice adopt the same tone. They were not, however, without literary importance. Their exuberances and peculiarities register for the literary historian some of the less admirable qualities of popular taste; and they really contain much work of value. At a time when most of the literary magazines were living but a precarious existence many of the annuals were well established and financially successful. It was the annuals and not the magazines that were able to pay what was considered a lavish price for a few verses or a short tale by a popular author. It is too true that they often depended on the names of one or two distinguished contributors to sell a volume composed largely of cheaper material; but men like Poe, Irving, Bryant, Whittier, Emerson, Longfellow, Lowell, and Holmes were not ashamed to contribute to annuals, and often furnished some of their best work. The better editors were also alert for modest and unknown merit. It was in annuals that most of Hawthorne's *Twice Told Tales* first saw the light, and these were all printed without the author's name. Change of taste has left the twentieth century reader sadly out of sympathy with the annuals, but they invite from the student more attention than they have yet received.

Few of the annuals deserve individual consideration. *The Atlantic Souvenir*, already mentioned as the earliest of its kind in America, was published by H. C. Carey and I. Lea of Philadelphia from 1826 to 1832. It was a small and not a very elaborate volume, but it contained poems, essays, and tales by some of the most popular writers of the day. After the issue for 1832 it was merged with *The Token*, published by Gray & Bowen, of Boston, and later volumes of the latter bore the title *The Token and Atlantic Souvenir*. *The Token* was first issued in 1828 with Samuel G. Goodrich as both editor and publisher, and Goodrich continued to edit it until its demise in 1842, except the second volume, which bore the name of N. P. Willis on the title-page. *The Token* was one of the best of the earlier annuals as regards literary content, and though less showy than many of its later rivals it contained illustrations of high merit. A large number of Hawthorne's tales and sketches were first published in *The Token*, and among the contributors were N. P. Willis, Miss Sedgwick, Longfellow, Mrs. Child, and other writers whose names are less impressive now than they were in their own day. John Cheney was for a time employed exclusively on work for *The Token*, and throughout the quality of the engraving was good. The popularity and the intrinsic merit of *The Token* offered temptations to piratical publishers. After the abandonment of the legitimate series, *The Token* for 1838, one of the best volumes, appeared in at least ten re-issues by different publishers, with changes of title and of plates, and in some instances with abridgment of contents. The volume for 1840 was similarly treated at least five times. The name was also adopted by a New York publisher for the reprint of a cheap annual which appeared without date in the later fifties.

*The Rose of Sharon, a Religious Souvenir* (Boston, 1840 to 1858) boasted a longer continuous existence than any of the other American annuals. The first ten volumes were edited by Miss Sarah C. Edgarton, the last eight by Mrs. Caroline M. Sawyer. The volume for 1857 was reissued, merely with change of date, "for 1858"; and a publisher at Auburn, New York, borrowed the title for a wholly different work in 1849. *The Rose of Sharon* was somewhat showy in binding, but was good in typography and illustrations, and in literary contents was an average example of the better grade of annuals. *The Opal, A Pure Gift for the Holy Days*, published by John C. Riker, New York, survived only from 1844 to 1849 inclusive, but it was made attractive by contributions from Poe, Willis, Longfellow, and Whittier, and by plates by Cheney and Sartain.

Among annuals that differ a little from the ordinary was *The Talisman*, which was published at New York for 1828, 1829, and 1830. The literary contents were prepared in collaboration by William Cullen Bryant, Robert C. Sands, and Gulian C. Verplanck, and the illustrations were by artist friends of the authors, among them Henry Inman and S. F. B. Morse. The volumes were unpretending in appearance, but the literary quality was high. *The Boston Book* (Boston, 1836, 1837, 1841, 1850) is, in the words of the editor, "a compilation of specimens,—or, essentially, a specimen, in the aggregate—of the modern literature of the metropolis of the North." *The Liberty Bell, by Friends of Freedom*, published nearly every year from 1839 to 1858 for the benefit of the annual anti-slavery fair or anti-slavery bazaar in Boston, contained contributions from all the leading anti-slavery writers of New England.

Others of the better known annuals were *The Amaranth, The Christmas Blossoms and New Year's Wreath, The Diadem, The Forget-Me-Not, Friendship's Offering, The Garland, The Gem of the Season, The Gift, The Gift of Friendship, The Hyacinth*

*The Keepsake, The Keepsake of Friendship, Leaflets of Memory, The Lily, The Lily of the Valley, The Magnolia, The Mayflower, The Odd-Fellows' Offering, The Religious Souvenir, The Remember Me.* These and others had each its especial admirers, and the critic of today hardly need attempt the task of deciding on their respective merits.

# CHAPTER XXI

# Newspapers, 1775–1860

THE turbulent years between 1775 and 1783 were a time of great trial and disturbance among newspapers. Interruption, suppression, and lack of support so checked their growth that at the close of the war they were in most respects less thriving than at the beginning of it. Although there were forty-three newspapers in the United States when the treaty of peace was signed, as compared with thirty-seven on the date of the battle of Lexington, only a dozen had had continuous existence between the two events, and most of those had experienced delays and difficulties through lack of paper, type, and patronage. Not one newspaper in the principal cities, Boston, New York, and Philadelphia, continued publication throughout the war. When the colonial forces were in possession, royalist papers were suppressed, and at times of British occupation Revolutionary papers moved away, or were discontinued, or they became royalist, only to suffer at the next turn of military fortunes. Thus there was an exodus of papers from the cities along the coast to smaller inland places, where alone it was possible for them to continue without interruption. Scarcity of paper was acute; type worn out could not be replaced. The appearance of the newspapers deteriorated, and issues sometimes failed to appear at all. Mail service, never good, was poorer than ever; foreign newspapers, an important source of information, could be obtained but rarely; many of the ablest writers who had filled the columns with dissertations upon colonial rights and government were now otherwise occupied.

News from a distance was less full and regular than before; yet when great events happened reports spread over the country with great rapidity, through messengers in the service of patriotic organizations. The newspapers made use of such assistance, and did service in further spreading the tidings, though they seldom overtook the flying word of mouth. Naturally, reporting was still imperfect. The Salem *Gazette* printed a full but coloured account of the battle of Lexington, giving details of the burning, pillage, and barbarities charged to the British, and praising the militia who were filled with "higher sentiments of humanity." The Declaration of Independence was published by Congress, 6 July, 1776, in the Philadelphia *Evening Post*, from which it was copied by most of the papers; but some of them did not mention it until two weeks later, and even then found room for only a synopsis. When they were permitted to do so they printed fairly full accounts of the proceedings of provincial assemblies and of Congress, which were copied widely, as were all official reports and proclamations. On the whole, however, a relatively small proportion of such material and an inadequate account of the progress of the war is found in the contemporaneous newspapers.

The general spirit of the time found fuller utterance in mottoes, editorials, letters, and poems. In the beginning both editorials and communications urged united resistance to oppression, praised patriotism, and denounced tyranny; as events and public sentiment developed these grew more vigorous, often a little more radical than the populace. Later, the idea cf independence took form, and theories of government were discussed. More interesting and valuable as specimens of literature than these discussions were the poems inspired by the stirring events of the time. Long narratives of battles and of heroic deaths were mingled with eulogies of departed heroes. Songs meant to inspire and thrill were not lacking. Humour, pathos, and satire sought to stir the feelings of the public. Much of the poetry of the Revolution is to be found in the columns of dingy newspapers, from the vivid and popular satires and narratives of Freneau[1] to the saddest effusions of the most commonplace schoolmaster.

The newspapers of the Revolution were an effective force working towards the unification of sentiment, the awakening of a consciousness of a common purpose, interest, and destiny

[1] See Book I, Chap. IX.

among the separate colonies, and of a determination to see the war through to a successful issue. They were more single-minded than the people themselves, and they bore no small share of the burden of arousing and supporting the often discouraged and indifferent public spirit. Many of the papers, however, which were kept alive or brought to life during the war could not adapt themselves to the new conditions of peace.

Perhaps a dozen of the survivors held their own in the new time, notably the Boston *Gazette*, which declined rapidly in the following decade, *The Connecticut Courant* of Hartford, *The Providence Gazette*, and *The Pennsylvania Packet* of Philadelphia, to which may be added such representative papers as *The Massachusetts Spy*, the Boston *Independent Chronicle*, the New York *Journal* and *Packet*, the Newport *Mercury*, *The Maryland Gazette* of Annapolis, *The Pennsylvania Gazette* and *The Pennsylvania Journal*, both of Philadelphia. Practically all were of four small pages, each of three or four columns, issued weekly. *The Pennsylvania Packet*, which appeared three times a week, became in 1784 the first daily paper. In the same year the New York *Journal* was published twice a week, as were several of the papers begun in that year. There was a notable extension to new fields. In Vermont, where the first paper, established in 1781, had soon died, another arose in 1783; in Maine two were started in 1785. In 1786 the first one west of the Alleghanies appeared at Pittsburg, and following the westward tide of immigration *The Kentucky Gazette* was begun at Lexington in 1787.

Conditions were hardly more favourable to newspapers than during the recent conflict. The sources of news were much the same; the means of communication and the postal system were little improved. Newspapers were not carried in the mails but by favour of the postmen, and the money of one state was of dubious value in another. Consequently circulations were small, rarely reaching a thousand; subscribers were slow in paying; and advertisements were not plentiful. Newspapers remained subject to provincial laws of libel, in accordance with the old common law, and were, as in Massachusetts for a short time in 1785, subject to special state taxes on paper or on advertisements. But public sentiment was growi:ng strongly against all legal restrictions, and in general the papers practised freedom, not to say license, of utterance. With independence had come the consciousness of a great destiny. The collective spirit aroused by the war, though clouded by conflicting local difficulties, was intense, and the principal interest of the newspapers was to create a nation out of the loose confederation. Business and commerce were their next care; but in an effort to be all things to all men, the small page included a little of whatever might "interest, instruct, or amuse." Political intelligence occupied first place; news, in the modern sense, was subordinated. A new idea, quite as much as a fire, a murder, or a prodigy, was a matter of news moment. There were always a few items of local interest, usually placed with paragraphs of editorial miscellany. Correspondents, in return for the paper, sent items; private letters, often no doubt written with a view to such use, were a fruitful source of news; but the chief resource was the newspapers which every office received as exchanges, carried in the post free of charge, and the newspapers from abroad.

The newspaper continued to compete with the magazine by supplying moral, descriptive, and sentimental essays, poetry, anecdotes, reflections, and articles on trade, education, and conduct. Imitators of the English writers of periodical essays, the beginning of whose activities almost coincided with that of American newspapers,[1] multiplied in numbers, until towards the close of the century it was a poor paper that did not maintain at least one series. The "Lay Preacher" essays of Joseph Dennie[2] gave *The Farmers' Museum* of Walpole, New Hampshire, as wide a reputation as that of any paper in its day.

The editor, usually reflecting the sentiment of a group or a faction, began to emerge as a distinct power. He closely followed the drift of events and expressed vigorous opinions. But as yet the principal discussions were contributed not by the editors but by "the master minds of the country." The growing importance of the newspaper was shown in the discussions preceding the Federal Convention, and notably in the country-wide debate on the adoption of the Constitution, in which the

[1] See Book I, Chap. VII, and Book II, Chap. III.
[2] See Book II, Chap. III.

newspaper largely displaced the pamphlet. When Hamilton, Madison, and Jay united to produce the *Federalist* essays,[1] they chose to publish them in *The Independent Journal* and *The Daily Advertiser*, from which they were copied by practically every paper in America long before they were made into a book. When the first Congress assembled 4 March, 1789, the administration felt the need of a paper, and, under the influence of Hamilton, John Fenno issued at New York, 15 April, the first number of *The Gazette of the United States*, the earliest of a series of administration organs. The seat of government became the journalistic centre of the country, and as long as party politics remained the staple news interest the administration organs and their opponents were the chief sources of news for the papers of the country.

One question of great importance to the press was early raised and settled. Reports of state legislative proceedings had always been permitted in the colonies, though in Massachusetts the reporters had been denied the use of the chaplain's pulpit as a desk. As soon as the first Congress assembled, the newspapers began to print the proceedings and debates, whereupon, in September, a Mr. Burke moved that representatives of the press should be excluded from the sessions. After a warm debate the resolution was withdrawn, never again to be revived, at a time when the taking of notes in the British Parliament was still forbidden.

Partisan bitterness increased during the last decade of the century. New England papers were generally Federalist; in Pennsylvania there was a balance; in the West and South the anti-Federalist press predominated. Though the Federalists were vigorously supported by such able papers as Russell's *Columbian Centinel* in Boston, Thomas's *Massachusetts Spy*, *The Connecticut Courant*, and, after 1793, Noah Webster's daily *Minerva* (soon renamed *Commercial Advertiser*) in New York, *The Gazette of the United States*, which in 1790 followed Congress and the capital to Philadelphia, was at the centre of conflict, "a paper of pure Toryism," as Thomas Jefferson said, "disseminating the doctrines of monarchy, aristocracy, and the exclusion of the people." To offset the influence of this, Jefferson and Madison induced Philip Freneau, who had been

[1] See Book I, Chap. VIII.

editing *The Daily Advertiser* in New York, to set up a "half weekly," to "go through the states and furnish a Whig vehicle of intelligence." Freneau's *National Gazette*, which first appeared 31 October, 1791, soon became the most outspoken critic of the administration of Adams, Hamilton, and Washington, and an ardent advocate of the French Revolution. Fenno and Freneau, in *The Gazette of the United States* and *The National Gazette*, at once came to grips, and the campaign of personal and party abuse in partisan news reports, in virulent editorials, in poems and skits of every kind, was echoed from one end of the country to the other.

This decade of violence was nevertheless one of development in both the quality and the power of newspapers. News reporting was extended to new fields of local affairs, and the intense rivalry of all too numerous competitors awoke the beginnings of that rush for the earliest reports which was to become the dominant trait in American journalism. The editor evolved into a new type. As a man of literary skill, or a politician, or a lawyer with a gift for polemical writing, he began to supersede the contributors of essays as the strongest writer on the paper. Much of the best writing, and of the rankest scurrility, be it said, was produced by editors born and trained abroad, like Bache of the *Aurora*, Cobbett, Cooper, Gales, Cheetham, Callender, Lyon, and Holt. Of the whole number of papers in the country towards the end of the decade, more than one hundred and fifty, at least twenty opposed to the administration were conducted by aliens. The power wielded by these anti-administration editors impressed John Adams, who in 1801 wrote: "If we had been blessed with common sense, we should not have been overthrown by Philip Freneau, Duane, Callender, Cooper, and Lyon, or their great patron and protector. A group of foreign liars encouraged by a few ambitious native gentlemen have discomfited the education, the talents, the virtues, and the prosperity of the country."

The most obvious example of that Federalist lack of common sense was the passage of the Alien and Sedition laws in 1797 to protect the government and its chief officers from the libels of politicians and editors. The result was a dozen convictions and a storm of outraged public opinion that threw the party from power and gave the radical Republican press renewed confidence and the material benefit of patronage when the anti-Federalists took control of the government. The passing of the Federalist party made a radical change in journalistic supremacy, but for a third of a century the newspapers were to continue primarily party organs; the tone remained strongly partisan, though it gradually gained poise and attained a degree of literary excellence and professional dignity.

The number and geographical distribution of newspapers grew apace. Whereas in 1800 there were between 150 and 200 all told, by 1810 there were 366, and during the next two decades the increase was at least equally rapid. With astonishing promptness the press followed the sparse population as it trickled westward and down the Ohio or penetrated the more northerly forests. By 1835 papers had spread to the Mississippi River and beyond, from Texas to St. Louis, throughout Ohio, Indiana, Illinois, Michigan, and into Wisconsin. These pioneer papers, poorly written, poorly printed, and partisan often beyond all reason, served a greater than a merely local purpose in sending weekly to the seat of government their hundreds of messages of good and evil report, of politics and trade, of weather and crops, that helped immeasurably to bind the far-flung population into a nation. Every congressman wrote regularly to his own local paper; other correspondents were called upon for like service, and in some instances the country editors established extensive and reliable lines of intelligence; but most of them depended on the bundle of exchanges from Washington, Philadelphia, and New York, and reciprocally the city papers made good use of their country exchanges.

Meanwhile the daily newspapers were increasing in number. The first had appeared in Philadelphia and New York in 1784 and 1785; in 1796 one appeared in Boston. By 1810 there were twenty-seven in the country—one in the city of Washington, five in Maryland, seven in New York, nine in Pennsylvania, three in South Carolina, and two in Louisiana. As early as 1835 the Detroit *Free Press* began its long career.

The political and journalistic situation made the administration organ one of the characteristic features of the period. Fenno's *Gazette* had served the purpose for Washington and

Adams; but the first great example of the type was *The National Intelligencer* established in October, 1800, by Samuel Harrison Smith, to support the administration of Jefferson and of successive presidents until after Jackson it was thrown into the opposition, and *The United States Telegraph*, edited by Duff Green, became the official paper. It was replaced at the close of 1830 by a new paper, *The Globe*, under the editorship of Francis P. Blair, one of the ablest of all ante-bellum political editors, who, with John P. Rives, conducted it until the changing standards and conditions in journalism rendered the administration organ obsolescent. *The Globe* was displaced in 1841 by another paper called *The National Intelligencer*, which in turn gave way to *The Madisonian*. Thomas Ritchie was in 1845 called from his long service on *The Richmond Enquirer* to found, on the remains of *The Globe*, the Washington *Union*, to speak for the Polk administration and to reconcile the factions of democracy. Neither the *Union* nor its successors, which maintained the semblance of official support until 1860, ever occupied the commanding position held by the *Telegraph* and *The Globe*, but for forty years the administration organs had been the leaders when political journalism was dominant. Their influence was shared and increased by such political editors as M. M. Noah[1] and James Watson Webb of the New York *Courier and Enquirer*, Solomon Southwick of the Albany *Register*, Edwin Croswell, who edited *The Argus* and who, supported by Van Buren and others, formed what was known as the "Albany Regency." The "Regency," the Richmond "Junta," which centred in the *Enquirer*, and the "Kitchen Cabinet" headed by the editor of *The Globe*, formed one of the most powerful political and journalistic cabals that the country has ever known. Their decline, in the late thirties, was coincident with great changes, both political and journalistic, and though successors arose, their kind was not again so prominent or influential. The newspaper of national scope was passing away, yielding to the influence of the telegraph and the railroad, which robbed the Washington press of its claim to prestige as the chief source of political news. At the same time politics was losing its predominating importance. The public

[1] See also Book II, Chap. II.

had many other interests, and by a new spirit and type of journalism was being trained to make greater and more various demands upon the journalistic resources of its papers.

The administration organ presents but one aspect of a tendency in which political newspapers generally gained in editorial individuality, and both the papers and their editors acquired greater personal and editorial influence. The beginnings of the era of personal journalism, the chief figures in which will be discussed in later paragraphs, were to be found early in the century. Even before Nathan Hale had shown the way to editorial responsibility, Thomas Ritchie, in the Richmond *Enquirer* in the second decade of the century, had combined with an effective development of the established use of anonymous letters on current questions a system of editorial discussion that soon extended his reputation and the influence of his newspaper far beyond the boundaries of Virginia. Washington Barrow and the Nashville *Banner*, Amos Kendall and *The Argus of Western America*, G. W. Kendall and the New Orleans *Picayune*, John M. Francis and the Troy *Times*, and Charles Hammond and the Cincinnati *Gazette*, to mention but a few among many, illustrate the rise of editors to individual power and prominence in the third and later decades. Notable among these political editors was John M. Daniel, who just before 1850 became editor of the Richmond *Examiner* and soon made it the leading newspaper of the South. Perhaps no better example need be sought of brilliant invective and literary pungency in American journalism just prior to and during the Civil War than in Daniel's contributions to the *Examiner*.

Though it could still be said that "too many of our gazettes are in the hands of persons destitute at once of the urbanity of gentlemen, the information of scholars, and the principles of virtue," a fact due largely to the intensity of party spirit, the profession was by no means without editors who exhibited all these qualities, and put them into American journalism. William Coleman, for instance, who, encouraged by Hamilton, founded the New York *Evening Post*[1] in 1801, was a man of high purposes, good training, and noble ideals. The *Evening Post*, reflecting variously the fine qualities of the editor,

[1] See also Book II, Chap. v.

exemplified the improvement in tone and illustrated the growing importance of editorial writing, as did a dozen or more papers in the early decades of the century. Indeed the problem most seriously discussed at the earliest state meetings of editors and publishers, held in the thirties, was that of improving the tone of the press. They tried to attain by joint resolution a degree of editorial self-restraint which few individual editors had as yet acquired. Under the influence of Thomas Ritchie, vigorous and unsparing political editor but always a gentleman, who presided at the first meeting of Virginia journalists, the newspaper men in one state after another resolved to " abandon the infamous practice of pampering the vilest of appetites by violating the sanctity of private life, and indulging in gross personalities and indecorous language," and to " conduct all controversies between themselves with decency, decorum, and moderation." Ritchie found in the low tone of the newspapers a reason why journalism in America did not occupy as high a place in public regard as it did in England and France. The editorial page was assuming something of its modern form. The editorial signed with a pseudonym gradually passed away, but unsigned editorial comment and leading articles did not become an established feature until after 1814, when Nathan Hale made them a characteristic of the newly established Boston *Daily Advertiser*. From that time on they grew in importance until in the succeeding period of personal journalism they were the most vital part of the greater papers.

As the magazines were still few and offered poor pay, if any at all, the newspaper became the means of support of innumerable authors, and even in this age of the political press there were as many literary as political editors. In contrast with the situation today, when the magazines are generally conducted by men whose tastes and ideals have been formed in journalism rather than in literature, and assume more and more the characteristics of timeliness, until the middle of the century the newspapers owed their character to men of literary tastes and pursuits. When Bennett the elder referred slurringly to the "poets of the *Post*" and the *Post* declared that Bennett was not a journalist, a momentous divergence and change of ideals was indicated.

Changes which came about in the thirties well-nigh re-volutionized the newspapers. Within a decade the cheap newspaper was begun; steam presses were introduced; a radical alteration took place in the idea of news values, reporting, and correspondence; freedom from party control was found possible; and important modifications took place in the party press.

Several of these changes are exemplified in the work of James Gordon Bennett (1794-1872), though he originated few of them. In more than ten years of unsuccessful effort as a political journalist he had become familiar with the increasing enterprise in news-gathering that had already distinguished American methods. He despised the journalism of the day— the seriousness of tone, the phlegmatic dignity, the party affiliations, the sense of responsibility. He believed journalists were fools to think that they could best serve their own pur-poses by serving the politicians. As Washington correspondent for the New York *Enquirer*, he wrote vivacious, gossipy prattle, full of insignificant and entertaining detail, to which he added keen characterization and deft allusions. Bennett saw a public who would not buy a serious paper at any price, who had a vast and indiscriminate curiosity better satisfied with gossip than discussion, with sensation rather than fact, who could be reached through their appetites and passions.

The idea which he did much to develop rested on the success of the one-cent press created by the establishment of the New York *Sun* in 1833. To pay at such a price these papers must have large circulations, sought among the public that had not been accustomed to buy papers, and gained by printing news of the street, shop, and factory. To reach this public Bennett began the New York *Herald*, a small paper, fresh, sprightly, terse, and "newsy."

"In journalistic débuts of this kind," he wrote, "many talk of principle—political principle, party principle—as a sort of steel trap to catch the public. We . . . disdain . . . all principle, as it is called, all party, all politics. Our only guide shall be good, sound, practical common sense, applicable to the business and bosoms of men engaged in every-day life."

News was but a commodity, the furnishing of which was a busi-ness transaction only, which ignored the social responsibility of the press, "the grave importance of our vocation," prized of the elder journalists and of the still powerful six-cent papers. The *Herald*, like the *Sun*, was at once successful, and was remarkably influential in altering journalistic practices.

This idea of news and the newspaper for its own sake, the unprecedented aggressiveness in news-gathering, and the blatant methods by which the cheap papers were popularized aroused the antagonism of the older papers, but created a competition which could not be ignored. Systems of more rapid news-gathering and distribution quickly appeared. Sporadic attempts at co-operation in obtaining news had already been made; in 1848 the *Journal of Commerce, Courier and Enquirer, Tribune, Herald, Sun,* and *Express* formed the New York Associated Press to obtain news for the members jointly. Out of this idea grew other local, then state, and finally national associations. European news, which, thanks to steamship service, could now be obtained when but half as old as before, became an important feature. In the forties several papers sent correspondents abroad, and in the next decade this field was highly developed.

The literary departments of newspapers were being stimulated by the rise of literary or semi-literary weeklies. Some of these, such as *The Notion* in Boston, and *The New World* and *Brother Jonathan* in New York, were devoted mainly to the reprinting of English novels and other literary successes. Others, like *The New York Mirror*, contained sketches of life and manners, society verse, stories, and essays, as well as some news. The *Mirror* and its kind were a source of much material for newspapers. N. P. Willis's[1] *Pencillings by the Way*, for instance, were copied by five hundred newspapers. Another class of weeklies of general circulation contained much literary material combined with a larger proportion of politics and affairs. Such a paper was Greeley's *New Yorker*, "devoted mainly to current literature, but giving regularly a digest of all important news," and maintaining a good editorial page. Neither magazine nor newspaper, these weeklies were something of each. From the former they doubtless took away a good many readers; to the latter they were an incentive to the

[1] See also Book II. Chap. II.

maintaining of literary departments which in a few papers, like the *Tribune*, became important.

Newspapers in foreign languages, especially the German, multiplied rapidly about the middle of the century. Some of the ablest journalists of the middle of the century, not only of papers in the German language but also of papers in English, were liberal-minded Germans who sought in America the freedom of speech which was denied them in their native country.

The telegraph, in 1844 shown to be practical, and put to successful use during the Mexican War, led to numerous far-reaching results in journalism. Telegraphic columns became a leading feature; news associations grew as the wires lengthened; but the greatest effect on the journalism of the country at large was to decentralize the press by rendering the inland papers, in such cities as Chicago, Louisville, Cincinnati, St. Louis, and New Orleans independent of those in Washington and New York. A change made in the postal laws in 1845 favoured the local circulation of newspapers. The country circulation of most of the large Eastern papers was so curtailed that only one or two, like the New York *Tribune*, were able to maintain through their weekly editions something of their national character; the organs in Washington, even Niles's *Weekly Register*, which had been a most useful vehicle for the disseminating of political information, were still further shorn of their usefulness and soon eliminated; and the already vigorous provincial press became numerous and powerful.

In a period of wide-spread unrest and change many specialized forms of journalism sprang up—religious, educational, agricultural, and commercial, which there is no space here to discuss. Workingmen were questioning the justice of existing economic systems and raising a new labour problem; the socialistic ideas of Cabet and Fourier were spreading; Unitarianism and Transcendentalism were creating and expressing new spiritual values; temperance, prohibition, and the political status of women were being discussed; abolition was a general irritant and a nightmare to politicians. The subject of controversy most critically related to journalism was abolition. The abolitionist press which began with *The Emancipator* of 1820, and had its chief representative in William Lloyd Garrison's *Liberator*, first issued 1 January, 1831, forced the slavery question upon the newspapers, and there ensued a struggle for the freedom of the press more acute than any since that caused by the Alien and Sedition laws. Many abolitionist papers were excluded from the mails; their circulation was forcibly prevented in the South; in Boston, New York, Baltimore, Cincinnati, Alton, and elsewhere, editors were assaulted, offices were attacked and destroyed; rewards were offered in the South for the capture of Greeley and Garrison; in a few instances editors, like Lovejoy at Alton, lost their lives at the hands of mobs.

Out of the period of restless change in the thirties there emerged a few great editors whose force and ability gave them and their newspapers an influence hitherto unequalled, and made the period between 1840 and 1860 that of personal journalism. These few men not only interpreted and reflected the spirit of the time, but were of great influence in shaping and directing public opinion. Consequently the scope, character, and influence of newspapers was in the period immensely widened and enriched, and rendered relatively free from the worst subjection to political control.

Naturally, the outstanding feature of this personal journalism was the editorial. Rescued from the slough of ponderousness into which it had fallen in its abject and uninspired party service, the editorial was revived, invigorated, and endowed with a vitality that made it the centre about which all other features of the newspaper were grouped. It was individual; however large the staff of writers, the editorials were regarded as the utterance of the editor. "Greeley says" was the customary preface to quotations from the *Tribune*, and indeed many editorials were signed. James Gordon Bennett, Samuel Bowles (1826–78), Horace Greeley (1811–72), and Henry J. Raymond (1820–69) are the outstanding figures of the period. Of Bennett's influence something has already been said; especially, he freed his paper from party control. His power was great, but it came from his genius in gathering and presenting news rather than from editorial discussion, for he had no great moral, social or political ideals, and his influence, always lawless and uncertain, can hardly be regarded as characteristic of the period. Of the others named, and many besides, it could be said with approximate truth that their ideal was "a full presentation and a liberal discussion of all questions of public concernment, from an entirely independent position, and a faithful and impartial exhibition of all movements of interest at home and abroad." As all three were not only upright and independent, but in various measure gifted with the quality of statesmanship at once philosophical and practical, their newspapers were powerful moulders of opinion at a critical period in the history of the nation.

The news field was immeasurably broadened; news style was improved; interviews, newly introduced, lent the ease and freshness of dialogue and direct quotation. There was a notable improvement in the reporting of business, markets, and finance. In a few papers the literary department was conducted by staffs as able as any today. A foreign news service was developed which in intelligence, fidelity, and general excellence reached the highest standard yet attained in American journalism. A favourite feature was the series of letters from the editor or other member of the staff who travelled and wrote of what he heard or saw. Bowles, Olmsted, Greeley, Bayard Taylor, Bennett, and many others thus observed life and conditions at home or abroad; and they wrote so entertainingly and to such purpose that the letters—those of Olmsted and Taylor, for instance—are still sources of entertainment or information.

The growth of these papers meant the development of great staffs of workers that exceeded in numbers anything dreamed of in the preceding period. Although later journalism has far exceeded in this respect the time we are now considering, still the scope, complexity, and excellence of our modern metropolitan journalism in all its aspects were clearly begun between 1840 and 1860.

The highest development in provincial journalism during this period is typified in the Springfield *Republican*. Established by Samuel Bowles in 1824 as a country weekly, it was converted into a daily in 1844 by his energetic and ambitious son, who bore the same name. From the beginning it was a clean, well written, honest, independent, and conservative paper that reported all of the happenings of its own vicinity, with brief mention of the gist of important events generally.

As rapidly as possible its news-gathering was extended until within a few years its columns contained departments of items from every town and hamlet along the Connecticut valley, as well as from Springfield. Bowles believed that the newspaper should be a power in the moral, religious, and literary, as well as the political life of the community, and he tried to make his paper fulfill those functions, not for the world at large but for the people of western Massachusetts. With the aid of J. G. Holland and others who joined the staff the paper attained excellent literary quality and a high moral tone. Probably its success rested most of all upon its political discussions. The excellence of its short, crisp, pithy editorial paragraphs and longer discussions, free from pedantry and heaviness, based always on fundamental ideas and principles, made the *Republican* widely known and respected. Its opinions soon reached all New England, and after the formation of the Republican party they extended far beyond the limits of any section. But in spite of the extent of its influence, the *Republican* held steadily to its purpose as a provincial newspaper; it told all the news, gave all sides a fair hearing, preserved its self-respect and independence, frowned on all "isms," and presented invariably the personal opinions of its editor, whom all its readers knew.

The New York *Tribune* under Horace Greeley exhibited the best features of the new and semi-independent personal journalism based upon political beginnings and inspired with an enthusiasm for service that is one of the fine characteristics of the period. In editing the *New Yorker* Greeley had acquired experience in literary journalism and in political news; his *Jeffersonian* and *Log Cabin*, popular campaign papers, had brought him into contact with politicians and extended his acquaintance with the masses. Being with all his independence a staunch party man, he was chosen to manage a party organ when one was needed to support the Whig administration of Harrison, and the prospectus of the New York *Tribune* appeared 3 April, 1841. Greeley's ambition was to make the *Tribune* not only a good party paper, but also the first paper in America, and he succeeded by imparting to it a certain idealistic character with a practical appeal which no other journal possessed. His sound judgment appeared in the unusually able staff which he gathered about him. Almost from the first, the staff which made the *Tribune* represented a broad catholicity of interests and tastes, in the world of thought as well as in the world of action, and a solid excellence in ability and in organization which were largely the result of the genius of Greeley and over which he was the master spirit. It included Henry J. Raymond, who later became Greeley's rival on the *Times*, George M. Snow, George William Curtis, Charles A. Dana, Bayard Taylor, George Ripley, William H. Fry, Margaret Fuller, Edmund Quincy, and Charles T. Congdon. It is easy to understand how with such a group of writers the idea of the literary newspaper, which had been alive from the beginning of the century, should have advanced well-nigh to its greatest perfection.

The great popular strength of the *Tribune* doubtless lay in its disinterested sympathy with all the ideals and sentiments which stirred the popular mind in the forties and fifties. "We cannot afford," Greeley wrote, "to reject unexamined any idea which proposes to improve the moral, intellectual, or social condition of mankind." He pointed out that the proper course of an editor, in contrast to that of the time-server, was to have "an ear open to the plaints of the wronged and suffering, though they can never repay advocacy, and those who mainly support newspapers will be annoyed and often exposed by it; a heart as sensitive to oppression and degradation in the next street as if they were practiced in Brazil or Japan; a pen as ready to expose and reprove the crimes whereby wealth is amassed and luxury enjoyed in our own country as if they had only been committed by Turks or Pagans in Asia some centuries ago." In conformity with these principles Greeley lent his support to all proposals for ameliorating the condition of the labouring men by industrial education, by improved methods of farming, or even by such radical means as the socialistic Fourier Association. He strongly advocated the protective tariff because he believed that it was for the advantage of the workingman; and the same sympathy led him to give serious attention to the discussion of women's rights with special reference to the equal economic status of women. There were besides many lesser causes in which the *Tribune* displayed its spirit of liberalism, such as temperance reform, capital punishment, the Irish repeals, and the liberation of Hungary. On the most important question of the time, the abolition of slavery, Greeley's views were intimately connected with party policy. His antipathy to slavery, based on moral and economic grounds, placed him from the first among the mildly radical reformers. But his views underwent gradual intensification. Acknowledged the most influential Whig editor in 1844, he had by 1850 become the most influential anti-slavery editor—the spokesman not of Whigs merely but of a great class of Northerners who were thoroughly antagonistic to slavery but who had not been satisfied with either the non-political war of Garrison or the one-plank political efforts of the Free Soil party. This influence was greatly increased between 1850 and 1854 by some of the most vigorous and trenchant editorial writing America has ever known. The circulation of the *Tribune* in 1850 was, all told, a little less than sixty thousand, two-thirds of which was the *Weekly*. In 1854 the *Weekly* alone had a circulation of 112,000 copies. But Rhodes has pointed out that even this figure is not the measure of the *Tribune's* peculiar influence, "for it was pre-eminently the journal of the rural districts, and one copy did service for many readers. To the people in the Adirondack wilderness it was a political bible, and the well-known scarcity of Democrats there was attributed to it. Yet it was as freely read by the intelligent people living on the Western Reserve of Ohio," and in Wisconsin and Illinois. The work of Greeley and his associates in these years gave a new strength and a new scope and outlook to American journalism.

Henry Jarvis Raymond, who began his journalistic career on the *Tribune* and gained further experience in editing the respectable, old-fashioned, political *Courier and Enquirer*, perceived that there was an opening for a type of newspaper which should stand midway between Greeley, the moralist and reformer, and Bennett, the cynical, non-moral newsmonger. He was able to interest friends in raising the hundred thousand dollars which he thought essential to the success of his enterprise. This sum is significant of the development of American daily journalism, for Greeley had started the *Tribune* only ten years earlier with a capital of one thousand dollars, and Bennett had founded the *Herald* with nothing at all. On this sound financial basis, Raymond began the career of the New York *Times*, 18 September, 1851, and made it a success from the outset. He perfected his news-gathering forces and

brought into play his intimate acquaintance with men of af
fairs to open up the sources of information. Above all he set
a new standard for foreign service. The American public never
had a more general and intelligent interest in European affairs
than in the middle years of the nineteenth century. The leading papers directed their best efforts toward sustaining and
improving their foreign service, and Raymond used a brief
vacation in Europe to establish for his paper a system of correspondence as trustworthy, if not as inclusive, as that of the
*Herald* or *Tribune*. If our newspapers today are immeasurably in advance of those of sixty years ago in almost every
field of journalism, there is only here and there anything to
compare in worth with the foreign correspondence of that
time. The men who wrote from the news centres of Europe
were persons of wide political knowledge and experience, and
social consequence. They had time and ability to do their
work thoroughly, carefully, and intelligently, innocent of superficial effort toward sensation, of the practices of inaccurate
brevity and irresponsible haste which began with the laying
of the Atlantic cable.

The theory of journalism announced by Raymond in the
*Times* marks another advance over the party principles of his
predecessors. He thought that a newspaper might assume the
rôle now of a party paper, now of an organ of non-partisan,
independent thought, and still be regarded by the great body
of its readers as steadily guided by principles of sincere public
policy. An active ambition for political preferment prevented
him from achieving this ideal. Although he professed conservatism only in those cases where conservatism was essential to the
public good and radicalism in everything which might require
radical treatment and radical reform, the spirit of opposition
to the *Tribune*, as well as his temperamental leanings, carried
him definitely to the conservative side. He was by nature
inclined to accept the established order and make the best of
it. Change, if it came, should come not through radical agitation and revolution, but by cautious and gradual evolution.
The world needed brushing, not harrowing. Such ideas, as he
applied them to journalism, appealed to moderate men, reflected the opinions of a large and influential class somewhere
between the advanced thinkers and theorists and the mass of

men more likely to be swayed by passions of approbation or protest than by reason.

It was the tone of the *Times* that especially distinguished it from its contemporaries. In his first issue Raymond announced his purpose to write in temperate and measured language and to get into a passion as rarely as possible. "There are few things in this world which it is worth while to get angry about; and they are just the things anger will not improve." In controversy he meant to avoid abusive language. His style was gentle, candid, and decisive, and achieved its purpose by facility, clearness, and moderation rather than by powerful fervor and invective. His editorials were generally cautious, impersonal, and finished in form. With abundant self-respect and courtesy, he avoided, as one of his coadjutors said, vulgar abuse of individuals, unjust criticism, or narrow and personal ideas. He had that degree and kind of intelligence which enabled him to appreciate two principles of modern journalism —the application of social ethics to editorial conduct and the maintenance of a comprehensive spirit. As he used them, these were positive, not negative virtues.

Raymond's contribution to journalism, then, was not the introduction of revolutionizing innovations in any department of the profession but a general improving and refining of its tone, a balancing of its parts, sensitizing it to discreet and cultivated popular taste. Taking the London *Times* as his model, he tried to combine in his paper the English standard of trustworthiness, stability, inclusiveness, and exclusiveness, with the energy and news initiative of the best American journalism; to preserve in it an integrity of motive and a decorum of conduct such as he possessed as a gentleman. To his success American journalism is deeply indebted.

# CHAPTER XXII

# Divines and Moralists, 1783–1860

THE writings of the American clergy between the Revolution and the Civil War have Jonathan Edwards[1] for their point of departure, and carry onward the tendencies he brought to a focus. Let us rather say two focuses: for Edwards is great precisely in the intensity with which he manifests a tough-mindedness and a tender-mindedness that are universal. He is at once dogmatist and mystic; he works out his theology into dualistic metaphysics, yet he knows himself to be one with God; though he philosophizes away the Freedom of the Will, and preaches Hell for sinners, yet he meditates also the Benevolence of the Deity, and is translated into mystical rhapsodies upon the divine love and upon Nature as its symbol and emanation. The primacy he gives to motivation places him with those who insist that reward and punishment must be held up before depraved mankind to keep it even outwardly decent; his insistence upon an inner light and a love for universal being faces him toward the believers in man's essential goodness and perfectibility. He never reconciled these tendencies in his own thinking; nor have they been reconciled since in that American literature which in various phases, mixtures, and proportions they have continued to colour.

Historically, at the close of the American Revolution the tender-minded derive from the Cambridge Platonists and their successors the English deists. Their thought is developed by Shaftesbury and the "benevolists"; favoured by Berkeley; much re-enforced by the works of Paley, and by Butler's

---

[1] See Book I, Chap. IV for Edwards. For divines other than Congregational and Unitarian see Book III, Chap. XVII.

*Analogy;* and developed again in various directions by Rousseau, William Godwin, and, later, Kant and Coleridge. They are the liberals, transcendentalists, and romantics, and Plato is their ultimate master, though he contributes his realism to their opponents. The tough-minded derive from Aristotle, St. Augustine, and, of course, Calvin; find themselves close kin to Hobbes and Locke, to the "motivists," and, later, to Reid and Dugald Stewart; and are the classics—the orthodox. In the large, the thought of American divines and moralists from Edwards to Beecher moves from tough to tender, parallel with the romantic movement in secular literature; while Beecher's contemporary, Mark Hopkins, toughly reacting against romanticism, anticipates the present secular return toward greater sharpness in realizing evil and the fundamental cleavages in things.

Our secular and our theological literature, thus closely akin in ideas, have also a strong personal connection, almost a family connection. With us, divinity has seldom been more, and has usually been less, than a generation removed from literary scholarship or the literary imagination. Andrews Norton is father to Charles Eliot Norton, William Henry Furness to Horace Howard Furness, Abiel Holmes to Oliver Wendell Holmes, Charles Lowell to James Russell Lowell. James Russell Lowell and Robert Traill Spence Lowell are brothers; so are Henry Wadsworth Longfellow and Samuel Longfellow. There is something filial in the scholar Ticknor's pious task of editing the sermons of the Rev. Joseph Stevens Buckminster, one generation before him. Emerson's forefathers had been clergymen for seven generations; and within his single life the early days as preacher and the later days as *sacer vates* were "bound each to each by natural piety." So were those of John Gorham Palfrey, George Ripley, and Octavius Brooks Frothingham, and of such clerical families as the Channings, the Abbotts, the Wares, the Beechers, the Muhlenbergs, and the Dwights, whose *pietas*, priestly, educational, juristic, and literary, has extended unto the third generation and beyond. It would be easy, but needless, to multiply examples in proof of the close and various personal connections between our divinity and our scholarship and literature.

The family tradition is evident at once in Edwards's disciples.

The sons of Jonathan, whether after the flesh or after the spirit, included Jonathan Edwards the younger (1745–1801), a systematic theologian, President of Union College, Schenectady, from 1799 to his death; David Brainerd (1718–47), author of a diary of his mystical experiences; Joseph Bellamy (1719–90); Samuel Hopkins (1721–1803); and Edwards's grandson Timothy Dwight (1752–1817). Of these, Hopkins and Dwight are for many reasons the most important. The younger Edwards, after graduating at Princeton in 1765, was Hopkins's disciple; Bellamy's chief works were all published before the Revolution; and Brainerd, a young consumptive, who was to have been Edwards's son-in-law, died before him. Hopkins, moreover, exercised an influence which went beyond theology into literature; and Dwight produced something uncommonly like literature itself.

Hopkins was born of Puritan stock at Waterbury, Connecticut. Roused to religious conviction at Yale by his college mate, David Brainerd, and by the revivalist Tennent, he heard Edwards before graduating in 1741, and, still not sure that he was a Christian, "concluded to go and live with Mr. Edwards" at Northampton as a student of divinity—which he did off and on till 1743. Then he was settled and ordained at Housatonic (later Great Barrington), where he had to contend with Indian attacks, malaria, and the Dutch settlers in his congregation; taking comfort, however, in a second intimate contact with Edwards while the latter was conducting the mission to the Stockbridge Indians. In 1769 the poverty of Hopkins's congregation, together with their opposition to his stiff doctrine, led to his dismissal.

In the next year he accepted a call to the First Congregational Church at Newport. The Rev. Ezra Stiles, then minister of the Second Congregational Church and later (1777–95) President of Yale, opposed the call, but preached a learned sermon at Hopkins's installation, and remained on friendly terms with him despite radical differences in doctrine and temper. In Newport, too, Hopkins became acquainted with the Channing family: William Ellery Channing, then a boy, heard him preach and was repelled by his harsh doctrine. Though the Revolutionary War wrecked his church, he remained with it, and in the lean years following wrote his

*System of Doctrines Contained in Divine Revelation Explained and Defended* (1793). After 1770 he also produced his sermons and pamphlets against slavery, probably the most readable of his works, being somewhat less impeded than the others by the pitiless iteration and verbose pedantry of his style. He seems to have aided in procuring the passage of the Rhode Island laws of 1774 and 1784, respectively forbidding the importation of negroes and declaring free all children born of slaves after the next 1 March. In failing health and with a dwindling congregation, he ministered faithfully until his death in 1803.

The formula associated with Hopkins's name, and most definitely set forth in his posthumous *Dialogue between a Semi-Calvinist and a Calvinist*, is "Willingness to be damned for the glory of God." It is the upshot of all his strict Calvinist theory of decrees, election, and evidences. Rejecting the benevolists' belief in a mild Deity, he transfers "universal benevolence" from God to man—of whom he then requires it. The germs of the doctrine are to be found in Edwards's theory of virtue as consisting in love for universal being; and some of Mrs. Edwards's own religious experiences while Hopkins resided at her house might well have suggested to him his extension of the doctrine. For with him the willingness to be damned is not merely the acme of mystical devotion, but an indispensable evidence of grace—a necessary, though not a sufficient, condition of salvation. If you are not willing to be damned, then you are sure to be.

Hopkins thus carried onward and reduced to a system the materials which Edwards left unco-ordinated. So tough-minded was he that in his hands what might otherwise have been an efflorescence of tender mysticism became a dogma of terror. Naturally it roused intense opposition, but this, together with the logical completeness of the system, focussed attention upon it; so that it remained a powerful influence until the time of general emancipation from theological terrors.

Hopkins personally met his own requirements of benevolence. His combination of terrific doctrine with a kindly and self-denying personal life among his Newport parishioners is the underlying theme of Harriet Beecher Stowe's novel,

*The Minister's Wooing.*[1]  His philanthropic opposition to the slave trade, said to be the first open opposition by an American clergyman, rendered him so unpopular among the prosperous traders of Newport that he was left to die in poverty with the feeling that his work was unaccomplished.  Futile, he must have felt, was his letter of remonstrance and admonition (1802) to his revered master's grandson, Aaron Burr, upon the latter's dangerous courses; and his *Farewell to the World* is a pathetic review of the state of man as he then beheld it in all portions of the globe, particularly in Newport among his congregation. It is not a hopeful view.  Hopkins could not foresee the success of his opposition to slavery; and he could scarcely have believed, even if told, that his doctrine of disinterested benevolence had so impressed young Channing with the boundlessness of human generosity and the infinite worth of man that it became with him one of the points of departure for a new hopefulness.

Timothy Dwight (1752–1817) could have had no such doubts of his present success.  After a varied experience as student (graduated 1769) and tutor at Yale, as an army chaplain during the Revolution, as a farmer, as a member of the Connecticut legislature, and as preacher, schoolmaster, and writer of verse[2] at Greenfield, Connecticut, he became, at the age of forty-three, Dr. Stiles's successor in the presidency of Yale.  He seems to have been the prototype of the modern college president,—appreciative of scholarship, but primarily a practical administrator. He raised the college to financial prosperity; he broadened the curriculum, especially by introducing courses in science; and to the infidels then numerous among the student body he brought religious conviction.

His divinity (*Theology Explained and Defended*, 1818–19), though schematic, is also controversial, aiming perhaps less to systematize than to convince, and establishing orthodoxy by refuting heresy.  It consists of the sermons—essentially Hopkinsian—which he delivered from the college pulpit week after week and year after year, repeating the full set every four years so that each student generation might have the benefit of the whole course.

[1] The romance indicated by the title was suggested in part by an incident of Hopkins's ministry at Great Barrington.

[2] For his verse see Book I, Chap. IX.

As a contribution to American prose it is much less important than his four posthumously published volumes of *Travels in New England and New York* (1821–22). These record a series of journeys, on horseback or in a gig or "sulky," which Dwight undertook for his health, usually during college vacations, beginning in September, 1796, and continuing at intervals until 1815. The book is the upshot of his experience of life; he was engaged upon the manuscript within nine months of his death, and probably within a few days of it.

He professes as his motive for writing, the humanistic desire to vivify the past; he had wished to know "the manner in which New England appeared or to mine own eye would have appeared eighty or one hundred years before"; and, finding this impossible for himself, he resolved to make it possible for posterity. A second professed motive was the desire to refute foreign misrepresentations of America; and with this in view he cast his material into the form of letters and topical essays addressed to an imaginary Englishman.[1]

These definite purposes do not prevent the book from being an *omnium gatherum*. For Dwight does not use them as a basis of selection or exclusion of material, but admits anything that happens to interest him; and as he is interested in anything he sees and thinks of, the unity of his book is far to seek. Now, in emulation of the early New England annalists, he chronicles a great storm or an egregious murder; now, in a vein reminiscent of White's *Selborne*, he tells of the habits of birds, of the fitness of trees for particular soils, or of the right weather for maple sap; now, for chapter after stodgy chapter, he repeats and summarizes the Connecticut constitution and laws, the system of land tenure, the powers and duties of officers of government, and the penal system, even down to the fines imposed for

[1] Thomas Jefferson's *Notes on Virginia* (1786) has these points in common with Dwight's *Travels:* it purports to answer questions asked by a foreigner; it gives information about the constitution and laws, religion and manners, public revenue and expense, manufactures, commerce, money, histories, and memorials; it refutes the views of Buffon and of the Abbé Raynal upon the bad climate and soil of America, and upon the degeneracy of its animals and men. (See also Book II, Chap. 1.) An immediate predecessor of Dwight in this *genre* was Ezra Stiles, who bequeathed to Dwight his *Literary Diary*, and whose *Itineraries* Dwight may well have seen in MS. Investigation would probably show that Dwight owed much to Jefferson and to Stiles.

various offences. Yet his commentary upon this tedious
material—shrewd and lucid, well-balanced both in judgment
and in style, and above all practical—places it in a kind of
Blackstonian tradition. For the rest, he mingles topographical
accounts of the regions he passes through with sketches of the
characters and lives of distinguished residents, descriptions of
scenery, estimates of inns and innkeepers, bits of historical
narrative, and statistics of industry, wealth, religion, and
climate.

Dwight's descriptive powers are high but unsustained.
At Canajoharie, he tells us, the Mohawk runs below, in a
gorge, while above is a

long narrow stripe of azure seen overhead. On both sides rise
stupendous walls of a deep black, awful with their hanging precipices,
which are hollowed with a thousand fantastical forms. . . . As
you advance up the stream . . . you suddenly arrive at a cascade
sixty feet in height, where the water descends with a sufficient
approximation to perpendicularity to convert the current from a
sheet into a mass of foam perfectly white and elegant.

The passages that he does not thus spoil, as, for example, his
description of the Notch of the White Mountains, of a view in
the Catskills, or of the "oak openings" of the Genesee River,
are very few. His narratives, too, while interesting as raw material of literature, are seldom more. The woman one hundred
and two years old who, when "the bell was heard to toll for a
funeral, . . . burst into tears and said, 'When will the bell
toll for me? It seems that the bell will never toll for me,'"
might have appealed poignantly to Hawthorne. Dwight's
traveller, who rode across a bridge in the dark, and only in the
morning discovered that the bridge had not a plank on it and
that his horse had found his way across the naked frame, was
in fact used by Henry Ward Beecher as an illustration rather
less effective than the original. Dwight's tale of how the
regicide Goff, then a venerable man in concealment in the
house of the minister at Hadley, had suddenly appeared during
an Indian raid upon the congregation, rallied them, and disappeared, may well have actually suggested Hawthorne's story
of *The Gray Champion*. But Dwight has no *flair* for imaginative material; nor is he content to leave even his expository

effects unspoiled. His narrative of the Saratoga campaign is solid historical writing; but alas, hard at its heels follows the judgment that Saratoga was more important than Marathon.

In description, in narrative, in its dry controversial humour, Dwight's style is a sound eighteenth-century style, very serviceable in conveying his keen judgments upon statecraft and college management; an administrator's style, clean in structure, sharp and low-toned in diction, modelled upon Johnson and Burke, but with an occasional richer rhythm. "The bloom of immortality, already deeply faded, now withered away." The apostle Eliot, when he died, "undoubtedly went to receive the benedictions of multitudes, who, but for him, had finally perished." Sometimes there are short passages of a sober eloquence not unlike Edwards's own. Of the congregation to whom Dr. Swift had been a faithful pastor Dwight observes: "Many of them will probably remember him with gratitude throughout eternity." But such pieces of Attic diction or noble rhythm may be followed in the very next sentence by a banality. As in his descriptions and narratives, so in the general body of his prose, the passages of power or beauty are not sustained. He has merely stumbled upon them.

From first to last Dwight has either no æsthetic standards or only the standards of cocksure provincialism. "Longitude from Yale College," the legend upon the map prefixed to each of his volumes, might be their motto. His opinions upon Elizabethan writers, upon architecture, upon the drama, upon Greek and Roman literature, would be incredible if they did not stare us in the face from cold type. His genuine powers are rendered nugatory by his incompetence in the realms of taste and imagination. He is the complete Puritan, inhospitable to art but thoroughly efficient in dealing with things; and—to modify Arnold's formula concerning the Philistine—a maker of farms that produce, of sermons that edify, of a college that educates, and of characters that wear. His want of adequate standards leaves his book a miscellany, not so much because there are all sorts of things in it as because of their huge artistic incongruities; not so much because of the variety of its contents as because of the unplumbed gaps between their literary levels.

Yet this is not to say that after some acquaintance with the *Travels* the reader does not perceive a dominant interest emerge. This is Dwight's interest in watching the world confirm his creed. Streams erode their banks, waterfalls recede, puddingstone is compounded, in order to support the Mosaic chronology, which infidel geologists had been heard to assail. Insects found alive in wood known to be eighty years old, seeds that germinate after centuries, frogs found alive by diggers far under ground, are not mere curiosities: they prove that a species supposed to be new may well have been the offspring of such durable creatures, and hence that there is no new species and no spontaneous generation. Dwight chronicles them to support the Biblical account of the origin of all species by creation at the beginning, an account which even in his time was being questioned by precursors of the evolutionary philosophy. His interest in other marvels, again, such as floating islands and mysterious bright spots in the clouds, is much the same as Cotton Mather's interest in *magnalia*— What hath God wrought! Every detail of the creation is full of manifest providences. The rich vegetable mould on the surface of new lands, for example, which yields an abundant crop to the pioneer almost without effort on his part, has been placed there for that very purpose, to support him during the first years of his settlement, when his energies, being required to build his house and clear more land, are diverted from the soil. Then, when the beneficent mould has disappeared, the poor soil has its providential purpose too, for by now the settler has time to cultivate it, indeed, must cultivate it if he is to live; so that he has a motive for industry and the other virtues which make him respectable. Thus both the presence and the absence of vegetable mould are effects of the final causes which make the world for man.

Carrying his theology into his judgments upon life, Dwight is interested above all, then, in seeing how a depraved humanity actually gets along in the world. His picture of the trim green New England landscape, with its white spires and prosperous villages, and his picture of the unkempt and sprawling German settlements along the Mohawk, though they may at first seem intended to produce an imaginative contrast, at length reveal his purpose of showing what it is that makes people become respectable. In fact the whole book is a collection of materials toward a genetic psychology of respectability.

Dwight's observations of certain portions of Long Island and Westchester County, of the whole of Rhode Island (which he considers "missionary ground"), of the Indian settlements in parts of Connecticut, of the Irish settlements in central New York, and, generally speaking, of the world outside New England Congregationalism, all strengthen his conviction of the general depravity of man, and help him to confute the doctrines of Rousseau and William Godwin that men are good by nature but have been corrupted by civilization. His theology here coincides with his politics—his inveterate abhorrence of French "atheistic" democracy and Jeffersonianism in general. The *Travels* is a Federalist document, exhibiting in its most sensible consequences the view that men are presumably bad until something makes them good. Bent therefore upon discovering and applying the incentives that will make them good—for Dwight is a convinced motivist—he exemplifies everywhere the sanctions furnished by thrift, by education, by strong government, and by strong religion. Probably there exists no completer application of Calvinistic principles to secular life. Dwight is the last of the Puritans.

The term "Unitarian" was accepted by the leaders of the movement only after much reluctance and delay. The doctrine designated by it is not perhaps the characteristic note of the movement at all, for it suggests mere static belief or disbelief in a proposition; whereas Unitarianism was a dynamic tendency, and to be designated rather by some such term as "Liberal Christianity." Liberty, tolerance, the free play of the intellect, the enfranchisement of the soul from its terrors, faith in the possibilities and the worth of man,—these are more characteristic of it than the denial of the divinity of Jesus, though its high concept of humanity, indeed, renders its humanization of Christ no derogation.

Thus interpreted, Unitarianism has points of contact with whatever is liberal and hopeful in any religion. Its affiliation with Deism, Natural Religion, Benevolism, and other liberal tendencies of eighteenth-century Europe, need not be traced here. It is sufficient to observe that in America the Unitarians drew strength from the liberal wing of any or all of the Protestant churches. The less strict Calvinists, like Ezra Stiles,

Jonathan Mayhew, and Charles Chauncy, are thus accounted
to have been upon the verge of Unitarianism. Mayhew (died
1766)[1] had been a champion not more of civil than of religious
liberty. Stiles exhibited the Unitarian tolerance: he was the
friend not only of Hopkins but of the Boston progressives and
of the Newport rabbis. His administration at Yale is said to
have broadened and secularized the college. In his pursuit of
the intellectual life he touched another side of Unitarianism:
he and Cotton Mather were the two American scholars whom
Timothy Dwight considered able to stand comparison with
British scholars. Chauncy[2] had condemned the more violent
manifestations of the Great Awakening of 1740. In the pre-
Revolutionary controversy concerning the establishment of
Episcopacy in America, he had opposed the Anglican views of
William White of Philadelphia (afterward the first Bishop
of Pennsylvania), asserted that the English Church had best
leave the American to develop independently, and contended
for the right of the congregation to ordain its own minister.
He leaned also toward the Arminian emphasis upon human
choice as a genuine factor in salvation, thus falling in with the
Unitarian tendency to magnify man. At the same time he is
credited with "high" Arianism, and with a touch of Universalism. He had written, too, upon the benevolence of the
Deity. He is thus found upon several characteristic Unitarian
pathways.

It was the Boston Episcopalians, however, rather than the
Congregationalists, who took the first decisive step. In 1785,
the congregation of King's Chapel, having adopted a modification of the Anglican liturgy, from which all Trinitarian
doctrine had been omitted, ordained and installed as its rector
James Freeman, who, together with William Hazlitt (father
of the essayist), had performed the revision. This ordination is
usually held to mark the formal beginning of Unitarianism in
New England.

The Rev. Joseph Buckminster (1751–1812) of Portsmouth,
New Hampshire, a strict Calvinist, from first to last was doomed
to lift up his voice against the liberal movement in vain. He
protested against the Rev. Mr. Foster's Sermon at New Brain-
tree (1788), which, he thought, offered salvation upon too easy

---

[1] See also Book I, Chap. v.                         [2] See *ibid.*

terms; in a series of letters (1811) to the Rev. Hosea Ballou (1771–1852)[1] he protested against that pioneer Universalist's preaching the final salvation of all mankind; and above all he protested against the defection of his own son, the Rev. Joseph Stevens Buckminster (1784–1812), whose ordination sermon (1805) he nevertheless preached, not without a note of fatherly foreboding.

The Buckminsters were of the Edwards stock. The staunch and earnest father was a contemporary of Dwight, Barlow, and Trumbull at Yale; the scholarly, eloquent, and saintly son was an immediate predecessor of Andrews Norton, and a contemporary of W. E. Channing, Charles Lowell, and Washington Allston at Harvard. But for his father's opposition, he might have become assistant to James Freeman, whom he heard with admiration at King's Chapel. He taught Daniel Webster Latin at Phillips Exeter, and tried to persuade his pupil to take part in the school exercises in public speaking. His work, in fact, is full of seeds which the future brought to fruition. Its new note of secular culture, against which his father had warned him—its allusions to art, to foreign books and travel (he was abroad in 1806–07), and to classical philosophy and literature — becomes increasingly characteristic of nineteenth-century clerical writing. In quietly removing emphasis from the staggering conditions of salvation to the process of religious training, Buckminster anticipates Jacob Abbott and Horace Bushnell. He anticipates Andrews Norton both in attaching prime importance to philology and history, as evidences of Christianity, and in a large conception of theology as including the widest range of scholarship,—as bounded, in fact, only by the limits of human knowledge. Buckminster realized Norton's idea of a "learned and able theologian—disciplined in habits of correct reasoning—[and] informed by extensive learning." Norton seems to have laid upon himself the task of continuing the work that his admired friend had "died too young to do." "Hearing Buckminster," said Norton, "one seemed to be walking in the triumphal procession of Truth."

Despite warning and opposition, then, "liberal Christian-

---

[1] Great-uncle of Hosea Ballou 2d, who was a founder and the first President of Tufts College.

ity" continued to flourish, until in 1805 the Rev. Henry Ware, an outspoken Unitarian, was appointed to the Hollis Professorship of Divinity in Harvard College. This invasion of the school whose initial purpose had been the production of Congregational ministers roused the Congregationalists of every shade of opinion to the defence of their discipline; and from extreme Hopkinsians to moderate Calvinists, they combined to establish at Andover a new theological seminary, which was opened in 1808.

During the era of orthodoxy Andover Seminary published *The Andover Review*, and had its famous teachers, such as Leonard Woods, Moses Stuart, Austen Phelps, and Edwards A. Park; yet in the course of time even this stronghold yielded to the irresistible trend toward liberalism. In 1886, five of its professors who had published a volume of advanced theological thought were tried for heresy, and acquitted. The legal proceedings for their removal also failed. By a bit of historical irony, the counsel for the defence was Theodore William Dwight, a grandson of Timothy. In 1908, the wheel having come full circle, Andover Seminary removed to Cambridge and became affiliated with Harvard University.

The Princeton Theological Seminary, founded by the Presbyterian branch of the Calvinists, was opened in 1812, and had its strong men also: Archibald Alexander (1772–1851) and his sons James W. (1804–59) and Joseph A. Alexander (1809–60); Charles Hodge (1797–1878), who in 1825 established the organ of the Seminary, afterwards named *The Princeton Review*; and James McCosh (1811–94), President of Princeton College 1868–88. Princeton has always remained Presbyterian.

These conservative reactions in the early nineteenth century widened the cleavage between the Calvinists and the Unitarians, which by 1819 had become so marked that William Ellery Channing, who in that year preached the ordination sermon of Jared Sparks at Baltimore, adopted for it the title *Unitarian Christianity*. Thenceforth the separate establishment of the Unitarians was unquestioned.

As Channing[1] was their great mild preacher, so Andrews Norton was their hard-headed champion. Descended from

[1] See Book II, Chap. VIII.

the Rev. John Norton, the notable minister of Ipswich and of Boston, Andrews Norton was born in 1786 at Hingham. In 1804 he graduated at Harvard, and spent the next fifteen years as graduate student, tutor, and lecturer, there and at Bowdoin. In 1819 he was appointed Dexter Professor of Sacred Literature in Harvard College, acting also from 1813 to 1821 as the College Librarian. His *Statement of Reasons for Not Believing the Doctrine of Trinitarians*, first published in 1819 in a controversy with Professor Stuart of Andover, soon became a Unitarian classic. In 1833 and 1834 he was engaged with Charles Folsom in editing *The Select Journal of Foreign Periodical Literature*, one of the numerous magazines of that period of growing international culture. The first number contains Macaulay's *Essay on Hampden*, reprinted from *The Edinburgh Review*; Paulin Paris's *Letter upon the Romances upon the Twelve Peers of France*, from Férussac's *Bulletin Universel* ("translated from the French with notes by Professor Longfellow"); and reviews from *The Foreign Quarterly Review* and elsewhere. For a number of years Norton contributed also to *The North American Review*, and was influential in its management.

Emerson's celebrated *Divinity School Address*[1] in 1838 brought to a head Norton's distaste for the Transcendental movement. A year later he addressed to the alumni of the Harvard Theological School at their Commencement reunion his *Discourse on the Latest Form of Infidelity*, which, by opposing Spinoza, Schleiermacher, Strauss, and Hegel, whom apparently Norton considered responsible for much Transcendental error, refutes Emerson by indirection, without mentioning him or taking explicit issue with his views. Yet the clash of their opinions is uncompromising. Where Emerson insisted upon intuition, Norton requires an outer revelation evidenced by historical documents. Where Emerson insisted that genuine religion cannot be received at second-hand, but is intuitive and immediate, Norton emphasizes the dependence of laymen upon expert authority and mediation in difficult matters of research and exegesis. Where Emerson rejected any conception of a miracle that would oppose it to the ordinary course of nature, implying that nature is miraculous enough,

[1] See also Book II, Chap. IX.

and that miracles are happening all the time, Norton reiterates that miracles are suspensions of the course of nature, are historical, and are evidence of the divine mission of Christ. George Ripley's answer to Norton's *Discourse* led to a controversy which belongs to the history of the Transcendental movement.[1]

Norton's opposition to intuitionalism appears throughout his works. His *Views of Calvinism* scores the proposition (which had found support even at Andover Seminary) that "The truths of Christianity have always been addressed to the intuitive perceptions of the common mind." Norton points out the inconsistency between the Calvinist doctrine that the common mind is naturally so depraved as to be unable to perceive religious truth, and the new Andover doctrine, adopted from Transcendentalism, that the common mind has absolute intuitions of religious truth. He thus hits out in opposite directions, against both the orthodox and the Transcendentalists, but on the same ground, namely, his rejection of intuitions. The violence of this rejection, indeed, carried him too far; so that when in the warmth of controversy he rejected all but the historical or external evidences of Christianity, he laid himself open to George Ripley's charge of narrowness.

From the very first, however, for example in his *Defence of Liberal Christianity* (1812), Norton had been consistent in pleading for the historical and linguistic interpretation of the Bible, and the consideration of dogma less as prescribed by authority than as developed by history. His final contributions to scholarship, the *Evidences of the Genuineness of the Gospels* (1837–44), and the *Translation of the Gospels* and *Internal Evidences of the Genuineness of the Gospels* (both published posthumously in 1855), take the same line. Even by "internal evidences" Norton does not mean evidences of spiritual truth. He is concerned not with establishing Christianity but with the genuineness of certain documents; thus his remarks are limited generally to matters of historical and linguistic exegesis and logical probability. Least of all does he consider what might by some be defined as internal evidence, the adaptability of Christianity to the character of man, or the intuition that Christianity is true.

[1] See Book II, Chap. VIII.

Norton is the representative Unitarian in taking the position, typical of that body, precisely half-way between Calvinism and Transcendentalism, engaging impartially in controversy on the one hand with Moses Stuart and on the other with George Ripley. The common basis of his opposition to both is his opposition to Plato. Platonism, his researches led him to believe, had in its Neo-Platonic avatar at Alexandria produced, among other doctrines of emanation, the doctrine of the Trinity. Platonism also, believing the soul to have been in contact with ideal archetypes whose memory it retained in this life, was the very fountain of the doctrine of intuitions. Norton's opposition to Emerson and Ripley was thus of a piece with his opposition to Philo Judæus and Moses Stuart, the opposition of an exact scholar to what he considered loose, effusive, and sentimental thinking. Indeed, though Norton never says so in so many words, he seems to have recognized the Platonism of the Transcendental movement, and to have condemned it upon the same grounds as those upon which he condemned Plato himself. Anti-Platonism is the key to Norton's position.

Norton's teaching is praised by his disciple William Henry Furness (1802–96), who carried it to the First Unitarian Church in Philadelphia; and it must, in fact, have been a powerful stimulus to anyone who could taste his austerity and his intellectual keenness. He is not wholly free from banalities, those devils that stand ever ready at the clerical elbow; he prefers Mrs. Stowe to Goethe; but the great body of his work is ascetically pure in taste as in style. It can still be read with pleasure, indeed with a certain intellectual thrill.

The work of enfranchisement was carried on in their several modes by three notable contemporaries: Horace Bushnell (1802–76), Henry Ward Beecher (1813–87), and Mark Hopkins (1802–87), each in his way a liberator.

Superficially, Bushnell may seem to have been a reactionary. Born in Litchfield. Township, Connecticut, he graduated at Yale in 1827, whither, after a short experience in journalism, he returned as tutor, student of law, and finally student of theology. In 1833 he was ordained pastor of the North Congregational Church in Hartford, where he remained until 1859. In 1856, while in California for his health, he was active in organizing at Oakland the "College of California," which in 1869 was merged in the University of California, and the presidency of which he declined. He thus belongs by birth, by training, and by professional activity to that hinterland— consisting of the valleys of the Connecticut and the Housatonic, and of the Litchfield and Berkshire Hills—whose orthodoxy has stood out against the liberal movements of the coast line from Boston to Newport.

Bushnell disliked what to his richly mystical temperament seemed the baldness of Unitarianism, and he re-established on a new basis many of the institutes of orthodoxy, notably the Trinity and the Atonement. Yet he consistently opposed all dogma, not because it was bigoted on the one hand or lax on the other, but because of the inadequacy of language as such to convey the religious mysteries which his piety bade him hold fast despite their logical contradictions. Mere logic he distrusted so deeply that its contradictions, dilemmas, anti-nomies were to him no arguments against a belief. According to a well-known anecdote, Bushnell, finding a college-mate stropping his razor all in one direction, bade him oppose his strokes to each other, a procedure which has been accepted as typical of Bushnell's dialectic, and which is not unlike Hegel's. Contradictories merely led him to a higher resultant—a mystical synthesis and a sort of *credo quia impossibile*. He saved impossible dogmas by turning them into sacraments.

At the same time, the rationalist in him offered to weaker faiths a *modus vivendi*. The Trinity, whose essence was a mystery inexpressible in language, was reconcilable with the divine unity in that it was a mode and an instrument by which the Absolute revealed itself to and worked upon finite souls. This epistemological view, which is said to go back to Sabellius, was perhaps a novelty in American theology; its pragmatism and distrust of logic seem even to be anticipations. In much the same way Bushnell retained the doctrine of the Atonement by attributing to it a moral effect upon the human soul, instead of the old-fashioned governmental or legalistic function of paying a debt, expiating a crime, or mending a broken law. These positions he promulgated in his *God in Christ* (1849), with its introductory *Dissertation on the Nature of Language as Related to Thought and Spirit*, in *Christ in*

*Theology* (1851), and in *The Vicarious Sacrifice* (1856). For the old revivals, with their sudden superemotional conversions, he also substituted the concept of a gradual education in Christianity; *Christian Nurture* (1847), like Jacob Abbott's *The Young Christian* (1832), directs the attention of those who would be of the faith toward the possibility of growing in it by a process open to all mankind, the process of training. In his attitude toward the abolition of slavery, Bushnell was likewise detached from the extremists. Here, too, he believed less in drastic measures than in education and in the gradual workings of nature under Providence. In the same way he assumed toward the scientific movement of the mid-nineteenth century an attitude at once decisive and concessive. Whatever science might have to say about the rigour of causation and necessity within the physical world, man was always to be recognized as an essentially free supernatural being, placed literally above nature by his alliance with the divine. Yet the two realms, of necessity and of freedom, were held together by a Deity immanent in both (*Nature and the Supernatural*, 1858).

Without being a compromiser, Bushnell thus works *rapprochements* everywhere. His thought holds all subjects suspended in a sort of Platonic solvent, conciliating opposites—not without sometimes confusing them. Yet he continues with vigour the tradition of Plato, Hegel, and Coleridge, and is a genuine religious thinker, whose importance in the history of American thought has perhaps not been generally recognized. In many ways he suggests William James. Moreover, he has a style, nervous, clean, and racy. Kept fresh by its " antiseptic " virtue, his *Literary Varieties*—the volumes of essays entitled *Work and Play* (1864), and *Moral Uses of Dark Things* (1868) and *Building Eras in Religion* (1881)—will still richly reward a reader. Indeed, all of Bushnell's prose, though manifestly influenced by Emerson, by Carlyle, and by Ruskin, yet possesses its own peculiar vitality, a pulsation that at its best may be likened, to use a metaphor of his own, to the beat of wings.

Henry Ward Beecher, too, was born in the orthodox uplands of Litchfield, and of a strictly Calvinistic sire. Lyman Beecher (1775–1863) had studied theology under Timothy Dwight at Yale; had occupied, after 1798, first the Presby-

terian pulpit at Easthampton, Long Island, next the Congregational pulpit at Litchfield, and lastly that of the Park
Street Church in Boston; until in 1832 he became President
of the newly established Lane Theological Seminary in Cincinnati. He is best known, perhaps, for his *Six Sermons on
Intemperance*, but he was a dogmatist as well as a moralist,
staunchly supporting the Calvinism of his native tradition.

His son Henry, graduating at Amherst in 1834 in no
doubt as to his vocation, at once entered the Lane Theological
Seminary, and studied under his father and under Calvin
Stowe (1802–86), an Oriental scholar of real attainment,
who in 1836 married Beecher's sister Harriet. Beecher served
his apprenticeship in the pulpit at Lawrenceburg and Indianapolis, whence in 1847 he was called to the new Brooklyn
congregation of Plymouth Church. The liberal movement
of his thought paralleled his geographical wanderings from
the region of orthodoxy, through the region of culture,
to the practical West, and back to the metropolitan East.
He had had his fill of dogmatic theology in youth, and never
took much further interest in it. He became more and more
a minister, looking rather to the needs of humanity than
to the theory of divinity. In the West, under the stress of
primitive conditions, he soon threw overboard a system of
doctrines in which, he found, plain people were not interested;
so that by the time he took the Brooklyn pulpit, which soon
became a national platform, he was preaching straight at
human nature, and touching it with a more and more liberating
hand as he advanced in years.

From his *Seven Lectures to Young Men* (1844) to his *Evolution and Religion* (1885) he came a long way. The *Lectures* are
addressed apparently not to young men in general, but to young
employees—clerks, mechanics, salesmen, and apprentices.
Hence their flavour of *Poor Richard* and the *Industrious
Apprentice*. Guided to his audience by Franklin and Hogarth,
Beecher combines allegory with vivid eighteenth-century
realism; bigoted invective against the theatre and novels, with
"characters," the Sluggard, the Busybody, the Dandy, the
Pleasure-Loving Business Man, the Cynic, the Libertine.
This antique literary material explains the excessively old-
fashioned flavour of the book. Though Beecher grew im-

measurably away from it, he seems never to have disavowed or changed it, and for fifty years it remained perhaps his most popular work.

To Beecher's Western period also belong short pieces which first appeared in an Indiana agricultural paper and were later (1859) reprinted as *Plain and Pleasant Talk about Fruit, Flowers and Farming*. Of no intrinsic literary importance, they are of interest as showing the sources of much of Beecher's imagery. He was always close to the soil, and he drew from natural phenomena some of his most effective "illustrations." The *Star Papers* (1855 and 1859) and the *Eyes and Ears* (1862), collections of short essays, are good reading even now. With naïveté and self-depreciation, Beecher records his impressions of his first tour in Europe, tells of holiday outings among the Connecticut hills and trout streams, and gives plainly and modestly his very sensible opinions upon such subjects as sudden conversion, mischievous self-examination, and total depravity. The latter doctrine he rejects, accepting the doctrine of men's sinfulness and the necessity of their atonement not because Adam fell but because sin is actual and present. With regard to conversion, he takes the empiricist view that only in rare cases does the inner clock strike twelve when men have found grace; they may have it, yet not have infallible evidence. Hence he deprecates excessive introspection and hesitation, and says "Go ahead." His reminiscences, too, of old Litchfield at a time when that lucky town held Miss Pierce's Female Seminary and the celebrated Law School of Judge Gould and Judge Tapping Reeve, are discursive essays of permanent interest. His story of how, having as a boy of thirteen visited the Charlestown Navy Yard, he stole a cannon ball and went away with it in his hat, is as enjoyable as Franklin's apologues of *The Axe to Grind* and of *Paying too Dear for One's Whistle*. The *Essay on Apple Pie* is not *toto cælo* removed from the *Essay on Roast Pig*. *Home Revisited*, the record of a few days in Indianapolis, recalls the first of his sermons which he considered a success because it was aimed at his hearers; and tells by the way of his awe of Jonathan Edwards. "I never could read . . . *Sinners in the Hands of an Angry God* . . . at one sitting. I think a person of moral sensibilities, alone at midnight, reading that awful discourse, would well nigh go crazy." Through many of these pieces there breathes a frank sensuous enjoyment of physical beauty, which passes easily into religious exaltation. Beecher revels in the form and colour of great painting, and in the sounds, sights, and colours of landscape; the pictures in the Louvre and the glories of a sunset are to him literally revelations. These volumes testify once more to the richness of his mental imagery, and to its decided growth in range and in culture after his removal to the East.

Meanwhile, during all the years from his first pulpit to the beginning of the Civil War, his opposition to slavery had been deepening. He never joined the Abolitionists, but untiringly opposed the extension of slavery, and during the decade from 1850 to 1860, in lectures and in contributions to periodicals, denounced the various compromises and outrages that led up to the conflict. *Freedom and War* (1863), a volume of spirited sermons and addresses from the Brooklyn pulpit, exhibits the growth of his opinions up to the moment when he began to advocate immediate abolition—a moment just before the Emancipation Proclamation itself.

In educating public opinion upon slavery, Beecher had been unconsciously preparing his own armament for uses which he could not have guessed. While upon a vacation in England in the autumn of 1863 he was asked to speak on the war, and in the course of eleven days delivered almost impromptu, at Manchester, Glasgow, Edinburgh, Liverpool, and London, the series of addresses which gave him perhaps his greatest celebrity. Some of his audiences, notably those at Liverpool and Glasgow, were most tumultuous, and had actually to be conquered by the speaker. He conquered them, and won over the English middle class to sympathy with the Union cause. The determination of the British government to maintain strict neutrality is said to have been largely due to Beecher's effect upon public opinion. As literature, the addresses in England, though of course they bear the marks of their hasty composition and contested delivery, yet reveal the easy mastery of his material which Beecher had been storing up in his years of preparatory writing and speaking. Their lucidity and humour are still delightful; they still throw off visibly the live sparks that were struck out in the original clash between the speaker and his hearers; they reproduce the time in its very form and pressure; and in their way, too, they are classics of argumentation, for Beecher realizes the essential Aristotelian form of rhetoric—the orator's persuasion of an audience confronting him. The history of slavery and of secession could hardly be read in a more interesting form.

In *Norwood, or Village Life in New England* (1868), advertised as "Mr. Beecher's only novel," Beecher attempted an excursion into imaginative literature, but failed for want of breath. He had no power of construction and very little power of characterization. The personages are lay figures moving through an action prescribed for them by the author, and speaking his language, not their own. The general woodenness of the book, and several delightful absurdities, lay it open to easy parody. So much allowed, *Norwood*, if taken not as a novel but as a series of sketches of New England types, descriptions of New England scenery, and discussions not too profound of topics in religion, politics, and æsthetics, has distinct merit. This is much the same merit that is exhibited, under much the same limitations, by Beecher's short essays: though he had imagination, he had no architectonic.

Beneath the routine activities of the next twenty years— his regular sermons, the public addresses for which he was more and more in request, and his sentimental *Life of Jesus the Christ* (1871), Beecher was quietly conducting an earnest study of the evolutionary philosophy. From the very beginning of his acquaintance with the new way of thinking, he seems to have felt that it would be his latest and his last instrument for enfranchising the soul; and when he had accomplished his task of educating public opinion at home and abroad toward the abolition of slavery, he turned to this other task of spiritual emancipation. "If I had preached thirty years ago," he says in one of the sermons of his *Evolution and Religion* (1885), "what I preach now, it would have been a great mischief to you; but for thirty years I have been cautious, and have fed you as you could bear it."

Beecher did not, it would seem, understand the full power of the instrument he was employing, and as he was a man of images and not of ideas he never brought his own self-contradictions to a clear issue. In his prevailing mood he makes the assumption, which comes down to him from Platonism, natural religion, and Transcendentalism, that nature is a symbol of God and the moral order, is a continuing revelation of God, is sympathetic with humanity, and is parallel, analogous, and favourable to religion and morals.  Often, however, he realizes to some extent, and frankly declares, as far as he realizes it, the inevitable implication of the theory of natural selection, that nature is alien to the moral strivings of man, and is thoroughly unmoral if not immoral.  When he is conscious of his self-contradiction at all, Beecher seems merely puzzled by it as by one mystery among many.  It would of course be fatal to his work if that work were a philosophical system—which it is not.

Despite his indecision upon this central problem, really the problem of evil itself, Beecher succeeds in giving sight and freedom to souls weighed down and blinded by the old unhappy dogma of depravity.  Without denying man's sinfulness, he reverses the whole prospect of humanity by simply declaring that it is not true that men were created innocent but fell and incurred a debt which they could never hope to pay; but rather that the human race began low down, has not come up very far, and has the opportunity for limitless development upward.

Beecher's close contact with his audience and the abundance of his imagery are the sources of his peculiar power. They keep his style homely and racy (Robert South he declared to have been his chief model), and hold his thought and feeling near to human needs.  He deliberately cultivated both. He carried pocketfuls of gems, which he loved to turn over and examine; he haunted picture-galleries and jewellers' shops. Like Whitman, whom he is said to have influenced, he walked the streets, spent whole days among the docks and ferry boats, made himself familiar with all sorts of trades, and talked with all sorts of people.  These sources of power were also at times sources of weakness.  Beecher came to depend upon hearers rather than readers; his hand faltered when he felt himself out of contact with an audience; and as he could not bring himself to revise with any degree of care the reports of his oral discourse, the form in which much of it has come to us is distinctly sub-literary.  His exuberance of imagery also upon occasion betrayed him into incongruity and bathos.  Yet his writings as a whole produce a deepening impression of merit. Here was a large personality, all of a piece, singularly free from repressions, and with no closet for a skeleton to lurk in. Beecher's openness of soul—exhibiting frankly his delight in beautiful things and in human contacts—is perhaps his characteristic note, and together with the great historical interest of his work will probably go far to render it permanent.

Mark Hopkins was one of a group of clerical college presidents and teachers in whom the old interest in systems was transferred from theology to "anthropology." The group includes men like Francis Wayland (1796–1865), President of Brown University (1827–55); Archibald Alexander (1772–1851), professor at Princeton; James McCosh (1811–94), President of Princeton (1868–88); and Noah Porter (1811–94), President of Yale (1871–86). All of these turn from dogmatic theology to psychology, ethics, and the relations of the human mind to Christianity. They produce textbooks on "Christian Evidences," "Moral Science" or "Moral Philosophy," and "Mental Philosophy," for the most part in a vein of Scottish dualistic realism modified by Sir William Hamilton's Kantian importations.

Mark Hopkins, like Beecher, came of tough-minded stock in a tough-minded region. He was the grandson of Mark, one of three younger brothers who were reared by the benevolent Samuel Hopkins. He was born at Stockbridge, graduated in 1824 at Williams College, and spent the next two years there as tutor. In 1829 he took a degree in medicine at the Berkshire Medical College in Pittsfield, but in 1830 returned to Williamstown as Professor of Moral Philosophy and Rhetoric. Though licensed in 1833, he did not accept a pulpit, but in 1836 became President of Williams College, where he did main service until his resignation in 1872. He remained at Williamstown as President Emeritus, and as a general counsellor to the college and to the very wide community of his pupils.

The influence to which they testify is accounted for not only by his strong, gentle, and sympathetic personality, but also by his mastery of those pregnant generalizations which interest growing minds. He was from first to last a man of ideas. It would be too much to expect that among so many ideas even the majority should be original, and in point of fact

Hopkins derived nearly all from his Calvinistic tradition and from his reading. His works refer explicitly to an exceedingly large number of authors. But the success with which, as a teacher, he caused his pupils to wheel his ideas into action, is surely originality enough. Those ideas, if not themselves a liberal education, gave to the education of hundreds its coherence, articulation, and aim. The winged word of his pupil James A. Garfield, variously reported, asserts that the essence of a college is a student at one end of a log and Mark Hopkins at the other.

Literary quality was only a by-product of a mind thus primarily engaged in forming character. Hopkins's prose is exceedingly uneven. Probably nothing in it was obscure when he spoke it aloud with his own significant intonations; but as a text for the eye it abounds in pitfalls. Yet he so reiterated, developed, illustrated, and enforced his ideas as to produce a total effect of lucidity. He has moments, too, of eloquence and charm.

From the Edwardean tradition Hopkins received the concept of universal benevolence, the dogmatic side of which interested him, however, much less than its usefulness as a basis of ethics. From his very early essay on *The Connection between Taste and Morals* down to his latest volume on *The Scriptural Idea of Man*, he so used it. In his mind it coincided fruitfully with the Aristotelian notion of a scale of things in which each lower member is the condition of a higher; the State, for instance, in which the best life for the citizen is conditioned upon the existence of slaves. Hopkins combined these or kindred ideas into a scale of forces and beings each member of which had a worth higher than that of the one upon which it was conditioned. Thus he established at once a series of ethical values and a series of physical phenomena, each built upon all the preceding and all leading up to the highest, which took up all the lower, and benevolence toward which was the basis of morals. As early as 1857 Hopkins's baccalaureate sermon, *The Higher and the Lower Good*, explained gravity as conditioning cohesion, cohesion as conditioning chemical affinity, and so on up through regularity of form, organic life, sensitive life, rational life, and moral life. Thenceforward this conception reappeared in all his more important works.

Essential to its working also was the assumption that each stage was lifted into the next higher stage by the addition of some external force. It will be observed that this gave Hopkins a full-fledged evolutionary process, worked, however, not from within but from without, by means of accessions of matter and force effected by an external artificer. It was this last phase of his theory that gradually drew to itself the chief emphasis and the most important functions of the whole, and became in Hopkins's hands his great instrument of liberation.

To Hopkins's thinking, the evolutionary philosophy threatened the destruction of personality, the personality of God and of man, both of whom seemed about to be swallowed up in a mechanistic nature. Hopkins has no illusions on the subject. Charm she never so wisely, Nature cannot persuade him of her virtue. She is not, except in some very early Platonistic effusions of his, the symbol of a divine moral order, but is rather a machine grinding out uniform cycles under mechanical necessity, and making no answer to the human demand for purpose and freedom. These elements must be supplied from without; and it is a detached Deity who supplies them.

The germ of this portion of Hopkins's system appears in one of his earliest published works, that entitled *On the Argument from Nature for the Divine Existence* (1833), a review of Whewell's Bridgewater Treatise on *Astronomy and General Physics Considered with Reference to Natural Theology*. Here Hopkins already discredits the "argument from design" and finds evidence of the existence of God much less in nature than in man. Nature, though full of "contrivance," is often irrational and neither wise nor good; only in man is there found a glimmering of wisdom and goodness, only there a moral valuation,—which must be the effect of a cause not different in kind, and hence of the Deity. This argument, too, runs throughout Hopkins's system, parallel with his use of the scale of conditioning and conditioned; so that when he beholds the menace of the evolutionary philosophy, he has his weapons ready.

Tyndall's *Belfast Address* (1874), with its assertion of the complete immanence of all the developing forces within matter itself, realized Hopkins's worst fears; and thenceforth he held evolutionism to this its extreme logic. With a flexibility that was little short of marvellous in one well past his threescore years and ten and confronted by a new and complex hypothesis, he seized at once the fundamental issue between evolutionism and Christianity. This, he saw, was essentially the old issue of immanence against transcendence. Many a younger mind even now fails to grasp this ultimate implication as Hopkins grasped it the moment Tyndall pointed it out; many a Christian even now thinks himself a thorough-going evolutionist when he believes that a detached God created the universe and left it thenceforth to evolve. Hopkins perceived and turned to account with much acumen these same intellectual compromises, futilities, and divisions within the camp of the evolutionists themselves. Spencer, with his utterly detached transcendent Absolute; Fiske, with his old argument from nature to his new unknowable power distinct from matter; and, Hopkins might have added, Wallace, with his several special creations of "higher faculties," one every little while;—these, clearly enough, not only were divided among themselves, but were not carrying the evolutionary argument "whithersoever it led." They were only clouding the issue. All such compromises he refused, and with an intellectual honesty and courage even more admirable than his flexibility, pushed the question to its ultimate form and squarely faced it there. About each professor of evolution he asks, in effect: "Does he, or does he not, say that this power is inherent in matter? If he does, he is properly an evolutionist. If he does not, . . . but says that the results are due to the action of a being . . . that is separable from matter and uses it, then he is not properly an evolutionist." So facing the question, Hopkins had no need of the Bishop of Oxford's weapons. For at least a generation his own mind, as if anticipating the struggle to come, had been forging its sword.

Hopkins, then, uncompromisingly groups together evolutionism, with its mechanistic nature, its continuity, uniformity, necessity, law, monism, immanence, and tendency to pantheism, over against a scale of being that rises into personality, with its freedom, its choice of ends, its discontinuity, its movement *per saltum,* its realism as to species, its supernatural man, and its transcendent Deity. The sum of God's attributes, indeed, is that he is a person; and for Hopkins religion is faith in a person. This order of ideas, suggested as early as the Williams College Semicentennial Address of 1843, grows stronger and stronger in the series of his works; with deepening earnestness he declares that, deprived of personality and of the scale of moral values conditioned by it, the world will go forever circling through mechanical revolutions, but that progress is impossible.

It is a matter for serious inquiry whether the future is not with him. The world has of course moved beyond a denial of the facts of evolution; but it may have to admit that from the accepted and undeniable facts it has been drawing the falsest inferences. The romantic "return to Nature" has led man into the suicidal fallacy that he ought to imitate her in the conduct of his own affairs, and that because he has been evolved by natural selection he must continue its wild work. A reaction against these romantic horrors is now in sight. Many are feeling that romanticism, having given us its best, has had its day; and that "as the Nineteenth Century put man into nature, so it will be the business of the Twentieth to take him out." If man shall indeed acknowledge that he has been following the law for thing rather than the law for man, if he shall understand how it was by following nature's senseless competitive ways, instead of subjecting his self-assertiveness to man's ethical scale, that he betrayed his race to mutual slaughter, and how it was a pseudo-scientific philosophy that brought him to this *doloroso passo*, he will turn from his ghastly naturalism to a controlling humanism such as has never yet been realized.

CHAPTER XXIII

# Writers of Familiar Verse

## I. HOLMES

ONE of the best known passages in *Elsie Venner* is that in which Holmes asserted the existence of an aristocracy in New England, or at least a caste, which "by the repetition of the same influences, generation after generation," has "acquired a distinct organization and physiognomy." This caste is composed of those whose ancestors have had the advantage of college training and have practised one or another of the three learned professions. The young man born in this selected group is commonly slender, with a smooth face and with features regular and of a certain delicacy. "His eye is bright and quick,—his lips play over the thought much as a pianist's fingers dance over their music,—and his whole air, though it may be timid, and even awkward, has nothing clownish." Teachers discover that he "will take to his books as a pointer or setter to his field work." He may be intended for the bar while his father was a minister and his grandfather a physician; and by the very fact of this heredity he "belongs to the Brahmin caste of New England."

The man who thus described this caste was himself a Brahmin of the strictest sect, endowed with its best qualities, and devoid of its less estimable characteristics,—the tendency to anæmia and to the semi-hysterical outlook of the dyspeptic reformer. He was energetic, wholesome to the core, sound and sane, unfailingly alert, fundamentally open-minded, never tempted to crankiness or freakishness. He was born in an illustrious year, 1809, which saw the birth of Darwin and Lincoln, of Tennyson and Gladstone, of Chopin, Mendelssohn, and Edgar Allan Poe. It was toward the end of August that the Rev. Abiel Holmes, author of the *Annals of America*,[1] made a brief entry at the foot of a page in his almanac, "—29. son b." The son was named Oliver Wendell Holmes, the Wendell being the maiden name of his mother, descended from an Evert Jansen Wendell who had been one of the early settlers of Albany; and thus her son could claim a remote relationship with the Dutch poet Vondel:

And Vondel was a Wendell who spelt it with a V.

Through his father, the Calvinist minister, and his grand-father, a physician who had served in the Revolution with the Continental troops, Holmes was descended from Anne, daughter of Thomas Dudley, governor of Massachusetts Bay, and wife of Simon Bradstreet, twice governor of the province.[2] The author of the *Autocrat* shared with R. H. Dana, author of *Two Years before the Mast*, the honour of descent from this literary ancestress. Holmes was born in Cambridge, in an old gambrel-roofed house that had served as General Ward's headquarters at the outbreak of the Revolution: "The plan for fortifying Bunker's Hill was laid, as commonly believed, in the southeast room, the floor of which was covered with dents, made, it is alleged, by the butts of the soldiers' muskets." Holmes's mother, it may be recorded here, to account in a measure for the veracity and the vigour of his *Grandmother's Story of Bunker-Hill Battle*, was only a little girl of six when she was hurried off from Boston, then taken by the British, who were preceded by rumours that "the redcoats were coming, killing and murdering everybody as they went along."

It was in Cambridge that Holmes grew to boyhood, playing under the Washington Elm. He was sent to what was then known as a "dame's school." He had an early inclination to verse, and composed rhyming lines in imitation of Pope and Goldsmith before he knew how to write; and Pope and Goldsmith remained his masters in metrical composition to the end of his long life. His father had a library of between one and two thousand volumes, and in this the son browsed at

[1] See Book II, Chap. XVII.
[2] For Anne Bradstreet, see Book I, Chap. IX.

will, reading in books rather than through them. "I like books," he told us later; "I was born and bred among them and have the easy feeling when I get into their presence, that a stable boy has among horses." When he was fifteen he was sent to Phillips Academy at Andover; and at sixteen he entered Harvard, graduating in 1829, eight years after Emerson and nine before Lowell. Among his classmates were James Freeman Clarke[1] and S. F. Smith, the author of *America* (1832). He wrote freely for the college papers, both in prose and verse, preserving in his collected works only a very few of his earlier humorous lyrics.

Upon his graduation he hesitated as to his profession, spending a year at the Dana Law School without awakening any liking for the law, and confessing later that "the seduction of verse-writing" had made this period "less profitable than it should have been." Yet it was while he was supposed to be studying law, and when he was just twenty-one, that he wrote the first of his poems to achieve an immediate and lasting popularity. This was the fiery lyric on *Old Ironsides*, protesting against the breaking up of the frigate *Constitution*, victor in the naval duel with the *Guerrière*. The glowing stanzas were written in a white heat of indignation against the proposed degradation of a national glory; they were published in 1830 in the Boston *Advertiser;* they were copied in newspapers all over the country; they were reprinted on broadsides; and they accomplished their purpose of saving the ship, which did not go out of commission for more than half a century after Holmes had rhymed his fervent appeal for its preservation.

At last he turned from the law to medicine, the profession of his grandfather. He studied for a while at the private school of Dr. James Jackson; and then he crossed the Atlantic to profit by the superior instruction to be had in Paris. Half a century later he recorded:

I was in Europe about two years and a half, from April, 1833, to October, 1835. I sailed in the packet ship " Philadelphia " from New York to Portsmouth, where we arrived after a passage of twenty-four days. . . . I then crossed the channel to Havre, from

[1] See Book II, Chap. VIII.

which I went to Paris. In the spring and summer of 1834 I made my principal visit to England and Scotland. . . . I returned in the packet ship "Utica," sailing from Havre, and reaching New York after a passage of forty-two days.

On his return to America he settled in Boston as a practising physician, taking as his motto "the smallest fevers thankfully received." He was twenty-seven when he obtained the degree of doctor of medicine and when he issued his earliest volume of poems. Nothing that he had written before or that he was to write later was more characteristic than one of the lyrics in this book,—*The Last Leaf*. He won several prizes for dissertations upon medical themes, published together in 1838; and the next year he was appointed professor of anatomy and physiology in the medical school of Dartmouth College, a position which he held for only a brief period. In 1840 he married Amelia Lee Jackson. He had resumed his practice in Boston, and he continued to contribute freely to the literature of his profession. He was always justly proud of his share in diminishing the danger from puerperal fever and of his trenchant attack upon *Homeopathy and its Kindred Delusions* (1842). Then in 1847 he was called to Harvard as professor of anatomy and physiology; and this position he was to fill with distinction for thirty-five years.

The career of Holmes was placid and uneventful even beyond the average of literary careers. Nothing happened to him other than the commonplaces of life; he took part in nothing unusual; he practised medicine for a few years and he taught medical students for many years; he wrote prose and verse in abundance; and in the fulness of years he died. The only dates that call for record here are those of the publication of his successive books. Until he was almost at the summit of his half-century he was known to the general public only as a writer of verse. He used prose for his discussions of medical questions; and whenever he was moved to express his opinions on other themes he chose the medium of metre. Those were the fertile years of the Lyceum System, and Holmes went the rounds of the lecture-halls like many others of the New England authors who were his contemporaries; but even as a lecturer he preferred rhyming verse to the customary colloquial prose.

Then quite unexpectedly, when he was forty-eight, an age when most men shrink from any new departure disconcerting to their indurated habits, he revealed himself in an entirely new aspect. *The Atlantic Monthly* was started in 1857 with Lowell as its editor; and to its early numbers Holmes contributed *The Autocrat of the Breakfast-Table.* Lowell had insisted as a condition precedent to his acceptance of the editorship that Holmes should be a constant contributor, awakening him "from a kind of lethargy in which" he was "half-slumbering."

Much of the vogue of the new magazine was due to the novel flavour of Holmes's series of papers; and he was persuaded to follow up his first success with kindred volumes entitled *The Professor at the Breakfast-Table* (1860), *The Poet at the Breakfast-Table* (1872), and *Over the Teacups* (1890). For the same monthly he wrote many disconnected essays, some of which he sent forth in 1863 under the appropriate name *Soundings from the Atlantic.* In the several volumes of the Breakfast Table series there is a thin thread of story and the obligatory wedding winds them up at the end; and in his three attempts at fiction, *Elsie Venner* (1861), *The Guardian Angel* (1867), and *A Mortal Antipathy* (1885), the thread is only a little strengthened and there is no overt abandonment of the leisurely method of the essayist. From the telling of fictitious biographies to the writing of the lives of two of his friends was only a step; and he published a memoir of John Lothrop Motley in 1878 and a study of Emerson in 1884.

It was in 1883, when he was seventy-four, that he resigned his professorship; and it was in 1886, when he was seventy-seven, that he paid his second visit to Europe. He spent the summer mainly in England, and in London he was "the lion of the season." It was almost exactly half a century since his first voyage across the ocean; and on his return from this second voyage he wrote out a pleasantly personal narrative of *Our Hundred Days in Europe.* At intervals, for nearly sixty years, he had sent forth volumes of verse; the latest to appear (in 1888) was aptly entitled *Before the Curfew,*—as Longfellow had called his final volume *In the Harbor* and Whittier had felicitously styled his last book *At Sundown.* On 7 October, 1894, Holmes died at the ripe age of eighty-five, unusual even among the long-lived American poets of his generation, of whom he was the last to survive.

During his second visit to London, Holmes was the guest of honour at a dinner of the Rabelais Club, founded to cherish the memory of an earlier humorist who was also a practitioner of medicine; and in his letter accepting the invitation he took occasion to confess his regard for another physician-author, Ambroise Paré, whom he termed "good, wise, quaint, shrewd, chatty." And all five of these characteristics he possessed himself. He was a gentleman and a scholar—to revive the fine old phrase—who was also a physician learned in the lore of the healing art and keenly interested in its history. He was a gentleman and a scholar, who was also a man of the world, in the best sense of that abused term,— a man of the world holding a modest place as a man of science. And at bottom he was a Yankee, with a true Yankee inventiveness,—the hand-stereo-scope he devised being the outward and visible sign of this native gift, which was exhibited incessantly in his writings, notably in *The Physiology of Verse* and in *The Human Wheel, its Spokes and Felloes*. In prose and in verse he disclosed an unfailing Yankee cleverness, whittling his rhymes and sharpening his phrases with an innate dexterity.

"The secret of a man who is universally interesting is that he is universally interested," William Dean Howells has told us; "and this was above all the secret of the charm Doctor Holmes had for every one." There is zest and gusto in all that he wrote, and the reader can share the writer's own enjoyment. Especially was the writer interested in himself, as the true essayist must be. His delight in talking about himself was complacent, contagious, and innocent. "I have always been good company for myself," Holmes once confessed; and this is one reason why he has been pleasantly companionable to countless readers who found in him a friendly quality which took them captive. His egotism was as patent as Montaigne's, even if it was not so frank in its expression nor so searching in its analysis. The more of himself he revealed, the more he won the hearts of his fellow men, who relished the gentleness and the firmness of the character so openly disclosed, its kindliness, its urbanity and amenity, its lack of all acerbity or acridity, its total freedom from the rennet of meanness which curdles the milk of human kindness.

In a letter which Whittier wrote for a celebration of Holmes's seventy-fifth birthday, the Quaker poet singled out for praise the Boston bard's "genial nature, entire freedom from jealousy and envy, quick tenderness, large charity, hatred of sham, pretence and unreality, and his reverent sense of the eternal and permanent." This is keen criticism. Holmes was a wit, but there was no bitterness in his laughter, because it lacked scorn; and there was in it no echo of the cruel sterility of Voltaire's irony. We can say of Holmes what Moore said of Sheridan, that his wit

> ne'er carried a heart-stain away on its blade.

We can say this with the weightier emphasis when we recall the cheerful courtesy with which he met the vindictive and virulent retorts evoked by his dissolvent analysis of the abhorrent and horrible aspects of Calvinism, a disestablished code inherited from a less civilized past. Holmes's influence was civilizing and humanizing; and it was more important than we are likely now to recognize. He had in a high degree the social instinct which has given grace to French life and which was perhaps accentuated in him during his two years' stay in Paris in his malleable youth. He was the constant exponent of good manners and of right feeling, at a period in the evolution of American society when the need for this was even more evident than it is now.

It was in a score of his poems and in the successive volumes of the *Breakfast-Table* series that Holmes most completely disclosed himself. His two biographies and his three novels are far less important,—in fact, these other prose writings are important chiefly because they are the work of the "Autocrat"; and it may be well to deal with them briefly before considering his major work, in which he is expressing the essence of his cheerful optimism. The less significant of his two memoirs is that of Motley, a labour of love undertaken in the months that followed hard upon the death of the historian. "To love a character," said Stevenson, "is the only heroic way of understanding it." Possibly an author could write a vigorous life of a man he hated, since hatred is the other side of love. But no author could paint a vital portrait of a personality which left him indifferent; to his biographer at least a man must be a hero; and no valet has yet written an acceptable account of his master's life. But love needs to be controlled by judgment; and Holmes, at the time he composed his memoir, felt too keenly the injustice from which Motley had suffered to be able to survey the career and to estimate the character of the eminent historian with the detachment necessary to the painting of a portrait for posterity. What he did was to put forward an apology for Motley, with undue insistence upon the temporary griefs of the man and with less adequate consideration of the histories by which his fame is supported.

The biography of Emerson is far better, even if it also is not wholly satisfactory. It is in no sense an apology, for there was nothing in Emerson to extenuate. It is less personal, more detached, more disinterested, more comprehensive. It is admirably planned, with the adroitly articulated skeleton which we have a right to expect from a professor of anatomy. It is rich in appreciation and abundant in phrases of unforgettable felicity, for Holmes was ever the neatest of craftsmen. But when all is said, we cannot repress the conviction that he was out of his natural element when he undertook to deal with a figure so elusive as Emerson's. Holmes's very qualities, his concreteness, his sense of reality, his social instinct, tended to unfit him for interpreting an intangible personality like Emerson. He was characteristically witty when he compared Emerson to those "living organisms so transparent that we can see their hearts beating and their blood flowing through their transparent tissues"; but he did not altogether succeed in making us feel the ultimate purpose for which Emerson's heart beat and his blood flowed. The interest of the biography— and it has its full share of the interest which animated all that Holmes wrote—is kept alive rather by the adroitness of its author than by the revelation of its subject.

Such also is the interest of his three novels; they appeal to those who relish the flavour of Holmes's personality rather than to those who expect a work of fiction to be first of all a story, and secondly a story peopled with accusable characters.

In one of the prefaces to *Elsie Venner* Holmes cited the remark of a dear old lady who spoke of the tale as "a medicated novel"; and he declared that he was "always pleased with her discriminating criticism." It is not unfair to say that all three novels were conceived by a physician and composed by an essayist. Holmes, so Leslie Stephen asserted, lacked the "essential quality of an inspired novelist," which is "to get absorbed in his story and to feel as though he were watching instead of contriving the development of a situation."

Of *Elsie Venner* Holmes himself said that the "only use of the story is to bring the dogma of inherited guilt and its consequences into a clearer point of view"; and he declared that his "heroine found her origin not in fable or romance, but in a physiological conception, fertilized by a theological dogma." In other words, *Elsie Venner* is a novel-with-a-purpose; it is a fiction devised by a nineteenth-century physician to attack eighteenth-century Calvinism. Perhaps a born story-teller could have so constructed his narrative as to fascinate the reader in spite of the argument it was intended to carry, but Holmes was not a born story-teller. He described characters and places, not for their bearing on the story itself, and not even for suggesting the appropriate atmosphere of the action, but mainly if not solely for their own sake, and quite in the manner of the character-writers who had blazed the trail for the early essayists. By the side of figures thoroughly known and delicately delineated, there are others, not a few, outlined in the primary colours and trembling on the very verge of caricature. In this we can discover the unfortunate influence of Dickens, as we can perceive the fortunate influence of Hawthorne in the treatment of the abnormal heroine. And equally obvious is the influence of Thackeray, who also began and ended his career as an essayist. Thackeray, even if he had a bias toward moralizing, confessed to the Brookfields that he found his ethical lectures very convenient when he had to pad out his copy to fill the allotted number of pages in the monthly parts in which his larger novels originally appeared. But Thackeray, after all, was a born story-teller, an inspired novelist, who got absorbed in his story and felt as though he were watching and not inventing his situations. Holmes lingered by the way and chatted with the reader, not from any external necessity, but because digression and even disquisition is to the essayist the breath of life.

In *The Guardian Angel*, the heroine is a composite photograph of half a dozen warring ancestors of whom now one and now another emerges into view to insist upon the reappearance of his or her identity in Myrtle Hazard. Yet, when all deductions are made, both *Elsie Venner* and *The Guardian Angel* have many a chapter that only Holmes could have written, rich in wisdom, in wit, in whimsy, and in knowledge of the world. But this can scarcely be said of *A Mortal Antipathy*, the latest of the medicated fictions and the feeblest, written when its author had long passed threescore years and ten. The physiological theme is too far-fetched, too unusual, too abnormal, to win acceptance even if it had been handled by a master of fiction; and we may doubt whether even Balzac could have dealt with it triumphantly. As Holmes dealt with it, it did not justify itself; the narrative was too fragmentary for fiction and too forced, while the intercalary papers lacked the freshness of view and the unpremeditated ease of Holmes's earlier manner as an essayist.

"The prologue of life is finished at twenty; then come five acts of a decade each, and the play is over, with now and then a pleasant or a tedious afterpiece, when half the lights are put out, and half the orchestra is gone." When Holmes wrote this, he could not foresee that he would be able to keep in their seats more than half of the spectators, if not the most of them, to the very end of his pleasant afterpiece. He was not forty when he first discoursed as the "Autocrat" and he was twice forty when he gossiped "Over the Teacups." In the octogenarian book he may be a little less spontaneous and a little more self-centred than in its predecessor of twoscore years earlier; and the shadowy figures who take part in its conversations may seem to talk a little because they are aware that they were created on purpose to converse, instead of talking freely for the fun of it as the solider persons who met around the breakfast table were wont to do. Yet the latest of the group, even if its wit be less pungent, has almost as many samples of shrewd sagacity as adorned the two books that came after the *Autocrat*. "Habits are the crutches of old age," Holmes tells us; and he never lost the habit of cheerfulness. There is no hypocritic praising of past times; on the contrary there is a blithe and buoyant recognition of the gains garnered in eighty years.

*Over the Teacups* may be a little inferior to *The Poet at the Breakfast-Table* but only as the *Poet* is a little inferior to the *Professor* and the *Professor* to the *Autocrat*, because the freshness had faded and because we were no longer taken by surprise. The *Autocrat* struck the centre of the target and the hit was acclaimed with delight; the later books went to the same mark, even if they were not winged by an aim as unerring. No doubt, a part of the immediate success of the *Autocrat* was due to its novelty,—novelty of form and novelty of content. Holmes was characteristically shrewd when he declared that "the first of my series came from my mind almost with an explosion, like the champagne cork; it startled me a little to see what I had written and to hear what people said about it. After that first explosion the flow was more sober, and I looked upon the product of my wine-press more coolly"; and he added, "continuations almost always sag a little." Perhaps the novelty of form was more apparent than real, since Steele and Addison had given us a group of characters talking at large as they clustered about Sir Roger de Coverley. But there is this salient difference, that in *The Spectator* the talk is mainly for the purpose of creating character, whereas in the *Autocrat* the characters have been created that they might listen.

Yet in so far as the *Autocrat* has a model, this is plainly enough the eighteenth-century essay, invented by Steele, improved by Addison, clumsily attempted by Johnson, and lightly varied by Goldsmith. Steele is the originator of the form, since the earlier essay of Montaigne and of Bacon makes no use of dialogue; it has only one interlocutor, the essayist himself, recording only his own feelings, his own opinions, and his own judgments. Steele was probably influenced by the English character-writers, perhaps also by the lighter satires of Horace, and quite possibly by the comedies of Molière,— notably by the *Précieuses Ridicules* and the *Femmes Savantes*. The outline Steele sketched the less original Addison filled with a richer colour. As Holmes had begun when a child by imitating the verse of Pope and Goldsmith, so as a man when he wrote prose he followed the pattern set by Steele and Addison. Although he was not born until the ninth year of the nineteenth century, he was really a survivor from the eighteenth century; and his prose like his verse has the eighteenth-century characteristics, despite the fact that he himself was ever alert to apprehend the new scientific spirit of the century in which he lived.

The real novelty of the *Autocrat* was in its content, that is to say, in Holmes himself, the master talker of the Breakfast-Table, in the skill with which the accent of conversation is caught. The other characters are responsible for an occasional remark not without individuality and point; but the Autocrat himself tends to be a monopolist and to intermit his discourse only that his adversary in the verbal combat may lay himself open to a series of sharp thrusts in retort. This is as it should be, since the others who gather about the breakfast table were but ordinary mortals, after all, whereas the Autocrat was an extraordinary mortal, an artist in conversation, gifted by nature and trained by long experience, a man who had thought widely if not deeply about life, who had read the records of the past and who could revive them to shed light on the present, a physician abreast of modern science and swift to bring its new discoveries to bear on the old problems of life. In reading the *Breakfast-Table* series in swift succession the reader cannot help remarking the frequency with which Holmes draws on his professional experience; he sees men and women through the clear spectacles of the family physician;—and perhaps one reason why he arrogates to himself the major part of the conversation is in revenge for the silence imposed on the practitioner by the tedious and interminable talk of his patients about themselves to which the family physician has perforce to submit. Holmes used medical analogies and dropped into the terminology of the anatomist and physiologist with the same frequency that Shakespeare employed the vocabulary of the theatre, even in incongruous situations finding material for figures of speech in his own experience on the stage.

Holmes is not only a man of science and a man of the world, he is also a humorist and a wit,—a wit who has no antipathy even to the humble but useful pun,—a humorist abounding in whimsy. And as a result of this fourfold equipment his talk is excellent merely as talk. It has the flavour of the spoken word; it is absolutely unacademic and totally devoid of pedantry. Therefore it is not only delightful but stimulating; it continually makes the reader think for himself and turn back upon himself. Despite its acuteness, its liveliness, its briskness, its vivacity, it never lacks seriousness, without ever becoming ponderous.

It may be that Holmes does not attain to the high seriousness, the deep seriousness, of enduring philosophy; and it cannot be denied that there are pages here and there which are not as valid today as when they were written. It would be doing the Autocrat an ill-service to compare him with his remote and mighty predecessors Montaigne and Bacon. And it may be admitted that there is more or less warrant for the remark of John Burroughs, to the effect that Holmes always reminded him "of certain of our bird songsters, such as the brown thrasher or the cat-bird, whose performances always seem to imply a spectator and to challenge his admiration." Holmes seems "to write with his eye upon his reader, and to calculate the advance upon his reader's surprise and pleasure." To admit this would be only to acknowledge the truth of the French saying that every man has the defects of his qualities. But it cannot be admitted if it implies that Holmes was unduly self-conscious or affected or pretentious. In fact, much of the charm of the Autocrat is due to the entire absence of affectation and to the apparent spontaneity of the talk which pours so easily from his lips and which discloses so abundantly the winning personality of Holmes himself. "Every book is, in an intimate sense, a circular letter to the friends of him who writes it," so Stevenson has told us; and Holmes was fortunate in that his circular letter made a friend of every one who received it.

The qualities which give charm to Holmes's prose are those which please us also in his verse. He has left a dozen or a score of lyrics secure in the anthologies of the future. But he wrote too easily and he wrote too much to maintain a high average in the three hundred double-columned pages in which his complete poems are collected. No poet or prose man can take down to posterity a baggage wagon of his works, and he is lucky if he can save enough to fill a saddle-bag. Holmes's reputation as a poet will rise when his verses are winnowed and garnered into a thin volume of a scant hundred pages wherein *Old Ironsides* and *The Last Leaf*, *The Chambered Nautilus* and *Homesick in Heaven*, *The Wonderful "One-Hoss Shay"* and *The Broomstick Train*, *Grandmother's Story of Bunker-Hill Battle*, and a handful more are unincumbered by the hundreds of occasional verses which were each of them good enough for its special occasion and yet not good enough to demand remembrance after the event.

There are a few of Holmes's loftier poems in which we feel that the inspiration is equal to the aspiration; but there are only a few of them, with *The Chambered Nautilus* at the head, accompanied by *Homesick in Heaven*,—not overpraised by Howells when he called it one of the "most profoundly pathetic of the language." And Stedman was right also when he suggested that Holmes's serious poetry had scarcely been the serious work of his life. Even at its best this serious poetry is the result of his intelligence rather than of his imagination. It lacks depth of feeling and largeness of vision. It has a French felicity of fancy, a French dexterity of craftsmanship, a French point and polish; and also a French inadequacy of emotion. "Assuredly we love poetry in France," said Anatole France when he was discussing the verse of Sainte-Beuve; "but we love it in our own fashion; we insist that it shall be eloquent, and we willingly excuse it from being poetic." *Old Ironsides*, fiery as its lines ring out, is eloquent rather than truly poetic.

Here again Holmes declares himself as a survival from the eighteenth century, when English literature conformed to French principles. His favourite reading as a child was Pope's *Homer*, the couplets of which "stimulated his imagination in spite of their formal symmetry." And even their formal symmetry was not displeasing to his natural taste:

> And so the hand that takes the lyre for you
> Plays the old tune on strings that once were new.
> Nor let the rhymester of the hour deride
> The straight-backed measure with its stately stride;
> It gave the mighty voice of Dryden scope;
> It sheathed the steel-bright epigrams of Pope;
> In Goldsmith's verse it learned a sweeter strain,
> Byron and Campbell wore its clanking chain;
> I smile to listen while the critic's scorn
> Flouts the proud purple kings have nobly worn.

The even merit of its occasional verse is one of the obvious qualities of the eighteenth century which we find also in Holmes. Late in life he admitted that he had become rather too well known in connection with "occasions." He was intensely loyal to Boston; and he felt that he had no right to refuse the summons to stand and deliver whenever the city received an honoured guest or when an honoured citizen died or went away or came back. As he explained in one of these occasional pieces,

> I'm a florist in verse, and what *would* people say
> If I came to a banquet without my bouquet?

Late in life Holmes admitted that "many a trifling performance has had more good honest work put into it than the minister's sermon of that week had cost him"; he confessed to strenuous effort over his copy of verses, insisting that "if a vessel glides off the ways smoothly and easily at her launching, it does not mean that no great pains have been taken to secure the result"; and he proudly reminded his readers that "Pindar's great odes were occasional poems . . . and yet they have come down among the most precious bequests of antiquity to modern times." The noblest example of English prose in the nineteenth century, Lincoln's Gettysburg address, was also evoked by an occasion. Even if Holmes's occasional verse has not the lofty elevation of Pindar's odes or the pathetic simplicity of Lincoln's little speech, it has almost always an exquisite propriety to the event itself, an unfailing happiness of epithet, a perfect adequacy to the moment of local importance. Its chief fault, if not its only defect, is that there is too much of it, even if its average is higher than might reasonably be expected.

In a letter to Lowell, Holmes declared, speaking of Bostonians in particular and yet perhaps also of Americans in general, that "we Boston people are so bright and wide-awake . . . that we have been in danger of thinking our local scale was the absolute one of excellence—forgetting that 212 Fahrenheit is but 100 centigrade." There is one department of poetry in which Holmes can withstand without any danger of shrinking the application of the centigrade scale; this is the department of *vers de société*, so called, although it is never merely society verse. Perhaps Cowper's term best describes it, "familiar verse," the lyric commingled of humour and pathos, brief and brilliant and buoyant, seemingly unaffected and unpremeditated, and yet—if we may judge by the infrequency of supreme success—undeniably difficult, despite its apparent ease. Dr. Johnson, who was himself quite incapable of it, too heavy-footed to achieve its lightness, too polysyllabic to attain its vernacular terseness, was yet shrewd enough to see that it is

less difficult to write a volume of lines, swelled with epithets, brightened with figures, and stiffened by transpositions, than to produce a few couplets, grand only by naked elegance and simple purity, which require so much care and skill that I doubt whether any of our authors have yet been able for twenty lines together nicely to observe the true definition of easy poetry.

In this "easy poetry," which is the metrical equivalent of the essay in its charm, in its grace and in its colloquial liberty, Holmes has few rivals in our language. It was with strict justice that Locker-Lampson, in the preface to the first edition of *Lyra Elegantiarum* (1867)—to this day the most satisfactory anthology of *vers de société*,—declared that Holmes was "perhaps the best living writer of this species of verse." It may be recorded also that Locker-Lampson paid Holmes the even sincerer compliment of imitation, borrowing for two of his delightful lyrics not only the spirit but also the stanza Holmes had invented for *The Last Leaf*. With characteristic frankness the London lyrist once told an American admirer that this stanza might seem easy but it was difficult, so difficult that no one had handled it with complete success—except Holmes and himself.

Locker-Lampson derived directly from Praed, whose verses have an electric and dazzling brilliance, whereas in Holmes the radiance is more subdued and less blinding. Of all the writers of familiar verse no one has ever surpassed Holmes in the delicate blending of pathos with humour, as exemplified most strikingly in *The Last Leaf*, in which fantasy plays hide and seek with sentiment. Scarcely less delightful in its eighteenth-century quaintness is the family portrait, *Dorothy Q;* and close to those two masterpieces are lesser lyrics like *Contentment, Bill and Joe*, and the lines *On Lending a Punch Bowl* and *To an Insect:*

> I love to hear thine earnest voice,
>   Wherever thou art hid,
> Thou testy little dogmatist,
>   Thou pretty Katydid!
> Thou mindest me of gentlefolks,—
>   Old gentlefolks are they,—
> Thou say'st an undisputed thing
>   In such a solemn way.

These are only a few of the best of his lighter lyrics, now sprightly and sparkling, and now softer and more appealing, often evoking the swift smile, although never demanding the loud laugh, and sometimes starting the tear on its way to the eyelid; and in them Holmes proved that Stedman was only just when he declared that familiar verse may be "picturesque, even dramatic," and that it may "rise to a high degree of humor and of sage and tender thought."

## II. Minor Writers

It is in a half dozen of the ineffably graceful lyrics of the Greek anthology and in a like number of the more personal songs of Horace that we may find the earliest analogue of English familiar verse, better and more abundant than the French *vers de société*, even though the native English form has been compelled to borrow a French name for itself. The Greek anthology has the freedom of the fields and of the solitary hillside, and therefore it lacks a little of the social tone which is the dominating quality of familiar verse. Yet Horace is never rustic—he belongs to the town; and Stevenson is right in saying that Horace is urban, even when read outdoors; he has the abundant urbanity and the total absence of rusticity which familiar verse must ever reveal. Familiar verse is a species of poetry which can flourish only where men and women meet frequently, without undue parade, not wearing their hearts on their sleeves, and hiding their deeper feelings behind the semi-transparent mask of conventional detachment from the serious duties of life.

Familiar verse can develop only when men congregate in cities; it is a town-product; and Boston can claim a share in Holmes's success in this difficult department of song. Other

Americans in other cities have been inspired to risk the dangers of familiar verse and to rhyme the sayings and doings of their fellow citizens. Sometimes they give to their airy nothings a local habitation and a name as easily recognizable as the background of *Dorothy Q.* Could *Nothing to Wear*, detailing the sad plight of Miss Flora McFlimsy of Madison Square, and the *Visit from Saint Nicholas* on

> the night before Christmas, when all through the house,
> Not a creature was stirring, not even a mouse

—could either of these have been composed elsewhere than in New York? And could *The Truth about Horace* have been told with such stern veracity anywhere else than in Chicago?

In the first century of the American republic there were only a few large cities, and yet urban amenity was to be discovered here and there in towns where the social organization had advanced beyond its elementary stages. Benjamin Franklin, a pioneer in so many different departments of human endeavour, seems to have been the earliest American to adventure himself among the difficulties of this lighter poetry, so closely akin to prose in its directness and in its seeming lack of effort; and perhaps his lines on *Paper* could open an American selection of familiar verse only by favouritism. Philip Freneau[1] essayed it more than once; so did Royall Tyler,[2] our first writer of comedy; so did John Quincy Adams[3] and James Kirke Paulding[4] and Washington Irving,[5]—prose men all of them, dropping into rhyme only occasionally, and only when the spirit moved them. And it is a significant fact, supported by a host of examples in both branches of English literature, British and American, that it is in familiar verse that the expert essayist is most likely to be successful when he risks himself in the realm of rhyme.

Yet it is possible also to select specimens of this special type from the major poets, the sport of their frolicsome moods, and no adequate anthology would fail to include Bryant's *Robert of Lincoln*, Emerson's *Humble-Bee*, Whittier's *In School Days* and Longfellow's *Catawba Wine*. From Lowell the

[1] See Book I, Chap. IX.    [2] *Ibid.*
[3] See Book II, Chap. XV.    [4] See Book II, Chap. V.
[5] See Book II, Chap. IV.

VOL. II — 16

examples would be half a dozen at least, with *Auf Wiedersehen* and *Without and Within* as the first flowers to be picked. Indeed, Lowell is Holmes's only chief rival among American poets in the limited field of familiar verse, but he is less meticulous in finish and polish and more likely to charge his lines with a meaning too large for the lyric which aims above all else at lightness and brightness.

Three other American poets of high ambition, Stedman,[1] Aldrich,[2] and Bret Harte,[3] gave a more abundant share of their attention to the poetry which is blithe and buoyant; and in any selection of the best in this kind, it would be inexcusable to omit Stedman's *Pan in Wall Street*, Aldrich's *In an Atelier*, or Bret Harte's *Her Letter*. Nor would any competent editor exclude from such a collection Weir Mitchell's *Decanter of Madeira*, George Arnold's *Jolly Old Pedagogue*, or Charles Henry Webb's *Dum Vivimus Vivamus*. Nor would it be difficult largely to increase this list of examples chosen from the verse of men whose reputation has been won mainly in other fields.

Three of our lighter lyrists demand a little more detailed consideration,—John Godfrey Saxe (1816–87), Eugene Field[4] (1850–95), and Henry Cuyler Bunner[5] (1855–96), though the last two belong to a period somewhat later than that chiefly considered in this chapter. Of these Saxe is the earliest and the least important. He is not only the earliest, he is also the most old-fashioned in his method and the least individual in his outlook. His verse is modelled upon Praed's, to whose dazzling brilliance he could not attain; and he borrowed also the pattern of Hood in his more broadly comic lyrics. He was clever and facile; but he was a little too easy-going to achieve the delicate fineness which we have a right to demand in familiar verse. He does not understand that the thinner the theme the more care must be exercised to redeem its exeguity by certainty of touch and by infinite solicitude in execution. The immanent difficulty of familiar verse is due to the fact that poetry of this type at its best ought to be humorous without broadening into mere fun, while it ought also to be pathetic without slopping over into sentimentality. Saxe is quite free from senti-

[1] See Book III, Chap. x.       [2] *Ibid.*
[3] See Book III, Chaps. v. and vi.     [4] See also Book III, Chap. ix.
[5] See also Book III, Chap. vi.

mentality, in fact he does not often succeed in suggesting sentiment. His defect is that his verse tends to be frankly laughter-provoking. It is in *Little Jerry* that he has hinted the sentiment which sustains humour, as it is in *The Mourner à la Mode* that he has echoed the more worldly manner of mere society verse.

Eugene Field is like Saxe in one respect at least,—that his verse is frankly comic more often than not. His humour is bold, exuberant, energetic, spontaneous, and easy; and there is cause for wonder, therefore, that he was able to restrain himself on occasion and to curb his comic verse within the strictest bounds of familiar verse, endowing it with genuine sentiment without foregoing either blitheness or brilliancy. He had far more freshness than Saxe, a more fertile originality, and knowledge of men and of books both wider and deeper. He is superior also in technical dexterity, in variety of rhythm, and in fertility of rhyme. His feeling is more spontaneous, his sentiment more abundant and finer in feeling. He can when he chooses hint at the tear which trembles above the lips that seem to smile. There is warrant for the wide popularity of his *Little Boy Blue*, in which the pathos is pure and tender, without any taint of mawkish sentimentality. Only a little narrower in its appeal is *Old Times, Old Friends, Old Loves*. Field's command of sentiment is so certain that he can impart true feeling even to stanzas as frolicsome and as rollicking as those which delight us in *Apple Pie and Cheese*.

The youngest of these three younger practitioners of familiar verse, Henry Cuyler Bunner, could also be broadly comic; he had an ample outlook on literature and on life; and he was truly a poet, who won a memorable position among our lyrists by lyrics of a loftier flight than mere comic verse. His lyre was a winged instrument on which he could strike at will the resonant note of patriotism or the gentler strain of peaceful sentiment. *The Way to Arcady* is almost too poetical, its spirit is almost too ethereal, to let it fall within the narrow circle of social verse; it has a simple grace and a light freedom not often discoverable since the songs of the Elizabethan dramatists. In certain of his brisker and brighter poems Bunner reveals himself as a disciple of Austin Dobson; in others he is treading the trail of Herrick or following in the footsteps of Heine. He sat at the feet of many masters and learned what they had to teach him, standing forth in time upon his own feet and giving voice to a note of his own. No one of his predecessors in social verse could be credited with the suggesting of *Forfeits* or *Candor*, the *Chaperon* or *One, Two, Three*, exquisite in its certainty of execution, in the skill with which the sadness of the theme is relieved by the joyousness of the treatment. It is the abiding quality of Bunner's familiar verse that it discloses the spirit of the true poet, even while it confines itself within the bounds of the brevity, the brilliancy, and the buoyancy which are the hampering limitations of familiar verse.

# CHAPTER XXIV

# Lowell

NEITHER Lowell's poetry nor prose has that obvious unity of effect which characterizes the work of so many nineteenth century writers. His work does not recall, even in the minds of its admirers, a group of impressions so distinct and fixed as those summoned by the poetry of Whittier, Poe, or Whitman, or by that of Swinburne, Morris, or Browning, or by the prose of Thoreau or Emerson, of Ruskin or Arnold. His work, indeed, does not have the marks of a dominant or of a peculiar personality; nor does it add to literature a new group of ideas or a new departure in workmanship. Though its volume is large, and though a number both of his poems and his essays have won a wide familiarity, there is difficulty in summarizing their qualities of form or matter in a way that will indicate with justice his importance in American literature.

This somewhat miscellaneous appeal made by his writing may be ascribed in part, no doubt, to a lack of literary power that prevented him from winning the triumphs that belong to the great conquests of the imagination, but it is also due in large measure to the variety of responses which his rich personality made to the changing movements of American life. Other writers were surer of their message or of their art, but perhaps the career of no other affords a more varied and interesting commentary on the course of American letters, or responds as constantly to the occasions and needs of the nation's experience. It is impossible to consider him apart from his time and environment, or to judge his writing apart from its value for the United States. It has left something for posterity, but its best energy was expended in the manifold tasks which letters must perform as a builder of national civilization. It is this service which makes him an eminent and in some ways our most representative man of letters.

The briefest summary of the events of his life will indicate the variety of his interests and occupations. Born in 1819 in Cambridge, Massachusetts, in the colonial house where he was to spend most of his life, he went to Harvard College, studied law—and abandoned it for a career of letters. He contributed verses and sketches to the magazines, edited a few numbers of an unsuccessful literary journal, *The Pioneer*, brought out his first volume of poems, *A Year's Life*, in 1841, a second volume in 1843, and a collection of essays, *Conversations on Some of the Old Poets*, in 1844.

In December of this year he was married to the poetess Maria White. The nine years of their married life until her death in 1853 mark a distinct period in Lowell's literary work. He contributed constantly both prose and verse to various journals, at first largely for those of the anti-slavery propaganda; and the Mexican War gave the opportunity for *The Biglow Papers*, the first of which appeared in *The Boston Courier* of 17 June, 1846. In 1848 appeared a second collection of poems, the completed *Biglow Papers*, and *The Fable for Critics*. Lowell had won, in both popular and critical regard, an assured place in what was already an important national literature. The fifteen months which the family spent in Europe in 1851–52 seem to have increased his desire to widen the range of his poetry, but the ambitions that thronged with the return to America were interrupted by the death of his wife. A period of uncertainty followed his bereavement, and circumstances gave him a new occupation.

In 1855 he delivered in Boston a course of twelve lectures (unpublished) on English poetry, and as a result of their success was appointed to succeed Longfellow as Smith Professor of the French and Spanish Languages and Literatures and Professor of Belles Lettres in Harvard College. A few months were spent in Dresden in preparation for a course on German literature, and in the fall of 1856 he began twenty years work as a teacher. In the following year he was married to Frances Dunlap and resumed life in Elmwood. His professorship turned his mind to criticism and scholarship, but did not hasten that stronger poetic flight for which he had felt himself preparing. A brief-lived literary magazine, *Putnam's Monthly*, in 1853–54 had given place to one or two of his best known essays, and a new literary enterprise, *The Atlantic Monthly*, in 1857 gave further opportunity for his prose. Lowell was editor of the new magazine for two years and a regular contributor of reviews and articles until 1863, when he joined with Charles Eliot Norton in editing *The North American Review*. For the next dozen years his essays both political and literary appeared mainly in this review.

During the Civil War, Lowell's chief contributions to poetry were the new series of *Biglow Papers* which began in the *Atlantic* in 1861. It was not until the war was over that the great themes of national triumph through sacrifice called forth the four memorial odes. Miscellaneous verse of the preceding twenty years was collected in *Under the Willows* (1868); but the odes and longer poems, as *The Cathedral* (1870), *Agassiz* (1874), best represent both the emotional impulses that followed the war and the maturity of Lowell's art.

The political interests which had engaged much of his prose writing before and during the war had not interrupted his increasing devotion to the study and criticism of literature. He had been directing his attention less to contemporary letters and more to the masters of English and to a few of the masters of foreign literature, notably Dante. The result of these studies was a long succession of essays which make up the volumes *Among My Books* (1870), *My Study Windows* (1871), and *Among My Books, Second Series* (1876). It is these books which are his main contributions to literary criticism.

Lowell and his wife spent two years (1872–74) in Europe, and after a brief resumption of his professorship he was appointed minister to Spain in 1877, and in 1880 was transferred to England. After his retirement in 1885 he spent a considerable part of his time in England until his death in 1891. The mission was a recognition of his distinction not merely as a man of letters but as a representative of the best American culture, and this distinction Lowell maintained in a number of addresses on both literary and political themes, represented by the volume *Democracy and Other Addresses* (1886). Although his poetry became infrequent there was enough for a final volume, *Heartsease and Rue*, in 1880.

To all these varied activities as poet, essayist, humorist, editor, teacher, scholar, and diplomat, must be added that of letter writer. For Lowell's letters, in addition to their annals of his personal experiences and friendships, contribute something to literature and history which perhaps has ceased with the day of the typewriter—a record of the intimate association of the high-minded. His work as a man of letters may be considered most readily by the main divisions of verse and prose; but the separation is not always significant. The poetry is mostly bounded by the years 1840 and 1870, and the best of the essays by 1860 and 1890; but there is hardly a year of his half century which did not see both prose and verse. Nor can the subject matter be divided by the two forms, for both require attention from the historian of either the literary or the political progress of the half-century. Both respond to the changing events of his own life, and to the greater changes that transformed the nation of 1840 into that of 1890.

Lowell's youth was spent among books. Before he left college he had become a wide if desultory reader, and the study of law failed to detach him from what was to become a life-long devotion to the easy chair and the library. To the inheritance of English blood, law, language, and religion that bound New England to the mother country, he added an enthusiastic appreciation for English literature. Naturally this appreciation was directed by the Romanticism which had reached its full flower in English letters, by its leaders, Wordsworth, Keats, Lamb, or by the gods of its idolatry, Shakespeare, Spenser, and Dante. His feeling was like that which Keats had experienced twenty years before, when English poetry had opened out a new world inviting to fresh beauty and new enterprise. And this world of British letters had added since then the clarion voice of Carlyle and the exquisite art of Keats himself and of Tennyson. It is easy to trace in Lowell's early verse imitation and reminiscence of the English poets of the preceding half-century; but even more important was his acceptance of their faith in poetry. With Wordsworth he believed that it was to be the moral guide and spiritual inspirer, with Keats he saw it opening new doors to the abode of beauty. He shared the assurance of *Sartor Resartus* that literature was to supply the new priesthood that was to direct the new age.

There were also new ideas and impulses astir in the New England of Lowell's youth. The narrow Puritanism had given way to Unitarianism and Transcendentalism[1] and literature. During the first twenty years of Lowell's life, American literature had taken a bulk and character which might risk comparison with the literature of any European nation during that period. In his teens he was reading Emerson, Longfellow, Holmes, Whittier, Hawthorne, and Prescott, and most of these men were his neighbours and ready to welcome and direct his first attempts at letters. There is a sense of an intellectual and imaginative dawn to be found in Lowell's essays and verse, a dawn that is to gladden the granite and pines of his native land. With a loving admiration for the old literature, there is a loyal national pride in the new; or, rather, there is a sectional pride; for the patriotism is mainly a sectional patriotism, a fervour for the New England hills and men. Boston was then a long way from New York and Philadelphia—although Lowell's literary adventures carried him to both cities—and the rest of the nation was separated by barriers of manners and habit. He was patriotically American because his beloved and awakened New England was expected to lead the nation.

Lowell's early poems do not show much novelty of theme or manner. They are on about the same subjects that all men were writing verse upon in the forties, and written with the same vocabulary, images, and rhythms. Love, nature, liberty, idealism, classic story, personal moods are the themes, but there is some novelty in the ingenuity of the phrases and in the new fauna and flora. If he was following the English romanticists he was transferring their worship of beauty to a New England landscape and their religious musings to the turmoil of idealism that stirred the youth of Massachusetts. He writes of the dandelion and the pine-tree, and his seasons are the riotous June or the Indian summer of Cambridge, his landscape that of Beaver Brook. All is descriptive or reflective; there is no narrative except when it is the mere text for sentiment and moral.

Some union of art and morality, of Keats and Carlyle, Poe and Emerson—that was the poet's endeavour. He wrote to Briggs in 1846:

[1] See also Book II, Chaps. VIII and XXII.

Then I feel how great is the office of Poet, could I but even dare to hope to fill it. Then it seems as if my heart would break in pouring out one glorious song that should be the gospel of Reform, full of consolation and strength to the oppressed, yet falling gently and restoringly as dew on the withered youth-flowers of the oppressor. That way my madness lies.[1]

It is easy to smile at this youthful fervency, as Lowell himself smiled a year or two later in *The Fable for Critics*.

> There is Lowell, who's striving Parnassus to climb
> With a whole bale of isms tied together with rhyme.
> The top of the hill he will ne'er come nigh reaching
> Till he learns the distinction 'twixt singing and preaching.

But, with most nineteenth-century poets, Lowell was a preacher as well as a singer. Poverty, tyranny, doubt, industrialism, are the themes that for England distracted the attention of the Muse; in the United States, the mid-century vision of beauty was clouded by the presence of slavery. And if Lowell was conscious that the isms, even that of the anti-slavery cause, burdened his climb up Parnassus, there was never any doubt of the imperative nature of the summons of moral reform.

The American reader should indeed have a special sympathy for this avowal of high purpose; for is not this gospel of reform the better genius of our nation? The material advance which has conquered a continent has made us self-confident, disregardful of the past, and careless of reflection, but it has inspired us with a faith in our power to rebuild and move on. The evils which beset us do not daunt us, and the virtues we possess we would fain impose upon others. We believe in propaganda, we are uneasy without some cause to further, some improvement to promote. If we ever determine what the American idea is, we shall evangelize the world.

It was perhaps this spirit of reform which Lowell had sought to express in his *Prometheus* and which he had in mind when in another letter to Briggs he declares "I am the first who has endeavoured to express the American Idea, and I shall be popular by and by."[2] Popularity came first, however, when

---

[1] Scudder, *Life*, Vol. I, p. 267.  [2] *Ibid.*

fervour was linked with wit and humour in *The Biglow Papers* with their racy Yankee dialect and their burning zeal against the aggressiveness of the slave-holding South.

The art of these verses has no resemblance to the art of Keats, and their gospel of reform is not a glorious song of consolation; but their rapid fire of wit and common sense was perhaps a better expression of Lowell's temperament than any of his more studied measures. Certainly no poems have ever more distinctly revealed the New England temper. When collected they were imbedded in a paraphernalia of apparatus in which the wit is often laboured, and some of them are no more than clever journalism; but the best have become a lasting part of our popular literature. If this is due in part to their vernacular homeliness, and in part to their wit, it is also due to the moral fire of their democracy. As Horace Scudder insisted, there is a connection between them and another popular success of a different kind, *The Vision of Sir Launfal*. There "it is the holy zeal which attacks slavery issuing in this fable of a beautiful charity."[1]

In 1850 Lowell wrote to Briggs:

I begin to feel that I must enter a new year of apprenticeship. My poems have thus far had a regular and natural sequence. First, Love and the mere happiness of existence beginning to be conscious of itself, then Freedom—both being the sides which Beauty presented to me—and now I am going to try more after Beauty herself. Next, if I live, I shall present Life as I have seen it.

But, as often, Life proved a jealous mistress who would not yield the field to Beauty. Change and bereavement followed, and his professorship and editorship gave little incentive for verse. The moral exaltation which had seemed the promise of America found itself involved with all the turmoil of emotions that accompany terrific war. For these, Hosea's dialect was scarcely an adequate vehicle of expression, and the second series of *Biglow Papers*, if not inferior in skill, somehow lacks the entire sufficiency of the first; even when, as in the tenth paper, both the pathos and valour of the great conflict sound through the verse. The passions that the war aroused were

[1] Scudder. *Life*. Vol. I. p. 268.

too overpowering for poetry except the brief expression of dominant feeling, as in the fine stanza written in October, 1861.

> God, give us peace! not such as lulls to sleep,
> But sword on thigh, and brow with purpose knit!
> And let our Ship of State to harbor sweep,
> Her ports all up, her battle-lanterns lit,
> And her leashed thunders gathering for their leap!

In the poems written in the decade after the war there is a greater depth of thought and a maturity of feeling. The cause which he served broadened into the issue of the life of a national democracy; and he was called upon to sing its victories and the sacrifice by which they were won. The odes are so noble in sentiment and so splendid in parts that one cannot forbear to regret that they do not bring an even more perfect beauty to their great theme. The far-fetched figure, the halting measure, the forced rhythm occasionally intrude on verse where the feeling demands all the majesty of poetic mastery. And yet, national anniversaries have rarely if ever aroused such pæans as these in which New England mourns her slain but passes on her heritage to the larger nation. Eloquence rises again and again to passionate melody, yet the feeling never loses the restraining guide of thought. Lowell never attains greater mastery than in the thoughtful analysis and noble beauty of the stanzas on Lincoln in the *Commemoration Ode*.

The war and its aftermath left Lowell's poetic faculty somewhat spent. Now and then a theme would arouse his imagination to its earlier spontaneity. Chartres revisited summoned back the recollections of its first impressions and stirred him to search again the mysteries and confusions of faith. The death of Agassiz recalled the Cambridge of old and its brave spirits. But the visits of the Muse grew rarer, and Lowell came to find his most characteristic expression in the prose essay. As the close of the war relieved him from the pressing necessity of political writing, he naturally returned to literature.

Mrs. Browning, in one of her letters to her husband, complains of the *Conversations on Some of the Old Poets*, which she has just been reading, that Lowell is saying over again the same things that every one knows. There is, no doubt, a certain truth in the charge, even when applied to his maturer essays. Lowell introduces no new principle or methods into literary criticism and he makes no search after novelties. In these respects and in the part that his essays have played in changing the direction of literary criticism, they may be regarded as less important than those which Matthew Arnold was writing during the same decade. But this is mainly due to the fact that Arnold's literary criticism was a part of a definite propaganda. When he gave up poetry and turned to prose, it was with the pronounced intention of getting at the British public, of entering on controversy, of preaching a new gospel, that of Culture, which was to have its main ally in criticism. Lowell's increasing use of prose was made from no such incentive. The great cause to which he had been devoted had been won. It was in part as a relief from controversy and propaganda that he turned from political subjects to the leisurely appreciation of his favourite authors. The essays have no reforms to propose. They are the summing up of many hours spent in his library and his class-room.

The influence of the college makes itself felt in various ways. Agassiz in science and Child in letters were among Lowell's colleagues, and his years as a professor had given him both an opportunity for wide reading and an acquaintance with the sterner exactions of scholarship. In some cases, as in the careful review of Richard Grant White's edition of Shakespeare, the criticism is precise and textual. In all cases the reflections about the great masters formed through years of intimacy have undergone the seasoning discipline of a broad and adequate scholarship. Lowell did not write on a subject unless he knew a good deal about it, nor did he fail to avail himself of the best that scholarship had accumulated; and such habits have not been matters of course among literary critics. Not only Lowell's thoroughness and accuracy, but his very freedom from the bias of propaganda and from the desire for novelty give his criticism an enduring sanity, a sanity which is happily united with a rich and discriminating sympathy.

Lowell's essays indeed may be warmly defended from any charge of ineffectuality. If he did not proclaim a definite evangel, yet scarcely less potently than Arnold he preached the gospel of culture. To a nation torn by war and largely engaged in the indispensable work of economic reconstruction, he taught by both precept and example the value of criticism. In the renewed task of making a nation, he turned confidently to literature as the record of human activity that contains most that is vital for the spirit. The cause of culture, indeed, called for a different service in the two countries. For Arnold in England, literature was to be given a renewed allegiance in the face of industrialism and science, and literature itself was to be directed away from the dangers of romanticism into a wiser and better poised criticism of conduct. For Lowell in the United States, the nation was to be reminded of the value for it of the great traditions of the old world and the need of linking both conduct and letters to the best that the past could offer.

One example may further suggest the different tasks of literary criticism in the two countries. It was unnecessary for Arnold to preach the value of medieval art. The Middle Ages were still very much present in England, and they had been summoned for various purposes by Scott, Carlyle, Tennyson, Ruskin, and Morris. In the United States, the Middle Ages are as remote as Persia or Egypt, and their significance for us discernible mainly through literature. Lowell took occasion later to defend his land against the implication in Ruskin's remark that he could not live in a country that had neither castles nor cathedrals. But for "our past well-nigh desolate of æsthetic stimulus" his essays were supplying the past of Milton and Spenser, of Chaucer and Dante. The essays on the two medieval poets are among his best and have done their part in stimulating among thoughtful Americans a study and appreciation of the great centuries of human progress that preceded Columbus's discovery.

The personal essay as a literary form seems to require maturity of mind, breadth of experience and reading, a responsive humour, and intensity and discrimination in taste. These qualities Lowell brought to his essay writing, whether the subject be drawn from nature or society or the world of books. Nowhere else, unless in his letters, is his personality more fully and charmingly revealed. The essays are full of good things. Allusion and quotation, epigram and description, whimsical epithet and graphic phrase crowd one another along the page, but all move in the train of Wit and Wisdom, our constant companions along the way.

The glimpses of New England village life that one receives in the essays will appeal to some readers with a charm like that of personality. The village has often been celebrated in literature from Sweet Auburn to Spoon River, but full justice has scarcely been done to the individuality and distinction of the New England village of the mid-nineteenth century. Cambridge was one of the best representatives of the type, but there were many of them. Each was likely to have a college, or at least an academy, one orthodox and one Unitarian church, a few pleasant colonial houses, and many elms. Everyone who lived in the village had been born there, was proud of that accident, loved whatever natural beauty its trees and meadows afforded, and enjoyed a conscious satisfaction that it was not like other places. Among the residents there might be a great personage, or even a poet, and there were certain to be enough teachers, ministers, doctors, judges, and writers to make up a coterie where ideas circulated. During the long winters, in fact, every one did considerable reading and thinking.

It was for the cultivated men and women of these villages that Lowell wrote. They of all persons delighted in his essay *On a Certain Condescension in Foreigners*, with its urbane reproof of criticism of our lack of urbanity; for the village cherished some dignity of manners and would accept a predestined hell easier than condescension from anybody. The old villages have faded, but their June gardens and winter nights, their serious talk and eager reading, their self-reliance, mitigated by a sense of humour, live again in Lowell's prose.

Wit becomes less exuberant and sagacity is the leading spirit in Lowell's later writing. Village society is disappearing, Cambridge is becoming a large city and Harvard a university, and Lowell is in Europe. Both as a poet and an essayist, he had appeared in part as a mediator or ambassador between the culture of the old world and the new, between the ideals of England and of the United States. In continuing this function as a foreign minister, he did not escape some censure that he was losing his faith in American democracy. To the reader today of his later addresses, that criticism must seem groundless. To be sure, his long residence abroad increased his liking for England and Englishmen; and the course of American politics was a rather dismal sequel to the *Gettysburg Address* and the *Commemoration Ode*. After vanquishing slavery, the nation found itself facing still more dangerous evils, and was somewhat loth to gird its loins for the struggle. Lowell had greeted the dawn that was brightening the New England of his youth, and had seen the noonday of heroic effort in the Civil War. Now, as his own days were lengthening, he could be excused if he saw only a dubious twilight in the America of the eighties.

As a matter of fact there is little doubt and no indifference in these later writings. The maturing years had widened Lowell's perspective without vanquishing the idealism of his youth. He could look back on the course of the industrial revolution which had transformed his New England as well as older lands; and he could foresee the impending revolution that science had already begun in men's standards and processes. The effect of these movements on his own thought are manifest in his poetry and essays mainly by implication and suggestion; but in the utterances of the last decade of his life he often looks upon both his own career and the American purpose directly from this more modern point of view.

In his address at Manchester, in 1884, on Democracy, he declared:

By temperament and education of a conservative turn, I saw the last years of that quaint Arcadia which French travellers saw with delighted amazement a century ago, and have watched the change (to me a sad one) from an agricultural to a proletary population.

Nevertheless, though opposing the single tax and State Socialism, he could see with hopefulness the portents in the air and even believe that democracy was to be the fulcrum for a Socialism possessing "the secret of an orderly and benign construction." He is willing to rebuild his house and believes that it can be builded better. The forward call is to be found in those speeches as well as in the ardent verse of youth, the call of "the radiant image of something better and nobler and more enduring than we are."

This moral earnestness, this desire for perfection, this zeal

to reform a changing but evil world, characterizes English
literature of the years 1830–1880, and American literature of
the same epoch. Literature in those years has preached many
creeds and many reforms, and it has lost something in simplicity and certainty because it has been so much in earnest.
So Lowell's writing loses in certainty of art and unity of effect
from its very responsiveness to the shifting opportunities for
usefulness. But its contribution to civilization is not lessened,
for it has done its best to teach a new people to guide their
steps by the great men and great ideas of the past.

In the address on Democracy, Lowell held forth as arguments in favour of our national institutions two of their
products, Lincoln and Emerson. We surely need not despair of
our democracy so long as it can produce men of letters like
Lowell and utilize them in the service of the common weal.

# Book III

## CHAPTER I

# Whitman

WALT WHITMAN once declared his *Leaves of Grass* to be "the most personal of all books ever published."

This is no book;
Who touches this, touches a man.

Thus he fits Hazlitt's description of Montaigne as one who dared to set down as a writer what he thought as a man. This being the claim of the volume, it becomes highly important to determine the character of the author. Evidently Whitman was not, in any conventional sense of the term, that "average man" whose praises he sang, else even his novel form of expression would hardly have sufficed to keep his poetry so long a time from the masses. He was a man and a writer who could be hated as an impostor or adored as a Messiah but who was in any case a challenge to discussion. Much light is thrown on his character, of course, by the autobiographical parts of his writings; but here it is frequently difficult to determine which incidents belong to his outward and which to his inner, or imaginative, life, so deftly do his vicarious mystical experiences blend with the sublimations of his own deeds, and so carefully have many of those deeds been mystified or concealed. [1]

[1] For instance, a poem, *Once I Pass'd Through a Populous City*, taken by many biographers to support the theory that Whitman had a romance with a lady of high social standing during his 1848 visit to New Orleans, proves to have been addressed, in the original draft of the poem, not to a lady but to a "rude and ignorant man";

Much remains for painstaking research to accomplish. This chapter attempts to set forth only the facts of his biography which are well established or establishable.

Born in the same year as Lowell, Whitman may be said to represent the roots and trunk of democracy, while Lowell may be likened to its flowers or fruits. Whitman, for his part, could hardly have been, or wished to be, a flower; it was not in his ancestry, his education, or his environment. Blending in his own nature the courage, the determination, and the uncompromising Puritan idealism of good, if somewhat decadent, English ancestry with the placid slowness,[1] self-esteem, stubbornness, and mysticism of better Dutch (and Quaker) ancestry, Walt[2] Whitman was born 31 May, 1819, at the hamlet of West Hills, a few miles south of Huntington, Long Island. His father, Walter Whitman, was a farmer and later a somewhat nomadic carpenter and moderately successful housebuilder, who, although, like the poet's excellent mother, he had even less education than their nine children were destined to have, was something of a free thinker. The Whitmans moved to Brooklyn about 1823–25,[3] but Walt, until he went to live in Washington during the Civil War, continued to be more or less under the wholesome influence of the country. Throughout childhood, youth, and earlier manhood he returned to spend summers, falls, or even whole years at various parts of the Island, either as a healthy roamer enjoying all he saw, or as a school-teacher, or as the editor of a country paper, or as a poet reading Dante in an old wood and Shakespeare, Æschylus, and Homer within sound of the lonely sea, and mewing his strength for the bold flights of his

---

on the other hand, the poem *Out of the Rolling Ocean, the Crowd*, to which no biographer has attached particular personal significance, can be shown to have been addressed, about 1864, to a married woman with whom Whitman was in love and with whom he maintained for a time a correspondence notwithstanding the jealous objections of her husband.

[1] This description does not allow for a high temper, displayed on occasion, which Whitman seems to have inherited from his father.

[2] Shortened from Walter to distinguish the son from his father, but not used in connection with his published writings until 1855.

[3] The exact date is uncertain. Whitman gives 1822–3 once, 1823 twice, 1824 twice, and 1825 once; the earliest record in the directory of the city (Spooner) is 1825. At any rate Whitman was probably accurate in his statement that he was "still in frocks."

fancy. Perhaps it was a certain disadvantage that while he was thus "absorbing" and learning to champion the common people, the "powerful uneducated persons," among whom he moved on equal terms though not as an equal, he was little thrown, in any influential way, among people of refinement or taste. In his old age nobility and common humanity jostled each other in his hospitable little parlour—or kitchen; but during his youth the breadth of his view and the democracy of his sympathy were somewhat limited, not so much in theory as in fact, by the conditions that surrounded him. At the same time his native "egotism," as he frankly calls what Emerson would probably have softened to "self-reliance" had it been a trifle less arrogant, was being abnormally developed, even for a genius, by conditions little fitted to correct it. Nevertheless, he thus early learned lessons from nature and from human nature which were as indispensable to the inspiring and shaping of his liberating art and his democratic philosophy as was his outdoor life in developing his remarkably sensitive and healthy physical constitution.

Whitman's youth in Brooklyn, though full of interest, was uneventful. As a child of six he was flattered by Lafayette's chancing to lay his hands on him during a visit to the city in 1825. He attended the public school for a few years, impressing his teacher, Benjamin Buel Halleck, only with his good nature, his clumsiness, and his poverty of special promise. He ran with the boys of the street and was familiar with the city and its environs, especially with Fulton Ferry, whose slip was not far from his home. Not Irving, not Charles Lamb was more intimately or passionately fond of city life, with its opportunities for human contact and for varied sights, than was Whitman, both as boy and man. When about eleven years old he left school to become an office-boy, first to a lawyer and then to a doctor, the former of whom kindly afforded him opportunities for reading such books as the *Arabian Nights* and the poetry and romances of Scott. At twelve he was learning to set type, in a building once used as Washington's headquarters, under the instruction of a veteran printer who had many tales to tell of Revolutionary heroism. Next he went to set type for a few dollars a week on Aldin Spooner's *Star*. He had already felt the satisfaction of authorship when "sentimental bits" had appeared from his pen in the newspapers. Later he became a compositor on unknown journals in New York.

In May, 1836, Whitman went down to his father's farm at Hempstead, and then began a wandering career as a well-liked but not altogether successful country school-teacher. He taught somewhat after the fashion of the transcendentalists, substituting moral suasion for the ferule, and "boarding round" in at least seven different districts in Queens and Suffolk counties, but seldom remaining more than a few months at any one school. His mind was but half on his work, and after two years of teaching he sought (June, 1838), a more congenial occupation in starting a village newspaper, *The Long Islander*, at Huntington. On this he did all the work, even to delivering the papers on horseback; but he did it so irregularly that in less than a year his financial backers entrusted the little sheet to more punctual hands. Again teaching had to be resorted to. When living at Jamaica (1839–41) Whitman spent some of his time, apparently after school hours, in learning the printing business in the office of James J. Brenton's *Long Island Democrat*, to the pages of which he contributed a considerable number of sketches and essays replete with juvenile philosophy, as well as a number of patriotic and sentimental poems in conventional measures. The poet's tendency to dream—to loaf and invite his soul—to the neglect of more earthly duties, a tendency that was to become a tradition wherever he thereafter worked, had already marked him as an unusual person. He was even then dreaming of composing a ponderous and prophetic book to teach men, among other things, the danger of riches. The Quaker's attitude toward truth and the mystic's attitude toward nature were already discernible in his writings. But his life was unhappy, full of irresolution and unrest, and frequently given to a morbid brooding on death, while his enormous capacity for sentimental friendship, equalled only by his capacity for taking delight in external nature, had already taught him to sing of unreturned affection, and drove him, no doubt, to take refuge, like Narcissus, in self-admiration. Yet he took part in the sports and merry-makings of the village and was interested in the political campaigns of the day, himself attaining some prominence as a stump speaker in Queens County and even in New York City.

Then, in the summer of 1841, he definitely and finally threw in his lot with the city, and the second important period of his development began. Heretofore the highly sensitive youth had been almost ladylike in his sentiments, often morbid in his contrary moods, but puritanically strict in word and deed. At twenty-two his passionate nature demanded a sort of reaction. He "sounded all experiences of life, with all their passions, pleasures, and abandonments,"[1] and became, in another sphere of indulgence, something of a dandy. He was developing his personality meanwhile, and he was learning to write.

Whitman's early pieces written in New York reflect the wave of sentimentality which was, in the forties, sweeping over the country, and display, along with their humanitarian feeling, a fondness for melodramatic extravagance which caused him later to wish them all "quietly dropp'd in oblivion." He was a reformer pleading for the abolition of intemperance (including the use of tobacco, tea, and coffee), of capital punishment, and of slavery; and urging, as the constructive side of his reform, the need of a native American drama, opera, and literature. His interest in the theatre and the opera was a vital one, the constant satisfaction of which was made possible by his having a pressman's pass. Here he received many hints for his declamatory and rhythmical style of verse. Altogether more than a score of tales, sketches, essays, and poems have been found which belong to this period. To these must be added a crude and hasty dime novelette, *Franklin Evans,*[2] addressed, in the cause of temperance, not to the "critics" but to "THE PEOPLE," and evidently written to order. In this period Whitman was connected with some of the best city magazines and newspapers as contributor, compositor, or editor. The most important position that he held was that of editor of *The Daily*

---

[1] John Burroughs, in *Notes on Walt Whitman as Poet and Person,* 1867, p. 81. The substance, if not the phrasing, of this indefinite though suggestive passage was supplied by Whitman himself.

[2] This was republished, in compressed form, under the caption *Fortunes of a Country Boy,* by J. R. S. in *The Brooklyn Eagle* (November, 1846) as an "original novel." *Death in the School Room, The Child's Champion, Little Jane, The Death of Wind-Foot,* and a few poems were similarly twice published by Whitman, in the lax fashion of the day. See Bibliography.

[and *Weekly*] *Brooklyn Eagle*, a connection which extended from February, 1846, to January, 1848, when a "row with the boss," on account of Whitman's unreliability, and with "the party," on account of his progressive Barnburner politics, made it necessary for him to shift for a new position. This was readily found on *The Daily Crescent*, a paper about to be launched in New Orleans.

The trip which, with his favourite brother Jeff, Whitman made in the spring of 1848 by rail, stage, and Mississippi steamboat to New Orleans, his residence in that city for three months, and his return by way of the Mississippi and the Great Lakes[1] were rather less important than has commonly been supposed. It is doubtful whether the experience brought into his life a great but secret romance,[2] and it appears certain that he was not by it first made conscious of his mission as a poetic prophet. But the journey did give him a new and permanent respect for the undeveloped possibilities of his country, especially in the South and West, and it gave him opportunities for the study of the French and Spanish elements in New Orleans; while his observation of the South's "peculiar institution" caused him to remain, though a radical Free-Soiler, one careful not to be classed with the Abolitionists. But if this journey was of only measurable importance, perhaps others were of greater; for, though details are almost entirely unknown, it is practically certain that he made still other visits to the South.[3]

Notwithstanding the attractiveness that the new atmosphere had for all that was Southern in Whitman's temperament, he soon haughtily resigned his position, because of a

---

[1] Whitman's fullest and best account of the trip south was printed in the early numbers of the *Crescent*. This was not preserved in his collected prose editions, but a considerable portion of it was reprinted in *The Yale Review*, September, 1915.

[2] Whitman never married. In old age he confided to John Addington Symonds the information that, though unmarried, he had had six children, from intimate relations with whom he had been prevented by circumstances "connected with their fortune and benefit." For a fuller discussion of this confession and the questions arising out of it than is here possible the reader is referred to the biographies by Binns, Perry, Edward Carpenter, Bazalgette, De Sélincourt, and Traubel.

[3] Several lines of evidence point to this conclusion. Here it will be sufficient to refer to Whitman's autobiographical note published in *The Critic*, 28 February, 1885, over the pseudonym "George Selwyn." See Bibliography.

difference with his employers, and left for home 27 May. Almost immediately after his arrival he was engaged by Judge Samuel E. Johnson to edit (and nominally to own) a new Free-Soil paper, the weekly [1] *Brooklyn Freeman*, as the organ of those Democrats with whom Whitman, but not the party leaders behind the *Eagle*, had sympathized the year before. The new paper appeared 9 September, but it had the hard fortune to be burnt out, with no insurance, in a great conflagration that swept the city that very night. But the *Freeman* was revived in November, and, though a small and apparently a very outspoken sheet, it attained a large circulation. The nature of the political warfare in those days of personal invective may be suggested by Whitman's valedictory, published when, without explanation, he resigned the paper, 11 September, 1849, into the hands of those who would compromise, as he would not, with his political opponents:

To those who have been my friends, I take occasion to proffer the warmest thanks of a grateful heart. My enemies—and old hunkers generally—I disdain and defy the same as ever.

Of the next six years of Whitman's life comparatively little is known. He is said to have been connected with certain newspapers, [2] to have run a book-store and printing establishment, and to have assisted his aging father, now suffering from paralysis, in building small houses for sale. He had here an opportunity for money-making which, to the disappointment of the family, he allowed to pass unimproved. What is more important, he was growing rapidly in his inner life, as he attended lectures, read miscellaneous magazine articles, Shakespeare, Epictetus, the Hebrew and the Hindoo bibles, and Emerson, and loafed on the shores of Coney Island, timing the new poetry he was composing to the rhythmic beat of the sea. Somewhere in this period probably belongs the mystical experience, described in the poem *Song of Myself*, Section 5,

---

[1] Changed to a daily in April, 1849.

[2] An article in the Springfield *Republican*, 28 March, 1892, states that Whitman helped to edit Levi D. Slamm's *Plebeian;* and a letter from Whitman's friend, T. H. Rome, the first printer of the *Leaves of Grass*, to Wm. E. Benjamin (September, 1898) mentions the fact that after his return from New Orleans Whitman conducted for a short time an advertising sheet called *The Salesman*. See also Hearne's city directory for 1851 and 1852.

which clarified his vision "of the world as love" and fused his purposes in life, and which some biographers, attaching to it more significance than did Whitman himself and forgetting that he had other such experiences, are inclined to consider the most important fact in his biography. At any rate, the book of which he had dreamed since adolescence and of which he had as early as 1847[1] written many passages was now, in 1854–5, written and rewritten, and printed in Brooklyn, without a publisher, in July, 1855.

The purpose of the author in writing this unique volume may be stated in his own comprehensive words, written in 1876:

I dwelt on Birth and Life, clothing my ideas in pictures, days, transactions of my time, to give them positive place, identity—saturating them with the vehemence of pride and audacity of freedom necessary to loosen the mind of still-to-be-form'd America from the folds, the superstitions, and all the long, tenacious and stifling anti-democratic authorities of Asiatic and European past—my enclosing purport being to express, above all artificial regulation and aid, the eternal Bodily Character of One's-Self.

The plan for his poetic life-work was to have been completed, he tells us in the Preface to the 1876 edition, by composing

a further, equally needed volume, based on those convictions of perpetuity and conservation which, enveloping all precedents, make the unseen soul govern absolutely at last.

The perfecting of this latter work, dealing with the soul and immortality, had proved beyond his powers and failing health, but a fair idea of what it meant to set forth is to be found, no doubt, in *The Two Rivulets* (1876).

If Emerson's *American Scholar* address was the intellectual declaration of American independence, this first edition of *Leaves of Grass*, though only a thin imperial octavo of ninety-five pages with a hastily written but vigorous and far-sighted explanatory preface, was the first gun in a major campaign of the war that was to win that

[1] A Whitman manuscript notebook in the possession of Thomas B. Harned, one of the poet's friends and literary executors, preserves these earliest known specimens of modern free verse. They are shortly to be published by the present writer.

independence. Of the form taken by so audacious a message space is wanting for accurate description. It may be said, however, that, denying to itself rhyme, regular metre, stanza forms, literary allusions, and "stock 'poetical' touches" in general, it frequently achieved, nevertheless, a deep and satisfying rhythm of its own—sometimes pregnant gnomic utterances, sometimes a chant or recitative, occasionally a burst of pure lyricism. Just where, if anywhere, Whitman found the hint for this flexible prose-poetic form critics have not agreed. Perhaps Biblical prosody, *Ossian*, the blank verse of Shakespeare and Bryant, the writings of Blake, the prose of Carlyle and Emerson, and his own impassioned declamation all assisted; but full allowance must be made for the unquestioned originality of his own genius, working slowly but courageously for the fuller liberation of song.[1]

The book, expecting opposition, was met by almost complete disregard. Except for a few copies which found their way to England and were later to secure for Whitman ardent disciples and his first English editor, William Michael Rossetti, there was practically no sale. Most of the reviews in the periodicals that noticed the book at all were as scandalized as had been anticipated; but a highly congratulatory letter from Emerson, who evidently recognized in Whitman the disciple he then professed to be, compensated for all neglect or abuse from other quarters, and a sentence from it was put to good, if indelicate, use as advertising on the back of the second edition (1856), a volume much larger than the first and more open to criticism because of its attempt to combat prudery in America by a naturalistic but fragmentary treatment of the facts of sex. Of this patent and confessed indebtedness to

---

[1] In one of the anonymous reviews which Whitman saw fit to write, in 1855, of his own first edition, he disclaims any model: "The style of these poems, therefore, is simply their own style, just born and red. Nature may have given the hint to the author of 'Leaves of Grass,' but there exists no book or fragment of a book which can have given the hint to them." *In Re Walt Whitman*, p. 16.

The first poem known to have been published in this measure was *Blood-Money*, which appeared in Horace Greeley's *Tribune* (Supplement), 22 March, 1850. But *Isle of La Belle Rivière*, published in the Cincinnati *Post*, 30 April, 1892, was written, in what is now called imagist verse, at the age of thirty (1849–50), while *New Year's Day, 1848*, written in an album just before Whitman's departure for New Orleans, shows a tendency to break away from conventional forms. By far more important are the Harned manuscript notebook specimens already mentioned.

Emerson, who had brought the simmering pot of Whitman's literary and patriotic ambition to a boil, Whitman had no cause to feel ashamed; for though lacking Emerson's sanity and mature idealism, he had a greater sympathetic, active, and emotional equipment than had the Concord sage. If Whitman was, as he said, "a child, very old," Emerson was a man, very young. It was almost as if the older champion of individuality had meditated the philosophy by which the younger was to live; but whereas the Emersonian gospel, addressing itself to the idealism of its readers, "breeds the giant which destroys itself," Whitmanism, appealing strongly to the religious sentiment, has already had the ironical fate of developing something not unlike a cult, both at home and in other countries.

Of course such a book failed to bring in royalties, and Whitman again fell back on the drudgery of editing a newspaper, in this instance the bantling *Daily Times* (Brooklyn). Just when this editorship began (1856 or 1857) is not easily determined, but it ended probably in the early part of 1859, after the editor had repeatedly rebuked certain church officials for the, as he thought, unfair treatment they had accorded to one Judge Culver, then the defendant in an ecclesiastical trial. At odd times Whitman wrote the new poems, including that incomparable lyric, *Out of the Cradle Endlessly Rocking*, which appeared now and then in the pages of the Bohemian *Saturday Press*, and the many others which were to be included in the 1860 edition of the *Leaves*. The country was full of lecturers in 1858, and Whitman planned to become one, both to support himself and to supplement the *Leaves*, which could hardly as yet have been called a success. But though he disciplined himself in a style of oratory only less novel than that of his poetry, writing "barrels of lectures" on religion, democracy, language, æsthetics, and politics, and though the desire thus to present his message in a more personal fashion than any sort of authorship, even his own, could afford, persisted throughout life, only a few memorial addresses—such as the tribute to Lincoln—and a few public readings of his own poems written for college commencements or other special occasions ever came of it.

Meanwhile Whitman was widening the circle of his acquaintance. Emerson not only called on him frequently when in the city but sent Alcott, Moncure Conway, and Thoreau to do likewise. Lord Houghton also came, and Bryant crossed the river to share with him long walks into the country. These were the days of Whitman's Bohemianism. A negligent, open-throated attire and great soft hat that one might associate with a carpenter or a sailor he insisted on wearing, Richter-like, wherever he went. In the earlier years of his journalism he had worn a high hat, cane, and boutonnière; now the dandy had given place to a man dressed in a habit more in keeping with his new rôle as the national bard of democracy *en masse*. The affectations in his dress were, however, of less importance than the inner character of the man. And that character was one of great human sympathy and magnetism, possessing a charm which those who felt it most were least able to explain. He spent, as from childhood he had done, much time among the people—boatmen, pilots, omnibus drivers, mechanics, fishermen —going anywhere to "feed his hunger for faces." He visited prisons, attended the sick in hospitals, drove all one winter the stage of a disabled driver, and mingled as a meditative observer among the liberal-minded and light-hearted Bohemians at Pfaff's restaurant. In 1860 he went to Boston and published, through Thayer and Eldridge, his third edition, full of the echoes of this life, in which he had not always been a mere observer. Until the war drove its publishers to the wall, the book had a fair sale. The poems of two new groups— *Enfans d'Adam*, celebrating the love, usually physiological, between the sexes, and *Calamus*, celebrating that "adhesiveness" or "manly attachment" which Whitman then considered the true cement of a democracy—have in the past provoked much severe criticism and indignant defence, and the former were the occasion, at various times, of a threatened official prosecution, of a temporary exclusion of the book from the mails, and of the author's being dismissed from a government clerkship. Emerson had urged Whitman to be more tactful and worldly-wise, but the latter's inner conviction that he was right and his stubborn determination to go ahead in the chosen course blinded him to the value of tact and condemned him to suffer from a reputation that he did not really deserve. What-- ever may be the true interpretation of these poems, one finds it difficult to understand either the character or the writings of Whitman unless one's eye is kept on the chronology of his publications, a feat which his method of grouping has rendered rather difficult; for he was a growth, as his poems were, in which a heroic and loving soul gradually freed itself from the passions of a very human and earthly body. His reaction from the asceticism of his adolescence was strong, tumultuous, almost tragic, but it was only a reaction; and when the war had passed over him with its purification and its pain, and when he had suffered severely in his personal affections, he sang more and more of the soul.

Whitman's optimistic faith in democracy was put to the severest possible test by the outbreak of the Civil War. But he did not come into personal touch with its heroic and pathetic sides until, in December, 1862, he went down to the front at Fredericksburg to look after his younger brother, an officer in a volunteer regiment, who had received a slight wound in battle. Shortly after the outbreak of hostilities Whitman had begun writing (June, 1861) for the weekly *Brooklyn Standard* a serial history of the city, entitled *Brooklyniana*, based on his own reminiscences, his conversations with older citizens, and his rather desultory historical reading. He had likewise been composing a few of the vivid war poems in *Drum-Taps*. But as the war became more serious he suspended this writing and took a loitering trip through many of his old haunts on Long Island, fishing, sailing, meeting people in the unceremonious manner of the country, and doubtless pondering the gloomy problems of the war. The early Whitman, so inadequately reported in the biographies, was preparing to give place to the well-known serious and noble Whitman of the Washington hospitals; and this leisurely visit was, one chooses to think, a farewell to the light-hearted irresponsibility of his protracted youth. Returning to Brooklyn in the fall, he took up the *Brooklyniana* again and occupied himself with it almost until the accident to George Whitman called him to the Virginia battle-field.

Thence he casually drifted into the finest employment of his life, that of caring for sick and wounded soldiers on the field and, especially, in the many military hospitals in and about Washington. He lived frugally, supporting himself for a time by doing copying[1] and by contributing wonderfully vivid sketches of his

---

[1] It is probable that Whitman had been reduced to the necessity of doing copying before, for the Brooklyn city directory (Lain) for 1860 gives "Walt Whitman, copyist."

experiences to the Brooklyn *Eagle* and *Union* and the New York *Times*. [1] To supply the little comforts and necessities of the hundred thousand soldiers, Northern and Southern, to whom, as he estimated, he ministered courage and cheer, he privately raised several thousand dollars from friends and correspondents in the North. When he obtained a salaried position in 1865, a generous portion of his earnings went into the same fund. But chiefly he gave himself, in undisguised affection. The full tenderness, almost motherliness, of this large-hearted, self-sacrificing man can be fully understood only in the modest but realistic account of his daily activities preserved in the letters written to his mother at the time and in the hospital-notebook jottings printed in *Specimen Days*. It would be a questionable service to Whitman to affirm that these three years of slow martyrdom sanctified the whole of his life; but it is literally true that the deepest and best instincts in him never before had found such full and beautiful expression. Partly, at least, as a result of his hospital service his magnificent health was lost, and the last twenty years of his life were those of a paralytic cripple.

Whitman's poetic power was still at its height. *Drum-Taps*, —the poetic complement to *Specimen Days* and *The Wound-Dresser*,—a booklet charged with the pathos and the spirituality of the war, was published in 1865, with the profoundly moving dirge for the martyred Lincoln. In *Democratic Vistas* (1871) he made use of prose, though with unequal success.

This period was also important because of the friendships that it made or fostered. Perhaps the most important was that with William Douglas O'Connor. When, in 1865, Whitman had been employed for several months in the Interior Department under Secretary Harlan, the latter, on learning that he was the author of *Leaves of Grass*, had him summarily dismissed; then O'Connor came to his friend's defence in a brilliant and passionate, though ill-advised, polemic, *The Good Gray Poet*, the title of which gave the bard a fit and enduring sobriquet. The advertising value of such a polemic, or of such an incident, though it was rated highly by Whitman and by some of his friends, may now be questioned. Thanks to such

[1] Most of these letters were reprinted in *Specimen Days* or in *The Wound-Dresser*. See Bibliography.

staunch friends, however, Whitman was soon settled, for the eight following years, in a comfortable clerkship in the Attorney-General's Department.   Another close friend and enthusiastic disciple then and later was John Burroughs, who published in 1867 the first biographical and critical study of the poet.   An attachment more similar to those of the New York days was Whitman's singular friendship for Pete Doyle, an un-schooled young Confederate soldier, now a street-car conductor, with whom, notwithstanding the disparity in their ages and in-terests, the poet spent much of his leisure time.   To him Whit-man wrote the letters which were, after his death, published by one of his literary executors under the appropriate title *Calamus*. But this comfortable and congenial life was destined to a sud-den end.   Just when Whitman was beginning to make literary friends abroad—Rudolf Schmidt in Denmark, Freiligrath in Ger-many, Madame Blanc in France, Edward Dowden in Ireland, ·and in England William Rossetti, Swinburne,[1] Robert Bu-chanan, Roden Noel, John Addington Symonds, Tennyson, and Anne Gilchrist—and when he was beginning to become some-what favourably known abroad through Rossetti's expurgated selection, *Poems by Walt Whitman* (1868), and through frag-mentary translations in Continental countries, an attack of paralysis (January, 1873) compelled him first to suspend and finally to give up his clerical work.   Taking his savings, enough to tide him over the first few years of invalidism, he went to live with his brother, Colonel George Whitman, in Camden, New Jersey.   A leisurely trip to Colorado in 1879, a longer one to Canada in the following year, and various briefer visits and lecture journeys—now to New York, now to visit his friend Bur-roughs at his home on the Hudson, now to his own Long Island birthplace, but oftenest to recuperate and to write charming nature descriptions at his retreat on Timber Creek—except for these furloughs Whitman was to spend the remainder of his days, and to be buried, in Camden.   In March, 1884, he bought a little house (328 Mickle Street, now 330) with the proceeds from the very successful Philadelphia edition of the *Leaves* in 1882.

This period, the final act of Whitman's unique life, was natur-

---

[1] Swinburne, who had in *Songs before Sunrise* hailed Whitman as a new force in literature, considerably retracted his praise in later publications.

ally not a climax of achievement, though it was a severe test of his patience and optimism, a test which, on the whole, he stood with unassuming courage. He sent forth occasional contributions to various American and British magazines and newspapers, besides new editions of his works. The most notable of these latter was the autographed Centennial or Author's Edition in two volumes of prose and verse (1876), designed to be sold in England, his best market, in order to relieve the straitened circumstances of the author, who was then "paralyzed . . . poor . . . expecting death," and who had been fleeced by his New York publishers; *Specimen Days and Collect* (1882–3), a "diary of an invalid," which contains some of Whitman's most characteristic prose and is a storehouse of autobiographical data; and *November Boughs* (1888), containing reprints of short poems that Whitman had been writing regularly for the New York *Herald* and of miscellaneous prose essays that had appeared elsewhere, the most significant of these being *A Backward Glance O'er Travel'd Roads.*

New friends were made, as faithful as the old. One was Dr. Richard Maurice Bucke, of Canada, who, like Burroughs, hailed the *Leaves of Grass* as "the bible of democracy" and wrote (1883) the first comprehensive biography of its author, to set him forth as a mystical saviour of the modern world. Another was Thomas B. Harned, in whose hospitable home the poet met, during these later years, not a few American and foreign notables. A third was Horace Traubel, who until Whitman's death was his daily visitor, who, without pay, assisted him in his dealings with printers and publishers, and who has for some years been publishing a minute diary of his talks with the poet during 1888–92. These three friends became, by Whitman's will, his literary executors. Space is wanting to mention even the most prominent of that host of other visitors, American and foreign, who made Camden the object of their pilgrimages, some with a selfish desire to secure the poet's bold autograph, others with a reverent wish to pay homage to a liberator of the soul. One of the most sincere and unreserved of these tributes was that proffered by Mrs. Anne Gilchrist, the English author (then a widow), who through his poetry came to love the man [1] and who

---

[1] The love-letters of Anne Gilchrist and Walt Whitman are now being edited by Thomas B. Harned and will soon be published.

later with her children spent two years (1876–1878) in Philadelphia in order to be near him. Assistance of a substantial
nature from abroad, due in part to the efforts of Mrs. Gilchrist,
who had been the first woman to defend the *Children of Adam*
poems in print, together with similar if somewhat later help
from a growing number of friends and readers in America,
lightened the burdens of Whitman's last years, affording him
comforts that would otherwise have been denied him and giving him hope that the tide of disapproval and misunderstanding which he had been breasting for half a lifetime was beginning
at last to turn. When a complication of maladies finally resulted in his death, 26 March, 1892, he had "positively appeared," a prophet and a poet not without honour even in his
own country. He was buried, with unique but impressive
ceremony, beside a number of near relatives, in a massive and
costly tomb which he had built for the purpose the preceding
year. Most of his property, valued at a few thousand dollars,
was left for the support of an imbecile brother, to care for whom
Whitman had for many years saved money from his own
small income.

The influence of Whitman has in the past taken three
directions. Those of his readers who, like himself, attach most
significance to the revolutionary and the religious elements in
his writings have naturally been somewhat indifferent as to
whether a place could be found for Whitman among the recognized literary coteries. To them he has been a seer profound
enough and a lover sincere enough to render ordinary literary
criticism an impertinence—unless such criticism would content
itself with mere exegesis. On the other hand a growing number
of readers have seen in Whitman—quite aside from a personality which, for all its philosophical breadth and its friendly
sweetness, was hampered by an occasionally repellent sentimental egotism and a marked deficiency in taste—a genuine
artist and a true poet. All manner of liberal political, sociological, and religious movements have been fathered on Whitman
the seer and prophet; while Whitman the poet has become the
legitimate founder of the various forms of modern free verse.
Criticism that confounds this twofold claim and this twofold
appeal of Whitman's writings is destined to make little progress, as is also that criticism which considers the two methods

of approach to be necessarily exclusive. Still a third class of readers, uninterested in poets or prophets, as such, have gone to Whitman for the refreshing presence of a man and a writer who was entirely himself and who loved nature and his fellow men.

## CHAPTER II

# Poets of the Civil War I

### THE NORTH

WITH the opening of the Civil War the people of the loyal states were stirred to a more intense realization of the high responsibilities of citizenship in a republic. At once the country was confronted by the gigantic task of feeding and clothing the men in the field, of caring for the sick and wounded, of raising the crops, and keeping the shops and factories going. Such a radical readjustment of forces called out powers hitherto unsuspected either in the nation or in its individual citizens. The great present seemed to engulf the petty troubles and ill feelings, social and political, of the past, and the people of the North found themselves moved by a national spirit which knew few of the bounds of the old provincialism. Like the shot at Lexington almost a hundred years before, the guns at Sumter struck the note of a new era. The country marched to war with the gay step of youth; it came back solemnly, as if tried by fire. As it went, the bands played *Annie Laurie*, and the men sang the sentimental songs of adolescent America; they returned chanting

Mine eyes have seen the glory of the coming of the Lord.

Readers of poetry in the fifties had enjoyed the verse of Bryant[1] and Longfellow[2] and of others who modestly portrayed aspects of quiet nature, mildly moralized upon conduct, or willingly submitted to the spell of beauty. For not a few of the poets, poetry was something apart from the actuality of

[1] See also Book II, Chap. v.   [2] See also Book II, Chap. xii.

life, too often little more than commonplace sentiment inspired by earlier poets. It is interesting to find Longfellow writing in his diary in 1856:

> Dined with Agassiz to meet Emerson and others. I was amused and annoyed to see how soon the conversation drifted off into politics. It was not until after in the library that we got upon anything really interesting.

Longfellow, Taylor, Story, and Stoddard (in his early days) were practitioners of the poetic art rather than workers in the real material of human experience. There were other singers, however, who, though surrounded by much that was crude and raw, petty and vulgar, still had visions and felt pulses throbbing beneath the rude exterior of American life. Of such were Lowell, Whittier, Whitman, and various more ephemeral writers who felt the stirring times. To them it was not satisfying merely to dream of the past or yearn for the land of the Lotos Eaters. As if called to a great service, they saw a work to be done and prepared for its doing. Stedman at twenty-eight could write:

> I have cared nothing for politics—have been disgusted with American life and doings. Now for the first time I am proud of my country and my grand heroic brethren. The greatness of the crisis, the Homeric grandeur of the contest, surrounds and elevates us all. . . . Henceforth the sentimental and poetic will fuse with the intellectual to dignify and elevate the race.

Stedman[1] himself, brought up in an older school of lovers of beauty, turned to a more resonant lyre, and wrote such pieces as *How Old Brown Took Harper's Ferry*, *Kearny at Seven Pines*, *Wanted—A Man*, *Gettysburg*, and the stirring romance *Alice of Monmouth*—pieces full of metrical energy, strong, high spirit, and convinced devotion to the union. Stoddard,[2] writer of delicate "Melodies and Catches," rose to the grave, noble tones of his Horatian ode *Abraham Lincoln*, among the finest of all the poems commemorative of the chief personage of the War. Lowell[3] wrote a second series of *The Biglow Papers*,

[1] See also Book III, Chap. x.  [2] See *ibid.*
[3] See Book II, Chap. xxiv.

confirming his right to be called the great American satirist in verse; and Whittier,[1] already, like Lowell, no uncertain voice speaking against slavery, almost forgot his Quaker traditions in the eager strophes with which he encouraged the fighters for freedom and exulted over the victory of their aims.   Whitman,[2] already the prophet, though as yet hardly heard, of a mystical union of his people, composed, during the struggle to destroy the Union of the states, battle-pieces that are without rancour, and, after that Union had been assured, splendid hymns of triumph that contain no insults to the conquered, vying with Lowell for the honour of producing the loftiest and best Northern poetry of the War.

The purpose of this chapter is to tell not of the major poets of the mid-century period, most of whom, in the intervals of full poetic careers traced elsewhere in this history, lent powerful voices to the cause of anti-slavery and union, but of some of the lesser figures whose best or most significant work deals almost wholly with the conflict.   At least one of them has not received his due share of praise—Henry Howard Brownell (1820–1872), called by Holmes "Our Battle Laureate."   Born at Providence, he went with his family to Hartford, where he graduated from Trinity College in 1841.   After a short season of teaching in Mobile, he returned to Hartford, was admitted to the bar, and began the practice of his profession, while also joining his brother in literary work.   His early devotion to the sea, stimulated by frequent voyages, inspired him to sing of its awe and its beauty.   Like his brother, who lost his life in 1859 exploring South America, he had the spirit of an adventurer, but, though his little volume of *Poems* (1847) had contained some lines of verse ringing with denunciation of ease and lazy comfort at a time when such a question as slavery was pressing for answer, he had dealt, for the most part not originally or strikingly, only with the eternal themes of minor poets—love, disappointments, passing beauty, the hard fate of the poetical tribe—and did not really find expression for himself until the Civil War.   For a Hartford paper he composed a rhymed version of Farragut's orders to his fleet before the attack upon New Orleans.   The verses so pleased the Commodore that he wrote to Brownell in terms of hearty appreciation and afterwards made the poet

[1] See also Book II, Chap. XIII.          [2] See also Book III, Chap. I.

his secretary. Brownell thus had an opportunity, in actual service, to become acquainted with the details of warfare. The best of his pieces, all included in *Lyrics of a Day* (1864) and *War-Lyrics* (1866), still deserve praise as strong as that pronounced by Lowell and Aldrich in Brownell's own generation. His power lay in combining vivid detail with lyric exultation, accurate pictures of still life with fiery episodes of heroic action. No other Northern poet reported real warfare so accurately. Some of Brownell's lines read like rhymed journalism, but he had everywhere such intensity of visualization, such fiery passion, and such natural, racy language dignified by sincerity that he rarely suffered any descent into prose, though he tended to *longeurs*. Energy and swift movement are not his only qualities. In the midst of *The Bay Fight* he does not forget the actual men engaged. He can pass from scenes of fighting to the calm, sad picture of Lincoln watching from on high the troops that have not returned for the Grand Review in Washington. Perhaps nothing in his verse seems more striking, in the twentieth century, than his terrific confidence in the cause of the Union and equally terrific condemnation of all Southern "traitors." His moral energy is as much the secret of his power as are his poetical vigour and veracity.

Less important than Brownell as a war poet was George Henry Boker,[1] a native of Pennsylvania, who, though primarily a dramatist, was from 1861 to 1871 the efficient secretary of the Union League of Philadelphia, and prominent in patriotic activities throughout the struggle. His *Poems of the War* appeared in 1864. It contained a few pieces, some of them still remembered, which adequately represent the faith and deep feeling of that time. Most interesting are the *Dirge for a Soldier, On Board the Cumberland, The Ballad of New Orleans, Upon the Hill before Centreville, The Black Regiment, The Battle of Lookout Mountain*. Boker's lyrics, however, lack the passionate truthfulness of Brownell's, and play too much with allegory and ancient mythology for the best effect. The *Dirge*, called forth by the death of General Kearny, is spontaneous and haunting. Bayard Taylor,[2] a friend of Boker, while ardently sympathetic toward the Union cause, and a speaker in its behalf in America and England, shows a slighter imprint of the conflict

[1] See also Book II, Chap. II.        [2] See also Book III, Chap. X.

in his verse. Even his *National Ode*, delivered on a great occasion in 1876, failed to rise to the dignity and power expected of it. It seems, for all its large weight of thought and knowledge, unimportant when compared with Lowell's *Commemoration Ode*. Still a third Pennsylvanian, Thomas Buchanan Read,[1] wrote, in *Sheridan's Ride*, one of the most rousing of all the martial ballads called forth by the war.

Herman Melville,[2] who said in the preface to his *Battle-Pieces and Aspects of the War* (1866) "I seem, in most of these verses, to have but placed a harp in a window, and noted the contrasted airs which wayward winds have played upon the strings," suffered in his verse as in his minor romances from a fatal formlessness, but he had moments of contagious enthusiasm. He celebrated some of the most striking incidents of the war in *The Victor of Antietam*, *The Cumberland*, *Running the Batteries*, *Sheridan at Cedar Creek*, *The Fall of Richmond*, and *The Surrender at Appomattox*. Most intimately associated with hostilities of all was Charles Graham Halpine,[3] better known as Miles O'Reilly, who entered the Union army and became a brigadier-general. Although his verse lacks metrical skill, it is vigorous and full of feeling, generally free of animosities, and in the tone of the soldier rather than of the bitter poet who stays at home.

To get a really vivid idea of the lyric expression of the time one should look less to individual writers or groups of writers than to the subjects which were most commonly their themes. The John Brown affair found many poets: Stedman in *How Old Brown Took Harper's Ferry*, Brownell in *The Battle of Charlestown*, fiercely ironic, Whittier in *Brown of Ossawatomie*, and, above all, the anonymous author (he may have been Charles Sprague Hall) of *John Brown's Body*, which, set to the air of an old Methodist hymn, became the most popular marching song of the Union armies, and survived innumerable parodies and rival versions—to be sung not only by American but by British troops in the present war. The secession of South Carolina called forth the earnest, affectionate *Brother Jonathan's Lament for Sister Caroline* by Oliver Wendell Holmes. Stedman and Brownell were but two of the many stirred to

---

[1] See also Book III, Chap. x.   [2] See also Book II, Chap. vii.
[3] See also Book II, Chap. xix.

verse by the attack on Sumter. The spirit of the volunteers
was celebrated in *A Call to True Men* by Robert Traill Spence
Lowell, *Who's Ready?* by Elizabeth Stuart Phelps, *The Heart
of the War* by J. G. Holland; Theodore Tilton published in
*The Independent* for 18 April, 1861, his clanging and exciting
tocsin *The Great Bell Roland;* even Bryant had a strange fire in
*Our Country's Call:*

> Lay down the axe; fling by the spade;
> Leave in its track the toiling plough;
> The rifle and the bayonet-blade
> For arms like yours were fitter now;
> And let the hands that ply the pen
> Quit the light task, and learn to wield
> The horseman's crooked brand, and rein
> The charger on the battle-field.

Thereafter the passion of events is recorded in the poems of
the war, North and South. Bayard Taylor's *Through Baltimore* cried out against the opposition offered by Southern
sympathizers to the passage through Baltimore streets of the
Sixth Massachusetts. A. J. H. Duganne, in his impetuous
*Bethel*, sang of the heroism but not the blunders of that battle,
the chief victim of which, Theodore Winthrop,[1] was the subject
of Thomas William Parsons's lofty *Dirge for One Who Fell in
Battle*. Bull Run, theme of many exultant Southern ballads and
satires,[2] brought from Boker the impassioned *Upon the Hill before Centreville*. In the controversy with England which followed
the seizure of Mason and Slidell, Lowell wrote his spirited and
determined *Jonathan to John*, second in the new series of *Biglow Papers*. During September, 1861, Mrs. Ethelinda (Ethel
Lynn) Beers wrote *The Picket-Guard* (attributed in the South
to Lamar Fontaine or Thaddeus Oliver), a widely popular piece
expressing sympathy with the minor and unnoted victims of
the conflict. Also popular was the anonymous *Tardy George*,
that is, General McClellan, of whom the North demanded more
activity than he ever attained. In the same cause, though without the mention of names, was *Wanted—A Man*, by Stedman,
who shortly after had to write another elegy, *Kearny at Seven
Pines*, upon the gallant officer commemorated by Boker in the

---

[1] See also Book III, Chap. XI.　　　[2] See also Book III, Chap. III.

*Dirge for a Soldier.* Thomas Dunn English's *The Charge by
the Ford* and Melville's *Malvern Hill* deal with the later events
of McClellan's first campaign. Lincoln's call for new troops
gave rise to the sentimental but immensely effective *Three
Hundred Thousand More* by James Sloan Gibbons and to Bret
Harte's *The Reveille* (sometimes called *The Drum*), which is
said to have played a large part in holding California loyal.
The advance of Lee to Antietam, his repulse there, and his
retreat found a record in Whittier's *Barbara Frietchie*, Melville's
*The Victor of Antietam*, Boker's *The Crossing at Fredericksburg*,
John Boyle O'Reilly's *At Fredericksburg*, and Aldrich's exquisite
sonnets *Fredericksburg* and *By the Potomac*.

Meanwhile the war in the West was not without its poet-
annalists, of whom the most notable perhaps was Forceythe
Willson (1837–67), a native of New York who lived in Indiana
from 1852 to 1864 and wrote Union editorials for the Louisville
*Journal.* During the first year of the war he began his sombre,
disheartened *In State*, a poem which spoke of the Union as
dead and lying on its bier:

> The Sisterhood that was so sweet,
> The Starry System sphered complete,
> Which the mazed Orient used to greet,
> The Four and Thirty fallen Stars glimmer and glitter at her feet.

The next year he wrote *Boy Brittan* to commemorate a seven-
teen-year-old lieutenant killed in the attack on Fort Henry,
and the year after published his masterpiece, *The Old Sergeant*,
which Holmes thought "the finest thing since the war began,"—
the death-scene of a nameless soldier wounded at Shiloh.
Richer in melody than Brownell, Willson was like him in directness and realism; his output, however, was very slight. The
struggle for the possession of Missouri was recorded in Stoddard's *The Little Drummer*, Henry Peterson's *The Death of
Lyon*, and Boker's *Zagonyi*. During the Confederate attempt
to recapture Corinth in October, 1862, the Eighth Wisconsin
imaginatively carried, instead of a flag, a live eagle which circled
over the battlefield and which gave Brownell his occasion for
*The Eagle of Corinth*.

This same year on the sea the duel between the *Merrimac*
and the *Cumberland* stirred the poets as did almost no other

episode of the entire war. Thomas Buchanan Read wrote *The Attack;* Longfellow, *The Cumberland;* Boker, *On Board the Cumberland;* Melville, *The Cumberland;* Weir Mitchell, *How the Cumberland Went Down,*—all of them poems which, with a larger eloquence than then appeared, sounded the knell of the wooden battleship.  As might have been expected, defeat had more poets than victory; Boker, however, wrote *The Cruise of the Monitor*, and Lucy Larcom *The Sinking of the Merrimac.*  For the capture of New Orleans there were Boker's *The Ballad of New Orleans* and *The Varuna* (the name of a Federal ship sunk during the action), while Brownell's *The River Fight* was as triumphant as the attack.

> Do you know of the dreary land,
>     If land such region may seem,
> Where 'tis neither sea nor strand,
> Ocean nor good dry land,
>     But the nightmare marsh of a dream—
> Where the Mighty River his death-road takes,
> 'Mid pools, and windings that coil like snakes,
> (A hundred leagues of bayous and lakes,)
>     To die in the great Gulf Stream?
>
> .    .    .    .    .    .
>
> Would you hear of the River-Fight?
> It was two, of a soft spring night—
>     God's stars looked down on all,
> And all was clear and bright
> But the low fog's clinging breath—
> Up the River of Death
>     Sailed the Great Admiral.
>
> On our high poop-deck he stood,
>     And round him ranged the men
> Who have made their birthright good
>     Of manhood, once and agen—
> Lords of helm and of sail,
> Tried in tempest and gale,
>     Bronzed in battle and wreck—
> Bell and Bailey grandly led
> Each his Line of the Blue and Red—
> Wainwright stood by our starboard rail:
>     Thornton fought the deck.

And I mind me of more than they,
Of the youthful, steadfast ones,
That have shown them worthy sons
Of the Seamen passed away—
(Tyson conned our helm, that day,
Watson stood by his guns.)

Lord of mercy and frown,
Ruling o'er sea and shore,
Send us such scene once more!
All in Line of Battle
Where the black ships bear down
On tyrant fort and town,
'Mid cannon cloud and rattle—
And the great guns once more
Thunder back the roar
Of the traitor walls ashore,
And the traitor flags come down!

It was in New England that Emancipation was most eagerly acclaimed. Emerson's *Boston Hymn*, written in honour of Lincoln's Proclamation, can hardly be matched for pungency and pregnancy of matter by any other American poem for an occasion. Whittier, who had already hailed Frémont's action in freeing the slaves of secessionists in Missouri in the poem *To John C. Frémont*, and the abolition of slavery in the District of Columbia in his hopeful *Astræa at the Capital*, hailed the actual Proclamation with passion, and, later, the passage of the constitutional amendment abolishing slavery with the rapt exultation of *Laus Deo*. Stedman's *Treason's Last Device* glowed with anger at a proposal made, as late as 1863, to bar New England from the Union because of an opposition to slavery that made that section very obnoxious to the South.

Boker in the spring of 1863 greeted the news of the Federal advance with his *Hooker's Across;* and Chancellorsville, which called forth so many Confederate poems [1] on the death of Stonewall Jackson, led George Parsons Lathrop to write his dashing ballad, *Keenan's Charge*. Perhaps it was again because poets

[1] See also Book III, Chap. III

sing best in defeat that no Union poem on Gettysburg quite equals Will Henry Thompson's later *High Tide* (1888). Stedman, however, made a ringing ballad, *Gettysburg*, and Bret Harte preserved a real episode of the day in his *John Burns of Gettysburg*. Best of all, of course, was Lincoln's famous address at the battle-field on 19 November, 1863, which lacks nothing of poetry but its outer forms.

As Grant rose to fame the poets kept pace with his deeds: Melville with *Running the Batteries* and Boker with *Before Vicksburg* dealt with the struggle to open the Mississippi. Lookout Mountain was commemorated by Boker—*The Battle of Lookout Mountain*—and William Dean Howells—*The Battle in the Clouds*. Two poems this year honoured the negro soldiers that the Union army had begun to use. Boker's *The Black Regiment* concerns itself with the assault on Fort Hudson; Brownell's *Bury Them* is a stern and terrible poem on the slaughter of the Fifty-Fourth Massachusetts, with their Colonel, Robert Gould Shaw, at Fort Wagner, South Carolina. The Confederates buried Shaw in a pit under a heap of his men, and Brownell thought of them as dragon's teeth buried in "the sacred, strong Slave-Sod" only to rise—Southerners are supposed to be speaking—as sabres and bayonets:

> And our hearts wax strange and chill,
> With an ominous shudder and thrill,
>   Even here, on the strong Slave-Sod,
> Lest, haply, we be found
> (Ah, dread no brave hath drowned!)
> Fighting against Great God.

In the fourth year of the war the note of triumph passed from the Southern to the Northern poets. S. H. M. Byers's *Sherman's March to the Sea* and Halpine's *The Song of Sherman's Army* are almost gay, and Henry Clay Work's *Marching Through Georgia* if not gay is nothing else. Holmes's *Sherman's in Savannah* rhymed the name of the fallen city with "banner." Strangely haunting is Whitman's *Ethiopia Saluting the Colors*. Also haunting, but sad, is Melville's *A Dirge for McPherson*——

> *True fame is his, for life is o'er*
> *Sarpedon of the mighty war*——

while his *Sheridan at Cedar Creek*, *The Fall of Richmond*, and
*The Surrender at Appomattox*, though never widely known, are
full of that distinction which Melville, with all his irregularities, was never long without, in prose or verse. Thomas
Buchanan Read's famous *Sheridan's Ride* is a better ballad
than Melville's piece on the same theme, but purely as
poetry it is inferior. Henry Clay Work's *The Year of Jubilee*, supposed to be written by a slave full of delight in the
coming freedom, is too amusing and racy to need to have its
poetical merits estimated. Read's *The Eagle and the Vulture*
and Weir Mitchell's *Kearsarge* echoed the doom of the *Alabama*.
Farragut was so fortunate as to have two poets among his
officers at Mobile Bay: William Tuckey Meredith, who wrote
*Farragut*——

> Farragut, Farragut,
> Old Heart of Oak,
> Daring Dave Farragut,
> Thunderbolt stroke——

and Brownell, whose *The Bay Fight*, though perhaps too long,
can hardly be matched for martial energy.

In the armies themselves the most popular verses were
naturally less fine than those which have chiefly been remembered as the poetic fruits of the war. It was to furnish more
worthy words to the tune of *John Brown's Body* that Julia
Ward Howe wrote her noble poem *The Battle Hymn of the Republic*, but the words proved too fine to suit the soldiers, who
would not sing of "grapes of wrath" or "the beauty of the
lilies." They preferred instead such pieces as *Three Hundred
Thousand More*, *Marching Through Georgia*, and *The Year of
Jubilee*, which have been already mentioned, the equally favoured *The Battle Cry of Freedom*, *Tramp, Tramp, Tramp*, and
*Just Before the Battle, Mother*, of George Frederick Root, and
Walter Kittredge's *Tenting on the Old Camp Ground*. Now
forgotten, but famous in its day, was William B. Bradbury's
*Marching Along*, most frequently sung by soldiers of the Army
of the Potomac. The song perhaps most frequently heard
from soldiers of both sides in the conflict was *When This Cruel
War Is Over* by C. C. Sawyer. In the Northern version "blue"

rhymes with "true"; with cheerful unconcern for the rhyme, the Southerners substituted "gray." This song was sentimental, without poetic merit or rhythm, without even a trick of melody to recommend it, but it voiced the eager longing for peace and was heard in every camp many times every day. Other popular songs were the *Song of the Soldiers* by Halpine and

> I'd rather be a soldier,
> A tramping, camping soldier

by John Savage.

All these are primarily concerned with the military side of the conflict. Civil matters, too, found poetic voices: Bret Harte's *The Copperhead* and *The Copperhead Convention*, and Thomas Clarke's *Sir Copp*, stinging denunciations; F. W. Lander's *Rhode Island to the South*, full of prophetic challenge; Richard Realf's *Io Triumphe*, hopeful and resolute; W. A. Devon's *Give Me Your Hand, Johnny Bull*, a friendly, earnest bid for British sympathy. Still more interesting are the numerous pieces that reveal the feelings of sorrowing men and women at home, and of soldiers sick for home. Specially memorable are Lucy Larcom's *Waiting for News*, Kate Putnam Osgood's extraordinarily pathetic *Driving Home the Cows*, C. D. Shanly's *The Brier Wood Pipe*, Augusta Cooper Bristol's *Term of Service Ended*, Read's *The Brave at Home*, *The Drummer Boy's Burial* (anonymous), and William Winter's *After All*. From civil life came the tender and moving note of reconciliation in Francis Miles Finch's *The Blue and the Gray*, written in 1867 when the news came that the women of Columbus, Mississippi, had decorated the graves both of Northern and Southern soldiers.

To civil life, too, belongs the supreme poetry that the war called forth, associated, for the most part, with the name of Lincoln. Stoddard's *Abraham Lincoln*, Whitman's *When Lilacs Last in the Door-yard Bloomed* (not to be mentioned with the popular but less valuable *O Captain! My Captain!*), and Lowell's *Ode Recited at the Harvard Commemoration*. Whitman had written not a few vivid descriptions of war scenes, and he stands alone among all the poets of his time in his noble freedom from partisanship, but his chanting was never elsewhere so rapt or melodious. Lowell, a fiery partisan, had in his second series of *Biglow Papers* applied his satirical powers to every step of the conflict, and had at times risen to thrilling elevation, as in *Mr. Hosea Biglow to the Editor of The Atlantic Monthly*, but in his *Ode* he outstripped himself and brought American civic poetry to its highest point. An intensely pacific people had the happiness to have poets who sang peace better than they had sung war, when they had won, even at the price of war, a peace which left them purged of slavery and still a nation.

Much of this verse has naturally lost its appeal, but its national and historical significance cannot be overlooked. As Stedman afterwards wrote:

One who underrates the significance of our literature, prose or verse, as both the expression and the stimulant of national feeling, as of import in the past and to the future of America, and therefore of the world, is deficient in that critical insight which can judge even of its own day unwarped by personal taste or deference to public impression. He shuts his eyes to the fact that at times, notably throughout the years resulting in the Civil War, this literature has been a "force."

# CHAPTER III

# Poets of the Civil War II

## THE SOUTH

AMONG the many reasons that have been suggested for the lack of literature in the ante-bellum South—the absorption in politics, the pre-eminence of the spoken word as compared with the written, the absence of centres of thought and life—must be considered the failure of the people as a whole to appreciate the literary efforts of their writers, and, what is more important, the failure of writers of talent to devote themselves to literature as a profession. The popular orator, William L. Yancey, expressed the views of many when he said in a grandiose way: "Our poetry is our lives; our fiction wil! come when truth has ceased to satisfy us; as for our history, we have made about all that has glorified the United States." A. B. Meek, author of *The Land of the South*, in the preface to a volume of his poems (1857) said: "The author is not a poet by profession or ambition; he has written only at long intervals or at the instigation of trivial or transient causes. The present volume is composed of occasional effusions through many years of my life." Some years later Margaret J. Preston wrote to Hayne:

Poetry has been only my pastime, not the occupation or mission of my life, which has been too busy a one with the duties of wifehood, motherhood, mistress, hostess, neighbor, and friend. . . . I think I can truly say that I have never neglected the concoction of a pudding for the sake of a poem, or a sauce for a sonnet. Art is a jealous mistress and I have served her with my left hand only.

Of a great many Southern poets, then, it may be said that they were "amateurs quick to feel the poetic instinct and the influence of other poets, content with an occasional poem or a single volume, and thenceforth prone to lead a life of culture rather than of creative activity."

The result was that the South, in 1860, had found no adequate expression of her life, no interpretation of her ideals, not even a description of her natural scenery. What writing there was, with few exceptions, was not of the soil nor of the people. Poe,[1] Edward Coate Pinkney (1802-28), author of the exquisite love-compliment *A Health*, and Richard Henry Wilde (1789-1847), who wrote the fragrant *Stanzas* beginning "My life is like the summer rose," might have written anywhere. One poem of the War of 1812, one or two of the Mexican War, and some half dozen other lyrics constituted, despite the appearance of not a few volumes of well-meant verse,[2] the poetic output of the South before the Civil War.

The Civil War aroused intense emotions that found expression in a large body of lyric poetry, written by some men who were professedly poets and by more who were but occasionally such. It is difficult for one of the present generation to realize the unity and the fervour of the Southern people at the beginning of the war. Most intelligent Southerners would now agree with President Wilson that the principles for which the South fought "meant stand-still in the midst of change; it was conservative, not creative; it was against drift and destiny; it protected an impossible institution and a belated order of society; it withstood a creative and an imperial idea, the idea of a united people and a single law of freedom." But it was given to few men, if any, on either side to understand the issues thus clearly defined. In fact, as soon as Fort Sumter was attacked and Maryland was invaded there was no longer a question of political issues—it was rather, to Southerners, a struggle of human passions, of liberty against despotism, and of the invasion of the sacred rights of home and commonwealth. As Sidney Lanier,[3] himself then a young man just graduating at a Georgia college, said:

An afflatus of war was breathed upon us. Like a great wind it drew on, and blew upon men, women, and children. Its sound mingled with the serenity of the church organ, and arose with the earnest words of preachers praying for guidance in the matter. It

[1] See Book II, Chap. xiv.          [3] See also Book III, Chap. iv.
[2] See Bibliography.

thundered splendidly in the impassioned appeals of orators to the people, it whistled through the streets, it stole into the firesides, it clinked glasses in bar-rooms, it lifted the gray hairs of our wise men in conventions, it thrilled through the lectures in college halls, it rustled the thumbed book leaves of the schoolrooms, it arrayed the sanctity of a righteous cause in the brilliant trappings of military display, it offered tests to all allegiances and loyalties,—of church, of state; of private loves, public devotions; of personal consanguinities, of social ties.

Of this solidarity of Southern opinion and feeling no better evidence could be given than the fact that practically all those who wrote poetry during the Civil War were either participants in the actual struggle or were intimately connected with those who were. Theodore O'Hara, who had been in active service during the Mexican War and had written *The Bivouac of the Dead* in honour of those who died in that war, was colonel of an Alabama regiment and later a staff officer in the Confederate Army. Henry Rootes Jackson, who had also fought in the Mexican War and had written *My Wife and Child* and *The Red Old Hills of Georgia*, served under Hood in the battles around Atlanta, commanded a brigade in the Army of Tennessee, and was captured in the battle of Nashville. Their poems of the Mexican War were frequently quoted, and in fact were printed in nearly all the Southern anthologies of the Civil War. James Barron Hope, who had been Virginia's official poet at the Jamestown celebration and the unveiling of the Washington monument in Richmond (1858), was quartermaster and captain in the Army of Virginia, and came out of the struggle broken in fortune and in health. Albert Pike,[1] born in Massachusetts and author of *Hymns to the Gods* (1839), was Confederate Commissioner to the Indians and afterwards a brigadier-general. Margaret Junkin Preston, born in Philadelphia, revealed in *Beechenbrook*—a poetical transcript of her experiences and impressions of the war—what the war meant to a woman who was the wife of one of the most distinguished colonels of Lee's army, the sister-in-law of Stonewall Jackson, and the friend of Lee. John R. Thompson, successor to Poe as the editor of *The Southern Literary Messenger*, became assistant secretary to the Commonwealth of Virginia and was

[1] See also Book II, Chap. VII.

later sent to England in the hope that his poems and articles might help to win English sympathy for the Confederacy. Of the younger poets Paul Hamilton Hayne, Henry Timrod, and James Ryder Randall volunteered for service but were prevented by delicate constitutions from remaining in the army, though as staff officers, correspondents, or poets they followed the events of the war with the keenest interest. Henry Lynden Flash was on the staff of General Joseph Wheeler and was thus prepared by his experience to write his tributes to Zollicoffer, Polk, and Jackson. Dr. Francis O. Ticknor was in charge of the hospital work at Columbus, Georgia, and ministered to the needs of soldiers, among them the brave Tennessean whom he made immortal in *Little Giffen*. Abram J. (Father) Ryan could never have written *The Conquered Banner* and *The Sword of Robert Lee* if he had not visualized as a chaplain the heroism and tragedy of the long struggle. William Gordon McCabe, who went from the University of Virginia as one of the Southern Guards, was a poet of the trenches, giving expression in his *Dreaming in the Trenches* and *Christmas Night of '62* to the quieter and gentler aspects of a soldier's life. Sidney Lanier and John B. Tabb,[1] after living the romantic life of soldiers, sealed a memorable friendship by a common suffering in the prison at Point Lookout.

The feeling of the South as represented by all these poets first expressed itself in music. Southern soldiers were quick to seize upon *Dixie*, the words of which had been written by Dan D. Emmett for Bryant's minstrels in 1859. Except for the refrain and a few haunting phrases, the words were totally inadequate, but the music proved to be the chief inspiration of Southern armies throughout the long conflict. Sung for the first time by Mrs. John Wood in New Orleans late in 1860, it was taken up by the Louisiana regiments and was soon heard by the campfires and hearthstones of the South. From New Orleans, too, came *The Bonnie Blue Flag*, an old Hibernian melody, with words written by an Irish comedian, Harry McCarthy, a volunteer soldier in the Confederate Army from Arkansas. The enthusiasm aroused by its first rendition at the Varieties Theatre in 1861 is well described by a later writer. The

[1] See Book III, Chap. IV.

theatre was filled with soldiers from Texas, Arkansas, and
Louisiana on their way to the front. McCarthy appeared on the
stage accompanied by his sister waving a Confederate flag.
"Before the first verse was ended the audience was quivering
with excitement. After he sang the second stanza the audience
joined in the chorus and sang it over and over again amid the
most intensive excitement. It was wafted to the streets and in
twenty-four hours it was all over the Southern Army." For
the crude words of both these melodies were soon substituted
various versions more dignified and intellectually more worthy
of the Southern cause. Of all these, the most striking version
of *Dixie* was written by Albert Pike, and the most stirring
words for *The Bonnie Blue Flag* by Mrs. Annie Chambers
Ketchum. But not even these versions took the place in the
army, or have since taken the place in the affections of the
Southern people, held by the first forms.

If New Orleans may lay claim to the first popular melodies,
it was natural that from Charleston should come the first
notable expression in verse of the South's feeling with regard
to the war. Aside from the fact that this city was the meeting
place of the convention which proclaimed the secession of
South Carolina, aside from the fact, too, that the first incident
of the war was connected with Fort Sumter, Charleston, at the
outbreak of the war, was the one Southern city that might
have been considered a literary centre. Here for many years
Simms,[1] as the editor of many magazines and as a prolific
romancer, had made his brave fight for literary independence,
and here he had gathered about him in his later years a group
of young men, two of whom especially were to respond as poets
to the call of the new nation. He himself was now an old man,
moving among his friends "like a Titan maimed." As the
struggle tightened about Charleston in the later years of the
war, he wrote some fiery appeals against the besieging foe, but
there is in his verse excitement rather than inspiration, heat
rather than light.

Of the group of friends and younger men who gathered
about Simms, the most promising was Paul Hamilton Hayne
(1830–86). The descendant of several generations of Carolina gentlemen and gentlewomen, he had deliberately turned

[1] See also Book II, Chap. VII.

away from the attractive profession of law and politics and had definitely chosen literature as his profession. In his first published poem he had announced his dedication to the poet's life in words that are in striking contrast to the views of the Southern people in general, and even of Southern poets, who had looked on the writing of poetry as a pastime and not a passion. Before the war he had edited *Russell's Magazine* (1857–60) and had published three volumes of poetry—poems characterized by a certain imitativeness and yet a genuine love of nature and a feeling for idyllic life. When the war came he volunteered, only to find that his delicate health would not allow him to share the hardships of a campaign. From the first, however, he hailed his native state as his mother, who, like a priestess "blessed with wondrous vision of the things to come," would not wait till the sister nations would join her in the conflict. While he wrote constantly of many incidents of the war in other places, Charleston was the centre of his tenderest affections; perhaps his greatest poem of those years was *The Battle of Charleston Harbor*. In certain reminiscences that he wrote after the war, as well as in the poems written during the war, one realizes what a charm this city, with its distinct flavour and atmosphere, had for him. If to Henry James and Owen Wister Charleston is today "the most appealing, the most lovely, the most wistful town in America," how much more so was it to a sensitive soul who from infancy had known its legends and its history, and whose most tragic thought in his later life was that he was an exile from the City by the Sea.

Henry Timrod (1829–67), the friend of Simms and Hayne, had also definitely dedicated himself to the work of a poet, having already published a volume of poems in Boston (1860) and many individual poems in *Russell's Magazine* and *The Southern Literary Messenger*. A poet by natural temperament, he was a critical student of the classics and of the best English poetry. A poet hitherto of nature and of love, he was now to show himself the greatest Southern poet of the Civil War. Even before the Southern Confederacy was formed he wrote *The Cotton Boll*, which struck a new note in that it was almost the first Southern poem of local colour. The single boll of cotton which he holds in his hand as he reclines beneath an immemorial pine suggests the great plantation near Charleston from which it came, and then all the cotton fields of the South, from gray Atlantic dawns to the evening star; and not only cotton fields, but the rivers and mountains and forests of this land, which blesses the world with its mighty commerce, joining "with a delicate web remotest strands." In offices of peace and love his country's mission lies; but now the enemy is coming—war is inevitable. In words of passionate indignation and patriotism he exclaims:

> Oh, help us, Lord! to roll the crimson flood
> Back on its course, and, while our banners wing
> Northward, strike with us! till the Goth shall cling
> To his own blasted altar-stones, and crave
> Mercy; and we shall grant it, and dictate
> The lenient future of his fate
> There, where some rotting ships and crumbling quays
> Shall one day mark the Port which ruled the Western seas.

The closing lines—partly ridiculous and partly pathetic in the light of today—are typical of the absolute confidence of the South.

When the Confederate Congress met in Montgomery in February, 1861, Timrod hailed the birth of the new nation in his stateliest ode, *Ethnogenesis*. All nature's blessings are with the South and take part with her against the North, mad and blinded in its rage. The strength of pine and palm, the firmness and calm of the hills, the snow of Southern summers (cotton), the abundance of the harvests, the heart of woman, the chivalry of men are arrayed against materialism and fanaticism. To doubt the end were want of trust in God. The poem closes with a passage that still remains the most felicitous expression of the Southern temperament. Although the poet's vision of a separate nation was an illusion, there will never be a time when these words should not be quoted in any characterization of the natural warmth and cordiality of the Southern people:

> The hour perchance is not yet wholly ripe
> When all shall own it, but the type
> Whereby we shall be known in every land
> Is that vast gulf which lips our Southern strand,

And through the cold, untempered ocean pours
Its genial streams, that far off Arctic shores
May sometimes catch upon the softened breeze
Strange tropic warmth and hints of summer seas.

With the outbreak of hostilities in April, Timrod wrote his passionate lyric *A Cry to Arms*, and later, *Carolina*. But none of Timrod's poems had the lyric quality that fits them for popular music. The union of music and poetry in a splendid impassioned utterance came from James Ryder Randall (1839–1909). Seldom in history have the man, the moment, and the word met in such happy conjunction as in the composition of *My Maryland*. Randall, a native of Baltimore—just from college in Maryland, and, as he said, full of poetry and romance —was teaching English literature in Poydras College at Pointe Coupee, Louisiana, when he read in the New Orleans *Delta* an account of the attack on the Massachusetts troops as they passed through Baltimore:

This account [he said in later years] excited me greatly; I had long been absent from my native city, and the startling event there inflamed my mind. That night I could not sleep, for my nerves were all unstrung, and I could not dismiss what I had read in the paper from my mind. About midnight I arose, lit a candle, and went to my desk. Some powerful spirit appeared to possess me, and almost involuntarily I proceeded to write the song of *My Maryland*. I remember that the idea appeared to first take shape as music in the brain—some wild air that I cannot now recall. The whole poem was dashed off rapidly when once begun. It was not composed in cold blood, but under what may be called a conflagration of the senses, if not an inspiration of the intellect.

He read the poem the next morning to his students, and at their suggestion sent it to the New Orleans *Delta*, from which it was copied in nearly every Southern journal. The finding of an appropriate melody for the words was the achievement of the Cary sisters of Baltimore. A glee club, which was in the habit of singing at their home, sang the words to the tune *Lauriger Horatius*, well known as a college tune that had come from a modification of the German *Tannenbaum, O Tannenbaum*. A few weeks later, shortly after the battle of Manassas, the two sisters and their brother went through the Southern lines. One night while visiting the headquarters of General Beauregard they were serenaded by a regiment of soldiers from New Orleans, who in turn asked for a song. One of the sisters sang *My Maryland;* the refrain was speedily caught up and tossed back from hundreds of rebel throats, who shouted, "We will break her chains; she shall be free!" Soon the words which had been read far and wide were being sung in every part of the South—had become indeed a great national song, the Marseillaise of the Confederacy.

The words—too familiar to be quoted—suggest every aspect of the great struggle from the Southern standpoint. They summarize in passionate, concentrated lines the points of view that are scattered here and there throughout all the anthologies of Southern poetry. The feeling of an exiled son at the invasion of his home, the crushing of liberty under the despot's heel, the peerless chivalry of Maryland's former heroes of history and tradition, his love for the state as a mother, the appeal for a sister state's aid to Virginia, and, on the other hand, the fierce indignation at the "vandal," the "despot," the "Northern scum"—all these are suggestive of the passion of a people giving themselves entirely to the great struggle.

The popular melodies, the odes of Timrod, and the lyric cry of Randall—all of them the best illustrations of their various types—were prophetic of an outburst of poetry in all parts of the South. Such papers as the Charleston *Mercury*, the Richmond *Examiner*, the Louisville *Courier*, the New Orleans *Delta*, and such magazines as *The Southern Literary Messenger, The Southern Field and Fireside*, and *The Southern Illustrated News* published constantly poems written by men and women in all sections. As there were no general means of communication, many poems were attributed to various authors and many were published anonymously. On account of the lack of publishing houses practically no volumes of poetry were published during the war. The problem, therefore, of making anthologies of these poems was a difficult one—much more difficult than was the case in the North, where so many poets already famous were writing constantly during the war, and where there were so many means of communication and of publication. Southern readers had to be satisfied with scrap-books in which were treasured many of the poems that in this way became the common property of a good many people.

Of distinctly different quality from the poems already referred to, and all other "literary" poems, are certain crude vernacular verses. With some of the characteristics of popular ballads, they had much currency in the camps. A writer in the *Southern Bivouac* (July, 1885) recalls and characterizes some of these as follows:

As the long contest dragged on, and war, losing much of its earlier illusions, became a stern, bitter, and exceedingly monotonous reality, these "high-toned" lyrics were tacitly voted rather too romantic and poetical for the actual field, and were remitted to the parlor and the piano stool. The soldiers chanted in quite other fashion on the march or seated at the campfire. In these crude rhymes, some of them improvised for the moment, there was less of flourish but more of meaning, not so much bravado but a good deal more point. They were sappy with the homely satire of the camps, which stings friend and foe alike. Innumerable verses were composed and sung to popular refrains. The Army of Virginia and the Army of Tennessee had each its history rudely chronicled as fast as made in this rough minstrelsy. Every corps and command contributed some commemorative stanza. The current events of campaigns were told in improvised verse as rapidly as they occurred and were thereafter skillfully recited by the rhapsodist who professed to know the whole fragmentary epic.

Forms of such rhymed narratives may be seen in typical stanzas:

> Marse Robert said, "My soldiers,
>     You've nothing now to fear,
> For Longstreet's on the right of them,
>     And Jackson's in the rear."

.    .    .    .    .    .    .

> The Fourteenth Louisiana,
>     They charged 'em with a yell;
> They bagged them buck-tailed rangers
>     And sent 'em off to hell.

> O Morgan crossed the river,
>     And I went across with him;
> I was captured in Ohio
>     Because I could not swim.

No matter where this song was sung, or by whom, or which
of its multitude of stanzas happened to be selected by the
minstrel, the following verse always closed it:

> But now my song is ended,
>     And I haven't got much time,
> I'm going to run the blockade
>     To see that girl of mine.

Some of these poems are found in *Rebel Rhymes and Rhapsodies* (1864) edited by Frank Moore as a companion volume
to two other volumes of war poetry of the North.   In his
preface to this first anthology of Southern war poetry Moore
says:

It has been the purpose of the editor to present as full a selection of the songs and ballads of the Southern people as will illustrate the spirit which actuates them in their rebellion against the
government and laws of the United States.   Most of these pieces
have been published in the magazines and periodicals of the South,
while many are copies of ballad-sheets and songs circulated in the
Rebel armies, and which have come into the possession of the forces
of the Union in their various moves and advances during the present
conflict.

We find in the volume many humorous poems of the kind
just described.   The more serious include two poems each by
Randall and Ticknor, one each by Hayne, Hope, Flash, Meek,
Pike, Simms, and J. R. Thompson, Timrod's *A Cry to Arms*
and Palmer's *Stonewall Jackson's Way*, the last two published,
however, anonymously.   There are also many parodies of
famous songs such as *Annie Laurie, Gideon's Band, Bannock-
burn, Columbia, Wait for the Wagon, The Star Spangled Banner*,
etc.

It was probably this collection that formed the basis of the
selections from Southern poetry published as an appendix to

Richard Grant White's *Poetry, Lyrical, Narrative, and Satirical of the Civil War* (1866). In his preface White says:

I have read all that I could discover of the war poetry, written by the confederated enemies of my government, and have preserved here all that, in a most catholic spirit, I deemed of any intrinsic merit or incidental interest. It was my original purpose to embody them with the substance of the volume, giving each piece its place in the order of time; but finding so little of this poetry which possesses any kind of interest, instead of scattering it sparsely through the collection, I put it in an appendix. The secessionists fought much better than they wrote; and it is worthy of remark that the best poem on that side, "The Conquered Banner" was published in a New York newspaper, *The Freeman's Journal.*

Omitting the humorous poems published by Moore, White has only the ten or twelve of a more serious and important nature, and these, in the main, not the ones that might be considered the most important by the leading Southern poets. The selections are a good illustration either of the difficulty of getting hold oi Southern poems or of a provincial point of view that happily no longer exists.

Inadequate as these anthologies were, they were much better than the volume entitled *War Lyrics and Songs of the South*, published in London in 1866, and edited by "a faithful few Southern women" who had thrown "hastily together this book of poems," in the hope that

its sale to the charitable might secure a fund for the relief of the crippled and invalid men who fought as soldiers in the war in the South; the impoverished women and children, widows and orphans, as well as those who from sorrow, need, sickness, and other adversity have lost their health and their *minds.*

In this volume *The Virginians of the Valley*, by Ticknor, and *Stonewall Jackson's Way* and *The Conquered Banner*, both published anonymously, are the only poems of any value. An illustration of the carelessness of the editors is that Henry R. Jackson's *My Wife and Child* is attributed to General J. T. [T. J., or Stonewall] Jackson. More than half of the volume is given up to *Songs of the Southland and Other Poems* by "Kentucky."

In the following year Miss Emily V. Mason of Virginia edited *The Southern Poems of the Civil War*. She had from the beginning of the war conceived the design of "collecting and preserving the various war poems which (born of the excited state of the public mind) then inundated our public newspapers." With her collection, supplemented by those of her friends, she made an edition of 247 poems, not only as a memorial to the lost cause, but "to aid the education of the daughters of our desolate land" and especially to fit a certain number to be teachers. The volume proved popular, for by 1869 a third and enlarged edition was published, consisting of 288 poems. The first edition is notable for the large number of women writers selected from, 71 in all, the only noteworthy one being Mrs. Preston. There are thirteen poems on Stonewall Jackson, only two poems by Timrod, an indiscriminate list by Randall, and many anonymous poems. In the third edition we have eight by Timrod, four by Father Ryan, and good, though not the best, selections by Lucas, McCabe, Flash, and others.

The improvement in this edition may doubtless be attributed to William Gilmore Simms's *War Poetry of the South* (1866). It was a noble task undertaken by this "weary old Titan" of Southern letters to preserve the writings of the younger poets, many of whom had been inspired by his friendship or by his lifelong devotion to Southern letters. The spirit in which he made the book is indicated in the following words from the preface:

Though sectional in its character, and indicative of a temper and a feeling which were in conflict with nationality, yet, now that the States of the Union have been resolved into one nation, this collection is essentially as much the property of the whole as are the captured cannon which were employed against it during the progress of the late war. It belongs to the national literature, and will hereafter be regarded as constituting a proper part of it, just as legitimately to be recognized by the nation as are the rival ballads of the cavaliers and roundheads by the English in the great civil conflict of their country.

Not much can be said for the critical standards which allowed Simms to publish so much unworthy poetry, none more so than the seven poems from his own pen. His desire to give a place to representative poets of all states, and especially to his personal friends, is in part responsible. Furthermore, the book was thrown hastily together without any arrangement of the material with regard to authorship or chronology. When all has been said, however, we find in this volume the first anthology of practically all the important poems produced by the South during the war—seven each by Randall, J. R. Thompson, and Simms himself, six by Hayne, three by Ticknor, three by Flash, and, above all, eleven by Timrod. It is this recognition of Timrod's greatness as a poet, this first setting him forth as the poet of the South who expressed in adequate verse every aspect of the struggle, that increases the value of the book and our appreciation of Simms's critical judgment.

In 1869 appeared *The Southern Amaranth*, characterized by its editor, Miss Sallie A. Brock, as "a carefully selected collection of poems growing out of and in reference to the late war." In the preface of March, 1868, she expresses a wish to render to her Southern sisters "some assistance in gathering up the remains of the Confederate dead." Her regret is that "a vast number of beautiful and worthy productions are compelled for want of space to be crowded out of this volume." In florid style she exclaims:

The Muse of the Southland is one of tireless wing, and though her theme is lofty and glorious as the golden sunset splendor upon the purple sky of evening, her song is often as sad as the weary echoes of the winter wind through her matchless forests—the mournful wailings of broken hearts.

The most striking new features of the volume are Timrod's *Ode on the Confederate Dead* (written in 1867) and Dr. Ticknor's *Little Giffen of Tennessee*, which, though probably written in 1863, was not published until October, 1867, in *The Land We Love*. The latter poem is not given, however, as it appears in the revised form of later years, the last stanza being especially faulty.

All these anthologies had appeared with but little introductory material or notes regarding the lives of the writers or the circumstances under which the poems were written. They were all practically a conglomeration of poems with little to aid the student of literary history. In 1869 James Wood Davidson's *Living Writers of the South* was published in New York, with salient facts as to the biographies and bibliographies of some 241 writers—166 men and 75 women. Of these he puts down 112 as having written "verse" and eight as having written "poetry." He adds:

Some of these specimens are poor enough, in all conscience,— some inartistic of course; and some, it may be, frivolous,—but each in its way and all together have their use in the general design. Some of the writers have talents and character, with corresponding results, which enable them to stand in the front rank of American authorship. Some have limited ability. And some have none.

These words are typical of the judgment and sense that run through the volume. There are, for instance, critical estimates, biographical sketches, and bibliographies of Simms, Hayne, Mrs. Preston, Flash, and Randall, and surprisingly short ones of Ticknor and Lucas. It required courage on the author's part to characterize the poems of the veteran Simms as "prosaic, commonplace, and Tupperesque." After citing some sixty-five titles of his books of all kinds he remarks: "He has not written an epic; why, I have no idea, but we may be infinitely grateful that he has not."

In his criticism of Flash, for whom he shows much enthusiasm, Davidson puts his finger upon the cardinal defects of many of the Southern poets. Flash, he says, "has never written anything which was not finished at a single sitting, and has never been more than two hours writing anything he has ever published." He wrote his poem on Polk when his foreman told him that he lacked six or seven inches for the makeup of *The Daily Confederate.* "You have written about Zollicoffer and Jackson, you might as well write about Polk, who was killed the other day." Flash quickly responded to the suggestion, and in five minutes the poem was in the hands of the composer, and in twenty minutes was being printed. Paying full tribute to Flash's good qualities, the author warns him that without work there is not the remotest chance for an enduring reputation, and at the same time makes the same suggestion to others who may have acquired "a reverence for inspiration so called, and a contempt for the art of versification."

Apart from his critical judgment Davidson shows the ability of a careful editor in weighing evidence as to the authorship of *All Quiet Along the Potomac*—a poem that all Southerners had claimed as the work of Lamar Fontaine.[1] Davidson publishes Fontaine's letter claiming positively the authorship, but side by side with it is one from Joel Chandler Harris, who was at that time, according to the editor, planning an edition of Southern poems, and who after much deliberation expresses the opinion that Mrs. Beers is the author of the poem. He quotes also a letter to the same effect from the editor of *Harper's Magazine*. While he himself does not express an opinion, it is not difficult for the reader to be convinced by the reasoning submitted by Joel Chandler Harris. The mention of Harris suggests that in this volume he himself appears as the author of several poems which are as unlike his later writings as anything could well be. Davidson has the credit too of publishing for the first time in this volume McCabe's *Dreaming in the Trenches* and *Christmas Night of '62*, and certain recent poems of Maurice Thompson and Sidney Lanier. He also has much to say of poems that do not relate to the war.

In 1882 Francis F. Browne of Chicago carried out the purpose that Richard Grant White had expressed by publishing *Bugle Echoes*—a collection of poems of the Civil War, Northern and Southern. Drawing upon the anthologies that have been discussed and upon separate editions of Southern poets, such as Hayne's edition of Timrod (1873), of Ticknor (1879), of Hayne (1882), he finds a much larger number of Southern poems that fit into his plan of suggesting the story of the Civil War by poems written at the time. Thus for the first time a systematic arrangement was made of this material. The result is altogether striking. The Southern poems, while slightly fewer in number (the proportion is 60 to 85), measure up well with those of the North. Side by side in this volume appear Bryant's *Our Country's Call* and Timrod's *A Cry to Arms*, Whitman's *Beat, Beat Drums* and Randall's *My Maryland*, Pike's *Dixie* and *The Battle Hymn of the Republic*, Holmes's *Voyage of the Good Ship Union* and Ticknor's *Virginians of the Valley*, Lowell's *Commemoration Ode* and Timrod's *Ode to the Confederate Dead*, and at the very end Finch's *The Blue*

[1] Now by some ascribed to Thaddeus Oliver (1826–64).

*and the Gray* and Lanier's *The Tournament*—both of them prophetic of a new national era. Not only was Browne's idea happy and well executed; his introduction and notes are invaluable. He established the fact that the author of *Stonewall Jackson's Way* was Dr. J. W. Palmer. He printed in connection with the poems valuable letters as to the circumstances under which were written *My Maryland* and *The Conquered Banner*. The volume as a whole was so marked by a careful critical judgment and good taste as to distinguish it from the hastily prepared anthologies by Southerners.

Two books of similar nature are Eggleston's *American War Ballads* and Burton E. Stevenson's *Poems of American History*, in both of which the poems are published in chronological order, and in Stevenson's book with the historical setting which interprets many of the individual poems. In later years selections from Southern writers by Miss Manly and Miss Clarke and Professors Trent, Kent, and Fulton, and biographical sketches by Baskervill and Link, have brought the best poems and poets within the reach of a larger circle of students and readers. *The Library of Southern Literature* is a valuable mine of selections and biographical material.

When one tries to make a general estimate of this war poetry as a whole, there are three standpoints from which it may be considered. Judged from the standpoint of absolute criticism, it affords another illustration of the contention that war produces a quantity of mediocre poetry but little of enduring worth. Four or five poems at best have stood the winnowing process of time and judicial criticism. Randall's *My Maryland*, Ticknor's *Little Giffen of Tennessee*, and Timrod's *Ode* on the Confederate dead in Magnolia Cemetery might well be included in any anthology of lyric poetry, ancient or modern. If we consider the poems from the standpoint of either literary or social history, a larger number must be considered significant. They rightly find their place in such a collection as Stedman's *American Anthology* as affording material for the comprehensive survey of American poetry; or in the books of Stevenson and Browne, where the various stages of the Civil War are suggested in poems rather than in army orders, political tracts, or newspaper comment. When President Lincoln said at the end of the war that the Northern army had captured *Dixie* he might have extended his remarks to other poems that have become a part of our national heritage. Still another interest attaches to it. Much of it is an adequate, if not felicitous and final, expression of the ideas and emotions of Southerners at a time when they felt as one people. The emotional fervour that swept over the South was somehow the inspiration of a literature different from that of any other era in its history. Southern literature before the war had been marked by its absorption in politics, or its divorce from real life, or its amateurishness and sentimentalism. A people that had been all too inclined to underrate poetry and to discourage literary production found their deepest emotions expressed in martial strains, or in meditative lyrics. Written for local newspapers, preserved in scrap-books, collected in volumes like those of Simms and Miss Mason, sifted by the later editors and collectors, they preserve heroes and incidents, landscapes and sentiments that will always endear them to the Southern people.

If we consider the poems from this last point of view, they serve to suggest the principal events of the war in rapid review. The gauntlet was thrown down in the poems hitherto cited and also in Tucker's *The Southern Cross*, Miles's *God Save the South*, Randall's *Battle Cry of the South*, Mrs. Warfield's *Chant of Defiance*, Thompson's *Coercion*, and Hope's *Oath of Freedom*. Among the group of Virginia poets who wrote of the early battles on Virginia soil, John R. Thompson (1822–73) and Mrs. Preston (1820–97) stand out as the most conspicuous. Of distinctly higher quality than the crude rhymes already referred to were Thompson's humorous poems on some of the early Southern victories. His *On to Richmond*, modelled on Southey's *March to Moscow*, is an exceedingly clever poem. His mastery of double and triple rhymes, his unfailing sense of the value of words, and his happy use of the refrain ("the pleasant excursion to Richmond") make this poem one of the marked achievements of the period. Scarcely less successful in their brilliant satire are his *Farewell to Pope*, *England's Neutrality*, and *The Devil's Delight*.

The humour of these poems soon gave way, however, to the more heroic and tragic aspects of the war. Thompson himself wrote dirges for Ashby and Latané, both of them the finest types of Virginia gentlemen. Mrs. Preston wrote a still more beautiful tribute to Ashby, in which she expresses one of the favourite ideas of the South—that the struggle was between the cavaliers and men of low breeding. The tragic aspects of Virginia and the heroism of her people were visualized also by a Georgia poet, Francis O. Ticknor (1822–74), whose wife was one of the distinguished Nelsons of the Old Dominion. His *Our Left* is the most vivid account of the second battle of Manassas. *Virginia* is the best tribute we have to the commonwealth that bore the brunt of the struggle. The more popular *Virginians of the Valley* suggests the most romantic story of early years and adds that the same spirit pervades their descendants:

> We thought they slept! the men who kept
> The names of noble sires,
> And slumbered, while the darkness crept
> Around their vigil fires!
> But aye! the golden horse-shoe Knights
> Their Old Dominion keep,
> Whose foes have found enchanted ground,
> But not a Knight asleep.

One phase of the struggle ends with Lee's whole army crossing the Potomac into Maryland—an event celebrated by Hayne in his *Beyond the Potomac*. Then the fighting changed to the West, and we have Thompson's poem on Joseph E. Johnston in which he exhorts the West to emulate Virginia in its struggle for freedom. Requier's *Clouds in the West* is followed by Flash's tribute to Zollicoffer, Ticknor's poem on Albert Sidney Johnston, Hayne's *The Swamp Fox*—a spirited characterization of Morgan, who seems to the poet a re-incarnation of the South Carolina Revolutionary patriot Marion. Connected also with the battles of the West were Ticknor's *Loyal* and *Little Giffen of Tennessee*—the latter based on a story of real life and a striking illustration of the heroism with which the sons of the masses threw themselves into the Southern struggle. This poem, so dramatic in its quality, so concise in its expression, so vital in its phrasing, is destined to outlive all the tributes to the great leaders of the Confederacy. Mrs. Preston's *Only a Private* and Mrs. Townsend's *The Georgia*

*Volunteer* and the anonymous *Barefooted Boys* are poems of the same general tenor, but they lack the freshness and the vigour of Ticknor's poem.

With the publication of Hayne's poems on Vicksburg and the battle of New Orleans, the scene shifts again to Virginia, and especially to the dramatic death of Stonewall Jackson after some of the fiercest battles of the war. This event more than any other pierced the heart of the South and called forth scores of poems from all sections. One of the early collectors claimed to have found forty-eight of these; at least four or five rise to a high level of expression. No other poem gives anything like so adequate an expression of Jackson—his personal appearance, his religious faith, his impressive commands, his almost magical control of his men—as *Stonewall Jackson's Way* by John Williamson Palmer (1825–1906). Excellent also are Margaret J. Preston's *Stonewall Jackson's Grave* and *Under the Shade of the Trees*, Flash's *Death of Stonewall Jackson*, Randall's *The Lone Sentry*, and the anonymous *The Brigade Must Not Know, Sir*.

In 1863 Charleston was attacked by the Northern fleet and her group of devoted poets gathered about her in suspense. Timrod described the dawn of the eventful day as the city in the broad sunlight of heroic deeds waited for the foe. The hostile smoke of the enemy's fleet "creeps like a harmless mist above the brine." He knows not what will happen—the triumph or the tomb. With his *Carmen Triumphale* he sings the rapturous joy of the victory. Paul Hamilton Hayne sang a nobler song of victory, giving the details of the battle, ending in the triumphant victory of Sumter's volleyed lightning, and closing with an apostrophe to his native city:

O glorious Empress of the main, from out thy storied spires
Thou well mayst peal thy bells of joy and light thy festal fires,—
Since Heaven this day hath striven for thee, hath nerved thy
    dauntless sons,
And thou in clear-eyed faith hast seen God's angels near the guns.

This victory was short-lived, however, for on 27 August, by a land attack, Fort Sumter was reduced to a shapeless mass of ruin, though the city itself stood unshaken. As the fate of the city became more and more uncertain, William Gilmore

Simms, now in his old age, did all in his power to rouse the Spirit of the inhabitants. In a series of poems, *Do Ye Quail?* *The Angel of the Church*, and *Our City by the Sea*, he presents in passionate words the claims of the historic city upon its inhabitants. Especially vivid is his plea for St. Michael's church, whose spire for full a hundred years had been a people's point of light, and the sweet, clear music of whose bells, made liquid-soft in Southern air, had been a benediction in the life of the city.

But the words of her poets could not avail the doomed city when, in 1865, Sherman's army marched north from Savannah. Timrod, now a citizen of Columbia, wrote his greatest lyric, *Carolina*, which comes nearest to *My Maryland* of all the poems of the war in its indignation and power. He reproaches the idle hands and craven calm of the inhabitants, but calls upon the descendants of Rutledge, Laurens, and Marion to rouse themselves against the despot who treads their sacred sands. The answer to this appeal was the burning of Columbia. Hayne and John Dickson Bruns still had hope that Charleston might escape the doom. As Timrod from Charleston had given to the world the first expression of the new nation's hope, so his friend and fellow townsman, Dr. Bruns, was to utter the last appeal for Charleston in his *The Foe at the Gates*. There is nothing more tragic in the Civil War than the fall of Charleston—the proud, passionate, and romantic city that had issued her challenge to the South to join her in the conflict with the North. In her last despairing cry the poet calls upon her children to ring round her and catch one last glance from her imploring eye:

> From all her fanes let solemn bells be tolled;
> Heap with kind hands her costly funeral pyre,
> And thus, with pæan sung and anthem rolled,
> Give her unspotted to the God of Fire.

The fall of Charleston was the beginning of the end. Various poems on Lee, notably Ticknor's *Lee*, Thompson's *Lee to the Rear*, and the anonymous *Silent March*, suggest the last battles in Virginia. The dominant note of the later poetry is that of melancholy, now and then tempered by a sort of pathetic longing for peace. Eggleston tells us that the most popular poem on both sides came to be C. C. Sawyer's *When This Cruel War Is Over.*[1] The sentiment of the poem is echoed in poems on peace by George Herbert Sass, Ticknor, Bruns, and Timrod. Very different from the concluding lines of the *Cotton Boll* is Timrod's pathetic yearning for peace, in the poem entitled *Christmas:*

> Peace in the quiet dales,
> Made rankly fertile by the blood of men,
> Peace in the woodland, and the lonely glen,
> Peace, in the peopled vales!
>
> .    .    .    .    .    .    .
>
> Peace on the whirring marts,
> Peace where the scholar thinks, the hunter roams,
> Peace, God of Peace! peace, peace, in all our homes,
> And peace in all our hearts!

When peace came, the defeat of the South, its unconquerable loyalty to the lost cause, and its sad resignation at the inevitable found expression in Mrs. Preston's *Acceptation*, Requier's *Ashes of Glory*, Flash's *The Confederate Flag*, and, above all, Father Ryan's *The Sword of Robert Lee* and *The Conquered Banner.* Not until the end of the war did the last-named poet suddenly flash forth as the most popular of all Southern poets. *The Conquered Banner* was written under somewhat the same circumstance as *My Maryland*—written in less than an hour as he brooded over the thought of the dead soldiers and the lost cause. He wrote other poems, chiefly religious, but none that has ever stirred the hearts of the people like these two written in the shadow of defeat.

Somewhat different in tone and spirit is *The Land Where We Were Dreaming*, by Daniel B. Lucas. Written and first printed in Montreal, whither the author had fled at the end of the war, it is a striking expression of a Southerner's awakening from the illusions which had so long dominated the thought of the people. There is the same loyalty to the leaders and the principles of the South, but a glimpse of reality that augured a readjustment for the future.

Two years after the war, Timrod, suffering from tuberculosis and the direst poverty, wrote his greatest poem, the *Ode*

[1] See Book III, Chap. 11.

*Sung on the Occasion of Decorating the Graves of the Confederate Dead at Magnolia Cemetery, Charleston, S. C., 1867.* The poem is a fit ending to any consideration of Southern War Poetry, for it is the last word to be said of those who died and of those who would honour their memory.

I

Sleep sweetly in your humble graves,
    Sleep, martyrs of a fallen cause;
Though yet no marble column craves
    The pilgrim here to pause.

II

In seeds of laurel in the earth
    The blossom of your fame is blown,
And somewhere, waiting for its birth,
    The shaft is in the stone!

III

Meanwhile, behalf the tardy years
    Which keep in trust your storied tombs,
Behold! your sisters bring their tears
    And these memorial blooms.

IV

Small tributes! but your shades will smile
    More proudly on these wreaths to-day,
Than when some cannon-moulded pile
    Shall overlook this bay.

V

Stoop, angels, hither from the skies!
    There is no holier spot of ground
Than where defeated valor lies,
    By mourning beauty crowned!

The question inevitably arises as to how these poets developed after the Civil War. One would naturally suppose that many of the younger ones especially would grow in power and influence. But all the causes generally assigned for the lack of poetry in the ante-bellum South prevailed in the new era; and thereto were added poverty, widespread disaster, and an overwhelming confusion in the public mind. Lanier tersely expressed the chief limitation under which the writer laboured when he wrote to Bayard Taylor: "Perhaps you know that with us of the younger generation of the South since the war, pretty much the whole of life has been merely not dying." Simms wrote to Hayne just before his death in 1870: "I am rapidly passing from a stage where you young men are to succeed me," and inscribed for his tombstone the poignant words: "Here lies one who, after a reasonably long life, distinguished chiefly by unceasing labours, has left all his better works undone." Meek, O'Hara, John R. Thompson, and Henry Timrod were all dead by 1875. Randall spent many years in the drudgery of a newspaper office, never recapturing the first fine careless rapture of his great song. Ticknor and Bruns followed with devotion the life of a doctor, while McCabe became one of the best-known schoolmasters of Virginia—a position which seemed to deaden his poetic inspiration, though he remained an inimitable raconteur, and the friend of some of the most gifted poets of England and America. Mrs. Preston continued to write as late as 1887, when she published *Colonial Ballads*, but she added nothing to her fame. Flash became a merchant and lived for many years in the Far West.

Paul Hamilton Hayne alone made progress after the war. With magnificent courage and faith, after the destruction of his city and his home, he moved to a small cabin of his own building in the pine barrens near Augusta, Georgia. Here on a writing desk made out of a carpenter's work-bench he wrote poems for the remainder of his life. To Mrs. Preston he wrote: "No, no! By my brain—my literary craft—I will win my bread and water; by my poems I will live or I will starve." In 1872 he brought out a volume of *Legends and Lyrics;* in 1875 *The Mountain of the Lovers and Other Poems;* and in 1882, a complete edition of his poems. Two or three of his best poems were written in his last years, notably *A Little While I Fain Would Linger Yet*, and *In Harbor*. While Hayne did not strike a deeply original note, he cultivated faithfully the talents with which he was endowed. His best poems are characterized by delicacy of feeling, conscientious workmanship, and a certain assimilation of the best qualities of other poets. His magnanimous spirit after the war, as revealed in his tributes to Whittier and Longfellow, his revelation of the picturesqueness of the Southern landscapes and especially of the pine forests of Georgia, are the substantial features of his poetry. As a connecting link between Simms and Lanier he has a permanent place in the literary history of the South.

# CHAPTER IV

# The New South : Lanier

THE conditions of Reconstruction were inimical to the production of literature. The life of the South, always sluggish, now became stagnant. A country of farms and plantations, there were in it few large cities to foster an intellectual life. The large planters whose travel and whose experience in government and statesmanship rendered them the natural leaders were downcast by the sudden destruction of their wealth in slaves and soil. The poor whites lived too close to mother earth and were too densely ignorant to furnish a public for literary activity. The isolation of the whole South was heart-sickening. The roads were unfit for teams. The railroads had been destroyed Cities like Columbia, South Carolina, reputed to be the most beautiful on the continent, stood a wilderness of ruins, " like Tadmor alone in the desert." Not one of the railways that formerly entered it had so much left as the iron on its track.

The newspapers were few and ill-informed. For many years they devoted their meagre talents to vituperation of Republican acts and policies. There was, to be sure, a short-lived effort at literary activity, as if the section might make good with the pen what had been lost by the sword. But even so catholic a venture as *The Land We Love*, edited by General D. H. Hill, which was devoted to literature, military history, and agriculture, had soon to die of inanition. Journals of opinion, like *De Bow's Review*, in New Orleans, maintaining a precarious existence in scattered centres of the region, had at length to give up the struggle. Schools and colleges were few and far between. Even the will to attend them had to be fostered with perseverance and great care. In fine, the intellectual stagnation of the South made literature impossible except for those with an unquenchable longing for expression.

Worse even than stagnation was the hopelessness of the outlook. The leaders, the owners of plantations, were reduced from affluence to poverty. Many a family that had been comfortable or even rich was now thankful for a supper of cornmeal. Plantations were for sale at a song. The "richest estates" of North Carolina were at first to be bought for from one to ten dollars an acre. A hundred acres four miles from Macon, Georgia, the birthplace of Lanier, was offered for fifty cents an acre. The Southerner was convinced that the negro would not work in freedom. Two books give unforgettable pictures of the efforts of the planters to meet the new industrial situation. *Ten Years on a Georgia Plantation* by the daughter of Fanny Kemble, Frances Butler Leigh, details the childishness of the negro under the novel conditions of freedom. Mrs. Leigh can hardly be claimed as a Southern author, but Susan Dabney Smedes (1840—) must take high rank as one. Her *Memorials of a Southern Planter* is an artless but absorbing picture of a class made extinct by the war. Without any of the theatrical effectiveness common in the older Southern prose, she relates in simple, dignified words the history of her father, Thomas Dabney, a planter of Mississippi. The war brought out in him such lofty nobility as is seldom seen in actual life. On laying down the volume Gladstone exclaimed "Let no man say, with this book before him, that the age of chivalry is gone, or that Thomas Dabney was not worthy to sit beside Sir Perceval at the 'table round' of King Arthur." His struggle to keep the plantation ended in its sale. A like fate awaited others. It was only slowly through the years that the large holdings were broken up into small farms and reduced to a more intense cultivation by intelligent diversification of crops.

Hopelessness of the economic outlook was deepened to despair by political and social conditions. By 1870 the seceded states were nominally reconstructed. But the Republican measures were such as poured salt and iron filings into the open wounds of civil war. Negro soldiers were set over their former masters. The intelligent voters were disqualified. The state governments were handed over to Northern carpet-baggers and

Southern scalawags, and the ignorant freedmen were given the right to vote. These former slaves marched through legislative halls on plush carpets, sat with their feet on mahogany desks, and spat into imported cuspidors. In one capital they resorted to a free and continuous lunch, with ample food and drink. All these luxuries were paid for out of the pockets of their former masters. This proud race, accustomed to generations of autocratic government, ground its teeth in silent rage. But by 1876 it had by fraud or violence overturned the inverted pyramid, and once more placed the state governments in the hands of responsible men, and returned many of its former leaders to the national Congress. The reins of government had been restored to the white man.

This atmosphere of turmoil was not conducive to a fine or vigorous literary product. Even so late as 1880 in Alabama "the assessed value of guns, dirks, and pistols was nearly twice that of the libraries and five times that of the farm implements of the state." For there continued the race problem to set the Southerners apart as a peculiar people. In many neighbourhoods the blacks outnumbered the whites two to one, three to one, four to one, and in the Yazoo bottom lands of Mississippi as many as fifteen to one. Their presence was viewed as a peril. It continued to be viewed as a peril during the twenty years following 1880, though the South became more and more a modern industrial community.

During that period Northern capital flowed in to draw iron and coal from the South's mines, to build factories along its streams, to spin a web of railways over its territory, to gather more and more its population into the humming hives of cities. The stagnation of the years immediately following the war gave way to an alerter life. Hopelessness and despondency waned gradually. With leisure and an interest in literature came visions of new beauty, a new-found joy in life, an impulse to share with others the creations of one's mind and spirit. Yet it was even more due to the Northern periodical and the Northern publisher that in the seventies and still more in the eighties the South found a voice in literature. That voice, in prose, spoke at first in the sonorous accents of the antebellum orator. Only as means of publication were multiplied and made more available did it take on the natural tones of every-day use.　Poetry in the seventies tended to give way to prose fiction.[1]

Of course, those who had written before the war still tried to gain a livelihood from the pen, but they continued the manner and traditions of the Old South.　John Esten Cooke,[2] for example, carried on in Virginia the tradition of the school of Scott and Cooper, then elsewhere becoming archaic.　George William Bagby (1828–83),[3] also of Virginia, renewed his newspaper productions and added the lyceum to his resources.　But so intense a lover of the Old Dominion and its civilization could suffer no sea-change even in the fiery baptism of war.　He tried to deliver his lecture *The Virginia Negro* in New York, but the reception was unmistakably cool.　Life "befo' de war" had not yet become for the North a charming memory from a land of romance.

Richard Malcolm Johnston (1822–98)[4] in his various writings evinces an equal devotion to the earlier times before the railroad came to central Georgia.　They form a sympathetic record of the ways and characters of that humble but picturesque era.　Johnston, though a slave-holder, was unwaveringly opposed to secession and the war.　Nevertheless, reduced by the surrender at Appomattox from an estate of fifty thousand dollars to poverty, to him the situation seemed so hopeless that he removed, with the school he kept, to Baltimore.　The autobiography, the eighty stories, and the three novels which he there produced, it is interesting to note, were written largely to assuage a sad longing for his boyhood home.　These writings show him to have been, in spite of his political opinions, of the old school of Southern gentlemen.

More typical both in opinions and in fervour was Charles Colcock Jones, Jr. (1831–93).　Born in Savannah, he graduated from Princeton in 1852 and the Harvard Law School in 1855.　His Southern convictions, however, still intact, were intensified by his service in the artillery of the Confederate States.　When the guns were stilled by the surrender of Lee, he, like Johnston, joined that numerous caravan which, seeing no hope in its own section, sought fortune in other regions.　New York and the practice of law were his goals.

---

[1] See Book III, Chaps. VI and XI.　　　[2] See also Book III, Chap. XI.
[3] See also Book II, Chap. XIX.　　　　[4] See also Book III. Chap. VI.

Although he remained North twelve years, he moved no jot nor tittle from his early point of view. On his return south in 1877 to a suburb of Augusta, Georgia, he became at once conspicuous for his devotion to the Lost Cause, and when he died in 1893, his body, wrapped in the flag of the Confederacy, was given a soldier's burial.

The style and the spirit of his numerous public addresses may be seen in a single sentence taken from *Sons of Confederate Veterans*, delivered so late as 1891:

Under the absurd guise of a New South, flaunting the banners of utilitarianism,—lifting the standards of speculation and expediency, —elevating the colors whereon are emblazoned consolidation of wealth and centralization of government,—lowering the flag of intellectual, moral, and refined supremacy in the presence of the petty guidons of ignorance, personal ambition and diabolism,— supplanting the iron cross with the golden calf,—and crooking

"the pregnant hinges of the knee
Where thrift may follow fawning"

not a few there are who, ignoring the elevating influence of heroic impulses, manly endeavor, and virtuous sentiments, would fain convert this region into a money-worshiping domain; and, careless of the landmarks of the fathers, impatient of the restraints of a calm, enlightened, conservative civilization, viewing with indifferent eye the tokens of Confederate valor, and slighting the graves of Confederate dead, would counsel no oblation save at the shrine of Mammon.

This turgid style was much admired for the magniloquent swing of the phrases and the unending procession of lofty and sectional notions. It so well comported with his tall, stately figure and Chesterfieldian manners that he employed it even in his history of the aboriginal, colonial, and Revolutionary epochs of Georgia. The book was the product of careful research in the records then available, so that Bancroft hailed the author as "the Macaulay of the South." But he is a Macaulay muffled in a pompous dress. His *Antiquities of the Southern Indians, Particularly of the Georgia Tribes*, which appeared so early as 1873, along with many other monographs established his reputation as an archæologist. He was, indeed, the most fertile Southern author of the period. His publications num-

ber eighty, including fourteen books, ten pamphlets, twenty-
two magazine articles, and twenty-nine addresses. His indefatigable industry demonstrated the energy and the diligence
of the old order, yet his writings are characteristically aristocratic and grandiose when compared with the more scientific
researches of later scholars like John Bell Henneman (1864–
1908), whose voluminous editorial labours represent very well
the activity of the new generation.

Strange to say, the breath of the new era first faintly stirred
those who had been in the thick of the fight. It was, perhaps,
not so strange that men like Zebulon Baird Vance (1830–94)
and Benjamin Harvey Hill (1823–82) should be reconciled to
the outcome. Vance was not only a strong Union man but
he opposed secession with all the fire of his oratory until the
moment that he heard of the attack on Sumter. It seems natural, then, that after the war he should sing again the glories
of the Union, one and indivisible. His *Sketches of North
Carolina*, however, which had appeared serially in *The Norfolk
Landmark*, show much the same fond longing for the past which
charms in Johnston and Bagby. Hill in Georgia fought for
the preservation of national unity even in the secession convention, yet, once in the war, he was as fervent in the support
of the Confederacy. This fervour was intensified by the Reconstruction policy of the National Government. His *Notes
on the Situation* in 1869 were vitriolic in their denunciation.
Much of this belligerent attitude appears in his speeches in
Congress. They have a narrative quality which, though less
lofty, is more telling than the ringing rhetoric of some of his
peers.

The case of General John Brown Gordon (1832–1904) is
even more memorable. His brilliant record in the Confederate armies was closed by his generous address to his soldiers
after the surrender at Appomattox, in which he exhorted them
to bear their trials bravely, to go home in peace, to obey the
laws, to rebuild the country, and to work for the weal and harmony of the Republic. In spite of the iniquities of Reconstruction, his political career was instinct with the same chivalrous
spirit, which found its most widely echoing expression in that
speech in the Senate in 1893 when he pledged the South to maintain law and order. His *Reminiscences of the Civil War*, with

its oratorical swing and fluency, diffused throughout the North that generous recognition of the foe and that proud acceptance of the result which have overcome the passions of sectionalism on both sides of Mason and Dixon's line.

The noblest example of this reconciling spirit among ante-bellum leaders is Lucius Quintus Cincinnatus Lamar (1825–93). Born and reared in Georgia, and a strict disciple of Calhoun, he removed at the age of twenty-four to Mississippi, which eventually became his home. So thoroughly imbued was he with the justice of the extreme Southern attitude that, as chairman of the Committee of Fifteen, he brought in the ordinance of secession for Mississippi. He came out of the ordeal of war with the vision of a new heaven and a new earth, for the first heaven and the first earth had passed away. But the dark years of Reconstruction fell over his soul like a pall. Pondering on the supreme necessity of getting his people into harmonious relations with the Federal Government, he saw no hope except in their going to work to restore their material prosperity and to establish their institutions of education. In 1872 he was elected a representative of Mississippi, the first Democrat of the Old South to enter the halls of Congress. To one object he was consecrated: the perfect reconciliation of the North and the South. The opportunity to remove from the North a wellnigh universal suspicion of the South and to rescue the nation from the perils of an increasing sectional hate came to him sooner than he anticipated. The death of Charles Sumner was the occasion of resolutions in both houses of Congress. On 28 April, 1874, Lamar delivered that Eulogy of Sumner which melted the distinguished audience to tears, which rang through the nation in a day, and which echoes still. Filled with the patriot's pride and faith, it revealed the Southern people to their better selves and began in the North to mitigate the estrangements of a generation. Yet the loftiness of its sentiment is not the passport to posterity which it should be. The long Southern roll of the eloquence needs the revealing tones of a voice to bring out its majesty. Frequently the sentences become for the average modern reader too far prolonged or too intricately involved to surrender their meaning at once. The same drawback may be found in Lamar's other deliverances, even the carefully prepared oration at the unveiling of the Calhoun monument at Charleston. But with those who read speeches the Eulogy of Sumner will live as the noble expression of a patriot and a seer, whose gentleness and devotion will win him a bright and quiet niche in the dark and troublous vestibule of Reconstruction.

Another disciple of Calhoun, Jabez Lamar Monroe Curry (1825–1903), born in Georgia but reared in Alabama, learned at the University of Georgia to regard the Arch-Secessionist as second only to Aristotle. Going to Harvard in 1843 to study law, he was soon fired by Horace Mann with a passion for universal education. It was therefore natural, although he became a United States Congressman and a member of the Confederate Congress, that after the war he should enter educational work, in order that the youth of his section might be fitted to build worthily and helpfully in the tumble-down world that surrounded them. As agent of the Peabody and Slater Funds, he aided more than any other one man to develop an irresistible public opinion for the education of the whole people, both white and black, in the Southern States. Today the most valuable of his educational writings is the *History of the Peabody Education Fund*, which records the progress of one of the most beneficent philanthropies since the war. He is thus on the side of the constructionists as opposed to those forensic champions who revelled in the abstract notions of States' rights and liberty, but where he develops the theory of secession, as in *Civil History of the Government of the Confederate States* or *The Southern States of the American Union*, there is a pugnacious reiteration of outworn arguments which will appeal chiefly to the historical student or the partisan. His numerous other writings dealing with the South, even when they utter a national spirit or retail personal experiences, lack the colour and the vigour which render Gordon's reminiscences still interesting. His life of Gladstone lacks power to portray and to analyze.

But the figures we have passed in review, revered and stately though they be, and eloquently as they avowed the new spirit of allegiance to a common country, in reality belonged to an earlier generation than that of the Reconstruction period. Those who did not, like Bagby and Johnston, sing the glories of an aristocratic civilization resting on slavery, were at least imbued, like Vance and Hill and Gordon, with the elder spirit, which regarded politics as the only arena toward which ambition beckoned. Their writings are consequently concerned with lofty ideals of human rights and the limits of governmental action. They are rhythmic with the cadences of an oratory which too frequently forsook cold argument for fervid appeals to tradition and class interests. Rare was the apostle like Curry who preached the democratic necessity of developing both the black and the white races. Rarer still was the seer like Lamar who divined that the hope of the future lay in going to work to develop the material resources of the section.

Not till we reach the fascinating figure of Henry Woodfin Grady (1851–89) do we find a true representative of the new generation. He is recognized by common consent as the chief latterday orator of his section. Born in Athens, Georgia, he grew up in the turmoil of the Civil War, often visited the camp of his father's soldiers, and could never forget the scene when Major Grady's remains were brought back from one of the last battles around Petersburg. His sunny disposition and his inexhaustible flow of animal spirits made him a general favourite with the professors at the University of Georgia, where he developed that style which was later to win him fame both South and North. After graduation he became a journalist. The journalism of Georgia, like that of the whole South, was then in a deplorable state. The State governments were still in the hands of the carpet-baggers. The editors drew what comfort they could from denouncing the Republicans as the authors of all evil. Into this sullen circle came Grady with the bright, racy humour which had captivated his classmates, with a freshness and an individuality which caused many a Georgia editor to open his eyes. His own editorial ventures were brilliant in their audacity but dismal in their financial returns. By 1875 he had dissipated his fortune. Borrowing fifty dollars, he gave twenty to his wife, and with the remainder, with characteristic impetuosity, bought a ticket to New York. There, by a single article, he won the position of Southern correspondent of the New York *Herald*. His reports of the South Carolina riots of 1876 and of the Florida election frauds of the same year were so graphic and complete that they established his future. In 1879 he was enabled to purchase a quarter interest in *The*

*Atlanta Constitution*, a medium through which he impressed himself upon his state and his section.

In 1886, by reason of a speech on *The New South* delivered 22 December before the New England Society of New York City, he became the spokesman of the new era, and the title of that speech became the watchword of a vast movement. Though it aroused the ire of the old school, as seen above in the denunciation of "the banners of utilitarianism" by Charles Colcock Jones, Jr., it expressed a new sense of the economic basis of society and of the social conditions which must obtain more and more in the regenerated South. Some of his later speeches are notable. *The South and her Problem*, delivered in Dallas, 26 October, 1887, and *The Farmer and the Cities*, at Elberton, Georgia, in June, 1889, show him as the evangel of the new gospel to his own section. His treatment of the negro problem before the Boston Merchants' Association in December, 1889, was more cogent in argument than his other addresses, but less ardent in appeal. Yet one of the auditors characterized it as "a cannon-ball in full flight, fringed with flowers." Weakened by his exertions on this trip in the unexpected cold of the Northern winter, he returned to Atlanta to die 23 December, 1889.

One singular feature of Grady's career, and one significant of the new era, was that he never held public office. His ambition shows the change which had come over the spirit of the South:

My ambition is a simple one. I shall be satisfied with the labors of my life if, when those labors are over, my son, looking abroad upon a better and grander Georgia—a Georgia that has filled the destiny God intended her for—when her towns and cities are hives of industry, and her country-side the exhaustless fields from which their stores are drawn—when every stream dances on its way to the music of spindles, and every forest echoes back the roar of the passing train—when her valleys smile with abundant harvests, and from her hillsides come the tinkling of bells as her herds and flocks go forth from their folds—when more than two million people proclaim her perfect independence and bless her with their love—I shall be more than content, I say, if my son, looking upon such scenes as these, can stand up and say: "My father bore a part in this work, and his name lives in the memory of this people."

This ambition dictated the character of his journalism and the substance of his speeches. In his newspaper he endeavoured without shadow of turning to draw attention to the material resources of the South and to develop her industries. In his speeches he displayed even greater brilliancy, fervour, and versatility in presenting the various phases of the topic. Incapable of rancour himself, he with magnanimous sincerity and a whole heart endeavoured to remove the barriers to harmony and co-operation between the sections. In short, he became the orator of the peacemakers.

This purpose in part explains the form of those addresses. He was delivering an appeal to his public, not conducting a legal argument. He was moving his auditors to a new point of view, not convincing them of a scientific truth. He threw into the effort all the ardour of a generous and enthusiastic nature. The pictures of his fancy, the constant balancing of phrases and ideas, the play of wit and humour and pathos were employed with the instinctive effectiveness of one who has learned to sway audiences. They reflect, too, in many ways the sonorous models of Southern oratory that formed the pattern and ideal for his youthful attempts. Yet there is a greater definiteness of thought, a closer linking of word and idea, on the whole a simpler and more vivid style than obtained in the old school. To the ears of the sophisticated, of course, his periods are cloying in their fluency. To thousands of untutored youths all over the South, on the other hand, his words have seemed the echoes of a silver tongue flowing like the honey of Hybla. His picture of "a country home, a quiet, modest house, sheltered by great trees," his vision of the returning Confederate soldier, "this hero in gray with the heart of gold," have been declaimed from hundreds of school and college platforms all over the South. His continued popularity proves that his sentiment was not merely a device for moving an audience but was the outpouring of Grady's real nature, full of quick sympathy and unfathomed tenderness. In character and disposition Grady belonged with the Old South; in vision and purpose he was the herald of the New.

No account of the New South in literature would be complete without notice of the life and writings of Booker T. Washington[1]

[1] See also Book III, Chap. v

(1859–1915). He was not only a product of Reconstruction but he contributed much to the progress and prosperity of his section in the new era. Born two or three years before the war on a Virginia plantation, his mother a slave, his father he knew not who, he a few years after the war joined in that rush for an education which seized great numbers of the freedmen. The acuteness of that struggle, the inspiring tenacity with which it was maintained, form one of the bright pages in that dark period. When he had completed his studies in Hampton, he turned aside from the opportunities for political preferment which lured many of his race to destruction, and devoted his days and his nights to the upbuilding of his fellow freedmen. In 1881 he was called to the obscure village of Tuskegee in Alabama to take charge of what was to be a normal school for coloured people. Thereafter his name and Tuskegee became synonymous for negro progress. For he there worked out with dauntless persistence a scheme for education which would fit the negro to his actual surroundings. Consecrating all of his vast energy to that cause, he became long before his death the foremost representative of his race in the world, a writer known in every section of his own country, and one of the most eloquent speakers of his generation.

Of his addresses, typical is the five-minute speech delivered at the Atlanta exposition 17 September, 1895, which made him the recognized leader of his race. Aside from the fact that it presented a platform so simple, yet so fundamental in its assumptions, that both black and white could stand thereon, it illustrates well the guiding principles of his rhetoric, that every word shall mean something. There is in it little of that fatally easy use of superlatives, that sonorous succession of periods, which so tickled the ears of old-time audiences. There is little of the habitual resort to cunning balance and alliteration which even Grady constantly introduced to secure his effects. It is simple, direct, vivid, yet sustained by a high devotion to the future of his race. Not only in its message but in its style it speaks of the New South.

His writings display the same characteristics. Of these, his autobiography, consisting of *Up from Slavery* and *Working with Hands*, forms one of the noblest records America has to show. *Up from Slavery* in particular, the annals of his childhood and rise to fame, with its mingled pathos and humour, its etching of the past, its modest story of a quiet but heart-stirring achievement, has already become one of the classics of its type. Of his other voluminous writings, dealing almost exclusively with the colored race, weighty is *The Future of the American Negro,* which contains his views on the enigma which ever confronts the South. Not founding his argument on those lofty conceptions of right and justice which aroused such fanatical zeal before the war, but with a sanity of outlook upon the industrial situation in the South and an unclouded vision of the progress of his race in the past and of the necessary steps in future advance, he discusses the various aspects of the problem with a dispassionate but illuminating calm. Though his contact with the more steadfast and aspiring kind of negro may have filled him with undue hope, yet no reader can fail to admire his self-forgetful devotion to his race, or refuse to accord him a high place among the prose writers of the New South.

The poets, also, represent the effects of Reconstruction on literature in the South. They belonged to a younger generation. They felt in their own persons the wreck of their section. Their outlook upon life and their practice of their art were formed or deeply changed by the hopeless struggles of reconstruction and restoration. Their more sensitive souls felt and recorded the underlying attitudes of their generation. Both their lives and their writings merit close attention.

The first voices were proud and defiant. They echoed in more poignant phrases the Berserker rage of the Southern editorial columns. Most notable of these myriad voices of the press was Carlyle McKinley (1847–1904), of the Charleston *News and Courier.* At fifteen he forsook the quiet campus of the University of Georgia and distinguished himself by bravery in the trenches before Sherman at Atlanta. Like most Southern youths after the war, he drifted about for a time between two worlds, one dead, the other powerless to be born. In 1875 he joined the staff of the *News and Courier,* and after a brief excursion into commercial life in New York he returned in 1881 as associate editor, where in failing health he remained the rest of his days.

His prose was greatly admired, especially his *An Appeal to Pharaoh* (1889), an argument for deportation, a solution of the

negro problem to which thousands of Southerners in the early despair of Reconstruction turned with hope, until the enthusiasm
of Grady and the doctrine of Booker T. Washington brought to
light a more adequate economic and sociological basis.

Nevertheless, it is in poetry that the man and the period
are revealed. Not only did McKinley love the South with his
whole heart, but the Lost Cause was dear to him in a passionate degree. Early in Reconstruction his *At Timrod's Grave*
voiced the complaint of Southern poets:

> For singing, Fate hath given sighs,
> For music, we make moan.

His undaunted demeanour under the manifold injustices of
Reconstruction speaks for his state and his section. Typical
is his *South Carolina—1876:*

> They've wasted all her royal dower;
> They've wrought her wrong with evil power;
> And is she faint, or doth she cower?
> —She scorns them in her weakest hour!
>
> She bides her time—a patient Fate!
> Her sons are gathering in the gate!
> She knows to counsel and to wait,
> And vengeance knoweth no "too late."

In later years he came to take refuge in poetry from the dis-
tresses of life, to find in it an anodyne. Probably the best example of this mood, *Sapelo*, illustrates not only the finish of
his verse, which lifts him above the rhymesters of his section,
but at the same time the lack of that inspiration or individual power which would give him a secure place in the poetical
annals of our country.

It is individuality of style that strikingly distinguishes
another Reconstruction poet who could never forget the Lost
Cause and who sought solace in the realms of poesy. John
Banister Tabb (1845–1909) was born and reared at The Forest,
a plantation near Richmond. The only blemish on the bright
untroubled period of his boyhood with a loved mother and kind
tutors was weakness of the eyes, which at the age of twelve
an occulist pronounced incurable. His youthful passions were

poetry and music, yet when the conflict came he soon forsook these nymphs to fly to arms and war. In 1862 he entered the navy as a captain's clerk and after two years of service was captured on a blockade runner and confined to Point Lookout Prison. There Sidney Lanier's flute-playing made the two men firm friends for life. Unlike Lanier, however, Tabb could not forget the prison and the victorious Northern armies which dispersed his wealth. In the blank years following the war he first studied music and then resigned himself to teaching. He was ordained a Catholic priest in 1884, but remained in St. Charles College at Ellicott City, Maryland, till his death, for as teacher of literature, especially of his favourite poets, Poe, Keats, and Shelley, he was eminently successful. His total blindness in 1906 he bore with equanimity until his death in 1909.

His career reveals the character of his mind. He was detached from life and sought to pierce below its aspects to the soul beneath. Nature, to be sure, he loved. His memory dwelt fondly on the Virginia scenery of his boyhood, the rolling slopes and "smooth-sliding" streams, the kildee and the wood-robin of that Utopian period. In Maryland he liked to take walks and come back with flowers and leaves. More than thirty birds are celebrated in his poems. Yet even when they stir the deepest emotion these voices of nature speak to him of some facet of human life. The call of the robin in the waning daylight reminds him of the shadowy but inevitable approach of Death:

> Come, ere oblivion speed to me, flying
> Swifter than thou.

It is his underlying philosophy that God speaks to man through the multiform aspects of nature; that

> Love, of sweet Nature the Lord,
> Hath fashioned each manifold chord
> To utter His visible Word;

that the poet acts merely as interpreter. Indeed, so intent is Tabb on the thought symbolized that he comes to find loveliness in nature only as its aspects may be interpreted. More than that, everywhere in his unformulated but profoundly-felt philosophy,—and not in mere figure of speech,—all the outwardly beautiful objects in nature live and breathe and have their being in God as much as we.   Almost might St. Francis of Assisi have written *Brotherhood:*

> Knew not the Sun, sweet Violet,
>     The while he gleaned the snow,
> That thou in darkness sepulchred,
>     Wast slumbering below?
> Or spun a splendor of surprise
> Around him to behold thee rise?
>
> Saw not the Star, sweet Violet,
> What time a drop of dew
> Let fall his image from the sky
>     Into thy deeper blue?
> Nor waxed he tremulous and dim
> When rival Dawn supplanted him?
>
> And dreamest thou, sweet Violet,
>     That I, the vanished Star,
> The Dewdrop, and the morning Sun,
>     Thy closest kinsmen are—
> So near that, waking or asleep,
> We each and all thine image keep?

Quite in keeping with this detachment from mundane affairs, this preoccupation with the abstract relationships of life, is Tabb's absorption in the dogmas of the Church.   That they should have engaged his imagination so deeply reveals the strength of his other-worldliness, the extent to which he fled from the ordinary interests of men.   One human feeling, however, he displayed in a beautiful degree—friendship.   His affection for Sidney Lanier in particular was one of the bright strands in his life.   Their few months together in prison reveal an affinity between them that was not dimmed by the lapse of years.

Yet, as we shall see, their poetic styles were in sharp contrast.   An English critic has compared "the long, voluminous, rushing flow of Lanier with the minute, delicately carved work" of Tabb rather to the credit of Tabb, who, he says, "piping on his flute can do things which Lanier's great four-manual organ could never accomplish." It surely will be conceded that Tabb's poetic manner is as individual as Lanier's. Yet his first poems in 1883, some nineteen lyrics and a few sonnets, reveal little of this originality or indeed of poetical promise. The shortest poems were in ten lines, whereas his later style tends to quatrains. Working in such small compass, he has polished his technique to a point near perfection. The diction is of extreme simplicity. The measures flow on without a ripple. The figures are suggested in the most concise phrasing. In short, his poems are a series of the most delicate cameos. Contrast and endless comparison are the basis of his style, which is largely coloured by the frequency of scriptural allusions, the constant introduction and personification of abstract ideas, and the subtle intermixture of symbolism. He was so wrapped up in his poetic fancies that his figures often pass over into conceits. Who else could give to the spiritual inquiry "Is thy servant a dog?" such a turn as this:

> So *must* he be who, in the crowded street,
> Where shameless Sin and flaunting Pleasure meet,
> Amid the noisome footprints finds the sweet
> Faint vestiges of Thy feet.

In his *Child's Verse* the effect is natural enough, for his puns, no matter how far fetched they appear to the sober eye, there strike one as flashes of wit. But in serious poetry the effect is different. The mind hardly has time to link the symbol and the interpretation. The compression does not permit full grasp of the significance.

In spite of these shortcomings, however, we must concede that Father Tabb, though he lived constantly in a rarefied religious atmosphere, far removed from the daily interests of man, yet was endowed with an ear sensitive to those overtones which escape most men and that he was often visited with those intuitions which reveal nooks of beauty, aspects of cheer. Though his lute was of few strings, he played it with exquisite tone.

Another class of Reconstruction poets felt less keenly the sting of defeat. Some in fact came to catch the new national spirit and have even expressed in poetry their devotion to the common flag. Verse was for them not so much an avenue of escape from the cares and tribulation of this life as a means of self-expression. A humble and rather negative representative is John Henry Boner (1845–1903), whom North Carolina now claims as her chief poet of the period, although in Reconstruction times she drove him from her borders. Coming from a quite different class of society from that of Tabb or McKinley, he found it easy to become a Republican after the war. Not till his demise did his fellow citizens forgive him. In 1870, when, after a campaign that approached civil war, a Democratic governor was elected, the Republicans took care of Boner by placing him in the Government Printing Office in Washington, for which he was fitted by his earlier trade as printer; but when the Democrats again gained control of the national government, Boner was dismissed on the ground of offensive partisanship. Fortunately his poetry had won him the ear of Edmund Clarence Stedman, who obtained for him in New York various tasks of compilation. He eventually became editor of *The Literary Digest*, which he conducted with ability until his resignation in 1897.

All this time, however, he cherished memories of the South and the scenes of his boyhood. In particular, the theme that pleased Stedman, the music of the pines as the wind sighed through them or the moon rose beyond them, haunted him with a gentle yearning. *The Light'ood Fire* lightens his memory with fond pictures. *Crismus Times is Come* is an unusually faithful representation of the negro character and religion. These effusions are carefully finished. The versification is smooth, often liquid. The descriptive passages are clear and sometimes vivid. The tone of melancholy that pervades his best efforts casts the charm of subdued light over both the measures and the man. Nevertheless, Boner is deficient in imagination, and adds no new note, no original element, to American verse. He will consequently live as a poet of one poem—*Poe's Cottage at Fordham*. The subject enlisted a deeper interest than even the events of Boner's own life and much deeper than the swirling progress of his adopted section. The lines well up from a sympathy that interprets and enshrines. They flow with a haunting melody worthy of the magician in metre whom they celebrate.

Less sectional, more completely national in spirit, was Robert Burns Wilson (1850–1916). He was endowed with a double gift—the gifts of painting and poetry, each of them genuine. It must be conceded that he did not have to break the shackles of sectionalism. Born in Pennsylvania and moving early to Virginia, he looked back, not on memories of conflict, but on scenes of quiet peace. He early studied art. At barely twenty he received further impetus while on a canoe trip with John W. Alexander. Much of his later success may be attributed to Alexander's influence and assistance. In painting he sought "to catch the passing and elusive things in nature, which do not sit for their pictures." It is just the mood and feeling of these evanescent aspects of nature which form the substance of his poetry. Visions of Kentucky woods and fields float by on the wings of music, but there is usually some melancholy cadence or echo in the strain. The most famous, and probably the best of his poems, *When Evening Cometh On*, is characteristic of his method of presenting pictures suffused with emotion in order to create a dominant mood. In spite of the variety of measures which he employs, there is a weakness in his repetition of similar themes in successive volumes.

During the Spanish-American War Wilson made clear how truly the South had become national. His *Remember the Maine* not only occupied the front page of the New York *Herald* but was reprinted all over the country. His *Such is the Death the Soldier Dies*, which appeared originally in *The Atlantic Monthly*, was at once welcomed for the gentle pathos of its picture and its sentiment. Many stirring and martial poems by other Southerners attest the genuineness of the national spirit which had followed the dark and bitter days of Reconstruction. Not by any surcease of sorrow but by the genuine fire of a new vision did Southern poetry bud forth into a patriotic cry. The days of McKinley and his *South Carolina—1876* had given way to the new conception of a united country and eager, confident prospects for the future.

The most salient figure in this change, in fact the most distinguished man of letters of the New South, is Sidney Lanier, who, like Wilson, was endowed with a double gift—music and poetry. He was born in Macon, Georgia, 3 February, 1846.

His father was a lawyer of undistinguished abilities but of cultured and literary tastes. His mother was devotedly religious, and reared her family in the strict Presbyterian faith. His grandfather's hotel, the Lanier House, was the centre of a cordial, hospitable social life. The city of Macon, a prosperous commercial centre, counted among its citizens many wealthy plantation owners but few who aspired to higher education or intellectual achievement. Even his father's literary interests seem to have been confined to Shakespeare and Addison and Sir Walter Scott—to the items of that self-sufficient culture which reigned everywhere in the South before the Civil War.

Although Scott and Froissart fired Lanier's young mind with ideals of chivalry, the thing which set him apart from the Macon school boys was his remarkable musical ability. At seven he had made himself a reed flageolet, and on receiving a flute at Christmas he soon organized quartets and bands among his playfellows. Indeed, it was because of his leadership in serenading parties at Oglethorpe, which he had entered shortly before his fifteenth birthday, that his father brought him home to spend a year in the Macon post office. When he returned to Oglethorpe as a junior he began to play the violin with such effect that he would at times lose consciousness for hours. His father, fearing this stimulation, induced him to return to the flute and discouraged him as much as possible from devotion to music. The result is seen in the boy's journal:

The prime inclination—that is, natural bent (which I have checked, though) of my nature is to music, and for that I have the greatest talent; indeed, not boasting, for God gave it me, I have an extraordinary musical talent, and feel it within me plainly that I could rise as high as any composer. But I cannot bring myself to believe that I was intended for a musician, because it seems so small a business in comparison with other things which, it seems to me, I might do.

His later life seems to bear out the assumption that America, by his father's solicitude and the social pressure of Southern opinion at the time, was deprived of another distinguished name in music.

The life at Oglethorpe was a period of intellectual advance for Lanier.  The major influence was exerted by James Woodrow of the department of science, who took the boy on long rambles, or on long drives, when the two of them would talk about everything either of them was interested in.  Woodrow thought so much of Lanier that he secured for him an appointment as tutor.  Better still, he gave the future poet a zest for science that remained with him to the end, and a vision of the intellectual life which shaped his aspirations and his future conduct.  Giving up music as a possible career, Lanier resolved to spend two years in Heidelberg and to return to a professorship in some American college.

Then came the cataclysm of Civil War, and with it for Lanier a period of storm and stress that tossed him this way and that for a dozen years.  At the outbreak he was enthusiastic at the prospect of a South more wealthy than history had yet seen.  Macon, he thought, was to become a great art centre whose streets were to be lined with marble statues like unto Athens of old.  At the close of the college year he, like nearly all the other teachers and the students of Oglethorpe, enlisted for service.  The war itself was not an unmixed evil to Lanier.  Although he saw some exciting service as a signalman along the James River, he was for three years allowed ample time for study and for cherishing that passion for the very highest which grew with his years.  He now began to contemplate a literary life as his vocation.  To his father he wrote in 1864, "Gradually I find that my whole soul is merging itself into this business of writing, and especially of writing poetry."  He began his novel, *Tiger Lilies*, and sent several poems to his father for criticism.  In 1864, however, he was transferred to Wilmington, North Carolina, where he served as signal officer on the blockade runners.  In November he was captured in the Gulf Stream and sent to Point Lookout Prison in Maryland.  There he continued to play the flute, which won him the friendship of Tabb.  He busied himself with German poetry, but the prison conditions were so loathsome as to induce a breakdown in health.  He came out emaciated to a skeleton, and when he finally reached Macon in March he fell ill and lingered near death for two months.  Thereafter his life was an unavailing search for health.

The fact that members of his family "who used to roll in wealth are, everyday, with their own hands ploughing the little patch of ground which the war has left them, while their wives do the cooking and washing," did not disturb him. What he felt most keenly was the intellectual stagnation of the South. Already in 1866 he was, with characteristic breadth and lack of prejudice, writing thus to a Northern friend:

You are all so alive up there, and we are all so dead down here! I begin to have serious thoughts of emigrating to your country, so that I may live a little. There is not enough attrition of mind on mind here to bring out any sparks from a man.

Even among these untoward surroundings he continued to foster his literary ambitions. In another letter he continues:

We have no newspapers here with circulation enough to excite our ambition, and, of course, the Northern papers are beyond our reach. Our literary life, too, is a lonely and somewhat cheerless one; for beyond our father, a man of considerable literary acquirements and exquisite taste, we have not been able to find a single individual who sympathized in such pursuits enough to warrant showing him our little productions—so scarce is "general cultivation" here.

I am thirsty to know what is going on in the great art world up there; you have no idea how benighted we all are. I have only recently begun to get into the doings of literary men through "The Round Table" which I have just commenced taking.

That journal not only satisfied his thirst for the doings of the great world but helped to foster the national spirit which he was to voice more clearly than other poets of his section, and to fire his own ambition for a literary career. Several of his earlier poems appeared in its pages.

To the same inspiration may be traced his visit to New York in 1867 to find a publisher for *Tiger Lilies*. Possibly it was the reputation he gained from its publication which caused him to marry in the face of the precarious future. The setting up of the state governments under the Reconstruction Act of 1867 made the prospect for him, as for hundreds of others, even darker and more discouraging. Despairing of earning a living by his pen, and seeing that Southern colleges were so poor as "to hold out absolutely no inducement in the way of support to a professor," he yielded in January, 1869, to his father's solicitation and betook himself to the study of law.

The work in the law office kept him very busy. He did indeed write a few humorous dialect poems, published in various local papers, but in general his resignation was that expressed in a letter to Paul Hamilton Hayne in 1870:

> I've not put pen to paper, in the literary way, for a long time. How I thirst to do so, how I long to sing a thousand various songs that oppress me, unsung,—is inexpressible. Yet, the mere work that brings bread gives me no time. I know not, after all, if this is a sorrowful thing. Nobody likes my poems, except two or three friends,—who are themselves poets, and can supply themselves!

But music regained its ascendancy over him. Letters to his wife written in 1869, 1870, and 1871, on visits to New York, reveal the intensity of his pleasure in a violin solo, or the singing of Nilsson, or Theodore Thomas's orchestra, where he plunged into an amber sea of music and came away from what he felt might have been heaven.

The turning point of his life came in San Antonio, Texas, whither he went in the winter of 1872–3 for his health. He filled in part of his time there with literary projects, but the inspiration of his stay was found in a group of German musicians, who received "amid a storm of applause" his flute-playing before the *Maennerchor*. In February, 1873, he played before "a very elegant-looking company of ladies and gentlemen." He reported:

> I had not played three seconds before a profound silence reigned among the people. . . . When I allowed the last note to die, a simultaneous cry of pleasure broke forth from men and women that almost amounted to a shout, and I stood and received the congratulations that thereupon came in, so wrought up by my own playing with (hidden) thoughts, that I could but smile mechanically, and make stereotyped returns to the pleasant sayings, what time my heart worked falteringly, like a mouth that is about to cry.

Two weeks later he wrote:

I have writ the most beautiful piece "Field-larks and Black-birds," wherein I have mirrored Mr. Field-lark's pretty eloquence so that I doubt he would know the difference betwixt the flute and his own voice.

In the summer he confessed to Hayne:

Are you, by the way, a musician? Strange, that I have never before asked this question,—when so much of my own life consists of music. I don't know that I've ever told you, that whatever turn I have for art is purely musical; poetry being, with me, a mere tangent into which I shoot sometimes. I could play passably on several instruments before I could write legibly; and since then, the very deepest of my life has been filled with music, which I have studied and cultivated far more than poetry.

Inspired with this new faith, he again repaired to New York, this time determined to settle his future. He revelled in the musical associations which he quickly formed. By November he had been engaged by Asger Hamerik for the position of first flute in the new Peabody Orchestra forming in Baltimore. On 29 November he wrote his declaration of independence to his father:

Why should I, nay, how *can* I, settle myself down to be a third-rate struggling lawyer for the balance of my little life as long as there is a certainty almost absolute that I can do some other thing so much better. Several persons, from whose judgment there can be no appeal, have told me, for instance, that I am the greatest flute-player in the world; and several others, of equally authoritative judgment, have given me an almost equal encouragement to work with my pen. . . . My dear father, think how for twenty years, through poverty, through pain, through weariness, through sickness, through the uncongenial atmosphere of a farcical college and of a bare army and then of an exacting business life, through all the discouragements of being wholly unacquainted with literary people and literary ways—I say, think how, in spite of all these depressing circumstances, and of a thousand more which I could enumerate, those two figures of music and poetry have steadily kept in my heart so that I could not banish them. Does it not seem to you as to me, that I begin to have a right to enroll myself among the devotees of those two sublime arts, after having followed them so long and so humbly, and through so much bitterness.

Thus he entered upon the third and final period of his life, one of feverish activity. During the winter succeeding his great resolution he grew rapidly in the intellectual grasp of music. He had the soul of an artist, and gradually acquired the technical skill to bring the most out of his instrument. Still the strength of his renderings always resided in the emotion he imparted. His conductor testifies:

His conception of music was not reached by any analytical study of note by note, was intuitive, spontaneous; like a woman's reason: he felt it so, because he felt it so, and his delicate perception required no more logical form of reasoning. His playing appealed to the musically learned and unlearned—for he would mesmerize the listener; but the artist felt in his performance the superiority of the momentary living inspiration to all the rules and shifts of mere technical scholarship.

The next year he still yearned for a musical career. He told Dr. Leopold Damrosch, then conductor of the Philharmonic Society of New York, that music "is not a matter of mere preference, it is a spiritual necessity. I must be a musician, I cannot help it." But the conference with Damrosch impressed Lanier with the great handicap he suffered in lack of thorough technical training. Though he continued to gain intense joy from music, literature more and more occupied his thoughts and monopolized his time.

In February, 1875, *Corn*, which he had conceived the preceding summer and had rewritten during the winter, appeared in *Lippincott's Magazine*. It was one of the earliest Southern poems to receive publication in a Northern periodical. Notable, too, is the fact that the verses are not an effort to escape into some dreamland but the presentation of a widespread problem of Georgia agriculture.

*Corn* attracted favourable attention, notably from Gibson Peacock, editor of the Philadelphia *Evening Bulletin*. Within a month Lanier was at work on a second ambitious poem, *The Symphony*, which appeared in June, and which brought him the friendship of Bayard Taylor. The firm of Lippincott was able to fill Lanier's time with hackwork. The whole summer was spent in preparing "a sort of spiritualized guide-book" to Florida. Yet he was happy. He wrote of himself as one

who, after many days and nights of tribulation and bloody sweat, has finally emerged from all doubt into the quiet and yet joyful activity of one who knows exactly what his *Great Passion* is and what his God desires him to do. As for me, life has resolved simply into a time during which I must get upon paper as many as possible of the poems with which my heart is stuffed like a schoolboy's pocket.

When at the instance of Bayard Taylor he was appointed to write the cantata for the Centennial Exposition to be held in Philadelphia, he was jubilant. His patriotic fervour produced also *The Psalm of the West*. A place among American poets he challenged by bringing out a slender volume of poems late in the same year.

Because of a severe illness he was ordered South for the winter of 1876–7, but there he continued to throw off "a sort of spray of little songs" and to hope for "that repose which ought to fill the artist's firmament while he is creating."

The four remaining years of his life were spent in an unavailing search for that repose. He endeavoured to make sure where next week's dinners were coming from before carrying out his ambitions for creative work. He continued his connection with the Peabody Orchestra, but his chief endeavour turned him aside, this time into the field of scholarship. He wandered about in Old and Middle English, and ranged far in the Elizabethan period. These enthusiastic studies resulted in lectures at the Peabody Institute, and in 1879 in his appointment as lecturer in Johns Hopkins University. *The Science of English Verse* and *The English Novel* are the products of those two years, besides some books for boys and many poems. But consumption had made such advances that it was feared that he would not live to complete his last series of lectures. Indeed, those who listened to him momentarily feared that he would not survive to the end of the hour. In May, 1881, he was taken to the mountains of North Carolina, where he died 7 September.

often too much so for his own good, but none the less the rhetoric is not out of place. On the other hand, to put rhetoric, except in dramatic passages, into literary prose is almost as bad as to write metred prose, of which Dickens was guilty in the description of the death of Little Nell. But when we come to giving the literary touch to rhetoric the exact reverse is the case. The rhetoric is at once lifted up and illuminated. The only objection is that the art is as rare as it is difficult, to be found in only a few great masters of speech in human history. It was precisely in this rare and difficult art that Webster excelled. His rhetoric was always unimpeachable, but his peculiar power lay in the fact that he was able to give to it with ever-increasing ease the imperishable literary quality.

We detect the first gleams of this beautiful art in the Plymouth oration. It is not necessary to take as an example the celebrated passage about the slave trade, where the rhetoric predominates; less familiar sentences prove the point. He is speaking of Rome:

Although the time might come, when darkness should settle on all her hills; when foreign or domestic violence should overturn her altars and her temples; when ignorance and despotism should fill the places where Laws, and Arts and Liberty had flourished; when the feet of barbarism should trample on the tombs of her consuls and the walls of her Senate-house and forum echo only to the voice of savage triumph.

A little farther on, speaking of the human love of home and birth-place, a well-worn theme, he says:

When the heart has laid down what it loved most, then it is desirous of laying itself down. No sculptured marble, no enduring monument, no honourable inscription, no ever burning taper that would drive away the darkness of the tomb, can soften our sense of the reality of death, and hallow to our feelings the ground which is to cover us, like the consciousness that we shall sleep, dust to dust, with the objects of our affections.

The thought in these passages is simple, oft-recurrent, entirely familiar, expressed by many other orators with great effect and received by genuinely moved audiences with much applause. The first time one looks upon them, if one could